SoHo

Famous for its cast-iron buildings and for the artists who colonized its empty industrial lofts in the 1960s, SoHo today is the epitome of a gentrified neighborhood. The artists have left, but visitors flock here to shop, eat, and take in the atmosphere.

SoHo, the area SOuth of HOuston St (*map p. 620, C1; subway: N, R to Prince St; 6 to Spring St; B, D, F to Broadway-Lafayette; bus: M5*), enjoys the city's greatest concentration of cast-iron architecture and one of its denser concentrations of shopping opportunities, with stores ranging from high-end boutiques to sidewalk carts. Some of the side streets, particularly those in the southern end of the district, still have Belgian block paving, granite sidewalks, and iron loading platforms. Broadway swarms with tourists, especially on weekends; West Broadway is less frenzied. Greene St has the best cast-iron architecture.

HISTORY OF SoHo

Like most of Manhattan, what is now SoHo was farmland until the end of the 18th century. After the Revolution its large holdings were subdivided and the area developed as a quiet residential suburb. By 1825 it had become the most densely populated part of New York. By 1840 it had become fashionable, and in the 1850s expensive hotels and retail stores of sterling reputation lined Broadway while the side streets began sporting brothels, dance halls, and casinos, some of them glamorous. As the carriage trade moved on uptown, industry filled the vacuum. Between 1860 and 1890, most of the cast-iron architecture so admired today was constructed as factories or warehouses, often with shop fronts on the ground floor. Appealing as they seem now with their Corinthian columns, Palladian windows, or French Second Empire dormers, many functioned as sweatshops where immigrants, mostly European, endured twelve or more hours a day of tedious labor. The little that remains of the Italian population in SoHo is descended from those immigrants.

Although immigration quotas after World War I stanched the flow of abundant, uneducated, and hence acquiescent labor, SoHo remained industrial until the middle of the 20th century. Gradually the cast-iron buildings became outmoded, and SoHo's paper-box companies, tool and dye factories, and wool remnant companies moved elsewhere. In 1959 the City Club of New York published an influential report labeling the area—then known as Hell's Hundred Acres (because of its frequent fires) or The Valley (a lowland between the architectural highs of the Financial District and Midtown)—an industrial slum with no architecture of note.

In the early 1960s artists attracted by those same empty buildings began moving in, illegally converting manufacturing lofts to apartments. By the late 1960s SoHo was an artist's Eden. Rents were cheap, space was plentiful, and society was made up mostly of other artists. By 1970 SoHo had become a boomtown for real estate dealers, art dealers (some headed downtown from the Upper East Side), and artists who, if not becoming rich, were at least forming a coherent artistic community. Film, video, and "performance" art—the avant-garde media of the 1960s—became staple commodities of SoHo artistic life. Experimental dance and drama flourished. Cooperative galleries opened.

Today the SoHo of artistic legend is a victim of its own success. As the galleries brought in a moneyed clientele, rents soared. Artists, except for the most successful, moved elsewhere—to Brooklyn or the far edges of the Lower East Side. Gradually the galleries began their own exodus to Chelsea, to Brooklyn, and other locations throughout the boroughs.

BROADWAY: WEST HOUSTON TO BROOME

Broadway south of Houston St has become a shopping strip with a string of brand-name and upscale clothing stores. **Prada** (*575 Broadway at the corner of Prince St; map p. 619, D4*) occupies a Ruskinian brick and stone building (1882; Thomas Stent) built for a men's clothier. A century later, redesigned by Arata Isozaki (1992), the now-defunct SoHo branch of the Guggenheim moved in. Redesigned again by Rem Koolhaas in 2001, it has become a shrine of Italian fashion.

On the ground level of 560 Broadway, at Prince St, in another masonry building by Thomas Stent (1883), **Dean & DeLuca** sells luxury foods. The company arrived in SoHo in 1977, moved to its present location in 1988, and now, with branches nationwide, is headquartered in Kansas. The building was once a vertical shopping mall for art.

The **Singer Building**, also known as the "Little Singer Building" (1904; Ernest Flagg; restored 2008; Bone/Levine Architects), at 561-3 Broadway, is a twelve-story steel-framed, L-shaped building designed by the architect of the former Singer Tower downtown. The façade draws admiration for its terra cotta panels, curls of dark green wrought iron, large expanses of plate glass, and great arch rising beneath the cornice. The building wraps around the corner of Prince St, enveloping 565 Broadway next door (1859; John Kellum), whose carved marble Corinthian columns evoke the days when Ball, Black & Company purveyed jewelry to society.

Next door at 557 Broadway is the **Scholastic Building** (2000), the final work of Italian architect Aldo Rossi, who died in 1997 before construction began. It sits between the Singer Building and the Rouss Building, echoing the red terra cotta and green-painted cast iron of the former and the classical columns of the latter. A more severely industrial façade faces Mercer St.

Charles "Broadway" Rouss, whose name is emblazoned on the façade of the eponymous building at **555 Broadway** (1889; Alfred Zucker), came debt-ridden to New York
from Virginia and so flourished that he took the street's name as his own. He got his
start reselling "stale" goods—merchandise unsalable at full price—and with his profits
built this department store, which sold jewelry, Japanese goods, and carpets to the gentry.

In 2013, artist **Donald Judd's former home and studio**, a cast-iron warehouse at
101 Spring St (Mercer St), opened for guided visits (*by appointment, Tues, Thur, Fri,
and Sat; T: 866 811 4111, juddfoundation.org*). Judd moved to SoHo in 1968, the year
Paula Cooper opened the area's first major gallery. He bought this building (1870;
Nicholas Whyte) for $68,000, stripping it down to its architectural bones (jettisoning
such clutter as fire prevention systems), and turning it into an exhibition space for
himself and artists he admired. It is SoHo's only intact, single-use cast-iron building
and New York's third artist's residence preserved as a house-museum (after the Alice
Austen House in Staten Island and the Chaim Gross Museum in Greenwich Village).
Its 40 large windows make the façade remarkable (in SoHo) for the high proportion of
glass to metal. The building, a "permanent installation" in Judd's language, illustrates
his artistic principle that the placement of a work of art is critical to its understanding.
On view are Judd's paintings, sculpture, and furniture, as well as work by John
Chamberlain, Marcel Duchamp, Dan Flavin, Claes Oldenburg, Ad Reinhardt, and
Frank Stella. The auction of some of Judd's sculptures partly financed the remarkable
restoration (2013; Adam Yarinsky of Architecture Research Office).

Bloomingdale's SoHo (*504 Broadway near Broome St*), in a remodeled masonry
building with a cast-iron front (1860; John Kellum), opened in 2004 replacing the
iconic Canal Jeans, which sold vintage clothes, military wear, feather boas, and, of
course, jeans. Bloomies' arrival confirmed SoHo's gentrification.

THE HAUGHWOUT BUILDING

In the supremely elegant Haughwout Building (1857; John P. Gaynor) at 488–92
Broadway (*map p. 620, C1*), Eder V. Haughwout sold china, glassware, chandeliers, and
silver from a ground-floor showroom. In 1861 Mary Todd Lincoln shopped here for the
official White House china: a 190-piece Haviland dining service banded in hand-painted
solferino (reddish purple) with a gold rope border and an American eagle stretching its
wings in the center of each piece.

Designed in the then-popular Italianate palazzo style and perhaps modeled on
Sansovino's Libreria Marciana in Venice, the Haughwout Building is sometimes inap-
propriately called the Parthenon of Cast-Iron Architecture. It was one of the first New
York buildings whose floor loads were carried by a cast-iron skeleton instead of
masonry walls and the very first to feature a passenger elevator with a safety device, a
steam-driven, cable-and-drum contraption invented by Elisha Otis. The economy of
casting many forms from the same mold fostered the repetition of detail on cast-iron
buildings such as this one, whose basic motif—a round-arch window between slender
Corinthian colonnettes flanked by larger Corinthian columns—is repeated 92 times in
four tiers on two façades, creating the frequently invoked harmony of the building.

WEST BROADWAY & WOOSTER STREETS

SoHo's widest street, West Broadway (*map pp. 620, C1 and 619, D4*), like East Broadway, got its name from its intended function: relieving Broadway's congested traffic. The brick Romanesque Revival building near Houston St, at 468 West Broadway (1885–6; Oscar S. Teale), its round two-story arches decorated with the cast-iron floral swags, recapitulates SoHo's evolution. Originally a manufacturing loft, its tenants through the years produced safes, canes, umbrellas, and corrugated paper boxes. In the 1970s and '80s, it housed an art gallery and a cabaret; in the 1990s a clothing boutique leased ground floor space; today the upper floors are luxury condos.

THE *NEW YORK EARTH ROOM* AND *THE BROKEN KILOMETER*

Upstairs at 141 Wooster St, near Prince St, is the *New York Earth Room* (1977), one of two long-term SoHo projects of the Dia Art Foundation and an example of "Earth" or "Land" Art by sculptor Walter De Maria (*open mid-Sept–June, Wed–Sun 12–6; closed 3–3:30; ring bell to left of door for entry; free; T: 212 989 5566, diaart.org*). Inside the starkly white gallery, 280,000 lbs of dark damp soil are piled to a depth of 22 inches. Like some of De Maria's other works, the Earth Room explores the relationship between the natural world and the constructs of civilization. (It exudes a pleasant earthy smell.) Upkeep involves weekly watering and a drying out period during the summer months when the exhibition is closed.

The block between Spring and Prince Sts on West Broadway was once the hotspot of the gallery scene. The legendary Leo Castelli opened his gallery at 420 West Broadway in 1971. Castelli (1907–99), long acknowledged as the dean of the Pop Art movement, made his name representing Jasper Johns, Robert Rauschenberg, Roy Lichtenstein, and Andy Warhol.

Walter De Maria's second SoHo installation, **The Broken Kilometer** at 393 West Broadway between Spring and Broome Sts (*open mid-Sept–mid June, Wed–Sun 12–6; closed 3–3:30; free; T: 212 989 5566 or 212 925 9397*), has been on view since 1979. Mathematical and precise, its 500 polished, two-meter brass rods rest on the floor in five parallel rows of 100 rods apiece, each row 5mm further apart than the previous one.

THE DRAWING CENTER

35 Wooster St (Grand St). Subway: A, C, E, R to Canal St. Bus: M5. Open Wed and Fri–Sun 12–6, Thur 12–8. Admission charge, but free Thur 6–8. Bookstore. T: 212 219 2166, drawingcenter.org.

Founded in a warehouse in 1977 by Martha Beck, a former curator of drawing at the Museum of Modern Art, the center has attracted attention for mounting major shows on modest budgets. It has been a showcase for emerging artists and an unlikely venue for drawings by world-famous figures: Michelangelo, Donatello, Palladio, Christopher Wren, and Antonio Gaudí.

Most cast-iron façades sheathe conventionally structured interiors with brick load-bearing walls, wooden beams, and joists supporting wooden floors. This one (1866;

Samuel Curtiss Jr.) and a few others has a system of slender cast-iron columns supporting the floors, an arrangement that permits a very open interior, desirable for showing art.

SOHO'S CAST-IRON ARCHITECTURE

Cast-iron architecture, developed during the later decades of the 19th century, served as an alternative to masonry during a period when cast iron was inexpensive and steel was not yet readily available. SoHo's commercial buildings with their elegant, prefabricated cast-iron façades, once a source of personal and civic pride, later suffered the ravages of neglect—disfigured by ugly ground-floor modernizations or dulled by layers of paint. In 1973 the SoHo Cast-Iron Historic District was created to protect a 26-block tract—bounded by West Broadway, Houston, Crosby, and Canal Sts—with the largest concentration of cast-iron architecture in the world; the historic district was widened in 2010 to include the west side of West Broadway and the blocks east of Crosby St.

Early cast-iron architecture, adorned with the familiar quoins, columns, and consoles of the Classical tradition and painted tan, buff, or cream, imitated marble or limestone. Sometimes the iron plates were even grooved to resemble blocks of stone mortared together. Eventually iron-founders, many of whom had previously dealt in stoves, safes, and lawn furniture, began offering catalogues of ornaments from which the client could select, combining the elements in simple or lavish compositions. As long as patterns could be carved and molds made, elaborate ornaments could be cheaply reproduced, allowing businessmen who could not afford stonecutting to enjoy the prestige of fluted Corinthian columns or floral swags bolted onto their buildings and painted to look like stone. While the earliest cast-iron buildings hark back stylistically to Italy, later examples were based on French Renaissance, Second Empire, or Neo-Grec styles.

In one sense cast-iron architecture was standardized: the ornaments were machine-made, mass-produced, and as interchangeable as parts of a Winchester rifle, allowing the architect scope and originality, as the general exuberance of these SoHo buildings demonstrates. The elements of a façade were separately cast, the smaller pieces bolted together at the factory, and the whole façade laid out with pieces numbered and tested for fit. It was all then shipped to the construction site where the front was assembled and permanently bolted into place.

GREENE STREET

Greene Street (*map p. 619, D4*) is named after Nathanael Greene, the Revolutionary War general. At its northern end, near Houston St, it offers fine examples of cast-iron architecture. The brick Federal house (c. 1824) at **139 Greene Street**, its original dormers and lintels more or less intact, is one of the few buildings remaining from SoHo's early period of residential development. The house has been in an arrested state of renovation for decades. The elaborate building at **121–3 Greene St** (1883; Henry Fernbach), with its fluted pilasters, Corinthian columns, and ornate cornice, all painted a smooth cream color, is a fine example of this prolific architect's work. The sidewalks are monolithic granite slabs, some with their edges rounded to form curbing.

At the southwest corner of Greene and Prince Sts, no. **112–14 Greene St** has a faded and peeling *trompe l'œil* mural (1975) by Richard Haas. On the brick eastern wall of the building (1889; Richard Berger), the mural wittily reproduces the cast-iron detail of the northern façade. The cast iron in turn suggests masonry construction with its banded corner pilasters resembling masonry blocks and protruding cornices ending in decorative blocks supported by consoles. Thus the painted mural imitates cast iron imitating masonry.

On the sidewalk near 110 Greene St is Belgian artist Françoise Schein's steel subway map embedded in the pavement; created in 1986, its proper name is *Subway Map Floating on a New York Sidewalk*. The work combines the artist's interests in human rights and cartography since, according to her website, the subway "appeared to be the most democratic place [to] engrave philosophical concepts to address to the people."

AROUND SPRING AND BROOME STREETS

Spring Street (*map pp. 620, B1–621, D1*) takes its name from a spring tapped by Aaron Burr's Manhattan Water Company, whose ostensible purpose was to supply drinking water to the city but which quickly evolved into a banking company instead. A former well at Broadway and Spring St became the grave of one Juliana (or Gulielma) Elmore Sands, whose body minus shoes, hat, and shawl was found floating there on Jan 2, 1800. In a sensational murder case, her fiancé was acquitted of the crime (Aaron Burr and Alexander Hamilton were on the defense team). Another version of the legend locates the well beneath 129 Spring St, today a clothing store.

The building at **72–76 Greene St** (1872; J.F. Duckworth), with a monogram cast on the central pilaster between the doorways, was once a warehouse of the Gardner Colby Co. Most of the other buildings on this block between Spring and Broome Sts were designed by Henry Fernbach and John B. Snook in the early 1870s and used by firms dealing in rug clippings, wool rags, and fabric remnants, though **66 Greene St** (1873; John B. Snook) began as a store for the Lorillard tobacco company.

THE QUEEN OF GREENE STREET

The vista along the block between Grand and Canal Sts reveals the city's longest continuous row of cast-iron architecture, built between 1872 and 1896 when SoHo was rapidly industrializing. Known as the "Queen of Greene Street," **no. 28–30**—an ornate Second Empire building (1872; J.F. Duckworth) crowned with a stupendous mansard roof—is the *pièce de résistance* of the block. It offers a wealth of architectural ornament: tall broad windows flanked by half-round columns; keystoned segmental arches; a central two-window bay rising the full height of the building to a broken pediment; and elaborate dormers with balustrades, modillions, pediments, and finials.

During the 1850s, when nearby Broadway sparkled with theaters, hotels, and casinos, Greene and Mercer Sts were notorious for their brothels. Whereas the houses on the southern end of the streets near Canal St catered to sailors from ships docked in the Hudson, the houses further north appealed to a wealthier clientele. An 1859 *Directory to the Seraglios* in New York, written by an anonymous "Free Loveyer," recommends a Miss Clara Gordon at 119 Mercer St, "beautiful, entertaining and supremely seductive," patronized by Southern merchants and planters, and a Mrs. Bailey of 76 Greene St, whose comfortable and quiet "resort" is within a few moments' walk of Broadway and the principal hotels.

CANAL STREET

NB: For the section of Canal St in Chinatown, see p. 117.

Canal Street (*map p. 620, B1*) runs river to river connecting the Holland Tunnel with the Manhattan Bridge. Cars and trucks jam the roadway, their drivers often leaning on their horns. Pedestrians clog the sidewalks, their progress impeded by vendors, merchandise spilling from open storefronts, and in the sheer volume of foot traffic. Awnings, billboards, placards, and other signs posted on almost every available flat surface make the street visually chaotic. Canal St's western end meets northern Tribeca; its mid-section borders SoHo; further east it separates Chinatown to the south from what is left of Little Italy to the north, with the sidewalk scene changing appropriately.

Canal Street owes both its name and its width to a canal proposed by the city fathers in 1805 to serve as a storm drain, a household sewer, and a conduit siphoning off the waters of the Collect Pond near present Foley Square (*see p. 95*). By the 1820s both street and canal had been paved over: a mixed blessing, for while the covered sewer alleviated the mosquito problem, the stench it created depressed both property values and morale until adequate air traps were installed.

AROUND MERCER STREET

On the northeast corner of Canal and Mercer Sts stands the **former Marble House** (1856–65; Griffith Thomas; restored 2011), 307–11 Canal St, originally the Arnold Constable Dry Goods Store. During the 1850s and 1860s the neighborhood boasted other fine stores, including Lord & Taylor, then located a block north at Broadway and Grand St, ultimately the victor in its perennial rivalry with Arnold Constable.

Mercer Street, still paved with its 19th-century Belgian blocks, is named after Hugh Mercer, a surgeon and brigadier general in the Revolutionary War. **No. 11 Mercer St** (1870) retains its vault cover, also known as an illuminated sidewalk or light platform. The glass discs embedded in the iron stoop permit sunlight to reach the storage vault below, a system for which Thaddeus Hyatt, an abolitionist as well as an inventor, received patents in 1845 and 1858, but which had been previously used to illuminate below-deck areas in ships, where fire would be hazardous.

EATING AND DRINKING IN SoHo

When SoHo's galleries began drawing viewers, restaurants followed. Now most of the galleries are gone but the crowds are still here and so are some of the restaurants—surprising, perhaps, in a city where restaurants can be as fleeting as the clouds.

$$$ Aquagrill. ■ This favorite seafood place has appealed both to the eye and the taste buds for decades. Go for the oysters, cod, salmon, or those more exotic creatures of the sea: whelks, periwinkles, and sea urchins. Soups, chowders, and bouillabaisse. Also a few specialties from dry land. Award-winning wine list. Lunch and dinner daily. *210 Spring St (Sixth Ave). T: 212 274 0505, aquagrill.com. Map p. 620, B1.*

$$$ Balthazar. This SoHo legend draws downtown crowds to its classic bistro food with American touches. *Plats du jour* include rabbit, sole, and (seasonally) a soft-shell crab sandwich. The towering *plateaux de fruits de mer* are part of the legend. Reservations strongly recommended but you can join the bar crowd without them. Be warned, the noise level is high. **Balthazar Bakery** next-door has fine breakfast items, even a tasty concoction called green juice, surely packed with vitamins. Breakfast, lunch and dinner daily. *80 Spring St (Broadway and Crosby St). T: 212 965 1414, balthazarny.com. Map p. 620, C1.*

$$$ Blue Ribbon Sushi. ■ One of New York's first sushi bars, opened when the cuisine was a novelty but after almost 25 years still on everyone's short list. Dark and dim, with a long walnut sushi bar as well as tables. Long menu, with maki rolls, sushi and sashimi, vegetarian dishes, and fresh fish flown in from both oceans and the Sea of Japan. Open daily for lunch, dinner, and until late. *119 Sullivan St (Prince and Spring Sts). T: 212 343 0404, blueribbonrestaurants.com. Map p. 620, B1.*

$$$ David Burke Kitchen. One of star chef David Burke's several New York restaurants, stylishly located in the boutique James Hotel. Downstairs is a New American style restaurant with farm-to-table food, including cauliflower steak, prawn pappardelle, and heritage pork. Upstairs the Treehouse bar serves up good drinks and great views. Breakfast weekdays, brunch weekends, lunch and dinner daily, late night menu. *23 Grand St (Sixth Ave). T: 212 201 9119, davidburkekitchen.com. Map p. 620, B1.*

$$$ Lure Fishbar. Downstairs in the heart of SoHo, with porthole windows that suggest cruise-ship decor. Sushi counter and raw bar. Dishes include lobster ravioli, branzino with roasted fennel, even fish and chips. For landlubbers there are burgers and steak. Lunch and dinner daily. *142 Mercer St (Prince St). T: 212 431 7676, lurefishbar.com. Map p. 619, D4.*

$$$ Raoul's. The founders arrived in

the 1970s along with the gallery hoppers, recreating here the bistro food of their native Alsace. Favorites include skate, cod, organic free-range chicken, and that all-time bistro standard steak frites. A guidebook from the '70s calls it *cuisine française* with flair. It still is. Comfortable, cozy atmosphere draws crowds. Dinner nightly. *180 Prince St (Sullivan and Thompson Sts). T: 212 966 3518, raouls.com. Map p. 618, C4.*

$$ Blue Ribbon Brasserie. Flagship of a far-flung restaurant empire that includes a bakery, several sushi bars, and outposts in Las Vegas and London (Brooklyn Bowl), this American bistro serves simple, straightforward food late into the night. Soups, salads, and such bistro favorites as roast chicken and strip steak. You can even get matzo ball soup for real comfort. Open daily for lunch, dinner, and until 4am. *97 Sullivan St (Prince and Spring Sts). T: 212 343 0404, blueribbonrestaurants.com. Map p. 618, C4.*

$$ Ciccio. Simple Tuscan food by Florentine chef at fair prices. Soups, salads, *schiacciati* (sandwiches similar to panini), handmade pasta, and meatballs from a family recipe. Informal and pretty restaurant. Lunch Mon–Fri, dinner Tues–Sun. *190 Sixth Ave (Prince and Vandam Sts). T: 646 476 9498, ciccionyc.com. Map p. 620, B1.*

$$ L'École. The kitchen is run by students of the International Culinary Center, hence the name. Pleasant, cheerful room, with early and late dinner. Dishes range from the École burger with cheese, barbecue sauce and béarnaise, to horseradish crusted trout. Good value from well-taught students. Lunch Mon–Fri, brunch Sat, dinner Mon–Sat. *462 Broadway (Grand St). T: 212 219 3300, lecolenyc. com. Map p. 620, C1.*

$$ Snack. Small, authentic Greek café on a pleasant street. Contemporary twist on classic food, for snacks and more. Meze include *spanakopita* and *taramasalata*; for a sandwich try the braised lamb or the vegetarian *souvlaki* on pitta; dinner favorites include a vegetarian *moussaka*. Greek wines and desserts. Lunch and dinner seven days. *105 Thompson St (Prince St). T: 212 925 1040, snacksoho.com. Map p. 618, C4.*

Chinatown, Little Italy, & Nolita

Authentic ethnic and stylishly updated restaurants plus a burgeoning art scene around the Bowery draw crowds to these historic immigrant neighborhoods.

While many of Manhattan's ethnic enclaves are shrinking, Chinatown is expanding, eastward into the Lower East Side and northward into Little Italy, but the traditional core of the neighborhood around Mott and Mulberry Sts, south of Canal St, still surges with energy. Pedestrians elbow one another on the narrow sidewalks; merchandise crowds the display windows; signs in English and Chinese on virtually every storefront clamor for attention. Visitors come for the ambiance, for bargains, and for food.

Map p. 621, D2. Subway: 6, J, N, Q, R, Z to Canal St. Bus: M15, M103. The Museum of China in America (see overleaf) offers walking tours April–Dec on Sat at 1pm; reservations required; tickets at mocanyc.org or T: 212 619 4785. The Chinatown Information Center at Canal and Baxter Sts has maps and event info; open daily 10–6, holidays 10–3; explorechinatown.com.

HISTORY OF CHINATOWN

For the first two centuries of its existence, Chinatown grew slowly. Although the China trade brought sailors and merchants from the Far East in the late 18th century, only about 150 Chinese had established residence a century later, and only after the completion of the transcontinental railroad in 1869 did the population grow significantly. In the later 1870s peasant laborers imported to build the railroad found themselves without work, and increasing racial hostilities in the West drove many eastward.

National exclusionary laws and minuscule immigration quotas kept Chinatown's population small relative to other immigrant groups. Other regulations prevented the naturalization of Chinese already in this country and barred wives and families from entering, so that Chinatown long remained a "bachelor" society. Most of the immigrants during this period arrived from Guangdong (Canton) province in southeast China and settled in "old" Chinatown, maintaining their languages (Cantonese and

Taihanese) and cultural traditions, which included the Confucian ideals of filial piety and loyalty. English was not needed for the kind of jobs available—rolling cigars or working in laundries, restaurant kitchens, and garment factories—all low paying and labor intensive. Hand laundries are now obsolete, but the pillars of the Chinatown economy remain the restaurant and garment industries (though the latter is under pressure by imports from China). After World War II, the War Brides Act (1945) and the G.I. Fiancées Act (1946) helped improve the ratio of women to men.

When the quotas, set in 1943 at 105 Chinese per year, were lifted in 1965, a new surge of immigrants changed the political, geographical, and cultural makeup of New York's Chinatown; by 1980 it was the largest in the US. Arrivals from Hong Kong, Taiwan, and mainland China led to new Chinatowns in Queens, Brooklyn, and more recently East Harlem—all connected by subway to the "old" Chinatown hub.

Many of the newer immigrants in the early 1990s were rural Fujianese, and many arrived illegally. The 1993 fiasco of the *Golden Venture*, a ship carrying illegal immigrants that ran aground off Queens, revealed the scope of the problem and the plight of these often impoverished and poorly educated arrivals. The presence of the new immigrants, whose loyalties are to mainland China and whose language (one of the many dialects of Fujianese) is not understood by earlier settlers, has impacted Chinatown politics, long dominated by speakers of Cantonese. Around Mott St people, especially older immigrants, speak Cantonese and Taishanese, but Mandarin, the official language of China, is becoming dominant except along East Broadway, where Fujianese reigns. In recent years Chinatown has become ethnically more diverse, with arrivals from Burma, Bangladesh, the Philippines, and Malaysia.

Much of Chinatown remains plagued by poverty, overcrowding, and physical deterioration; its housing and commercial spaces are largely substandard. Chinatown supports an underground economy that includes sweatshop labor (in restaurants and garment factories), counterfeiting (of trademarked luxury items), and the smuggling of illegal immigrants. There are also intercity bus lines based in Chinatown that offer very low fares to Boston and other East Coast cities, as well as nearby casinos, but several have come under regulatory scrutiny (or been closed down) for safety issues.

THE MUSEUM OF CHINESE IN AMERICA (MoCA)

Map p. 620, C1. 211–15 Centre St (Grand and Howard Sts). Subway: N, R, Q, J, Z, and 6 to Canal St. Bus: M9, M15, M103. Open Tues–Sun 11–6, Thur 11–9. Closed Mon, New Year's Day, Thanksgiving, and Christmas. Admission charge but free on first Thur of month. Gift shop. T: 212 619 4785, mocanyc.org.

Located in a former machine shop redesigned (2009) by Maya Lin, the museum began (1980) as the Chinatown History Project, founded to preserve the memories of first-generation immigrants. The building centers around a brick-walled atrium, suggesting a traditional Chinese courtyard house. The core exhibit explores the arrival of Chinese in America, the Exclusion Acts and discrimination, and assimilation. On view are images of Chinese stereotypes, a recreation of a Chinese general store—truly general in that it also served as a pharmacy, travel agency, community center, and post office–an eight-pound iron, symbolic of a mainstay of the Chinese-American economy, a tiny shoe for a bound foot, and an exhibit on the history of "Chinese" food in America.

CANAL STREET

East of Broadway, Canal St (*map pp. 620, C1–621, D1*) is vividly Chinese. At the intersection of Canal and Centre Sts, the **former Golden Pacific National Bank** (1983), with its bright colors and sweeping tile roofs, was once the pride of Chinatown. The bank collapsed in 1985 and two of its high-ranking officers were convicted of fraud.

83–85 Mott Street (*corner of Canal St*) is an architectural mélange of East and West, housing the Chinese Merchants' Association and the headquarters of the On Leong Tong, a bakery and beauty parlor.

The eastern end of Canal St near the Bowery is the city's second largest jewelry district and still glitters with shops offering gold and diamonds. In the 1930s Jewish immigrants fleeing Nazi Germany opened stores here on the fringes of the Lower East Side, but after World War II many jewelers moved up to Midtown around West 47th St and many of the downtown merchants now are Asian. The imposing domed building at **58 Bowery** (*corner of Canal St*), now a branch of HSBC (Hong Kong and Shanghai Banking Corporation), was built in 1924 as the Citizen's Savings Bank.

The **Mahayana Buddhist Temple**, at 133 Canal St (*Manhattan Bridge Plaza*), is the largest Buddhist temple in Chinatown, with an imposing golden image of the Buddha.

THE TONGS OF CHINATOWN

Chinatown's tongs—neighborhood and business associations—were formed at the turn of the 20th century as immigrant aid societies. They offered legitimate services—language help, credit unions, loans, social outlets—and they mediated disputes among individuals and between rival groups of immigrants. The two strongest were Hip Sing and On Leong, which came to control many businesses and also became involved in crime, prostitution, gambling, and drugs. On Leong was said to control Mott St, while the Hip Sings' turf was Pell St. Until the 1970s the tongs and the gangs they controlled were unchallenged in Chinatown, but as the demographics changed, they lost power.

THE MANHATTAN BRIDGE

The Manhattan Bridge (1909; Leon S. Moisseiff; *map. p. 621, E2*), the third East River crossing, is notable for its ceremonial approach, arch, and colonnade (1912; Carrère & Hastings). Feelings ran high over the bridge even when on the drawing boards, for

MANHATTAN BRIDGE
A view of the bridge framing the Empire State Building.

though the Brooklyn Bridge (1883) was received enthusiastically, the Williamsburg Bridge (1903) was considered ugly. The disputing parties were engineers (technical), architects (aesthetic), and city officials (financial and political). Plans for the Manhattan Bridge thus went through several modifications.

An early plan was scrapped around 1901 and the bridge was redesigned by Gustav Lindenthal, NYC bridge commissioner at the time, and architect Henry Hornbostel, whose belief in "artistic" engineering resulted in a proposal that used eye-bars instead of wire cables to support the roadway. In 1904 Tammany-controlled mayor George W. McClellan Jr. came to power, scrapped the Lindenthal-Hornbostel plan, and appropriated money for a third design, this one by Leon Moisseiff. Over the long run the Moisseiff design, with its cable-borne roadway, has required repeated major repairs, unable to support the load it presently carries.

The World's Columbian Exposition in Chicago (1893), awakening public interest in Neoclassical architecture, gave birth to the City Beautiful movement and from these enthusiasms sprang plans for improving the approaches to the bridge. Carrère & Hastings, who had studied at the École des Beaux-Arts in Paris, the cradle of the Neoclassical movement, were well qualified for the undertaking.

The bridge's approach ends in a **monumental arch and colonnade**, the former modeled after the 17th-century Porte St-Denis in Paris, the latter after Bernini's colonnade at St. Peter's Square in Rome. The frieze over the arch opening by Charles Cary Rumsey is said to have been inspired by the Panathenaic procession on the Parthenon frieze. This Americanized version depicts four Native Americans on horseback hunting buffalo—a peculiar subject on a classical arch approaching a modern suspension bridge, perhaps; but such frontier themes were popular at the turn of the 20th century.

Two large **granite sculptural groups** by Carl Augustus Heber flank the arch opening: the *Spirit of Commerce* on the north side and the *Spirit of Industries* on the south. Above the arch opening (36ft by 40ft) is a cornice and a low attic story decorated with lions' heads. The interior of the arch is barrel-vaulted and coffered. The arch is set in the middle of a colonnade of Tuscan columns (31ft high) above which are cornices with balustrades that connect the columns to one another and to the arch.

MOTT & MULBERRY STREETS

Mott, Pell, and Doyers Streets form the center of "old" Chinatown. Mott St is named after Joseph Mott, a prosperous pre-Revolutionary butcher, who also ran a tavern at what is now 143rd St and Eighth Ave. The storefront **Eastern States Buddhist Temple** at 64 Mott St (*open daily 8–6; T: 212 966 6229*) was the first Chinese Buddhist temple on the eastern seaboard, founded in 1962. The **Community Center** at 62 Mott St is run by the Chinese Consolidated Benevolent Association, formed in 1883 by established merchants to help newly arrived countrymen survive in business and in America. It provided language aid, loans, and social contact for the early immigrants, mediated disputes, and served as a link between the Chinese and American communities.

At **32 Mott St** is Chinatown's oldest continuously operating store. Founded as Quong Yuen Shing around 1899, it originally sold herbs, groceries, and general merchandise; provided a safe where Chinese could store their valuables; and served as a mail drop. The store failed in 2003, victim of the economic downturn after 9/11, but reopened as Good Fortune Gifts a year later. Chinatown's economy was hard hit by the attacks, losing both tourists and World Trade Center workers. Because trucks could not make deliveries through the debris-clogged streets, many of the garment factories shut down for weeks. Today the shop sells items ranging from action figures of Dracula and sports stars to imitation jade Buddhas and Good Fortune coin banks.

CHURCH OF THE TRANSFIGURATION

Before Chinatown was Chinese, the Church of the Transfiguration (1801) at 29 Mott St (*at Mosco St; map p. 621, D2*) was built for a German-speaking Lutheran congregation. Nine years later, for reasons doctrinal, linguistic, and financial the congregation voted to become Episcopalian, renaming itself the Zion Episcopal Church. Then, in 1853, as neighborhood demographics changed and Protestant families decamped for uptown, the church was sold to the Roman Catholic archdiocese, becoming the Church of the Transfiguration. Father Felix Varela, who had founded the parish in 1827 after being exiled from his native Cuba for advocating Cuban independence from Spain, served a congregation of Irish and Italian immigrants. Today Masses are celebrated in Cantonese, Mandarin, and English. Transfiguration School, open to all faiths, serves local children, many of them Buddhist. The modest rubblestone building belongs to the Georgian tradition with its triangular pediment, simple tower, and unusual pointed-arch windows. The copper-clad spire was added in 1868.

COLUMBUS PARK

Chinatown's communal back yard, **Columbus Park** (opened 1897; *facing Mulberry St between Bayard and Worth Sts; map p. 620, C2*) owes its existence to the early reformers who spurred passage of the Small Parks Act in 1887. It replaced Mulberry Bend, a violent slum that reformer Jacob Riis called "the worst pigsty of all." Today people practice tai ch'i, play cards or Chinese chess, or simply rest. Elderly women gossip on plastic stools; children swing on the playground equipment; young men play basketball. Sometimes musicians with Asian instruments serenade passers-by. The grim bulk of "The Tombs" (*see p. 96*) looks down on the park and the statue of Dr. Sun Yat-sen (2011; Lu Chun-Hsiung), considered the father of modern China and chief engineer of the demise of the Qing Dynasty; he lived briefly on Mott St during periods of exile.

Chinatown Ice Cream Factory sells homemade ice cream in flavors ranging from prosaic vanilla to exotic red bean and green tea. (*65 Bayard St at Mott and Elizabeth Sts; cash only; open daily 11am–10/11pm; T: 212 608 4170, chinatownicecreamfactory.com*).

DOYERS STREET & CHATHAM SQUARE

Crooked, narrow Doyers St (*map p. 621, D2*) was originally a cart lane leading to Anthony Doyer's distillery. The bend in the street was once known as "Bloody Angle," recalling turn-of-the-20th-century tong wars between the Hip Sings and On Leongs. On the site of the present Post Office at **6 Doyers St** Irving Berlin, born Israel Baline, waited tables at the Chatham Club. Across the street at 5–7 Doyers St stood the original Chinese Opera House, acquired (1910) for a mission run by Tom Noonan, an ex-convict who dispensed charity to the Bowery bums until his death in 1935. So many barber shops line Pell and Doyers Sts that Pell has been nicknamed "Haircut Street."

The **former Edward Mooney house** at 18 Bowery (*Pell St*) is the city's oldest row house (c. 1785). Mooney, a butcher and amateur racehorse breeder, built it on land forfeited after the Revolution by Tory James De Lancey. It is thoroughly Georgian, with splayed keystones on the lintels and quarter-round and round-headed windows facing Pell St. The many windows reveal Mooney's wealth: glass, produced in the middle colonies only after c. 1740, was an expensive commodity. In the 19th century the building became a brothel; more recently it has housed a betting parlor and a mortgage lender.

Facing Chatham Square at Division St and the Bowery is Taiwanese sculptor Liu Shih's bronze **statue of Confucius**, presented c. 1977. It stands near Confucius Plaza (1976), the only new housing built in Chinatown between the 1960s and early 1980s. Division St marked the border between the farms of James De Lancey and Henry Rutgers in pre-Revolutionary New York.

CHATHAM SQUARE

Bounded by a tangle of intersecting streets, Chatham Square (*map p. 621, D2*) used to be the eastern edge of Chinatown. Before the Revolution it was named for William Pitt, Earl of Chatham and prime minister of Great Britain; because Pitt supported the colonies, the name remained after the British departed. The **Kim Lau War Memorial** (1962; Poy G. Lee), an arch with a pagoda-style top on one of the traffic islands, honors Chinese-Americans who died in the US armed services during World War II and is named for Lt. Benjamin Kim Lau (1918–44), a bomber pilot shot down over New Guinea.

In the area south and east of Chatham Square several landmarks predate Chinese immigration. The **Mariners' Temple** (1844–5; *12 Oliver St, corner of Henry St*) was built as the second house of worship for the Oliver Street Baptist Church (established 1795). The Mariners' Temple bought it in 1863 for a house of worship and a social mission for Swedish seamen who worked on the nearby docks, immigrants, and, later, Bowery derelicts. The building, roughly contemporary with nearby St. James Church, is of stone laid in random courses, plastered (where visible from the street), and grooved with false joints to give it the smooth appearance characteristic of the Greek Revival style. It has been attributed to Isaac Lucas and/or the more famous Minard Lafever.

SHEARITH ISRAEL GRAVEYARD AND ST. JAMES CHURCH
Between Oliver and James Sts, the forlorn **First Shearith Israel Graveyard** (1683) is the earliest known burial ground of the city's first Jewish congregation (*see p. 45*). In 1656 a cemetery was consecrated on land granted by Peter Stuyvesant outside the city, but its location is unknown. Among those buried here is Gershom Mendes Seixas, the first native-born Jewish congregational leader. An ardent patriot and philanthropist, Seixas later became the only Jewish incorporator of Columbia College. As Congregation Shearith Israel migrated uptown, it established two other cemeteries, one at West 11th St and another at West 21st St.

St. James Church (dedicated 1836), a severe brownstone Greek Revival building and one of the city's earliest Roman Catholic churches, served Irish immigrants. Alfred E. Smith, who rose to fame as a social reformer, four-time governor, and first Roman Catholic candidate for US president (1928), was baptized here and received his entire education at the former St. James School across the street.

EAST BROADWAY: "FOUZHOU STREET"
East Broadway, which runs east from Chatham Square, is sometimes called "Fouzhou Street" after the capital of the province of Fujian because many mainland Chinese have settled there, lining the street with Fujianese herbal shops, hair cutters, food markets, dating services, and driving schools. Gazing sternly down East Broadway a **statue of Lin Ze Xu** (1785–1850), a Fujianese government official known for his resistance to the opium trade, is identified on the base of the statue (1997) in English and Chinese as a "Pioneer in the War Against Drugs." Since New York's Fujianese have sometimes been stereotyped as drug dealers, the choice of Lin made an obvious point; his mere presence also suggests the political impact of the newer immigrants, generally sympathetic to mainland China, to whom Lin has come to be seen as a figure of anti-imperialism and national unity. The statue balances the older figure of Confucius, a block away, placed there by Cantonese-speaking, generally pro-Taiwanese earlier immigrants.

LITTLE ITALY

Map pp. 621, D1. Subway: J, N, Q, R, Z, 6 to Canal St. Bus: M1, M103.

Mulberry Street, from around Canal St to Kenmare St, is the spine of Little Italy, an ethnic enclave dating from the 1880s but today squeezed between Chinatown to the south and gentrifying Nolita to the north. Today there is a more truly Italian enclave in the Bronx (*see p. 512*); what's left of Little Italy in Manhattan survives on tourism: cafés; "red sauce" restaurants; red, green, and white banners strung overhead; and shops offering kitschy souvenirs (T-shirts that say "Fugeddaboudit" or "Kiss Me I'm Italian"). Throngs stroll the sidewalks on pleasant weekends and during the feast of San Gennaro (*see p. 571*), when a huge image of the saint is carried through the district and some three million people enjoy street food, music, and arcades of lights.

Da Gennaro's restaurant at 129 Mulberry St, named for the patron saint of Naples (San Gennaro, or St Januarius), occupies the site of the infamous Umberto's Clam House where mobster Joe "Crazy Joey" Gallo was shot down in 1972 while eating *scungilli* (whelks) on his 43rd birthday.

The small **Italian-American Museum** (*155 Mulberry St at Grand St; open Fri–Sun, noon–6; requested donation; T: 212 965 9000, italianamericanmuseum.org*) is dedicated to preserving the culture of this once-teeming neighborhood. Housed in the former Banca Stabile (1882–1932), a family-owned operation that offered banking, travel, and letter-writing services, the museum (chartered 2001; opened 2007) preserves the old bank vault, teller windows, and marble floor. The permanent collection, donated from Italian-American attics and closets, contains four-foot Sicilian puppets, photos, and personal memorabilia, as well as artifacts from the bank—pay stubs, steam ship tickets and telegrams, an adding machine. Changing exhibitions have documented Italian Americans in law enforcement, photos of Sicily, and immigrant volunteers during the American Civil War.

On **Grand Street** some Italian food shops and cafés offer sweets, fresh pasta, cheeses, cured meats, and olive oil. The **Alleva Dairy** (founded 1892) at 188 Grand St advertises itself as the oldest *latticeria* in the US; the **Ferrara Café** (also 1892) at 195 Grand St proclaims itself the city's first espresso bar and oldest *pasticceria*; **Di Palo's Fine Foods** at 200 Grand St, founded (1910) as a dairy store, today purveys all manner of regional Italian specialties.

The grand scale and Baroque flamboyance of the **Police Building Apartments** (1905–9; Hoppin & Koen), at 240 Centre St, set the former police headquarters apart from the surrounding tenements and loft buildings. Impassive stone lions flank the main entrance, which is further embellished by a large New York coat of arms and five statues representing the boroughs, all intended to enhance the image of the police force, which was relatively new and rapidly expanding at the time. The police moved out in 1973; in 1987 the building was converted into luxury condominiums.

LITTLE ITALY
Busts of San Gennaro, patron saint of Naples, whose feast is celebrated in September.

NOLITA

Map p. 620, C1. Subway: 6 to Spring St; N, R to Prince St. Bus: M5, M103, M21.

Nolita (NOrth of LIttle ITAly), bounded roughly by Houston, Broome, and Lafayette Sts, and the Bowery, has gentrified to become a kind of SoHo East. The southern Italian families who lived in its tenements have been replaced by urban professionals, and upscale boutiques and restaurants now line the quiet, tree-lined streets.

The **Storefront for Art and Architecture** (*map p. 620, C1; 97 Kenmare St at Centre St; open Tues–Sat 11–6; free; T: 212 431 5795, storefrontnews.org*) occupies a thin wedge of a building (1993, restored 2008) only five feet wide at its narrowest, designed by architect Steven Holl and artist Vito Acconci with front panels that flip up or down, left or right. Exhibitions are always avant garde and provocative. Among the many well-known artists, architects, and designers who have exhibited here are Jean Nouvel, Diller & Scofidio, Alfredo Jaar, Dan Graham, and Kiki Smith.

The **former Germania Bank Building** at 190 Bowery (Spring St) was built (1898; Robert L. Maynicke) when the neighborhood was known as *Kleindeutschland*. (The name was changed to Commonwealth Bank in 1917, during an era of anti-German sentiment.) More recently it became famous for the graffiti festooning the façade as high as the spray can could reach. Though it appeared abandoned, the 72-room building in fact belonged to a photographer, who bought it in 1966 (for $102,000) and lived and worked here with his family until 2015, when he finally sold it (for many times the purchase price). At the time of writing, 190 Bowery was evolving from bohemian artist's residence into a proposed mix of retail and office space.

THE BOWERY

One of Manhattan's oldest streets, the Bowery (*map p. 621, D1*) runs about one mile from Chatham Square to Cooper Square along the route of an old Indian trail. The name comes from the Dutch word for farm (*bouwerie*). During the 18th century it was part of the Boston Post Road, and in the early 19th century it traversed a fine residential area. Lorenzo da Ponte, Mozart's greatest librettist, briefly ran a grocery here in the early 19th century, a job he disdained because it forced him to deal with those below his social station. By mid-century, the Bowery glittered with theaters, which produced the city's first blackface minstrel show and the first stage version of *Uncle Tom's Cabin*.

After about 1870 as the slums encroached, the Bowery began its long slide into poverty, pocked by beer halls, distilleries, and flophouses, where lodgers slept on the floor, their spaces chalked out by the proprietor. During the Depression the Bowery's shoddy hotels, doorways, and all-night eateries offered the mass unemployed a place to spend the night or wait until times got better. Even after the Depression, in the 1940s and '50s, multiple bars per block offered the solace of alcohol, and until 1968 the Salvation Army operated a mission, doling out food, coffee, and the solace of religion.

Between Grand St and Delancey Sts a wholesale lighting district arose to supply the theaters with gas fixtures; further north, between Delancey and East Houston Sts, a restaurant supply district arrived in the 1930s. Bar stools and used commercial stoves still clutter the sidewalks here and there, and chandeliers glitter in a few showrooms; but higher rents and rising land values are squeezing out the remaining merchants.

THE NEW MUSEUM

Map p. 619, E4. 235 Bowery (Prince St). Subway: N, R to Prince St; 6 to Spring St. Bus: M103 to Prince St; M6 to Prince and Broadway. Open Wed and Fri–Sun 11–6, Thur 11–9. Admission charge; pay what you wish Thur 7–9pm. Sky Room open weekends. Tours Wed and Fri at 12:30, Sat and Sun 12:30 and 3pm. Café. Shop. T: 212 219 1222, newmuseum.org.

At its inception (1977), the New Museum was Manhattan's only institution devoted exclusively to living artists, nurturing the carreers of Jeff Koons, Keith Haring, Bruce Nauman, and Jenny Holzer among others, and bringing to their work the attention and scholarly research that museums usually devoted to artists of the past. Founding director Marcia Tucker, former curator at the Whitney Museum, mounted forward-looking shows that drew critical applause and occasionally incited people to action. Part alternative art space and part traditional museum, it has become a cultural destination and the anchor of the downtown art scene. Still committed to innovation and information, its emphasis is on the presentation of art in its political and social contexts.

The museum opened in cramped quarters on Hudson St, moved to a few rooms in the New School, then to SoHo and, in 2007, to this arresting modern space. Tokyo-based architects Kazuo Sejima and Ryue Nishizawa, relatively unknown in the US at the time, designed the much-admired seven-story building that suggests a teetering stack of shimmering boxes. A startling modern presence on this once dingy street, it is the first art museum ever constructed from the ground up in downtown Manhattan.

NOLITA
The aluminum façade of the New Museum at 235 Bowery.

ON AND AROUND PRINCE STREET

Diagonally across Bowery from the New Museum is the downtown home of the **International Center of Photography** (*see p. 271*). John Gotti (1940–2002), longtime boss of the Gambino crime family, frequented the **former Ravenite Social Club** (*247 Mulberry St*), now a boutique. Known as the Teflon Don and the Dapper Don, he raised thuggery to celebrity status and sometimes posed with tourists in the street. Information caught on FBI wiretaps here was instrumental in sending him to prison.

At 32 Prince St (*Mott St*) stands the **former Roman Catholic Orphan Asylum** (1825–6), an unusually large Federal-style building with brownstone trim, its handsome doorway framed by slender Corinthian columns and a fanlight. It accepted girls only after 1851 but later became St. Patrick's Convent and Girls' School. Sold by the church in 2013, it is being converted to condos. Another remnant from the area's slum past, the Gothic Revival **former 14th Ward Industrial School of the Children's Aid Society** (1888–9; Vaux & Radford) at 256–8 Mott St, was one of many such charitable schools teaching reading, writing, and the rudiments of citizenship to immigrant children. Calvert Vaux, who collaborated on the design of Central Park, designed the beautiful terra cotta ornament. The school has been converted to condos.

BASILICA OF ST. PATRICK'S OLD CATHEDRAL

Map p. 619, D4. Corner of Prince and Mott Sts. Subway: N, R to Prince St; 6 to Spring St. Bus: M5, M103. Open daily 9–5 except Wed. T: 212 226 8075, oldcathedral.org.

Built for a burgeoning Irish Catholic population, St. Patrick's Old Cathedral is the oldest Roman Catholic building in the city (though the parish of St. Peter's in Lower Manhattan is older). Designed by Joseph François Mangin (co-architect of City Hall), it was begun in 1809 and finished six years later. In 1836 an anti-Irish mob marched up the Bowery, intent on sacking the cathedral, but Irish defenders cut gun ports in the surrounding wall, posted armed men along Prince St, and stockpiled bricks on the upper stories of surrounding buildings, dissuading the would-be attackers.

When the present St. Patrick's Cathedral on Fifth Ave was completed in 1879, Old St. Patrick's became a parish church. The original Gothic-style building was gutted by fire in 1866; its appearance now only hints at its former self. The smooth, windowless façade on Mott St is dignified in its severity; rubblestone side walls contain pointed-arch stained-glass windows. A low wall surrounds the churchyard (*usually locked; best view from Mulberry St*), the original burial place of Pierre Toussaint (1766–1853), born a slave in Haiti, revered for his ministrations to the poor, and presently under consideration for canonization as the nation's first African-American saint. Since 1990 his remains have rested in the crypt of St. Patrick's on Fifth Ave.

BOOKS AND PRINTING

McNally Jackson (*52 Prince St between Mulberry and Lafayette Sts; T: 212 274 1160, mcnallyjackson.com*) is an independent bookstore with a pleasant café and an Espresso Book Machine that can print on demand.

Housing Works Used Books Café (*126 Crosby St, between Houston and Prince Sts; T: 212 335 3324, housingworks.org*) offers a great stash of used books in a homey store with a friendly café. Profits support the homeless and people living with HIV/AIDS.

Filling the block at 295–309 Lafayette St is the imposing brick Romanesque Revival **Puck Building** (1885–6), which long served the printing industry, first as the home of the humor magazine *Puck*. At the corner of Houston St and above the main entrance on Lafayette St are figures of Puck, top-hatted and cherubic, by Henry Baerer (whose statue of Beethoven stands in Central Park).

THE BAYARD-CONDICT BUILDING

Map p. 619, D4. 65–69 Bleecker St (Broadway and Lafayette). Good view from Crosby St.

This is New York's only building (1899) by Louis H. Sullivan, often considered the creator of the skyscraper. Known for his work in Chicago, he attracted attention for his radical theories on skyscraper design, which stressed their function as a determinant of form and was influenced by new building materials.

Sullivan's first plan for this building incorporated a free-standing steel skeleton with 14-inch structural columns and exterior brick walls only twelve inches thick, but the conservative city building code insisted on thickening the lower walls and columns. With the loss of floor space and rental income, the original investors could no longer afford the building and sold it to Silas and Emmeline Condict. The terra cotta decoration of leafy forms, seed pods, tendrils, vines, and gargoyles culminates in an ornate cornice beneath which six angels hover with outspread wings. According to a story in the *New York Times*, Condict, a lawyer who long had wanted to enter the ministry, insisted that Sullivan add the ten-foot angels, because he wanted everyone who entered the building to "realize that the true spirit of fair dealing among men can and should prevail during the six business days of the week, as well as on the Sabbath."

During restoration (2002) many of the terra cotta pieces were cleaned and re-glued, the original storefronts were replaced, and the capitals of the ground-floor columns recreated from originals stored at the Brooklyn Museum.

EATING AND DRINKING IN CHINATOWN, LITTLE ITALY AND NOLITA

Restaurants in these neighborhoods reflect the Asian and Italian populations who lived (and live) in its tenements, the well-heeled newcomers, and the spillover from the Bowery with its new arts colony. **Chinatown** offers sit-down eateries, noodle shops, dim sum and dumpling places, and bakeries; other Asian cuisines, such as Malaysian and Vietnamese, also have a presence here. Some think the best Chinese restaurants have migrated to Queens, but Chinatown still has much to offer. **Little Italy** is tourist town and most of its restaurants feature frill-free, Southern Italian red-sauce dishes. In warm weather it can be fun to sit at the outdoor tables, especially on Mulberry St, and absorb the scene.

CHINATOWN

$$ 456 Shanghai Cuisine. Soup dumplings are excellent here, as are cold noodle dishes and stir-fries. Shanghai specialties include fried yellow fish, scallion pancakes, pan-fried pork dumplings. Chinatown décor, i.e. plain. Lunch and dinner daily. *69 Mott St (Canal St). T: 212 964 0003, no website. Map p. 621, D1.*

$$ Peking Duck House. More ambiance than most Chinatown restaurants, and a bit more expensive. There are seafood specialties and other dishes, but go for the classic Peking duck. Beer and wine. Lunch and dinner daily. *28 Mott St (Pell St and Chatham Square). T: 212 227 1810, pekingduckhousenyc.com. Map p. 621, D2.*

$ New Malaysia. ■ Popular, crowded restaurant in the Chinatown Arcade. Classic Malaysian food (*nasi lemak*, coconut shrimp), classic Chinatown service (brusque). Lunch and dinner daily. *46–48 Bowery (Bayard and Canal Sts. T: 212 964 0284, newmalayasia restaurant.com. Map p. 621, D2.*

$ Nom Wah Tea Parlor. The city's oldest dim sum parlor. The waiters formerly came around with carts and you pointed at what you wanted; today there is a menu and an upgraded kitchen. Lunch and dinner daily. *13 Doyers St (Bowery and Pell St). T: 212 962 6047, nomwah.com. Map p. 621, D2.*

$ Royal Seafood. Busy restaurant; specializes in seafood, as the name implies, but also classic Cantonese with some updated dishes. Communal tables. Lunch and dinner daily. *103 Mott St (Canal and Hester Sts). T: 212 219 2338, no website. Map p. 621, D1.*

$ Tasty Hand-Pulled Noodle Shop. Hand-pulled and knife-cut noodles, also dim sum and regular entrées. Small, simple, very popular. Lunch and dinner daily, cash only. *1 Doyers St (Pell St). T: 212 791 1817, tastyhand pullednoodlesnyc.com. Map p. 621, D2.*

$ Thai Son. Probably the best of the Vietnamese places on this stretch of Baxter St. Small, busy, clean; it serves lunchtime refugees from the Civic Center and Asian locals. *89 Baxter St (Bayard and Canal Sts). T: 212 732 2822, thaisonnyc.com. Map p. 620, C2.*

LITTLE ITALY

$$ Il Cortile. ◼ This pleasant place with a brick-walled courtyard dishes up hearty portions of linguine with clam sauce, baked *ziti* and *scaloppini*. It's a bit more expensive than most. Lunch and dinner daily. *125 Mulberry St (Canal and Hester Sts). T: 212 226 6060, ilcortile.com. Map p. 620, C1.*

$$ Vincent's Clam Bar. Seafood, pasta, and red sauce, since 1904. Photos of celebrity diners on the walls. If you like the famous sauce (hot or sweet), you can buy it to take home. Lunch and dinner every day; closed Thanksgiving and Christmas. *119 Mott St (Hester St). T: 212 226 8133, no website. Map p. 621, D1.*

$ Ferrara. A venerable family-owned café known for *cannoli*, ricotta cheesecake, gelato, and other sweets, offers all kinds of coffee, also beer and wine. Open 8am to midnight every day except Christmas. *195 Grand St (Mott and Mulberry Sts). T: 212 226 6150, ferraracafe.com. Map p. 621, D1.*

NOLITA

$$$ Cherche Midi. Newish place from Keith McNally (Balthazar, Odeon, and uptown Café Luxembourg). Comfortable professional service, French-tinged menus with such standbys as frogs' legs and foie gras, skate and salmon, and, if you feel like splurging, a dry-aged prime rib served with caramelized onions and soufléed potatoes. For dessert, such old friends as *île flottante*, *crêpes suzette*, and *tarte tatin*. Lunch and dinner daily, brunch weekends. *282 Bowery (East Houston St). T: 212 226 3055, cherchemidiny. com. Map p. 619, E4.*

$$$ Estela. ◼ Upscale contemporary restaurant at the SoHo-Nolita border. Menus change frequently. Snacks and appetizers might include homemade matzoh with sardines and gnocchi, or *burrata* with salsa verde. Uruguayan-born chef with good NY credentials. Small, sometimes loud. Dinner weekdays, brunch weekends. *47 East Houston St (Mulberry St). T: 212 219 7693, estelanyc.com. Map p. 619, D4.*

$$$ The Musket Room. New Zealand is not famous for cuisine, but in the hands of chef Matt Lambert, it has garnered kudos and awards, for food and for design. The menu recalls the history of New Zealand eating, from its European beginnings, through its Asian influences, to its local-seasonal focus. Oysters with mignonette dressing, salmon with quinoa, and venison with fennel and juniper. Order *à la carte*, or try one of the two tasting menus. Good wine list. Dinner only, every evening. *265 Elizabeth St (East Houston St). T: 212 219 0764, musketroom.com. Map p. 619, E4.*

$$$ Pearl & Ash. Contemporary wine bar; small, globally influenced plates. Intriguing décor of open-faced wooden boxes filled with antiques and other little curiosities. Extensive wine list. Fairly priced. Dinner nightly. *220 Bowery (Prince St). T: 212 837 2370, pearlandash.com. Map p. 619, E4.*

$$$ Peasant. Rustic Italian food in generous portions. Brick pizza oven, grilled specialties. Closed Mon, dinner other days. *194 Elizabeth St (Prince and Springs Sts). T: 212 965 9511, peasantnyc.com. Map p. 619, E4.*

$$$–$$ Nyonya. Comfortable but not atmospheric Malaysian place with authentic food. Curries, roti, rice dishes, and seafood. Sauces made from coconut milk, tamarind seeds and freshly pounded curry pastes. Branches in Brooklyn. Lunch and dinner daily. *199 Grand St (Mott and Mulberry Sts). T: 212 334 3669, ilovenyonya.com. Map p. 621, D1.*

$$ Delicatessen. Beautiful people and high-style deli-diner food. Specials range from soft shell crabs (seasonal) to humble spaghetti and meatballs. Open breakfast to late night. *54 Prince St (Lafayette St). T: 212 226 0211, delicatessennyc.com. Map p. 619, D4.*

$$ Emporio. A Roman eatery that remains popular with the locals. The attractive open kitchen features a wood-burning oven, requisite for the thin-crust pizzas. Many of the cheeses are imported from Italy, while most of the pastas are handmade on site. Lunch and dinner daily. *231 Mott St (Prince and Spring Sts). T: 212 966 1234, emporiony.com. Map p. 619, D4.*

$$ Spring Street Natural. Founded in 1973, when organic food was not yet "a thing," and still in business because the food is good and the setting is pleasant. Eggs, salads, tacos, chicken, and fish. Delicious hummus; kale salad. Open daily from breakfast through dinner. *62 Spring St (Lafayette St). T: 212 966 0290, springstreet natural.com. Map p. 620, C1.*

$$ Uncle Boons. Atmospheric downstairs restaurant with dim lighting. Thai food by imaginative and sophisticated chefs. Beer, wine, and cocktails to tame the heat. Dinner nightly, weekend brunch. *7 Spring St (Bowery and Elizabeth St). T: 646 370 6650, uncleboons.com. Map p. 621, D1.*

$$–$ Lombardi's. One of several pizzerias claiming to be the nation's oldest, licensed in 1905. Regardless, it is one of the best, with its coal-fired oven and thin-crust pies. Classic Neapolitan pizza Margherita and white pizza; also calzone, but no slices. Cash only. Lunch and dinner daily. *32 Spring St (Mott St). T: 212 941 7994, firstpizza.com. Map p. 620, C1.*

$ Pho Bang. Popular Vietnamese. The mainstay is *pho*—herb-spiced rice noodle soup with meat—but also curries. Simple, easy on the wallet. Cash only. Open daily 10–10. *157 Mott St (Broome and Grand Sts). T: 212 966 3797, no website. Map p. 621, D1.*

The Lower East Side

The Lower East Side was once the most densely populated patch of ground on Earth, a place where hundreds of thousands of immigrants struggled to lay down American roots.

The traditional Lower East Side (*map p. 621*) once encompassed today's East Village, Little Italy, and Tompkins Square, and the neighborhood is still called the Lower East Side—south of Houston St from the Bowery to the East River. Once predominantly Jewish, its profile is changing as Chinatown expands and developers snap up desirable sites for new structures or convert 19th-century tenements to luxury apartments. Here flossy new buildings stand next to six-floor walk-ups. Other traces of the district's past include a handful of ethnic food stores and a few synagogues, some of them active houses of worship, others adapted to alternative uses. Long-standing social service institutions, for example the Educational Alliance and the Henry Street Settlement, once dedicated to the largely Jewish population, continue to serve neighborhood residents, now mostly black, Latino, and Asian.

Visiting the Lower East Side

The Lower East Side Visitor Center at 54 Orchard St (Hester and Grand Sts) has publications to help you explore the area on your own, as well as organized walking tours (open Mon–Fri 10–6, Sat–Sun 12–5; T: 212 226 9010, lowereastside.org). Several other organizations offer specialized or general neighborhood tours; some are free: the Lower East Side History Project (232 East 11th St; T: 347 465 7767, leshp.org) and the Lower East Side Jewish Conservancy (235 East Broadway; T: 212 374 4100, lesjc.org). Also check the listings of the Museum at Eldridge Street (see p. 133) and the Lower East Side Tenement Museum (see p. 134).

HISTORY OF THE LOWER EAST SIDE

In the 18th century much of what is now the Lower East Side belonged to wealthy land-owners—the Stuyvesant and Rutgers families (Dutch) and the De Lanceys (French Huguenot). After the Revolution, loyalist James De Lancey saw his estate confiscated, broken up, and sold off as building lots, in part to butchers, grocers, cartmen, and oth-

THE LOWER EAST SIDE
Tenement houses.

ers who had formerly worked as tenants on his land. Henry Rutgers, whose allegiances put him on the winning side of the war, parceled out his riverside land and leased it to shipwrights, sail-makers, and rope-makers.

By 1850 immigrant arrivals were altering the character of the neighborhood. Former captains' mansions on East Broadway became shops; single-family row houses were sold off for a quarter of their value of 30 years earlier or were knocked down and replaced by tenements. Between 1846 and 1860 large numbers of Irish immigrants settled here. Many joined the building and maritime trades and later became municipal workers, policemen, firemen, and eventually politicians and lawyers. At mid-century Germans, both Jews and gentiles, arrived, among them skilled workers and craftsmen who formed trade unions and working men's associations, assimilated with relative ease, and took their places in society as merchants, jewelers, clothing manufacturers, furriers, and bankers.

When Czar Alexander II of Russia was assassinated by revolutionaries in 1881, the ensuing political repression led to a wave of Russian and Eastern European Jewish immigration. Many came to the Lower East Side and their legacy still affects the ethnic makeup of New York. Of the 2.5 million Jews who came from Russia and Eastern Europe between 1880 and 1924, about 85 percent arrived in New York City and about 75 percent of those settled at least temporarily on the Lower East Side. By the end of the 19th century it was the most densely populated place on Earth. Most of the Jewish immigrants found work peddling or in the needle trades, toiling 12–14 hours a day under miserable conditions for meager wages.

In the early years of the 20th century, while new arrivals were pressing at the barricades of Ellis Island, those who had managed to thrive were moving on. They rode out to Brooklyn across the East River bridges or on the subway; they took the elevated railway uptown or to the Bronx. The immigration laws of 1924 halted new arrivals from Eastern Europe, and the existing population of the Lower East Side trickled away.

THE "OLD" NEIGHBORHOOD

Writers of the late 19th century considered **Hester Street** (*map p. 621, D1*), site of a busy pushcart market, the heart of the ghetto, cacophonous with the shouts of vendors, the haggling and chattering of women, and the cries of children who darted through the crowds, playing and making swift raids on the pushcarts. One reporter from the *Times* in 1898 found the scene touching and attractive; another described it as the filthiest place on the western continent, whose inhabitants were slatternly, lawless, and indecent.

During the same period **Allen Street**, darkened and dirtied by the Second Avenue El, became a haven for prostitution. A local minister complained of women openly soliciting from the stoops of tenements adjoining his church. Michael Gold in his autobiographical novel *Jews Without Money* (1930) recalled the prostitutes sunning themselves in sidewalk chairs, their legs sprawled in the way of passers-by.

THE MUSEUM AT ELDRIDGE STREET

Map p. 621, D1. 12 Eldridge St (Canal and Division Sts). Subway: B or D to Grand St; F to East Broadway. Bus: M15. Open Sun–Thur 10–5, Fri 10–3; closed Sat and on major national and Jewish holidays. Admission charge, but free on Mon. Tours, concerts, interactive and other exhibits. Shop. T: 212 219 0302, eldridgestreet.org.

Dominating a cramped street of tenements, the former **Eldridge Street Synagogue** (1886–7) has been returned (2007) to its original splendor and is now a museum. Built by Congregation Kahal Adath Jeshurun (the People's Congregation of the Just), an Orthodox Romanian congregation founded in 1852, which later merged with Anshe Lubz ("the People of Lubz,"), the synagogue was the first great house of worship in the United States built from the ground up by Eastern European Jews.

By 1886, the congregation could afford architects; Peter and Francis William Herter, German Catholic immigrants, designed a synagogue that dramatically mixed Gothic, Romanesque, and Moorish Revival styles. (The more famous Herter Brothers, Gustave and Christian, designed interiors and furniture for the Vanderbilts and other uptown families; Peter and Francis William specialized in tenements.) The upstairs sanctuary is lit by stained-glass windows and brass chandeliers with Victorian glass shades. The towering ark is carved of walnut. The walls are stenciled or painted in *trompe l'œil* wood or marble. The blue barrel-vaulted ceiling is decorated with hundreds of gold-leaf stars—a magnificence that surely dazzled humble immigrant worshipers.

Unlike other *shuls*, which drew members from the founders' towns of origin, Eldridge St welcomed Jews from all over Eastern Europe and from every economic level. It was so enthusiastically attended in the early years that the police sometimes wielded clubs to control the crowds. But in the Depression it fell on hard times. In 1933, the main sanctuary was sealed off. The roof sprang leaks; the sanctuary deteriorated.

In 1971 Gerard R. Wolfe, an architectural historian and NYU professor, implemented a rescue effort completed in 2010 with the dedication of the luminous blue, star-spangled stained-glass window on the east wall, designed by artist Kiki Smith and architect Deborah Gans. The small Orthodox congregation Kahal Adath Jeshurun still meets on the lower level, where the small museum displays personal effects and historical documents, including the ashes of the synagogue's mortgage papers. (Children will enjoy the interactive games that evoke the quality of life on the Lower East Side.)

JARMULOWSKY'S BANK

The former bank at 54–58 Canal St (*Orchard and Allen Sts*), founded 1873, was one of several private Jewish banks established when financial conditions eased enough for local residents to save a few dollars. Its founder, Sender Jarmulowsky, was a Russian immigrant who was instrumental also in founding the Eldridge Street Synagogue. The bank brokered steamship tickets and provided loans and savings accounts. In the days before savings account insurance, bank runs were common, but Jarmulowky's survived until 1917, when depositors withdrew $3 million to send to relatives in Europe during World War I. It closed with assets of $600,000 and liabilities of $1.25 million, and Jarmulowsky's sons, by then managing the bank, were indicted for fraud. At the time of writing the landmarked building was being converted to a boutique hotel.

ORCHARD STREET

Named for James De Lancey's apple orchards, Orchard St (*map p. 621, D1*) is now a shopping street, the descendant of a pushcart market. For unskilled immigrants with little English, the pushcarts were one of few ways to eke out a living, but to Mayor Fiorello La Guardia they were "a blemish on the face of the city" and a target of his reforming zeal. For many years Orchard St was the place to go for discount clothing, fabrics, luggage, even girdles; now boutiques, galleries, and cafés have supplanted most of the mom-and-pop stores. Gone too are the "schleppers" who stood on the sidewalks "pulling in" customers, often by their coat sleeves. On Sunday the street becomes a pedestrian mall.

The **Lower East Side Tenement Museum** (*97 Orchard St, Visitor Center at no. 103; visits by guided tour only, usually late morning through afternoon; admission charge; tickets online, in person, or by phone; reservations recommended on weekends; neighborhood tours (admission charge); shop; T: 212 431 0233, tenement.org*) was founded (1988) to preserve the heritage of the nation's urban immigrants, especially the millions who lived on the Lower East Side. Several apartments in the six-story former tenement have been restored to their 19th-century appearance; a visit recreates the experience of living here. No. 97, built in 1863, predates the earliest housing reform laws and so was not required to conform to the 1879 Tenement House Act (*see box opposite*). Running water and flush toilets arrived only about 1905.

Congregation Kehila Kedosha Janina (Holy Community of Janina) at 280 Broome St near Allen St (*open Sun 11–4; admission by donation*) is the only Greek-Jewish synagogue in the Western Hemisphere, founded in 1906 by immigrants from Ioannina in northwest Greece. Romaniote Jews, who settled in Greece after being expelled from Spain in 1492, date back to Roman period. The little two-story building (1927–8; Sidney Daub), decorated with Tablets of the Law and an incised Star of David, was originally a tenement with a ground-floor store front. In the balcony a small museum displays photos, family heirlooms, and ritual objects that recount the history of Jewish communities in Greece including the period of Nazi domination during World War II.

ESSEX STREET MARKET AND RIVINGTON STREET

The **Essex Street Market** occupies the block of Essex St from Delancey to Rivington Sts (*map p. 621, E1; open Mon–Sat 8–7, Sun 10–6; individual stall hours vary; essexstreetmarket.com*). Built in 1940 for pushcart peddlers, it offers food for many palates—Latino, Jewish, and upscale urbanite: chicken gizzards, *nopales* (cactus stems), sherry vinegar, fish cheeks, prime cuts of beef, and artisanal cheeses. Close by at 105 Norfolk St (*Delancey St*), the 16-story **Blue Tower** (2007; Bernard Tschumi) soars above its modest neighbors. Clad in rectangular panels of dark and lighter blue, the building evokes, for some, the energy of Mondrian's *Broadway Boogie Woogie*. For others it symbolizes unwelcome gentrification, especially since it sits on the former parking lot of Ratner's legendary kosher dairy restaurant, which closed in 2002.

Rivington St (*map p. 621, D1*) is named after James Rivington (1724–1803), publisher of *Rivington's New York Gazetteer*, a Tory newspaper that attacked the American revolutionary movement. Rivington's sentiments and abrasive personality earned him the hostility of American patriots, who destroyed his presses and stole his type fonts, a serious drawback since no American foundries produced type of the same high quality as Rivington's imported English fonts. Undaunted, he returned to England and got new equipment, came back to New York, and started another Loyalist newspaper. In 1781, he had a change of heart, and became a spy for General Washington.

At 126 Rivington St is the **site of Schapiro's Kosher Wines**. From 1908 until 2001 the Schapiro family shop sold wine produced according to traditional methods from grapes grown in upstate New York and stored here in nine cellars filled with oak and redwood casks. Founded by Sam Schapiro, a Polish immigrant, the firm touted its products as "The Kosher Wines You Can Almost Cut With a Knife."

For 90 years **Streit's Matzo Company**, at 150 Rivington St, remained a mainstay of the Jewish community, its ovens hourly turning out as many as 900 tons of matzo, an unleavened bread used especially during Passover. In 2015, pressured by increasingly difficult business conditions, Streit's departed the Lower East Side for New Jersey, where it remains the nation's only family-owned matzo bakery.

TENEMENTS

Built to exploit all available space and maximize the return for the landlord, tenements were one of the horrors of immigrant life. The earliest, "Pre-Law" tenements, dated back to the 1860s, completely filling their 25 by 100-ft-building lots. Subdivided into four apartments per floor, they had communal outdoor toilets and only one room per apartment with windows onto daylight. The floor plans—three rooms strung together in a row—suggested their nickname, "railroad" tenements.

In 1867 the city passed its first Tenement House Act mandating fire escapes and windows in every room, but the law was usually ignored. The next attempt at amelioration came in 1878 with a contest for a design that would afford "safety and convenience to the tenant" and profit for the landlord. The prize-winner, the "dumbbell" tenement, soon became synonymous for all that was miserable in tenement design: two buildings side by side facing onto a narrow airshaft, which gave them their characteristic dumbbell shape. The airshafts, sometimes as narrow as a foot and a half, provided virtually no air or light to the lower rooms and acted like flues, spreading fires from apartment to apartment. Residents of the upper floors tossed garbage and human waste into the shafts, which had no outside access, making them impossible to clean. However, the Tenement House Act of 1879 (the "Old Law") did require running water either in the house or yard, one toilet for every two apartments, and windows that faced outward.

In 1902, reformer Lawrence Veiller helped enact the New York State Tenement House Act (the "New Law") forbidding further construction of dumbbell tenements, requiring a light court at least 4½ ft wide, a toilet in each apartment, and a window with natural light in each room. The law came too late since nearly 20,000 dumbbell tenements had already been built in Manhattan and the Bronx, thousands of them on the Lower East Side.

EAST BROADWAY & ITS NEIGHBORHOOD

The David Sarnoff Building, at 197 East Broadway near Jefferson St (*map p. 621, E1*), is the flagship of the **Educational Alliance** organized in 1889, an agency formed to help Eastern European Jews adapt to America's alien culture. The Alliance was founded by German-Jewish philanthropists, many of them "uptown" Jews, former immigrants who had prospered, moved out of the ghetto, and now saw Americanization as the key to freedom from want. The Alliance held classes for immigrant children to prepare them for the public school system and gave English language and civics courses to adults to prepare them for naturalization. It also provided showers, important in a tenement-ridden slum, where few apartments had bathtubs.

Relations between the "uptown" Jews who founded the Alliance and the "downtown" Jews whom it served long remained prickly. The assimilated uptowners found the new immigrants backward, "oriental" and slovenly, in need of instruction in hygiene as well as English. The "greenhorns," or new immigrants, found the German Jews condescending and insensitive to their desire to perpetuate their culture. Today the Alliance offers early childhood education, housing for the elderly, drug treatment, and cultural programs to people of many ethnicities.

Opposite Jefferson St at 192 East Broadway, the **Seward Park Branch of the New York Public Library** (1909; Babb, Cook & Welch; restored 2004) was founded in 1886 as the downtown branch of the independent Jewish Aguilar Library. It was incorporated into the NY Public Library system, the present building constructed with funds given by Andrew Carnegie. The library offered a large collection of books in Yiddish as well as a canopied rooftop reading room, where Nathan Straus, another philanthropic "uptown" Jew (*see opposite*), funded a milk bar. In its early years the branch broke circulation records, lending books to immigrants thirsting for education. Leon Trotsky used the library during his brief New York stay in 1917. Today the collection includes books in Yiddish and Hebrew, as well as in Russian, English, Chinese, and Spanish.

Seward Park is named after William H. Seward (1801–72), governor of the state of New York, US senator, and secretary of state under Abraham Lincoln. In 1898, settlement workers Lillian Wald (*see p. 138*) and Charles Stover founded the Outdoor Recreation League to build playgrounds on city-owned land for children who otherwise played in the streets. The playground at Seward Park (1903) was the first permanent, municipally-built play facility in the US.

Across from Seward Park is the **Forward Building** (1912; George A. Boehm; *173–5 East Broadway between Jefferson and Rutgers Sts*), built for the *Jewish Daily Forward*, the country's most influential Yiddish daily newspaper. The first-floor frieze includes portraits of Karl Marx and Friedrich Engels. In the later years of the 19th century the Lower East Side was a hotbed of left-wing political activity, with the Yiddish Communist daily *Freiheit* and Emma Goldman's anarchist *Mother Earth* also published in the neighborhood. The *Jewish Daily Forward* (founded 1897) rose to prominence under Lithuanian immigrant Abraham Cahan (1860–1951), who dictated the editorial policy and also reported on the whole spectrum of immigrant Jewish experience. Intimate in tone and straightforward in diction, the *Forward* recounted everyday life on the Lower East Side. Cahan wrote about the iniquities of bosses who imposed unbearable working conditions; his paper explained baseball to the greenhorn and offered advice on the use of the pocket handkerchief. The *Forward*'s most famous feature was the *Bintel Brief* ("Bundle of Letters"), a column in which readers unburdened themselves of personal problems. A mother writes that her adult daughter ridicules the old-country modes of dress, speech, and cooking. A working father worries because his daughters hang around with street boys, no better than gangsters. In 1974, the paper moved to 49 East 33rd St. In the 1930s the circulation was 275,000; in 2000, published as a weekly, it had 26,000 readers in English and about 7,000 in Yiddish.

Straus Square (*the triangle bordered by East Broadway, Canal St, and Rutgers St*) memorializes Nathan Straus (1848–1931), co-owner of Macy's; he became a leading proponent of the pasteurization of milk, donated to libraries and disaster relief, and championed the cause of a Jewish state in Palestine.

A couple of blocks north, at 367 Grand St, **Kossar's Bialys**, said to be the country's oldest *bialy* bakery (founded in the early 1940s) survives and thrives (*open Sun–Thur 6am–8pm, Fri 6–3, closed Sat*). *Bialys* (thinner than bagels with ground onions patted into the dough and poppy seeds sprinkled on top), were reputedly invented by the bakers of Bialystok in Poland. Also at Kossar's are *pletzels* (onion flatbreads), *bulkas* (small loaves), and sesame sticks.

Between 1856 and 1919, the old Essex Market Court House and Ludlow Street Jail occupied the block bounded by Ludlow, Essex, Broome, and Grand Sts, where the Seward Park Campus of the NYC Department of Education now stands. Violators of federal laws and criminals whose offenses came under the jurisdiction of the Sheriff of the County of New York were incarcerated here. Prisoners with enough money could buy upgraded accommodations. William M. Tweed (*see p. 89*), serving time for defrauding the city, availed himself of this privilege, occupying the warden's parlor with flower pots on the window sills and a piano to ease the tedium of prison life (though it is unlikely that Tweed played). He died in the jail in 1878.

EAST OF CLINTON STREET

The congregation of **St. Mary's Church** (*440 Grand St, west of Pitt St*) dates back to 1826. It is the city's third Catholic parish after St. Peter's on Barclay St (1786) and the Church of the Transfiguration on Mott St (1801). For seven years the congregation—mostly Irish and working class, including workers from the nearby docks—worshipped in a former Presbyterian church on Sheriff St, but in 1831, anti-Catholic, anti-immigrant nativists torched the building; the present church was completed in 1833. In 1864 Patrick C. Keely, pioneer architect of Catholic churches in the US, replaced the Greek Revival façade with the more stylish brick Romanesque Revival front, though the original fieldstone walls remain on the sides. John Drumgoole served as sexton (janitor) of the church and for 21 years sheltered street children in the basement. Today the congregation is largely Puerto Rican and Dominican.

The Orthodox **Bialystoker Synagogue** (1826; *7 Bialystoker Pl., also called Willett St*), originally the Willett Street Methodist Episcopal Church, occupies a plain late Federal building with walls of random Manhattan schist quarried nearby on Pitt St. A Jewish congregation from Bialystok bought the building in 1905 and as a sign of hope during the Depression glorified the interior with stained-glass windows and ceiling paintings. (*Tours by arrangement; T: 212 475 0165, bialystoker.org.*)

The buildings of the **Henry Street Settlement** (1827 and later additions; *map p. 621, E1; 263–7 Henry St near Montgomery St*) began as late-Federal houses on the outskirts of town, built for shop-owners, ships' captains and others who had prospered in the maritime trades. Only the central building has survived with original details intact: the wrought-iron stoop railing with open box newel posts, the areaway fence with knobby finials, the paneled door. The Settlement began as a nursing service, founded by Lillian Wald and Mary Brewster, which cared for the poor in their own homes and became known as the Visiting Nurse Service of New York. But it grew to include a co-op food store, clubs for boys and girls, a kindergarten, and a savings and loan fund; today the Henry Street Settlement has branches throughout the city and serves some 60,000 people annually.

LILLIAN WALD

Founder of the Henry Street Settlement, Lillian Wald (1867–1940) was a compassionate, gentle, yet shrewd and worldly woman who devoted her life to the poor. Awakened to a sense of vocation by a visit to a sick immigrant mother, she moved to a fifth-floor walk-up at 27 Jefferson St and began her rounds, fighting ignorance, disease, malnutrition, rats, and bigotry. Wald had the gift of persuasion and raised funds from moneyed friends including philanthropist Jacob Schiff, who donated two of the Henry Street buildings to the settlement. Coming from a bourgeois German-Jewish family, educated in an English and French day school for young ladies, and then trained as a nurse, Wald became an important liaison between the "uptown" and "downtown" Jews, who often found themselves at odds with one another. As an organizer she dealt with insurance companies, the public schools, the city bureaucracy, and the Red Cross. When she died, an editorial in the *Times* remarked that "she made the loftiest ideals of America articulate in words and acts," that "she was never consciously tolerant because she never admitted that the infinite differences in human nature called for tolerance." At a memorial service in Carnegie Hall, thousands gathered and listened to tributes including those from the mayor and the nation's president.

The modest Georgian-Gothic **St. Augustine of Hippo Episcopal Church** (1827–9) at 290 Henry St is one of four approximately contemporary churches built of local Manhattan schist. It began as the All Saints' Free Church—"free" because worshippers didn't have to rent their pews. Above the balcony are two "slave galleries" where, according to tradition, black worshippers were segregated from the rest of the congregation. Although New York State legally emancipated slaves in 1827, many were not actually free until decades later. The congregation, now largely African-American, began as a chapel, an outpost, of Trinity parish located on East Houston St, then a wild and dangerous neighborhood. St. Augustine's joined with All Saints' in 1945 and moved here, becoming independent of Trinity in 1976.

AROUND EAST HOUSTON STREET

Russ & Daughters (*map p. 619, E4; 179 East Houston St between Allen and Orchard Sts; open Mon–Fri 8–8, Sat 9–7, Sun 8–5:30; T: 212 475 4880, russanddaughters.com*) was founded by Joel Russ, an immigrant from an Eastern European *shtetl*. He began selling herring from a wagon in 1911 and settled into his first store on Orchard St in 1914. His three daughters Ida, Anne, and Hattie became partners the business, allegedly because they were more pleasant to the customers than their father was. The store, known in New York as an "appetizing store," sells caviar, smoked and salted fish, salads, dried fruit and nuts, and sweets. In 2014 the present owners, great-grandchildren of the founder, opened a popular sit-down restaurant, Russ & Daughters Café (*see overleaf*).

Katz's Delicatessen (*205 Houston St at Ludlow St*) is an old-style deli with a large dining room (*see p. 141*). Founded in 1888, it is famous for its jaw-stretching, mouth-watering pastrami sandwiches, and for its slogan, "Send a salami to your boy in the army," coined during World War II.

On the roof of **Red Square** (1989), an apartment building at 250 East Houston St (*Aves A and B*) whose name aptly describes its color and shape, a statue of Lenin salutes downtown Manhattan with a stiffly upraised arm. Commissioned by the Soviet government but never put on display because the Soviet Union unraveled, the statue was recovered from a dacha outside Moscow and installed here in 1994. A randomly numbered clock covers the water tower.

The **former Congregation Anshe Chesed** (1850; Alexander Saeltzer; *172 Norfolk St between Stanton and East Houston Sts*) is the city's oldest purpose-built synagogue, the original home of New York's third Jewish congregation (after Shearith Israel and B'nai Jeshurun). Designed by the architect of the Astor Library (now the Public Theater), it was once resplendent with Gothic Revival pointed-arch windows and delicate tracery. Its sanctuary, the city's largest at the time, seated 700 men on the ground floor and 500 women in the balcony. Its various owners reflect the successive waves of Jewish immigration in the neighborhood: built by a German congregation, Anshe Chesed ("People of Kindness"), it later housed a Hungarian immigrant group, and eventually became Congregation Anshe Slonim ("People of Slonim"), named for a fondly-remembered village in Poland. Anshe Slonim, dwindling in size and resources, abandoned the building in 1974. In the early 1980s it was sealed against vandalism and threatened with demolition. Sculptor Angel Orensanz bought the building (1986) and restored it; today as the **Angel Orensanz Foundation and Center for the Arts**, it hosts performances and exhibits, weddings, bar mitzvahs, and other events. Actors Sarah Jessica Parker and Matthew Broderick were married here in 1993.

EATING AND DRINKING ON THE LOWER EAST SIDE

New restaurants in this gentrifying neighborhood tilt toward the small and crowded and—more perhaps than in other areas—may have short shelf lives.

$$ Ápizz. In this pizzeria-plus, the kitchen offers traditional pizzas (Margherita, *quattro formaggi*) and the L.E.S. Special with chorizo. Other dishes include meatballs with ricotta, baked skate, and an oven-seared prime rib-eye steak. Dinner Tues–Sun, closed Mon. *217 Eldridge St (Rivington and Stanton Sts). T: 212 253 9199, apizz.com. Map p. 619, E4.*

$$ Cata. Among the tapas at this handsome Spanish restaurant are prawns, oysters, charcuterie with Spanish hams, artisanal cheeses, and braised duck ravioli. The drinks menu offers more gin-and-tonic combinations than you might have thought possible. Bring 8–12 friends and you can order a whole roasted suckling pig. Dinner nightly. *245 Bowery (Stanton St). T: 212 505 2282, catarestaurant.com. Map p. 619, E4.*

$$ Dirt Candy. ■ This attractive vegetarian restaurant, so popular that it moved from smaller quarters in the East Village, still pulls in the crowds, who enjoy battered cauliflower reformed as a waffle, or Portobello mushrooms as a mousse. Dinner Tues–Sat, closed Sun, Mon. *86 Allen St (Grand and Broome Sts). T: 212 228 7732; dirtcandynyc.com. Map p. 621, D1.*

$$ The Fat Radish. This pleasantly designed shabby-chic restaurant in a one-time sausage factory draws a young, good-looking, arty crowd. It serves fashionable dishes, plus a few British specialties—Scotch eggs, oysters, and heritage pork—all from the finest purveyors. Casual service; the noise level can rise. Dinner nightly, lunch Tues–Sun, weekend brunch. *17 Orchard St (Canal and Hester Sts). T: 212 300 4053, thefatradishnyc.com. Map p. 621, D1.*

$$ Russ & Daughters Café. ■ As soon as this offshoot of the venerable appetizing store opened, crowds lined up for the smoked fish, caviar, knishes, and noshes. Sweets include blintzes, challah bread pudding, and chocolate caviar (somewhat akin to chocolate mousse). Cocktails and wine. No reservations, so try weekdays or off hours. Lunch and dinner daily (opens at 10am weekdays and 8am weekends). *127 Orchard St (Delancey and Rivington Sts). T: 212 475 4881, russanddaughterscafe.com. Map p. 621, D1.*

$$ Schiller's Liquor Bar. This popular lower-priced relative of Balthazar in retro surroundings serves bistro food with some English specialties. Breakfast, lunch, and dinner daily; open late weekends. *131 Rivington St (Norfolk St). T: 212 260 4555, schillersny.com. Map p. 619, F4.*

$$-$ Clinton St. Baking Co. & Restaurant. Hugely busy for breakfast/brunch when it draws long lines of hopeful diners. It's easier to get in later, and the restaurant offers the same food at dinner plus burgers and buttermilk fried chicken. Full bar. Open Mon–Sat 8am–11pm (but closed 5–6pm), Sun 8–6 (but takeout only 8–9am on weekends). Credit cards accepted only at dinner. Restricted reservations policy, check the website. *4 Clinton St (Houston and Stanton Sts). T: 646 602 6263, clintonstreet baking.com. Map p. 619, F4.*

$$–$ Katz's Delicatessen. This Kosher deli has never forsaken the food and the attitude of bygone days—an assertive staff, modest surroundings, and crowds; go for the overstuffed pastrami, corned beef, or Reuben sandwiches, and the traditional garlicky full-sour pickles. Or the hot dogs and matzo ball soup. Open weekdays from 8am until late; Fri all night; Sat all day; Sundays 12–10:45. *205 East Houston St (Ludlow St). T: 212 254 2246, katzsdelicatessen.com. Map p. 619, E4.*

$ Congee Village. Despite its off-putting name, Congee Village offers very good Cantonese food at very good prices: dim sum, scallion pancakes, steamed chicken with black mushroom, and baked rice dishes. The encyclopedic menu also has true Chinese specialties such as duck's blood with ginger and scallion or baked fish intestine in a clay pot. Congee, a rice porridge, comes in a full range of varieties, with seafood, chicken, and pork. Lunch and dinner daily. *100 Allen St (Delancey St). T: 212 941 1818, congeevillagerestaurants. com. Map p. 621, D1. Another location at 207 Bowery (Rivington and Spring Sts), T: 212 766 2828.*

$ Kuma Inn. Up a flight of tenement stairs, this unadorned restaurant serves exceptional Thai and Filipino food in close quarters, with a small-plate format. The chef is a veteran of top fine-dining restaurants. On the menu: tuna tartare with a rice noodle crisp, squid salad with rice vinegar and mushrooms, pickled vegetables, and Chinese sausage with fiery Thai chili-lime sauce. No liquor license; bring your own bottle. Cash only. Dinner nightly. *113 Ludlow St (Delancey and Rivington Sts). T: 212 353 8866, kumainn.com. Map p. 621, D1.*

$ Morgenstern's. A "new American" ice cream parlor, i.e., small-batch ice cream, natural ingredients, and interesting flavors including some with sugar and salt. Opens daily at 8am, Sun–Thur until 11pm, Fri and Sat until midnight. Cash only. *2 Rivington St (Bowery and Chrystie St). T: 212 209 7684, morgensternsnyc.com. Map p. 621, D1.*

Greenwich Village

*Greenwich Village still charms with its 19th-century domestic architecture
and quiet streets, managing to retain its former artistic atmosphere,
though the old bohemian haunts are mostly gone.*

In the 20th century Greenwich Village (*map p. 618*) was America's bohemia, its Left Bank, a cradle of creativity, individuality, and artistic fulfillment. Novelists pounded out their masterworks here; the Little Theater movement began here; Abstract Expressionists developed a new kind of painting in Village studios; musicians found their groove in its clubs. "Beat" poets, anarchists, advocates of birth control and free love expounded their ideas in its cafés and coffee houses. Today, the bars and coffee houses where Dylan Thomas, Eugene O'Neill, Jack Kerouac, and their friends imbibed, spouted poetry, and observed the human condition are largely gone, but the Village's crooked streets and small-scale buildings retain their charisma.

HISTORY OF GREENWICH VILLAGE

When Washington Square was still marshland traversed by Minetta Brook, a Native American settlement stood in present-day Greenwich Village. The Dutch later divided the land into farms. The British called it Greenwich (Green Village), a name that first appears in city records in 1713. A few large landholders dominated the landscape: Trinity Church and such established families as the De Lanceys, Lispenards, and Van Cortlandts; Sir Peter Warren, whose naval exploits won him a seat in Parliament, owned a country estate of some 300 acres. By the 1790s, however, the big holdings were being broken up as the city spread northward, in part fleeing epidemics of yellow fever, and its irregular streets were being mapped.

Between 1825 and 1850 the population of the Village quadrupled. Since its inhabitants at that time were predominantly native born, the area became known as the "American Ward," a title that lost its accuracy toward the end of the century. By 1870 the southern part of the Village had become a backwater, the departure of fashionable commerce leaving a vacuum soon filled by immigrants. First came the Irish and a black population who settled south of Washington Square; then came the Italians in the 1890s and a second, poorer, wave of Irish who settled around Sheridan Square.

EXITVS ACTA PROBAT

WASHINGTON SQUARE PARK
Sculpture (1918) of George Washington by A. Stirling Calder on the western
pier of Washington Arch.

Federal, Greek Revival, and Italianate row houses gave way to tenements, while shops and hotels became warehouses or manufacturing lofts suitable for exploiting immigrant labor.

Around the turn of the 20th century, the Village entered its halcyon period. Because of its relative isolation, its historic charm, and the indifference of a foreign population occupied with its own problems, the Village attracted a radical, avant-garde element of American society. Here were cheap rents and freedom from the late-Victorian sexual and material values that dominated middle-class America. The place swarmed with radical activity: Max Eastman edited *The Masses* (1911), known for its socialist politics, brutally realistic graphics, and relentless criticism of bourgeois values; its publication was suppressed in 1917 for opposing World War I; a similar fate befell the *Seven Arts* (founded 1916), whose contributors included D.H. Lawrence, Sherwood Anderson, and Robert Frost. Clubs like the "A" Club and the Liberal Club became forums for female suffrage, birth control, anarchy, and free love.

Among the theater groups flourishing in the opening decades of the 20th century were the Provincetown Players, whose productions displayed the talents of Eugene O'Neill, Edna St. Vincent Millay, and Bette Davis among others. Resident Village writers included Sherwood Anderson, Theodore Dreiser, John Dos Passos, and Van Wyck Brooks as well as poets E.E. Cummings, Hart Crane, and Marianne Moore.

The isolation of the Village ended when Seventh Avenue South was carved through it in the second decade of the 20th century, and in the 1930s a second subway line linked the neighborhood to the rest of the city. Real estate developers replaced row houses with apartments, a process that accelerated after World War II. Still, for about a decade after the war, the Village remained central to the city's counterculture. In its bars—the Minetta Tavern and especially the San Remo Café (*see p. 150*)—the founding members of the Beat generation hung out. (Jack Kerouac, Allen Ginsberg, and Gregory Corso lived elsewhere because the Village was already too expensive; William Burroughs, whose parents sent him a monthly allowance, had a place on Bedford St.) Others who drank at the San Remo during its heyday were James Agee, Merce Cunningham, John Cage, William Styron, and W.H. Auden.

Avant-garde painters also congregated in the Village. Willem de Kooning, Jackson Pollock, and Franz Kline caroused at the working-class Cedar Street Tavern (originally on Cedar St but later at 24 University Place). During the folk revival of the 1960s, Simon and Garfunkel, Joan Baez, and Bob Dylan followed an older generation of folk musicians (Woodie Guthrie and Pete Seeger) to the Village. Jimi Hendrix arrived in 1966 and established the Electric Lady Studios four years later.

The Village also attended the birth of Off Off-Broadway, whose ethos rejected the values of the commercial theater. Beginning in 1958 Joe Cino, a dancer whose enlarging waistline shortened his career, produced experimental plays in his Caffé Cino (*31 Cornelia St*) on a minuscule homemade stage. A few years later, Al Carmines, the charismatic assistant minister of Judson Memorial Church, established an experimental theater in the church's sanctuary.

Today the Greenwich Village is populated by professionals and a few celebrities instead of struggling painters and poets. Nevertheless, Villagers have maintained the neighborhood's time-honored sense of community and continue to exercise themselves in political and social causes.

AROUND WASHINGTON SQUARE

Map pp. 618, C4–619, D4. Subway: A, C, E, F, to West 4th St-Washington Square. Bus: M1, M2, M3, M5.

Washington Square Park is often considered the heart of Greenwich Village. The area's first inhabitants, after the Native Americans, were black slaves freed by the Dutch (from 1644) and granted farmland. Toward the end of the 18th century the future park was a potter's field (burial place for paupers and strangers) and possibly a hanging ground. In 1826 it became a parade ground and in 1827 the park was laid out, attracting the well-to-do, whose houses rose along its perimeter.

In the early 1950s Robert Moses, then Parks' Commissioner and always a highway advocate, decided to push a highway over, under, or through the square to ease downtown traffic on Fifth Avenue, a project that Villagers defeated in 1963 after a bitter, decade-long struggle. In the 1950s and '60s, the park, a center of the folk music revival, attracted stars of the counterculture and police surveillance, initiating several decades of neglect, when it became dirty, druggy, and sometimes dangerous. Today, after a major renovation, the park is safe and clean.

The clumsy bronze **statue of Garibaldi** east of the fountain (1888; Giovanni Turini) was funded by donations from the working-class Italian-American community. Turini's original design, according to an 1896 interview with the *New York Times*, called for a stone "mountain" with Garibaldi on top flanked by a bugler and a bayonet-wielding soldier. Money ran out after the Garibaldi figure had been cast, and the other two figures never materialized. Worse yet, Garibaldi's legs didn't fit the granite pedestal that replaced the stone "mountain," so they were bent to accommodate it.

WASHINGTON ARCH AND ITS SCULPTURE

Washington Arch (dedicated 1895), designed by Stanford White and modeled on the Arc de Triomphe, frames the northern entrance to Washington Square Park, replacing a temporary wood and plaster arch (1889) that commemorated the centennial of George Washington's inauguration. Henry James, seeing it after a long sojourn in Europe, described it as "the lamentable little Arch of Triumph which bestrides these beginnings of Washington Square—lamentable because of its poor and lonely and unaffiliated state."

Sculpted against the north side of the eastern pier is *Washington in War* (1916; Hermon A. MacNeil), the commander-in-chief flanked by *Fame* (right) and *Valor*. On the west pier *Washington in Peace* (1918; A. Stirling Calder), shows the statesman in the company of *Justice* and *Wisdom*, holding a book inscribed "Exitus acta probat" ("The end justifies the deed"). The sculptor was the father of Alexander Calder.

NEW YORK UNIVERSITY (NYU)

New York University (*map p. 619, D4*) was founded in 1831 by business and professional men including Albert Gallatin, secretary of the Treasury under Thomas Jefferson. The university, nonsectarian and "modern" in its curriculum, offered practical as well as classical courses to a middle-class student body, providing an alternative to Episcopalian, conservative Columbia College. Among its early faculty members was Samuel F.B. Morse, painter, sculptor, and inventor of the telegraph and Morse code. NYU is now the largest private university in the US, with a total enrollment of almost 60,000 students, of whom 40,000 attend 14 schools and colleges at six different locations in Manhattan. Its more than 19,000 employees make it one of New York's largest employers. Since opening its first building on Washington Square East in 1835, NYU has became by far Greenwich Village's largest landowner, which has prompted confrontations with residents over expansion. The **Brown Building** (*29 Washington Pl. at Greene St*), is named for Frederick Brown, a realtor and art patron who gave it to NYU—but it is infamous as the site of a disastrous industrial fire.

WASHINGTON SQUARE NORTH

Throughout the 19th century row houses faced the square on three sides; today only Washington Square North (*Fifth Ave to MacDougal St*) retains the old gentility. By 1889 William Dean Howells, editor and critic, had noticed the economic gulf between the "international shabbiness which has invaded the southern border" (he meant immigrants), and the "old-fashioned American respectability which keeps the north side in vast mansions of red brick."

The houses (late 1820s–'50s) on the west side of Washington Square North were developed individually, the mix of Federal, Greek Revival, and Italianate styles reflecting the owners' personal tastes. **Nos. 21–23** (1835–6) are Greek Revival, with columned doorways and long parlor windows. The square's earliest house, **no. 20** (1828–9), one of the city's few remaining Federal mansions, was converted into apartments in 1880 by Henry Hardenbergh, architect of the Plaza Hotel. The keystone and blocks in the arched doorway and the panels on the lintels are decorated with a vermiform design.

The original buildings between 18 Washington Square North and Fifth Ave have been demolished, including Henry James's grandmother's Greek Revival house (no. 18), which provided the setting for his 1880 novel *Washington Square*. In 1951 the site was sold for an apartment house, dismaying the locals, who waged a losing battle against what they considered wanton development.

Known as **The Row**, extending east from Fifth Ave to University Place, nos. 1–13 occupy land that belonged to Snug Harbor (*see p. 534*). Built in 1833 and now owned by NYU, they form one of the city's first examples of controlled urban design. The fronts are red brick; the basement stories, trim, porches, and huge balustrades are marble. Along the street runs an iron fence with anthemia, lyres, and Greek key motifs. Famous residents have included Edith Wharton, William Dean Howells, John Dos Passos (who wrote *Manhattan Transfer* at no. 3), and architect Richard Morris Hunt, who lived at no. 2 from 1887–95. From 1913–67, Edward Hopper had a studio at no. 3.

A half-block north on the east side of the avenue is **Washington Mews** (*Fifth Ave and University Pl.*), a private alley with converted 19th-century stables (north) and small houses (1930s) built on former back gardens (south).

EAST OF WASHINGTON SQUARE

GREY ART GALLERY
Silver Center: 100 Washington Square East (Washington Place); entrance at 33 Washington Place. Subway: A, B, C, D, E, F, or M to West 4th St; N or R to 8th St; 6 to Astor Pl.; 1 to Christopher St. Bus: M1, M2, M3, M5. Open during exhibitions Tues, Thur, Fri 11–6; Wed 11–8; Sat 11–5; closed Sun, Mon, Thanksgiving weekend, Memorial Day weekend, Independence Day. Suggested admission. T: 212 998 6780, nyu.edu/greyart.
The Grey Art Gallery, NYU's university gallery, is located on the site of NYU's original home, the University Building (1835–92). Here Winslow Homer, Daniel Huntington, Samuel Colt, George Innes, and Henry James all lived and worked, as did Professor Samuel F.B. Morse, a painter before he became an inventor. The gallery mounts exhibitions from its own collection and elsewhere, many of which emphasize historical, cultural, and social contexts. The permanent collection is strong in American paintings from 1940 onward, including work by Romare Bearden, Elaine de Kooning, Helen Frankenthaler, Arshile Gorky, Adolph Gottlieb, Kenneth Noland, and Ad Reinhardt.

THE TRIANGLE SHIRTWAIST COMPANY FIRE

Built in 1900, the ten-story Asch Building (now the Brown Building) cost $400,000. The owners declined to pay another $5,000 for a sprinkler system because they considered the building fireproof. On March 25, 1911, fire broke out at about 4:30pm in the upper stories where the Triangle Shirtwaist Company employed some 500 workers, mainly Jewish and Italian immigrant girls. Most of the stairwell doors had been locked to prevent employees from sneaking out or stealing; the few available stairways were narrow and winding; the fire escape, unable to bear the weight of the fleeing workers, tore away from the wall; and the fire department ladders reached up only six stories. Before the fire was brought under control, perhaps 20mins later, 146 workers had died, most jumping out the windows and perishing on the pavement ten floors below. The owners, acquitted of manslaughter, received some $65,000 more in insurance than they paid out in claims (a profit of $6,445 per victim), but the tragedy eventually brought about stricter fire codes and led to the rise of organized labor.

WASHINGTON SQUARE SOUTH

NYU's massive red sandstone **Bobst Library** (1973; Philip Johnson and Richard Foster), built as part of an unfinished master plan to unify the campus architecturally, dominates the south side of the square. The newest campus addition is the Kimmel

JUDSON MEMORIAL CHURCH
Stained-glass window of St. George, designed by John La Farge.

Center for University Life (2001; Roche, Dinkeloo and Associates), containing the Skirball Center Theater, the largest performing arts space south of 42nd St.

JUDSON MEMORIAL CHURCH

Map p. 619, D4. 55 Washington Square South (Thompson St).

The Judson Memorial Church, affiliated with the Baptist Church and the United Church of Christ, was founded by Edward Judson to honor his father Adoniram Judson (1788–1850), first Baptist missionary to Burma and compiler of an English-Burmese dictionary. The younger Judson focused his missionary zeal closer to home, building the church with its main portal facing the bluebloods of Washington Square North across the park but its back door opening onto an immigrant neighborhood, thus setting the congregation on the path of social and political activism it still follows. The adjoining campanile and Judson Hall were intended as fundraisers for the church ministry. In recent years the church has sold off real estate to support its programs and revitalize its historic building.

With the help of contributions from eminent Baptists, including John D. Rockefeller, the church hired Stanford White to design the complex (1888–93) and chose leading artists to decorate the interior. The building and adjoining square bell-tower, amber Roman brick with terra cotta moldings and panels of colored marble, are generally Romanesque Revival in style, influenced by White's Italian travels.

The simple style of the Meeting Room inside (*open during services and events*) reflects the emphasis of Baptist worship on preaching and baptism. The 17 stained-glass windows, by John La Farge, the largest collection in the country, are remarkable in technique and design. La Farge pioneered opalescent glass, which Louis Comfort Tiffany and others exploited, here used to imitate marble and stone. La Farge's images of saints in the tall round-arched windows suggest the niche sculptures of Italian Renaissance masters. Though Judson had hoped to commemorate Baptist missionaries in the stained glass, the realities of fundraising curtailed that plan, and at least some of the windows are said to depict donors.

MACDOUGAL STREET, MINETTA LANE & BLEECKER STREET

The **Provincetown Playhouse** (*133 MacDougal St near West 4th St; map p. 618, C4*), the storied theater that produced Eugene O'Neill's first plays and nurtured the careers of Paul Robeson, E.E. Cummings, Bette Davis, and others, has been largely demolished for NYU's Law School building. A group of struggling actors and writers, the Provincetown Players founded a Cape Cod summer theater in 1915 and a year later opened a New York season. In 1917 they moved here, remodeling an existing stable and bottle works. Among the plays first produced were *The Emperor Jones* and *The Hairy Ape* by Eugene O'Neill, whose work changed the shape of American drama. The company went under after the 1929 stock market crash, though the theater continued to host independently produced plays.

Next-door (also subsumed by the NYU building) was the Liberal Club, with Polly Holliday's restaurant downstairs, a famous eating and meeting place for artists and intellectuals in the early 20th century. Polly's lover, the anarchist Hippolyte Havel, who cooked and waited tables, gave the place its own cachet, shouting "bourgeois pigs!" and other insults at the patrons, who nonetheless remained loyal. The **Golden Swan Garden** (*2000; southwest corner of West 4th St and Sixth Ave*) is the site of another watering hole: the Golden Swan bar, known by its intimates as the Hell Hole. With a clientele of thugs as well as playwrights, it provided the setting and some characters for O'Neill's *The Iceman Cometh*. The **West 4th Street Courts** (aka "The Cage"), famous for pickup basketball games, draw players from all over the city.

The **Café Wha?** (*115 MacDougal St at West 3rd St*) dates back to the 1960s when Bob Dylan, Janis Joplin, and Jimi Hendrix performed here, before fame sent them to larger venues.

Minetta Lane recalls the Minetta Brook, which flowed from former hills near Fifth Avenue and 21st St to the Hudson River near Charlton St. Some sources say the name comes from a Native American name, *Manetta* ("devil water"); others say the Dutch called it *Mintje Kill* ("little stream"). Minetta Street, which intersects Minetta Lane a half-block west, follows the course of the brook. The walls of the **Minetta Tavern** (*113 MacDougal St at Minetta Lane*), which opened in 1937, are covered with pictures of illustrious clients. The most famous was the legendary Joe Gould, whose exploits and eccentricities were chronicled by writer Joseph Mitchell. A Harvard graduate, Gould lived in the Village by his wits and on the charity of friends for three decades, gathering material for his magnum opus, "An Oral History of Our Time." The work, consisting of innumerable conversations, was reputed to have reached eleven million words when Gould died in a mental institution in 1957. It was never found.

MACDOUGAL-SULLIVAN GARDENS HISTORIC DISTRICT

The MacDougal-Sullivan Gardens Historic District embraces 22 houses (1844–50) south of Bleecker St (*MacDougal St and Sullivan St*) that share a common back garden. In the mid-19th century Nicholas Low, a banker, land speculator, and legislator, subdivided the plot and built the houses as an investment. Although the immigrant population altered the social makeup of the neighborhood in the late 19th century, the Low family resisted the temptation to replace the houses with more lucrative tenements. In 1920 William Sloane Coffin, scion of the W. & J. Sloane furniture company, modernized the old row houses as moderate-cost housing; although the façades have been altered, the district remains an example of early urban renewal with a common garden created from small individual plots.

BLEECKER STREET

Bleecker Street (*map pp. 618, C4–619, D4*) is named after Anthony Bleecker, an early 19th-century man of letters who ceded the land to the city. The main street of the immigrant Italian neighborhood in the 19th century, it became the boulevard of bohemia in the 1950s. The San Remo Café (1925; *93 MacDougal St, corner of Bleecker St*), frequented by Beat generation superstars, closed in 1967; Le Figaro (*186 Bleecker St*), a favorite coffee house, went under in 2008. The legendary Bleecker St Cinema (*144 Bleecker St*), where viewers saw such then-avant-garde films as Kenneth Anger's *Scorpio Rising* and Jonas Mekas's *The Brig*, fell victim to real estate pressures and closed in 1990. Of the street's famous entertainment venues, only the aptly named **Bitter End** (*147 Bleecker St*) remains in business, more than half a century after its 1961 opening.

    The Atrium (*160 Bleecker St at Thompson St*) started out as Mills House No. 1 (1896; Ernest Flagg), a philanthropic low-income housing project. Flagg designed houses for the wealthy, including the Scribner family, but also high-density dwellings for the poor. This building, palatial in scale but cut up into tiny single rooms, was named for Darius Ogden Mills, who financed it hoping for a modest five percent profit. With some justification *Scribner's Magazine* described Mills House as "A Palace at Twenty Cents a Night." Its 1,500 rooms faced either the streets or the grassy interior courts; residents could enjoy modern bathrooms, lounges, restaurants, and smoking rooms. Eventually it deteriorated into the seedy Greenwich Hotel, a flophouse that catered to a down-and-out clientele. In 1958 the ground floor and basement became the home of the Village Gate, where the great jazzmen of the 1960s and '70s played. The club closed in 1994, but basement space re-opened in 2008 as **Le Poisson Rouge**, a high-art cabaret for classical music, jazz, rock, and pop, and poetry readings, with performers who range from drag queens to divas.

LA GUARDIA PLACE

On the east side of La Guardia Place (*Bleecker and West 3rd Sts; map p. 619, D4*) is Neil Estern's **statue of Fiorello La Guardia** (1994), who was born at 177 Sullivan St in a building that collapsed in 1987. The statue depicts the short, stocky mayor open-mouthed in mid-sentence, gesticulating with his hands, and striding forward. As the sculptor said, "He was always railing against something, some injustice or corruption."

FIORELLO LA GUARDIA

Mayor from 1934–45, Fiorello H. La Guardia (1882–1947) was renowned for his fighting spirit and ferocious temper, his boundless energy and ambition, and his facility in seven languages. Born in 1882 to a Jewish mother from Trieste and an agnostic Italian father, raised as an Episcopalian, married first to a Catholic and then a Lutheran, La Guardia was a living example of the city's ethnic diversity. He was a liberal, a reformer, and an irate opponent of dishonesty in government.

A shrewd politician himself, he nonetheless professed contempt for politicians, calling them "tin horn gamblers," but was usually able to turn his political independence to his own advantage. When he campaigned in Little Italy he carried a copy of *Il Progresso* and spoke Italian; on the Lower East Side he spoke Yiddish and carried *The Daily Forward* (*see p. 136*). Elected during the Depression as a reformer, La Guardia gained the confidence of President Roosevelt and was able to secure federal aid for public clinics, housing developments, parks and playgrounds, sewers, bridges, and La Guardia Airport, while providing jobs for thousands of the unemployed. He was the only reform mayor to be re-elected, proving his dominance over Tammany Hall, the entrenched Democratic party machine (*see p. 185*). He considered his greatest achievement to be the increased honesty and efficiency in municipal government that he brought about in New York through his own actions and throughout the country by force of example.

La Guardia has been called the most colorful mayor since Peter Stuyvesant. His flamboyant personality and unbounded energy were the stuff of legend. During a newspaper strike, he read the comics over the radio. On occasion he conducted symphony orchestras (his father was a musician). He followed firefighters into burning buildings and went on raids with the police. He died of pancreatic cancer at the age of 64 and is buried in Woodlawn Cemetery in the Bronx.

The Renee & Chaim Gross Foundation (*526 La Guardia Pl., near Bleecker St; open Sept–June Thur–Fri 1–5; by appointment only July and Aug; free; T: 212 529 4906, rcgrossfoundation.org*), founded in 1995, four years after the sculptor Chaim Gross's death, in his former home and studio, preserves both his artworks and the studio complete with mallets and chisels. On view are wood and stone carvings from the early

1920s onward, including his final wood sculpture (1988–9), preparatory maquettes, watercolors, and objects from his own collections of African and modern art.

The New York chapter of the American Institute of Architects is located in the **Center for Architecture** (*536 La Guardia Pl.*), which offers exhibitions, lectures, films, tours, and events about the built environment, design, and sustainability. The building (1911, redesigned 2003; Andrew Berman), a skillfully reconstructed storefront, exemplifies the principles espoused by the organization—filled with natural light, geothermally heated, and enlarged by cutting an opening through the floor slab of the old store to create usable space. A great place for anyone interested in architecture or the nature of cities (*open Mon–Fri 9–8, Sat 10–5; closed Sun; T: 212 683 0023, aiany.org*).

Filling a five-acre superblock (*Mercer St and La Guardia Pl., Bleecker St and W. Houston St*), the cast-in-place concrete **Silver Towers** (1967; I.M. Pei) serve as NYU housing. The buildings reflect the architectural thinking of Le Corbusier, whom Pei admired. In the central courtyard, the 60-ton, 36-ft concrete *Bust of Sylvette* replicates on a giant scale the 2-ft profile of a pony-tailed teenager Picasso painted on a piece of bent metal. The Norwegian sculptor Carl Nesjar executed the concrete enlargement (1967) with slight alterations appropriate to the now-monumental scale, remarking the he must be "the only person in the world who has corrected a Picasso."

AROUND SHERIDAN SQUARE

Subway: 1 to Christopher St-Sheridan Square; A, B, C, D, F to West 4th St; N, R, or W to 8th St-NYU. Bus: M5 (uptown), M20.

Christopher Park (*Christopher St at Seventh Ave South; map p. 618, C3*) is often mistaken for Sheridan Square—understandably since it contains a statue (1936; Joseph Pollia) of General Philip Sheridan (1831–88), a successful Union general during the Civil War and a ruthless exterminator of Native Americans thereafter. The park also contains George Segal's *Gay Liberation* (1992), two same-sex couples, cast in bronze and painted stark white, appropriately sited across the street from the Stonewall Inn (*see opposite*). **Sheridan Square** itself, actually a triangle (bounded by Washington Place, Barrow St, and West 4th St), contains a small garden maintained by volunteers, but is otherwise undistinguished.

THE NORTHERN DISPENSARY AND GAY STREET

The austere brick **Northern Dispensary** (1831), bounded by Waverly Place, Grove St, and Christopher St, a triangular building on a triangular plot, is the only remaining public building from the Federal period. The dispensary offered free medical care to the poor for more than 150 years (Edgar Allan Poe was treated for a cold in 1837). The vagaries of Greenwich Village geography allow the building to have two different sides facing one street and one side facing two streets, since Waverly Place forks at its southeast corner and Christopher St joins Grove St along its northern façade. It has remained empty for more than two decades, partly because a deed restriction requires that it be used to serve the poor and infirm.

Crooked, block-long **Gay St**, between Waverly Place and Christopher St, is still graced by several small, dormered Federal houses. In the 19th century Scottish weavers lived here; off and on until about 1920 the area was a residential enclave for the Village's black population. During Prohibition it harbored the Pirate's Den, a speakeasy where the waiters reputedly refused to give change. Novelist Ruth McKenney, who lived at no. 14, put Waverly Place on the cultural map with her play *My Sister Eileen*, later adapted as the musical comedy *Wonderful Town*, which recounted her adventures in the bohemia of the 1930s.

THE STONEWALL RIOTS

The 1969 riots at the Stonewall Inn (*53 Christopher St*) marked the turning point in the struggle for gay civil rights. The Stonewall Inn, in the heart of a gay neighborhood, operated without a liquor license as a "bottle club" where "members" brought their own alcohol. It was a claptrap sort of place with no running water behind the bar and no fire exits, but it did allow gay patrons to dance together, which in some circles made it *the* gay bar. The Mafia-connected owner regularly paid off the police to announce raids ahead of time so that customers could escape before the lawmen arrived. If arrested, gay patrons usually submitted passively, afraid of publicity. In the pre-dawn hours of June 28, police unexpectedly raided the bar. Patrons refused to comply with police orders; an angry crowd gathered outside on Christopher St; hostilities intensified; customers and passers-by threw paving stones and bottles at the police and tried to firebomb the bar as the outnumbered police barricaded themselves inside. The rioting, which continued for several days, presaged a new militancy among gays. Gay Pride parades, held toward the end of June in many cities, commemorate the uprising.

ST. JOSEPH'S CHURCH

St. Joseph's Church (*371 Sixth Ave at Waverly Pl. and Washington Pl.*) is the city's second oldest purpose-built Roman Catholic Church building (after Old St. Patrick's in 1815) and one of its earliest (1834) Greek Revival churches. It was designed by John Doran, about whom little is known. The main façade belongs to the then-emerging Greek Revival tradition, with its smooth surface, two large Doric columns, low pediment, and frieze. The corner quoins and the rubblestone masonry on the side walls hark back to the Federal period; the arched windows on the front date from 1885, during restoration after a fire. John McCloskey (1810–85), an early rector, became America's first cardinal. Father Thomas Farrell (pastor from 1857–80) bequeathed $5,000 for a church for blacks, stipulating that if such a church was not established in three years the money was to go to a Quaker orphan asylum; in 1883 the Church of St. Benedict the Moor opened its doors on Bleecker St.

THE WEST VILLAGE

Block-long, gingko-lined **St. Luke's Place** (*Leroy St between Hudson St and Seventh Ave South; map p. 618, C4*), named for the nearby chapel, exudes the aura of settled repose that characterizes much of the West Village. Built in the early 1850s for prosperous merchants, many of whose livelihoods were tied to the Hudson River, the Italianate row houses incorporate such fashionable details as brownstone trim, bold cornices, tall stoops with elaborate cast-iron railings, high rusticated basements, and deeply recessed doorways with double doors. Poet Marianne Moore, artist Paul Cadmus, and psychedelic guru Timothy Leary have all lived here, but the block's most notorious resident was James J. ("Jimmy") Walker, the popular, high-living mayor who resigned under a cloud of fiscal scandal in 1932. He lived at no. 6.

James J. Walker Park, across the street, was originally St. John's Burying Ground of Trinity Parish (which owned the West Village up to Christopher St under a 1705 land grant from Queen Anne). The sarcophagus on the north side of the park, dedicated in 1834 to three fallen firemen, is the only reminder of the former cemetery.

BEDFORD STREET

Bedford Street (*map p. 618, C4*) was mapped before 1799 and named after its precursor in London. James Vandenburgh, master mason of Trinity Church, lived at no. 68 in 1821, another reminder of Trinity's influence in the West Village. William Burroughs lived briefly at no. 69 during World War II, before he achieved fame as a Beat novelist. The house at **75½ Bedford St**, only 9½ft wide, is distinguished both as the Village's narrowest house and as a residence (1923) of Edna St. Vincent Millay. Built in 1873, it was wedged into a former carriage alley. Millay (1892–1950), Pulitzer-prize-winning poet, playwright, and actress, arrived in Greenwich Village in 1917, illuminating bohemian society with her beauty and personality. She is probably one of very few people named after a hospital: her middle name honors the former Greenwich Village hospital, where the staff had saved a relative's life. The **Isaacs-Hendricks House** (*77 Bedford St at Commerce St*), the oldest house in the Village (1799) has been significantly altered. Around the sharp bend on Commerce St, two remarkable houses, **nos. 39 and 41 Commerce St** (1831 and 1832), face one another across a central courtyard. Although legend says a sea captain built them for two feuding daughters, records attribute them to a local milk seller. The mansard roofs were added in the 1870s.

Chumley's bar and restaurant (*86 Bedford St at Grove and Barrow Sts*), once a speakeasy, is a hangover from Prohibition days. It opened in 1927 disguised as a garage, catering to Edna St. Vincent Millay, John Steinbeck, Willa Cather, and other literary types whose thirst was not quenched by the Volstead Act. A "secret" entrance through an alley door allowed patrons to come and go unobtrusively. In commemoration of those clandestine times, the restaurant never advertised its presence with a sign. (The façade collapsed in 2007; the building is now structurally sound, but at the time of writing it had not reopened, deterred by a lawsuit brought by neighboring homeowners.)

AROUND GROVE STREET

The clapboard house at **17 Grove St** was built in 1822 by William Hyde, a window-sash maker. A Greek Revival doorway was added in the 1830s or 1840s and a third story in 1870, but it is the best preserved of the Village's few wood-frame houses. Behind it at 100 Bedford St stands Hyde's workshop (1833). The bizarre house known as "**Twin Peaks**" (*102 Bedford St at Grove St*) was built in 1830 as an ordinary frame house but was given a total makeover (1925) as a stuccoed, gabled, and half-timbered extravagance by Clifford Daily, a designer and amateur architect. Daily, who believed that artists needed inspirational surroundings to court the muse, persuaded financier Otto Kahn to bankroll the renovation so that painters, writers, and actors could live there free from financial pressures. The resulting house was reported to contain bricks from a former Madison Square Garden, a Second Avenue tenement, and an Upper West Side apartment. At the opening ceremonies, the novelist Princess Amélie Troubetzkoy, a Virginian married to a Russian aristocrat, sat on a platform on one peak making a burnt offering of acorns to Pan while actress Mabel Normand sat on the other baptising the building with the customary bottle of champagne.

Grove Court (*visible from Grove St between Bedford and Hudson Sts*), a hidden architectural enclave of shuttered brick houses, was constructed (1853–4) for workmen. Remarkable today for its serenity, the court's boisterous past earned it such names as "Mixed Ale Alley" and "Pig's Alley."

ST. LUKE IN THE FIELDS

487 Hudson St (Grove St). Map p. 618, B4. Church open Mon–Fri 10–3; T: 212 924 0562, stlukeinthefields.org. Gardens: Barrow Street and North Gardens open daily from 8am until dusk; the Rectory Garden open Mon–Thur 10–5.

St. Luke's began in 1820 as an independent Episcopal institution on land donated by Trinity Church. Because it became a refuge for downtown New Yorkers fleeing yellow fever, it was named for Luke the Evangelist, a physician. In the late 19th century, as immigrants overwhelmed the neighborhood, the congregation built a new church on Convent Ave at West 141st St, and in 1891 St. Luke's became a chapel of Trinity Parish, which it remained until 1976. Built of brick rather than the more customary rubblestone, St. Luke's, with its low, square tower lacking a steeple, reflects the austerity of the Federal style. Badly damaged by fire in 1981, it was reconstructed and expanded (1981–5). The parish has a long history of tolerance and community service, including a dole of bread to the poor a century ago and activism for HIV sufferers more recently. Early on, 14 townhouses flanked the church, providing rental income. Six remain (**nos. 473–7** and **487–91 Hudson St**, all built in 1825), as does the handsome vicarage in the churchyard. The gardens are an unforeseen pleasure.

A block west, the ten-story dark brick building at **666 Greenwich St** (*Christopher and Barrow Sts*), the former US Appraiser's Stores (1899), first served as a warehouse for goods passing through customs and later as a federal archives and post office. Renamed "The Archive" when converted to apartments in 1988, it sturdily typifies the

Romanesque Revival style, with strong brick arches at ground level, rounded corner turnings, and successive bays of arched windows.

LUCILLE LORTEL THEATRE

The Lucille Lortel Theatre (*121 Christopher St between Hudson and Bleecker Sts; map p. 618, B4*), honors "the Queen of Off-Broadway," whose 70-year career demonstrated a commitment to new plays and young talent. Lortel (1900–99), born Lucille Wadler, gave up acting in 1939 in deference to her wealthy husband. She had a barn moved to their Connecticut estate, intending to raise horses, but the scarcity of feed during World War II scuttled that plan; instead Lortel founded the White Barn Theater in 1947, far from the commercial pressures of Broadway, where she produced plays by fledgling and unfamiliar playwrights, challenging actors and directors to move in new directions. Her husband, tired of her spending so much time in Connecticut, bought this theater, then called the Theatre de Lys, as an anniversary gift. She opened it (1954) with a revival of *The Threepenny Opera* starring Lotte Lenya, which ran for seven years. Over her long career, Lortel mounted more than 500 productions, including work by Edward Albee, Ugo Betti, Eugene Ionesco, Athol Fugard, Sean O'Casey, Terrence McNally, and Langston Hughes.

THE FAR WEST VILLAGE

The unlikely wooden house at **121 Charles St** (*at Greenwich St; map p. 618, B4*) with wide clapboards, double-hung windows, and unexpected angles and proportions sits tucked away on a small triangular plot. It may date from the 18th century, but was brought here in 1968 from York Ave and 71st St, where it sat on a back lot with no street frontage. When the little farmhouse was threatened with demolition, its owner purchased this small piece of land and had the house trucked here.

At 567 Hudson St on the corner of West 11th St, the **White Horse Tavern** was built for a bookseller but is remembered as a saloon for writers in the 1950s and 1960s—Norman Mailer and Jack Kerouac, among many. Dylan Thomas's prodigious drinking bouts have made it a destination for his admirers, and for many tourists. On November 3, 1953, Thomas announced that he'd had "eighteen straight whiskies. I think that's the record," probably an apocryphal remark, but one that became an urban legend anyhow. The next day the poet fell into a coma, and on November 9 died in the (now-defunct) St. Vincent's Hospital.

AROUND BANK AND BETHUNE STREETS

Bank Street (*map p. 618, B3*) became an important financial center when the Bank of New York on Wall St, threatened with quarantine for yellow fever, established (1798) an emergency branch on a nameless Greenwich Village lane; during the smallpox epidemic of 1822 other banks arrived for similar reasons. Attractive homes line the block and cobblestones line the street.

Westbeth at 55 Bethune St (*block bounded by Bank and Bethune, Washington and West Sts*) offers living and working space for artists in a bulky industrial building formerly used by the Bell Telephone Laboratories (1900; Cyrus L.W. Eidlitz). The transistor and transatlantic telephone came into being here, but the building's greatest artistic contribution was the production on its sound stage of parts of *The Jazz Singer*, the first commercially successful "talkie."

Towering above its ordinary lower stories, **Palazzo Chupi** (*360 West 11th St between Washington and West Sts*), a pink, pseudo-Mediterranean condo-palazzo (2007), houses painter Julian Schnabel, his studio, and five luxury units he built on speculation. The name derives from a term of endearment Schnabel used for his second wife.

Bethune Street leads to **Abingdon Square** (*map p. 618, B3*)—named for Charlotte Warren, who married the Earl of Abingdon. Although many British place names were jettisoned after the Revolution, Abingdon Square remained Abingdon Square because the earl and his wife had sympathized with the American cause. Charlotte's father, Admiral Sir Peter Warren, one of Greenwich Village's great 18th-century landholders, went to sea as a twelve-year-old, rose to his own command at age 24, made a fortune as a privateer, and married Susannah De Lancey, eventually acquiring some 300 acres. He returned to England before the Revolution, became a member of Parliament, and acquitted himself brilliantly in society. He died in 1752 at the age of 49 and is buried in Westminster Abbey. Abingdon Square contains the Greenwich Village War Memorial (1921; Philip Martiny), a bronze figure of an American soldier carrying a flag.

WEST 8TH TO WEST 14TH STREETS

In 1914 Gertrude Vanderbilt Whitney (*see p. 203*) founded the **former Whitney Studio Club** at 8 West 8th St (*map p. 618, C3*) as an exhibition space and meeting place for artists. Whitney had already remodeled a stable at 19 MacDougal Alley as her own sculpture studio and had generously supported artists in need, even those whose work offended the era's genteel taste. In 1929, she offered the Metropolitan Museum her collection of more than 500 contemporary works plus an endowment to maintain them. The director rejected her offer outright, saying the museum already had a "cellar full of that kind of painting"; thereafter Whitney established the Whitney Museum of American Art in this building, which now houses the New York Studio School of Drawing, Painting, and Sculpture.

The **former Lockwood de Forest residence** (1887), at 7 East 10th St near Fifth Ave (*map p. 619, D3*), now NYU's Center for Jewish Life, has unusual East Indian decorative details, including a teakwood bay window and carved door frame. A celebrated designer, De Forest worked in India where he developed an interest in traditional woodcarving. He also designed the teakwood trim for the library in Andrew Carnegie's mansion and donated a room from an Indian Jain temple to the Metropolitan Museum of Art.

THE SITE OF THE MABEL DODGE HOUSE

At 23 Fifth Ave, on the northeast corner of West 9th St, stood the house—well known in Village lore—where Mabel Dodge held her famous "evenings." In 1912 Mrs. Dodge and her wealthy husband rented the second floor, whose salon she decorated with a white bearskin rug in front of a white marble fireplace. Inviting anarchists, poets, artists, sculptors, and journalists, she organized her evenings around themes—psychoanalysis, birth control, the labor movement. Featured speakers included "Big Bill" Haywood (leader of the "Wobblies" or Industrial Workers of the World) and anarchist Emma Goldman. In 1919 Mrs. Dodge moved to Taos, New Mexico, where she instituted another salon, had an affair with D.H. Lawrence, and married a Pueblo Indian named Antonio Luhan.

CHURCH OF THE ASCENSION

33–36 Fifth Ave (West 10th St). Open weekdays 12–1; tours of artistic heritage after some Sun services and by appointment. T: 212 254 8620, ascensionnyc.org.

The Church of the Ascension (Episcopal), founded in 1827, moved to this fine brownstone Gothic Revival building (1840–1) after its Canal St church burned. Richard Upjohn designed it, five years before turning his hand to Trinity Church. In 1844 President John Tyler was married here to Julia Gardiner, whom a contemporary diarist described as "one of those large fleshly Miss Gardiners of Gardiners Island." In 1885–8, Stanford White "modernized" the church, an early project by the firm of McKim, Mead & White. McKim designed the pulpit; John La Farge painted the altar mural, *The Ascension of Christ*, considered one of his best works, and designed four of the stained glass windows; Louis Saint-Gaudens (brother of the better-known Augustus) designed the marble reredos. Next-door (*7 West 10th St*), the Gothic Revival Rectory (1839–41) was daringly innovative for its day, with asymmetrical massing, drip moldings, a steep roof and large chimney, and a rough brownstone façade.

WEST 10TH STREET

Some of the houses of this architecturally outstanding street have interesting social and artistic connections. Etiquette expert Emily Post (1873–1960) lived at no. 12 (1846), built by her architect father, Bruce Price. Mark Twain lived at no. 14 (1900–1). Emma Lazarus wrote "The New Colossus" ("Give me your tired, your poor...") while living at no. 18. The houses at nos. 20–38 (1856–8) are known either as Renwick Terrace, since attributed to James Renwick, or as the English Terrace, since influenced by rows or "terraces" of townhouses in London. Stylistically these Anglo-Italianate or "English basement" houses depart from the usual New York brownstone in having low stoops (three or four steps instead of ten or twelve) and round-arched single windows and doorways on the ground floor. Like other mid-19th-century brownstones, Renwick Terrace was planned as a unified streetscape, with cornices, rooflines, and window levels aligned to create an impressive vista. Dada artist Marcel Duchamp, a chess aficionado, moved to no. 28 in 1959, across the street from the Marshall Chess Club, still at no. 23. Over the central carriage door at 50 West 10th St, a sign reads "Grosvenor Private Boarding Stables." The brick stable, built sometime between 1863 and 1879, was remodeled in 1887 by the brother of the Metropolitan Museum's first president; later playwright Edward Albee lived here and still later, Jerry Hermann, who wrote *Hello, Dolly!* and *Auntie Mame*.

JEFFERSON MARKET LIBRARY AND GARDEN

Map p. 618, C3. 425 Ave of the Americas (10th St). Open Mon and Wed 10–8, Tues and Thur 11–6, Fri and Sat 10–5. T: 212 243 4334, nypl.org/locations/jefferson-market.
The former Jefferson Market Courthouse dates to 1877, designed by Frederick Clarke Withers with assistance from Central Park architect Calvert Vaux. Turreted, towered, gabled, carved, and further embellished with stained glass and ironwork, the building exemplifies Victorian Gothic architecture at its most flamboyant. Voted the nation's fifth most beautiful building in 1855, it stood empty from 1945 until 1967, when (after a struggle by preservationist Villagers) Giorgio Cavaglieri remodeled it as a branch of the New York Public Library system.

The courthouse stands on the site of the Jefferson Market (meat and produce). The old market (founded 1833) had a tall wooden fire-tower with a bell to alert volunteer firefighters, the precursor of the present main tower originally used for the same purpose. Assembly rooms above the market sheds doubled as courtrooms, and when the present building was constructed, it became part of a complex that included a brick jail and a reconstructed market building. Harry K. Thaw, who murdered the architect Stanford White (*see p. 197*), was tried here and found insane. Mae West was tried here on obscenity charges, paid a $500 fine, and spent one day in jail and nine more in the workhouse on Welfare (now Roosevelt) Island.

In the late 1920s the jail was demolished and replaced by the infamous Women's House of Detention (1931), a massive Art Deco building, long a village landmark (or eyesore, depending on the beholder's point of view). When it opened, the *New York Times* praised it as a model prison, breathlessly describing the "blocks of light, airy rooms," the roof garden "where games of handball and miniature tennis" would be played, and the special Sunday uniforms, "not of drab gray but of some brighter color." But as the prison grew more crowded, conditions deteriorated: its grim bulk darkened the street and the noise of inmates shouting and cursing disturbed the neighborhood day and night. In 1973–4 the jail was demolished and the site converted to the **Jefferson Market Garden** (*open afternoons except Mon, weather permitting, April–Oct; free; jeffersonmarketgarden.org*), a flower-filled patch maintained by volunteers.

PATCHIN PLACE, MILLIGAN PLACE, AND THE SECOND SHEARITH ISRAEL CEMETERY

Gated and locked, **Patchin Place** at West 10th St (*Sixth and Greenwich Aves*) is a secluded mews with ten brick houses built in 1848 by one Aaron D. Patchin. Theodore

Dreiser lived here in 1895 while still an obscure journalist, and E.E. Cummings, the occupant of no. 4, enjoyed its serenity for some 40 years.

Also visible through its fence, **Milligan Place** (*on Sixth Ave between West 10th and West 11th Sts*) is another enclave of 19th-century houses clustered around a tiny courtyard. Samuel Milligan purchased farmland here in 1799. The houses (c. 1852) are said to have accommodated Basque waiters from the former Brevoort Hotel on nearby Fifth Avenue and French feather workers who dealt in millinery plumes.

Behind a crumbling wall about a quarter of a block along the south side of West 11th St (*near Sixth Avenue*), the small triangular **Second Cemetery of the Spanish and Portuguese Synagogue**, also known as the Second Shearith Israel Synagogue Cemetery, remains from a larger, rectangular plot. This graveyard opened in 1805 when the synagogue's first burial ground at Chatham Square was full. It was used until West 11th St was cut through in 1830, obliterating much of it. Most of the bodies were removed to West 21st St near Sixth Avenue, where the congregation established its third graveyard, used until 1852 when a new law prohibited burials within the city limits. The present Shearith Israel Cemetery is on Long Island.

In the same block, but closer to Fifth Avenue, **no. 18 West 11th Street**, a newish brick townhouse with a jutting façade (1978; Hardy Holzman Pfeiffer Assocs) replaces one (1845) destroyed by an explosion in 1970. Members of the Weather Underground, a radical sect born in the politicized 1960s, were concocting pipe bombs in the basement when the dynamite went off, severing gas lines, killing three of the bomb makers, and sending the others into hiding.

FIRST PRESBYTERIAN CHURCH AND SALMAGUNDI CLUB

The **First Presbyterian Church** (1846, Joseph C. Wells; south transept, 1893, McKim, Mead & White; chancel 1919) on Fifth Ave at West 12th St (*map p. 619, D3*) replaces an earlier one on Wall St, whose congregation moved north when Wall St became commercial. In 1846 the Gothic Revival style reigned supreme in New York church architecture, and English-born Joseph C. Wells created here a fine example based on English models. The crenellated central tower recalls those of Magdalen College, Oxford, and the Church of St. Saviour in Bath. George Templeton Strong, the 19th-century diarist and a congregant of Trinity Church, declared the building "a travesty of a Gothic church;" as it rose higher, Strong found that it grew "uglier and uglier, and when its tower is finished it will resemble a corpulent Chinese gander with its neck rigid, stout, and tall." Today the *AIA Guide to New York City* calls it "stately" and "bold" in form.

Inside are stained-glass windows by the masters of the period: Louis Comfort Tiffany, Francis Lathrop, D. Maitland Armstrong, and Charles Lamb. In 1922 Harry Emerson Fosdick lost his job here for preaching a sermon entitled "Shall the Fundamentalists Win?," which questioned the literal truth of the Bible, stressed tolerance, and suggested that science and religion were compatible. The Park Avenue Baptist church, whose most influential parishioner was John D. Rockefeller Jr., quickly hired him and he went on to establish a long career as pastor of the Riverside Church (*see p. 434*).

Across the street at 47 Fifth Ave (near 12th St) the **Salmagundi Club** occupies the only surviving mansion (1852–3) on lower Fifth Avenue. The house, built for the president of a coal company, belongs to the Italianate tradition, with a boldly rusticated basement, high stoop, ornate door hood, and cast-iron work. The Salmagundi Club was founded in 1871 as a sketching club, numbering among its members John La Farge, Louis Comfort Tiffany, and Stanford White. The name "Salmagundi" (whose origins cannot reliably be traced back beyond the French *salmigondis*—a salad of minced veal, anchovies, onions, lemon juice, and oil) was adopted by Washington Irving and his collaborators as the title of a periodical whose pages satirized New York life. The club offers art classes and exhibitions (*open during exhibitions daily 1–5; free; gift shop; T: 212 255 7740, salmagundi.org*).

THE NEW SCHOOL

The New School, originally the New School for Social Research, occupies several blocks between Fifth and Sixth Avenues, from West 10th St to West 14th St, though the campus extends to other parts of the city. The school, founded in 1919 to offer college-level courses for all "intelligent men and women," remains one of the city's innovative educational institutions.

In the 1920s the New School broke ground by introducing psychoanalysis to the American public and was the first college to offer courses on black culture (taught by W.E.B. DuBois). Teachers who lectured in the school's six rented brownstones in Chelsea included Lewis Mumford, Franz Boas, and Bertrand Russell. During the following decades it became a "university in exile" for intellectuals fleeing Europe before World War II, and after the war the school welcomed returning veterans and others whose lives had been disrupted. During the 1950s Hannah Arendt, W.H. Auden, and Robert Frost offered lectures. In recent decades, the Mannes College of Music and the Parsons School of Design have become part of the New School, which has also added a school of management and urban policy, a drama school, and a program in jazz and contemporary music.

In 1930 the New School commissioned Joseph Urban to design its first permanent home, now **Alvin Johnson/J.M. Kaplan Hall**, at 66 West 12th St (*map p. 618, C3*). Known for his sometimes extravagant stage sets and theater designs, Urban tried to make this Modernist building unobtrusive on a street where most of its surroundings are small in scale. After trying various color schemes, he chose rows of black and white brick alternating with bands of windows set in black frames. The upper stories are recessed to de-emphasize the building's bulk. Inside (*student ID required for admission*) is Urban's landmarked egg-shaped auditorium. Works in the New School art collection reflect the school's diversity and commitment to freedom of expression; most famous are the city's only murals by José Clemente Orozco (1931), *A Call for Revolution and Universal Brotherhood*, which explore themes of exploitation, revolution, and the dignity of labor. Thomas Hart Benton's *America Today*, also commissioned by the New School, now belongs to the Metropolitan Museum of Art (*see p. 340*).

EATING AND DRINKING IN GREENWICH VILLAGE

$$$$ **Blue Hill**. ■ Chef Dan Barber, at the forefront of the farm-to-table movement and owner of Stone Barns in Westchester County, serves food that expresses his philosophy about sustainable agriculture and food policy. Delicious food, much of it from the farm at Stone Barns, prepared to bring out inherent flavors: Stone Barns pastured chicken, Blue Hill pig with eggplant and tomato. Dinner only, seven days. *75 Washington Place (Sixth Ave And Washington Square Park). T: 212 53 9 1776, bluehillfarm. com. Map p. 618, C4.*

$$$$ **Carbone**. Upscale red-sauce restaurant on a street of former tenements that were once home to immigrant Italians. All the dishes you would expect at a Little Italy hangout, but prepared with supreme skill and top-quality ingredients. Such old-time delights as *zuppa di pesce, pasta fagioli*, veal parmesan, lobster *"fra diavolo."* Lunch weekdays, dinner nightly. *181 Thompson St (Bleecker and Houston Sts). T: 212 254 3000, carbonenewyork.com. Map p. 619, D4.*

$$$$ **Gotham Bar and Grill**. ■ Well-known and well-loved for three reasons: its warm, welcoming atmosphere, its classic dishes, and its professional service. Roast chicken, Maine lobster, Nova Scotia halibut; plus the irresistible Gotham chocolate cake served with salted almond ice cream Lunch weekdays, dinner nightly. *12 East 12th St (Fifth Ave and University Pl.), T: 212 620 4020, gothambarandgrill.com. Map p. 619,* D3.

$$$$ **One If By Land, Two If By Sea**. Often cited as one of the city's (or world's) most romantic restaurants, this classic in the heart of the West Village has fireplaces, chandeliers, and, in some of the rooms, views of a leafy courtyard. Subdued piano music heightens the mood. Classic American dishes. Full bar, including a Coupe d'Amour cocktail. Only *prix fixe* unless you sit at the bar. Dinner seven days, brunch weekends. *17 Barrow St (7th Ave and Bleecker St). T: 212 255 8649, oneifbyland.com. Map p. 618, C4.*

$$$ **Annisa**. The surroundings are civilized, even a little formal, with soft lighting and quiet music, but the food is bold, inventive and multicultural, created by chef Anita Lo, one of Annisa's founders around the turn of the 21st century. The wine list features products of women vintners. Dishes include seared foie gras soup dumplings and grilled marinated pork loin. Dinner every evening. *13 Barrow St (Seventh Ave South and West 4th St). T: 212 741 6699, annisarestaurant. com. Map p. 618, C4.*

$$$ **Babbo**. Occupying the first two floors of an 1826 Federal townhouse on a busy street, Babbo has been a Village staple since 1998, serving up indulgent Italian and Mediterranean food. An early outpost of chef Mario Batali's food empire, it can be loud (both the clientele and the music) and boisterous; the rooms can be crowded, but the food more than compensates. Variations on the Italian theme

include beef cheek ravioli, or a mixed grill with lamb chops, sweetbreads, and beef tongue. Lunch and dinner Tues–Sat, dinner only Sun–Mon. *110 Waverly Pl. (MacDougal St and Sixth Ave). T: 212 777 0303, babbonyc.com. Map p. 618, C3.*

$$$ **Minetta Tavern**. Once the scruffy haunt of such writers and drinkers as Ernest Hemingway, E.E. Cummings, Eugene O'Neill, and Joe Gould (*see p. 150*). Made over by Keith McNally, the tavern, which opened during the Depression, has has risen to earn a Michelin star and a reputation as one of the city's finest steakhouses. Among the manly cuts of meat are a *filet mignon* with Roquefort and an admirable dry-aged *côte de boeuf* for two, along with the traditional sides. Imbibers will find plenty to slake their thirst. Lunch Wed–Fri, brunch weekends, dinner nightly. *113 MacDougal St (Minetta Lane). T: 212 475 3850, minettatavernny.com. Map p. 618, C4.*

$$ **Kesté Pizza & Vino**. Narrow brick-walled pizzeria with an imposing wood-fired oven that turns out Neapolitan pizzas, some that cater to special diets. Among the specials are pistachio and sausage, ricotta and walnuts, and several white pizzas; home-made mozzarella. Lunch and dinner seven days. *271 Bleecker St (Cornelia and Jones Sts). T: 212 243 1500, kestepizzeria.com. Map p. 618, C4.*

$$ **Lupa**. Lupa Osteria Romana, to call it by its given name, is a Roman-style *trattoria* with traditional fare made from fresh, local ingredients. Try the octopus with Swiss chard or the *saltimbocca*. Pastas include *casarecce* (folded and twisted litte tubes) with short rib ragù and *bavette cacio e pepe* (skinny fettuccine with cheese and pepper). Convivial and noisy. Lunch and dinner seven days. *170 Thompson St (Bleecker and Houston Sts). T: 212 982 5089, luparestaurant.com. Map p. 619, D4.*

$$ **Murray's Cheese Bar**. This modest tiled eatery, a stone's throw from the famous shop, is to cheese what the Russ & Daughters Café is to smoked fish. Choose from an encyclopedic selection ripened in Murray's own caves, or pick a familiar American favorite: mac and cheese (with pimento and Tickler English cheddar), wedge salad (with Roquefort and blue cheese dressing), or a three-cheese melt. Also fondue and raclette, and charcuterie. Beer and wine. Lunch Tues–Fri, brunch weekends, dinner every day. *264 Bleecker St (Morton St). T: 646 476 8882, murrayscheesebar.com. Map p. 618, C4.*

NoHo & East Village

Bordered by SoHo, the East Village, and the Broadway-Astor Place district with its educational institutions, NoHo bears witness to all these influences. The East Village, like the rest of downtown Manhattan, is becoming steadily more affluent.

NoHo (North of Houston), rebranded in the 1970s as it began to shed its shabbiness, was first developed for the upper crust in the 19th century by the enterprising John Jacob Astor. Its economic and social history cycled from riches to rags and has now swung back again. After the Civil War, factories and warehouses replaced the sedate residences of the 1830s and '40s, but a century later these open industrial buildings attracted artists, who were then followed by developers (as previously in SoHo); today they are being reinvented as condos and office space, once again for the well-to-do.

AROUND HOUSTON STREET

The intersection of East Houston St and the Bowery (*map p. 619, E4*) now being marketed as "the Four Corners of Downtown," epitomizes the neighborhood. On the northeast corner, the Liz Christy Community Garden recalls the grass roots activism of an earlier East Village. On the northwest corner the Bowery Mural gives a rotating cast of street artists the opportunity to work large. On the south side of Houston St (and therefore in SoHo) an upscale food market and a French restaurant hold down the intersection.

LIZ CHRISTY BOWERY-HOUSTON COMMUNITY GARDEN
110 East Houston St (Second Ave and the Bowery). Subway: F, V to Second Ave. Bus: M15, M21, M103. Open Sat all year 12–4; also Sun and Tues May–Oct 6pm–dusk. Free. lizchristygarden.org.
Community gardens have grown in New York since 1736 when the inmates of the first almshouse grew vegetables for their own subsistence, but the movement has flowered more recently in bleak, weedy vacant lots throughout the city. This garden is one of the most famous, founded by artist Liz Christy (1945–85), who was spurred to action

when she saw a child in a vacant lot playing in an abandoned refrigerator. Christy and fellow volunteer gardeners hauled out rubble and garbage, carted in topsoil, installed a fence, and planted. Today the garden thrives, with raised vegetable beds, trees, perennials, even a fish pond. The Dawn Redwood (*Metasequoia glyptostroboides*), the garden's largest tree, planted by Liz Christy herself, has grown to over 100ft. Until the 1940s, when it was discovered by a forester in a remote area of China, the species was known only from fossil records and thought to have become extinct; ironically, dawn redwoods, resistant to Asian longhorn beetles and tolerant of drought, are now being planted as street trees.

THE BOWERY MURAL

Since 2008 the wall on the northwest corner of the Bowery and East Houston St has become famous as a canvas for muralists who decorate the space with satirical, lyrical, and sometimes confrontational murals. The reproduction of a joyous Keith Haring mural (1982) inaugurated the series, initiated by Tony Goldman, a real estate entrepreneur, preservationist, and supporter of the arts. The nearby **Hole Gallery** (*312 Bowery, between Houston and Bleecker Sts, T: 212 466 1100, theholenyc.com*) curates the murals in conjunction with the Goldman firm, which owns the wall.

At no. 315 Bowery (*intersection of Bleecker St*), the **former home of CBGB**, the famous punk rock club, now houses a men's designer boutique featuring punk rock inspired clothing. The club was founded in 1973 as CBGB & OMFUG, an acronym for Country Blue Grass Blues and Other Music for Uplifting Gormandizers, though its offerings shifted away from the owner's intentions. Artists associated with the club include Sonic Youth, the Ramones, Blondie, Talking Heads, and Patti Smith. When the club closed in 2006 after a rent dispute, Smith remarked that its departure was "a symptom of the empty new prosperity of our city." The tattered and dirty awning is in the Rock and Roll Hall of Fame in Cleveland, Ohio.

BOND STREET TO FOURTH AVENUE

No. 1–5 Bond St, the **Robbins & Appleton Building** (1879; Stephen D. Hatch), now residential, was built for the proprietors of the American Waltham Watch Co. and also held the headquarters of publisher D. Appleton & Co., whose torches of learning remain above the main doorway. The mansard-roofed cast-iron building dramatically exemplifies the French Empire style, the large expanses of plate glass made possible by the strength of iron under compression, so that a few widely spaced columns could support a sizable façade.

On the block between Lafayette St and the Bowery, two newish residential buildings have attracted attention. Nouveau-cast-iron **40 Bond Street** (2008; Herzog & de Meuron) faces the street with a convoluted aluminum gate, sometimes described as "Gaudíesque," which the architects intended to suggest 3D graffiti. At **48 Bond Street**

Deborah Berke's limestone-and-steel condo makes a quieter statement—which is not to say it's not luxurious: inside is a 60-ft lap pool with an underwater sound system.

GREAT JONES STREET
Samuel Jones, a prominent lawyer and the city's first comptroller (1796–9) ceded the land for Great Jones St to the city stipulating that the street bear his name. New York already had a Jones St; for a while it had two, until Samuel Jones suggested calling his street "Great Jones St." At no. 42 is the firehouse of **Engine Company 33** (1898; Ernest Flagg and W.B. Chambers), a satisfyingly flamboyant Beaux-Arts building dominated by a monumental three-story arch. The bold Romanesque Revival **Schermerhorn Building** on the northwest corner of Great Jones and Lafayette Sts (*376 Lafayette St*) was built (1888) as a warehouse by Henry J. Hardenbergh, better known for the Plaza Hotel and the Dakota Apartments. On the northeast corner of the intersection, at 399 Lafayette St, is the **former De Vinne Press Building** (1885; Babb, Cook & Willard), a stark Romanesque Revival building of dark brick with terra cotta trim. Massive and simple, it is remarkable for its appearance of weight and strength. Theodore De Vinne (1828–1914) was a successful printer and scholar of the history of printing.

MERCHANT'S HOUSE MUSEUM
Map p. 619, D4. 29 East 4th St (Lafayette St and the Bowery). Subway: N or R to 8th St; 6 to Astor Place; F, B to Broadway-Lafayette. Bus: M5, M6 to Broadway-4th St; M103 to 4th St; M1 to Broadway and 8th St. Open Fri–Mon 12–5, Thur 12–8; last entry at 4:30; closed major holidays. Guided tour at 2pm; neighborhood walking tour March–Oct second Sun at 12:30pm. T: 212 777 1089, merchantshouse.org.
This remarkably preserved Greek Revival house is an authentic relic of Old New York. Inside the museum (1936) are the furnishings and possessions of the Tredwell family, who lived here for almost 100 years. A hat merchant dabbling in real estate built the three-story brick townhouse (1832; Joseph Brewster) on speculation and sold it in 1835 for $18,000 to Seabury Tredwell, a prosperous hardware merchant and importer. It remained in the family until the death of Tredwell's eighth and last child, Gertrude (1840–1933). Fortunately, Gertrude threw nothing away.

The slanted dormer roof and handsomely detailed doorway are typical of the late Federal period. The interiors are Greek Revival in style, with beautiful moldings and plasterwork. Three floors of period rooms showcase the family's furniture ranging from a Federal sofa with hand-carved eagles to such Tredwelliana as needlework, gloves and hats, underclothes, and chamber pots. In the ground-floor kitchen the cast-iron stove remains installed in the original cooking hearth. Behind the house a narrow walled garden blooms with plants, some of which were chosen from albums of pressed flowers left by the Tredwell daughters.

LAFAYETTE STREET
In 1804 John Jacob Astor paid $45,000 for land near present Lafayette St (*map p. 619, D4*). While waiting for its value to rise, Astor leased it to a Frenchman who created Vauxhall Gardens, a pleasure ground with pavilions for light refreshments and a

remodeled greenhouse for heavier drinking. In 1825 Astor reclaimed his land, carved out the street, and sold lots for more than $45,000 apiece, the price of the entire parcel two decades earlier. John Jacob Astor never lived on Lafayette St, but his son William B. Astor did—opposite Colonnade Row, in a house described by a contemporary as a "plain but substantial-looking brick mansion."

On the west side of Lafayette St (nos. 428–34) the four remaining houses of **Colonnade Row** (1833; Seth Geer, builder), once desirable, are now dingy. Originally named La Grange Terrace after the country home of the Marquis de Lafayette, Colonnade Row's original nine houses were joined by a monumental two-story Corinthian colonnade and faced with white Westchester marble cut by Sing Sing prisoners. Notables including Franklin Delano, grandfather of Franklin Delano Roosevelt, snapped up the luxury dwellings, but Colonnade Row enjoyed only a brief moment of social splendor as the juggernaut of commerce rolled up Broadway. By the 1860s the plain but substantial Astor mansion had become a restaurant; a neighborhood church had been converted to a boxing ring; and the five southernmost houses of the row had devolved into the Colonnade Hotel. When Lafayette St was extended south to the City Hall area in the 1880s, its remaining houses became tenements and rooming houses or were torn down for warehouses and factories.

THE PUBLIC THEATER AND ASTOR PLACE

Map p. 619, D3. 425 Lafayette St (4th St and Astor Pl.). Subway: N, R to 8th St; 6 to Astor Place. Bus: M2, M3, M5, M15, M101, M102.

The **Public Theater** (*T: 212 539 8500, publictheater.org.*) grew out of the New York Shakespeare Festival, founded by Joseph Papp (1921–91) to bring free Shakespeare to New Yorkers. Papp, a larger-than-life figure whose entrepreneurial skills and artistic courage changed the face of the American theater, was born in Brooklyn to Jewish immigrant parents, his early love for music mutating into an attraction for Shakespearean language. The Public Theater has consistently championed new and challenging work; nurtured the careers of black, Asian, and female playwrights; and cast actors of color in classic roles. The theater opened (1967) with the musical *Hair*, which moved to Broadway a year later. Profits from *Hair* and later *A Chorus Line* underwrote more adventurous plays, and in this, too, Papp broke new ground. The theater has introduced new work by David Mamet, John Guare, Sam Shepard, Vaclav Havel, David Hare, Suzan-Lori Parks, and others.

The theater building was built in three separate sections and then remodeled when threatened with demolition in the mid-20th century (south wing 1849–53, Alexander Saeltzer; center wing 1856–9, Griffith Thomas; north wing 1879–81, Thomas Stent; remodeled 1966, Giorgio Cavaglieri). It originated (1854) as the Astor Library, the only major public benefaction of tight-fisted John Jacob Astor, who dedicated it to working people, but kept it open only on weekdays when workers couldn't use it. When the Astor Library merged with the Lenox and Tilden collections in 1912 to form the nucleus of the New York Public Library system, the Hebrew Immigrant Aid Society took over and used it (1921–65) in its work of resettling Eastern European immigrants. In 1966 Joseph Papp convinced the city to buy it and remodel the interior under the guidance of Giorgio Cavaglieri, who also brilliantly recycled the Jefferson Market Library in Greenwich Village.

On the traffic island on the east side of **Astor Place**, a weathering steel cube (1966) by Bernard (Tony) Rosenthal balances on one apex. The 15-ft work, *Alamo*, got its name from a remark by the sculptor's wife that the piece had the visual strength of a fortress.

The **Astor Place subway** entrance across the street (*Fourth Ave and East 8th St*) is a cast-iron reproduction (1985) of an original subway kiosk. The station below (1904; Heins & LaFarge) is one of the city's best subway restorations, with murals by Milton Glaser.

The newest neighborhood arrival is glassy **51 Astor Place** (2013; Fumihiko Maki), an office building whose lobby sports a 14-ft, 6,600-lb pert *Balloon Rabbit (Red)* by Jeff Koons. Outside is Keith Haring's *Self-Portrait* (1989).

THE ASTOR PLACE RIOT

The building at 13 Astor Place stands on the site of the Astor Place Opera House, now remembered chiefly for the Astor Place riot (May 10, 1849). The arrival of the opera house (1847), at the intersection of then-elite Broadway and the proletarian Bowery, inflamed existing class tensions. The dress code for men attending the opera ("freshly shaven faces, evening dress, fresh waistcoats, and kid gloves") emphasized the social gulf, as did the seating arrangements. An already bitter theatrical rivalry between the English actor William Macready and his American counterpart Edwin Forrest, fanned by anti-British and anti-aristocratic sentiments, erupted into violence during a performance of *Macbeth*. The audience hurled garbage at Macready while a mob outside assaulted the building with bricks and paving stones. The militia summoned from a nearby armory was eventually ordered to fire into the crowd. Estimates of casualties differ, but the usual count is 22 dead and 150 wounded.

COOPER UNION

The Cooper Union for the Advancement of Science and Art is a private college recognized for programs in art, architecture, and engineering. Occupying the block bounded by Third Ave, 7th St, the Bowery, and Astor Place (*map p. 619, D3*), the brownstone Italianate **Cooper Union Foundation Building** (1859; Frederick A. Peterson) embodies the innovative genius of its founder both in its physical plant and in the institution it houses. The building incorporates some of the first wrought-iron beams used anywhere, beams Cooper developed from train rails and for which he built the necessary rolling machinery in his ironworks. Cooper's beams eventually evolved into I-beams, which when translated into steel became the bones of modern skyscrapers. The upper stories, added in the 1890s, once housed the collection of decorative arts that later became the nucleus of the Cooper-Hewitt Museum. In the small park across from the main entrance, the bronze **statue of Peter Cooper** (1897) is the work of Augustus Saint-Gaudens, who had received early training as a night student at Cooper Union; Stanford White, a friend of the sculptor, designed the canopy.

PETER COOPER

Cooper (1791–1883), a self-educated genius, designed the first American locomotive, promoted the Atlantic cable, and helped develop the telegraph. His fortune, however, came largely through his ironworks in Trenton, New Jersey, and a glue factory in Baltimore. Unlike others of his breed, Cooper recognized that his wealth had come from the "cooperation of multitudes" and turned his millions to philanthropy. By establishing Cooper Union as a free educational institution to give poor students the equivalent of a college degree while stressing also the practical arts and trades, Cooper provided for others the education he would have wished for himself. Requiring no other credentials than a good moral character, Cooper Union opened its doors to women as well as men, to adults as well as young people.

Another of Cooper's aims was to establish a forum where great issues of the day could be freely discussed. In the Foundation Building's Great Hall, Henry Ward Beecher, William Cullen Bryant, and William Lloyd Garrison spoke against slavery. Abraham Lincoln made his famous "right makes might" speech in 1860, winning the support of the New York press and hence the presidential nomination.

41 Cooper Square (2009; Thom Mayne), Cooper Union's new engineering building, has dramatically altered the streetscape with its glittering metal façade and its bold, slashed-open design. Environmentalists have recognized its first-class environmental credentials with a platinum LEED rating; neighborhood residents seem to have accepted its scale—reduced following local protests from a more ambitious proposal that would have obliterated little Taras Shevchenko Place behind it.

GRACE CHURCH

Map p. 619, D3. 802 Broadway (East 10th St). Generally open Mon–Sat 12–5. Free. Guided tours Sun at 1pm. Check website for organ recitals. T: 212 254 2000, gracechurchnyc.org.
Grace Church (Protestant Episcopal) lifts its delicate spire at the bend in Broadway at East 10th St. Often praised as New York's finest Gothic Revival church (1843–7; James Renwick Jr.), it was also once its most socially desirable. Although the original church stood across from Trinity Church, Grace Church was always an independent congregation, not a chapel of Trinity. James Renwick Jr., son of Trinity's architect, was 24 years old when chosen for the commission and had little experience (his sole design credit was a fountain at Bowling Green), but he would go on to design St. Patrick's Cathedral.

The façade, of white marble quarried by Sing Sing convicts, is known for its delicate stonework and fine proportions. The octagonal marble spire (1888), which cost two-thirds as much as the church, replaced a simple wooden steeple. Facing Broadway on the lawn, the large terra cotta Roman urn, possibly dating from the time of Nero, was presented to an early rector by a parishioner.

Inside, the "Te Deum" window in the chancel (1878) is by the English firm of Clayton and Bell (1878). The Pre-Raphaelite windows by Henry Holiday (also English) in the north and south aisles represent an attempt to fuse medieval and 19th-century sensibilities. The rectory (north of the church), designed by Renwick at the same time as the church, is one of the city's earliest Gothic Revival dwellings.

Book Row on Fourth Ave once comprised some seven blocks of used-book stores. **The Strand Bookstore** (1927), a family-owned business (*828 Broadway at 12th St; open Mon–Sat 9:30am–10:30pm, Sun 11am–10:30pm; T: 212 473 1452, strandbooks.com*), is a lonely survivor, offering readers "18 miles of new, used, and rare books."

THE EAST VILLAGE

The East Village, bounded by Houston St and Fourteenth St, the Bowery and Third Ave, and the East River, has embraced the immigrant poor, working-class families, middle-class hippies, artists and writers, squatters, the homeless, and more recently young professionals, and a surging population of students. Within its borders lie the Bowery; St. Mark's Historic District, with its faded ties to a long-gone aristocracy and more vivid ones to the punk rock scene of the 1970s; Little Ukraine and the former Yiddish Rialto; and Alphabet City.

HISTORY OF THE EAST VILLAGE

Until the 1960s the East Village did not exist as a distinct neighborhood. In the 19th century, considered part of the sprawling Lower East Side, its tenements housed Irish, German, Eastern European and Slavic immigrants. Its western sector, around St. Mark's Place and Astor Place, a formerly aristocratic neighborhood, declined.

In the 1950s a few beatniks moved in—Jack Kerouac and Allan Ginsberg among them—and during the next decade artists, writers, musicians, and other exponents of the burgeoning counterculture were drawn here by low rents. By the mid-1960s the area had acquired its new name, the East Village, capitalizing on the offbeat reputation of Greenwich Village. The blocks around St. Mark's Place pulsed with energy, its cafés, bookstores, theaters, coffee houses, and "head shops" catering to the intellectual, emotional, and spiritual needs of the psychedelically inclined. By the 1970s the counterculture had faded along with the city economy, and by the 1980s drug abuse, crime, and racial/cultural tensions surfaced, erupting in the 1988 Tompkins Square Park riots (*see p. 177*).

Since the 1990s, the city has recovered economically and the East Village has gentrified; condos rise above deteriorating tenements; a deluxe grocery store replaces a crack mart; chic restaurants have arrived. Even the far east of the Village, Alphabet City, is moving upscale, its reputation as an urban frontier fading like old graffiti.

TWO PRIVATE CEMETERIES

Monuments visible through the handsome iron fence of the **New York City Marble Cemetery** (*52–74 East 2nd St between First and Second Aves; subway: 6 to Bleecker St or F to 2nd Ave-Lower East Side; check website for designated visiting days; T: 212 228 6401, nycmc.org*) mark the marble underground vaults of a burial ground established in 1831, when the city's repeated yellow fever and cholera epidemics had convinced many that only burial in sealed marble vaults could contain the miasmic vapors thought to be responsible for the spread of disease. President James Monroe and John Ericsson, designer of the ironclad *Monitor*, were interred here but later moved to more prestigious pastures; still resting here in peace are the earthly remains of early mayor Marinus Willett; several Roosevelts; and Preserved Fish, a sea captain, merchant, and eventually banker, whose given name reflects the hoped-for state of his soul. The cemetery name includes the word "city" to distinguish it from its nearby predecessor, the **New York Marble Cemetery** (*41½ Second Ave; entrance halfway up the block between East 2nd and East 3rd Sts; open at least once a month April–Sept; check website for schedule, marblecemetery.org*), the city's first nonsectarian graveyard, built in 1830 as a money-making venture after burials were outlawed south of Canal St. The names of families who bought the underground vaults are inscribed in plaques on the wall: among them are Beekmans, Van Zandts, Varicks, and Scribners. In 2014 the cemetery offered two reclaimed and empty vaults at $350,000 each.

George and Ira Gershwin lived in a second-floor apartment at **91 Second Ave** (*East 5th and 6th Sts*) until 1909. East 6th St between First and Second Aves, sometimes called **Curry Row**, has a lineup of inexpensive Indian and Bangladeshi restaurants.

LITTLE UKRAINE

The remnants of the city's Ukrainian enclave stretch along Second Ave from about East 4th to East 14th Sts, with East 6th and 7th Sts at its heart. Ukrainians began immigrating to New York in the 1880s along with other Eastern Europeans; after World War II Little Ukraine reached a population of about 60,000 as immigrants fled Soviet control, but dwindled thereafter until the collapse of the Soviet Union when the tide turned again. Although many younger Ukrainians have left for the suburbs or Brooklyn, the neighborhood retains vital cultural institutions.

THE UKRAINIAN MUSEUM
Map p. 619, E4. 222 East 6th St (Second and Third Aves). Subway: 6 to Astor Place; N, R to 8th St-Broadway; F to 2nd Ave-Houston St. Bus: M15, M101, M102, M103. Open Wed–Sun 11:30–5; closed Mon, Tues, major national holidays, and some Ukrainian religious holidays; check the website. Admission charge; guided tours. Shop. T: 212 228 0110, ukrainianmuseum.org.

The handsome four-story museum building (2005), designed by Ukrainian-American George Sawicki, came to fruition after 15 years of planning. When the museum was founded in 1976, Ukraine was a republic of the Soviet Union. To preserve its traditional past, the museum collected Ukrainian folk art, including costumes, embroidered textiles, metalwork, kilim rugs, and *pysanky*—brilliantly decorated Easter eggs whose origin dates back to pre-Christian fertility rituals—as well as fine arts. The collection includes work by Ukrainian-American Jacques Hnizdovsky, Modernists Alexander Archipenko and Alexis Gritchenko, and the primitive artist Nikifor, among whose favorite subjects were the Orthodox churches and wooden buildings of his native Krynica. Changing exhibitions incorporate loans from here and abroad.

ON AND AROUND EAST 7TH STREET

Onion-domed, Byzantine-style **St. George's Ukrainian Catholic Church** (1977; Apollinaire Osadca) at 30 East 7th St is the largest institution in the community. On the north side of the street, **Surma** at 11 East 7th St, a family business since 1918, sells traditional Ukrainian handicrafts, books, and music, as well as authentic dyes for making your own *pysanky*. Nearby Ukrainian establishments include the Ukrainian National Home (*140–2 Second Ave; T: 212 614 3283*), a community center with an inexpensive, home-style Ukrainian eatery. **Veselka** at 144 Second Ave has served handmade *pierogi* and goulash to generations of locals (*T: 212 228 9682, veselka.com*).

One of the most venerable saloons in the city, **McSorley's Old Ale House**, originally McSorley's Saloon, opposite St. George's church at 15 East 7th St, claims 1854 as its opening date. The walls are covered with memorabilia and the floor with sawdust. Joseph Mitchell and E.E. Cummings wrote about the place; John Sloan painted scenes of the bar-room and the back room; Hippolyte Havel, Village anarchist, imbibed here, as did Babe Ruth, Will Rogers, Woody Guthrie, and generations of working men. Women were not permitted until 1970, when it became illegal to exclude them.

The **former Fillmore East** (1968–71) at 105 Second Ave (*East 6th and East 7th Sts*), began as the Commodore Theater (c. 1925–6; Harrison Wiseman), a venue for vaudeville and movies, its narrow façade fronting a 2,800-seat auditorium. A couple of decades later, rock impresario Bill Graham bought the then-derelict theater, which became "the best showplace for rock music in New York," presenting Jimi Hendrix, The Grateful Dead, The Doors, and other stars. Today a bank occupies the former lobby and the auditorium has been replaced with apartments.

ST. MARK'S PLACE

St. Mark's Place (*8th Street from Third Ave to Avenue A; map p. 619, E3*) was developed in the early 19th century as a fashionable street, its houses set back from the sidewalks to suggest spacious elegance. It lost its cachet as waves of immigrants colonized the Lower East Side but a century later became a countercultural destination, drawing thousands during the punk rock scene of the 1970s. Today it has a retro shopping strip with tattoo parlors, head shops, restaurants, and a few street people, though traces of its rich history remain. The venerable **St. Marks Comics** (*11 St. Mark's Pl., near Third Ave; T: 212 598 9439, stmarkscomics.com*) arrived in 1984 and continues to draw aficionados to its trove of comics, graphic novels, action figures, and collectibles.

Built in 1831, the **Hamilton-Holly House** (*4 St. Mark's Pl.*) was from 1833–41 the home of Elizabeth Schuyler Hamilton, widow of Alexander Hamilton since 1804. When Hamilton was shot by Aaron Burr, he left Elizabeth with seven children and the heavy debts he had incurred building and furnishing Hamilton Grange (*see p. 448*). Two other houses in this block, nos. 20 and 25, date from the same period.

The building at **no. 12 St. Mark's Place** (1888–9; William C. Frohne) was originally the social hall of the Deutsch-Amerikansiche Schuetzen Gesellschaft, a German shooting club, its identity marked by the ornamental terra cotta target and crossed rifles on the upper façade. A basement shooting gallery and bowling alley and an upstairs saloon and restaurant provided newcomers with opportunities to meet and socialize with their fellow countrymen.

Beginning in the 1920s, Polish immigrants flocked to **no. 19–25 St. Mark's Place**, the Polish National Home (*Polski Dom Narodowy*), a social club with a dance floor. In the 1960s "the Dom," with a bar downstairs and a ballroom upstairs, became a nightclub and discotheque called the Electric Circus. Andy Warhol rented it for his multimedia extravaganzas, films accompanied by light shows and music by the Velvet Underground. In 1970, a small bomb exploded on the dance floor, injuring at least 15 people, and by 1971 the Dom had become a community house with an addiction treatment center.

At the corner of Second Ave and St. Mark's Place (*131 Second Ave*) the **Gem Spa**, a famous newsstand since the 1920s, is often mentioned as the birthplace of the urban-legendary egg cream, a soda fountain beverage of obscure origins. Egg creams contain neither eggs nor cream, making even the name a subject for speculation, though the "egg" part may come from German/Yiddish *echt* ("genuine"). Some sources say that one Louis Auster, a Brooklyn candy-store owner, invented the concoction in the 19th century. Others give the honor to Yiddish actor Boris Thomashefsky who brought back *chocolat et crème* from Paris. What people do agree upon, however, is that egg creams must be made fresh (preferably at the soda fountain of your corner drugstore), and they must contain milk, chocolate syrup, and seltzer.

The **Ottendorfer Branch of the New York Public Library** (1884; William Schickel) at 135 Second Ave (*between St. Mark's Place and East 9th St*), originally the Freie Bibliothek und Lesehalle, was founded as a free public library by newspaper publishers Oswald and Anna Ottendorfer, who donated the bright red-brick building and the original collection of 8,000 books. To help their countrymen to assimilate and to encourage English-speaking Americans to acquaint themselves with German language and culture, half the books were in English, the other half in German. Next door at 137 Second Ave is the **former Stuyvesant Polyclinic Hospital** (1884; William Schickel), also founded (1857) by the Ottendorfers; as the German Dispensary it provided free health care to the poor. The building is noteworthy for its terra cotta ornament, which includes portrait busts of William Harvey, Antoine-Laurent Lavoisier, Galen, and Christoph Wilhelm Hufeland, a German physician.

ST. MARK'S HISTORIC DISTRICT

Historic ties bind St. Mark's Historic District to the Stuyvesant family. This residential neighborhood, with fine Greek Revival, Italianate, and Anglo-Italianate row houses, lies within the boundaries of Peter Stuyvesant's original farm (*bouwerie*), purchased from the Dutch West India Company in 1651, its fields and woods stretching from the East River to present-day Fourth Ave, from East 5th (*map p. 619, F4*) to about East 20th Sts.

In the late 1780s, the governor's great-grandson, Petrus Stuyvesant, land poor at the time, subdivided some of his property into lots along a grid oriented to the points of the compass. Construction began around 1800 but the City moved to impose its own grid in 1811, with streets oriented to the long axis of Manhattan. Although the City closed most existing streets and tore down buildings in the way, the Stuyvesant Street neighborhood was allowed to remain, in deference to the powerful family.

RENWICK TRIANGLE AND THE STUYVESANT-FISH HOUSE

The houses at 112–28 East 10th St and those directly behind them (*23–35 Stuyvesant St*) comprise **Renwick Triangle** (1861; attrib. James Renwick Jr.), built on land inherited by Hamilton Fish, whose mother was a Stuyvesant. Fish sold the lots encumbered by a restriction against future "noxious or offensive establishments"—breweries, slaughter houses, soap or glue factories, tanneries, cattle yards, or blacksmith shops. Before the advent of restrictive zoning laws, such covenants were the sole means of ensuring residential tranquility. The houses are red Philadelphia pressed brick with brownstone trim, bold cornices, and (many of them) fine cast-iron railings.

At 21 Stuyvesant St near Third Ave, the earlier **Stuyvesant-Fish House** (1803–4; *see also p. 191*), today the residence of Cooper Union's president, was built by Petrus Stuyvesant as a wedding gift for his daughter Elizabeth and her husband, Nicholas Fish. The unusual height and width (28¾ ft) of this brick Federal building suggest the Stuyvesant wealth. Hamilton Fish (1808–93), born in the house to Elizabeth and Nicholas and freed by his inheritance from the need to earn a living, went on to become governor of New York, US senator, and US secretary of state.

THE YIDDISH RIALTO

Second Ave from Houston St to East 14th St, once called the Yiddish Rialto (*map p. 619, E4–E3*), was the center of a vital theatrical tradition beside whose dramas the rest of the theater community paled. The plays, written for an unsophisticated audience, implausibly coupled tragic events with song-and-dance routines, low comedy, and extravagant tableaux. For Eastern European immigrants who spoke no English, the Yiddish theater offered escape from a tough reality, virtually the only entertainment available; journalist Hutchins Hapgood noted in 1902 that people whose weekly wage was only $10 willingly spent half their income on the theater. The Yiddish theater thrived until the 1930s, when the Depression and the decline in Yiddish speakers brought its glory years to a close.

The building that houses the **Village East Cinemas** (*189 Second Ave at East 12th St*) was constructed as the Yiddish Art Theater (1926), later becoming the Yiddish Folks Theater (?1929), the Phoenix Theater (1953), and a movie theater (1991). Seating 1,236, it was one of the last Yiddish theaters designed in a multicultural Moorish-Byzantine-Middle Eastern style.

Although it postdated the great years of the Yiddish Rialto, the Second Avenue

Delicatessen (1954–2005) at 156 Second Ave (*10th St*) became a Lower East Side legend. The deli is gone but the Hollywood-style **"Yiddish Theater Walk of Fame"** remains embedded in the sidewalk, its once-famous names eroded by footsteps. Among the bygone luminaries are Boris Tomashefsky, who billed himself as "America's Darling," and Jacob Adler, the best dramatic actor of his generation, who performed Shylock on Broadway in Yiddish while the other actors spoke English. The original delicatessen owner, Abe Lebewohl, was murdered in 1996; his nephew has re-opened the restaurant, which now has two locations, neither on Second Ave (*2ndavedeli.com*).

ST. MARK'S-IN-THE-BOWERY

131 East 10th St. Map p. 619, E3. Sanctuary open Mon–Fri 10–4, but usually viewable only from balcony level due to classes and rehearsals. T: 212 674 6377, stmarksbowery.org.

St. Mark's-in-the-Bowery (1799) is the second-oldest church in the city after St. Paul's Chapel. Built on the probable site of Peter Stuyvesant's own chapel, St. Mark's, which originally served an affluent, conservative congregation, has long been one of the city's most socially active Protestant Episcopal churches and an important cultural center.

The building
After modest, late-Georgian rural beginnings, visible in the rubblestone walls and simple triangular pediment, St. Mark's enjoyed the services of prominent architects. The Greek Revival steeple was added in 1828 (attrib. Martin E. Thompson and Ithiel Town) and an Italianate cast-iron portico was built in 1854, keeping the church abreast of architectural fashions. The brick Sunday School building (1861) was designed—or at least supervised—by James Renwick Jr. The rectory (1899), now the Neighborhood Preservation Center, was designed by Ernest Flagg. Flanking the main doorway are two marble lions (one a copy of Donatello's *Marzocco*, the emblem of Florence) and, outside the portico, two granite statues of Native Americans based on drawings by Solon Borglum, brother of the more famous Gutzon Borglum. Commissioned by the church, they were executed by the Piccirilli brothers (*see p. 400*) and are said to symbolize Aspiration and Inspiration. At the west end of the porch is a bust (1939; O. Grymes) of Daniel Tompkins (1774–1825), a governor of New York State known for liberal reforms in education, the criminal code, and human rights. He is buried in the graveyard.

The interior, steeple, and roof were severely damaged in 1978 when a worker's torch ignited the wooden gallery on the second floor. In 1980 a new bell was installed, dedicated to the workers who rebuilt the church, many of them young local laborers.

The churchyard
Divided in two by the church building, the churchyard suffered a ghoulish grave robbery in 1878 when the body of department store millionaire A.T. Stewart (*see p. 90*) was exhumed and carted off for ransom. A bag of bones—possibly Stewart's—was recovered two or three years later, in a dark lane at dead of night, after the payment of $20,000. Resting undisturbed are Commodore Matthew Perry, Daniel Tompkins and members

of the prominent Fish, Goelet, Schermerhorn, Stuyvesant, and Livingston families.

In the eastern sector stands the old bell, cracked by the 1978 fire, which tolled the deaths of John F. Kennedy, Robert F. Kennedy, and the Rev. Dr. Martin Luther King; after Dr. King's assassination it was rung only to celebrate the end of the Vietnam War. Plaques on the parish house wall commemorate poets W.H. Auden (a parishioner of the church), Ted Berrigan, and Allen Ginsberg and novelist John O'Hara. Entombed in the church wall are the remains of Peter Stuyvesant; the statue of the governor was sculpted in the Netherlands (1911) by Toon Dupuis.

THE EASTERN EAST VILLAGE & ALPHABET CITY

The 10.5-acre **Tompkins Square Park** (*map p. 619, F3*) is named after onetime governor and US vice president Daniel D. Tompkins.

HISTORY OF TOMPKINS SQUARE PARK

The 1811 Commissioners' Plan designated 54 acres including what is now the park as open space for a wholesale market, one of the few areas on Manhattan not divided into small rectilinear plots. The City acquired the then-marshy land in 1834, graded it, and landscaped it as a public square, which eventually (1878) became a park. In 1936 Robert Moses had it laid out in its present configuration—small patches of green interrupted by curving walkways. In 1992 the park and its monuments were restored and the city's first official dogrun was added.

As one of the few open areas and gathering spaces in the increasingly crowded Lower East Side, Tompkins Square Park has witnessed two historic riots and many lesser demonstrations, sparked by poor economic conditions, oppressive labor relations, and the Vietnam War, among other causes. During the first riot (1874), mounted police wielding clubs suppressed a gathering of thousands of unemployed workers who were hoping for financial relief during a severe economic depression. The tinder that ignited the second (1988) was the enforcement of a park curfew. The ensuing street battle exposed underlying hostilities and fears and reflected the changing demographics of the neighborhood, which included squatters, hippies, remnants of the Old World immigrant population, young white affluent professionals, and newer Puerto Rican and black immigrants.

PARK MONUMENTS

Near the 9th St entrance is the **Temperance Fountain** (1888; Albert Bertel Thorvaldsen), its canopy bearing a statue of Hebe (cup-bearer to the Olympian deities) beneath which a drinking fountain encourages the healthful consumption of water. The fountain's donor, Henry D. Cogswell, a dentist who made a fortune fixing prospectors' teeth during the Gold Rush and investing the proceeds in San Francisco real estate, donated several of these elaborate water fountains to cities he thought in need of moral guidance. The fountains were not always well received.

On the north side of the park near the restrooms stands the *General Slocum memorial* (1905; Bruno Louis Zimm), a 9-ft marble stele depicting a boy and girl gazing into the distance, their features eroded by time.

THE *GENERAL SLOCUM* DISASTER

The *General Slocum*, a coal-fired wooden sidewheeler, burned and sank in the East River on June 15, 1904. The 1,021 victims, virtually all of them women and children from this predominantly German neighborhood, had been on their way to a church picnic on Long Island. Less than 20 minutes after embarking, the steamer was on fire. Instead of immediately beaching the ship, the captain continued upwind to North Brother Island. The safety equipment failed spectacularly—the rotted canvas fire hoses and crumbled cork life preservers proved worse than useless. The crew, unprepared for the panic aboard, acted to save themselves. Less than a half hour after the fire was discovered, the *General Slocum* lay a charred wreck on the beach of North Brother Island. Bodies washed up for days. Funerals continued longer than a week, one of them a procession with 156 hearses. Many men, who had been kept from the outing by their jobs, lost their entire families; for the bereaved, the Tompkins Square neighborhood became too painful and most survivors moved to other German communities. It was the city's single largest loss of life until 9/11.

In the center of the park an old American elm known as the **Hare Krishna Tree** marks the spot where Bhaktivedanta Swami Prabhupada introduced the Hare Krishna religion to the US in 1966.

Near the southwest entrance to the park a **statue of Samuel Sullivan Cox**, "the letter carrier's friend," memorializes an Ohio congressman who sponsored legislation that raised wages and gave salaried vacations to postmen. The statue (1891; Louise Lawson) was first erected in Cooper Square, where it occasioned the criticism that the figure resembled a department-store floor-walker beckoning an approaching customer. When Saint-Gaudens's figure of Peter Cooper was installed in the square (*see p. 170*), Congressman Cox came here.

AROUND THE SQUARE

Facing the park at 228 East 10th St (*Avenue A*) is **St. Nicholas of Myra Orthodox Church** (1883; James Renwick Jr. and W.H. Russell), a congregation founded by immigrants from Carpathian Ruthenia, now in western Ukraine. The Rutherford-Stuyvesant family built the church as a missionary chapel of St. Mark's-in-the-Bowery.

Half a block west of the church, in a former tenement, the **Russian & Turkish Baths** (*268 East 10th St*) are the oldest (1892) such baths in Manhattan. In 1897 the borough had 62 Russian (steam) and Turkish (hot air) baths which served immigrants keeping their traditions. The assimilated younger generation shunned them as old-fashioned, but today as the Tenth Street Baths they serve a varied clientele.

Along the north side of the park stands a row of houses built in 1846 when the Tompkins Square neighborhood looked toward an auspicious future. The houses on the south side, built a year later, were described at the time of completion as "new and desirable tenements," but their ground floors were designed as storefronts which could be rented for $200 a year, an indication of a less optimistic outlook. By the 1850s, as German immigrants began crowding into the neighborhood, the one- and two-family dwellings were subdivided into rooming houses or razed to be replaced by more profitable tenements. By the 1860s the area was described as dirty, seedy, and dusty; East 4th Street between Avenues A and B was called "Ragpickers' Row," while East 11th Street from First Avenue to Avenue B became "Mackerelville."

ALPHABET CITY

Avenues A through D, lying in the eastward bulge of Manhattan Island (*map p. 619, F3*), were laid out and named by the Commissioners' Plan of 1811 so that First Ave could run almost the full length of the island instead of ending where the island narrows around 14th St.

East of Tompkins Square Park at 151 Avenue B (*East 9th and 10th Sts*) is the **former Charlie Parker House** (c. 1849; *map p. 619, F3*), where the great sax player lived (1950–4) in a ground-floor apartment with his companion, Chan Richardson (she called herself Chan Parker, but the couple never married). Parker was recognized as a major jazz innovator but his life was spinning out of control. He died in 1955, his death hastened by drug abuse. The house itself is modestly remarkable as one of the city's few remaining Gothic Revival townhouses retaining its original pointed-arch entranceway and double wooden doors.

La Plaza Cultural de Armando Perez (*632–50 East 9th St at Ave C; open summer Sat and Sun 12–5, laplazacultural.org*) flourishes in what was once a rubble-filled vacant lot. Two huge willow trees planted c. 1976 shade an amphitheater made of reclaimed railroad ties and building materials. Playful sculptures of flattened cut-up tin cans decorate the surrounding fence. Armando Perez was a community activist murdered in 1999.

THE MUSEUM OF RECLAIMED URBAN SPACE (MoRUS)

Map p. 619, F3. 155 Avenue C. Open Tues and Thur–Sun, 11–7, but call ahead. Suggested donation. Guided neighborhood tours. T: 973 818 8495, morusnyc.org.

Housed on the ground floor of a five-story brick walk-up, the Museum of Reclaimed Urban Space (2012) documents the history of the eastern East Village's recent past, its political activism, and its role in such now-mainstream activities as bicycling, recycling, and community gardens. The formerly abandoned City-owned tenement known as C-Squat (or See Squat) became a legendary preserve for punk rock bands and graffiti artists, but has survived as one of the eleven squatted buildings the City turned over to residents. The museum offers photos, documents, and videos of the memorable days of radicalism, including an energy bike that helped power Zuccotti Park during the Occupy Wall Street siege and provided cell-phone power to locals during Hurricane Sandy.

EATING AND DRINKING IN NOHO AND THE EAST VILLAGE

In these districts you can expect student hangouts, local eateries, and various cuisines. Around St. Mark's Place and 10th St, an area sometimes called "Little Japan" or "Little Tokyo," are ramen shops, karaoke bars, and Japanese gift shops.

ASTOR PLACE AND NOHO

$$$ Jewel Bako. This established high-end sushi restaurant serves a wide selection of exotic and local fish. The tables are close together in an elegantly designed space with bamboo and mirrored glass, and the sushi appears on hand-crafted Japanese and French plates. Wines and many sakes. Dinner Mon–Sat. *239 East Fifth St (Second and Third Aves). T: 212 979 1012, jewelbakosushi. com. Map p. 619, E4.*

$$$ Prime & Beyond New York. The upscale Korean-inflected steakhouse and butcher shop offers meat from the purveyor used by Peter Luger and other top NY steakhouses. Not your usual steakhouse décor: the room is cool and spare. Sides include kimchi and fermented cabbage, and there is a vegetarian entrée; even better are the dry- and wet-aged steaks and lamb chops. Dinner nightly. *90 East 10th St (Third and Fourth Aves). T: 212 505 0033, primeandbeyond. com. Map p. 619, D3.*

$$ Mermaid Inn. So many varieties of oysters are available in this enjoyable seafood place that it provides an app for your phone to help you order. During the happy hour there are fish tacos, shrimp corn dogs, and other bite-sized snacks. Dinner features seafood in many guises and one or two earthbound entrées. Specials include the Sunday "lobsterpalooza" and Taco Tuesdays. Dinner nightly. *96 Second Ave (5th and 6th Sts). T: 212 674 5870, themermaidnyc.com. Map p. 619, E4.*

$$ Porsena. The chef describes this small, casual eatery as a pasta restaurant, but there are excellent salads and a few appetizers, along with such irresistible pastas as *anelloni* with spicy lamb sausage and mustard greens, and *pennette* with roasted cauliflower, anchovies, capers, and black olives. Serious carnivores can go for the dry-aged rib eye. Many Italian wines. Dinner nightly; check website for weekend brunch hours. *21 East 7th St (Second and Third Aves). T: 212 228 4923, porsena.com. Map p. 619, E3.*

$ ChikaLicious Dessert Bar. The menu in this 20-seat restaurant changes daily with delicacies spun from sugar, butter, flour, and chocolate: brulées, sorbets, tarts, cakes, and fruit-and-cheese plates. For drinks there are teas and coffees, dessert wines, and non-alcoholic beverages. Across the street the Dessert Club offers takeout. Open Thur–Sun 3–10:45, closed Mon–Wed. *203 East 10th St (First and Second Aves). T: 212 475 0929, chikalicious. com. Map p. 619, E3.*

$ Mighty Quinn's. This barbecue

joint made its debut at Smorgasburg in Brooklyn, but Manhattanites can now enjoy it without crossing the river. The battered tables came from the Puck Building (*see p. 126*); the service is casual but the barbecue is what barbecue should be. Traditional sides include slaw and *frites*. Lunch and dinner daily. *103 Second Ave (East 6th St). T: 212 677 3733, mightyquinns bbq.com. Map p. 619, E4.*

$ **Zabb Elee**. Small, inexpensive Thai restaurant featuring Northern specialties from the Isan region bordering Laos and Cambodia. Unusual dishes include green papaya salad, and pork and beef *larb*—a spicy combination of ground meat with roasted rice—as well as grilled and fried dishes. Lunch and dinner daily. *75 Second Ave (4th and 5th Sts). T: 212 505 9533, zabbelee.com. Map p. 619, E4.*

EAST VILLAGE

$$$$ **Kyo Ya**. Small downstairs restaurant, beautifully designed in the Japanese tradition. Known for its intricate multi-course *kaiseki* meals (order at least a day ahead), there is also an *à la carte* menu with fine sushi, tempura, soups, and familiar and exotic Japanese dishes. Dinner nightly, open late. *94 East 7th St (First Ave and Ave A). T: 212 982 4140, no website. Map p. 619, E3.*

$$$$–$ **Momofuku**. (*For reservation info on all Momofuku restaurants, visit momofuku.com.*) When chef David Chang, veteran of fine dining restaurants and Japanese noodle shops, opened **Momofuko Noodle**

Bar (*171 First Ave between 11th and 12th Sts; lunch and dinner daily, weekends open late*) in 2004, its irreverent, in-your-face attitude changed the course of NYC dining, immediately attracting the hip crowd as well as the establishment. Chang has since expanded to a veritable empire. Small, intimate **Momofuku Ko** (*8 Extra Pl. off East 1st St between Bowery and Second Ave; dinner Wed–Sun*) serves a chef's tasting menu: what you see is what you get, though it is said to be spectacular. (The Noodle Bar is larger and offers contemporary comfort food.) **Momofuku Ssäm Bar** (*207 Second Ave at 13th St; lunch Mon–Fri, dinner Tues–Sun, brunch weekends*) also references Chang's Asian heritage. Its signature dish is steamed pork buns. The extreme arduousness of getting reservations adds to the mystique. Also at 207 Second Ave (*entrance on 13th St*) is **Booker and Dax**, Momofuku's walk-in bar, with snacks; some tables with reservations; lunch and late dining daily (*207 2nd Ave at East 13th St*). **Momofuku Milk Bar** serves Chang's take on traditional bakery goods: soft-serve ice cream, whimsically named pies, cakes, and savories (*251 East 13th St at Second Ave plus other locations; open 9am–midnight; T: 347 577 9504*).

$$ **Bianca**. Charming low-key rustic restaurant with an open kitchen, wooden tables, and curtained windows. The cooking, from Emilia-Romagna, offers such treats as gnocchi with gorgonzola, lasagna with béchamel and ragù, and *gramigna*, a twisted pasta traditionally served

with a creamy sausage sauce. Dinner every evening; cash only. *5 Bleecker St (Bowery and Elizabeth St). T: 212 260 4666, biancanyc.com. Map p. 619, E4.*

$$ DBGB Kitchen & Bar. Chef Daniel Boulud's modest downtown satellite near the site of long-gone rock club CBGB. The menu includes burgers, chopped salad, charcuterie, and tuna crudo, and the prices are reasonable. Full wine list. Dinner nightly, lunch Fri, brunch weekends. *299 Bowery (1st and Houston Sts). T: 212 933 5300, dbgb.com. Map p. 619, E4.*

$$ Prune. This simple, modest, small restaurant with skillful cooking and a frequently changing menu, has attracted a loyal clientele since 1999. Open to the street on warm sunny days. Dinner nightly, brunch weekends. *54 East 1st St (First and Second Aves). T: 212 677 6221, prunerestaurant.com. Map p. 619, E4.*

$ Lil' Frankie's. Classic East Village décor—small, brick-walled, a little shabby-chic—with fine pizza baked in a wood-burning oven. The restaurant also offers fresh *antipasti* and pastas. No reservations, so you may have to wait. Cash only. Lunch weekends, dinner nightly (open late). *19 First Ave (1st and 2nd Sts). T: 212 420 0040, lilfrankies.com. Map p. 619, E4.*

$ Sigiri. Good, authentic Sri Lankan food near the Sixth St "curry row." Lunch and dinner daily. *91 First Ave (6th St). T: 212 614 9333; sigirinyc.com. Map p. 619, E4.*

BLUE GUIDE

NEW YORK

CAROL von PRESSENTIN WRIGHT

SOMERSET • LONDON

CONTENTS

PRACTICAL INFORMATION

MAPS & PLANS

About the Blue Guides
The BLUE GUIDES were launched in 1918, founded by two Scottish brothers, James and Findlay Muirhead. The guides remain the leading series in the English language for art, architecture, culture, and history, designed, as a past editor expressed it, "for the traveler who desires to understand more fully what he or she sees."

Fifth edition 2016
Reprinted 2022

Published by Blue Guides Limited, a Somerset Books Company

Unit 2, Old Brewery Road, Wiveliscombe, Somerset TA4 2PW

www.blueguides.com
'Blue Guide' is a registered trademark.

ISBN 978-1-905131-93-8

A CIP catalogue record of this book is available from the British Library.

The author and the publishers have made reasonable efforts to ensure the accuracy of all the
information in *Blue Guide New York*; however, they can accept no responsibility for any loss,
injury, or inconvenience sustained by any traveller as a result of information or advice
contained in the guide.

Statement of editorial independence: Blue Guides, their authors and editors,
are prohibited from accepting any payment from any restaurant, hotel, gallery or other
establishment for its inclusion in this guide, or for a more favorable mention than
would otherwise have been made.

Every effort has been made to contact the copyright owners of material reproduced in this
guide. We would be pleased to hear from any copyright owners we have been unable to reach.

Your views on this book would be much appreciated. We welcome not only specific
comments, suggestions, or corrections, but any more general views you may have: how
this book enhanced your visit, how it could have been more helpful. Blue Guides authors
and editorial and production team work hard to bring you what we hope are the best-
researched and best-presented cultural guide books in the English language. Please
write to us by email (editorial@blueguides.com), via the comments page on our website
(www.blueguides.com) or at the address given above. We will be happy to acknowledge
useful contributions in the next edition, and to offer a free copy of one of our titles.

Series editor: Annabel Barber
Assistant editor: Katie McKain.

Maps: Dimap Bt. Floor plans: Imre Bába
Architectural line drawings: Michael Mansell RIBA & Gabriella Juhász
All maps, plans, and drawings © Blue Guides.
Cover: 40 Wall St, by Michael Mansell RIBA & Gabriella Juhász © Blue Guides.

Image research by Hadley Kincade, pre-press by Anikó Kuzmich.
Images by Gábor Fényes (pp. 3, 75, 84, 125, 131, 148, 233, 246, 253, 265, 275, 305, 308, 343,
479), Annabel Barber (p. 47), © blackwaterinamges/iStock (p. 37), © leadinglights/iStock
(pp. 44, 409), © Nigel Francis/Robert Harding/World Imagery/Corbis/Profimedia (p. 63)
© H. Armstrong Roberts/ClassicStock/Corbis/Profimedia (p. 67), © Nathan Benn/
Ottochrome/Corbis/Profimedia (p. 80), © Atlantide Phototravel/Corbis/Profimedia (p. 114),
© Songquan Deng/iStock (p. 118), © Ramin Talaie/Corbis/Profimedia (p. 123),
© Mark Thomas/iStock (p. 143), © Gail Mooney/Corbis/Profimedia (pp. 211, 243),
© Percy Feinstein/ Corbis/Profimedia (p. 165), © MarkdeOliveira/iStock (p. 193),
© Dutchnatasja/iStock (p. 202), © Najlah Feanny/Corbis/Profimedia (p. 287), © Rudy
Sulgan/Corbis/Profimedia (p. 292), © Donald Nusbaum/Robert Harding/World Imagery/
Corbis/Profimedia (p. 372), © samdiesel/iStock (p. 399), © LehaKoK/Shutterstock (p. 406),
© mjbs/iStock (p. 420), © Farrell Grehan/Arcaid/Corbis/Profimedia (p. 455), © Bettmann/
Corbis/Profimedia (p. 457), © Danny Lehman/Corbis/Profimedia (p. 460),
© Andrew Gosling/iStock (p. 469), © Ben Russell/iStock (p. 503),
© Russel KORD/Photononstop/Corbis/Profimedia (p. 525).

All material prepared for press by Anikó Kuzmich.

Author's acknowledgements:
Grateful thanks especially to Jean M. Taylor, and to Annabel Barber, Kristen Braun,
Hilary Buchanan, Paula Glatzer, Pat Jaeger, Amy Jaffe, Katie McKain, Julie Meyers,
Rosey Perron-Kaniecki, Pedro F. Rodriguez, and Fred Wright
for their suggestions, generosity, and knowledge of the city.

Printed and bound by Lightning Source.

CAROL VON PRESSENTIN WRIGHT has been writing and revising editions of *Blue Guide New York* since 1976 and has also authored *Blue Guide Museums and Galleries of New York*, *art/shop/eat New York*, and *Staten Island: A Blue Guide Travel Monograph*. She has published on women's health and cooking and has contributed to the *Encyclopedia of New York City*. Her work has appeared in *The New York Times*, *Ceramics*, and other periodicals and has been translated into Chinese, Hebrew, and Romanian. She was born on Staten Island and received a graduate degree from Columbia University as a Woodrow Wilson Fellow.

FRANCIS MORRONE is an architectural historian and writer, and the author of eleven books, including *Guide to New York City Urban Landscapes* (W.W. Norton, 2013) and, with Henry Hope Reed, *The New York Public Library: The Architecture and Decoration of the Stephen A. Schwarzman Building* (W.W. Norton, 2011), as well as of architectural guidebooks to Philadelphia and Brooklyn.

Union Square to Madison Square

Union and Madison Squares, among the city's most historic, bookend a diverse commercial and residential neighborhood. Landmarks include the Flatiron Building, the former grand department stores of Ladies' Mile, and the dignified mansions and clubs around Gramercy Park.

Once surrounded by fine homes, later a hotbed of political activism, and still later a bedraggled open-air drug mart, **Union Square Park** is today home to the city's best-known farmers' market. Theaters and destination restaurants line the side streets. The park swarms with energy—children cavorting in the playground, chess players strategizing, street dancers, ball players, and people simply watching the passing scene.

Map p. 619, D2–D3. Subway: L, N, Q, R, 4, 5, 6 to 14th St-Union Square. Bus: M1, M2, M3, M7, M9, M14. Walking tours Sat at 2pm depart from the Abraham Lincoln statue at the 16th St transverse. Pavilion Café (seasonal) at north end of park; T: 212 677 7818, thepavilionnyc. com. For park events, see unionsquarenyc.org.

HISTORY OF UNION SQUARE PARK

Union Square, formerly called Union Place, gets its name from its location at the union of the two main roads out of town: the Bowery Road (part the Boston Post Road, now Fourth Avenue and beyond), and the Bloomingdale Road (part of the Albany Post Road, now Broadway). One of the few open squares designated by the Commissioners' Plan of 1811, it served as a potter's field until 1815 and was bought by the City for a park in 1833. In 1839 when the park opened, upscale homes, restaurants, theaters, and hotels abutted the square. Toward the century's end, it became the heart of Ladies' Mile, a promenade of fashionable stores along Broadway (*see p. 186*), followed later by factories of related industries including sewing machine companies. On September 5, 1882, cigar makers, jewelers, bricklayers, and other laborers marched up Broadway to the square in the first

Labor Day Parade while seamstresses waved handkerchiefs from windows along the route. By the 1890s, the stores and theaters had given way to tall office buildings.

As a forum for radical politics, the park has hosted anarchists, socialists, "Wobblies" (members of the Industrial Workers of the World), and communists. Unions including International Ladies' Garment Workers Union and the American Civil Liberties Union established headquarters nearby. Mass meetings sometimes degenerated into confrontations with the police, most notably a gathering protesting the execution of anarchists Nicola Sacco and Bartolomeo Vanzetti (1927) and a Depression-era labor demonstration (1930) attended by 35,000. In 1965 pacifists burned their draft cards in protest against the Vietnam War to a crowd of supporters and hecklers.

By the 1970s the park had become seedy and infested with drug dealers, and in the 1980s the City began to rehabilitate it, adding the plaza at the southern end and replanting the lawns and gardens. After 9/11, because the public was barred south of 14th St, Union Square became a makeshift outdoor shrine with candles, pictures of loved ones, messages of hope or sorrow, and tributes to the missing.

MONUMENTS IN THE PARK
The heroic bronze equestrian **statue of George Washington** (dedicated 1856) near 14th St is the work of Henry Kirke Brown, a master of equestrian sculpture. Between 14th and 15th Sts, near Union Square West, is Kantilal B. Patel's bronze (1986) **statue of Mohandas Gandhi**. Also on the western side of the park is the **Union Square Drinking Fountain** (1881; Karl Adolph Donndorf), donated by Daniel Willis James (his fortune came from mining and railroads). It depicts *Charity*, represented allegorically by the sculptor's wife and children.

On the other side of the park, near East 15th St, a bronze **statue of the Marquis de Lafayette** (dedicated 1876; Frédéric-Auguste Bartholdi) offers his sword to the cause of American independence. France presented the work in gratitude for American support during the Franco-Prussian War; the sculptor's fame would be assured with that larger monument to Franco-American friendship, the Statue of Liberty. On the imposing base (36ft diameter, 9½ft high) of the 40-ft **Independence Flagstaff** (cast 1926, dedicated 1930; Anthony De Francisci), bronze reliefs contrast democracy with tyranny. Formerly called the Charles F. Murphy Memorial after a Tammany Hall boss (*see opposite*), the flagpole was financed by Tammany money collected on the 150th anniversary of the signing of the Declaration of Independence. After Murphy's death in 1924, Tammany power players had wanted to transform an existing flagpole into a memorial for their leader, a desire many New Yorkers opposed, not wanting a monument honoring Murphy towering over the statues of Washington and Lincoln.

If the statue of George Washington was considered Henry Kirke Brown's best work, the bronze **Abraham Lincoln** (cast 1868, dedicated 1870) at the north end of the park was judged his worst, criticized as ugly, lacking in heroic spirit. An anonymous *New York Times* writer ridiculed the combination of modern dress and Roman toga, though other sculptors of the period sometimes combined realism with Neoclassical idealism.

A colossal public sculpture, ***Metronome*** (1999), by Kristin Jones and Andrew Ginzel, covers ten stories of the façade of 1 Union Square South (*14th St between Fourth Ave* *and Broadway*). The work is said to be a meditation on time—geological, astronomical, historical, and "real." Among its elements are a pendulum, a piece of rock, and a 15-place digital clock that simultaneously measures the time passed since midnight (left to right) and the time remaining until the next midnight (right to left)—in hours, minutes, seconds, and tenths of a second; the middle digit records hundredths of a second whirling by at illegible speed.

EAST AND NORTH OF THE PARK

The **former Union Square Savings Bank** (1907) at 20 Union Square East (*East 15th St*), with its handsome Corinthian colonnade, recalls architect Henry Bacon's most famous accomplishment, the Lincoln Memorial in Washington, D.C. Today the Daryl Roth Theatre, one of several Off-Broadway houses in the neighborhood, occupies the building. The Union Square Theatre (*100 East 17th St between Union Square East and Park Ave South*) and the New York Film Academy offer performances and courses in film-making in the Colonial Revival **former headquarters of Tammany Hall** (1929).

TAMMANY HALL

Later synonymous with the corrupt Democratic Party machine, Tammany Hall began in New York as the Tammany Society, incorporated in 1789. Earlier Tammany societies had been instituted in Philadelphia and elsewhere, named for a legendary Native American, Tamanend, whose deeds assumed heroic proportions (for example, creating Niagara Falls during an epic battle with an evil spirit). Tamanend became symbolic of the new republic and was sometimes feted as St. Tammany, patron saint of America.

After the Revolution, the Tammany societies supported republicanism (and opposed the revival of an aristocratic elite), accepting anyone who paid a small membership fee. The ordinary members, "braves," were drawn largely from the ranks of artisans and tradesmen; the leaders were "sachems." They met monthly at their "wigwam," to eat, drink, and talk politics. During celebrations, braves and sachems paraded through the streets wearing approximations of Native American garb.

The society quickly became politicized. William M. "Boss" Tweed owed his start in politics to Tammany, which recruited him from a volunteer firefighters' company whose snarling tiger logo later became the symbol of Tammany Hall. As immigration surged, Tammany expanded its power base by helping the new arrivals find jobs, easing their way to citizenship, and eventually controlling their votes. The powerful sachems ran the Democratic Party, rewarding loyalty with government contracts.

After Tweed's fall in 1871, John Kelly headed Tammany Hall, converting it from a rabble of competing interests to a disciplined political apparatus. Kelly, the first of ten Irish bosses, introduced a hierarchical system that involved every unit of electoral politics from the city precincts up to the highest levels of state government. Ethnic groups within Tammany included the Irish principally, but also Jews and Germans.

The organization peaked in 1928, when its candidates filled the offices of governor (the respected Al Smith) and mayor (the high-living James J. Walker). The following year Tammany opened this building on Union Square. Only three years later the once powerful Democratic machine had lost its stranglehold on city politics. In 1932, after the Seabury Commission publicly revealed government corruption, Walker resigned. Newly elected Franklin D. Roosevelt, an anti-Tammany Democrat, took control of federal patronage and promoted Fiorello La Guardia over the Tammany candidate. Tammany's membership dwindled; in 1943, unable to meet the mortgage payments, the sachems sold the building to the Ladies' Garment Workers Union.

The **Union Square Greenmarket** (*open Mon, Wed, Fri, Sat 8–6, grownyc.org*) brings city dwellers farm-fresh produce, potted plants, baked goods, and flowers from "the country," i.e. anywhere outside the five boroughs. Its arrival in 1976 helped spur the redevelopment of the park and neighborhood; today in peak season some 140 farmers, fishermen, and bakers offer their products to a devoted clientele.

WEST & NORTH OF UNION SQUARE

THE CENTER FOR JEWISH HISTORY
Map p. 618, C2. 15 West 16th St (Fifth and Sixth Aves). Some of the galleries are free: these are open Sun 11–5, Mon and Wed 9:30–8, Tues and Thur 9:30–5, Fri 9:30–4. The Yeshiva University Museum galleries are open Sun, Tues, Thur 11–5, Wed 11–8. Admission charges to YUM galleries except free Wed 5–8 and Fri 11–2:30. All exhibition spaces closed Sat, Jewish holidays, and major national holidays. T: 212 294 8301, cjh.org.

The Center for Jewish History (2000) brings together five institutions formerly scattered throughout Manhattan: the Yeshiva University Museum (1973), the Leo Baeck Institute (1955), the American Jewish Historical Society (1892), the American Sephardi Federation (1973), and the YIVO Institute for Jewish Research (founded 1925 in Wilno, Poland, now Vilnius in Lithuania), the only pre-Holocaust scholarly institution that successfully transferred its work to the Western Hemisphere. The collections, shown in changing exhibitions, include 100 million archival documents, half a million books, more than a thousand family trees, and the largest collection of Yiddish-language materials in the world. The tens of thousands of artifacts include Emma Lazarus's handwritten sonnet "The New Colossus"; a box of Brillo soap pads with an ad in Yiddish explaining that using Brillo is acceptable in kosher kitchens; a letter by Thomas Jefferson denouncing anti-Semitism; personal correspondence from Anne Frank's father to his friend Nathan Straus Jr., hoping for help escaping Amsterdam; and Sandy Koufax's first baseball uniform (signed).

LADIES' MILE

In the later decades of the 19th century the blocks between Union Square and West 23rd Sts along Broadway became known as Ladies' Mile, a shopping district where palatial department stores occupied prominent intersections and dominated the avenues, with lesser establishments on the side streets. A second stretch of historic stores on Sixth Ave, where the Sixth Avenue "El" (elevated railway) arrived in 1878 making the stores accessible to a wider clientele, was named "Fashion Row." The stores not only offered "the perfection of everything," according to an 1893 guidebook, but introduced amenities that changed shopping from a domestic task to an amusement—restaurants, art galleries, fountains, divans, and skylit rotundas. These department stores, descendants of modest "dry goods" stores, reflected an increasingly affluent society, in which women were becoming the chief household consumers. Several of the grand emporia remain, though altered both in appearance and function: look at the upper stories to get an idea of how they looked in their prime.

The **former Arnold Constable Dry Goods Store** (*881–887 Broadway between East 18th to East 19th Sts*) was designed in 1868–76 by Griffith Thomas, architect of the earlier Arnold Constable store on Canal St (*see p. 111*). Thomas clad the Broadway façade of the new store with marble—the only suitable material according to Aaron Arnold—and as the store expanded, duplicated the Broadway façade in cast iron along Fifth Ave, wrapping the imposing mansard roof around the whole building. Arnold Constable & Co., physically one of the largest business establishments in the world, sold the latest fashions to the ladies of the Carnegie, Edison, Rockefeller, and Vanderbilt families.

The **former W. & J. Sloane Store** (1882; William Wheeler Smith), across the street at 880–6 Broadway (*East 18th to East 19th Sts*), a six-story brick building with cast-iron decoration, wide windows, and classical detailing, served as a showplace for the Sloane brothers, first William and then John, who immigrated from Kilmarnock, a center of Scottish weaving. William got his start selling carpets and oilcloth floor coverings but expanded into oriental rugs, lace curtains, upholstery fabrics, and even furniture. Eventually the Sloanes became full-service decorators, fitting out the mansions of the wealthy, even intermarrying with Vanderbilts and Whitneys. W. & J. Sloane's migrated uptown in 1912. Today ABC Carpets and Home—risen from pushcart beginnings on the Lower East Side—occupies both the former Constable and Sloane buildings.

The **former Gorham Manufacturing Co. Building** (*889–891 Broadway between East 19th and East 20th Sts*), constructed of brick in the Queen Anne style with a chamfered corner that once rose to a tower, was built (1883; Edward Hale Kendall) as an investment by the Goelet family. Its lower-level showrooms displayed Gorham silver and ecclesiastical metalwork, while the upper floors were fitted out as bachelor apartments. The Goelet family began as ironmongers and hardware merchants but their real estate holdings propelled them into the upper strata of New York society. Across the street at the northeast corner of the intersection, no. 890–892 Broadway occupies the **site of the Peter Goelet mansion**, remembered less for its architecture than for the eccentricities of its owner. Peter Goelet, a penny-pinching bachelor, wrote rental receipts on one-inch scraps of paper, fabricated household articles on a forge in the basement, and kept guinea pigs and a milk cow in the back yard along with storks, pheasants, and at least one peacock. Passers-by would stop and gaze through the iron fence at the "unwonted sight" of these creatures peacefully enjoying life in a busy commercial district. Early tenants included dealers in millinery, curtains, lace, and corsets.

Another family investment, the **former Goelet Building** (*900 Broadway at East 20th St*), is conspicuous for its fine brickwork and sweeping arches. Built (1887) by McKim, Mead & White, it is considered an outstanding example of their early work.

The best view of the **former Lord & Taylor store** (*901 Broadway at East 20th St*), built in 1869–70, is from the east side of Broadway. It is the fourth and grandest Lord & Taylor emporium, a cast-iron French Second Empire confection by architect James H. Giles, known for working in this style. The original two-story arched entranceway is gone, but the imposing corner tower and high mansard roof remain. During its first three days of operation, ten thousand shoppers rode its steam-powered elevators. Ladies could rest on cushioned seats next to the counters and enjoy a reception room in the dressmaking department staffed by "polite little pages in uniform."

THEODORE ROOSEVELT BIRTHPLACE NATIONAL HISTORIC SITE

Map p. 619, D2. 28 East 20th St (Broadway and Park Ave South). Subway: 6 to 23rd St; 4, 5 to 14th St-Union Sq.; R to 23rd St. Bus: M1. Open Tues–Sat 9–5 except New Year's Day, Thanksgiving, and Christmas. Free. Period rooms accessible by guided tour only. Under renovation at the time of writing; for updates, T: 212 260 1616, nps.gov/thrb.

Theodore Roosevelt (1858–1919), the 26th president of the United States, was born at this address and lived here until he was 14. The only US president born in New York City, TR looms large in local history as a crusading police commissioner and indefatigable supporter of the American Museum of Natural History.

The present four-story brownstone (1923; Theodate Pope Riddle) reconstructs the birthplace, rebuilt from its former neighbor and mirror image, which belonged to Roosevelt's uncle. The interior has been restored to the era when Roosevelt lived here, with furnishings from the original house or from family members. On view are a parlor, bedroom, library, and the outdoor porch on which the teenage Roosevelt exercised to improve his health. Among the memorabilia are Roosevelt's christening gown and a shirt pierced by bullet holes from a failed assassination attempt, examples of youthful taxidermy, a large lion he shot in Africa, his Rough Rider uniform, and his diaries.

STUYVESANT TERRITORY

Map p. 619, E2–E3. Subway: L to 1st or 3rd Ave; 4 to Union Square. Bus: M15, M101, M102, M103.

Stuyvesant Square, once part of Peter Stuyvesant's farm, is today a quiet four-acre park (1847) bisected by busy Second Avenue and bordered by the institutional buildings of Beth Israel Medical Center. Gertrude Vanderbilt Whitney sculpted the bronze statue (1941) of peg-legged Peter Stuyvesant in the park's western section. In the northeast corner of the park's eastern section, Ivan Meštrović's statue (1963) recalls the Czech composer Antonín Dvořák, who lived at 327 East 17th St from 1892–5.

In 1836 Peter Gerard Stuyvesant, the governor's great-great-grandson, sold the land to the city for $5, with the understanding that the city would fence and landscape it as a park, enhancing the value of his own surrounding property but also ensuring open space in an area that would later be heavily developed. The City procrastinated and only after years of litigation (Stuyvesant was a lawyer) did it come through with the fence, trees, and fountains. By the 1850s the area was attracting sedate religious institutions and well-to-do residents. The fence is the second oldest in the city after the Bowling Green fence.

DVOŘÁK IN THE NEW WORLD

In 1891 the philanthropist Jeannette Meyers Thurber hired Dvořák to teach at the National Conservatory of Music of America, which she had founded to provide New York with something similar to the Paris Conservatoire, where she had studied. To lure Dvořák to New York from Prague, she offered him a dream contract: first-class steamship tickets, a salary of $15 thousand (more than 25 times what he was making in Europe), four-month summer vacations, and 18 hours of weekly conducting and teaching the school's "most talented pupils only." Though he was conflicted about coming—he'd heard mixed reviews of America—the composer wrote some of his finest music during his stay, including the *New World Symphony* and the *Cello Concerto*. The baritone Harry T. Burleigh, grandson of slaves, who sang for many years in the choir of St. George's Church (*see below*), introduced Dvořák to Negro spirituals (Burleigh's arrangement of "Swing Low, Sweet Chariot" is said to have inspired the theme of the second movement of Dvořák's famous symphony). The Conservatory, well ahead of its time, accepted African-American and female students, but during the economic Panic of 1893, the Thurber fortune dwindled and with it Dvořák's salary; the composer and his wife returned to Bohemia in 1895.

AROUND STUYVESANT SQUARE

Facing the square on the north, Protestant Episcopal **St. George's Church** (*Rutherford Pl. between East 16th and East 17th Sts*), a formidable Romanesque Revival brownstone (1846–8; Otto Blesch and Leopold Eidlitz), was originally a chapel of Trinity parish but is remembered as the church of J. Pierpont Morgan. The church burned in 1865, weakening the steeples which were subsequently taken down; the interior was rebuilt in an evangelically simple style replacing the former Episcopalian Gothic one. By the 1880s, facing increasing debts as Jewish and Catholic immigrants filled the neighborhood and its parishioners drifted away uptown, the church hired the Rev. William Stephen Rainsford, who believed that urban Protestant churches should minister to the poor. Under his leadership (and with Morgan's financial resources), the church instituted social programs including an industrial school, soup kitchens, and clubs for boys and girls. In the 20th century St. George's became one of the first churches to shelter the homeless. Once again facing dwindling resources it merged with Calvary parish church at 273 Park Ave South and the former Holy Communion Church at 47 West 20th St (deconsecrated in 1976).

STUYVESANT TOWN

Stuyvesant Town (*First Ave to Avenue C, 14th–20th Sts; map p. 619, F2*), constructed on onetime Stuyvesant land, is an immense housing project. Undertaken (1942–7) by the Metropolitan Life Insurance Company—but with the benefit of public incentives—it was intended as affordable housing, largely for returning servicemen. In 1947 the waiting list numbered some 110,000, and for many years the complex remained home to firefighters, teachers, nurses, and other middle-income tenants. During its early years "Stuy Town" accepted only white married couples, a policy that changed in 1950. Together with Peter Cooper Village, its slightly upscale neighbor to the north, the complex has 11,231 apartments in 110 brick buildings on 80 acres, and a population of about 28,000. MetLife sold it for $5.4 billion in 2006. Privately owned, its future as a bastion of middle-income housing is cloudy.

GRAMERCY PARK

Map p. 619, D2. Subway: 6 to 23rd St.

Gramercy Park is New York's only private residential square, a quiet enclave enclosed by an old iron fence and surrounded by townhouses, 19th-century clubs, mature trees, and, more recently, a luxury apartment hotel. Inside the park is a **statue of Edwin Booth in the character of Hamlet** (dedicated 1918; Edmond T. Quinn). Booth was the founder of the nearby Players club (*see opposite*).

The name "Gramercy" harks back to the Dutch colonial period when settlers called it *Krom Moerasje* ("little crooked swamp"), later anglicized as "Cromessie" or "Crommeshie" and eventually "Gramercy." A spring-fed brook, Cromessie Fly, meandered through the area emptying into the East River near 18th St. In 1831 Samuel Bulkley Ruggles, a well-connected lawyer who foresaw the coming land boom, began buying land. Ruggles drained the marshland, dumped almost a million cartloads of fill into a gully created by the brook and laid out a park, which he surmised would boost the value of his real estate. He designated 66 lots around it and sold them stipulating that only lot owners could use the park. His wishes remain in force: except for a brief period during the Draft Riots of 1863 when troops camped inside the eight-foot iron fence, the park trustees have resisted all intrusions, including a proposed cable car line (1890) and an extension of Lexington Avenue (1912). Only residents facing the square who pay a yearly maintenance fee are granted keys.

GRAMERCY PARK WEST

The Greek Revival and Italianate townhouses along Gramercy Park West include the former home of Dr. Valentine Mott (d. 1865), a prominent surgeon and founder of Bellevue Hospital, who lived at no. 1 (1849). At no. 4, a pair of Mayor's Lamps marks the home of James Harper (mayor 1844–5), a founder of Harper & Bros. publishers. Nos. 3–4 (c. 1844–50; attrib. Alexander Jackson Davis) are distinguished by their lacy cast-iron verandas. This ironwork, more familiar in such southern cities as Charleston and New Orleans, was considered a rustic touch appropriate to houses facing parks.

GRAMERCY PARK SOUTH

The **National Arts Club** (*15 Gramercy Park South near Irving Place; open occasionally for exhibitions and lectures; T: 212 475 3424, nationalartsclub.org*) occupies a brownstone created for Samuel J. Tilden from two houses (1845, remodeled 1884). Tilden was a successful lawyer, scourge of the Tweed Ring (*see p. 89*), governor of New York State, and the Democratic presidential candidate in 1876 (he won the popular vote but lost the presidency by a single electoral vote). His will, fiercely contested by relatives, stipulated that his 20,000 books and the bulk of his estate be used "to establish and maintain a free library and reading room in the City of New York." His bequest formed part of the core of the New York Public Library collection. The flamboyant Victorian Gothic-style building's attractions include medallions portraying Goethe, Dante, Franklin, Shakespeare, and Milton. The National Arts Club bought the property in 1906.

The Players (*16 Gramercy Park South near Iriving Place; T: 212 475 2116, theplayersnyc.org*), originally a club for actors and men in the arts, was founded by Edwin Booth, Mark Twain, and William Tecumseh Sherman among others. The house was a simple Gothic Revival brownstone (1845) until Booth, one of the finest actors of his time, bought it and hired Stanford White to remodel it (1888). The drip moldings on the upstairs windows remain from its earlier days, but the iron railings and the two-story porch based on an Italian Renaissance prototype are known to be by White. Booth's elder brother, John Wilkes Booth, assassinated Abraham Lincoln, an event that overshadowed the last three decades of Edwin's sad and rootless life; he lived on the top floor overlooking the park in a room that has been reputed to remain as it was when he died.

The **former Stuyvesant Fish House** (*19 Gramercy Park South at Irving Pl.*), five stories of red brick (1845) topped off with a stylish mansard roof, was built by an obscure Whig politician and purchased (1887) by financier Stuyvesant Fish, whose interests included railroads, insurance, and banking. Mrs. Fish launched her spectacular social career here, making her mark by "aggressive independence rather than by tact," according to a contemporary observer. After the Fishes decamped for the Upper East Side, the house declined until celebrity publicist Benjamin Sonnenberg bought and restored it (1931). Sonnenberg came from humble Russian stock but, like the well-born Mamie Fish, he promoted himself boldly, filling the house with antiques and guests for whom he threw dinners and teas and receptions large and small. When Sonnenberg died in 1978, Sotheby's auctioned his collections for a then-enormous $4.7 million.

Once threatened with demolition, the **former Friends' Meeting House** (*28 Gramercy Park South at East 20th St*), an austere Italianate building (1859), has been renovated as the Brotherhood Synagogue (1975; James Stewart Polshek).

IRVING PLACE

Irving Place was named (1831) by Samuel B. Ruggles for his friend Washington Irving, writer and diplomat, who never lived there. Between Irving Place and Third Avenue, East 19th St was known as "The Block Beautiful" for its charming 19th-century houses and converted stables. The artists' colony that flourished here during the 1930s included muckraker Ida Tarbell (*The History of Standard Oil*) and painter George Bellows.

Pete's Tavern (*129 East 18th St at Irving Pl.*) claims to be the oldest continuously operating saloon in the city, but seems to have arrived in this 1829 building no earlier than 1864; other contenders are the Ear Inn, the Bridge Café (*temporarily closed since Hurricane Sandy*), and McSorley's Old Ale House. Its most illustrious client, writer O. Henry (William Sydney Porter), who lived at 55 Irving Place, described it in *The Lost Blend*. It survived Prohibition disguised as a flower shop.

THE FLATIRON DISTRICT

Map p. 619, D2. Subway: N, R, or 6 to 23rd St. Bus: M2, M3, M5, M7.

Bounded roughly by Sixth and Lexington Aves, 20th and 26th Sts, this neighborhood acquired its name in the 1980s when it became increasingly residential. Formerly known for its concentration of photographers' studios, camera shops, and wholesalers of toys and gifts, the area today offers an abundance of high-end restaurants and shops.

The **former Scribner Building** (*153–157 Fifth Ave between 21st and 22nd Sts*), small and classically elegant, was the first commercial effort (1894) of Ernest Flagg, who also obliged the Scribners (his in-laws) with a printing plant, an uptown store, and two Manhattan townhouses. The building once had a salesroom reminiscent of a private library and a metal and glass entrance canopy reminiscent of *fin de siècle* Paris.

THE FLATIRON BUILDING

The Flatiron Building (*175 Fifth Ave at 23rd St*), which fills the triangle where Broadway crosses Fifth Ave, owes its status to its location, a plot of land known as "the flat iron" even before the building existed. It is the only New York work (1901–3) of Chicago-based architect Daniel H. Burnham, clad in white limestone and lavishly ornamented with terra cotta from Staten Island's Atlantic Terra Cotta Works. H.G. Wells (1906), memorably described its "prow...ploughing up through the traffic of Broadway and Fifth Avenue in the afternoon light" (the rounded corner-turning at the north end is only six feet wide). Photographers Edward Steichen and Alfred Stieglitz and painter Childe Hassam created iconic images of the building, its outlines softened by mist. John Sloan painted it during a dust storm, its top masked in clouds. In the early days, winds swirling around its base lifted women's skirts to reveal their ankles, so that a policeman was posted to keep men from loitering nearby (probably a sought-after assignment, according to Sloan).

MADISON SQUARE PARK

Map p. 619, D2. Event info: madisonsquarepark.org. Neighborhood walking tour, Sun 11am (rain or shine); meet at southwest corner of the park, 23rd St and Broadway, in front

FLATIRON DISTRICT
The iconic Flatiron Building at the intersection of Broadway and Fifth Avenue.

of the William Seward statue. The Shake Shack, near Madison Ave and 23rd St, is open 11–11 in summer; hours adjusted seasonally (T: 212 889 6600, shakeshack.com).

This 6.2-acre park, between 23rd and 26th Sts, Fifth and Madison Aves, is a much-loved haven in a busy commercial area. Visitors flock to its playground, dogrun, and environmentally-friendly Shake Shack refreshment stand, and enjoy its gardens, site-specific art, and music events.

Before the Commissioners' Plan of 1811 set aside the land, what is now Madison Square was—like other downtown parks—successively a marsh, a potter's field, and, when the street grid was imposed, a parade ground. In 1844 the city fathers named it after President James Madison; it opened officially in 1847. For a while after 1870 when Ignatz Pilatz landscaped the grounds, Madison Square Park was the centerpiece of a glamorous neighborhood, a garden of pleasure for the socially elite. This happy time ended in 1902 with the arrival of the skyscraping Flatiron Building, the harbinger of commerce. The park was restored in 2001, its gardens replanted under the direction of Lynden Miller.

MONUMENTS IN MADISON SQUARE PARK

Near the southwestern corner of the park is a bronze statue (1876) of **William Henry Seward**, US senator and secretary of state under Lincoln and Andrew Johnson, best known for purchasing Alaska from Russia. Initially admired, the statue drew scorn when a rumor falsely suggested that the artist, Randolph Rogers, had recast the body from an existing figure of Lincoln and attached Seward's head to Lincoln's neck. South of the fountain, a tall stump remains from an English elm older than the park. A bronze of **Roscoe Conkling** (1893; John Quincy Adams Ward) commemorates the US senator and presidential candidate who died of exposure after walking from his downtown office to his club on 25th Street during the blizzard of 1888.

West of the park, on the traffic island between Fifth Ave and Broadway (technically Worth Square), the **Worth Monument**, a 51-ft granite obelisk, towers over the grave of Major-General William Jenkins Worth (dedicated 1857; James Goodwin Batterson), hero of the Mexican War, whose mortal remains lie surrounded by a 19th-century cast-iron fence and a rush of traffic.

Toward the north end of the park, the **Admiral David G. Farragut Monument** (1880; Augustus Saint-Gaudens; pedestal design by Stanford White) stands whipped by an imaginary wind, gazing off at the horizon from his pedestal on which two low-relief female figures, *Courage* and *Loyalty*, emerge from a swirl of ocean currents. In the northeast corner is an unremarkable **statue of Chester A. Arthur** (1898; George E. Bissell), the unremarkable 21st president of the United States.

AROUND MADISON SQUARE PARK

West of the park at 200 Fifth Avenue (*23rd St*), **Eataly**, an upscale food hall stuffed with Italian edibles, attracts foodies from all over the world. Enormous—and enormously popular—it offers everything from antipasti to zucchini, as well as wine, kitchen gadgets, cookbooks, cooking classes, and several sit-down and stand-up eateries. (*Open seven days 10am to 11pm; check website for hours of specific vendors; closed Thanksgiving and Christmas Day; T: 212 229 2560, eataly.com.*)

In front of 200 Fifth Ave, the gilded **sidewalk clock** (installed 1909; Hecla Iron Works), one of few remaining in the city, recalls the days when wristwatches were less common and advertisements (which the clocks bore) were less ubiquitous.

South of the park at East 23rd St (*Broadway and Park Avenue South*), **One Madison** (2013; CetraRuddy), a 50-story skinny tower, dominates the skyline. Conceived at the height of a real estate bubble in 2006 by two developers who had never built in the city before, for a long time it remained unfinished, plagued by cost overruns and proliferating lawsuits, and was eventually pushed into bankruptcy. It finally opened in 2014, its multimillion-dollar, full-floor apartments with 360-degree views attracting celebrities and billionaires.

THE NATIONAL MUSEUM OF MATHEMATICS (MoMATH)

Map p. 619, D1. 11 East 26th St (Fifth and Madison Aves). Subway: N or R to 28th St or 23rd St; 6 to 28th St-Park Ave South or 23rd St; F, M to 23rd St. Bus: M1, M2, M3, M23. Open 10–5 seven days (but closes at 2:30 the first Wed of every month); closed Thanksgiving. Admission charge. Gift shop. T: 212 542 0566, momath.org.

Geared to children but equally entertaining for adults, MoMath (opened 2012), the only mathematics museum in the country, proves even to arithmophobes that "math" and "fun" are not mutually exclusive. The entrance doors have pi-shaped handles; the two levels of the museum are numbered 0 (the ground floor) and -1 (the basement level). Interactive exhibits invite you to ride a tricycle with square wheels that roll smoothly over a grooved platform; or stand in front of a video camera that creates fractal images with more and smaller images of yourself blossoming from your outspread fingertips.

THE MUSEUM OF SEX (MoSEX)

Map p. 619, D1. 233 Fifth Ave (27th St). Open to adults (18+) Sun–Thur 10–8, Fri–Sat 10–9, closed Thanksgiving and Christmas. Admission charge. Café. Gift shop. T: 212 689 6337, museumofsex.com.

The museum, also known as MoSex, opened in 2002 and has since expanded. Despite its avowedly educational mission—to document, study and display all aspects of human sexuality in historical and cultural contexts—it was denied not-for-profit status by the state, and the exhibits are sufficiently hard core to have ignited the fire of the Catholic League for Religious and Civil Rights. The permanent collection, begun when the museum was founded, includes erotic art, devices for enhancing (or deterring) sexual activity, and historical documents such as a *Guide to the Harem*, or *Directory to the Ladies of Fashion in New York and Various Other Cities for the years 1855–56*.

ALONG MADISON AVENUE

Buildings constructed for the Metropolitan Life Insurance Company, now MetLife, dominate the blocks along Madison Ave (*map p. 619, D2*). When completed in 1909, the **former Metropolitan Life Insurance Company Tower** (*1 Madison Ave between 23rd and 24th Sts*) became the world's tallest building, only to be topped by the Woolworth Building four years later. The 700-ft tower, designed by Napoleon Le Brun & Sons, was inspired by the campanile of St. Mark's in Venice. Each face of the clock is 26.5ft in diameter, each minute hand weighs half a ton, and each numeral is four feet high. The southern block of the building on 23rd St, also built by Le Brun (1893) has been considerably altered. The tower is being converted into a boutique hotel.

The limestone **North Building** (*11–25 Madison Ave between 24th and 25th Sts*), praised as one of the city's best Art Deco buildings, was intended as a 100-story skyscraper, designed by Harvey Wiley Corbett, who left the Rockefeller Center architectural team to take on the job, but the Depression curtailed plans and only the base (451ft) was built (1932), denying Corbett any shot at being the architect of New York's tallest building.

APPELLATE DIVISION OF THE NEW YORK STATE SUPREME COURT

Map p. 619, D2. 27 Madison Ave (East 25th and East 26th Sts). Lobby open weekdays 9–5, but the courtroom may be visited only when court is in session. For information, T: 212 340 0400.

The courthouse of the Manhattan Appellate Division built in 1900 under the influence of the City Beautiful movement is noteworthy inside and out for its sculpture and lavish decoration. The architect, James Brown Lord, enlisted some of America's most renowned sculptors, muralists, and craftsmen for the task of embellishing it. Built of white marble with a Corinthian portico facing East 25th St and four more columns along Madison Ave, the courthouse cost $633,768 of which more than one-third was spent on the statuary and murals. In the **interior** are beaded chandeliers, marble, wood paneling, and in the courtroom a stained-glass skylight bearing the names of then-famous American jurists.

Exterior of the building

Flanking the steps **along 25th St** are *Wisdom* and *Force* (Frederick Wellington Ruckstuhl). The pediment above the main doorway bears a sculptural group, *The Triumph of Law* (Charles H. Niehaus). The central group on the roof balustrade is *Justice with Power and Study*, by Daniel Chester French.

Along **Madison Avenue** (*best seen from the park across the street*), at the third-floor level, are four caryatids by Thomas Shields Clarke representing the seasons. Karl Bitter's *Peace* flanked by figures representing *Wisdom* and *Strength* is the central group on the balustrade.

The **roof balustrade** supports large figures of famous lawgivers, including Moses, Solon (Athenian reformer and one of the Seven Sages of ancient Greece), and Lycurgus (lawgiver of Sparta and founder of its military power), each by a different sculptor. A statue of Mohammed was removed and destroyed (1955) at the request of the governments of Egypt, Pakistan, and Indonesia, because Islamic law forbids such portraiture.

On the **Annex**, at street level facing Madison Ave, is Harriet Feigenbaum's **Memorial to the Victims of the Injustice of the Holocaust** (installed 1990), a six-sided pilaster rising 27ft above its base, with a relief of flames and an incised plan of Auschwitz based on a 1944 aerial reconnaissance photo. The inscription reads "Indifference to Injustice is the Gate to Hell."

THE NEW YORK LIFE INSURANCE BUILDING

The third and last (1926–8) of Cass Gilbert's neo-Gothic skyscrapers, the New York Life Insurance Company building (*51 Madison Ave at 26th and 27th Sts*) rises from a limestone base to a tower capped with a bright gold-colored pyramid, a feature Gilbert also used on the Woolworth Building and the Federal Courthouse at Foley Square. The grandiose lobby with its imposing scale, coffered ceiling, bronze appointments, and great staircase, suggests the wealth of the company that commissioned the building. It occupies the site of the first two Madison Square Gardens.

THE FIRST AND SECOND MADISON SQUARE GARDENS

The first Madison Square Garden began as an unused railroad depot, leased to P.T. Barnum (c. 1871) when the New York and Harlem Railroad moved its station uptown. The great showman operated it variously as Barnum's Monster Classical and Geological Hippodrome and Barnum's Great Roman Hippodrome, with spectacles that ranged from chariot races to waltzing elephants. In 1879 William Kissam Vanderbilt, who had become head of the railroad, took back the former depot and changed the name to Madison Square Garden, using the venue primarily as a sports arena.

In 1890, the second Madison Square Garden replaced the first, by then a money-losing "grimy, drafty, combustible old shell." The architect, Stanford White, financed by a syndicate that included J. Pierpont Morgan and William Waldorf Astor, constructed a new pleasure palace with a restaurant, theater, and roof garden in addition to a sports arena. The walls were yellow brick and white terra cotta; the sidewalks were arcaded; and the roof was ornamented with six open cupolas, two small towers, and a large tower modeled after the Giralda in Seville. On top stood Augustus Saint-Gaudens's gilded *Diana*, whose nudity distressed the prudish even though the goddess's anatomical charms could be glimpsed only remotely since she stood more than 300ft above the sidewalk.

In the roof garden theater in June 1906, the deranged Pittsburgh millionaire Harry K. Thaw fatally shot Stanford White. White had previously had an affair with Thaw's young and beautiful wife Evelyn Nesbit; his Madison Square Garden was torn down in 1926 to make way for the present building.

THE FORMER 69TH REGIMENT ARMORY

Nearby on Lexington Ave (*East 25th and 26th Sts*), the former 69th Regiment Armory was built (1904–6; Hunt & Hunt) for New York's "Fighting 69th" regiment of the National Guard, and is the only armory in the city that doesn't look like a medieval fortress. Behind the Lexington Ave façade extends an imposing barrel-vaulted drill hall, where the infamous Armory Show, officially the International Exhibition of Modern Art, stunned the New York art world in 1913.

THE ARMORY SHOW

Generally credited with introducing the American public to modern European art, the Armory Show opened on February 17, 1913 and, before it traveled to Boston and Chicago, drew as many as 75,000 people, a significantly larger audience than most art exhibitions of the day. With at least 1,250 works by 300 artists, the show was a broad survey, the oldest piece a miniature by Goya, the most recent created within the year of the show. About two-thirds of the works were American, but it was the European Modernists who provoked the most intense response.

Two artists in particular drew scorn. The first was Marcel Duchamp, whose Cubist-Futurist *Nude Descending a Staircase* (1912) depicted a moving figure as a series of fractured planes, painted with a restricted palette of brownish and reddish tones that simulated wood. It was parodied as "Rude Descending a Staircase: Rush Hour in the Subway" or "Food Descending a Staircase," and likened by one critic to an "explosion in a shingle factory."

Henri Matisse took second place in the high dudgeon sweepstakes, condemned by students at the Chicago Art Institute, among others, for such transgressions as "artistic murder" and "criminal misuse of line." Even the sculptor William Zorach confessed to being disturbed by Matisse's *Luxe II*, one of whose nudes has only four toes.

Nonetheless, the Armory Show brought modern art into major collections. A California dealer purchased Duchamp's *Nude* sight unseen; Lillie P. Bliss bought paintings by Cézanne, Redon, and Vuillard among others, which she later bequeathed to the Museum of Modern Art; and the Metropolitan Museum bought Cézanne's *Hill of the Poor (View of the Domaine Saint-Joseph)*. The Amory Show's achievement was not so much that it taught individual artists the mystique of Cubism, but it that drew a wider audience of collectors and gallery owners to Modernism, creating a market and laying the foundation for new directions in American art.

EATING AND DRINKING AROUND UNION AND MADISON SQUARES AND THE FLATIRON DISTRICT

As well as being famous for Eataly and the Shake Shack, this area is known for several luxurious establishments, as well as the more modest eateries of Curry Hill along Lexington Ave north of Gramercy Park, and some classics.

$$$$ **Eleven Madison Park**. ■ One of New York's best and most expensive restaurants, where everything is beautifully done, provides an experience to remember. Neo-classic cooking with luxury ingredients—foie gras, truffles—as well as a fine wine list and creative cocktails. Lunch Thur–Sat, dinner nightly. Reserve two months in advance. *11 Madison Ave (East 24th St). T: 212 889 0905, elevenmadisonpark.com. Map p. 619, D2.*

$$$ **A Voce**. Seasonal, regional,

upscale Italian cooking, including homemade pastas, in a sleek modern setting. There is a *prix fixe* option for a three-course lunch and a two-course version if you are in a hurry. Lunch Mon–Fri, dinner Mon–Sat. *41 Madison Ave (near 26th St). T: 212 545 8555, avocerestaurant.com. Map p. 619, D1.*

$$$ Aldea. Iberian cuisine is a relative rarity in a city crowded with Italian and French restaurants, but Aldea is a stellar example. The name, Spanish for "village," suggests rusticity, but the décor is modern, with a handsome wood bar. Charcuterie, snacks (called *petiscos* here), seafood, pork dishes; best value, the four-course *prix fixe*. Dinner Mon–Sat. *31 West 17th St (Fifth and Sixth Aves). T: 212 675 7223, aldearestaurant.com. Map p. 618, C2.*

$$$ Gramercy Tavern. ■ A Danny Meyers restaurant and a New York favorite, with *prix fixe* menus, a first-come-first served tavern menu for informality, and a more formal dining room for elegance. The menu offers very good, unfussy seasonal dishes, with a selection of farmstead cheeses. Lunch and dinner daily. *42 East 20th St (Broadway and Park Ave South). T: 212 477 0777, gramercytavern.com. Map p. 619, D2.*

$$$ NoMad. In the NoMad Hotel, named for the up-and-coming (or maybe it's already arrived) district north of Madison Square. One of the city's best hotel restaurants, NoMad draws a young, attractive crowd to its upscale, updated American cuisine. The roast chicken with foie gras, black truffle, and brioche is famous

(insanely good, according to some). Breakfast, lunch, and dinner daily; brunch weekends. The 24-ft mahogany Elephant Bar has been voted one of the world's best. Try one of the classic cocktails or opt for a microbrew. *1170 Broadway (28th St). T: 212 796 1500, thenomadhotel.com. Map p. 618, C1.*

$$ Boqueria. This Spanish spot modeled after the tapas bars of Barcelona draws crowds for its tempting light bites—squid with fried chickpeas, seared lamb skewers, *patatas bravas* with roasted garlic aioli. Convivial, which sometimes is equivalent to "loud." Spanish wines and several varieties of sangria. Lunch and dinner daily. Branches on the Upper East Side and in SoHo. *53 West 19th St (Sixth Ave). T: 212 255 4160, boquerianyc.com. Map p. 618, C2.*

$$ Bread & Tulips. Downstairs in the Hotel Giraffe building, this rustic Italian eatery is a good choice for a casual meal. For lunch consider the brick-oven pizzas and pastas; dinner entrées include a Long Island duck breast with polenta and marinated concord grapes. The atmosphere is cozy and relaxed. Lunch weekdays, dinner Mon–Sat, closed Sun. *365 Park Ave South (East 26th St). T: 212 532 9100, breadandtulipsnyc.com. Map p. 619, D1.*

$$ John Dory Oyster Bar. Located in the Ace Hotel, the John Dory offers nautical-themed décor and laudable food: Nantucket Bay scallops, stuffed squid, oyster pan roasts. Lunch and dinner daily. *1196 Broadway (29th St). T: 212 792 9000, thejohndory.com.*

Map p. 618, C1.

$$ Laut. Some of Manhattan's best Malaysian food, with a focus on seafood (*laut* means "sea"). The small, attractive space can be crowded. Dishes on the long menu feature regionally authentic spices, with choices that include street foods (rice crêpes with shrimp, Indian flatbread with curry dippings), curries, satays, noodles, and rice dishes. Lunch and dinner daily. *15 East 17th St (Broadway and Fifth Ave). T: 212 206 8989, lautnyc.com. Map p. 619, D2.*

$$–$ Eataly. An upscale extravaganza of Italian food, Eataly opened in 2010 to great fanfare. The many stalls of this vast but often crowded marketplace offer cheese, pasta, bread, groceries, gelato, and produce. There are cafés and sit-down eateries where you can enjoy Italian specialties—but seating can be hard to come by. The stalls open at different hours, but the marketplace is open 10am–11pm. *200 Fifth Ave (West 25th and West 26th Sts). T: 212 229 2560, eataly.com. Map p. 618, C2.*

$ Bhatti. Simple, unpretentious Northern Indian restaurant in Curry Hill where you can watch your kebab sizzling on the *bhatti*, the traditional open fire grill. Lunch and dinner daily. *100 Lexington Ave (East 27th St). T: 212 683 4228, bhattinyc.com. Map p. 619, D1.*

$ Saravana Bhavan. This Curry Hill standout, part of a worldwide chain, offers excellent choices for vegetarians, with its range of curries and Indian breads (chappathis, parathas, and pooris). The dosas (crêpes made of rice batter) and vadas (deep-fried rings of lentil flour) probably account for the lines that sometimes form out the door. Lunch and dinner daily. *81 Lexington Ave (East 26th St). T: 212 679 0204, saravanabhavan.com . Map p. 619, D1.*

$ Shake Shack. This is the first of a chain of high-quality fast-food venues that draws long lines of hungry eaters for delicious burgers and fries, as well as signature milkshakes. Lunch and dinner daily. *In Madison Square Park: East 23rd St (Broadway and Madison Aves). T: 212 889 6600, shakeshack. com. Map p. 619, D2.*

The Meatpacking District & Chelsea

In the Meatpacking District, the High Line and the new Whitney Museum of American Art have become major destinations. Chelsea's art district, with its galleries in former lofts and warehouses, also boasts upscale condos and cutting-edge architecture.

The Meatpacking District runs from Gansevoort St to West 15th St along the river and inland to Hudson St. The old loading platforms overhung by metal canopies and the cobbled, uneven streets still give the neighborhood a whiff of its working-class past, but it is no longer gritty and greasy during the day or empty and menacing after dark. A restaurant and club scene along with pockets of upscale shopping attract visitors and locals.

Map p. 618, B3. Subway: A, C, E to 14th St; walk south to 13th St and west along Gansevoort St. Bus: M11, M14D.

HISTORY OF THE MEATPACKING DISTRICT

The name of the district's original Gansevoort Market honors Peter Gansevoort (1749–1812), descendant of the Dutch elite, an officer in the American Revolution and the maternal grandfather of Herman Melville. At the end of the 19th century the City established two municipal markets: the West Washington Market (1889) at the foot of West 12th St, for meat, poultry, dairy products, and oysters; and across from it, the open-air Gansevoort Market (1879), also known as the "Goose Market," which drew New Jersey and Long Island farmers with wagons of produce to await the pre-dawn beginning of the workday. Herman Melville, his literary career apparently in ruins, worked as a customs inspector on the former Gansevoort dock for 19 years from 1866.

In the late 1920s when the Ninth Avenue El was torn down, the City decided to restructure the area as a meatpacking and distribution center, which at its peak numbered some 200 companies. As maritime traffic decreased in the 1960s, however, the waterfront declined and with it the meatpacking industry, dwindling to just seven companies by 2011. A raucous underground club scene filled the void: first the Zoo

THE MEATPACKING DISTRICT
Empty meat hooks outside a former meat market.

(1970), followed by clubs catering to wide-ranging sexual tastes—the Anvil, the Mineshaft, the Hellfire Club. Rumors hinted at Mafia involvement and police corruption, and in the late 1980s, anti-AIDS laws shut down the sex clubs. The area became a historic district in 2003; the luxury Gansevoort Hotel arrived in 2004; the High Line opened in 2009. Since then, development has accelerated, with the arrival of glass towers, luxury condos, and high-end shops.

THE WHITNEY MUSEUM OF AMERICAN ART

Map p. 618, B3. 99 Gansevoort St (Tenth Ave and Washington St). Subway: A, C, E, and L to 14th St. Bus: M1, M15, M11, M12. Open Mon, Wed, and Sun 10:30–6; Thur–Sat 10:30–10; closed Tues. Admission charge (expensive) but ground-floor galleries free. Exceptional restaurant and café. Book and gift shop. T: 212 570 3600, whitney.org.

The Whitney Museum of American Art, generally known as "The Whitney," holds a special place in the New York art world for its emphasis on contemporary American art. Since its inception in 1931, it has championed innovative work and emerging artists following its founder's vision. The Whitney Biennial, an invitational show of recent work, offered in even-numbered years, is a major event that often provokes strong opinions. In 2015, after more than three decades of planning, the museum opened downtown in the long-awaited Renzo Piano building.

GERTRUDE VANDERBILT WHITNEY AND HER MUSEUM

The great-granddaughter of Cornelius "Commodore" Vanderbilt, Gertrude Vanderbilt (1875–1942) was an heiress and a bohemian. Her marriage at 21 to Harry Payne Whitney piled her Vanderbilt inheritance (railroads and shipping) onto her husband's Whitney fortune (oil, tobacco, and banking)—but the life of luxury and social privilege this huge wealth provided failed to occupy her energies and talent. Mrs. Whitney established herself early as a patron of the arts and, to a lesser degree, as a sculptor.

In 1907 she converted a stable at 19 MacDougal Alley (*see p. 157*) into a working studio and started buying paintings from radical and sometimes starving young artists for whom there was virtually no market. During this period she met Juliana Rieser (later Juliana Force), a self-made woman who would become her lifelong associate, ultimately serving as the founding president of the Whitney Museum.

At a time when galleries were dominated by European painting, Mrs. Whitney took American art seriously, opening the Whitney Studio gallery at 8 West 8th St near her studio in 1914, then purchasing neighboring properties to establish, in 1918, the Whitney Studio Club, which became a gathering place for artists.

In 1929 she offered her collection to the Metropolitan Museum of Art, whose ultra-conservative trustees turned her down flat. By 1931 when she opened the Whitney Museum, she had accumulated some 500 works, including pieces by Edward Hopper, Stuart Davis, Reginald Marsh, George Bellows, Thomas Hart Benton, and Charles Sheeler. In 1954 the museum moved to a new building next to the Museum of Modern Art, a move that vastly increased its attendance. Overshadowed by MoMA and gasping for space, the Whitney opened (1966) the much admired Marcel Breuer building on Madison Ave at 74th St (*see p. 339*). Less than two decades later, the museum again began wrestling with problems of expansion. Various plans for the Breuer building were considered and abandoned; celebrity architects were hired and let go; key museum personnel left and were replaced. Finally in 2006 the museum acquired the land on Gansevoort St for the present building designed by Renzo Piano, whose work includes the New York Times Building (*Eighth Ave between 40th and 41st St*) and the expansion of the Morgan Library (*see p. 237*), as well as The Shard (2012) in London.

THE BUILDING

Renzo Piano's new Whitney building not only brings a powerful architectural presence to the Meatpacking District, but also culminates the Whitney's almost 40-year quest for a bigger, more modern home. Together with an 18,200-sq-ft, column-free fifth-floor gallery offering rotating exhibitions, four outdoor sculpture terraces as well as conventional exhibition spaces allow the museum to display more of its collection than ever before, and to accommodate supersized works of art. On the top floor a "studio" gallery and another café are lit by a saw-tooth skylight system that recalls the shed roofs of old industrial buildings. A huge floor-to-ceiling window at the east end overlooks the High Line; on the western side more expanses of glass bring the river into view. After Hurricane Sandy flooded the construction site with 30ft of water (2012), the building was retrofitted as a bulwark of storm protection, with watertight lower doors and a barrier system.

THE COLLECTION

Gertrude Vanderbilt Whitney appreciated the work of urban Realists from the Ashcan School—John Sloan, George Luks, and Everett Shinn. She befriended Arthur B. Davies and Robert Henri, the most influential members of The Eight (who challenged the traditions of the National Academy) and bought four of the seven paintings sold at their initial show in 1908. She collected works by American Regionalist painters John Steuart Curry and Thomas Hart Benton and early Modernists Stuart Davis, Charles Demuth, and Charles Sheeler. She admired and bought the work of Edward Hopper and Reginald Marsh, both of whom she helped so much financially that gifts from their widows gave the Whitney unparalleled holdings in their works.

Since then the collection has expanded to some 21,000 works by 3,000 artists, representing all the major movements in 20th-century American art. Areas of strength include Modernism and Social Realism, Precisionism, Abstract Expressionism, Pop Art, Minimalism, Postminimalism, art from the 1980s and 1990s focused on identity or politics, and contemporary work. Artists especially well-represented include Alexander Calder (a longtime visitor favorite is his whimsical *Circus*; 1926–31), Jasper Johns, Glenn Ligon, Brice Marden, Reginald Marsh, Agnes Martin, Georgia O'Keeffe, Claes Oldenburg, Ed Ruscha, Cindy Sherman, Lorna Simpson, and David Wojnarowicz. The exhibition program includes historical surveys, group shows, and one-person, in-depth explorations of American artists.

THE HIGH LINE

Gansevoort St to West 34th St between Tenth and Eleventh Aves. Subway: 1, 2, 3, A, C, E to 14th St; walk west to Tenth Ave. Bus: M11, M23. Open daily April–Nov 7am to 10 or 11pm; Dec–March 7am–7pm. Access at Gansevoort St, West 14th, and odd-numbered streets up to 30th St, but West 23rd St instead of West 22nd St; elevator access at 14th, 16th, 23rd, and 30th Sts. Free. Tours Tues 6:30pm and Sat 10am May–Sept, weather permitting. Food trucks (seasonal), nearby cafés and restaurants. Gift shop. Restrooms. T: 212 500 6035, thehighline.org.

The High Line (2009–14; James Corner of Field Operations, landscape architect; Diller Scofidio + Renfro, master plan; Piet Oudolf, garden designer), a park on an abandoned railroad viaduct 30ft above the street, stretches from the Meatpacking District to Midtown West. The walkway is romantically landscaped with grasses, trees, vines, and flowering plants. The unkempt, weedier northern section recalls the days when the rail line stood empty, abandoned by all except for graffitists, urban adventurers, and occasionally the homeless. Site-specific works of art appear here and there, and artist-designed billboards display arcane messages from nearby buildings. Near 13th St the Standard Hotel straddles the walkway, its plate glass windows encouraging guests to give in to their exhibitionist urges. (The hotel has been dubbed the "eyeful tower.") A block or so further north, water slides across the pavement inviting barefoot dabbling. The viaduct also passes through the former Nabisco Factory, shadowed by the massive old building. At West 30th St, the walkway swings west above rows of trains marshaled for the next commute and ends at West 34th St, surrounded by the rising skyscrapers of the Hudson Yards Redevelopment project.

HISTORY OF THE HIGH LINE

In the mid-19th century, the New York Central Railroad ran down the middle of Eleventh and Tenth Avenues. The trains spewed coal dust; the avenues were dirty, dangerous, and clogged with traffic. "West Side Cowboys" on horseback preceded the engines waving flags, but accidents were so frequent that Eleventh Ave became known as "Death Avenue."

The High Line viaduct for freight trains was constructed in the 1930s to solve these problems. To avoid darkening the avenue below, it ran mid-block, sometimes through buildings. Freight cars shunted into the elevated warehouse loading bays could roll out and head straight up the New York Central tracks to Albany and beyond.

During the 1950s rail freight gave way to trucking, and the last train, carrying frozen turkeys, rolled south to Gansevoort St in 1980. Because no one wanted to pay for demolition, the High Line was left to rust. Time passed. Wild plants sprouted from the rail bed giving the line the haunted quality of a Piranesi ruin. Among the urban explorers attracted to its melancholy beauty were artist Robert Hammond and writer Joshua David, who formed the not-for-profit Friends of the High Line, defeated proposals for demolition, and advocated recreating the viaduct as a linear park. Enormously popular, the High Line now attracts some five million visitors yearly and—for better or for worse—has boosted real estate values in the area.

CHELSEA

Map p. 618, B2. Subway: 1 to 18th St; A, C, E to 14th St. Bus: M11.

Chelsea lies between West 14th St and West 30th Sts, from the Hudson River to Sixth Ave. Once dominated by the river and the New York Central Railroad, it has become a major district for contemporary art, with galleries occupying former warehouses and manufacturing lofts. Celebrity architects have made their mark on the streetscape, and Hudson River Park has restored the waterfront to the public. Silicon Alley, New York's answer to Silicon Valley, has outposts here, with large firms including Google and IAC arriving in the early 21st century. Also in Chelsea are wine bars and clubs, restaurants of all varieties, and designer boutiques.

HISTORY OF CHELSEA

Chelsea owes its name and approximate boundaries to Captain Thomas Clarke, a retired British army captain who, in 1750, named his estate after London's Royal Hospital, Chelsea, a refuge for old and disabled soldiers. Clarke's grandson, Clement Clarke Moore (1779–1863), developed Chelsea's residential potential and is responsible for some of its most attractive streets. Foreseeing that the city's northward growth would engulf his hills and meadows, he shrewdly donated land to the General Theological Seminary (*see p. 208*) and guaranteed himself a genteel neighborhood by selling building lots with design and use controls attached: a mandatory ten-foot setback for all houses, no stables, and no "manufactures." Clarke, erudite as well as astute, taught Classics at Columbia, complied a Hebrew lexicon, and published on subjects ranging from history to agriculture, but is remembered for his poem "A Visit from St. Nicholas" ("'Twas the night before Christmas..."), though a few scholars dispute his authorship.

Western and eastern Chelsea have developed along different paths. The Hudson River Railroad, later absorbed by the New York Central, laid tracks down Eleventh Ave (c. 1847), attracting breweries, slaughterhouses, and glue factories (the "manufactures" Moore wanted to avoid), which in turn attracted job-hungry immigrants. Ethnic groups who settled here include Scottish weavers, a Spanish community, the once-predominant Irish, a French colony, Greeks, and, after World War II, Puerto Ricans. The Ninth Avenue El plunged the avenue into shadow, further depressing the area, and although it was dismantled before World War II, western Chelsea did not recover for many years.

Eastern Chelsea fared better. During the 1870s and '80s a theatrical district flourished on West 23rd St. Although the theater district moved uptown later in the century, Chelsea enjoyed a brief artistic revival around World War I as the center of early moviedom, before sunshine and open space lured the industry to California.

WESTERN CHELSEA

In the past 25 years, Western Chelsea has developed into a nouveau SoHo, its 19th-century industrial architecture repurposed as art galleries (more than 350), restaurants, bars, and hotels. The High Line has attracted development, as "starchitects" have gifted the neighborhood with their highly visible work.

CHELSEA MARKET

Map p. 618, B2–B3. 75 Ninth Ave, West 15th and 16th Sts. Subway: A, C, E to 14th St; L to Eighth Ave. Bus: M11. Open Mon–Sat 7am–9pm, Sun 8–8; individual businesses may have different hours. Tours available through Foods of NY Tours (T: 212 913 9964, foodsofny.com). T: 212 652 2110, chelseamarket.com.

Anchored by the former Nabisco (National Biscuit Company) factory, Chelsea Market opened in 1997 as a blockbuster food hall with restaurants and cookery shops. The redesigned building, its piping and brickwork exposed, includes a smattering of industrial artworks—a waterfall belching from a metal pipe, a sculpture made of machine parts.

In the 1920s Nabisco, the world's biggest baking factory, occupied some five blocks in the market district, "inventing" Oreos and Mallomars, and turning out Fig Newtons, Barnum's Animal Crackers, and Vanilla Wafers by the ton. When freight trains rolled along the High Line, the company routed a siding to a second-story viaduct, now part of the park. In 1958 Nabisco departed for New Jersey.

GOOGLE NEW YORK

Until 2010, the former Port of New York Authority Commerce Building (1932; Lusby Simpson of Abbott, Merkt & Company), a massive 15-story block-through at 111 Eighth Ave (*West 14th to West 15th St*), served the Port Authority as warehousing, exhibition space, and offices. It now houses the **East Coast headquarters of Google**, which bought it for $1.8 billion; at 2.9 million sq ft, it has more floor space than the Empire State Building. Behind its severe façade are the lavish, unorthodox perks associated with working for Google: scooters, limitless free dining, game rooms, terraces, and some New-York-styled meeting spaces that look like old subway cars, or the inside of a regular apartment. Outside, SUV limos line the curb, awaiting departing executives.

WEST 19TH STREET

Between the High Line and the Hudson, West 19th St is a showcase of glass- and metal-clad contemporary architecture, including Annabelle Selldorf's (2008) restrained **520 West Chelsea** and Shigeru Ban's (2010) **Metal Shutter Houses** at no. 524, with motor-ized roll-up-roll-down shutters that can block out the streetscape or open the interiors to the outside world. Nearby is the northern façade of Frank Gehry's first (2007) New York effort, the **IAC Building** (InterActiveCorp Building), a ten-story glass-clad office block (*555 West 18th St*) with sharp-edged swelling surfaces ballooning like sails. Unmistakable from the West Side Highway, it shines in the sunlight, glows at night, and almost disappears into the mist on cloudy days. Finally, Jean Nouvel's **100 Eleventh Avenue** (2009) wraps around the corner of West 19th St, suggesting a Mondrian paint-ing in blue and gray with its metal grid outlining windows of different sizes and shapes.

The Kitchen (*512 West 19th St at Tenth and Eleventh Aves; box office open Tues–Sat 2–6 and 1hr before each show; gallery open Tues–Fri noon–6 and Sat 11–6; free; T: 212 255 5793, thekitchen.org*), a not-for-profit arts organization, pioneered video and per-formance art, and today also serves up interdisciplinary and experimental work in many genres. Founded in 1971 in the kitchen of the long-gone Broadway Central Hotel, it launched the careers of Vito Acconci, Laurie Anderson, Bill T. Jones, Robert Mapplethorpe, Cindy Sherman, and Kiki Smith, among others.

CHELSEA ROW HOUSES

Clement Clarke Moore's intentions remain visible in the gracious Greek Revival and Italianate row houses along **West 20th St** (*between Ninth and Tenth Aves*). **No. 404** West 20th St is the oldest house in the historic district, built in 1829–30. **No. 402** West 20th St (1897; C.P.H. Gilbert) is remarkable for the concave façade that curves back from the corner tenement to the setback of the adjoining older houses. The initials DONAC above the door refer to Moore's friend Don Alonzo Cushman, a dry-goods merchant, parish leader, and developer who made a fortune building in Chelsea. **Cushman Row** (*406–418 West 20th St*) is named for him. Completed in 1840, these brick, brownstone-trimmed Greek Revival houses sport cast-iron wreaths around their small attic win-dows. Nos. 416–418 have pineapple newel posts. Further west are exceptional Italianate houses (nos. 446–450) dating from 1853; the round-headed ground-floor windows and doorways were expensive to build, and thus a feature restricted to upscale houses.

WEST 20TH TO WEST 24TH STREETS

The **General Theological Seminary** (*175 Ninth Ave between 20th and 21st Sts; gated entrance on West 21st St about halfway down the block; photo ID required; open to visitors weekdays 11–3; closed religious holidays and when school is not in session; T: 212 243 5150, gts.edu*) is the oldest Episcopalian seminary in the US (1817). At one time occupying the full city block, it was founded by Trinity Church and supported by Clement Clarke Moore, who donated land from his apple orchard. The late 19th-century buildings face a serene central courtyard with the Gothic Revival Chapel of the Good Shepherd (1886–8; Charles Coolidge Haight). In 2007, facing financial difficulties, the seminary sold several of its assets, including a 1960s building on Ninth Ave (replaced by condos) and 19th-century dormitories facing Tenth Ave (now the High Line Hotel).

Printed Matter (*195 Tenth Ave between West 21st and West 22nd Sts; open Mon–Wed and Sat 11–7, Thur–Fri 11–8; T: 212 925 0325, printedmatter.org*), a pleasantly cluttered store, is the retail outlet of a non-profit organization founded (1976) by artist Sol LeWitt and Lucy Lippard to foster appreciation of artists' books (books by artists which are themselves works of art). If the sign outside is accurate, the store offers 15,000 books, "zines," and posters; in the back room is a small historical exhibit area.

Long a Chelsea landmark, the **Empire Diner** (*210 Tenth Ave at West 22nd St; breakfast, lunch, and dinner daily; T: 212 596 7523, empire-diner.com*) has appeared in films, advertisements, and on TV. Built by a railroad-car company (?1943; Carl Laanes), it was refurbished in 1976 with Art Deco chrome and black detailing. The menu offers historic (meat loaf) and updated (salmon paillard) diner fare.

Between Tenth And Eleventh Aves, **West 22nd Street** offers a lineup of contemporary art galleries, several in handsomely converted industrial spaces. The building at **no. 522** was formerly the exhibition space of the Dia Art Foundation (now in Beacon, New York), one of whose installations occupies the southern side of the street.

7,000 OAKS

Joseph Beuys's *7,000 Oaks* (*West 22nd St between Tenth and Eleventh Aves*) consists of 23 basalt columns, each paired with a tree (not all of them oaks), thus having a part that grows and changes and a part that stays the same. Beuys, whose work also included sculpture and performance, was obsessed with the transformative powers of art, and for him the installation of the original 7,000 trees (begun 1982) in Kassel, Germany, initiated a worldwide tree-planting project to effect social and environmental change. The Dia Art Foundation planted the trees in 1988 and 1996.

The **London Terrace Apartments**, filling an entire block (*West 23rd to West 24th Sts, Ninth to Tenth Aves*), are an early modern apartment project (1930; Farrar & Watmaugh) named for the row (i.e. terrace) of 19th-century colonnaded townhouses that was torn down to make way for the present 14 buildings. Such amenities as a central garden, swimming pool, solarium, gymnasium, and doormen dressed as London bobbies attracted tenants to the 1,670 apartments. On the top level was the Marine Roof, fitted out like the deck of a transatlantic liner, complete with lifebuoys and folding deck chairs.

CENTRAL CHELSEA

St. Peter's Church (Protestant Episcopal; *346 West 20th St between Eighth and Ninth Aves*), a modest early Gothic Revival fieldstone church (1836–8), was constructed from designs by Clement Clarke Moore with stone quarried at Spuyten Duyvil and barged down the Hudson. According to legend, the foundations for the present church had already been laid when a vestryman returned from England so enthralled with the Gothic parish churches there that he persuaded his colleagues to redesign the new church. The Greek Revival rectory (1832), at the west end of the tract, first served as the church.

The **Joyce Theater** (1941; *175 Eighth Ave at 19th St*), formerly the Elgin Theater, started as a movie house but by the 1970s was reduced to showing pornography. In 1982 the firm of Hardy Holzman Pfeiffer gutted the building, rebuilt the interior for dance performances, and dramatically restored the exterior with its elaborately patterned brickwork. The Joyce is now one of the city's principal dance venues. (*For schedules of events and ticket information, T: 212 242 0800, joyce.org.*)

The Third Shearith Israel Cemetery (*West 21st St between Sixth and Seventh Aves*) is a tiny graveyard that served the city's earliest Jewish congregation (*see p. 45*) from 1829–51, as the synagogue moved uptown.

THE RUBIN MUSEUM OF ART

Map p. 618, C2. 150 West 17th St (Seventh Ave). Subway: 1 to 18th St; 2, 3 to 14th St. Bus: M7, M20. Open Mon, Thur 11–5; Wed 11–9; Fri 11–10; weekends 11–6. Closed Tues, New Year's Day, Thanksgiving, Christmas Day. Admission charge, but free Fri 7pm–10pm. Café, shop. T: 212 620 5000, rubinmuseum.org.

Devoted to the art of the Himalayas, this jewel of a museum (opened 2004) holds an important collection of art from Tibet, Nepal, Mongolia and Bhutan, much of it gathered by the founders, Shelley and Donald Rubin. The museum, which occupies a former Barneys clothing store, re-designed and with its dramatic central staircase intact, is spacious, elegant, and serene.

The permanent collection is shown in rotation, with two long-term exhibits introducing this generally unfamiliar art. On the second floor "Masterworks: Jewels of the Collection," organized geographically, introduces Buddhist and Hindu gods, depicted in stone, metal, and wood, on paper, ivory, silk, and papier-mâché. Also on view are lifesize facsimiles of murals from the Dalai Lama's Secret Temple near the Potala Palace in Lhasa, Tibet, inaccessible until the 20th century. On the third floor, "Gateway to Himalayan Art" elucidates the materials and techniques used to create these works and the purposes for creating them. Changing exhibitions from the permanent collection and other sources supplement the long-term exhibits.

THE CHELSEA HOTEL

At 222 West 23rd St *(Seventh and Eighth Aves; map p. 618, B2)*, the landmark Chelsea Hotel (1883–5; Hubert, Pisson & Co.) is architecturally notable for its cast-iron balconies with row upon row of sunflowers stretching across the long façade. As a hotel, it has been more notable for its hospitality to artists, writers, and musicians than for its creature comforts.

Originally a grand apartment building, The Chelsea was the first to reach twelve stories and to have a penthouse. It became a residential hotel in 1905, with its artistic heyday coming after the 1930s, when many writers, composers, and painters lived here. Dylan Thomas lapsed into a fatal coma in room 205 *(see p. 156)*; Andy Warhol portrayed it as wild and impetuous in his movie *Chelsea Girls*, and Sid Vicious, bass player of the punk rock band the Sex Pistols, was indicted in 1978 for murdering his girlfriend with a hunting knife, allegedly in the hotel. (He died of a heroin overdose before standing trial.) The hotel's most eccentric resident, perhaps, was George Kleinsinger, a composer who wrote the children's musical *Tubby the Tuba* and who is said to have been fond of composing at the piano with his pet boa constrictor encircling his body. Husband-and-wife artists Christo and Jeanne-Claude, today famous for their mega-scale art installations, stayed there in the 1960s, sometimes borrowing money for dinner when they ran short. At the time of writing, the hotel was being renovated.

CHELSEA ON THE HUDSON

Cross the West Side Highway at 22nd–23rd St to view **Chelsea Piers** *(map p. 618, A2)*. The original deepwater Piers 54–62 (1902–10) stretched from about West 12th to West 20th Sts and were designed by Warren & Wetmore, architects of Grand Central Terminal, to accommodate the transatlantic liners of the early 20th century. The 800-ft finger piers were finished just in time to receive the *Mauretania* and the *Lusitania*, then the pride of the Cunard Line. When the White Star line's *Titanic* sank, the passengers rescued by the Cunard *Carpathia* docked at Pier 54; the *Lusitania* left from there on its fatal final voyage to England in 1915. (The rusted metal arch near the foot of West 13th St is all that remains of the Cunard pier house).

The Depression debilitated the Atlantic trade, but the piers served as an embarkation point in World War II and during the late 1950s and early 1960s handled cargo. With the decay of New York as a port in succeeding decades, this segment of Chelsea's economy atrophied and the piers fell into disuse, with many of the dockworkers who lived nearby moving to New Jersey, where the piers remained active. By the 1990s, five of the original nine piers had burned or been destroyed.

CHELSEA PIERS SPORTS CENTER

Chelsea Piers, 23rd St at the Hudson River. T: 212 336 6666, chelseapiers.com.
Beginning in 1994, Piers 59–62 were rebuilt as an impressive and successful commercial sports complex. It includes an ice rink, a golf driving range, a skate park, a competition pool, and facilities for basketball, boxing, and fitness training.

CHELSEA
The Chelsea Hotel, former haunt of artists, before renovation.

HUDSON RIVER PARK

Battery Park to West 59th St along the Hudson River. Open daily from 6am to 1am; restrooms open dawn to dusk; hours for commercial sites vary. Sports include a skate park, mini golf, tennis, kayaking, biking; check website for locations. Walking tours, carousel, concerts, events; hudsonriverpark.org.

Stretching four miles along the far West Side, from Lower Manhattan to Midtown, Hudson River Park opens the waterfront to the public after generations of being cut off by piers, warehouses and, later, the West Side Elevated Highway. It has been touted as the most important park constructed in Manhattan since Central Park. Many of its 550 acres are landscaped naturally, with grasses, boulders, and berms, but there are also more formal gardens. Some of the old piers have been restored; others have been left to rot and today appear as melancholy pile fields. Along its length are recreational facilities and, here and there, works of art. The views both west and east are spectacular.

Before there was a park, there was the Miller Elevated Highway (1929–51), named for a Manhattan borough president but generally known as the West Side Highway. Built as part of the West Side Improvement project to make the docks accessible to trucks, it was admired at first (the *WPA Guide to New York City* called it a "magnificent express drive") but soon became obsolete, its deterioration hastened by heavy use and indifferent maintenance. On December 15, 1973, a passenger car and a dump truck loaded with ten tons of asphalt intended for road repairs dropped through the elevated section near Gansevoort St. Planning began for a mammoth high-speed replacement called Westway, but after years of campaigning by environmentalists, the project was defeated in 1985, opening the way for creating a park. In 2000 the Army Corps of Engineers issued a permit for reconstructing the piers, and the first section of Hudson River Park opened in 2003.

CHELSEA COVE

This is one of the most pleasant areas of the park, stretching from 22nd to 25th St. Designed by Michael Van Valkenburgh, it has a skate park for the athletically daring, a lawn for the sedentary, and public gardens (Lynden B. Miller, designer) for the horticulturally inclined. The solar-powered, green-roofed carousel offers children a ride on hand-carved creatures indigenous to the Hudson River and its valley: an Atlantic sturgeon, a horseshoe crab, and a coyote among them.

ART IN THE PARK

Permanent public works of art scattered through the park reflect its history and environment. Here are some highlights, from south to north:

West of Vestry and Desbrosses Sts (*in Tribeca; cross at Watt St*): The three *Serpentine Structures* (2008; Mark Gibian)—"Twister," "Torque," and "Offshoot"—are constructed of rolled and welded industrial pipe, modeled after fish skeletons and ship ribbing, and infiltrated with trumpet vines.

Pier 40 (*Houston St in Greenwich Village*): In the lobby of the pier house, formerly a terminal for passenger ships, the ceramic *Holland-American Line Shipping Mural* (1963; Frank Nix) recalls the days when the piers were the center of America's shipping industry.

Pier 46 (*near Charles St in Greenwich Village*): Recreating a familiar icon for the city, *The Apple* (2004; Stephan Weiss)—a nine-foot, three-ton bronze sculpture—sits on a circular bronze bench supported by bronze apple cores. Designer Donna Karan, Weiss's widow, donated the work in his memory.

Near Bank St (*in Greenwich Village*): A 42-ft curved stone bench on a landscaped knoll, the AIDS Memorial (2008) bears an inscription from a Swedish folk song: "I can sail without wind, I can row without oars, but I cannot part from my friend without tears."

West 24th St: *Stonefield* (2009; Meg Webster), an installation of boulders chosen for their "individual being-ness" according to the artist, conjures the geological history of the Hudson River.

Pier 66 (*at West 26th St in Chelsea*): *Long Time* (2007; Paul Ramirez Jonas), a 26-ft water wheel turned by the ebb and flow of the tide evokes the old sidewheelers that plied the Hudson River; the wheel was designed to turn indefinitely, or until "inevitable circumstances stop the wheel from spinning."

West 29th St: *Two Too Large Tables* (2006; Allan and Ellen Wexler) consists of one table seven feet off the ground supported by 13 very tall-backed chairs and another table 30 inches tall, supported by 13 ordinary but immobile chairs.

West 40th St (*in Midtown*): *Senes* (1973; William Crovello) is an 8ft welded stainless steel sculpture of interlocking links by a native New Yorker.

OTHER POINTS OF INTEREST

From the park there are good views of the 19-story **Starrett-Lehigh Building** (1931), at 601–625 West 26th St (*Eleventh and Twelfth Aves*), an imposing Modernist industrial building admired for its dramatic exterior—horizontal bands of glass, concrete, and brown brick wrapped around curved corners—and its innovative concrete column-and-slab construction. Built over a railroad spur and equipped with powerful elevators to lift boxcars from the tracks to the warehouse above, the building's marketing slogan trumpeted "Every floor a first floor." Because rail freight, which had to be ferried across the Hudson on railroad-car floats, could not compete with government-supported highways, the indoor upper-story railroad tracks were never built. The elevators still hoist 15-ton trucks into the vast interior.

No. 263–273 Eleventh Avenue, a massive fortress (*West 27th to West 28th St, Eleventh to Twelfth Aves*), was originally the **Central Stores of the Terminal Warehouse Company** (1890–1; George B. Mallory, Otto M. Beck), 25 storage buildings with 24 acres of warehousing walled into one space. The great arched doorway formerly admitted locomotives from a New York Central Railroad spur, while the west façade opened onto the deepwater Hudson River piers. Cool cellars running beneath the entire structure stored wines, liquors, rubber, and furs.

The **Protestant Episcopal Church of the Holy Apostles** (*296 Ninth Ave at West 28th St*), a small, brick, country-style church (1846–8, Minard Lafever; transepts 1858, Richard Upjohn & Son) with a copper-covered, slate-roofed spire, is an anomaly in a neighborhood of overscaled modern housing projects. William Jay Bolton, one of America's earliest stained-glass artists, and his brother John designed the windows. The scenes on the round sepia-toned panes are said to have been drawn from the Bolton family Bible. After a devastating fire in 1990, the church removed the pews to provide more flexible space. Today it hosts the dining area for the church's soup kitchen, which may serve as many as 1,200 meals a day.

EATING AND DRINKING IN THE MEATPACKING DISTRICT AND CHELSEA

As well as the restaurants listed below, **Chelsea Market** (*map p. 618, B2; Ninth Ave between 15th and 16th Sts; open Mon–Sat 7am–9pm, Sun 8–8; T: 212 652 2110, chelseamarket.com*) has stalls and eateries offering bread, chocolate, coffee, fish, street food, seafood, and more.

$$$$ Del Posto. ◼ Located in the gray area between the Meatpacking District and Chelsea, this destination restaurant sports a Michelin star and has become a favorite hangout for expense-account diners. Del Posto attracts for its handsome but opulent setting and fine Italian cooking. Several *prix fixe* menus and *à la carte*. Superb service and excellent wine list. Lunch weekdays, dinner nightly. *85 Tenth Ave (16th St). T: 212 497 8090, delposto.com. Map p. 618, B2.*

$$$ Buddakan. Loud, pulsing with energy, this glittering Asian restaurant in Chelsea Market occupies a great oak-walled two-story space with chandeliers that would have easily supported Quasimodo. And, the food is very good. Dinner

nightly. *75 Ninth Ave (15th and 16th Sts). T: 212 989 6699, buddakannyc. com. Map p. 618, B3.*

$$$ Santina. Before landfill, the restaurant site would have been on the shoreline, so "coastal Italian" is the theme. The menu features vegetables and seafood. Breakfast and lunch weekdays, brunch weekends, dinner nightly. *80 Washington St (Gansevoort St). T: 212 254 3000, santinanyc.com. Map p. 618, B3.*

$$$ Standard Grill. On the ground floor of the Standard Hotel straddling the High Line. Contemporary food, sidewalk tables, raw bar, grilled meat and fish. Lunch and dinner daily, open late. The **Biergarten** purveys beer, wurst, and kraut. *848 Washington St (Little West 12th and 13th Sts). T: 212*

645 4100, thestandardgrill.com. Map p. 618, B3.

\$\$\$ Txikito. ■ Popular Spanish Chelsea Market restaurant with outstanding *pintxoak*, the Basque equivalent of tapas. Cocktails, beer, cider, and wines, some of them Basque. Dinner nightly. *240 Ninth Ave (24th and 25th Sts). T: 212 242 4730, txikitonyc.com. Map p. 618, B2.*

\$\$\$–\$\$ Cookshop. At the foot of the High Line, this tried and true restaurant serves seasonal, farm-to-table straightforward American cooking; outdoor dining sometimes. Breakfast weekdays, brunch weekends, lunch and dinner daily. *156 Tenth Ave (20th St). T: 212 924 4440, cookshopny.com. Map p. 618, A2.*

\$\$\$–\$\$ Spice Market. Long-running, popular place housed in a former warehouse, serving pan-Asian street food. Lunch Wed–Sun, dinner nightly. *403 West 13th St (Ninth Ave). T: 212 675 2322, spicemarketnewyork.com. Map p. 618, B3.*

\$\$ The Red Cat. Warm, established restaurant with Mediterranean and American food, handy both for the High Line and the nearby art district. Lunch and dinner daily, brunch weekends. *227 Tenth Ave (23rd and 24th Sts). T: 212 242 1122, theredcat. com. Map p. 618, A2.*

\$\$ Untitled. In the Whitney Museum, part of the Danny Meyer group, offering minimalist, contemporary American cooking in a beautifully designed space. No need to pay the museum entrance fee. Lunch and dinner daily except Tues. The eighth-floor **Studio Café** offers light fare, beautiful views, and outdoor seating in fine weather. *Entrance at 99 Gansevoort St (Tenth Ave). T: 212 570 3670, untitledatthewhitney.com. Map p. 618, B3.*

\$ Artichoke Basille's Pizza. This outpost of a small chain costs more than a standard pizzeria but is still moderate. Full pies and slices, also salads, a couple of sandwiches, and stuffed artichokes. Lunch and dinner daily, open late. *114 Tenth Ave (17th St). T: 212 792 9200, artichokepizza. com. Map p. 618, A2.*

\$ The Half King. Named for an 18th-century Seneca Native American, this restaurant/bar has weekday breakfast for the late riser, weekend brunch, lunch, dinner, and late night snacking, along with a full bar. To feed the mind as well as the body, the Half King sponsors literary readings. Morning to late night, daily. *505 West 23rd St (Tenth Ave). T; 212 462 4300, thehalfking.com. Map p. 618, A2.*

\$ Num Pang. In Chelsea Market, this well-priced Cambodian sandwich place has few frills but well-designed sandwiches by a chef who has worked in the fine dining scene. Quick service, despite the crowds. Other locations. Lunch and dinner daily. *75 Ninth Ave (15th and 16th Sts). T: 212 390 8851, numpangnyc.com. Map p. 618, B3.*

The Garment District & Herald Square

Once the center of the country's clothing and newspaper industries, the Garment District and Herald Square are now home to the Fashion Institute and Macy's department store.

Subtitled "Fashion Ave," the street signs along Seventh Avenue pay tribute to the Garment District—once the source of 90 percent of the nation's clothing. (*Map p. 618, B1–C1. Subway: 1 to 28th St; B, D, F, N, Q, R to 34th St-Herald Sq. Bus: M2, M3, M4, M5, M7, M20.*) Around World War I, the Garment District followed the major department stores uptown from the sweatshops of the Lower East Side. The entire industry—designers, cutters, button makers, seamstresses, even marketing professionals—was crammed into the district, which was subdivided geographically according to specialty: the fur industry from West 27th to West 30th St near Seventh Ave; children's-wear around 34th St; and women's apparel north of 36th St. Allied industries on the fringes of the district dealt in millinery, hosiery, buttons, thread, trimmings, and fabrics. Although most manufacturing (including illegal sweatshops) has moved to cheaper quarters elsewhere or has been outsourced, some showrooms remain: Donna Karan, Ralph Lauren, Michael Kors, Betsey Johnson, and Carolina Herrera. The American clothing industry has shrunk in the face of cheaper imported goods; today there are about 24,000 fashion jobs in the area, including 6,500 production jobs—down from 200,000 in the 1960s. (*Garment District information kiosk at 553 Seventh Ave-West 39th St; open Mon–Fri 8:30–4; T: 212 398 7943, garmentdistrictnyc.com.*)

FASHION AVENUE TRIBUTES

Judith Weller's statue ***The Garment Worker*** (*1984; near 555 Seventh Ave between West 39th and West 40th Sts*) sits on the sidewalk working a treadle sewing machine. Weller's father, a tailor, inspired the bronze figure. Weller exhibited a 24-inch model of the statue in an exhibition in 1978, where a member of the International Ladies' Garment Workers Union saw it and, working with the artist, raised money from companies in the Garment District to create the present version.

Embedded in the eastern sidewalk of Seventh Ave (*East 41st to East 35th Sts*), the bronze discs of the **Fashion Walk of Fame** (dedicated 1999) honor New York's most influential designers.

In the plaza facing Seventh Ave and 27th St is Robert M. Cronbach's hammered brass *Eye of Fashion* (1976).

THE FASHION INSTITUTE OF TECHNOLOGY AND MUSEUM AT FIT

Map p. 618, C1. Seventh Ave at West 27th St. Subway: 1, N, R to 28th St; A, C, E, F to 23rd St. Bus: M20, M23. Open Tues–Fri noon–8; Sat 10–5; closed Sun, Mon, legal holidays. Free. T: 212 217 4558, fitnyc.edu.

The Fashion Institute of Technology offers degrees in fashion design, fragrance, computer animation, cosmetic marketing, and entrepreneurship. The **Museum at FIT** (1975) mounts stylish exhibits, fascinating to anyone interested in fashion, textiles, design, and social history. The permanent collection began as a research facility in conjunction with the Brooklyn Museum when World War I isolated American designers from developments in Europe. It now numbers some 50,000 garments and accessories.

AROUND HERALD SQUARE

Herald and Greeley Squares (*map p. 618, C1*) occupy respectively the northern and southern triangles created by the intersection of Sixth Ave and Broadway at West 34th St. The surrounding neighborhood, also called Herald Sq, was once a center of the newspaper and garment industries; today the flagship Macy's store is its star attraction.

Before the arrival of the newspapers in the late 19th century, the neighborhood was part of the vice-ridden Tenderloin district, which stretched from West 20th to 40th Sts, from Fifth to Seventh Aves. Reformers called it "Satan's Circus," but police inspector Alexander S. "Clubber" Williams, whose nickname described his favored means of dispensing justice, gave the place its more common name. Transferred to this precinct from quieter streets he remarked, "I've had nothing but chuck steak for a long time, and now I'm going to get a little of the tenderloin." He supplemented his modest salary with protection money extorted from the proprietors of saloons, gambling houses, and brothels, eventually owning a city home, a Connecticut estate, and a yacht. Through the efforts of reformers, the involvement of public officials in vice and crime became a source of indignation, and Williams was retired in 1895, "for the good of the force."

Herald Square takes its name from the *New York Herald* (1835–1924), founded by William Gordon Bennett, whose coverage of crime and scandal fattened his paper's circulation, surpassing even the *Times* of London only four years after the first edition rolled off the press. The paper's editorial offices occupied a McKim, Mead & White palazzo on the northern side of 35th St, whose bell and clock still stand as a memorial to Bennett and his son James Gordon Bennett Jr. Two muscular bronze figures (1894; Jean-Antonin Carles) "hammer" out the hours on the bell (actually rung from within), while a bronze Minerva and her owl observe the proceedings.

At **Greeley Square** is Alexander Doyle's bland statue (1892) of *New York Tribune* editor Horace Greeley. The eagles on the gateposts recall those on the *Tribune*'s masthead.

MACY'S

Map p. 618, C1. 151 West 34th St. Open Mon–Sat 9–9:30, Sun 11–8:30; T: 212 695 4400, macys.com.
Macy's flagship Herald Square store, with 2.2 million sq ft of selling space, was once the world's largest department store and is still one of the most famous. The building facing Broadway dates from 1901, while those along the side streets were appended in 1931. Its moderate to upscale clothing, housewares, gourmet foods, and accessories make Macy's a shopping destination for New Yorkers as well as visitors; its Thanksgiving Day parade and Fourth of July fireworks are red-letter events in the city's calendar.

HISTORY OF MACY'S

Rowland Hussey Macy, a Nantucket Quaker, went to sea at the age of 15 and returned four years later with $500 and a red star (Macy's logo) tattooed on his hand. After failures in merchandising and further disappointments in real estate and the stock market, Macy founded (1858) his New York store on Sixth Avenue near 14th St, an enterprise he expanded to the point where he could bill it as "the world's largest store." In 1887, a decade after he died, the store passed to Isidor and Nathan Straus, who had leased space in the basement (1874) to run a china-and-glassware department. Macy's moved to its current location in 1902, ten years before Isidor and his wife Ida perished on the *Titanic*, but the Straus family remained associated with Macy's for generations. In 1994 it merged with Federated Department Stores. Among spectacular past sales have been plumbing fixtures for Liberia's presidential palace and a length of silk to outfit a Saudi Arabian harem.

WEST 32ND AND WEST 33RD STREETS

The **Manhattan Mall** (*Broadway, West 32nd to West 33rd St*) occupies the much-altered former home (1908–12; Daniel H. Burnham) of the Gimbel Brothers Department Store, Macy's arch rival. Adam Gimbel, a Bavarian immigrant who started his American career as a pack peddler, founded the store in 1842 in the Midwest and brought it to New York in 1910. "Gimbels" rose to fame for its "feud" with Macy's, romanticized in the film *Miracle on 34th Street*. The rivalry profited both stores, but Gimbels fell on hard times, was bought out in 1973, and closed in 1987. A sky bridge across West 32nd St connects the former store to its former warehouse.

The **Hotel Pennsylvania** (*401 Seventh Ave at West 33rd St*) is probably the world's only hotel famous for its telephone number. Financed by the Pennsylvania Railroad and designed by McKim, Mead & White (1918), it was immortalized by Glenn Miller in his song "Pennsylvania 6-5000" (from the days when telephone exchanges had names). During the 1930s the hotel was a center for big bands as well as a gathering place for out-of-town Garment District buyers who arrived at Pennsylvania Station. The future of the building, today owned by a real estate trust, is cloudy.

PENNSYLVANIA STATION AND
THE FOURTH MADISON SQUARE GARDEN

Until it was destroyed in 1963, Pennsylvania Station (1906–10; *map p. 618, C1*) was McKim, Mead & White's masterpiece, a symbol of the power of the Pennsylvania Railroad, and a fitting entrance to a city rising in economic importance. The eagle-crowned façade with its imposing Doric colonnade found precedents in the Acropolis, St. Peter's Basilica, and the Brandenburg Gate; the General Waiting Room with its vaulted ceiling was modeled on the Baths of Caracalla in Rome; the steel and glass arches, domes, and vaults covering the concourse belonged to the tradition of crystal palaces and glass exhibition galleries. Novelist Thomas Wolfe called it "vast enough to hold the sound of time."

In 1961–2 the financially troubled Pennsylvania Railroad sold the air rights above the station for a new Madison Square Garden, to sit above a smaller station underground. The demolition of the old station spurred the enactment of landmark preservation laws across the nation. Architectural historian Vincent Scully lamented that in McKim, Mead & White's grand building "one entered the city like a god," while in the present subterranean station "one scuttles in like a rat." Among the glories of the destroyed building were 22 granite eagles on the cornice and a great stone clock framed by two classical figures, which were dumped in a landfill in Secaucus, New Jersey; you can see part of a column and one of the figures at the Brooklyn Museum.

The current subterranean Penn Station still gives access to the old tracks laid down by the Pennsylvania Railroad. The city subway system, two commuter lines (the Long Island Railroad and New Jersey Transit), and the long-distance Amtrak line pass through the station, making it the busiest transit hub in the country, traversed by a half-million commuters daily. The present graceless **Madison Square Garden** (1968; Charles Luckman Assocs) includes a 20,000-seat arena enclosed in a precast concrete-clad drum, a theater (up to 5,600 seats), and an office building (29 stories). The New York Rangers (ice hockey) and the New York Knicks (basketball) call the Garden home.

Founded in 2012, the small **Houdini Museum** (*421 Seventh Ave at West 33rd St, 3rd floor; open Mon–Sat 11–6; Sun 11–5; free; T: 212 244 3633, houdinimuseumny.com*) brings together rare Houdini posters, a straitjacket and other things from which the famous magician regularly escaped, including a full complement of handcuffs and his "metamorphosis" trunk. Also on view (and on loan) is a bust that formerly presided over his gravesite (but which was repeatedly smashed or stolen).

The **General Post Office** (*map p. 618, B1*; 1913, McKim, Mead & White) is officially the James A. Farley Building, named to honor a former postmaster general. Its two-block colonnade of 53-ft Corinthian columns was intended to match that of the former Penn Station, built by the same architectural firm. Around the frieze marches the postal workers' motto, loosely adapted from Herodotus: "Neither snow nor rain nor heat nor gloom of night stays these couriers from the swift completion of their appointed rounds." In the early 1990s Senator Daniel Patrick Moynihan proposed transforming the post office into a grand annex to Penn Station, but the plan faltered. At the time of writing, plans were creeping forward, albeit at a petty pace, and may actually come to fruition.

THE THIRTIETH STREET YARDS AND JAVITS CONVENTION CENTER

Once the hub of the city's freight distribution system, the **Thirtieth Street Yards of the New York Central Railroad** (*West 30th and West 37th Sts, Eleventh and Twelfth Aves*) were connected to additional rail yards at 60th St via a surface line on Eleventh Ave and to the downtown waterfront via the elevated High Line and a terminal around Houston St. At the time of writing, 26–28 acres, renamed Hudson Yards, were being rebuilt as a massive mixed-use real estate project conceived after New York lost its bid for the 2012 Olympics, when a stadium was proposed for the site. The final section of the High Line wraps around the project.

The **Jacob Javits Convention Center** (1986; I.M. Pei & Partners; *West 34th St between Eleventh and Twelfth Aves*), named for a former senator, occupies the northern part of the yard. It is the city's primary venue for trade shows, conventions, and large-scale events.

EATING AND DRINKING AROUND THE GARMENT DISTRICT AND HERALD SQUARE

This is a restaurant-challenged neighborhood, though there are some good Korean restaurants in Little Korea, centered around Lexington Ave in the 30s.

$$$ **Keen's Steakhouse.** ■ Go for the history (*see p. 268*) as well as the meat. Steakhouse classics, aside from the steak and mutton chop, are the oysters, shrimp cocktail, iceberg wedge salad with blue cheese dressing, and creamed spinach. For dessert, flaming bananas Foster. Lunch weekdays, dinner nightly. *76 West 36th St (Fifth and Sixth Aves). T: 212 947 3636, keens.com. Map p. 617, D4.*

$$ **Lugo Cucina Italiana.** Close to Penn Station, this busy café has moderately priced Italian food, with homemade mozzarella, pasta, salads, and pizza. Breakfast and lunch weekdays, dinner nightly. *1 Penn Plaza* (*entrance on West 33rd St*). *T: 212 760 2700, ldvhospitality.com/brands /lugo-cucina-italiana. Map p. 618, C1.*

$$ **Szechuan Gourmet.** Better than the décor and the service are the spicy regional dishes and the prices. Branches in Flushing and the East 70s. *21 West 39th St (Fifth and Sixth Aves). T: 212 921 0233, no website. Map p. 617, D4.*

$ **Cho Dang Gol.** Korean restaurant notable for its homemade bean curd. If it gets busy, expect Chinatown-style service. Lunch and dinner daily. *55 West 34th St (Fifth and Sixth Aves). T: 212 698 8222, chodanggolny.com. Map p. 618, A1.*

Times Square Theater District & Hell's Kitchen

Times Square, the heart of the city's entertainment district, glows nightly with Broadway's fabled lights. Hell's Kitchen to the west, once the turf of warring street gangs, has become home to a respectable upwardly mobile middle class.

Times Square (*map p. 616, C3*) is not a square at all, but two triangles created by the intersection of Broadway and Seventh Avenue (the "Crossroads of the World"), as the streets merge, cross, and diverge. The neighborhood of Times Square stretches from about West 40th to West 54th Sts between Sixth and Eighth Aves. It is a glitzy Mecca for tourists, and a symbol of urban renewal. Crowded and chaotic by day, it is spectacular after dark, illuminated by lighting displays famous the world over. Directly west, nearby Hell's Kitchen has rapidly gentrified since the 1980s and is sometimes known by the more salubrious name of Clinton.

HISTORY OF TIMES SQUARE

Before 1904 Times Square, then known as Longacre Square, was dominated by horse exchanges, carriage factories, stables, and blacksmiths' shops. John Jacob Astor owned a great deal of real estate in the area and enlarged his fortune selling off lots for hotels and other ventures. In 1904 the subway arrived along with the *New York Times*, whose publisher persuaded the city to rename the area for his newspaper, perhaps in competition with Herald Square to the south, named for the *New York Herald*, then the dominant newspaper.

O.J. Gude, an advertising man, is said to have coined the name "the Great White Way" in 1901, when he realized the commercial potential of electrically enhanced billboards, which through the years have given way to neon and then to giant LED screens. Viewers have marveled at a gigantic smoker exhaling smoke rings, a shower of golden peanuts cascading from an illuminated bag, and a giant electric Kleenex made of some 25,000 light bulbs. That pales, however, in comparison to an eight-story billboard (2014) with nearly 24 million LED pixels, which reaches from West 45th to West 46th

St.; at the time of installation, it was estimated to rent for $2.5 million a month, during which time an estimated nine million people would pass through Times Square.

The city's theater district developed around Times Square during the first three decades of the 20th century. Among the pioneering theaters to leave Herald Square for further up Broadway were Charles Frohman's Empire Theatre (1893) at 40th St, and the former Metropolitan Opera House (1883) between 39th and 40th Sts. Oscar Hammerstein—opera impresario, composer, cigar-maker, and grandfather of the famous lyricist—first forged north of 42nd St; his Olympia Theatre (1895) on Broadway between 44th and 45th Sts lasted only two years, but Hammerstein rebounded from bankruptcy and built three more theaters, earning himself the reputation of "the man who created Times Square."

Advances in transportation made the district widely accessible. Theaters were built either by speculators aware that a hit show could gross a million dollars in a single year—roughly the price of building a theater in the 1920s—or by financial backers working with independent producers, including Charles Frohman and David Belasco. Times Square began attracting agents, producers, theatrical publications, restaurants, hotels, and theatrical clubs. New York's best season came in 1927–8, when 80 theaters were in operation. (Today there are about half that number.)

The Depression devastated Broadway. The Federal Theater Project kept some actors and writers in work, but the theater district began a long process of attrition, abetted by rising land values and the inroads of the movies and, later, television. Many legitimate theaters were converted to burlesque theaters or to movie houses whose films deteriorated from Hollywood hits, to second-run movies, to X-rated pornography. By the 1970s, the area was notorious for sleaze—crime, drug dealing, and prostitution.

The turnaround began in the late 1980s with new commercial real estate development in the West 40s and 50s. In 1990 the state took over several historic theaters on 42nd St and formed a non-profit organization to oversee their redevelopment. The Walt Disney Company came to town in 1993, refurbishing the New Amsterdam Theatre for wholesome Disney-style entertainment. The Times Square Alliance, a business improvement association (founded 1992), improved public safety, bolstered economic development, and dealt with quality-of-life issues.

Today Times Square is clean, safe, profitable, and visitor- and pedestrian-friendly. While no one wishes for the return of crime and squalor, some observers lament the neighborhood's homogeneity, its bland lineup of chain-stores (albeit grandly scaled and beautifully illuminated), and its sense of being for tourists, not New Yorkers.

THEATER DISTRICT

Map p. 616, C3. Subway: 1, 2, 3, 7, N, Q, R, S to Times Square-42nd St. Bus: M7, M10, M20, M27, M42, M104. NB: Since many of the theaters have been landmarked, their façades may not be significantly altered, but giant marquees often obscure the original architectural features, so they are usually best viewed from a distance.

ON AND AROUND 42ND STREET

The New Amsterdam Theatre.
The showgirls of the Ziegfeld Follies once strutted their stuff in this elaborate Art Nouveau theater (1903, Herts & Tallant; restored 1997, Hardy Holzman Pfeiffer Associates)—the oldest on Broadway, along with the Lyceum (*p. 226*). During the Depression, it become a movie theater (1937), and closed in 1985, reopening eventually in 1997. *214 West 42nd St (Seventh and Eighth Aves). T: 212 282 2900.*

The New Victory Theater. Built as the Republic by Oscar Hammerstein (1900; J.B. McElfatrick & Co.), who sold it to impresario David Belasco, who added decorative touches. Now a center for children's entertainment. *207 West 42nd St (Seventh and Eighth Aves). T: 646 223 3010, newvictory.org.*

Ripley's Believe It or Not! Odditorium (*234 West 42nd St at Seventh and Eighth Aves. Open daily 9am–1am; earlier winter closing, check website; sizeable admission charge; T: 212 398 3133, ripleysnewyork.com*) and **Madame Tussauds wax museum** (*234 West 42nd St at Seventh and Eighth Aves; open Sun–Thur 10–8, Fri–Sat 10–10; extended holiday hours; sizeable admission charge; T: 212 512 9600, madametussauds.com/newyork*): these attractions arrived in Times Square in 2007 and 2000 respectively.

MADAME TUSSAUD AND ROBERT RIPLEY

Madame Tussaud, née Marie Grosholtz (1761–1850), was apprenticed as a child to Philippe Curtius, a Swiss doctor who created wax models for teaching anatomy. When Curtius moved to Paris, opening an exhibit of wax figures, Marie, his star pupil, followed. She sculpted Voltaire and Benjamin Franklin among other celebrities, and tutored the sister of Louis XVI. During the French Revolution, compromised by her ties to the royal family, she was imprisoned and, to show loyalty to the republic, was forced to make death masks of guillotined aristocrats including Louis XVI and Marie Antoinette. When Curtius died in 1794, he bequeathed his wax figures to Marie, by now Madame Tussaud. She fled to England (1802), taking along the models, and opened her first museum in 1835. Today the internationally franchised museums feature waxen stars of stage and screen, comic-book heroes, sports' stars, and politicians.

Robert Ripley (1890–1949) was a Renaissance man of sorts—an indefatigable cartoonist, athlete, writer of books on boxing and handball, world traveler, radio personality, and entrepreneur. His fame was assured in 1929 when William Randolph Hearst syndicated his newspaper column "Believe It or Not." Like Madame Tussaud, Ripley has become the figurehead of a franchise, with museums of oddities worldwide.

The Port Authority Bus Terminal.
Vast, confusing, and drab, this terminus for commuter and long distance lines is the nation's largest and busiest bus

station, built in 1950 and expanded thereafter. In front stands a two-ton statue of Ralph Cramden (2000; Lawrence J. Nowlan), television's big-mouthed bus driver from Bensonhurst, Brooklyn—actually the statue portrays comedian Jackie Gleason, who played the role in *The Honeymooners* (1955–6). The terminal has once again reached peak capacity and several plans have been proposed to relieve the congestion in the surrounding streets. *625 Eighth Ave, West 40th to 42nd Sts. For automated bus information, T: 212 502 2200.*

The former McGraw-Hill Building. This 33-story tower is the last of Raymond Hood's New York skyscrapers. Revolutionary when constructed (1931), it outraged critics, who found it heavy and unbeautiful. Because the building originally contained printing presses (for trade magazines including the *American Journal of Railway Appliances* and later Marvel Comics), it was relegated to the fringes of Midtown by the Zoning Resolution of 1916. Its sheath of blue-green terra cotta helps it blend into the sky; the horizontal bands of strip windows once illuminated the factory floors (good view from 42nd St between Seventh and Eighth Aves). *330 West 42nd St (Eighth and Ninth Aves).*

Theatre Row. The Off- and Off-Off-Broadway theaters of West 42nd St between Ninth and Tenth Aves are known as Theatre Row. Opened in 1978 on this then-derelict strip, the Row was housed in dreary buildings with primitive air conditioning and minimal amenities for audiences and actors. The 42nd Street Redevelopment Corporation invested some $12 million, sold the air rights to the apartment tower that rises above the theaters, and reopened the present Theatre Row building (*no. 410*) in 2002, with rehearsal studios and state-of-the-art stage technology. Also on the block are **Playwrights Horizons** (*no. 416*), devoted to supporting contemporary American playwrights, composers, and lyricists since 1971; and the **Little Shubert** (*no. 422*), built by the powerful Shubert Organization (*see p. 227*) for developing large-scale works.

The newest addition to the Row is the **Pershing Square Signature Center** (*no. 480*), designed by Frank Gehry (2012), with a glittering marquee, three theater spaces, two studios, and a lobby with a bookshop, bar, and café. The Signature Theater (1991) celebrates traditional American playwrights and supports new ones by offering residencies and sometimes presenting full seasons of a single writer.

TIMES SQUARE

One Times Square. Built as the Times Tower (1903–5), the original building is virtually unrecognizable today. When the *New York Times* arrived in December 1904, the 25-story trapezoidal tower, sheathed in ornamental terra cotta over a granite base, became an instant visual landmark. In the 1960s, long after the *Times* had moved to West 43rd St, a featureless slick marble surface replaced the terra cotta and granite. Today the building serves mainly as a skeleton on which to hang advertisements and a platform from which to drop the celebratory ball on New Year's Eve. Three floors up, the "zipper," a wraparound moving sign that first announced the presidential electoral results of 1928 (Herbert Hoover won) still informs passers-by of breaking news and sports scores. *West 42nd St (Broadway and Seventh Ave).*

Knickerbocker Hotel. This red-brick Beaux-Arts building (opened 1906), the only survivor of several ritzy hotels that graced the area at the turn of the 20th century, was commissioned by John Jacob Astor IV, whose family had long owned the land. Its marble-floored dining rooms could seat 2,000 guests; gentlemen frequenting the bar could enjoy Maxfield Parrish's 30-ft-long Old King Cole mural (*see p. 300*). Enrico Caruso, who regularly stayed here, sang "The Star Spangled Banner" out of his window to the crowd gathered below on Armistice Day in 1918. The hotel closed during the Depression and was converted to offices, but reopened in 2015. *1466 Broadway (West 42nd St).*

4 Times Square. This building helped kick start the renaissance of Times Square when it arrived in 1999. On the northwest corner a seven-story rounded tower with an electronic billboard flashes financial news and ads. The giant antenna on top was built to accommodate broadcasters whose facilities were destroyed with the World Trade Center. Condé Nast, publisher of stylish magazines including *The New Yorker* and *Vogue*, was long its primary tenant, until it began its move to One World Trade Center in 2014. *Broadway (West 42nd and 43rd Sts).*

The Paramount Building. This skyline landmark (1927; Rapp & Rapp) was originally the headquarters of Paramount Pictures. Its setbacks converge on a clock tower and an illuminated glass globe. On the clock's face, a circle of stars (instead of numbers) echoes Paramount's logo. Benny Goodman, Tommy Dorsey, and Frank Sinatra performed here; though the palatial theater is long gone, the original lobby remains, its heavily ornate ceiling, marble walls, chandeliers and bronze elevator doors the quintessence of old-fashioned theatricality. A Hard Rock Café occupies the ground floor. *1501 Broadway (West 43rd and West 44th Sts).*

WEST 44TH STREET

Belasco Theatre. Built (1906–7; George Keister) for playwright and producer David Belasco to showcase his technical innovations, it boasted an elevator stage, a sophisticated lighting system, and a grandly furnished apartment for Belasco himself. The murals inside are by Ashcan school painter Everett Shinn. Author of many forgettable plays, Belasco is remembered today for *Madame Butterfly* and *Girl of the Golden West*, granted longevity as operas by Giacomo Puccini. *111 West 44th St (Sixth Ave and Broadway).*

Discovery Times Square. Occupying the sub-basement of the former *New York Times* building, where huge presses once rolled out all the news fit to print, this 60,000 sq ft space presents presents exhibitions that are too large or perhaps too unconventional for traditional museums. Shows have been commercial (featuring such pop culture icons as Harry Potter), unsettling (flayed bodies preserved with plastic and resin), and quietly informative (the Dead Sea Scrolls). *226 West 44th St (Seventh and Eighth Aves); open Sun–Tues 10–7, Wed–Thur 10–8, Fri–Sat 10–9; admission charge (expensive); café; T: 866 987 9692, discoverytsx.com.*

Sardi's. The walls of this restaurant, the one-time haunt of actors, writers, and theater people, who gathered here on opening night awaiting the newspaper reviews, sport caricatures of showbiz celebrities. *234 West 44th St between Broadway and Eighth Ave.*

Shubert Theatre. The Shubert (1913; Henry B. Herts; *225 West 44th St)* has been resoundingly prosperous, beginning with its opening production of *Hamlet* and including *A Chorus Line*, which won the Pulitzer Prize in 1976 and ran until 1990. Lavishly built, perhaps because it was a memorial to Sam Shubert (*see opposite*), the theater has unusual Venetian-style *sgraffito* decoration. A medallion of architect Herts looks down from above the main entrance. The interior includes elaborate plasterwork and murals by J. Mortimer Lichtenauer.

Shubert Alley, midblock between West 44th and West 45th Sts, now a promenade for theatergoers, was formerly a gathering place for singers and actors hoping for roles in Shubert-produced plays. Fire laws mandated the alley as space for fire equipment behind the formerly adjacent Astor Hotel. At the north end of the alley, the **Booth Theatre** (1913; Henry B. Herts) was built as a companion to the Shubert; less opulent, it was intended for intimate drama or small-scale musicals and is named for actor Edwin Booth (*see p. 191*).

WEST 45TH TO WEST 47TH STREETS

Marriott Marquis Hotel. An early arrival (1985) in the "new" Times Square. In 1982, despite public protests, the historic Helen Hayes and Morosco Theatres, as well as the Gaiety, the Bijou, and the Astor, were demolished to make way for it. In return the developer had to build a theater (the 1,600-seat Marquis) within the hotel. On top, a revolving restaurant allows diners to give their regards to Broadway. *1535 Broadway.*

Lyceum Theatre. The oldest continuously operating legitimate theater in New York, is still one of the grandest (1902–3). It boasts an extravagant Beaux-Arts façade with an undulating marquee, elaborate banded Corinthian columns, and a high mansard roof pierced with oval windows. Its designers, Herts & Tallant, who had studied at the École des Beaux-Arts in Paris, were New York's premier theater architects. *149 West 45th St (Broadway).*

Former I. Miller Building. High up on the façade (*1552–4 Broadway*), marble statues celebrate onetime darlings of the theater: Ethel Barrymore (as Ophelia, drama), Marilyn Miller (as Sunny, musical theater), Mary Pickford (as Little Lord Fauntleroy, film), and Rosa Ponselle (as Norma, opera). Israel Miller, a shoemaker who arrived from Poland in 1892, via a stint in Paris with an exclusive shoe manufacturer, got his start making footwear for Broadway shows. Actresses soon asked him to design shoes for their own wardrobes, and in 1911 Miller opened a shop. As his clientele grew to include society women, he established factories in Brooklyn and Massachusetts, distributing to 228 branch stores. In 1926, Miller had this former tenement redesigned, adding the niches for statuary and balloting the public on the "enormously important" issue of which four of the country's best-loved actresses should fill the alcoves. Alexander Stirling Calder, father of Alexander Calder, sculpted the figures.

On the traffic island near the intersection of West 46th St and Broadway stands a bronze **statue of George M. Cohan** (1878–1942), the song-and-dance man best known for writing "Give My Regards to Broadway."

Duffy Square, the northern part of the traffic island, honors Father Francis P. Duffy (1871–1932), the "Fighting Chaplain" of New York's 69th Regiment during World War I. A figure of Duffy (1937; Charles Keck) stands near West 47th St. As pastor of nearby Holy Cross Church (*333 West 42nd St*), Father Duffy served a parish that embraced the slums of Hell's Kitchen, the burlesque houses and dance halls of Times Square, and the legitimate theaters of Broadway. He is depicted wearing his World War I uniform and holding the New Testament, his back to a granite Celtic cross.

THE SHUBERT BROTHERS

The flagship Sam S. Shubert Theatre is named after the eldest Shubert brother, who with his younger siblings Lee and Jacob (known as J.J.) came to the city around the turn of the 20th century and founded a theatrical empire, besting the ruling monopoly of the day, the Klaw and Erlanger Syndicate. Sam died at 26 from injuries received in a train wreck, and his brothers named the theater in his memory. In their heyday the Shuberts controlled the production, booking, and presentation of shows, dominating the out-of-town try-out circuits, and forcing producers to book exclusively through their organization. A decree issued in 1956 as the result of a federal antitrust action required them to stop their restrictive booking practices and to sell 12 theaters in six cities. Nevertheless, the Shubert Organization is still a power on Broadway.

WEST 49TH TO WEST 53RD STREETS

Brill Building. Built in 1931 by Abraham E. Lefcourt, a clothing manufacturer turned real estate entrepreneur, the building was named for Samuel, Max, and Maurice Brill, who held the lease and ran a haberdashery on

the ground floor. During the Depression, before the building was completed, the Brills foreclosed on Lefcourt and renamed the building after themselves. The bronze bust above the door is believed to represent Lefcourt's son

Alan, who died of anemia in 1930. The Brill Building became famous for the music written there during the early 1960s by Carole King, Neil Diamond, and other young singer-songwriters who blended rock and roll with the older Tin Pan Alley tradition popularized by Irving Berlin, the Gershwin brothers, et al. *1619 Broadway.*

Winter Garden Theatre. Back when the horse-and-carriage trade dominated this neighborhood, the building was a horse exchange financed by William K. Vanderbilt, founder of the Jockey Club and an avid racehorse breeder.

The Shuberts leased it from Vanderbilt in 1911 and converted it to a theater, decorating it with a garden theme and changing the show ring into the auditorium. *1634 Broadway.*

Ed Sullivan Theater. Home of the legendary *Ed Sullivan Show* (1948–71), and now *The Late Show*. A sports writer and columnist before becoming a powerful figure in the nascent world of television, Sullivan is remembered for introducing The Beatles to American audiences (1964) and for "making" the careers of many performers. *1697 Broadway (53rd and 54th Sts).*

THE THIRD MADISON SQUARE GARDEN

The third Madison Square Garden (1925; Thomas Lamb), undistinguished architecturally, was developed as an institution by John Ringling, a circus entrepreneur, and Tex Rickard, sometime gambler, cattleman, and promoter of prizefights. The Garden's staple offerings were boxing matches, ice hockey and basketball games, ice shows, the circus, rodeos, and expositions. Its social peak came with the annual horse show, for which a box cost $315 in 1939; its social nadir was probably the Six-Day Bicycle Race, for which in the same year a one-week admission cost a dollar.

HELL'S KITCHEN

Hell's Kitchen (*map p. 616, A3–B3*) is also known as Clinton, a dichotomy that suggests both the neighborhood's past as a low-scale, blue-collar district and its present as a gentrifying part of the far West Side of Midtown. The neighborhood stretches from the Hudson River to Eighth Ave, from about West 34th to West 57th Sts.

HISTORY OF HELL'S KITCHEN

During the mid-19th century Hell's Kitchen's proximity to the Hudson River and the railroad on Eleventh Avenue attracted slaughterhouses, gas plants, and glue and soap factories. These industries provided jobs for immigrants, particularly the Irish, who were willing to work in them and who were forced to live in some of the city's worst tenements. Local gangs preyed on the railroad yards and so terrorized the neighborhood that policemen from the nearby 20th Precinct would venture out only in groups. Bearing such colorful names as the Hudson Dusters, the Gophers, the Gorillas, and Battle Row Annie's Ladies' Social and Athletic Club, the gangs gave Hell's Kitchen a reputation as one of the most dangerous spots on the American continent. An urban legend, probably apocryphal, suggests that two policemen watching a street fight on a muggy summer night gave the district its name. Said one, "This neighborhood is hot as hell." "Hell is cool," corrected the other, "This here's Hell's Kitchen." After 1910, when the New York Central Railroad hired a strong-arm squad who clubbed, shot, arrested, and otherwise incapacitated most of the gangsters, life in the area mellowed for a while, only to resume its former violence with the arrival of bootleggers during the Prohibition era.

Although the waterfront flourished after World War II, containerized shipping sapped the economic vitality of the Hudson River piers. The Italians and Greeks who had worked as stevedores along with the Irish could no longer find jobs and departed. In the 1950s new immigrant groups, blacks from the South and Puerto Ricans, moved in. Racial tensions during that era provided the inspiration for Leonard Bernstein's *West Side Story*, whose Jets and Sharks contested turf in the West 60s where Lincoln Center now stands.

Plagued by drugs and crime in the 1970s, Hell's Kitchen began to gentrify in the 1980s. Today the process is accelerating, as large rental and condominium towers with upscale amenities and prices to match are changing both the appearance and the demographics of the neighborhood. Ethnic restaurants still line Ninth Avenue, the site of the annual **Ninth Avenue International Food Festival** (usually mid-May) when crowds wander the avenue from West 57th to West 37th Sts, sampling food from around the globe.

THE INTREPID SEA, AIR & SPACE MUSEUM

Pier 86 (West 46th St at 12th Ave). Subway: A, C, E, N, R, S, 1, 2, 3, 7 to 42nd St; walk or take the M42 bus to Hudson River (12th Ave); walk north four blocks. Ferry: New York Water Taxi from South Street Seaport and other locations (nywatertaxi.com/ tours/hop). From New Jersey, New York Waterway (nywaterway.com). Open April–Oct Mon–Fri 10–5, weekends and holidays until 6; Nov–March daily 10–5. Last tickets 1hr before closing. Closed Thanksgiving, Christmas. Admission charge; extra fees for guided tours and simulator. Café on Mess Deck. Shop. T: 877 957 SHIP (7447) or 212 245 0072, intrepidmuseum.org.

The aircraft carrier USS *Intrepid* (launched 1943, decommissioned 1974, opened to the public 1982) is the centerpiece of this museum of technology and naval history. In World War II, the Intrepid survived four kamikaze hits and a torpedo attack to launch fighter planes that destroyed 650 enemy planes and 289 enemy ships; thereafter she served in the Cold War and Vietnam, and as a NASA recovery vessel. On view are the USS *Growler*, a diesel-powered strategic missile submarine whose close quarters are not for the claustrophobic; the Concorde (on loan from British Airways), whose fastest transatlantic flight took only 2hrs and 52mins; and the space shuttle *Enterprise*. Below-deck exhibits emphasize technology and the experience of life aboard. You can "pilot" the space shuttle in a simulator or "submerge" in a 40-ft submarine. Rotating exhibits explore such topics as the use of camouflage, women in aviation, and the *Apollo I* tragedy. But the real draw remains the windswept 900-ft flight deck with its lineup of historic planes and helicopters and its exhilarating, vertiginous view of the water.

EATING AND DRINKING IN THE THEATER DISTRICT

Restaurant Row, on the block of West 46th St between Eighth and Ninth Aves, is the center of Theater District dining. Reserve well ahead.

$$$$ **Aureole**. Winner of a Michelin star, this fine-dining option in the base of the Bank of America tower offers mid-towners creative American cuisine and a fine wine list, with *prix fixe* in the dining room for dinner and a less expensive menu in the bar. Lunch weekdays, dinner nightly. *135 West 42nd St (Broadway and Sixth Ave). T: 212 319 1660, charliepalmer.com/aureole-new-york. Map p. 616, C4.*

$$$$ **The Lambs Club**. Formerly a men's theater club and now a public restaurant, it still feels both theatrical and clubby, with red banquettes and theater memorabilia on the walls. Upscale modern American food popular for business lunches, and a fantastic breakfast. Also lunch Mon–Fri, dinner nightly. *132 West 44th St (Broadway and Sixth Ave) in the Chatwal Hotel. T: 212 997 5262, thelambsclub.com. Map p. 616, C3.*

$$$ **Barbetta**. Since 1906, this family-owned Italian restaurant has served devotees of the theater. Classic Italian cooking in a formal setting, complete with crystal chandeliers. Lunch and dinner daily. *321 West 46th St (Eighth and Ninths Aves). T: 212 246 9171, barbettarestaurant.com. Map p. 616, B3.*

$$$ **Blue Fin**. Established updated seafood restaurant, with a weekday *prix fixe* lunch. Sushi, a raw bar, and a caviar menu round out the choices. Breakfast, lunch, brunch and dinner daily. *In the W Hotel, 1567 Broadway (47th St). T: 212 918 1400, bluefinnyc.com. Map p. 616, C3.*

$$$ **db Bistro Moderne**. This upscale bistro started the craze for elite burgers; the db (Daniel Boulud) version is sirloin filled with braised short ribs, foie gras, and black truffle on a Parmesan bun. Other choices are seafood, steak, and kale salad. Breakfast daily, lunch Mon–Fri, dinner nightly, brunch weekends. *In the City Club Hotel, 55 West 44th St (Sixth Ave). T: 212 391 2400, dbbistro.com. Map p. 616, C3.*

$$$ **Esca**. ■ A southern Italian *trattoria* with wonderful fish dishes and a wine cellar that does the Bastianich family proud. The raw fish appetizers are special. Dinner every day, lunch daily except Sun. *402 West 43rd St (Ninth Ave). T: 212 564 7272, esca-nyc.com. Map p. 616, B4.*

$$ Becco. Prime dining territory for theatergoers in a hurry, with menu choices that will get you in and out quickly. Familiar Italian dishes with seasonal specials. Lunch and dinner daily. *355 West 46th St (Eighth and Ninth Aves). T: 212 397 7597, becconyc.com. Map p. 616, B3.*

$$ Carmine's. Italian dining, family-style—think large portions, red-sauce specials, and a hectic atmosphere. Lunch and dinner daily. *200 West 44th (Seventh and Eighth Aves). T: 212 221 3800, carminesnyc.com. Map p. 616, C3.*

$$ La Masseria. ■ A *masseria* is a traditional Italian farm, a notion conveyed by the wood beams, stone walls, and roaring fireplace. Puglia-influenced food. Lunch and dinner daily. *235 West 48th St (Broadway and Eighth Ave). T: 212 582 2111, lamasserianyc.com. Map p. 616, C3.*

$$ Orso. This Restaurant Row veteran, serving Italian classics, is a favorite with Broadway actors after the show and is deservedly popular with theatergoers. Lunch and dinner daily. *322 West 46th St (Eighth and Ninth Aves). T: 212 489 7212, orsorestaurant.com. Map p. 616, B3.*

$$ West Bank Café. A beloved old-timer (since 1978) in Theater Row. Comfortable American food in a pleasant setting, while the world around changes. Lunch and dinner daily. *407 West 42nd St (9th Ave). T: 212 695 6909, westbankcafe.com. Map p. 616, B4.*

The Empire State Building & its Environs

The Empire State Building, while not the tallest, is probably the most famous skyscraper in the world, and the view from the top, day or night, is unforgettable.

At ground level (and indeed, reaching far underground), the other major draws of this neighborhood are the Morgan Library and Museum and the most important research branch of the New York Public Library. The Morgan, a Neoclassical "little museum building" constructed to house financier J. Pierpont Morgan's collections, has been expanded, most recently with a glass and steel addition by Renzo Piano that brings it into the 21st century. Further north, the world-famous New York Public Library building opens onto the pleasant landscape of a refurbished Bryant Park.

THE EMPIRE STATE BUILDING

At 1,250ft the Empire State Building (1931; Shreve, Lamb & Harmon) is no longer the world's tallest building—the World Trade Center's Twin Towers surpassed it in 1970 and many others have done so since—but for many people it has always been the quintessential skyscraper, a symbol of the city, the dominant silhouette on the skyline. On a clear day, visibility reaches 80 miles and the view is spectacular, by day or by night.

Visiting the Empire State Building

Map 618, C1. 350 Fifth Ave (33rd and 34th Sts). Subway: B, D, F, M, N, Q, R to 34th St-Herald Square. Bus: M1, M2, M3, M4, M5. Open daily 8am–2am, last elevator at 1:15am. Admission charge (expensive), online discount; surcharge for Express Pass Tickets, which put you at the head of the line. Lines for security check, tickets, and elevators can be daunting; consider going early or late. On the second floor the independently owned New York Skyride, a big-screen, motion-simulated aerial ride

BRYANT PARK
The park's famous bistro chairs near the New York Public Library.

through the city, probably appeals most to younger visitors (open daily 8am–10pm; admission charge (expensive); T: 212 279 9777 or 888-SKYRIDE, skyride.com). Shop. Restaurants on ground floor. No phone number for general information; esbnyc.com.

HISTORY OF THE EMPIRE STATE BUILDING

The fevered optimism of the 1920s engendered the notion of constructing the world's tallest skyscraper, but the building itself was a child of the Depression. Just two months before the 1929 stock market crash, wreckers demolished the Victorian Waldorf-Astoria and Astor Court, which then occupied the site. None of the chief investors was experienced in real estate development but remarkably, the Empire State Building was finished $5 million under budget and 45 days ahead of schedule, rising an average of 4½ stories a week and 14 stories during the ten peak working days. Steel was set in place sometimes only 80 hours after leaving the furnaces of Pittsburgh.

Because of the Depression, actual costs came to only $40,948,900, but the economic climate prevented full occupancy until shortly before World War II, a period during which the building was nicknamed the "Empty State Building." It became profitable only in 1950. Today tourism has become a prime money-maker, with the observation decks generating some $60 million in profits annually. In 2010 each of the 6,514 windows was removed and replaced to increase energy efficiency and decrease the annual $11 million utility bill.

The building's most famous visitor was King Kong: in the classic 1933 film, the mythical giant ape climbed the tower and swatted at a squadron of army planes buzzing around his head. The building has also known its share of tragedy: on February 13, 1935, Irma P. Eberhardt leapt from the top, becoming its first suicide. A decade later on a foggy July 28, 1945, an Army B-25 threaded its way among the pinnacles of Midtown and crashed into the 79th floor, killing 14 people.

Design and exterior of the Empire State Building

The façade consists of a limestone curtain wall trimmed with vertical strips of stainless steel running the height of the building, a design chosen after 15 discarded attempts, in part because it would facilitate rapid construction. Everything possible—windows, spandrels, steel strips, even slabs of stone—was fabricated at the site of origin and shipped for installation requiring no further hand fitting or stonecutting. Originally the building was to end at the 86th floor, but one of the backers determined that it needed a mast for mooring zeppelins, which added more than 150ft to the projected height. Several zeppelins did attempt to dock there, but the mast was never a successful mooring place, though a Navy blimp managed to dock long enough in 1931 to dump its ballast—water—on pedestrians several blocks away.

Since 1976 the façade has been illuminated with colored lights to commemorate holidays, the city's ethnic communities, important victories by New York sports teams, such causes or events as World Diabetes Day (blue) or the death of Frank Sinatra (also blue, for Ol' Blue Eyes), and such oddities as National Angel Food Cake Day (white). To honor Queen Elizabeth's Golden Jubilee, the building was bathed with purple and gold; to honor the death of actress Fay Wray, who played the woman loved by King Kong, the lights were dimmed for 15mins. In 2012 the building received a programmable LED lighting system that can flash millions of color combinations.

Lobby of the Empire State Building

The three-story lobby is faced with marble imported from France, Italy, Belgium, and Germany. A marble panel with an aluminum relief of the skyscraper superimposed over New York State faces the main entrance, next to it a 1938 scale model ($^1/_{16}$ inch = 1ft) of the building. Art Deco ceiling murals designed by Leif Neandross and executed in 24-karat gold and aluminum leaf depict a Machine Age sky, whose stars and planets resemble gears and wheels.

THE MORGAN LIBRARY & MUSEUM

Map p. 617, D4. 225 Madison Ave (East 36th St). Subway: 6 to 33rd St;, 4, 5, or 7 to Grand Central; B, D, F, Q to 42nd St. Bus: M2, M3, M4, Q32. Open Tues–Thur 10:30–5, Fri 10:30–9, Sat 10–6, Sun 11–6. Closed Mon (except some holiday Mons), Thanksgiving, Christmas, and New Year's Day. Admission charge but free Fri 7pm–9pm. Admission to Mr. Morgan's Library and Study, the Rotunda, and the Librarian's Office (but not the changing exhibits) also free Tues 3–5 and Sun 4–6. Pleasant dining room and café. Shop. T: 212 685 0008, themorgan.org.

The Morgan Library and Museum holds the core of an astonishing collection gathered by financier J. Pierpont Morgan (1837–1913), supplemented by more recent acquisitions. J.P. Morgan Jr. established the museum in 1924 according to the wishes of his father's will. Morgan's personal study and library remain much as they were during his lifetime and parts of the collection are always on view in changing exhibitions. In 2007 the office of Morgan's librarian, Belle da Costa Greene, was opened to the public.

THE BUILDINGS: EXTERIORS

The original library

NB: The best view of the original building is from East 36th St.

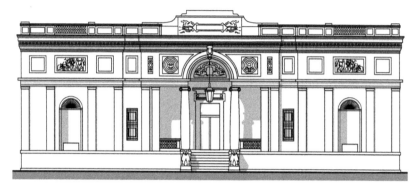

THE ORIGINAL MORGAN LIBRARY

In 1902 Morgan, then 65 years old, hired Charles Follen McKim of McKim, Mead & White to design a "little museum building" for his books and collections, which had outgrown his brownstone home on the northeast corner of East 36th St and Madison Ave. The library was completed in 1906, and though its modest proportions were consistent with the residential scale of the neighborhood, the building is often considered the pinnacle of McKim's career. He and his partner Stanford White were leading exponents of the American Renaissance style, which sought models in the monuments of the past and embodied the notion that America had inherited the intellectual and material energies of the Renaissance. Morgan, unsurprisingly, subscribed to these notions.

This small Neoclassical building is faced with marble blocks fitted closely together without mortar. Knowing that money was no great object for Morgan, McKim confessed his desire to construct a building this way, realizing a dream apparently born when, touring the monuments of ancient Athens, he had tried and failed to stick his penknife into the cracks between the stones of the Erechtheion. The exquisitely accurate stone-cutting added only about $50,000 to the total construction cost of $1,154,669.

McKim chose to adorn the library with pinkish Tennessee marble and a Palladian-style loggia. Sculptured panels (Adolph A. Weinman) below the frieze represent (right to left) *Truth Leads Literature, Philosophy, History, Oratory, Astronomy,* and *Music (or Apollo), accompanied by Fame, inspires the arts of Architecture, Sculpture, Painting, Ceramics, and Textiles.* The marble lionesses guarding the doorway are by Edward Clark Potter, who later placed a more famous pair in front of the New York Public Library.

Additions to the building

J. Pierpont Morgan died in 1913, and in 1924 the Morgan Library opened to the public. As the years passed and the collections grew, the "little museum building" no longer sufficed, so an **Annex** (1928; Benjamin Wistar Morris) was added at the corner of Madison Ave and East 36th St, on the site of Morgan's brownstone home.

In 1988 the Library purchased the **former home of J.P. Morgan Jr.** ("Jack" Morgan), on the southeast corner of Madison Ave and 37th St. Built in 1852 for copper king Anson Phelps Stokes, the 45-room brownstone (with its 2,000-bottle capacity wine cellar) had been acquired (1904) by Morgan for his son, for a million dollars. Morgan had already bought the house between his own more modest dwelling and the Phelps Stokes house for half of that; this middle house was torn down to make space for a garden. The modern entrance stands in the former garden, while the bookstore and restaurant occupy part of the son's home.

Renzo Piano's **expansion** (2006) links the three existing buildings with glass and steel. The windowless "cube" between the Annex and the original library often displays medieval and Renaissance treasures, mostly small in scale and some sensitive to light. The entrance facing Madison Ave opens into a 52-ft glassy atrium with glass-walled elevators and ficus trees sprouting through the floor, with views of all the buildings in the complex, the sky, and neighboring buildings. A concert hall and storage vaults have been drilled into bedrock below the building, keeping the above-ground scale appropriate to its surroundings.

THE ORIGINAL LIBRARY: INTERIORS

Charles Follen McKim designed a suite of three rooms for Pierpont Morgan: a study, a library, and an office for Morgan's librarian. A rotunda links the library and study.

Mr. Morgan's study: This was once called "the most beautiful room in America"; and even now, though dim and heavy to modern taste (the velvet curtains are kept drawn to protect the walls), it is surely one of the most sumptuous. At one end is Morgan's custom-made desk, on whose surface weighty transactions in finance and art were consummated. The red silk damask on the walls replicates the original armorial pattern that decorated the walls of the Chigi Palace in Rome. Morgan purchased the antique carved ceiling in Florence and brought it here in pieces. Displayed are some of Morgan's favorite paintings and *objets*

d'art in bronze, faïence, and metalwork, many of them notable for their intricate workmanship. They suggest Morgan's preference for small, precious objects.

The Rotunda (vestibule): The murals are by H. Siddons Mowbray, inspired by Raphael. The lunettes over the main entrance and the doors to the east and west rooms represent the great ages of poetry. The floor marbles came from ancient quarries in Africa and Italy. Morgan especially liked the deep purple of Imperial porphyry and had the large disc in the center of the room carefully delivered by Wells Fargo. The columns include beautiful grey-green Italian *cipollino* marble, whose striations may indeed suggest the rings of an onion.

Mr. Morgan's library: The triple tiers of rare books rise to an elaborately decorated ceiling. Treasures on display here always include one of the Library's three (of the 49 known) Gutenberg Bibles. The 16th-century Brussels tapestry above the mantelpiece depicts *The Triumph of Avarice*, perhaps an unintended ironic comment on the life of a man who accumulated such astonishing wealth. The Latin inscription warns that as Tantalus is ever thirsty in the midst of water, so the miser is always desirous of riches. It belongs to a series of the Seven Deadly Sins, designed by the Flemish tapestry master Pieter van Aelst, father-in-law of Pieter Brueghel the Elder.

The zodiacal signs in the ceiling decoration, again by Mowbray, refer to important dates in Morgan's life. Flanking the door are his birth sign, Aries, and that of the date of his second marriage in May 1865: Gemini, with Mercury signifying that it was a Wednesday. Directly across is Aquarius with the Muse of Tragedy, marking the death of Morgan's young first wife in February 1862, an event from which Morgan, prone to depression, never fully recovered.

The Librarian's office: The smallest of the McKim rooms, this was built for Belle da Costa Greene, first director of the Morgan Library and an important force in shaping the collection after Morgan's death. It contains original furniture as well as a bronze candelabrum with figures of Juno, Minerva, and Venus by Antoine-Louis Barye and a bronze sculpture of John Ruskin by Gutzon Borglum.

HIGHLIGHTS OF THE COLLECTION

Belle da Costa Greene once remarked that the library "apparently contains everything but the original tablets of the Ten Commandments," an understandable exaggeration considering the range and scope of the Library's holdings. Strengths include medieval and Renaissance manuscripts, prints and drawings, autograph manuscripts and letters, printed books, music manuscripts, and ancient cylinder seals.

Among the illuminated manuscripts are the *Farnese Hours* (1546) by Giulio Clovio, probably the last great Italian illuminated manuscript. The *Dutch Hours of Catherine of Cleves* (c. 1440) is remarkable for showing humble scenes from daily life, for example the Holy Family at supper, with Joseph sitting by the fire eating porridge. The *Reims Gospel Book*, the collection's finest Carolingian manuscript, was written in gold (c. 860) at the Abbey of St-Rémi, and bought by Morgan's son. Among the early printed books, in addition to the Gutenberg Bibles, are works by Gutenberg's associates, Fust and Schoeffer; by England's first printer, William Caxton; and by the great Venetian printer Aldus Manutius. Later works include the First Folio edition (1623) of Shakespeare's collected plays; the first printing, first state, of the American Declaration of Independence; and William Morris's *The Works of Geoffrey Chaucer* (1896), printed by the Kelmscott Press.

Master drawings include work by artists from Leonardo and Michelangelo to Degas and Matisse. The Library owns eight drawings by Albrecht Dürer, including *Adam and Eve* (1504), a celebrated work made in preparation for the engraving *Fall of Man*. William Blake is represented by a series of watercolor illustrations for the *Book of Job* as well as illustrations for Milton's *L'Allegro* and *Il Penseroso*. There is an outstanding collection of etchings and drawings by Rembrandt, including two drawings of his wife Saskia asleep.

J. PIERPONT MORGAN AS COLLECTOR

At a time when other millionaires hankered for French landscapes or Old Master paintings, J. Pierpont Morgan used his fortune to amass (in the true sense of that word) not only paintings and sculpture, but rare books and manuscripts, porcelains, majolica, faïence, fine goldwork and enamel, Mesopotamian cylinder seals, cuneiform tablets, even papyrus rolls. Morgan's passion for collecting began early: at age 14, he asked President Millard Fillmore for an autograph and received it in an envelope personally franked by the president. As a student in Switzerland and Germany, Morgan picked up bits of stained glass from the grounds of old churches and cathedrals; some of these shards are now embedded in the windows of his study.

However, it was not until his father died in 1890 and left J. Pierpont Morgan $15 million (a huge sum in those days) that Morgan's collecting began in earnest. During the next decade he purchased a Gutenberg Bible on vellum, the 1459 Mainz Psalter, the 9th-century Lindau Gospels with their spectacular jeweled binding, four Shakespeare Folios, and original autograph manuscripts by Keats and Dickens, among others. In the last 20 years of his life he spent an estimated $60 million on his collections (perhaps a billion dollars today), buying individual works, collections, and sometimes entire estates, and later selling off what he did not want.

Some of Morgan's motivation may have been personal, but larger forces were also at work. New York had become the center of world finance. European aristocrats, whose pedigrees were assured but whose cash flow was not, began to sell artworks to cash-rich, culture-poor Americans. Encouraged by new authentication techniques, the great American collectors of the period—Benjamin Altman, Henry Clay Frick, and Morgan—became more adventuresome in their choices, looking beyond Salon painting to other periods and media.

At first Morgan concentrated on autographs. Later he was advised in his choices by his scholarly nephew, Junius Spencer Morgan, who loved books and manuscripts, perhaps accounting for the emphasis on objects that document the history of the printed book: Egyptian, Greek, and Latin papyri; medieval works printed on vellum; incunabula; and later examples of beautifully printed and bound books. The acquisition of the Lindau Gospels, Morgan Manuscript 1, marks the beginning of Morgan's career as the nation's greatest collector of medieval manuscripts. His interest in cuneiform seals was unusual, and his collection is one of the finest in the world.

Among the musical manuscripts are autographs of Brahms's First Symphony, Beethoven's Violin Sonata in G major (op. 96), four Schubert Impromptus, the *Winterreise*, and Stravinsky's *Perséphone*.

Highlights among the autograph manuscripts include Charles Perrault's *The Tales of Mother Goose* (1695) and Charles Dickens's *A Christmas Carol* (1843). In 2004 the Morgan acquired watercolor studies and drafts from Jean de Brunhoff's *The Story of Babar*, including the earliest plan for the Babar book with 44 pages of pencil and watercolor sketches. John Milton's autograph manuscript of *Paradise Lost*, Book I, in the hand of various amanuenses, is the sole remnant of the manuscript from which the first edition was printed, and one of the most important British literary manuscripts in America. The collection of American manuscripts includes Twain's *Pudd'nhead Wilson*, Thoreau's *Journal*, and Steinbeck's *Travels with Charley*. There are letters autographed by Elizabeth I, Napoleon, George Washington, Thomas Jefferson, and an eclectic array of artists from Piranesi to Picasso.

In 1992 the Library received the Gilder Lehrman Collection of American historical manuscripts, whose treasures include a letter written by George Washington, a 1493 printing of Columbus's letter announcing his discovery, signed copies of the Emancipation Proclamation and the Thirteenth Amendment, and a signed copy of Gerald Ford's pardon of Richard Nixon.

MURRAY HILL

The Morgan Library lies in upscale Murray Hill, bounded roughly by 34th St, Third Ave, 42nd St, and Madison Ave. The neighborhood takes its name from Robert Murray, whose country home stood near present East 37th St and Park Ave during the Revolutionary War. In the mid-19th century real estate values soared as Morgans, Havemeyers, Phelpses, Delanos, Belmonts and Tiffanys built brownstone mansions along Fifth, Madison, and Park Avenues. Although most have been torn down or stripped of detail, a few homes, clubhouses, and carriage houses remain to suggest Murray Hill in its glory days.

The Protestant Episcopal **Church of the Incarnation** (*map p. 617, D4; 209 Madison Ave at East 35th St; open Sun 8–1, other days 11:30–2; T: 212 689 6350, churchoftheincarnation.org*) was founded as a mission chapel of Grace Church (*see p. 170*). The building (1864, rebuilt 1882; Emlen T. Little) is in the English Gothic style often favored by Episcopalians, here brownstone with lighter sandstone trim. During the 19th century, many of the city's Episcopal churches raised money by renting pews rather than collecting tithes, keeping a few pews open for visitors and those who could not afford the rent. To accommodate the latter, some congregations spun off chapels with free or low-rent pews. Incarnation was founded as such a chapel in 1850, becoming independent two years later and in 1863 establishing its own mission chapel.

Famous artists of the Gilded Age designed the stained-glass windows and other decorative work: Louis Comfort Tiffany (*The Pilgrim*, south side of chancel); the

Tiffany Glass Company (*Angel of Victory over Death* and *The 23rd Psalm*, both in the north wall); and John La Farge (*Calling of Peter and Paul* and *God the Good Vintner*, south wall). Other windows are by the William Morris Company and some are based on designs by Edward Burne-Jones. The altar rail has carved oak angels by Daniel Chester French. Admiral David Farragut was a congregant; Eleanor Roosevelt was confirmed here; and the funeral of Franklin Delano Roosevelt's mother took place here, the sanctuary made accessible to the crippled president with a purpose-built ramp.

The **Consulate General of the Polish People** (*233 Madison Ave at East 37th St*) was built as the Joseph Raphael De Lamar mansion. Born in Amsterdam, De Lamar worked as a merchant seaman before owning a marine salvage business. After being trapped underwater in a ship he was trying to recover or else because he was bitten by the gold bug, he went West in 1878 and made a fortune in mining, later enhancing his wealth on Wall Street, where he was known as a close-mouthed "man of mystery." The mansion, one of the city's grandest Beaux-Arts confections, was designed in 1905 by C.P.H. Gilbert, known for housing very wealthy clients, and represents De Lamar's hoped-for entrée into society. Crowned with a staggering mansard roof, ornamented with copper cresting, it is extravagant in every detail inside and out, originally featuring a subterranean garage with an elevator to the sidewalk. De Lamar, a fine organist, equipped the mansion with an instrument appropriate to his wealth and talent, and for good measure had another installed on his yacht.

THE NEW YORK PUBLIC LIBRARY

Map p. 617, D4. Fifth Ave at 42nd St. Open Mon and Thur–Sat 10–6, Tues–Wed 10–8, Sun 1–5. Closed holidays and Sun during the summer. Hours vary for special collections. Guided tours of the building and exhibitions Mon–Sat at 12.30 and 3.30, Sun at 2; meet at the reception desk in Astor Hall. Introductory film. Shop. Apps for mobile devices. T: 917 ASK NYPL (917 275 6975), nypl.org. NB: At the time of writing the Catalogue Room and the Reading Room were closed for restoration.

Officially the Stephen A. Schwarzman Building, but generally known either as the Main Branch or simply the New York Public Library, the building is admired for its architecture; inside are world-famous collections, shown in exceptional exhibitions on literary, artistic, and historical subjects.

The building

The building (1911; Carrère & Hastings) sits on a wide terrace running the length of the Fifth Avenue façade. The steps, which attract tourists, pigeons, footsore shoppers, and office workers on lunch break, are flanked by two famous marble lions by Edward C. Potter (1911). Originally criticized as mealy-mouthed, complacent creatures, they seemed undeserving of the nicknames Mayor Fiorello La Guardia would later give them names: *Patience* (south side) and *Fortitude* (north side), virtues the mayor thought important for New Yorkers struggling during the Depression. In niches behind the fountains are two statues (1913; Frederick W. MacMonnies): *Truth* (a man leaning against a sphinx) and *Beauty* (a woman seated on the winged horse Pegasus). Above the entrance on the frieze six allegorical figures by Paul Wayland Bartlett (1914) represent areas of knowledge (left to right): *History, Romance, Religion, Poetry, Drama,* and *Philosophy.* The pediment figures at the ends of the façade are *Art* (south) and *History* (north) by George Grey Barnard.

The entrance hall is finished in white Vermont marble, with an elaborate vaulted ceiling, heroic marble candelabra, and wide staircases. Behind it is **Gottesman Hall**, a venue for major exhibitions. To reach the **Rotunda**, take the elevator at the end of the right corridor to the third floor, or walk up the marble stairs. Visible from the stairway are the large interior courts that provide natural light for the catalogue and reading rooms. The Rotunda is decorated with murals (1940) by Edward Laning depicting the story of the recorded word. The Public Catalogue in Room 315 formerly held more than ten million cards, which are now logged onto the Library's digital catalogue system.

Beyond is the monumental **Main Reading Room**, about two blocks long, whose beautifully decorated ceiling, tall, arched windows, and furniture designed by Carrère & Hastings make it one of the city's great interiors; today its free internet access draws as many readers of laptops as of reference books.

The collections

The collections developed from the consolidation of two privately endowed libraries (the Astor and Lenox Libraries) and the Tilden Trust, a bequest of $2 million and 20,000 books from Samuel J. Tilden, lawyer, governor, and unsuccessful presidential candidate. John Jacob Astor, not himself a bookish man, was persuaded by Joseph Green Cogswell, bibliographer for the Astor Collection, to establish a public library as a testimonial to his adopted country instead of the huge monument to George Washington he had earlier favored. Astor bequeathed $400,000 and a plot of land for its foundation. The books, largely chosen by Cogswell, were in the fields of greatest public interest, including the "mechanic arts and practical industry," and languages, since Cogswell saw the American nation coming "into near relation with countries formerly the most remote." James Lenox, on the other hand, was a scholar whose interests included American literature and history, the Bible, Milton, Shakespeare, Bunyan, and Renaissance literature of travel and discovery. Lenox built his own library (1875) on the site of the present Frick Collection but at his death in 1880 left his 85,000 peerless books and an endowment of $505,000 to the New York Public Library. In 1895 the three gifts were united as the New York Public Library, Astor, Lenox, and Tilden Foundations.

In 1901 Andrew Carnegie, realizing that New York had nothing comparable to the public circulating systems of other American cities, gave $52,000,000 for the construction of branch libraries. Today the library has 88 neighborhood branches in the Bronx, Manhattan, and Staten Island and four research libraries. (Brooklyn, once an independent city, has its own system.) The circulating collections are publicly supported while the research libraries depend upon endowment and contributions.

NEW YORK PUBLIC LIBRARY
One of two marble lions flanking the library steps on Fifth Avenue.

Among the collections are the **Berg Collection** with printed books and manuscripts mainly related to American and English literature—from William Caxton's 1480 edition of *The Chronicles of England* to the countercultural poets of New York's Lower East Side (1960–80). Rarities in the **Prints Collection** include an engraving by Paul Revere of the British landing in Boston in 1768. The **Arents Collection** focuses on books published in serial form and on documents (1507–present) concerned with tobacco. In the **Rare Book Division** are a Gutenberg Bible; the only known copy of the original folio edition (in Spanish) of Christopher Columbus's letter describing his discoveries (dated 1493); the first full folio of Shakespeare (1623); and a Bay Psalm Book (1640) from Cambridge, Massachusetts, the first book printed in America in the English language.

BRYANT PARK

Map p. 617, D4. Subway: B, D, F, or M to 42nd St; 7 to Fifth Ave. Bus: M1, M2, M3, M5. Open 7–midnight in summer (Fri–Sat until 11pm); otherwise 7–10. Restaurant, café, food kiosks. Winter ice rink, wifi. bryantpark.org.

Directly behind the New York Public Library is Bryant Park, named in 1884 after William Cullen Bryant (1794–1878), editor, writer, abolitionist, and proponent of Central Park and the Metropolitan Museum, among other projects. After a turn as a potter's field, these 9.6 acres held the Croton Distributing Reservoir (1839–1900), a 50-ft-high granite mass with a promenade on top. For 200 years before the reservoir opened in 1842, New York City, dependent on increasingly polluted shallow wells and springs for its water supply, endured frequent cholera outbreaks and uncontrollable fires. The Croton system brought pure water from the mainland, 40.5 miles through an aqueduct, across High Bridge into Harlem, then through pipes and a tunnel into the reservoir. Enlarged and updated, it still functions.

West of the reservoir, a world's fair opened in 1853, complete with a Crystal Palace containing technology exhibits: pumps, hardware, sewing machines. It burned in 1858; the reservoir was demolished in 1899; and the New York Public Library rose in its stead.

In the 1930s Robert Moses, as Parks Commissioner, executed a redesign that raised the interior four feet above street level and laid out the central lawn and walkways. After deteriorating into a haven for drug dealers and muggers in the 1970s and '80s, the park was restored, redesigned, and re-landscaped. It reopened in 1992, the restored landscape inconspicuously doubling as a green roof for the New York Public Library's underground stacks (connected to the main library via a 62-ft tunnel). Today Bryant Park's kiosks, restaurants, and full schedule of events draw people to its pleasant open spaces.

MONUMENTS IN THE PARK

Statues include William Cullen Bryant (1911; Herbert Adams) depicted as an elderly sage (just behind the library); a bronze statue (1922; Jo Davidson) of a ponderous Gertrude Stein sitting cross-legged, and a bronze bust of Goethe (1932; Karl Fischer) near the carousel. Facing Sixth Avenue the statue of José Bonifacio de Andrada commemorates a scholar, poet, and patriarch of Brazilian independence. The statue, by José Lima, was cast from an original (1889) and presented to the US in 1954 as a gift from Brazil. The Josephine Shaw Lowell Memorial Fountain (1912; Charles Platt) is the city's first public memorial dedicated to a woman. Shaw, born to a wealthy Boston family, became a reformer who sought social justice and improved working conditions, especially for women. Also at the west side of the park, the statue of Benito Juárez (2004; Moises Cabrera Orozco) is the city's first monument honoring a Mexican. On the West 42nd St side of the lawn stands William Earl Dodge (1885; John Quincy Adams Ward), commemorated here not for founding the mining company Phelps Dodge, but for his philanthropy. Among other good works, he served as president of the National Temperance Society for 18 years.

EATING AND DRINKING NEAR THE EMPIRE STATE BUILDING

With the exception of Wild Edibles Oyster Bar, most restaurants listed here are within easy walking distance of the Empire State Building.

$$$ Artisanal. A cheese lover's delight, with many varieties stocked in the onsite cheese cave. Fondue, brasserie dishes, hamburgers, daily specials, plus takeout. Breakfast, lunch, and dinner daily. *2 Park Avenue (entrance on 32nd St). T: 212 725 8585, artisanalbistro.com. Map p. 619, D1.*

$$$ Wolfgang's. ■ Traditional steaks, fish and jumbo lobster tails; masculine décor. The owner, Wolfgang Zwiener, worked at Peter Luger's for years, which may account for his know-how. Other branches in NY and beyond. Lunch and dinner daily. *4 Park Ave (33rd St). T: 212 889 3369, wolfgangssteakhouse.net. Map p. 619, D1.*

$$ Café China. Outstanding Szechuan cooking in a romantic, 1930s Shanghai setting. The service can be slow. Lunch and dinner daily. *13 East 37th St (Fifth and Madison Aves). T: 212 213 2810, cafechinanyc.com. Map p. 617, D4.*

$$ Don's Bogam. Busy Koreatown barbecue with a festive atmosphere. Traditional Korean menu, *à la carte* or barbecue platters, lunch specials. Lunch and dinner daily. *17 East 32nd St (Fifth and Madison Aves). T: 212 683 2200, donsbogam.com. Map p. 619, D1.*

$$ Hangawi. Tranquil vegetarian and vegan restaurant in Koreatown; remove your shoes at the door. Lunch Mon–Sat, dinner nightly. *12 East 32nd St (Madison and Fifth Avenues). T: 212 213 0077, hangawirestaurant.com. Map p. 619, D1.*

$$ Les Halles. Tried and true French bistro that has fed a generation *steak frites, choucroute garni*, and sausages. Breakfast, lunch and dinner daily. Another branch downtown. *411 Park Ave South (28th and 29th Sts). T: 212 679 4111, leshalles.net. Map p. 619, D1.*

$$ The Morgan. The museum's atrium houses an informal café; eating here, under the glass, feels like dining al fresco. The Morgan Dining Room, where Jack Morgan and his family ate, offers lunch weekdays and brunch weekends. Some of the menus tie into current exhibits. No need to pay the museum entrance fee. *225 Madison Ave (36th and 37th Sts). T: 212 683 2130, themorgan.org. Map p. 617, D4.*

$$–$ 2nd Ave Deli. Reincarnated in 2007 from the Second Avenue original, the new deli has expanded the menu but still offers huge pastrami, corned beef, and Reuben sandwiches, plus soups, knishes, noshes, and entrées. Open daily 6am–midnight. *162 East 33rd Street (Third Ave). T: 212 689 9000, 2ndavedeli.com. Map p. 619, D1.*

$ Wild Edibles Oyster Bar. Formerly a fish wholesaler, now a restaurant with a raw bar: fish and chips and lobster rolls to linguine with clams. Lunch and dinner daily. *535 Third Avenue (36th St). T: 212 213 8552, wildedibles.com. Map p. 617, E4.*

GRAND CENTRAL TERMINAL
Vanderbilt Hall, the former waiting room leading to the Main Concourse.

Grand Central Terminal, Park Avenue, & the Far East Side

Grand Central Terminal, a destination for both tourists and commuters, anchors a district dominated by its presence. To the north lies corporate Park Avenue; to the east, the United Nations. Near the East River are several elegant residential enclaves.

Rail travel in the US may have declined in scope and grandeur since Grand Central Terminal was built—but there is no doubt that it remains one of the world's great railroad stations, and an enduring symbol of the city. Grand Central remains outwardly unchanged, although the surrounding neighborhood has moved with the times: Park Avenue's character has evolved from industrial (19th century) to elite residential (1920s), before becoming a corporate heartland post-World War II. Architectural highlights abound: the magnificent vaulted Main Concourse of the terminal itself; the Art Deco Chrysler Building; and later, gleaming examples of 20th- and 21st-century vertical thinking.

GRAND CENTRAL TERMINAL

Grand Central Terminal (1903–13; Reed & Stem and Warren & Wetmore) stands proudly astride Park Avenue covering three city blocks—East 42nd to East 45th Sts—between Vanderbilt and Park Aves, with passages extending to Lexington Ave. Beneath it are electric power facilities; steam, water, sewage, and electric mains; and loops of track where trains can turn around without backing out of the station. At one time Grand Central served long-distance trains: the New York Central, which stretched to the Mississippi River, and the New York, New Haven, and Hartford, which served New England. Today it is largely a commuter station, with 82 million people a year trekking through its corridors.

Visually less dramatic (perhaps) than those other emblems of New York's pre-eminence—the Empire State Building, Brooklyn Bridge, and the Statue of Liberty—it is nonetheless a magnificent piece of architecture, and a marvel of engineering and urban planning, bringing the railroad into the heart of the city and gathering into its environs office buildings, hotels, and (during the heyday of rail travel) private clubs. Its Main Concourse is one of New York's finest interiors.

Visiting Grand Central Terminal

Map p. 617, D4. East 42nd St at Park Ave. Subway: 4, 5, 6, 7, S to 42nd St-Grand Central. Bus: M1, M2, M3, M4, M101, M102, M103, M104. Open daily 5:30am until 2am. Shops and food market open daily Mon–Fri 8–8, Sat 10–8, Sun 11–6. Tours of building (admission charge), daily at 12:30pm; tickets online or at the "GCT Tours" ticket window in the Main Concourse. Paid audio tours also available from here or via iTunes app. Free neighborhood tours Fri at 12:30pm; meet in the sculpture court of 120 Park Ave on the southwest corner of 42nd St. T: 212 883 2420, grandcentralpartnership.nyc. Free app; see grandcentralterminal.com.

HISTORY OF GRAND CENTRAL TERMINAL

By 1869 Cornelius Vanderbilt, who began his spectacular career as a ferryboat captain, had seized control of all the railroads into New York City by a series of bold financial maneuvers. He resolved to do physically what he had done fiscally by erecting a Grand Central Depot at Fourth (now Park) Avenue and 42nd St, a location chosen because in 1854 the City had mandated that steam trains, which belched smoke, terminate at 42nd St. Grand Central Depot was ambitiously named, since at the time 42nd St was far from central, though the station was indeed grand. Ever the shrewd operator, Vanderbilt also bought land along Fourth Ave for storage and marshaling yards, real estate that constitutes almost all of the present Grand Central complex. The depot's "head house," designed (1869–71) by John B. Snook, was the nation's largest—a sprawling, elaborate brick and granite building with waiting rooms and offices, inspired in part by the grand Second Empire wing of the Louvre. The "car house" or train shed to the rear, with an arched glass roof, was the largest indoor space in North America, making the depot the world's second largest train station after St. Pancras in London.

As rail traffic quadrupled between 1880 and 1900, the station, its yards, and its sheds were enlarged and rearranged. The redesigned head house, by now called Grand Central Station and heightened to six stories, was designed (1898) by Bradford Lee Gilbert, a veteran railroad architect. Among its features were waiting rooms equipped with rocking chairs and fireplaces. A separate immigrant waiting room in the basement relieved the main waiting room upstairs "of this class of passengers." Behind the station the tracks were sunk in a tunnel beneath Park Avenue, which improved the flow of surface traffic, but steam, smoke, and cinders polluted the tunnel and obscured visibility, and in 1889 the City demanded that railroads be electrified.

It was William J. Wilgus who suggested tearing down Grand Central Station, electrifying the tracks as far as the southern Bronx, and introducing the two present levels of trackage. Wilgus, the brilliant self-taught chief engineer of the New York Central Railroad, also suggested a new terminal that would use the air rights over the tracks (*Madison to Lexington Aves, 42nd to 50th Sts*) for new, revenue-producing office and apartment buildings.

A competition for the design of a new station was won by architects Reed & Stem (Charles Reed was Wilgus's brother-in-law); their innovative plan called for wrapping Park Ave around the station on viaducts. After Reed & Stem had been chosen, the firm of Warren & Wetmore submitted an alternative plan. Whitney Warren was a cousin of William K. Vanderbilt, chairman of the board of the New York Central, and had already designed the New York Yacht Club (*see p. 272*). The railroad brokered a marriage of the two firms, clearly a fraught situation as Reed & Stem had already won the design competition. Though Warren & Wetmore seem to have triumphed in the ensuing power struggle, basic design premises, including the viaduct and the placement of piers for future office buildings along Park Ave, originated with Reed & Stem.

SAVING GRAND CENTRAL

Many assaults have been made on the architectural integrity of the terminal, which sits on prime Midtown real estate. Most have fizzled, with the exception of the MetLife Building, which towers above the terminal from the north (*see p. 259*). Among the less sensible of the failed schemes was a plan (1960) to divide the main waiting room horizontally into four 15-ft stories, the upper three containing bowling alleys. This proposal surely hastened designation of the terminal as a landmark in 1967, a status resented by the financially troubled Penn Central Railroad, which was operating the terminal at the time. The railroad, recognizing the soaring prices of surrounding real estate, proposed a 54-story tower over the waiting room, a design rejected by the Landmarks Commission. After several other plans to circumvent the designation failed, the railroad sued to have the landmark status withdrawn on the grounds of economic hardship, but in 1978 the US Supreme Court upheld the City's right to landmark and thus protect architecturally or historically valuable buildings.

The building

Whitney Warren, who was primarily responsible for the Beaux-Arts **south façade** (*best view from Park Avenue south of the station*), envisioned it as a gateway to the city, designing three great arched windows framed by pairs of columns to recall the triumphal arches of Rome. The terrace supporting the building is faced with Stony Creek granite; the façade is clad with Indiana limestone. The French sculptor Jules-Félix Coutan created the group that crowns the façade (1914). Entitled *The Glory of Commerce*, and sometimes called *Transportation*, it depicts Mercury (Commerce) flanked by Hercules (Physical Energy) and Minerva (Intellectual Energy). The Beaux-Arts-trained Coutan had the statue made here but never visited the US, because, as he explained to the *New York Times*, the sight of "some of your architecture would distress me."

Underneath the 13-ft **clock** stands a heroic bronze of Cornelius Vanderbilt (1869), sketched out by Albert De Groot, one of his former boat captains, and finalized by Ernst Plassmann; it was moved here from the former Hudson River freight station in 1929, where it had been the centerpiece of a huge frieze depicting the glories of his career. The cast-iron bald eagle over the Lexington Ave entrance originally perched on the roof of the earlier Grand Central Station, one of a flock of eleven; it alighted here in 1999.

The station interior was beautifully restored and refurbished in 1994–8 (Beyer Blinder Belle): escalators, air-conditioning, and the Grand Central Market were added, as was the staircase at the east end of the concourse—possibly planned in the original design but never built. The quarry that supplied the marble for the western staircase was reopened so that the two staircases would match perfectly.

Directly behind the Main Waiting Room, now called Vanderbilt Hall, is the famous **Main Concourse** (120ft wide; 375ft long). Sheathed in marble and simulated Caen stone, it rises to a cerulean elliptical vault (125ft high), decorated with the constellations of the zodiac designed by Whitney Warren with Paul Helleu (Warren's friend from his student days in Paris) and Charles Basing. The constellations are reversed, north to south, an error discovered by an angry commuter in 1913. Various explanations have been given: that the painters got it wrong because the diagram was placed on the floor; or that the painters were using a medieval manuscript that showed the stars from a point beyond the heavens. Worked into the ornamentation throughout the building are clusters of oak leaves and acorns, the Vanderbilts' chosen emblem.

The corridors are vaulted with Guastavino tile, with a **"Whispering Gallery"** outside the Oyster Bar; stand facing the wall in one corner and you can whisper across the arch to a friend.

NEW YORK TRANSIT MUSEUM GALLERY ANNEX AND STORE

Open Mon–Fri 8–8, Sat–Sun 10–6. Closed major holidays. T: 212 878 0106.
Just off the Main Concourse, in the Shuttle Passage, this outpost of the Transit Museum in Brooklyn (*see p. 473*) offers changing exhibitions on the art and history of public transit. The gift shop carries transit-related items as well as books on Grand Central and related subjects.

AROUND GRAND CENTRAL & EAST 42ND STREET

Across 42nd St from Grand Central (*110 East 42nd St*) is the **former Bowery Savings Bank**, now a catering hall. It was designed (1923) by York & Sawyer, the deans of New York bank architects, as an Italo-Romanesque-Byzantine neo-basilica with a dramatic deep-arched entrance. York & Sawyer saw the basilica form—used by the Romans for courts and adapted by early Christians for places of worship—as appropriate to a house of thrift, a virtue with almost sacred overtones. The former banking hall (*not open to the uninvited public*), monumental in scale and opulent in its finishing materials, was intended to convey the wealth of the bank as it expanded from its beginnings on the Bowery. The carvings in the frieze below the beamed and coffered ceiling suggest an allegorical bestiary: the squirrel for thrift, the rooster for punctuality, the bull and bear representing Wall Street.

The **Chanin Building** (1927–9; Irwin S. Chanin with Sloan & Robertson; *122 East 42nd St*) is an Art Deco delight, decorated with geometric and floral bas-reliefs. René Chambellan, best known for his work at Rockefeller Center, collaborated on the design of the interior, including the lobby, whose theme is "City of Opportunity." The bas-reliefs and grillwork express, respectively, the active and the intellectual life of the individual, with the geometric patterns, in Chambellan's conception, also symbolizing emotions and abstractions of thought. The whole design tells the story of a city where a man, through the exertion of his mind and hands, could rise from humble beginnings to wealth and power. The theme was especially applicable to Irwin Chanin (1891–1988). In 1919 he borrowed $20,000 to build two houses in Bensonhurst, Brooklyn. Ten years later he had developed 141 buildings including hotels and Broadway theaters.

VANDERBILT TERRITORY

In bygone days the neighborhood around Grand Central was the focal point of the New York Central Railroad's vast real estate empire. Handsome, staid hotels rose around the station using the air rights above the railroad tracks: the former Hotel Biltmore (1913; Warren & Wetmore) on Vanderbilt Avenue (*44th St*), named after George Washington Vanderbilt's château in North Carolina, has now become office space; the former Commodore Hotel (*42nd St at Lexington Ave*), named after the railroad's founder, was stripped to the bones and refleshed as the Hyatt Regency; the Yale Club (1915; James Gamble Rogers) stands at 50 Vanderbilt Ave, welcoming students and alumni of the university attended by several Vanderbilt descendants.

THE CHRYSLER BUILDING

The beautiful Chrysler Building (*405 Lexington Ave at East 42nd St; map p. 617, E4*) expresses the luxury and mechanical precision of the automobile in its Jazz Age incarnation. Designed by William Van Alen and completed in 1930, it is one of New York's most romantic Art Deco buildings.

History of the building
The building was undertaken by William H. Reynolds, a former state senator with ties to Tammany Hall (*see p. 185*) and a developer of the financially ruinous Dreamland amusement park (1904) at Coney Island. Like other ambitious men reaching back to the builders of the Tower of Babel, Reynolds aspired to erect the world's tallest tower, hiring maverick architect William Van Alen to design it. Reynolds defaulted on his lease and in 1928 the automobile manufacturer Walter P. Chrysler bought it, paying

out of his own pocket and getting the plans and the services of Van Alen in the deal. By that time the race for height had degenerated into a bitter rivalry between Van Alen and his former partner H. Craig Severance, at work on the headquarters of the Bank of the Manhattan Company (now 40 Wall St). Van Alen announced plans for a Chrysler Building of 925ft. In 1929 Severance one-upped him by topping off 40 Wall St at 927ft, appending a 50-ft flagpole and a lantern above the bank's 60 stories and ten penthouses. Meanwhile a team of steelworkers inside the fire shaft of the Chrysler Building was swiftly constructing its 185-ft spire. When Severance declared himself the victor, the workmen slid the spire through a hole in the roof, an operation that took just 90mins. The spire brought the building to 1,048 ft, 64ft higher than the Eiffel Tower, previously the world's tallest structure. A year later the Empire State Building soared above them all to 1,250 ft.

Architecture and interior

The Chrysler Building's slender tower rises to a shining **stainless-steel spire** above concentric arches pierced by triangular windows. There is probably more stainless steel on the façade of the Chrysler Building than on any other in New York, since the material—sleek, mirror-like, and vastly appealing to Art Deco designers—was too expensive for all but the most lavish builder. Below the spire, winged gargoyles suggesting automobile hood ornaments stare off in four directions and a brickwork frieze of wheels studded with radiator caps encircles the building.

Don't miss the **lobby** (*open Mon–Fri 8–6; closed weekends; free*), one of the best Art Deco interiors in the country. The walls are veneered with sensuously veined Rouge Flamme Moroccan marble in warm reddish tones; yellow Siena marble paves the floor; the elevator doors and walls are inlaid with exotic woods in intricate floral designs: Japanese ash, English gray hardwood, Oriental walnut, myrtle burl, curly maple, Cuban plum pudding, and satinwood.

Overhead a mural by Edward Trumbull depicts two favorite Art Deco motifs—transportation and human endeavor—its title bursting with Art Deco enthusiasm: "Energy, Result, Workmanship, and Transportation."

FORMER SOCONY-MOBIL AND DAILY NEWS BUILDINGS

The **former Socony-Mobil Building** (*150 East 42nd St between Lexington and Third Aves*) was built (1955) by Harrison & Abramovitz, a firm with ties to the Rockefeller family. Socony was an acronym for the Standard Oil Company of New York; Mobil was a successor to the original Standard Oil, founded by John D. Rockefeller and broken up in 1911 by the Supreme Court. At the time of the building's completion it was the world's largest metal-clad office tower. In 1988, the third edition of the *AIA Guide to New York City* labeled it "the ultimate architectural tin can," a view the most recent edition (2010) has qualified, comparing it favorably to the more recent spate of "cans" made of glass.

Between Third and Second Avenues (*220 East 42nd St*) is another Art Deco beauty: the **former Daily News Building** (1930), designed by Raymond Hood, often considered the quintessential architect of the Age of Commerce. A vertical extension of

THE CHRYSLER BUILDING
Viewed from the west, with the Queensboro Bridge and East River behind it.

the building conceals the water tower and other machinery on top—a radical notion at a time when such anachronisms as Greek temples often served as camouflage. Handsome brickwork and a bas-relief around the entrance form the only decoration of this austere building, which appeared in the 1970s *Superman* movies as the home of the mythical *Daily Planet*. Take a look at the lobby with its meteorological displays, including a two-ton globe (featuring some countries that disappeared long ago)—though the publisher at one point thought the public would prefer "murder charts," maps of the city with crime locations pinpointed.

THE FAR EAST SIDE

The neighborhood of Turtle Bay, along the East River (*about 43rd to 53rd Sts*) and inland to Third Ave (*map p. 617, F3–F2*), is named for a cove in the shoreline now obliterated by the gardens of the United Nations, the area's most important institution. In the vicinity are the UN missions of many nations and several charitable foundations. On the side streets, quiet residential enclaves preserve the ambiance of earlier times. In the Sutton Place neighborhood are fine views of the East River and Roosevelt Island.

THE UNITED NATIONS

On the east side of First Ave are the four principal United Nations buildings: the low **General Assembly Building**, the tall **Secretariat Building**, the **Dag Hammarskjöld Library**, and the **Conference Building** (*not visible from First Ave*). Le Corbusier established the original design of the complex: a tall slab with offices for the bureaucracy, a low horizontal building for conferences, and a functionally shaped though imposing assembly building, all to be set on a landscaped site—a scheme, according to critic Lewis Mumford, that demonstrated architecturally that "bureaucracy ruled the world."

Visiting the UN
Map p. 617, F3. Subway: 4, 5, or 6 to 42nd St-Grand Central. Bus: M15, M42, M50, M104. Visitors' entrance on First Ave at East 47th St. You can visit UN HQ only by guided tour (ages 5 and up). Admission charge. Purchase tickets online in advance (book well ahead) through website (visit.un.org) or at Visitor Center with official photo ID. Tour info: T: 212 963 8687. Tours (about 1hr) Mon–Fri 10:15–4:45 except holidays (check website or call) and during General Assembly debate (late Sept–early Oct). Shop. Delegates' dining room open for lunch (T: 917 367 3314, ddr-reservations.com).

LANDMARKS OF THE UN NEIGHBORHOOD
In front of the Secretariat Building, English sculptor Barbara Hepworth's bronze abstraction ***Single Form*** (1964) stands in the circular pool honoring Dag Hammarskjöld, the UN secretary-general killed (1961) in a plane crash on a peace mission to the former Belgian Congo.

The **United States Mission to the United Nations** (*799 United Nations Plaza at 45th St*), a 22-story concrete bunker with a less formidable but well-guarded entrance (2009; Gwathmey, Siegel & Assocs), clearly meets the stringent blast and security criteria of a post-9/11 world.

Visible inside the UN fence from the First Ave sidewalk north of the Visitor Center is *Good Defeats Evil* (1990) by Zurab Tsereteli, an immense St. George slaying the dragon of nuclear warfare. The dragon's body incorporates parts of an American Pershing II missile and a Soviet SS20 missile. A half-block further north, still inside the fence, stands the notorious *Bull Elephant* (1990), donated by Nepal, Kenya, and Namibia. Cast by Bulgarian-born artist Mihail Simeonov from a tranquilized male elephant on a ranch in Kenya, the statue originally offended some by the size of its male anatomy, today discreetly concealed behind the hedge that has grown up around it.

The west side of First Ave from East 42nd to East 49th Sts was renamed (1985) **Raoul Wallenberg Walk** to honor the Swedish diplomat who saved thousands of Hungarian Jews during World War II. In 1945 Wallenberg disappeared from Soviet-controlled Budapest; he is reported to have died in 1947 in the Lubyanka prison, but questions about the circumstances of his death remain unresolved. Sculptor Gustav Kraitz, an art student in Budapest in 1945, designed the *Hope* **monument** (1998), which stands on the traffic island at East 47th St. A blue ceramic sphere symbolizing hope caps one of the five black Swedish granite pillars. A bronze replica of Wallenberg's attaché case rests on a pavement of stones from the Budapest ghetto.

Dag Hammarskjold Plaza along East 47th St (*map p. 617, E3; open dawn–11pm*) has been landscaped and turned into a park with benches, fountains, and steel pergolas. Leading from the south side of the park is **Katharine Hepburn Garden**, planted with plants that thrive in the shade, and paved with stepping stones engraved with quotations on life and gardens from the famous actress, who lived nearby.

The black concrete-faced building at 333 East 47th St (1971; Junzo Yoshimura and George S. Shimimoto; expanded 2002) serves as headquarters of **Japan Society**, founded in 1907 to promote cultural exchange. A quiet blend of Modernism and traditional Japanese architecture, the building, on land donated by John D. Rockefeller III, was constructed as the US was just becoming aware of Japanese structural design. Architect Yoshimura had strong connections with the Rockefeller family, having previously designed a teahouse and a residence for their estate at Pocantico. Inside are gardens, a pool and waterfall, and furniture designed by George Nakashima. Japan Society offers lectures, performances, films, and highly regarded exhibits of contemporary and traditional Japanese art (*gallery open during exhibitions Tues–Thur 11–6, Fri 11–9, weekends 11–5; closed Mon and major holidays; admission charge; T: 212 832 1155, japansociety.org*).

TURTLE BAY GARDENS AND ITS DISTRICT

The **Turtle Bay Gardens Historic District** comprises two rows of 19th-century brownstones whose back yards were combined (1920) into a common garden in an act of private urban planning (*East 48th and East 49th Sts between Second and Third Aves;*

map p. 617, E3; NB: the common garden is private). Ordinary New York row-house back yards, as described in an 1893 article, presented "a dreary monotone of gray board fences, ash and garbage barrels, slop pails and clotheslines." The wealthy, well-travelled Charlotte Hunnewell Sorchan bought 20 houses, had them remodeled so that the kitchens faced the street and the living areas looked inward to the garden, and sold them to friends with enough deed restrictions to keep the enclave as she had planned it. Famous residents have included Leopold Stokowski, Katharine Hepburn, Stephen Sondheim, and the essayist E.B. White, for whom an old willow tree in the garden symbolized the city—"life surviving difficulties, growth against odds." The **former William Lescaze Residence** (*211 East 48th St*) began as an ordinary 19th-century brownstone but was aggressively transformed (1934) by architect Lescaze. He pushed the façade forward to the building line, smoothed it with stucco, and made dramatic use of his trademark glass blocks, which let in the light but also maintained privacy. In its day the house caused such a stir that Lescaze and his wife set aside an hour on Mondays for public visitation.

Amster Yard (1870, remodeled 1945; *map p. 617, E3; 211–215 East 49th St between Second and Third Aves*) is an enclave almost entirely secluded from the street, a cluster of workshops and small houses built on the site of what may have been the terminal stop of the Boston–New York stagecoach route. After the Second Avenue El was demolished in 1942, James Amster, a designer who started the decorating and antiques department at Bergdorf Goodman, bought the property and developed it into shops, apartments, and offices around a central courtyard. Today the yard serves the Instituto Cervantes New York, a non-profit organization created by the Spanish government for the dissemination of Hispanic-American culture; the Institute offers lectures, exhibits, concerts, and language instruction (*gallery open to the public daily 9–6; free; T: 212 308 7720, nyork.cervantes.es*).

The **Efrem Zimbalist House** (1926; *225–227 East 49th St*), former home of the violinist and his wife, the soprano Alma Gluck, betrays its musical connections with a cartouche over the door showing a violin and an unidentified musical theme. Gluck's daughter from a previous marriage, the novelist Marcia Davenport, published a biography of Mozart and a more famous novel, *My Brother's Keeper* (1954), based on the Collyer brothers (*see p. 444*).

THE SUTTON PLACE NEIGHBORHOOD

Beekman Place (*map p. 617, F3*) runs along a high bluff overlooking the East River. Its controlled development by the Beekman family, whose New York roots date back to the heyday of Peter Stuyvesant, made it as socially desirable early in its history as it is now. Among its residents have been John D. Rockefeller III, Irving Berlin, Gloria Vanderbilt, and Rex Harrison. The Beekman mansion, Mount Pleasant (built 1765, demolished 1874), stood near the river at about 50th St and for a while during the Revolution served as British headquarters.

One of the more imposing prominences in this quiet, elegant neighborhood is **River House** (1931; Bottomley, Wagner & White), overlooking the water east of First

Ave (*433–437 East 52nd St; map p. 617, F3*). Completed the same year as the George Washington Bridge, the Empire State Building, and the Waldorf-Astoria Hotel, River House quickly became synonymous with privilege and wealth. The apartments in the tower were duplexes or triplexes with as many as 17 rooms (one had nine bathrooms), while those in the body of the building were only slightly more modest. The arrival of the Franklin Delano Roosevelt Drive after World War II disturbed the serenity of the setting and brought about the demise of the riverside landing where residents had been able to dock their yachts.

Sutton Place, which runs between East 53rd and East 59th Sts, was formerly and less glamorously known as Avenue A. It may have been renamed after one Effingham B. Sutton, a dry goods merchant who developed the area around 1875 with a fortune he had made in the California gold rush of 1849—not by striking the motherlode but by selling picks, shovels, and provisions to hopeful prospectors. His venture with Sutton Place came about 50 years too soon, and the street remained modest until Anne Morgan (daughter of J. Pierpont Morgan) and Mrs. William K. Vanderbilt (née Anne Harriman, Vanderbilt's second wife) arrived in 1921.

The townhouses on **Sutton Square**, the block between 57th and 58th Sts, share a common back garden, hence the name. At the foot of 57th St is a small park with wonderful river views and a bronze replica of Pietro Tacca's *Porcellino*, the famous sculpture of a wild boar from the Mercato Nuovo in Florence (its Hellenistic marble model is in the Uffizi).

The vest-pocket parks at the river ends of several streets are all called Sutton Place Park, but are not connected to one another. The small park at the end of East 58th St east of Sutton Place has, to the north of it, parallel to the river, a small, cobbled, private street—**Riverview Terrace**—with 19th-century houses looking out from the top of the ridge. The end of East 58th St offers a fine view of the **Queensboro Bridge** (1909; Gustav Lindenthal, engineer; Palmer & Hornbostel, architects; *see overleaf*) which joins Long Island City in Queens with 59th St in Manhattan.

Along the north side of the bridge runs the **Roosevelt Island Aerial Tramway**, at its peak 250ft above the East River. (*Manhattan tram station on Second Ave between 59th and 60th Sts; tram runs about every 15mins, more frequently during rush hours, Sun–Thur 6am–2am, Fri and Sat 6am–3:30am. Only MetroCards accepted; vending machines in station.*)

MOUNT VERNON HOTEL MUSEUM AND GARDEN

Map p. 617, F2. 421 East 61st St (First and York Aves). Subway: N, R, 4, 5, or 6 to 59th St. Bus: M15, M31, M57. Open Tues–Sun 11–4. Admission charge T: 212 838 6878, mvhm.org. Miraculously surviving in the midst of dull modernity, this museum (formerly the Abigail Adams Smith Museum) occupies a stone coach house (1799) built during the early years of the American republic. It has been painstakingly restored and refurnished, predominantly in the Federal style. A pleasant garden with herbs and plantings recalls horticultural styles popular when the house was in its prime.

In 1795 Colonel William Stephens Smith and his wife Abigail Adams Smith, daughter of President John Adams, bought the land, which Smith called "Mount Vernon" after the estate of his former commander George Washington. In 1798 Smith sold his 23 acres and its uncompleted buildings to merchant William T. Robinson, who completed the stable and the house. By 1808 the house had become a hotel for middle-class day trippers, renowned for its turtle soup; it burned in 1826 but was restored. As the neighborhood became industrial around the turn of the 20th century, the house became private once again, was sold to the Standard Gas Light Company (a precursor of ConEd) and seemed headed for demolition. In 1919 Jane Teller, an antiques dealer with a commitment to reviving the domestic arts (and concomitant virtues) of the colonial period, rented the house, furnished it in a colonial style, and offered classes in spinning and weaving. In 1924 the Colonial Dames of America bought the house from the gas company and eventually restored it as a museum. Today it recreates the ambiance of the 19th-century resort, with a tavern, a ladies' parlor, and a bedroom.

THE QUEENSBORO BRIDGE (59TH STREET BRIDGE)

The cantilever Queensboro Bridge (1909; Gustav Lindenthal, engineer; Henry Hornbostel, architect), officially the Ed Koch Queensboro Bridge (since 2011) and locally the 59th Street Bridge (as memorialized in the 1966 Simon and Garfunkel song), connects East 59th–East 60th Sts in Manhattan with Long Island City in Queens. The span is 1182 ft long and 135ft above mean high water. About 50,000 tons of steel were used in construction at a cost of $20.8 million. The Guastavino-tiled vaults beneath the Manhattan approach contain a grocery store.

As early as 1852 powerful Long Island City families—Steinways and Pratts—began lobbying for a bridge, an enterprise furthered by Long Island Railroad tycoon Austin Corbin and later by a Dr. Thomas Rainey, who foresaw the bridge as an aid to tourism, freight handling, and the funeral business (there were 15 cemeteries on Long Island at the time). Political and financial problems delayed construction for some 40 years and the collapse of the partially built cantilever Quebec Bridge (1907) called into doubt the safety of this one. There is a shared pedestrian-bicycle roadway across (*north side, entrance on 60th St between Second and First Aves*), but you can no longer descend to Roosevelt Island.

PARK AVENUE

Map p. 617, D4–D1. Subway: 4, 5, 6, 7, S to 42nd St-Grand Central. Bus: M1, M2, M3, M4, M5, M101, M102, M103, M104.

Park Avenue, called Fourth Avenue on the 1811 grid, long remained undeveloped because the underlying granite ridge discouraged excavation. When the New York and Harlem Railroad requested a right of way for its tracks and permission to run its coal-powered engines north of 14th St (1832), the City granted it Fourth Avenue. The railroad company eventually blasted out the granite and laid the tracks in a cut from which coal smoke and noise infiltrated the neighborhood. Fourth Avenue was renamed in sections, with the northern portion leading to the Harlem River, becoming Park Avenue in 1888. The only remnant of Fourth Avenue today is the downtown stretch between Union Square and Cooper Square (*map p. 619, D3*).

Park Avenue north of Grand Central is in its third stage of urban development. Before 1900, when the tracks and rail yards were above ground, the street attracted factories. As the Fourth Avenue Improvement Scheme of 1872–4 submerged the tracks below street level as far as 56th St, it began its rise to elitism, though remaining humble until the tracks were completely decked over during the construction of Grand Central Terminal (1903–13). By the 1920s all air rights over the tracks had been acquired by apartments and hotels, and luxury buildings began appearing along both sides of the avenue as far as 96th St, where the tracks emerge from the tunnel. Land values soared over 200 percent between 1914 and 1930. After World War II, however, the drop in passenger revenues led the railroad to re-examine its real estate empire and to take advantage of these enormously increased values. Starting in the 1950s, Park Avenue began changing from a fine residential neighborhood to a desirable commercial area, the heartland of corporate America.

Just north of Grand Central the **MetLife Building** (*200 Park Ave; map p. 617, D3*), originally the PanAm Building (1963; Emery Roth & Sons, Pietro Belluschi, and Walter Gropius), bulky and intrusive (59 stories, on a 3.5 acre site), blocks the former vista up and down Park Avenue.

The **Helmsley Building**, originally the New York Central Building (1929; Warren & Wetmore; *230 Park Ave between 45th and 46th Sts*), once served as headquarters for the railroad, a visible reminder of its power both in real estate and transportation. Don't miss the central lobby, opulently finished with marble and bronze. Burgundy and gold were the Vanderbilt "armorial" colors, and the oak leaf was one of the chosen family emblems—all are much in evidence here. When the building opened, the architectural critic of *The New Yorker* likened its dark red jaspé oriental marble trim to the "red meat" of an era when "kings were kings and architects were princes." Two vehicular portals pierce the northern façade to carry traffic on ramps around the railroad terminal.

THE WALDORF-ASTORIA HOTEL
The famous Waldorf-Astoria Hotel (1929–31; Schultze & Weaver; *301 Park Ave; map p. 617, E3*) is an Art Deco landmark. Faced in brick and limestone over a granite base, the hotel rises to two chrome-capped, 625-ft spires, the **Waldorf Towers**, whose private apartments, accessed from a separate entrance on 50th St, have attracted such tenants as the Duke of Windsor, President Herbert Hoover, and General Douglas MacArthur. Facing Park Avenue above the main door, a figure by Nina Saemundsson symbolizes the "Spirit of Achievement," though it is uncertain whether this applies to the clientele or the hotel management.

The first Waldorf-Astoria (1894) stood on the site of the Empire State Building, replacing two Astor mansions that were torn down because of a family feud. In a struggle for social supremacy, the ambitious Caroline Schermerhorn Astor offended her nephew William Waldorf Astor, who had inherited the southern mansion; in revenge William Waldorf tore down his house and built the Waldorf Hotel, named after the family's ancestral home in Germany. Caroline, affronted by the towering hotel, moved uptown, leaving her house to her son, John Jacob IV, who tore it down and built the Astoria part of the Waldorf-Astoria, named after an Oregon trading post of the original John Jacob Astor's fur empire. In 1929 the hotel moved uptown to its present location.

Interior of the Waldorf-Astoria

The **lobby** is half a flight up from street level since, like other Park Avenue buildings, the hotel (1,800 rooms) stands over the railroad yards and needs space above ground for mechanical equipment. While the tracks may have been irksome for the architects, they were a convenience for former guests arriving in private rail coaches, who could be shunted onto a special siding, bypassing the terminal altogether. When the hotel opened during the Depression, President Hoover lauded it as an "exhibition of... confidence to the whole nation," and surely its exquisite Art Deco interiors with marble, bronze, and matched woods suggested that the management foresaw better times. The centerpiece of the lobby is a clock made for the Chicago Columbian Exposition in 1893. On it are likenesses of George Washington, Abraham Lincoln, Queen Victoria, and other notables, as well as bronze plaques representing various sports.

The names of some public rooms recall the hotel's grand past. The **Starlight Roof** once had a ceiling that could be rolled back on balmy evenings. **Oscar's American Brasserie** bears the name of the legendary Oscar Tschirky, the Waldorf's *maître d'hôtel in* 1893–1943, said to have invented Waldorf salad and eggs Benedict, and who bequeathed his collection of menus to Cornell University's School of Hotel Administration.

THE VILLARD HOUSES

The public rooms of the luxury **New York Palace Hotel** (*455 Madison Ave, near 50th St; map p. 617, D3*) are housed in part of the extraordinary Villard Houses (1886), a U-shaped group of six sumptuous neo-Renaissance dwellings built by McKim, Mead & White for Bavarian immigrant-turned-railroad-baron Henry Villard (born Ferdinand Heinrich Gustav Hilgard). At the peak of his power in early 1883, Villard started building a group of houses that would convince the most casual passer-by of his success. By Christmas, however, he had lost his fortune (perhaps $5 million) as well as the presidency of the Northern Pacific Railroad. The unfinished houses, transferred to trustees to be completed, went on the market. Their buyers included Villard's lawyer Artemas Holmes, and Elizabeth and Whitelaw Reid (editor of the *New York Tribune*), who bought Villard's own house for $350,000 in 1886 with wedding money from her father, the millionaire Darius Ogden Mills.

The houses remained residential until after World War II, when social and economic changes eroded the style of life implied by their grandeur. Commercial firms and the Archdiocese of New York in turn used the buildings as offices, fortunately leaving them more or less intact. When the archdiocese no longer wanted the property, exhaustive negotiations led to the present project. One of the stipulations of the conversion of the houses to a hotel was the preservation of the most important interiors.

Finished in warm Belleville (New Jersey) brownstone—no longer fashionable, but Villard had insisted—the façade is modeled after the Palazzo della Cancelleria in Rome (1489–96) and was designed by Joseph Morrill Wells, first assistant in the office of McKim, Mead & White. The central courtyard was originally a carriage turnaround.

ST. BARTHOLOMEW'S CHURCH

Map p. 617, E3. Park Ave between East 50th–East 51st Sts. Open Sun 7:45–6, Mon–Sat 9–6 (Wed until 8pm). Free tours on Sun after the 11am service. T: 212 378 0222, stbarts. org. A café and restaurant occupies the terrace during warm weather and the community house during the winter (T: 212.593.3333, insideparknyc.com).

Protestant Episcopal St. Bartholomew's Church (1919; Bertram G. Goodhue), familiarly known as St. Bart's, is one of the oldest buildings along Park Ave. The congregation, formed in 1835, raised its first church on Lafayette Place near the then-fashionable Bowery, moving uptown first to Madison Ave (*East 44th St*) in 1902 to land purchased from William H. Vanderbilt, and then to Park Avenue, which was just blossoming as an elite residential neighborhood. St. Bartholomew's bought the site (now one of the city's most valuable real estate parcels), for $1.5 million in 1914 from the F. & M. Schaefer Brewing Co., which had been making beer by the railroad tracks since 1860.

Exterior of St. Bartholomew's

The present ornate carved portico had been added to the previous St. Bartholomew's Church on Madison Ave as a memorial to Cornelius Vanderbilt II, grandson of the Commodore, founder of the family fortunes. Architect Stanford White of McKim, Mead & White styled it after the Romanesque church at St-Gilles-du-Gard in southern France and hired prominent sculptors—Daniel Chester French, Philip Martiny, and Herbert Adams—to execute the statuary. The frieze connecting the three arches of the portal depicts events from the Old and New Testaments. The tympanum over the center doors contains a representation of the Coronation of Christ.

On the south side of the church the Community House (1927) and its terrace create an L-shaped complex with pleasing proportions and open space, providing a moment of grace along an avenue that is largely an unrelieved wall of glassy corporate towers.

The interior

The mosaics on the ceiling of the narthex by Hildreth Meière depict the Creation. The narthex opens into the three aisles of the east-facing nave, constructed in the traditional cruciform shape with a barrel-vaulted ceiling. The structural elements are stone and marble veneered over concrete, and much of the wall surface has been covered with rough-textured Guastavino acoustic tiles. The west window, its stained glass donated as memorials for the earlier Madison Avenue church, has figures of the

Evangelists and scenes from the New Testament. Dominating the interior a mosaic of glass and gold leaf (also by Meière) fills the ceiling of the apse. It represents the Transfiguration, with Christ in the center flanked by Elijah and Moses standing on the mountain and the disciples Peter (north side), James, and John (south side). Thin sheets of amber onyx covered with grilles of the same material fill the five tall windows in the apse. The five-manual Aeolian-Skinner pipe organ is the city's largest, a worthy accoutrement of the church's fine music program.

THE GENERAL ELECTRIC BUILDING

On the southwest corner of East 51st St, providing a dramatic background to the church is the reddish-orange brick and terra cotta of the General Electric Building (1931; Cross & Cross) also known as 570 Lexington Avenue. Its spiked Art Deco crown suggests the fantasies of science fiction, appropriate to the original tenant, the RCA Victor Company, which was wooed away to Rockefeller Center. The lobby, with terrazzo floors, pale purple marble panels, aluminum light sconces, and silvery barrel-vaulted ceiling openings, is as coolly elegant as anything in the city.

Along East 51st St near Park Avenue, Robert Cook's bronze **Dinoceras** (1971) recalls a multi-horned mammal of the Eocene period (21 million years ago).

THE SEAGRAM BUILDING AND ITS NEIGHBORHOOD

Map p. 617, E3–D2.

The iconic **Seagram Building** (1958) at 375 Park Ave (*52nd and 53rd Sts*) is the only New York work of Ludwig Mies van der Rohe (Philip Johnson designed some of the interior spaces). This elegant metal and glass curtain-wall building sits back 90ft from the building line and rises about 500ft on square columns; its arrival signaled a major shift from the stolid masonry buildings that had once walled Park Ave to the modernist corporate towers that give the street its present glassy ambiance. All the Seagram's materials—the wall of custom-made amber glass and bronze; the green Italian marble seating around the fountains on the plaza (innovative for its day) of pink Vermont granite; the brushed aluminum and stainless-steel hardware—were chosen for their quality. The Seagram's excellence stems largely from the interest of Phyllis Lambert, daughter of former Seagram board chairman Samuel Bronfman, who persuaded her father to erect a monumental building, not merely a serviceable one. Bronfman had already hired Charles Luckman, a successful business executive (Lever Brothers) turned less successful architect (the present Madison Square Garden and underground Penn Station). Bronfman fired Luckman and allowed his daughter to play a major role in choosing the architect: she chose Mies van der Rohe. The 38-story tower is considered to be the world's finest International Style skyscraper and is one of the most recently built of all New York's landmarked buildings.

The **Four Seasons Restaurant** (1959; Philip Johnson & Assocs) on the ground floor of the Seagram Building was a haunt of the power lunch set for more than half a century. At the time of writing the Four Seasons' lease was to expire. However, the restaurant's Modernist décor is landmarked and presumably will remain under a new tenant.

THE ROTHKO MURALS

The Four Seasons Restaurant was famous for its art collection—works by Picasso among others—and also for a series of paintings it did not have. In 1958 the owners commissioned Mark Rothko to paint 600 sq ft of murals for the restaurant walls. Why Rothko, left-wing and intellectual, accepted the commission for an establishment catering to the rich and powerful, is not clear. He later said, perhaps disingenuously, that he had thought the works would be placed where working-class people could see them. At any rate he told a friend that he wanted to create "something that will ruin the appetite of every son-of-a-bitch who ever eats in that room."

The painter and his wife had visited Michelangelo's claustrophobic vestibule to the Laurentian Library in Florence, which, said Rothko, captured the feeling he wanted: it made "viewers feel that they are trapped in a room where all the doors and windows are bricked up, so that all they can do is butt their heads forever against the wall."

Back in New York Rothko and his wife booked a table at the Four Seasons; apparently he did not enjoy the experience. Later that evening he called a friend to say he was returning the money and keeping the paintings. They are now owned by Tate Modern, the National Gallery in Washington, D.C., and Japan's Kawamura Memorial Museum of Art.

Across the street from the Seagram Building (*370 Park Ave*) is the brick-and-limestone **Racquet and Tennis Club** (1918; McKim, Mead & White), designed after White and McKim had died and Mead had retired. Beneath the cornice, a terra cotta frieze depicts racquets and netting. The men-only private club, incorporated in 1890 to "encourage the manly sports," still has one of the few remaining court-tennis courts.

Lever House (*390 Park Ave between 53rd and 54th Sts*), the first (1952) steel and glass building to insert itself into the unbroken file of stolid masonry apartment houses on Park Avenue, predates the Seagram Building by half a dozen years. Designed by Gordon Bunshaft of Skidmore, Owings & Merrill, the building takes its form from two slabs, one horizontal, one vertical. Once considered the ultimate corporate headquarters and widely recognized as an important example in the evolution of the International Style, it remains impressive partly because it fills only about one third of the legally allowed space, a gracious act of restraint on the part of Lever Brothers, makers of such historic soaps as Lux and Lifebuoy. The curtain wall and the ground-floor public spaces were restored in 2003, with a replanted sculpture garden by Isamu Noguchi in the interior courtyard. Changing exhibitions of contemporary art are mounted in the lobby.

An example of the ultra-luxury skyscrapers presently vying for the top spot on the skyline (and possibly the top price per square foot) is the flat-topped **432 Park**

Avenue (*East 57th St*). Designed by Rafael Viñoly, it rises to 1,396 ft, making it the tall-est residential building in the Western Hemisphere, and at the time of writing (if you discount spires or antennas), the tallest building in the city.

EAST OF PARK AVENUE

The former CitiGroup Center, now **601 Lexington Avenue** (*East 53rd St; map p. 617, E3–E2*), is as representative of 1970s architectural values as Lever House and the Seagram Building are of 1950s tastes. The building (1978; Hugh Stubbins & Assocs, Emery Roth & Sons), sheathed in gleaming white aluminum, rises 915ft from the street, resting on four 127-ft columns at the midpoints of the sides, not at the corners. The top of the building slants at a 45-degree angle; the large surface facing south, origi-nally intended as a solar collector, is conspicuous on the skyline among the flat tops of the previous generation and the domes, crowns, and spires of earlier skyscrapers.

ST. PETER'S CHURCH
Crouching under the tower of 601 Lexington Ave is St. Peter's Lutheran Church (*map p. 617, E2*). Founded in 1861, it has existed in a variety of guises, and has been on this site since 1904. The church allowed the First National City Bank to buy its old build-ing (and, more importantly, the site) on the understanding that it would erect a new church on the site, but physically separate from the office tower. The architect was the same as that of the tower, Hugh Stubbins & Assocs. Inside, the beautiful **Erol Beker Chapel of the Good Shepherd** is enhanced by Louise Nevelson's wall sculptures (1977): *Cross of the Good Shepherd* and three columns, *Trinity* (north wall); *Frieze of the Apostles* (east wall); *Sky Vestment–Trinity* (west wall); *Grapes and Wheat Lintel* (south wall); and *Cross of the Resurrection* (southwest wall).

Located near the former nightclubs of 52nd St (whose heyday as a center of jazz spanned the 1930s and 1940s), St. Peter's has long been known for its jazz programs—the legacy of pastor John Garcia Gensel, who ministered to the spiritual needs of New York's jazzmen. Duke Ellington dedicated his Second Sacred Concert to the pastor, and Billy Strayhorn willed him a Steinway (*chapel open for meditation Mon–Fri during the day; T: 212 935 2200, saintpeters.org*).

THE "LIPSTICK BUILDING"
A block east at 885 Third Ave (*East 53rd and 54th Sts*) is the "Lipstick Building" (1986; John Burgee with Philip Johnson), a reddish elliptical tower, always noteworthy for its shape, more recently notorious for containing the office of Bernard L. Madoff, who ran his Ponzi scheme (collapsed 2008) from the 17th floor.

CENTRAL SYNAGOGUE
Map p. 617, E2. 652 Lexington Ave (corner of East 55th St). Tours Wed at 12:45. T: 212 838 5122, centralsynagogue.org.

EAST OF PARK AVENUE
601 Lexington Avenue, the former CitiGroup Center (1978).

CENTRAL SYNAGOGUE

Designed by Henry Fernbach, the first Jew to practice architecture in New York and now known chiefly for his cast-ironwork in SoHo, this is the state's oldest synagogue (1872) in continuous use. While Judaism has never had an architectural heritage similar to the Gothic tradition in Christianity, the Moorish style, alluding to Jewish roots in the Middle East, dominated synagogue architecture in the mid-19th century. Central Synagogue is generally considered the city's finest example of Moorish Revival architecture, inspired by—but not precisely modeled on—the Dohány Street Synagogue (1854–9) in Budapest. The onion-shaped copper domes rise to 122ft. The interior stenciled decorations in red, blue, and ochre were repainted after a 1998 fire. The geometric designs are said to come from Owen Jones's influential *Grammar of Ornament* (1856).

The congregation was founded on Ludlow St as Ahawath Chesed ("Love of Mercy") by 18 men, most of them immigrants from Bohemia. The congregation moved northward in stages, acquiring the present site in 1870. The building suggests the optimism of the 150 families of the congregation at that time, who built a synagogue whose sanctuary can accommodate more than 1,000 worshipers.

EATING AND DRINKING AROUND GRAND CENTRAL AND ON THE FAR EAST SIDE

IN GRAND CENTRAL

Grand Central Market, between the Main Concourse and Lexington Ave, is a foodie's delight, its displays of top-of-the-line edibles worthy of a Dutch still-life *(open Mon–Fri 7am–9pm, Sat 10–7, Sun 11–6; map p. 617, D4)*. **Michael Jordan's Steakhouse** is on the balcony overlooking the Main Concourse *(lunch weekdays, dinner seven days; T: 212 655 2300, michaeljordansnyc. com)*. The **Grand Central Oyster Bar** is a classic seafood restaurant open since 1913 *(lunch and dinner six days, closed Sun and holidays; T: 212 490 6650, oysterbarny.com)*. On the Lower Concourse casual eateries offer snacks and fast food, much of it a cut above what is found in most food courts.

THE FAR EAST SIDE

$$$ Felidia. ■ The flagship of the Bastianich family restaurants, offering Italian food in a friendly atmosphere. Lunch weekdays, dinner nightly. *243 East 58th St (Second and Third Aves). T: 212 758 1479, felidia-nyc.com. Map p. 617, E2.*

$$ Al Bustan. Reasonably close to the United Nations and frequented by diplomats, this Lebanese restaurant serves meze and *prix-fixe* dinners. Lunch and dinner daily. *319 East 53rd St (First and Second Aves). T: 212 759 5933, albustanny.com. Map p. 617, E2.*

$$ Bukhara Grill. Northern Indian food in a dramatic setting. Lunch and dinner daily. *217 East 49th St (Second and Third Aves). T: 212 888 2839, bukharagrill.ypguides.net. Map p. 617, E3.*

$$ Ethos Gallery 51st. Not far from Beekman Place, a cheerful Greek taverna with friendly service and generous meze. Lunch and dinner daily. *905 First Ave (51st St). T: 212 888 4060, ethosrestaurants.com. Map p. 617, F3.*

$$ Land of Plenty. A pleasant Chinese place with an appealing bar and quick service. Lunch weekdays, dinner nightly. *204 East 58th St (Second and Third Aves). T: 212 308 8788, landofplenty58.com. Map p. 617, E2.*

$$ P.J. Clarke's. Has been offering beer and burgers along with other gastro-pub food for decades; it looks like an old tavern—but it did even when it was new. Also a branch at Lincoln Center. Lunch and dinner daily. *915 Third Ave (55th St). T: 212 317 1616, pjclarkes.com. Map p. 617, E2.*

$$ Rosa Mexicano. The original of a small chain and probably still the best. Family-friendly, and colorful, it is famous for the tableside guacamole and the tortillas made as you watch. Lunch Sat and Sun, dinner nightly. *1063 First Ave (58th St). T: 212 753 7407, rosamexicano.com. Map p. 617, E2.*

A WALK UP FIFTH AVENUE

Fifth Avenue is still New York's most famous promenade, the route of its grand parades, the site of some of its most iconic attractions. This walk begins north of the Empire State Building and continues past the landmark New York Public Library to St. Patrick's Cathedral and Rockefeller Center. Fifth Avenue was once the mecca of elegant shopping, where the great department stores settled after they left Ladies' Mile (*see p. 186*), and while most of the department stores have now departed, the neo-palazzi that once housed them remain, as do Lord & Taylor and Saks Fifth Avenue.

To reach the starting point by subway: B, D, F, N, Q, or R to 34th St-Herald Square;. Bus: M2, M3, M4, M5. Begin at Fifth Ave and 34th St.

THE FORMER B. ALTMAN & COMPANY store at **365 Fifth Ave** (1906; Trowbridge & Livingston) fills the entire block between Fifth and Madison Aves, East 34th and East 35th Sts. It now houses Oxford University Press and the CUNY Graduate Center (*entrance on Fifth Ave*). Altman's, the first department store to intrude on a previously sedate residential area, was designed in the same Italian palazzo style that many of New York's newly rich chose for their mansions, perhaps to soften the blow to disgruntled neighbors.

BENJAMIN ALTMAN

Son of a Lower East Side milliner, Benjamin Altman (1840–1913) opened his first shop (c. 1865) on Third Ave near 9th St and worked his way uptown via a stylish store in Ladies' Mile (*Sixth Ave and 19th St*), becoming a legendary retailer and a notable art collector. He bought his first parcel of land on this block in 1896 and the rest when Grand Central Terminal and Penn Station announced their new locations. Apparently a humorless workaholic, Altman was nevertheless a compassionate employer, providing rest rooms and a cafeteria for his workers, funding education for their children, and inaugurating Saturday closings in summer. When he died unmarried in 1913, he left his art collection to the Metropolitan Museum of Art and $20 million in Altman stock to a philanthropic foundation. The store, known for high-quality clothing, home furnishings, dishes, and glassware, went out of business in 1989.

Keen's Steakhouse (*72 West 36th St, between Fifth and Sixth Aves*) dates back to 1878, when the side streets west of Fifth Ave belonged to the Theater District and the restaurant, then called Keen's Chophouse, served as the dining room for The Lambs, a social club for theater people. In 1885 manager Albert Keen restructured the restaurant as an independent commercial venture and began feeding his masculine clientele massive cuts of meat in dining rooms

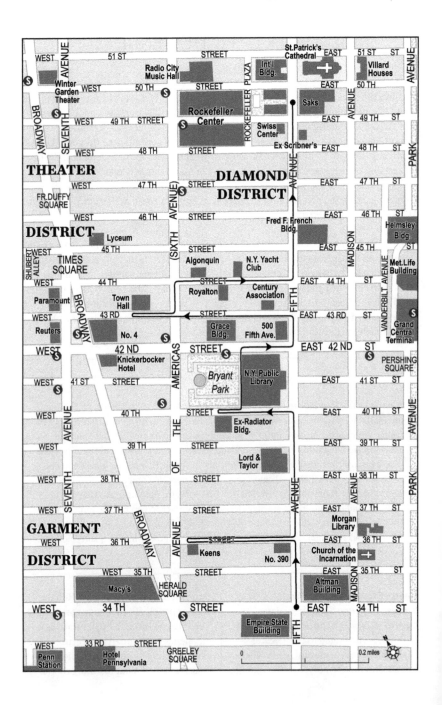

resplendent with dark wood and brass. Women were allowed only after 1901 when actress Lillie Langtry sued and won on grounds of discrimination. Although the restaurant changed its name from "chophouse" to the more modern "steak house" in 1995, the menu still features its "legendary mutton chop." Theater memorabilia decorate the walls, and on the ceiling are thousands of long-stemmed clay pipes, each numbered for its owner. Members of the "Pipe Club" have included Douglas MacArthur, Theodore Roosevelt, William Howard Taft, Babe Ruth, and Albert Einstein.

Return to Fifth Avenue. Nearby are the onetime homes of several more upscale stores that arrived at about the same time as Altman's but didn't last as long. At the corner of West 36th St, **no. 390 Fifth Ave** (1906; McKim, Mead & White) was built for the Gorham Company, jeweler and purveyor of table silver; the lower façade has unfortunately been altered. **No. 402 Fifth Ave**, with its fine terra cotta decoration, was for a while the Stewart Building, a department store and mail order company (not affiliated with the A.T. Stewart department store; see p. 90). Owned by the Goelet family, it was designed (1914) by Warren & Wetmore, the architects of Grand Central Terminal.

At 409 Fifth Ave is the **former home of Tiffany's** (1906; McKim, Mead & White), modeled after the Venetian Palazzo Grimani. In *The American Scene* (1907), Henry James, who lamented the crass materialism of American culture, nevertheless admired the building as "a great Palladian pile... a great nobleness of marble," while expressing gratitude

that instead of 25 stories it had only "three fine arched and columned stages above its high basement."

Between 38th and 39th Sts (*424 Fifth Ave*) is the only remaining department store on this stretch of the avenue: **Lord & Taylor** (1914; Starrett & Van Vleck), a conservative and gracious establishment, known for emphasizing American designers and traditional women's sportswear. Samuel Lord arrived in New York in April 1826 (when he was 22) on the packet *Constitution*, which listed his occupation as "iron moulder." He set up a dry goods shop on Catherine St and three months later invited his wife's cousin George W. Taylor into the business, each man contributing $1,000. They sold "heavy plaid silks for misses' wear" and "superior quality men's and women's silk hose," among other things, "at fair prices as usual."

A block further north and around the corner, the Bryant Park Hotel occupies the **former American Radiator Building** (1924; Hood & Fouilhoux), at 40 West 40th St, a striking black brick and gold terra cotta tower with a Gothic crown. When the building opened, the gold top was illuminated to suggest a glowing hot radiator, while the black brick suggested perhaps a heap of coal. Architect Raymond Hood later joined Rockefeller Center's design team.

Walk through Bryant Park (*see p. 243*) to the north, and then east on 42nd St to Fifth Ave. On the northwest corner of the intersection, **no. 500 Fifth Avenue** (1931), a 59-story Art Deco skyscraper, was designed by Shreve, Lamb & Harmon, who also designed the Empire State Building. Over the Fifth Ave entrance an allegorical relief by the sculptor Edmond Amateis symbolizes "the genius of the modern skyscraper." At the time of construction, this corner was considered the second most valuable in Manhattan, after the southeast corner of Broadway and Wall St.

The light-filled steel and glass box at 510 Fifth Ave (*corner of West 43rd St*), originally the **Manufacturers Hanover Trust building** (Gordon Bunshaft of Skidmore, Owings & Merrill), turned heads when completed in 1954, since at the time banks were heavy masonry affairs resembling palazzi or ancient temples. While the building was designed expressly so that it could be turned to other uses, the 30-ton Mosler safe in the window identifies its former life.

At 7 West 43rd St is the **Century Association** (1891; McKim, Mead & White). Founded in 1847 by William Cullen Bryant et al., the club was intellectual in scope, accepting "Artists, Literary Men, Scientists, Physicians, Officers of the Army and Navy, members of the Bench and Bar, Engineers, Clergymen, Representatives of the Press, Merchants and men of leisure." Mark Twain called it "unspeakably respectable." Within a decade most of the members were bankers, lawyers, physicians, and business executives, but the club is still known for its artistic and intellectual bent. Members Charles Follen McKim and Stanford White here designed one of their first neo-Italian Renaissance clubhouses, notable for its mixture of materials (terra cotta, granite, and yellow brick) and its second-floor ironwork beneath a Palladian window once part of an open loggia. The original plan was to have 100 members, but the roster has expanded to more than 20 times that number.

Continue west to Sixth Avenue. The **W.R. Grace Building** at 1114 Sixth Ave (*corner of 43rd St*), large and white with a self-important curvaceous concave façade, is the work of Gordon Bunshaft of Skidmore, Owings and Merrill (1974).

Across the avenue the corner of Sixth Ave and 43rd St (*1133 Sixth Ave*) was long the home of the **International Center of Photography**, founded in 1974 by photographer Cornell Capa to preserve the memory of four photographers who died in the course of their work. One of them was his older brother, Robert, a photo-journalist killed (1954) in Indochina. New York's foremost exhibitor of photography, ICP boasts a permanent collection that spans the history of photography and is rich in documentary works from 1930 to the 1960s; highlights include the Robert and Cornell Capa Collections, the Roman Vishniac and Weegee (Arthur Fellig) Archives, and the Life Magazine Collection. *NB: at the time of writing, ICP was moving its exhibition space to 250 Bowery, scheduled to open early 2016 (see icp.org). The Sixth Ave building will house the piano showroom of Steinway & Sons.*

Down the block to the west, red brick **Town Hall** (*113–23 West 43rd St between Sixth Ave and Broadway; box office T: 212 840 2824; thetownhall.org*) is acoustically one of the city's finest performance spaces. It was designed (1921) by younger partners in the firm of McKim, Mead & White (McKim and White had died) in a conservative neo-Federal style as a concert hall, meeting place, and club house. The League for Political Education, an organization of woman suffragists, commissioned it, expressing their democratic ideals in the absence of box seats. Margaret Sanger spoke here on birth control and got arrested onstage; Eleanor Roosevelt spoke on behalf of the New Deal; Andrés Segovia, Bob Dylan, Leontyne Price, Charles Mingus, and Charlie Parker enjoyed the hall's superb acoustics, and Joan Sutherland made her New York debut here—as have many aspiring musicians hoping for favorable reviews from New York critics.

Return to Sixth Ave and walk north to 44th St. The **Algonquin Hotel** (1902) at 59 West 44th St was once famous as a literary hangout. Frank Case, manager (1907) and later owner (1927), enjoyed rubbing elbows with celebrities, and over the years the Algonquin hosted Gertrude Stein, James Thurber, Sinclair Lewis, F. Scott Fitzgerald, Tennessee Williams, Graham Greene, and many others. Beginning in 1919, Robert Benchley, Dorothy Parker, and Robert Sherwood, all of whom worked at nearby *Vanity Fair* magazine, gathered for lunch in the hotel, amusing one another with their clever conversation. The press referred to the group as "The Round Table," but insiders called it the "Vicious Circle." Harold Ross founded *The New Yorker* partly to enshrine the sophisticated, incisive humor of his friends.

Further down West 44th St, at no. 37, the **New York Yacht Club** (1901; Warren & Wetmore) occupies land donated by J. Pierpont Morgan (commodore 1897–9). Limestone ropes, pulleys, anchors, and hooks adrip with limestone seaweed decorate the façade. Truly astonishing, however, are the three windows fashioned like the sterns of ships plowing through ossified seas whose stony waves curl over the sidewalk. The keystone above

the main entrance represents Poseidon. From 1857 until 1983, when its entry *Liberty* was defeated by the Australian challenger *Australia II*, the club housed the America's Cup, the ultimate prize in yachting, first given in 1851 by Queen Victoria.

Further east, at 27 West 44th St, is the **Harvard Club** (1894, McKim, Mead & White, with additions and extensions), one of several university clubs in the neighborhood. Harvard's clubhouse, neo-Georgian with a restrained brick and limestone façade, recalls the early architecture of the college itself.

Go back now to Fifth Ave. At no. 551, on the northeast corner of 45th St, is the 38-story **Fred F. French Building** (1927; John Sloan and H. Douglas Ives), probably the city's first flat-topped skyscraper and certainly a fine example of 1920s' exotic architectural design. The setbacks mandated by the requirements of the 1916 zoning code (*see p. 71*) found a corollary in the ziggurats of ancient Assyrian architecture, as do the colored faïence tiles that decorate the upper-story setbacks and the top of the building. The panels concealing the water tower on the roof are decorated with symbolic motifs chosen by Ives: on the north and south the rising suns (Progress) appear amid winged griffins (Integrity and Watchfulness) and golden beehives with bees (Thrift and Industry); on the east and west are heads of Mercury, god of commerce. The vaulted lobby with its bronze doors, chandeliers, and panels showing bearded Mesopotamian genii is worth a look.

Unimposing though it may be, the block of West 47th St between Fifth and Sixth Aves is the city's **Diamond**

District. In the 1920s and early 1930s the diamond business centered around the Bowery and Canal St on the Lower East Side and Fulton St in the Financial District, but the refugees who fled the ghettos of Amsterdam and Antwerp ahead of Hitler settled here and were joined by downtown jewelers who moved uptown. The glittering ground-floor shops are for the tourist trade, while the real business is transacted in trading clubs or upstairs in old buildings equipped with ultra-sensitive cameras and sophisticated alarm systems. Until recently virtually all the brokers and diamond cutters were Jewish, using skills passed down the generations from as far back as the 16th century, when stonecutting was one of the few trades open to Jews. Recently jewelers and stonecutters from Cuba, Puerto Rico, Russia, and East Asia have arrived. Ninety percent of the diamonds that enter the US are said to go through New York, and most of those through the 47th Street Diamond District.

Continue north on Fifth Avenue. After more than seven decades, the **former Charles Scribner's Sons bookstore** (*597 Fifth Ave at 48th and 49th Sts*) closed in 1989, but the building (1913; Ernest Flagg) remains, protected inside and out by landmarking. The black iron and glass storefront recalls *fin de siècle* Paris. Medallions on the piers two stories above the storefront portray famous printers: William Caxton, Johannes Gutenberg, Aldus Manutius, and Benjamin Franklin.

At 611 Fifth Ave (*49th and 50th Sts*) stands the flagship **Saks Fifth Avenue** (1924; Starrett & Van Vleck), a New York shopping icon. The business was founded in 1902 when Andrew Saks, who had begun his career as a peddler in Washington, D.C., established Saks Thirty-Fourth near Herald Square. In 1923 Saks's son Horace, a Princeton graduate, sold that less exclusive downtown store to the now-extinct Gimbels firm for $8 million in order to follow the carriage trade uptown. The next year he opened the present Saks with show windows offering a pigskin trunk ($3,000), raccoon coats ($1,000), and chauffeurs' livery.

Rockefeller Center

Rockefeller Center, a complex of commercial buildings, theaters, plazas,
underground concourses, and shops, has been hailed as the first architecturally
coordinated development in New York City, and a milestone in urban planning.

Rockefeller Center, which was developed principally during the Depression, is the world's largest privately-owned business and entertainment center. At one time steamship lines, airlines, tourist bureaus, and shipping firms, as well as representatives of the broadcasting and newspaper industries, tenanted its buildings, giving the center an aura of cosmopolitan glamour. Today, it remains a visual icon and a major tourist destination, embracing 19 buildings on 21 acres, offering shopping, restaurants, ice skating in season, and other diversions.

Visiting Rockefeller Center
Map 617, D3. Fifth to Sixth Aves (West 48th to West 51st Sts). Subway: 6 to 51st St;
B, D, F, M to 47th–50th Sts-Rockefeller Center; N, Q, R to 49th St. Bus: M1, M2, M3,
M4, M5, M7. Plaza and Concourse open daily 7am–midnight. Tours: Rockefeller
Center Tour (1hr 30mins) explores buildings and artworks, T: 212 698 2000; NBC
Studio tour (about 1hr 10mins) to studios and control rooms, T: 212 664 3700;
The Top of the Rock Observation Deck (see below). General info, T: 212 588 8601,
rockefellercenter.com.

HISTORY OF ROCKEFELLER CENTER

In 1927 the Metropolitan Opera, seeking to replace its outmoded house on Broadway between 39th and 40th Sts, became interested in the twelve acres of land owned by Columbia University between Fifth and Sixth Aves and West 48th and West 51st Sts. The land had blossomed briefly (1801–11) as the Elgin Botanic Garden, but now held speakeasies, rooming houses, and brothels. The opera company approached John D. Rockefeller Jr. (1874–1960) as a possible benefactor, hoping he might donate land for a plaza in front of the new opera house. Rockefeller began exploring the possibilities of leasing the land himself, making the central portion available to the opera, and then subleasing the rest to commercial interests who would construct their own buildings. Since real estate experts led him to believe that he could realize as much as $5.5 million

30 ROCKEFELLER PLAZA
Detail of Lee Lawrie's *Light* (1933).

ROCKEFELLER CENTER

Notable Artworks

1 *Prometheus*
2 *Wisdom* relief
3 Friedlander sculptures
4 Friedlander sculptures
5 *American Progress* mural (in the lobby)
6 Rainbow Room
7 *Intelligence Awakening Mankind*
8 Entrance to Top of the Rock
9 Hildreth Meière plaques
10 *News*
11 *Workers* panels
12 "International" screen
13 *The Immigrant*
14 *Atlas*
15 *Youth Leading Industry*

annually on the property, he signed a contract with Columbia University in 1928 to lease the property for a 24-year period with renewal options to 2019, later extended to 2069.

Then the stock market crashed (1929) and the Metropolitan Opera abruptly dropped its plans for a new house, leaving Rockefeller with a lease under which he owed more than $3.8 million a year on property that brought in only about $300,000. Rockefeller's only real choice was to develop the property without the opera house. He directed his planners to design a commercial center "as beautiful as possible consistent with maximum income," and work began on the city's first integrated commercial center, where skyscrapers could be planned in relation to one another with due consideration of open space, light, and traffic control. Largely responsible for the early project were developers Todd, Robertson & Todd, and three principal architectural firms: Reinhard & Hofmeister; Corbett, Harrison, and MacMurray; and Hood & Fouilhoux, who worked under the name of The Associated Architects, making it impossible nowadays to assign specific credit for individual buildings in the original development.

Between 1931 and 1940, 228 buildings were demolished and 4,000 tenants were relocated to make way for 14 new buildings; 75,000 workers were employed on the job. Architect Raymond Hood proposed that the Radio Corporation of America (RCA), still prospering during the Depression, should become the center's major tenant. For years most radio programs of NBC, a subsidiary of RCA, were produced here, and Rockefeller Center became known popularly as "Radio City."

Although Rockefeller drove the "last rivet" into the "last building," the United States Rubber Co. Building (now the Simon & Schuster Building at 1230 Sixth Ave) in 1939, development continued after World War II and again during the 1950s and '60s when Rockefeller Center expanded west to Sixth Avenue, replacing low buildings and small business tenants with stiff, ponderous office towers. In 1985 Columbia University sold its land under the center to the Rockefeller Group for $400 million, the largest price ever paid at the time for a single parcel of city real estate. On that 11.7-acre plot sit Radio City Music Hall, the skating rink, the Comcast Building (formerly the GE Building), and the other landmarked buildings of the original development. In 1989 the real estate arm of the Mitsubishi Group bought the center, provoking widespread indignation over what was seen as the sale of a prime piece of the American heritage to a foreign corporation. But when a recession squeezed profits, Mitsubishi walked away from its investment. In 2000 the real estate firm Tishman Speyer bought the property, restored the landmarked buildings, and upgraded the quality of the tenants. The Rockefellers are no longer directly involved with the landmarked office buildings, Radio City Music Hall, or the Rainbow Room.

ART DECO FAÇADES ON FIFTH AVENUE
The most dramatic approach to Rockefeller Center is from the east side of Fifth Ave between West 49th and West 50th Sts. The two low buildings flanking the central promenade (both completed 1933) are the British Empire Building (north) and La Maison Française (south), buildings whose modest scale reflects an earlier Fifth Avenue. By placing these low structures here, the developers gained rights to build the towering RCA Building (now the Comcast Building) in the center of the block (*30*

Rockefeller Plaza), simultaneously preserving neighborhood property values by leaving the side streets unshadowed.

Over the main door of **La Maison Française** an elaborate bronze panel by Alfred Janniot depicts Paris and New York joining hands above three female figures: *Poetry*, *Beauty*, and *Elegance*. Above the panel soars an Art Deco version, also by Janniot, of the traditional symbol of the French Republic, a woman holding the flaming torch of Liberty.

Over the main entrance of the **British Empire Building**, figures on a bronze panel (1933) by Carl Paul Jennewein represent nine major industries of the British Empire. At the bottom a bronze sun symbolizes the empire on which the sun was expected never to set. Above the panel a cartouche bears the Royal coat of arms and the mottoes of the British monarch and the Order of the Garter.

THE PROMENADE

A bronze strip in the sidewalk near the building line at the entrance to the Promenade marks the boundary of the property formerly owned by Columbia University. The Promenade (1933) was dubbed the "Channel Gardens" because it separates the British and French buildings; the walkway (60ft wide and 200ft long) is embellished with pools, seasonal floral displays, and fountains. The bronze fountain heads (1935), designed by René Chambellan, represent tritons and nereids riding dolphins. They symbolize (east to west) *Leadership, Will, Thought, Imagination, Energy*, and *Alertness*—qualities chosen by the earnest designers of the center's arts program as those contributing to human progress. Most of the themes of Rockefeller Center's artwork were chosen by Hartley Burr Alexander, a professor of philosophy at the University of Southern California, hired to impose thematic unity on the whole. Professor Alexander's general topic, "New Frontiers and the March of Civilization," resulted in artworks sometimes illustrating technology, sometimes suggesting values meaningful to the Rockefellers, and sometimes celebrating national pride—but often encumbered with unwieldy titles.

THE LOWER PLAZA AND SKATING RINK

The Promenade opens into the **Lower Plaza**. At the top of the stairway leading to the lower level a commemorative plaque recalls John D. Rockefeller Jr.'s personal credo: "I believe in the supreme worth of the individual... every right implies a responsibility, every opportunity an obligation..." The plaza is dominated by an 18-ft **figure of Prometheus (1)**, designed by Paul Manship (1934). The eight-ton gilded bronze statue, descending from a gilded mountain clutching a ball of fire in his right hand, is encircled by a ring containing the signs of the zodiac. The muscular model for Promethus, Leonardo Nole (d. 1998), the son of Italian immigrants, was "discovered" working as a lifeguard and recruited to pose for art classes at several women's colleges, which led to the commission. The red granite wall behind offers a quotation from Aeschylus: "Prometheus, teacher in every art, brought the fire that hath proved to mortals a means to mighty ends." During the Christmas season, thousands of lights illuminate a huge tree on the sidewalk behind the plaza, delighting the spectacular crowds who pack the area during the holidays. The **Skating Rink** is probably the most famous in the world, less than perfect for serious skating because of the crowds, but without equal in ambiance. During the summer it doubles as an outdoor café. (*Skating season usually begins in mid-Oct; skate rental available; for information, therinkatrockccenter.com.*)

ROCKEFELLER PLAZA

Three-block Rockefeller Plaza, one of the few private streets remaining in the city, separates the Lower Plaza from the western part of the center. Footsore visitors can sit and enjoy the spectacle of some 200 flags surrounding the rink and flapping in the breeze, their halyards clanking against the metal poles.

10 Rockefeller Plaza was completed in 1939, intended for Dutch commercial and cultural interests. When Germany invaded Holland in 1940, those plans were abandoned, though the building did briefly house the Dutch government-in-exile. Eastern Airlines became the major tenant, reflected in Dean Cornwell's lobby murals, *The Story of Transportation* (dedicated 1946). The silver goddesses of flight floating through the paintings were modeled on Cornwell's assistant, Wilmuth Masden Stevens. Today Christie's auction house is located in the building and in the northeast corner at street level is **NBC studio 1A**, where *The Today Show*, a popular news and talk program, is televised, drawing crowds of onlookers on weekday mornings.

30 ROCKEFELLER PLAZA

The first building constructed at Rockefeller Center is still its most imposing; 30 Rockefeller Plaza, also known as 30 Rock, whose changing menu of names reflects the corporate history of broadcast media in the US: originally the RCA Building (1933), it became the GE Building (1988), owned by the conglomerate General Electric (owner of NBC), and now the Comcast Building (2013). Because 30 Rock is landmarked, the changes in signage had to be approved by the Landmarks Preservation Commission. The building is roughly rectangular, with its narrow edge facing east–west, and broad slab-like walls on the north and south. It owes its disproportionate length to Rockefeller's desire to include within its walls some potentially unprofitable lots he owned on Sixth Avenue, at the time darkened by the elevated railway. Skillfully designed setbacks give the building the impression of soaring height. An eleven-story wrap-around structure houses television studios, constructed free from the rest of the building to minimize vibrations. Over the east entrance is **Wisdom (2)**, a technically challenging relief in stone and molded glass by Lee Lawrie, one of the foremost architectural sculptors of his era. Wisdom, a powerfully muscular giant with a remarkable Art Deco beard, spreads a compass above a glass screen made of 240 blocks of molded glass, whose texture the *WPA Guide to New York City* compared to crumpled cellophane. Only when the work was well underway did the art committee notice the embarrassing similarity between Lawrie's work and William Blake's frontispiece to *Europe: A Prophecy* (1794). On the left and right are images of **Sound** and **Light** (i.e. radio and television, industries in their infancy at the time), the means by which Wisdom is disseminated.

Flanking the 49th St entrance two limestone pylons bear sculptures by Leo Friedlander; the obscure symbolism of the two works collectively known as *Television*

(3) depicts (left of door) a large nude figure transmitting an image of dancers through the "ether" to another large figure (right of the door), who receives the image; the audience on the far right represents *Mother Earth* and her child, *Man*. Above the marquee at the 50th St entrance two more pylons, also sculpted by Friedlander, represent *Radio* (4); here a large figure conducts a chorus of singers, transmitting music to Mother Earth and Man via a loudspeaker before which stand a lyre player and another singer. Rockefeller found these works "gross and unbeautiful" and objected to the anatomical detail of the nudes; critics generally concur.

Indoors, directly in front of the main entrance, is *American Progress* (5), a huge mural by Catalan artist José María Sert. Abraham Lincoln, standing, represents the "Man of Action," while Ralph Waldo Emerson, seated, represents the "Man of Thought." The mural (1937) is famous in part for replacing the controversial Diego Rivera fresco destroyed by the Rockefellers (*see box*). For the conservative Sert, the commission was a triumphant moment, since he disliked Rivera personally, disavowed the Mexican muralist's strident anti-capitalist views, and envied his international reputation. The massive ceiling painting, again by Sert, is entitled *Time*, while the murals against the elevator banks in the north and south corridors, by Sert and the English painter Frank Brangwyn, illustrate themes of progress against such obstacles as disease, slavery, and crushing physical labor.

THE DIEGO RIVERA FRESCO FIASCO

Commissioned to paint a mural illustrating "man's new possibilities from his new understanding of material things," Rivera, already known for his radical politics and his reputation as a provocateur, submitted a sketch acceptable to his patrons—but then produced a fresco, *Man at the Crossroads*, that included a laudatory portrait of Lenin. Asked to substitute another face for Lenin's, Rivera replied that he would prefer to destroy the painting, at least preserving its integrity. The fresco remained shrouded in canvas during the opening ceremonies and eventually Rivera's wish was granted: the Rockefellers had the mural destroyed. In the recriminations that followed, cowboy humorist Will Rogers advised Rivera that he "should never try to fool a Rockefeller in oils." But Rivera had the last word: he painted a second version of *Man at the Crossroads* for the Palace of Fine Arts in Mexico City, including a portrait of John D. Rockefeller, a lifelong teetotaler, in a nightclub, cocktail glass in hand.

THE RAINBOW ROOM
In the Comcast Building (30 Rockefeller Plaza), 65th floor. Open to the public for dinner and dancing select evenings; Sun brunch. SixtyFive cocktail lounge open Mon–Fri 5–midnight. T: 212 632 5000, rainbowroom.com.
The elevator banks at 30 Rock contain the city's first high-speed elevators, including those to the Rainbow Room (6). The nightclub (opened 1934) is celebrated for its view and handsome decor. Noel Coward and Cole Porter came on opening day; the great

dance bands of the 1930s and '40s played there. Built as a two-story cylinder with no internal columns and originally called the Stratosphere Club, it was renamed the Rainbow Room for an organ that threw lights on the domed ceiling, the colors shifting with the musical pitches played. The landmarked dining room re-opened after renovation in 2014, the rainbow lights glowing once again.

THE CONCOURSE
Underground more than two miles of passages, lined with shops and restaurants, reach to Sixth Avenue and connect to every building in the complex.

SIXTH AVENUE

Less opulently decorated than the east façade, Rockefeller Plaza's Sixth Avenue entrance features a glass mosaic by Barry Faulkner, *Intelligence Awakening Mankind* (7), made of about one million pieces of colored glass. Four limestone panels by Gaston Lachaise higher on the façade depict *Genius Seizing the Light of the Sun, Conquest of Space, Gifts of Earth to Mankind*, and *Understanding—Spirit of Progress*.

THE ROCKEFELLER CENTER EXTENSION
On the west side of Sixth Ave loom four additions to the center, known as the Rockefeller Center Extension. Built during the 1960s and '70s by the successors of the Associated Architects (Harrison, Abramovitz & Harris), the buildings have been criticized for lacking a sympathetic human scale, their developers opting for maximum permissible rentable space at the expense of light, air, and pleasing proportions. The eminent critic Vincent Scully called them "an incoherent splatter of skyscrapers" marching along the west side of Sixth Avenue. The small mid-block park behind the McGraw Hill Building (*1221 Sixth Ave*), along West 49th St between Sixth and Seventh Aves, provides some relief from the overbearing architecture; its walk-through waterfall is a favorite with visitors.

TOP OF THE ROCK
Observation deck entrance on 50th St between Fifth and Sixth Aves, open daily 8am–midnight, last elevator at 11pm. Tickets at the box office, by phone, at self-service kiosk on concourse level of 30 Rockefeller Plaza, or online. Combination tickets available (Rock Pass and Rock MoMA), check the website. Admission charge (expensive). Gift shop. T: 212 698 2000 or toll free 877 NYC ROCK (877 692 7625), topoftherocknyc.com.

When the **Top of the Rock observation deck** opened in 1933, Adirondack chairs and a telescope gave it the ambiance of an ocean liner; its quaint, Gothic-style cast-iron perimeter fence was apparently a sop to Rockefeller's fondness for historic details. Closed for 20 years, the deck re-opened in 2005 after a $75 million restoration, with three levels of indoor and outdoor viewing and historical exhibits. On the 70th floor are 360-degree panoramic views that reach the Hudson River Valley to the north and the Verrazano Bridge to the south, with Central Park and the Empire State Building in the near distance. The view of the city by night is spectacular.

RADIO CITY MUSIC HALL

1260 Sixth Ave (West 50th St). Stage Door walking tour (about 1hr) daily 10–5, approximately every half hour. Admission charge (expensive). T: 212 247 4777, radiocity.com. Event tickets at the Radio City Music Hall box office and through TicketMaster.

The world's largest theater when it opened in 1932, Radio City Music Hall remains a masterpiece of Art Deco décor. Every holiday season since 1933 the theater has presented the Radio City Christmas Spectacular, an over-the-top entertainment with hundreds of lavishly costumed performers, high-tech special effects, and a chorus line of leggy Rockettes, the famous women's precision dance team. The Music Hall's principal designer was Edward Durell Stone, who also designed the Museum of Modern Art.

HISTORY OF RADIO CITY MUSIC HALL

Samuel Lionel Rothafel (1882–1936), better known as Roxy, began his career showing movies in the back room of a bar and rose to become a show business mogul, producing radio programs and stage shows and managing several theaters, including the opulent Roxy. His reputation of knowing infallibly what the public wanted earned him broad powers as director of the Music Hall. He contributed to the design of the theater and shaped its general policies, intending to revive vaudeville and produce spectacular variety shows.

Unfortunately Roxy's shows lost $180,000 in their first two weeks, and the format was changed. Until television began to pose a threat, the Music Hall thrived with the formula of wholesome movies paired with stage shows, drawing five million patrons a year at the end of 1967. By 1977 attendance had fallen to fewer than two million and the theater was in the red. In 1978 the Rockefellers announced they would demolish the Music Hall, but a wave of public support resulted in its interior being landmarked. In 1999 the hall was beautifully restored (Hardy Holzman Pfeiffer Associates).

The interior

The Music Hall with its great auditorium is a high point of American theater design and one of the city's grandest displays of Art Deco styling. The unity of the hall's decorative features—carpets, wall coverings, statues, murals, and furniture—was coordinated by Donald Deskey, who had been influenced by the Exposition Internationale des Arts Décoratifs in Paris. Deskey had attracted the attention of Abby Aldridge Rockefeller by the Braque-like abstractions he used in his Saks Fifth Avenue store windows, and had designed art galleries in the Rockefeller townhouse on West 54th St.

The **Grand Foyer** (140ft long, 45ft wide, and 60ft high) is decorated in warm, dark colors, and ornamented with brass and chrome. The carpet, designed by Ruth Reeves, who had studied with Fernard Léger in Paris, is executed in red, brown, gold, and black with abstract forms of musical instruments. Over the imposing staircase at the north end is a mural by Ezra Winter, *The Fountain of Youth*, its subject suggested by Professor Alexander (*see p. 278*) and drawn from an Oregon tribal legend. It depicts an old man gazing at a gleaming inaccessible mountaintop on which bubbles the elusive fountain; across the sky marches a cloudy procession representing the vanities of life. Gold mirrored panels reflect the light from two 29-ft glass chandeliers (two tons apiece). After the restoration, Stuart Davis's Modernist mural *Men Without Women* (1932) was returned to its original home after being sequestered for a almost a quarter of a century in the Museum of Modern Art.

The most impressive space in the Music Hall is the **auditorium** (seats 6,200). The ceiling is egg-shaped, a form Roxy demanded for its supposed acoustic superiority. The great proscenium arch (60ft high, 100ft wide) compels attention. Rising outward and forward from it are the successive overlapping bands of the ceiling, painted with perpendicular rays, whose effect has been compared to the aurora borealis, a sunburst, and the rays of dawn. Roxy liked to assert that a sunrise he had witnessed at sea inspired the design, but the model of the auditorium, complete with ceiling, had been photographed six days before he embarked on the inspirational voyage. The stage machinery includes sections that can be raised or lowered on elevators, a revolving central turntable, and a moveable orchestra pit. The stage can support twelve grand pianos, three Roman chariots with horses, or six elephants.

THE MIGHTY WURLITZER

Adding to the grandeur of Radio City Music Hall spectaculars is the "Mighty Wurlitzer" pipe organ. As the show opens, two organ consoles (each weighing 2.5 tons) roll out from curtained alcoves flanking the stage. The original plans called for elevators to lower the consoles into the basement after the organists had finished; when this proved unfeasible, the consoles were placed in alcoves, covered by electrically operated curtains. The organ operated by the consoles was built specifically for this theater and draws its huge and varied sound from 4,178 pipes in 58 ranks; the pipes range from the size of a pencil to 32ft and are housed in eleven separate rooms.

WEST 50TH STREET

On the wall of the Music Hall facing West 50th St are **plaques symbolizing *Dance*, *Drama*, and *Music* (9)**, designed by Hildreth Meière. Further east, at the corner of West 50th St and Rockefeller Plaza, is the former Associated Press Building (1938), at 50 Rockefeller Plaza. Above the main entrance is Isamu Noguchi's exemplary stainless-steel panel ***News* (10)** (1940), depicting five men with the tools of the reporter's trade: pad and pencil, camera, telephone, wirephoto, and teletype. Across from it, on the west side of the International Building, are Gaston Lachaise's panels depicting **workers (11)**, a tribute to the builders of Rockefeller Center.

THE INTERNATIONAL BUILDING

The International Building (*630 Fifth Ave*), which reflected Rockefeller's prescient view of a global economy, was built in a hurry in 1935, requiring only 136 working days of construction once the excavation was completed. The early tenants were steamship lines—the French Line, the Grace Line—rail lines, currency exchanges, travel agencies, and a US Passport Office.

Over the side entrance (*25 West 50th St*), a **limestone screen (12)** by Lee Lawrie symbolizes internationalism. The four figures in the central rectangle on the bottom row represent the four races of mankind; above them are a trading ship; figures representing art, science, and industry; and Mercury, messenger of trade. The upper side panels represent regions of the Earth (whale's fluke, palm trees, mosque, and Aztec temple), while the lower ones symbolize the old order (Norman tower and lion) and the new industrial, republican age (smokestacks and eagle). Two other panels by Lawrie are *Swords into Ploughshares* (over the doorway at no. 19), and (at no. 9) *St. Francis of Assisi*, with a halo of golden birds.

The main entrance is on Fifth Avenue, where a central doorway is flanked by two projecting wings. The south wing is known as the **Palazzo d'Italia** (1935), and like the British and French buildings demonstrates the developers' desire to attract foreign tenants at a time when Americans were suffering from the economic downturn. One relief panel by Giacomo Manzù depicts entwined wheat stalks and grapevines, symbolizing fruitfulness. A second, also by Manzù, ***The Immigrant* (13)**, showing a barefoot peasant woman and her child with their belongings tied to a stick, has been moved around the corner to a site near the 50th St entrance. These works, installed in 1965, replace Attilio Piccirilli's *Sempre Avanti Eterna Giovinezza*, a muscular youth energetically spading the earth, removed in 1941 when war with Italy was looming, because its imagery was considered fascistic.

In front of the central entrance a muscular bronze ***Atlas* (14)** (1937) shoulders an armillary globe studded with signs of the zodiac. Designed by Lee Lawrie and René Chambellan, this giant (height of figure, 15ft; diameter of sphere, 21ft; weight, 14,000 lb) impresses by his sheer size. The relief of ***Youth Leading Industry* (15)** above the north wing of the International Building (*636 Fifth Ave*) is by Attilio Piccirilli (*see p. 400*), the companion piece to the now-vanished *Sempre Avanti Eterna Giovinezza*.

Interior of the International Building

The central escalators, dominating the room like the grand staircases of 18th- and 19th-century public buildings, recall the fondness of Art Deco designers for machinery as a stylistic motif. It is worth a trip up and down to see the rose window and Gothic arches of St. Patrick's Cathedral across the street through the rings of Atlas's sphere.

For Eating and Drinking around Rockefeller Center, see p. 302.

Midtown: St. Patrick's, MoMA, & "the 50s"

St. Patrick's is the largest Roman Catholic cathedral in the US and the eleventh largest in the world. Nearby MoMA, established when modern art was not universally considered art, has remarkable holdings in 20th-century painting and sculpture. Nearby are fine stores, famous hotels, and at 59th Street, the southeast corner of Central Park.

Located in the heart of Midtown, **St. Patrick's Cathedral** is the seat of the Roman Catholic Archdiocese of New York—a city landmark, and a symbol of the achievements of New York's immigrant Irish Catholic population. The beauty of the cathedral and the power of its archbishops confer upon it an importance that goes beyond the city's boundaries.

Visiting St. Patrick's
Map p. 617, D3. Fifth Ave at East 50th St. Subway: B, D, F, M to 47th–50th Sts-Rockefeller Center; N, Q, or R to 49th St; 6 to 51st St. Bus: M1, M2, M3, M4, M5, M7, M50. NB: At the time of writing, the cathedral was undergoing major restoration; some areas may be closed to visitors. Open daily 6:30am to 8:45pm. Audio tour available through the Acoustiguide app (acoustiguide.com, or at the Cathedral); proceeds go restoration. Shops. T: 212 753 2261, saintpatrickscathedral.org.

HISTORY OF ST. PATRICK'S

In 1828 the two major Catholic churches of New York, St. Peter's on Barclay St (*see p. 82*) and St. Patrick's—now called "Old St. Patrick's" (*see p. 126*)—bought the plot where the present cathedral sits, intending it as a burial ground. The land turned out to be too rocky for easy digging and in 1850 Archbishop John Hughes announced his intention to build a new cathedral on the site. Hughes, who would become the cathedral's driving force, had arrived in America from Ireland in 1817, an uneducated 20-year-old eager to become a priest. He arrived in New York some two decades later, a bishop, a skillful administrator, and a flamboyant orator. By 1858 Hughes had raised the money to lay the cornerstone and begin construction; in 1879, the cathedral was dedicated, having cost twice as much as estimated and taken four times as long to build (partly because the Civil War intervened). It was consecrated, debt-free, in 1910.

When the cornerstone was laid, 200 priests and 100 choirboys attended the ceremony along with 100,000 onlookers—an astonishing turnout, since the population of the city was only about 814,000 in 1860. Some time in the last century, however, the cornerstone mysteriously disappeared.

Exterior of St. Patrick's

Designed by James Renwick (1879; towers, 1888) with William Rodrigue, brother-in-law of Archbishop Hughes, the building draws heavily on Cologne Cathedral (begun in the 13th century and completed in 1880 after a long hiatus). The general plan is a Latin cross with traditional east–west orientation. The façade is marble. Because the interior vaulting is brick and plaster, not stone, flying buttresses were unnecessary, but the pinnacles of the buttresses do exist, perhaps because Renwick originally called for stone interior vaulting supported by flying buttresses. The bronze doors at the west entrance (added 1949) were designed by Charles Maginnis with figures by John Angel. The figures represent (top to bottom, left to right): St. Joseph, patron of this church; St. Isaac Jogues, first Catholic priest in New York; St. Frances X. Cabrini, founder of the Missionary Sisters of the Sacred Heart and "Mother of the Immigrant"; the Blessed Kateri Tekakwitha, an Indian maiden called the "Lily of the Mohawks;" and St. Elizabeth Ann Seton, the first American-born saint.

Interior of St. Patrick's

Two rows of clustered columns divide the nave. Above the arches runs the triforium, divided into four sections by the arms of the cross, with clerestory windows above. The ceiling is groined with (plaster) ribs.

Chapels and aisle windows in the south aisle include a modern **Shrine of St. Elizabeth Ann Seton** (1975; sculptor Frederick Shrady) with the window above dedicated to St. Henry, 11th-century Holy Roman Emperor.

The **Stations of the Cross** in the south transept were designed by Peter J.H. Cuypers in the Netherlands. The window over the entrance, depicting scenes from the life of St. Patrick, was given by Old St. Patrick's Cathedral (*see p. 126*). In the west wall of the transept is another St. Patrick's window, this one given by architect Renwick, who appears in the lower panels. In the south ambulatory beyond the sacristy, the marble *Pietà* (1906; William O. Partridge) was inspired by Michelangelo's famous work in St. Peter's in Rome, but is three times larger.

The **Lady Chapel** at the east end of the church, begun in 1901 and completed in 1906, was designed by Charles T. Matthews and is based on 13th-century French Gothic architecture. The stained-glass windows (Paul Woodroffe) over this altar and the two flanking it depict the mysteries of the rosary. Directly opposite the Lady Chapel is the entrance to the **crypt** (*closed to visitors*), in which are buried the remains of Archbishop Hughes, the other cardinals of New York, and several rectors of this

ST. PATRICK'S CATHEDRAL
Based on the Gothic cathedrals of Europe, it was consecrated in 1910.

church, as well as Archbishop Fulton J. Sheen. Recent interments are those of John Cardinal O'Connor, archbishop 1984 until his death in 2000, Edward Cardinal Egan (died 2015), and Pierre Toussaint, the onetime Haitian slave who became a servant of the poor and is now a candidate for sainthood. His remains were exhumed in 1990 from Old St. Patrick's and reburied here.

In the north ambulatory, adjacent to the Lady Chapel on the north side, is the **altar of St. Michael and St. Louis**, designed by Charles T. Matthews and executed by Tiffany & Co. Beyond the usher's office and bride's room are the altar of St. Joseph and the chancel organ (1928) with 2,520 pipes. In the north transept, in front of the altar of the Holy Family, is the marble **Baptistery**.

The focal point of the sanctuary is the **high altar** with its bronze baldachin designed by Charles D. Maginnis, rising to a height of 57ft. From the crossing there is a good view of the west or **rose window**, 26ft in diameter and filled with stained glass in geometric patterns. In the loft beneath it is the Great Organ (1930), with 7,855 pipes, ranging from three inches to 32ft in length.

F. Scott Fitzgerald and Zelda Sayre were married in the sacristy in 1920. When Robert F. Kennedy's funeral mass was held here in 1968, lines of mourners stretched around the block. Andy Warhol's service (1987) filled the cathedral with artists, writers, designers, and Warhol's wealthy socialite admirers. Funerals for many police officers and firefighters who died at the World Trade Center on 9/11 took place here during the autumn of 2001.

"SWING STREET"

Between Fifth and Sixth Aves, **52nd St** (*map p. 617, D3*) has been designated "Swing Street" to commemorate its place in the history of jazz. Known simply as "The Street" among jazzmen, it attracted attention beginning in the late 1930s with its nightclubs, many of them former speakeasies in brownstone row houses, where the era's great innovators and performers worked: Art Tatum, Dizzy Gillespie, Thelonious Monk, Lester Young, and Charlie "Yardbird" Parker, for whom the Birdland jazz club would later be named. In particular the street has been identified with bebop, a style that emerged in Harlem between 1940 and 1944 and migrated downtown with black musicians, who could earn more and get wider exposure on 52nd St than in Harlem. The best known clubs were the Onyx, the Spotlight, the Three Deuces, the Royal Roost, and Bop City. The period was a golden age for jazz and for 52nd St, but by 1948, when heroin abuse was widespread among jazz musicians, the street had become the territory of prostitutes, strippers, and drug pushers. By 1950 only Jimmy Ryan's still played live music; ten years later the old brownstones gave way to office towers.

At 21 West 52nd St is the **21 Club** (1872)—a speakeasy during Prohibition and later a power-lunch spot. It is famous for its wine cellar and for the cast-iron jockeys above the entrance, said to be painted with the racing colors of patrons who donated them.

THE VANDERBILTS ON FIFTH AVENUE

In the late 19th century Vanderbilt buildings dominated Fifth Avenue in the low 50s. Between 1821 and 1885, William Henry Vanderbilt, son of the commodore, built three grandiose brownstones for himself and his two daughters on the west side of the avenue between 50th and 51st Sts. The socially ambitious Alva Smith Vanderbilt, first wife of his second son, William Kissam Vanderbilt (1849–1920), wanted something better than brownstone, and commissioned Richard Morris Hunt to design a limestone palace on the northwest corner of 52nd St, a mansion based on the château of Blois in the Loire Valley. All but one of those family mansions succumbed to the northward rolling juggernaut of commerce.

The single survivor stands on the east side of the street at **647 Fifth Ave**—constructed as part of a family effort to keep commercial establishments out of "their" part of town. The sons of Richard Morris Hunt built it in 1905 for George W. Vanderbilt II (1862–1914), who never lived there. George leased it to Robert Goelet (a relative by marriage), his wife and their son, who lived there with 14 servants. The Vanderbilt holding action failed: businesses encroached from downtown, and the house was altered to become a store for two art dealers. The current tenant is Versace.

Meanwhile, William K. Vanderbilt, alarmed by the northward creep of commerce, sold the corner lot, **651–3 Fifth Ave**, to millionaire banker Morton F. Plant on the condition that the site remain residential for 25 years. Plant, commodore of the New York Yacht Club, obliged with a five-story neo-Italian palazzo of marble and granite (1905) but by 1916 he, too, had become discouraged when a dressmaking business moved in across the street, and built a new mansion further uptown. Vanderbilt bought Plant's palazzo for a million dollars and quickly rented it to Cartier for $50,000 a year. Cartier is still the tenant.

THE PALEY CENTER FOR MEDIA

Map 617, D3. 25 West 52nd St. Open Wed–Sun 12–6 (Thur until 8); closed Mon, Tues, major holidays. Admission charge. Shop. T: 212 621 6600, paleycenter.org.

Formerly the Museum of Television and Radio and originally the Museum of Broadcasting, the Paley Center has a permanent collection of nearly 160,000 TV and radio programs, available on individual consoles or in special screenings. Launched in 1975 by William S. Paley, a pioneer in radio and television, the collection dates back to the dawn of radio, when station KDKA sent out its first signals in Pittsburgh in 1920. Documentary programs include decisive moments in 20th-century history, the earliest a 1920 speech by Franklin D. Roosevelt, then running for vice-president. Other broadcasts include an eyewitness account of the crash of the *Hindenburg* airship (1937), Adolf Hitler's 1939 address to the Reichstag, the Hiroshima news bulletin (1945), President Truman's dismissal of General Douglas MacArthur (1951), and coverage of the ticker tape parade that followed. The TV collection begins with such early pieces as an excerpt from a 1936 drama, *Poverty Is Not a Crime,* and continues to the present, including live coverage of the terrorist attacks on 9/11. The center also offers lectures and events that explore the impact of the media on contemporary life.

The **CBS Building** (1965; Eero Saarinen & Assocs; *51 West 52nd St at Sixth Ave*) is the only skyscraper designed by Saarinen, who had died in 1961. Known as "Black Rock" for its dark granite cladding, it is elegant and understated. Saarinen, who admired Mies van der Rohe, is said to have made this building as different as possible from the latter's Seagram Building.

THE AXA EQUITABLE CENTER

This complex (*map p. 616, C3*) comprises two office buildings that fill the entire block between Sixth and Seventh Aves (*West 51st and West 52nd Sts*). The atrium of the AXA Equitable Tower (*787 Seventh Ave*) is dominated by Roy Lichtenstein's *Mural with Blue Brushstroke* (1986), a 68-ft compendium of images from the artist's career, including his own familiar motifs plus visual references to the works of other 20th-century painters. The blue brushstroke is simultaneously a waterfall and a visual pun on the gestural style of the Abstract Expressionists. In the center is Scott Burton's *Atrium Furnishment* (1985), a marble settee and table-fountain. Burton began as a performance artist, and his chair sculptures evolved from performance works, though he was also inspired by Gerrit Rietveld and the designers of the Bauhaus. He once stated that art should "place itself not in front of, but around, behind, underneath (literally) the audience."

East of the AXA Tower is a covered gallery with several works on view: Barry Flanagan's wry *Hare on Bell* (1983) and *Young Elephant* (1985); and Sol LeWitt's *Wall Drawing: Bands of Lines in Four Colors and Four Directions, Separated by Gray Bands* (1984–5).

MoMA (THE MUSEUM OF MODERN ART)

Map p. 617, D2. 11 West 53rd St (Fifth and Sixth Aves). Subway: E to 5th Ave-53rd St; B, D, F, or M to 47–50th Sts-Rockefeller Center. Bus: M1, M2, M3, M4, or M5 to 53rd St. Open daily 10:30–5:30, Fri until 8; closed Thanksgiving, and Christmas. Admission charge (expensive), but free Fri evening 4–8; sculpture garden free daily 9–10:15 (enter from West 54th St). Purchase advance tickets online to avoid the crowds. Several cafés, restaurant. Shops in museum and across the street at 44 West 53rd St. Free app for mobile devices. T: 212 708 9400, moma.org. NB: The museum is often very crowded; try to go early or late.

MoMA (the Museum of Modern Art) is one of the city's premier cultural institutions, a great repository of modern painting and sculpture, drawing, design, photography, and film. Between 2.5 and 3 million visitors arrive yearly to gaze at the Picassos and Matisses, the Van Goghs and Cézannes, and the huge splattered canvases of Jackson Pollock that have made it a destination for lovers of modern art.

HISTORY OF MoMA

In 1929, when modern art was not considered art at all in many quarters, Abby Aldrich Rockefeller (1874–1948) and two wealthy, well-connected, and socially committed friends, Lillie P. Bliss (1864–1931) and Mary Quinn Sullivan (1877–1939), founded a small museum in rented space in what is now the Crown Building on Fifth Ave near 57th St. Their first exhibition featured Cézanne, Gauguin, Seurat, and Van Gogh, more daring choices then than they seem today. Although the stock market had crashed a few days earlier, the show succeeded wildly, drawing 47,000 visitors, with 5,300 on the last day crowding into the six-room rented apartment. The fledgling museum's initial collection, donated by a trustee in 1929, was less impressive—eight prints and one drawing—but two years later Lillie Bliss bequeathed masterworks by Cézanne, Gauguin, Matisse, Modigliani, Picasso, Seurat, and Degas.

The first director, Alfred H. Barr Jr., broadened the concept of the museum to include film, industrial design, prints, drawings, photography, and printed books as well as painting and sculpture. Barr quickly shaped MoMA into a major force. In 1932 the exhibit "Modern Architecture: An International Exhibition" was influential in introducing the International Style to the American public, and in 1935 an exhibition of Van Gogh proved, in the words of the *WPA Guide to New York City*, that "art can attract as many people as a prize fight."

In 1932 MoMA moved to the present site, leasing a brownstone from John D. Rockefeller Jr. (Abby Aldrich Rockefeller's husband), who later donated the land. Throughout the 1940s and '50s the museum blazed new territory, increasing its photographic collection, mounting exhibitions on Matisse, Nolde, Rodin, Magritte, Turner, Pollock, de Kooning, and Oldenburg, and sending abroad an influential exhibition devoted to Abstract Expressionism.

As its collection increased, the museum grew more conservative, preserving the past and offering a historical survey of art from Post-Impressionism to relatively recent times. To counteract this trend, MoMA merged in 1999 with P.S.1 in Long Island City (*see p. 519*), whose focus is avant-garde contemporary art.

THE BUILDING

After a decade at its temporary quarters in what is now the Crown Building on Fifth Ave at 57th St, the museum put up the core of the present building, an austere exemplar of the International Style designed by Philip L. Goodwin and Edward D. Stone. The façade, with its aluminum shell and canopied entrance, featured a new insulating material, Thermolux, whose two sheets of clear glass enclosed a layer of spun glass. The first sculpture garden, designed by John McAndrew, was planted behind the museum on land also donated by John D. Rockefeller Jr. and quickly became the urban oasis it remains today.

By the 1960s the museum had outgrown its space, and new wings designed by Philip Johnson (1964) were attached east and west of the 1939 building; at the same time Johnson redesigned the sculpture garden, renamed to honor Abby Aldrich

Rockefeller. As the collections and visitors increased, the museum again found its facilities inadequate and in 1976 announced that it would again expand. To develop new sources of revenue, the museum sold the air rights over its prime Midtown location to a developer for a condominium apartment tower, engineering an arrangement with the City whereby the museum receives the benefits of most of the municipal real estate taxes generated by the tower. Designed by Cesar Pelli & Associates, the expansion (1984) was admired more for the revenue it produced than for its interior spaces.

Twenty years later that expansion proved inadequate, and, in 2004 the museum reopened after a two-year sojourn in Queens. The $858-million expansion by Yoshio Taniguchi met with mixed reviews: while the building was acclaimed for its serenity and urbanity before the art was re-installed, the gallery space met with less enthusiasm. Ten years later, MoMA announced yet another expansion (?2018; Diller Scofidio + Renfro), adding another 54 thousand square feet of exhibition space, some of it in the former Museum of American Folk Art, which MoMA demolished to great public outcry (*it is now in its former satellite space; see p. 397*), and some of it in an 88-story skyscraper (architect Jean Nouvel) with luxury condos rising further west.

THE COLLECTIONS

MoMA's outstanding collection of 19th–20th-century painting and sculpture—the reason most people come to the museum—is installed chronologically, beginning on the fifth floor and continuing on the fourth. Works are occasionally rotated; what you see may differ from the description below.

FIFTH FLOOR: MODERN ART, 1880–1940
In the corridors of this floor are paintings beloved by MoMA visitors: Andrew Wyeth's *Christina's World* (1948), Edward Hopper's *House by the Railroad* (1925), Pavel Tchelitchew's *Hide and Seek* (1942), and Balthus's *The Street* (1933), as well as early American modernist works by Georgia O'Keeffe, Charles Sheeler, and Charles Demuth.

Gallery 1: Post-Impressionism and Fauvism. Along with several still-lifes and landscapes, works by Paul Cézanne include *The Bather* (c. 1885), whose central figure was described by director Alfred Barr as "rising like a colossus who has just bestrode mountains and rivers." Vincent van Gogh's *Portrait of Joseph Roulin* (1889) is one of five of the postman at Arles, who obliged the painter by sitting as a model and impressed him with his socialism and his warm domestic life as father of a large family. *The Starry Night* (1889) is justly loved as a visionary painting with a tumultuously radiant night sky. Van Gogh intended *The Olive Trees* (1889) as its daylight complement. Paul Gauguin is represented by *Seed of Areoi* (1892) and Henri Rousseau by *The Dream* (1910) and *The Sleeping Gypsy* (1897); Rousseau offered this painting to his home town but was refused, though his work was appreciated by other artists long before the public valued it. Also on view are Fauve landscapes and James Ensor's *Masks Confronting Death* (1888).

Gallery 2: Cubist Revolution. Here are early examples of Analytical Cubism, a radical style developed largely by Picasso and Braque, in which forms were analyzed into geometrical components and rendered, for the most part, in subdued colors. The focal point is Picasso's *Les Demoiselles d'Avignon* (1907), first imagined as a brothel scene including a sailor, a medical student, and the naked female figures. Gradually the work evolved into its present form, where the five prostitutes stare frontally at an unseen (and presumably male) viewer. *Les Demoiselles* is a seminal work in the history of modern art for its flattening and fracturing of conventional pictorial space, its inclusion of disjunctive elements—Egyptian, Iberian, African, European—and its expressionistic, even savage, rendering of the prostitutes, particularly the threatening masklike faces of the two women on the right. Picasso, who had visited the museum of African art at the Trocadéro while working on *Les Demoiselles*, referred to the painting as his "first exorcism picture."

Gallery 3: Futurism. Umberto Boccioni's apparently windswept *Unique Forms of Continuity in Space* (1913) in gleaming bronze dominates the room. The Futurists used Cubist techniques of spatial dislocation to render motion. Also on view are Robert Delaunay's *Windows* (1912), which established him as a committed abstractionist, and Marc Chagall's *I and the Village* (1911), a Cubist vision of the Hasidic community outside Vitebsk where Chagall was born.

Gallery 4: Vienna 1900. Along with furniture, silver, and glassware (Koloman Moser, Josef Hoffmann), the gallery offers Gustav Klimt's *Hope II* (1907–8). Klimt's ornamental, oriental stylization and the frequently erotic nature of his images, even allegorical ones such as this image of a pregnant woman, have made him the embodiment of *fin-de-siècle* Vienna. Also on view: Oskar Kokoschka's marriage portrait (1909) of two well-known art historians Hans Tietze and Erica Tietze-Conrat attempts to express their "closed personalities so full of tension."

Gallery 5: Dada. This provocative anti-bourgeois, anti-aesthetic, anti-rational movement arose in Europe as a reaction to the horrors of World War I. Marcel Duchamp, who moved to New York in 1915, is represented by *Fresh Widow* (1920), a "ready-made" French window whose panes of glass are obscured by black leather and *To Be Looked at (from the Other Side of the Glass) with One Eye, Close to, for Almost an Hour* (1918). Work by Francis Picabia, Man Ray, and important American Dadaists are also on display.

Gallery 6: Henri Matisse. Considered one of the major figures of 20th-century art, Matisse is well-represented at MoMA. *Dance (I)*, a study for a painting commissioned by Moscow collector Sergei Shchukin, is remarkable for a grace and energy that were not apparent to early audiences, who criticized the final picture for its flatness and simplified color. Also: *The Red Studio* (1911), *The Blue Window* (1913), *The Moroccans* (1915–16), and *Woman on a High Stand (Germaine Raynal)* (1914). MoMA owns several works from the end of Matisse's life including *The Swimming*

Pool (1952), the artist's largest cut-out, a 54-ft frieze of blue bathers silhouetted against a rectangle of white, and *Memory of Oceania* (1952–3).

Gallery 7: Art after World War I.

Notable here is Picasso's *Three Musicians* (1921), said to epitomize his "Synthetic" or decorative Cubism; the flat, rectilinear quality of the figures suggests a jigsaw puzzle or the Cubist technique of collage. The gallery includes examples of Giorgio de Chirico's metaphysical art including *Gare Montparnasse (The Melancholy of Departure)* (1914); and *The Song of Love* (1914), with its strange juxtaposition of objects: the surgical glove, the Greek statue, the train passing in the distance. Also on view are works by Constantin Brancusi: *The Cock* (1924), *Bird in Space* (1928), *Mlle Pogany* (1913), and *Blonde Negress* (1933), as well as one of Modigliani's elongated reclining nudes.

Gallery 9: Monet, Water Lilies.

Between the early 1890s and the end of his life in 1926, Monet was preoccupied with painting the pond in his garden at Giverny, rendering the surface of the water, the water lilies, and the reflections of the trees and sky as faithfully as possible under different conditions of light. The museum's triptych, *Water Lilies* (1914–26) and the additional panel are the largest holding of the *Water Lilies* outside France. Also on view are *The Japanese Footbridge* (c. 1920–2) and *Agapanthus* (1918–26).

Gallery 11: Picasso: The 1930s and 1940s.

In the 1930s Picasso turned to biomorphic shapes and softer colors; among his paintings of women

from this period are the Surrealistic and disturbing *Seated Bather* (1930), followed by *Girl before a Mirror* (1932) and *Interior with a Girl Drawing* (1935). Sculptures include *Head of a Woman* (1932) and *Head of a Warrior* (1933). Also on view: *Night Fishing at Antibes* (1939) and *The Kitchen* (1948), painted on the 30th anniversary of the death of his friend Apollinaire.

Galleries 12–14. These contain examples of mostly figurative work that challenged the status quo. In Gallery 12, devoted to Surrealism, are such iconic works as Salvador Dalí's *The Persistence of Memory* (1931), Joan Miró's *The Birth of the World* (1925), and Meret Oppenheim's fur cup, *Objet (Le Déjeuner en fourrure)* (1936). Sprawled on a low pedestal is Alberto Giacometti's insectivorous *Woman with Her Throat Cut* (1932), still shocking.

Gallery 13: Mexican Modernism.

Displayed here are paintings by Social Realists José Clemente Orozco and David Alfaro Siqueiros, and the less overtly political Rufino Tamayo.

Gallery 14: Expressionism. Ludwig Kirchner was a chief exponent of the modernism that developed in Germany and Austria during the early years of the 20th century. Like his contemporaries, Kirchner was drawn to urban life. His *Street, Dresden* (1908), with two women—presumably prostitutes—captures the city's nightmarish quality in its garish colors. Also on view are Kandinsky's four panels commissioned for the apartment of Edwin R. Campbell (a founder of Chevrolet Motor Company), abstractions painted in swirling vibrant color.

FOURTH FLOOR

Works displayed here roughly span the years 1940–80, emphasizing stylistic movements such as Abstract Expressionism, Pop Art, Minimalism, and Conceptual Art. MoMA's collection of New York painters from the 1940s and '50s is exceptional.

Galleries 15–17: New York Painters, 1940s. Here are works by painters from the era when the center of avant-garde art moved from Paris to New York. Among Jackson Pollock's earlier works is *Stenographic Figure* (1942), remarkably bright for an artist whose palette was generally somber; *Full Fathom Five* (1947) is the earliest of his "drip paintings," in whose thickly built-up surface small objects are embedded: a key, cigarette butts, buttons, and coins.

Helen Frankenthaler's *Jacob's Ladder* (1957) was painted in the manner of Pollock: canvas on the floor, paint poured from above—paint so thin, it soaked into the canvas giving the color a transparent quality. Franz Kline's *Chief* (1950) is a powerful black-and-white abstract of a locomotive remembered from childhood. Willem de Kooning's *Woman, I* (1950–2) is one of his best-known and most disturbing works, marking a return to figural painting after experiments with abstraction—for example *Painting* (1948), purchased by MoMA at de Kooning's first solo show.

Also here are works by Max Ernst, Roberto Matta, and Joseph Cornell. Mondrian's *Broadway Boogie Woogie* (1942–3), one of his last paintings, attempts to abstract the frantic energy of the urban scene—specifically New York, where Mondrian had arrived during World War II. The artist theorized that American jazz, with its de-emphasis of traditional melody and stress on rhythm, was the musical equivalent of what he was trying to achieve visually.

Gallery 17 displays Pollock's classic "drip" paintings. *Number 1A, 1948* is one of his largest. Pollock's contemporaries, classified as Abstract Expressionists but whose work illustrates a variety of approaches, include Ad Reinhardt, Barnett Newman, and Mark Rothko.

Galleries 18–19: Mid-1950s–early 1960s. Works here show a return to representational art, sometimes incorporating found objects or imagery. Included are Robert Rauschenberg's *"Combines": Bed* (1955) and *Canyon* (1959), which incorporates a stuffed bald eagle, found by a fellow artist in a hallway in the Carnegie Hall studio building.

New York City was the center of Pop Art, a subversive response to the elitism of Abstract Expressionism. MoMA has Andy Warhol's iconic *Gold Marilyn Monroe* (1962) and his *Campbell's Soup Cans* (1962); Roy Lichtenstein's *Drowning Girl* (1963) and *Girl with Ball* (1961), as well as soft sculptures by Claes Oldenburg and examples of the fragmented images of James Rosenquist.

Galleries 20–23: Minimalism and Conceptualism. On view here are works of impersonal austerity, often constructed of industrially processed or machine-made materials, sometimes incorporating language in the form of painted words. Included are the monochrome paintings of Robert Ryman, who by the 1960s restricted himself to white paint; Donald Judd's *Relief* (1961), a black rectangle with a metal baking pan inserted in the middle; and Sol LeWitt's *Standing Open Structure, Black* (1964), a wooden rectangle created by an artist who remarked that what a work of art looks like "isn't too important."

Conceptual Art includes Marcel Broodthaer's *General with Cigar* (1970), in which the artist poked a hole in a portrait found in the trash and inserted a half-smoked cigar into its mouth; and Carl Andre's *Equivalent V* (1966–9), an arrangement of 120 bricks on the floor.

Galleries 24–26

The first room shows art of Germany in the 1970s and '80s (Anselm Kiefer, Gerhard Richter). The next section, New Approaches to Painting in the 1970s, includes such disparate works as Sam Gilliam's color-washed *10/27/69* (1969), Lynda Benglis's wax reliefs, and Elizabeth Murray's boldly colored *Southern California* (1976). The third section is devoted to Joseph Beuys. Gallery 26 focuses on Latin American Artists 1951–81.

THIRD FLOOR

On this floor are changing selections from the collections of architecture and design, drawings, and photography, as well as special exhibitions. The design collection focuses on mass-produced utilitarian objects created to serve a specific need, while the architectural archives include models and photographs of buildings as well as architectural drawings, including the Mies van der Rohe Archive.

Objects in the design collection include pillboxes, nylon tents, vacuum cleaners, Tiffany lamps, self-aligning ball bearings, and an entrance arch to the Paris Métro (in the Sculpture Garden). Among the chairs are the Gerrit Rietveld "Red and Blue" chair and Le Corbusier's tubular steel armchair. Among the most memorable objects are a Bell-47D1 helicopter (in the main stairwell) and a World War II US Army Jeep.

Works on paper include drawings in pencil, ink and charcoal, as well as watercolors, gouaches, collages, and works in mixed media. The photography collection dates from c. 1840 to the present and includes work by artists, journalists, scientists, and amateurs.

SECOND FLOOR

The contemporary galleries, their 22-ft ceilings allowing for the installation of large-scale works, are devoted to artists working after about 1970. Shows here, changing about every nine months, may feature monumental works, extensive retrospectives, or performance art.

GROUND FLOOR

The **Abby Aldrich Rockefeller Sculpture Garden** (*closed during inclement weather*) is one of the city's beloved oases and a touchstone of American landscape architecture. Now restored to Philip Johnson's 1953 design, the 19,000 square-ft courtyard with reflecting pools, greenery, and seating, displays favorite examples of figurative and abstract sculpture, such as Picasso's *She-Goat* (1950, cast 1952), Gaston Lachaise's *Standing Woman* (1932), and Joan Miró's *Moonbird* (1966). According to Rodin, his massive, nine-foot *Monument to Balzac* (1898, this casting 1954) was intended to capture not the author's physical appearance but his artistic vitality.

IN THE NEIGHBORHOOD

ST. THOMAS CHURCH

Map p. 617, D2. 1 West 53rd St (Fifth Ave). Hours vary, but generally open Mon–Fri 7:30–6:30, Sat mornings and afternoons. Guided tour after the 11am Sun service. Self-guided tour pamphlets inside the Fifth Ave doors. T: 212 757 7013, saintthomaschurch.org.

Protestant Episcopal St. Thomas Church—picturesque, asymmetrical, and French Gothic in antecedents—triumphs over its cramped corner location. It was originally built (1914) without steel, following the principles of Ralph Adams Cram (architect of St. John the Divine), who believed that if a church were Gothic in style it should be Gothic in construction, its columns supporting its weight. However, eleven years after completion, with the unbuttressed north wall bulging dangerously, steel beams were placed across the columns above the ceiling. Later, during blasting for the subway under 53rd St, a steel beam was installed under the altar. The church is known for its exceptional music programs, including choral services and organ recitals. During the Gilded Age, wealthy people married one another at the first St. Thomas Church built on this site, most notably Consuelo Vanderbilt, who was forced by her socially ambitious mother to marry Charles Spencer-Churchill, the Ninth Duke of Marlborough.

The exterior

Bertram G. Goodhue (architect of St. Bartholomew's on Park Ave) planned the limestone façade, notable for its single corner tower. Above the double entrance doors a gilded relief depicts the four buildings in which the congregation has worshiped: on Houston St, on Broadway, and the last two here. The central figure between the two doors is St. Thomas, and above the left-hand door are depictions of his *Despair* and *Doubt*. Left of the main portal is the Bride's Entrance; above the doorway some observers have discerned a stylized dollar sign, whose presence recalls either medieval times, when carpenters and stoneworkers left social commentary in obscure corners; or the church's Gilded Age ambiance, when Fifth Avenue was still Vanderbilt territory.

The interior

Statues of more than 60 saints, apostles, churchmen, divines, and political leaders adorn the remarkable 80-ft reredos of ivory-colored Dunville stone (from Ohio). Lee Lawrie, known for his work at Rockefeller Center, Goodhue, the church's architect, designed it, though the central portion of kneeling angels adoring the Cross was copied from a smaller reredos by Augustus Saint-Gaudens in the previous church on this site (burned 1905). Below the Cross, in the central carved canopy immediately above the altar, is a kneeling figure of St. Thomas.

In the chancel, designs on the carved panels on the kneeling rail in front of the choir stalls represent historical events and fields of human endeavor. From the left they are: Christopher Columbus's ship, Theodore Roosevelt, Lee Lawrie (between the steamship and the telephone), a radio, and representations of *Finance* (with the initials of J. Pierpont Morgan) and *Medicine*.

PALEY PARK

At 3 East 53rd St small, serene **Paley Park** (1967; landscape architects Zion & Breen) is planted with ivy and honey locust trees. At its end the white noise of a "waterfall" obliterates the dissonance of traffic. Before William S. Paley donated the park in memory of his father Samuel, the Stork Club, a nightclub beloved of café society and gossip columnists, stood here.

In the lobby of **520 Madison Ave** stands a segment of the Berlin Wall, purchased in 1990 from the German government by Jerry I. Speyer, whose real estate firm owns the building. The monstrous red and yellow faces were painted during the 1980s by artists Thierry Noir and Kiddy Citny (*for another segment by Noir, see p. 60*).

WEST 54TH STREET

At 1 West 54th St, the **University Club of New York** (chartered 1865) occupies a grand McKim, Mead & White neo-Italian palazzo (1896–1900), built at a time when socially prominent men belonged to as many as 16 clubs (and spent in dues what the average worker earned in a year). Above the main door is a head of Athena modeled after a statuette owned by Stanford White. The interior (*not open to the public*) is remarkable for its opulent decoration: hallways paved with marble, ceiling paintings by H. Siddons Mowbray (of Morgan Library fame), pilasters of Italian walnut.

When St. Luke's Hospital vacated **West 54th Street** in 1896, new dwellings began to rise on both sides. Five adjoining houses (*nos. 5–14*) from this period, designed by prestigious architects in styles ranging from Georgian Revival to French Beaux-Arts, have been landmarked (most now occupied by businesses). Financier Robert Lehman lived at no. 7; his art collection is now exhibited in the Metropolitan Museum of Art in a wing that replicates some of the rooms (*see p. 352*). The Rockefellers owned houses at nos. 13 and 15; Governor Nelson Rockefeller installed his Museum of Primitive Art, much of it donated to the Metropolitan, at no. 15, and died in 1979 at no. 13.

The **Rockefeller Apartments** (1936) occupy the site of the senior John D. Rockefeller's townhouse at 17 West 54th St. An experiment in middle-class housing financed by John D. Rockefeller Jr., the buildings, designed by Harrison & Fouilhoux, run through the block, back to back, with a central garden between to admit light but not noise to the rear bedrooms. Because the cylindrical bays were designed as "dinettes," their windows face away from one another, insuring privacy.

WEST 55TH TO WEST 57TH STREETS

At 2 East 55th St is the **St. Regis Hotel** (1904; addition, 1925; Trowbridge & Livingston), a venture of John Jacob Astor IV (1864–1912), who realized from his experience with the Waldorf-Astoria that expensive hotels in fine residential neighborhoods could attract a clientele eager for proximity to social splendor. Astor is said to have named the place after Upper St. Regis Lake in the Adirondacks, where many of New York's elite had summer "camps"; St. Regis himself was a French monk and the patron saint of hospitality to travelers. The Beaux-Arts exterior is elaborated with stone garlands, a mansard roof with bull's-eye windows and copper cresting, and on 55th St, a brass and glass kiosk for the top-hatted doormen. Inside, Astor provided automatic thermostats in every room, a system for heating, cooling, moistening, or drying the air (predating air conditioning), 47 Steinway pianos, a service of gold-plated flatware, and other decorative touches that cost him $1.5 million. Once famous for its restaurants, including a palm room where members of both sexes could smoke publicly at all hours, the St. Regis is now known for the King Cole Bar with Maxfield Parrish's mural (1906) of the jolly old soul holding court (originally commissioned for another Astor enterprise, the Knickerbocker Hotel in Times Square).

At 718 Fifth Ave (*56th St*) is **Harry Winston, Inc.**, the famous jewelry store. Winston (1896–1978), the son of an immigrant who ran a modest jewelry sales and repair shop on Columbus Ave, eventually came to own some of the world's most famous jewels, including the 44.5-carat Hope diamond (a relic of the French Crown Jewels), which he donated to the Smithsonian Institution. He sent the diamond to the museum by registered mail. "If you can't trust the US mails," he asked, "who can you trust?"

Standing 58 stories tall at 725 Fifth Ave (*East 56th and East 57th Sts*) is **Trump Tower** (1983), a project of real estate entrepreneur Donald Trump. Designed by Der Scutt of Swanke Hayden Connell, the building's six-story marble-faced atrium provides an opulent setting for shops, including those selling Trump-branded items. The tower replaced Bonwit Teller, a women's apparel store that moved here in 1930.

A SIDE TRIP TO MADISON AVENUE

Just behind (and accessible from) Trump Tower is one of Midtown's most pleasant oases, the **atrium of the former IBM Building**. Sold by IBM 1994, the 403-ft block-long building (1983; Edward Larrabee Barnes, Assocs), also known as **590 Madison Avenue** (East 56th and East 57th Sts), is distinguished by its shape (a five-sided prism, like a triangle with two points sliced off), its dramatic cantilevered corner entrance, and its 68-ft atrium. Covered with a saw-toothed glass roof and brightened with greenery, the atrium offers seating, a kiosk for snacks (plus an Italian eatery), and changing art exhibits. Just outside, at the corner of 56th St and Madison Ave, is Michael Heizer's sculptural fountain, *Levitated Mass* (1982), under which sluices a torrent of water. At the corner of East 57th St and Madison Ave is Alexander Calder's bright red *Saurien* (1975).

The former Sony Building (1984; Philip Johnson & John Burgee) at **550 Madison Avenue** (*map p. 617, D2*), raised eyebrows when its design was made public in 1979, prompting jokes about its Chippendale top and questions about the architect's seriousness. Today the 648-ft tower is praised for its monumental proportions (the 131ft pedestal over which the building rises), its materials (the rose-gray granite masonry base), its majestic entrance (which originally showcased Evelyn Beatrice Longman's *Spirit of Communication*), and its public spaces. It is also considered a game changer—a pioneer of postmodernism—for its materials (stone, not glass and steel) and classically derived forms (the split pediment and the Renaissance-style arcaded base).

FIFTH AVENUE AND 57TH STREET

At the southeast corner of 57th St is **Tiffany & Company** (*727 Fifth Ave*), the famous jewelry store. It was founded by Charles L. Tiffany (1812–1902), father of the better-known Louis Comfort Tiffany, a designer of stained glass, jewelry, enamels, and interiors. The firm moved to this (relatively) modest granite palazzo from a fancier palace on 37th St and Fifth Ave. Famous for its window displays, it offers one-stop shopping for diamonds, jewelry, silver, china, and other luxury goods.

On the southwest corner of 57th St (*730 Fifth Ave*) the **Crown Building** (1921; Warren & Wetmore), originally the Heckscher Building, was the first tower (25 stories) to invade upper Fifth Avenue and the first office building constructed after the Zoning Resolution of 1916 (*see p. 71*). The Museum of Modern Art had its modest beginnings here in 1929, when its founders rented space on the 12th floor for loan exhibitions.

BERGDORF GOODMAN AND THE PLAZA

Cornelius Vanderbilt II, grandson of the Commodore and father of Gertrude Vanderbilt Whitney, built his mansion on the west side of Fifth Avenue (*57th and 58th Sts*), where Bergdorf Goodman now stands. The 137-room castle, filling the whole block with peaks, gables, dormers, and other Victorian extravagances, was the largest private residence ever built in New York City.

Like so many of the city's other luxury stores, Bergdorf Goodman had humble beginnings. Herman Bergdorf, a tailor skillful at adapting men's suits to the female figure, founded the firm, but Edwin Goodman, who bought out Bergdorf in 1901, raised the store to its present heights, moving it in 1928 to this white marble building. The store is known for its luxury clothing and accessories, its fur collection, and its service.

GRAND ARMY PLAZA

Popularly known as "the Plaza," Grand Army Plaza (*west side of Fifth Ave from 58th to 60th Sts*) commemorates the Union army during the Civil War. The open square, one of the few deviations from the city's gridiron plan, provides a site for the **Pulitzer Memorial Fountain** (Carrère & Hastings), built in 1916 with a $50,000 bequest from newspaper publisher Joseph Pulitzer (1847–1911), who wanted fountains "as far as possible like those in the Place de la Concorde." The fountain is surmounted by Karl Bitter's statue of Pomona, Roman goddess of orchards and, by extension, abundance—an appropriate virtue for a neighborhood dominated by the Plaza Hotel and Bergdorf's. Bitter, a protégé of Richard Morris Hunt, was killed by a car in 1915 as he was leaving the Metropolitan Opera; his studio assistants completed the statue from Bitter's clay model.

On the northern half of the Plaza, on the west side of Fifth Avenue and north of Central Park South, is the **Sherman Monument**, Augustus Saint-Gaudens's equestrian statue (1892–1903) of General William Tecumseh Sherman, remembered for his brutal "scorched earth" sweep through Georgia. An allegorical *Victory* walks before the conqueror waving a palm branch; the fallen pine branch on the granite pedestal (Charles Follen McKim) signifies Georgia.

The northernmost extension of Grand Army Plaza, **Doris Chanin Freedman Plaza**, named for the city's first Director of Cultural Affairs, frequently hosts exhibitions of contemporary sculpture. Freedman (1928–81), a pioneer supporter of public art and daughter of Irwin S. Chanin (*see p. 251*), spearheaded the Percent for Art legislation of 1982, whereby developers of certain city-funded construction projects must allocate one percent of the capital budget to art.

THE PLAZA HOTEL

Facing the plaza between 58th and 59th Sts is the Plaza Hotel (1907), the second on this site. Architect Henry J. Hardenbergh has long been admired for his skill in manipulating the details of its French Renaissance design—dormers, balustrades, high roofs, and rounded corner turnings—to create a harmonious whole. In the past two decades this celebrated hotel has changed ownership several times and has undergone several renovations and the conversion of some rooms to condos. The Plaza is as famous for its guests as for its site—overlooking Central Park and Fifth Avenue—its architecture, and its luxury. The first guests to sign the register were "Mr. & Mrs. Alfred G. Vanderbilt and servant"; since that day Mark Twain, Groucho Marx, and the Beatles have enjoyed its hospitality. Frank Lloyd Wright maintained a suite there for five years—he called it Taliesin East—while he supervised construction of the Guggenheim Museum. Truman Capote held his famous Black and White Ball there in 1966; and the six-year-old fictional Eloise, whose portrait hangs in the lobby, cavorted in its halls.

On the east side of Fifth Ave is the **former General Motors Building** (1968; Edward Durell Stone and Emery Roth & Sons), a 50-story, white marble-clad building. In front, a glass cube serves as a come-on to the Apple Store, which replaces an unloved sunken plaza.

EATING AND DRINKING IN MIDTOWN

$$$$ **Aquavit.** ■ Modernistic Scandinavian food in a sleek formal setting. Lunch weekdays, dinner Mon–Sat. *65 East 55th St (Madison and Park Aves). T: 212 307 7311, aquavit.org. Map p. 617, D2.*

$$$$ **Caviar Russe.** Any restaurant with "caviar" in the name is bound to be expensive, but this Michelin-starred upstairs hideaway does not disappoint with its European cooking and, yes, caviar. The tasting menus include a caviar version. Lunch and dinner daily, brunch Sun. *538 Madison Ave (54th and 55th Sts). T: 212 980 5908, caviarrusse.com. Map p. 617, D2.*

$$$$ **La Grenouille.** Founded in 1962, La Grenouille, with its legendary floral arrangements, is the last of New York's *haute-cuisine* restaurants and is still much admired. Its continued existence pays tribute to its fine French cooking and

patrician graciousness. Lunch and dinner Tues–Sat. *3 East 52nd St (Fifth and Madison Aves). T: 212 752 1495, la-grenouille.com. Map p. 617, D3.*

$$$$ Le Bernardin. A Michelin three-star restaurant, Le Bernardin has been serving exquisite, beautifully prepared seafood since 1986. The service equals the food. Lunch Mon–Fri, dinner Mon–Sat. *155 West 51st St (Sixth and Seventh Aves). T: 212 554 1515, le-bernardin.com. Map p. 616, C3.*

$$$ Bice. Part of the far-flung Bice empire founded in Milan in 1926, the New York outpost serves consistently good Northern Italian food in a chic setting. Lunch and dinner daily. *7 East 54th St (Fifth and Madison Aves). T: 212 688 1999, bicenewyork.com. Map p. 617, D2.*

$$$ Brasserie Ruhlmann. Good French food in Art Deco surroundings, with superb people-watching, especially from the patio. Lunch daily, dinner Mon–Sat. *45 Rockefeller Plaza (Fifth and Sixth Aves). T: 212 974 2020, brasserieruhlmann.com. Map p. 617, D3.*

$$$ Má Pêche. The big uptown cousin of the popular Momofuku restaurants in the East Village. Lounge, raw bar, and a branch of Momofuku Milk Bar. Breakfast, brunch, lunch, and dinner daily. *In the Chambers Hotel, 15 West 56th St (Fifth and Sixth Aves). T: 212 757 5878, momofuku.com. Map p. 617, D2.*

$$$ The Modern. MoMA's Michelin-starred restaurant combines a great location (overlooking the sculpture garden) with great design and outstanding food. The Bar Room is equally good (though without the view) and less expensive. Lunch Mon–Fri, dinner Mon–Sat. Bar Room also open Sun. *9 West 53rd St (Fifth and Sixth Aves). T: 212 333 1220, themodernnyc.com. Map p. 617, D2.*

$$$ Oceana. In the file of glassy skyscrapers just west of Rockefeller Center, Oceana draws an affluent crowd. Opinion is mixed on the modernistic décor, but the raw bar, the wine list, and the seafood draw applause. There's a pleasant bar, too. Breakfast and lunch weekdays, dinner nightly. *120 West 49th St (Sixth Ave). T:212 759 5941, oceanarestaurant.com. Map p. 616, C3.*

$$ Obicà. A welcome addition to the glassy atrium of the former IBM buiding, Obicà (the name means "Here it is!" in Neapolitan Italian) features fresh handmade mozzarella. Along with the cheese and its accompaniments, you can get pizza, salads, and sweets. Breakfast, lunch and dinner daily. *590 Madison Ave (56th St). T: 212 355 2217, obica.com. Map p. 617, D2.*

$$ PizzArte. Pizza and Neapolitan cooking in a gallery setting. Lunch and dinner daily. *69 West 55th St (Fifth and Sixth Aves). T: 212 247 3936, pizzarteny.com. Map p. 617, D2.*

$$ Remi. ■ Lively Italian restaurant with a glass-topped atrium not far from MoMA. Pasta made in-house, good salads. Lunch weekdays, dinner nightly. *145 West 53rd St (Sixth and Seventh Aves). T: 212 581 4242, remi-nyc.com. Map p. 616, C3.*

Central Park

The heartland of Manhattan, Central Park encompasses 843 acres set aside for New Yorkers and visitors, enjoyed by 40 million people annually.

Although Central Park seems "natural"—the largest surviving piece of Manhattan unencrusted with asphalt and masonry—its landscape and scenery are completely man-made, based on designs by Frederick Law Olmsted (*see p. 309*) and Calvert Vaux (*see p. 314*). Strolling around its peaceful, verdant lawns and slopes today, it is hard to believe that in the mid-19th century, before the adoption of Olmsted and Vaux's Greensward Plan, the area was desolate, covered with scrubby trees, rocky outcroppings, and occasional fields where squatters grazed their pigs and goats. A garbage dump, a bone-boiling works, and a rope walk added their own atmosphere.

Park information and maps
Open 6am–1am all year; park drives closed to vehicular traffic on weekends, major holidays, and weekdays during non-rush hours. For a map of the park, see pp. 310–11. Free Central Park Conservancy map available at the Visitor Centers or online at centralparknyc.org/maps; GPS-enabled app also available online. Information kiosks, open Apr–Nov, at Sixth Ave, West 72nd St, and East 72nd St entrances.

Visitor Centers
Chess and Checkers House: *Mid-park, 64th St. Open Nov–March Wed–Sun 10–5; April–Oct Tues–Sun 10–5; T: 212 794 4064.*
Dairy: *Mid-park, 65th St. Open daily 10–5, except Thanksgiving, Christmas, and New Year's Day; T: 212 794 6564.*
Belvedere Castle: *Mid-park, 79th St. Open daily 10–5, except Thanksgiving, Christmas, and New Year's Day; T: 212 772 0288.*
Charles A. Dana Discovery Center: *Inside the park at 110th St between Fifth and Lenox Aves. Open daily 10–5, except Thanksgiving, Christmas, and New Year's Day; T: 212 860 1370.*

Park tours
Free guided Welcome Tours cover park highlights; ticketed Premier Tours focus on

particular topics. The **NYC Department of Parks & Recreation** *offers information about park events: nycgovparks.org. For park info, T: 311 from New York City, or 212 639 9675 from outside New York City. The* **Urban Park Rangers** *patrol the park, assist visitors, and offer park tours and nature programs; T: 212 628 2345.*

Safety

Central Park is generally safe but avoid wandering in remote areas, especially at night. Be aware of speeding cyclists. Emergency call-boxes located throughout are connected directly with the Central Park Police Precinct on the 86th Street Transverse; T: 212 570 4820.

Finding your way

The first two digits on the metal plate attached to most park lampposts (some have disappeared) tell the approximate cross street: thus 06413 means 106th St and 70235 means 70th St. The odd-numbered final digits are on the west side of the park, and the even ones on the east.

Refreshments and restrooms

Informal restaurant service year round at **Loeb Boathouse** *and the* **Zoo**. *Full-service restaurants:* **Tavern on the Green** *(Central Park West at 67th St, T: 212 877 8684; tavernonthegreen.com) and* **Le Pain Quotidien** *(in the Mineral Springs pavilion, mid-park near 69th St, T: 646 233 3768; lepainquotidien.com). In warm weather refreshments available from carts, and at the Merchants' Gate Plaza, the Ballplayers' House, Harlem Meer, Lasker Rink, and North Meadow snack bars.* **Rest rooms** *are located throughout the park near playgrounds and recreational facilities. Open all year: Delacorte Theater, Charles A. Dana Discovery Center, Hesckscher Playground, Ramble Shed, North Meadow Recreation Center, Conservatory Garden, Ancient Playground (85th St near Fifth Ave).*

Sports and activities

Bicycling: *Bicycles for rent in season, weather permitting, at the Loeb Boathouse (northeast corner of the Lake at 74th St, rental bikes available daily 10–6; T: 212 517 2233, thecentralparkboathuse.com) or at Bike and Roll at Tavern on the Green and at Merchants' Gate Plaza near Columbus Circle (T: 212 260 0400, bikenewyorkcity.com). Or try the Master Bike Shop (265 West 72nd St between Broadway and West End Ave; T: 212 580 2355, masterbikeshop.com).*
Boating: *Rowboats for rent in season at the Loeb Boathouse; cash only, plus deposit. Gondola rides spring–fall; reserve at T: 212 517 2233, thecentralparkboathouse.com.*
Carriage rides: *Grand Army Plaza, 5th or 6th Aves at 59th St; or reserve online at centralpark.com.*
Ice skating: *Wollman Rink, also known as Trump Rink (mid-park near 63rd St), late Oct–early April. Open 10am, closing times vary. Admission charge. T: 212 439 6900, wollmanskatingrink.com. Lasker Rink, near 110th St and Fifth Ave, open seasonally 10am weekdays, later on weekends; for information, laskerrink.com.*

HISTORY OF CENTRAL PARK

In 1844 poet William Cullen Bryant (among others) began calling for a public park, observing that commerce was devouring great chunks of Manhattan and the population sweeping over the rest. Andrew Jackson Downing, an architect and the pre-eminent landscape designer of the period, added his voice as did several politicians, and in 1856 the City bought most of what is now the park for $5 million. Egbert Viele, a graduate of West Point and a civil engineer, was hired to survey the land and to supervise its clearing; he was aided by the police, who forcibly ejected the squatters and their livestock.

The board of Park Commissioners (established 1857) arranged a design competition for the park in part because Andrew Jackson Downing—who probably would have been chosen—had recently drowned in a steamboat accident. Among 33 entries, the Greensward Plan (1858) by Olmsted and Vaux was chosen, a plan based on enhancing existing land contours to heighten the picturesque, dramatic qualities of the landscape. During the initial 20 years of construction, ten million cartloads of dirt were shifted and half a million cubic yards of topsoil were spread over the existing poor soil (some of it recovered from the organic refuse of the garbage dump); four-to-five million trees, shrubs, and vines were planted—numbering almost 1,500 species between them. Sixty-two miles of ceramic pipe were laid to drain marshy areas and to supply water to lawns where hydrants were installed.

The Greensward Plan also incorporated the existing Arsenal and the Croton reservoirs, rectangular receiving pools for the aqueduct system that brought water from the Catskills. Curving drives were designed to keep would-be horse racers in check, while straight transverse roads recessed below ground level took crosstown traffic unobtrusively through the park. North of the reservoir site (later filled in to become the Great Lawn) the land was high and rocky with good views, and the designers chose to leave this area as wild as possible. South of the reservoir long, rocky, glacial ridges running north–south would be changed into open meadows, shady glens, and gently sloping hills. The formal element was to consist of a mall, an avenue of trees with a fountain at one end and statuary along its length.

Created at a time of increasing social unrest following the first great wave of immigration, the park was intended for the relief of working people as well as for the amusement of the wealthy. As a public works project it employed several thousand laborers, but unfortunately attracted politicians who saw in its labor-intensive landscape a golden opportunity for patronage (controlling immigrant votes) and for letting out lucrative contracts to cronies in the building trades.

Even before its completion the park was a target for unwanted encroachments, beginning with a racing track for horses, which Olmsted blocked. Whereas an airplane field (1919), trenches to memorialize World War I (1918), an underground garage for thousands of cars (1921 and frequently thereafter), and a statue of Buddha (1925) have not materialized, paved playgrounds, skating rinks, a swimming pool, a theater, and a zoo have taken up park land. Robert Moses, parks commissioner from the La Guardia era to 1960, advocated organized sports, accepted several buildings donated by

CENTRAL PARK
The ornate underpass at Bethesda Terrace, its ceiling decorated with
Minton tiles designed by Jacob Wrey Mould. The painted, round-arched recesses
in the side walls are also Mould's design.

philanthropists, and tore down structures of Olmsted's vintage, replacing them with boxy brick buildings. The present park environment thus represents a compromise between Olmsted's vision of pastoral serenity and modern interests in sports and recreation.

After the iron-fisted Robert Moses left office, the park—without an effective management strategy for maintaining either its landscape or its facilities—slid into disrepair, the Great Lawn trampled to Dust Bowl status, the Bethesda Terrace defaced with graffiti, and the Pond filled with beer cans. Crime, rising since the 1960s, was feverishly reported in the press so that in the minds of many, Central Park had become a forsaken and lawless place. The City's fiscal crisis in the 1970s only worsened matters.

In 1980 the Central Park Conservancy, a public-private, not-for-profit partnership, was founded to take control of an apparently hopeless situation. Since its inception the Conservancy has raised nearly $700 million and has restored major landscape areas—the Great Lawn, Harlem Meer, Reservoir, and Sheep Meadow—as well as buildings, bridges, and playgrounds. Today, under contract with the City, it maintains the park, raising 75 percent of the park's $58.3 million operating budget.

FREDERICK LAW OLMSTED

Frederick Law Olmsted (1822–1903) had trouble deciding on a career but when he did, he changed the face of the urban landscape—in New York and elsewhere. As a young man he moved from job to job: he sailed to China as an apprentice, clerked in a store, dabbled in scientific farming, and settled (he thought) on journalism. Between 1852 and 1857, he traveled the South, reporting on the moral and economic effects of slavery. By the time he embarked on his ultimate career, landscape design, his social views were well formed.

Olmsted's opposition to slavery extended to a belief in egalitarianism and faith in education as a tool for social equality. Education would not only give the "lower classes" the skills of reading and writing, but would teach "taste" as well, by which he meant civility and the attainment of a certain cultural level. This education "to refinement and taste" would improve "the mental and moral capital" of the learners.

In 1850 he had traveled to England where he visited Birkenhead Park, the first public park developed with government funds. In a magazine article thereafter, he noted that the park was enjoyed "about equally by all classes...some who were attended by servants...and a large proportion of the common ranks, and a few women with children... [who] were evidently the wives of very humble laborers." He also commented that "in democratic America there was nothing...comparable with this People's Garden."

The design of Central Park embodies Olmsted's social consciousness and his belief in a common green space accessible to all, a novel idea at a time when most parks were either former estates that had been given to a city, or gardens of the wealthy open occasionally to the public. Olmsted had noted the dehumanizing effects of the "modern" city, where many people were forced to live "with heart-hardening and taste-smothering habits." He saw the park as a counterpoise to the artificiality of the built-up city, a restorative to the stress of urban life, and an educational life force.

CENTRAL PARK: 59TH–72ND STREETS

Subway: 4, 5, 6 to 59th St; N, R to 5th Ave. Bus: M1, M2, M3, M4, M20, M104.

CENTRAL PARK SOUTH

Along the southern edge of the park (*Central Park South at Sixth Ave*) stand three **equestrian statues of South American liberators (1)**. Nearest Fifth Avenue is Simón Bolívar (1919; Sally James Farnham), who fought Spanish domination in South America. Facing straight down Sixth Avenue is Anna Hyatt Huntington's 1959 rendering of José Julián Martí, completed when the sculptor was 83 years old. Martí, a Cuban poet and intellectual (his "Versos Sencillos" were adapted as the popular song "Guantanamera"), organized Cuba's liberation from Spain while exiled in New York and returned to his homeland in 1895, where he was mortally wounded in a skirmish

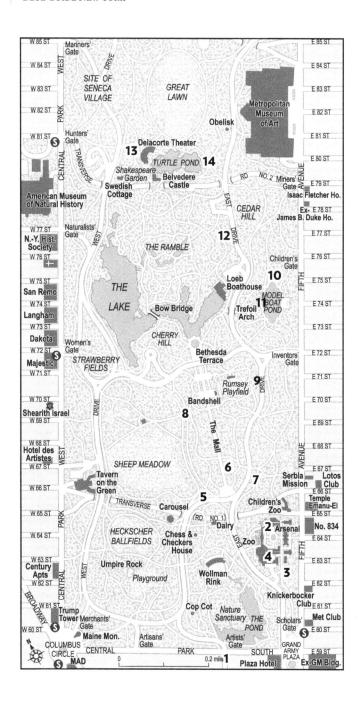

W 85 ST   Mariners' Gate   E 85 ST

W 84 ST

SITE OF SENECA VILLAGE

GREAT LAWN

Metropolitan Museum of Art

Obelisk

Hunters' Gate

Delacorte Theater

13

TURTLE POND

14

Shakespeare Garden

Belvedere Castle

Swedish Cottage

American Museum of Natural History

Miners' Gate

Isaac Fletcher Ho.

Ex- James B. Duke Ho.

CEDAR HILL

Naturalists' Gate

N.-Y. Hist. Society

THE RAMBLE

12

Children's Gate

San Remo

THE LAKE

Loeb Boathouse

10

Langham

Bow Bridge

MODEL BOAT POND

11

Trefoil Arch

Dakota

CHERRY HILL

Women's Gate

Majestic

STRAWBERRY FIELDS

Bethesda Terrace

Inventors' Gate

Shearith Israel

Rumsey Playfield

9

Bandshell

Hotel des Artistes

8

SHEEP MEADOW

The Mall

6

Tavern on the Green

7

Serbia Mission

Lotos Club

TRANSVERSE

Carousel

5

Children's Zoo

Temple Emanu-El

HECKSCHER BALLFIELDS

Chess & Checkers House

NO. 1

Dairy

2

Arsenal

No. 834

Zoo

4

Century Apts

Umpire Rock

Playground

Wollman Rink

3

Trump Tower

Maine Mon.

Merchants' Gate

Cop Cot

Nature Sanctuary

THE POND

Knickerbocker Club

Met Club

Scholars' Gate

COLUMBUS CIRCLE

MAD

Artisans' Gate

Artists' Gate

SOUTH

GRAND ARMY PLAZA

Plaza Hotel

Ex-GM Bldg.

0   0.2 mile   1

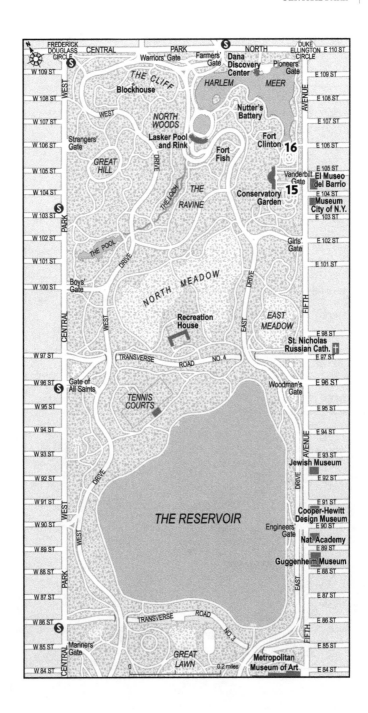

that marked the opening of Cuba's war for independence. Dressed in civilian attire, he clutches his wound, about to topple from his horse. To the west is José de San Martín (c. 1950; Luis J. Daunas), who led the revolt of Argentina, Chile, and Peru against Spain. The intersection of Central Park South and Sixth Avenue (officially renamed The Avenue of the Americas in 1945) is known (also officially) as Bolívar Plaza.

THE PARK ENTRANCES

In 1862 the Central Park Board of Commissioners issued a report that outlined a program for naming the park's 18 entrances after the industrial and intellectual pursuits of the day. Until the 20th century, the Inventors' Gate (*72nd St and Fifth Ave*), Mariners' Gate (*85th St and Central Park West*), Engineers' Gate (*90th St and Fifth Ave*), and one additional gate not planned in the original draft, the 76th St Gate, now the Children's Gate (*76th St and Fifth Ave*), were the only ones inscribed. During the fall and winter of 1999–2000, the Conservancy and City inscribed the remaining 14 blank entrances with the names originally proposed, including Merchants' Gate (*59th St and Central Park West*), Miners' Gate (*79th St and Fifth Ave*), Pioneers' Gate (*110th St and Fifth Ave*), Farmers' Gate (*110th St and Lenox Ave*), and others.

THE POND AND WOLLMAN RINK

The **Pond** at the southeast corner of the park was transformed by Vaux and Olmsted from swampland inhabited by a few impoverished immigrant families to a peaceful miniature lake. Real swans once glided across the waters, along with swan boats until 1924. The swans have largely been replaced by ducks, occasionally geese and egrets, and on the periphery, plenty of pigeons. **Hallett Nature Sanctuary**, just south of Wollman Rink, is a rocky landscape filled with native plants, and visited by birds (*open only for guided tours and during designated hours April through Oct, see the Park calendar of events on the Conservancy website: centralparknyc.org*).

In the winter **Wollman Rink** (1951) is a magical and popular place to skate, with views of the skyline and park landscape. The rink was restored in 1987 by real estate developer Donald Trump; in the summer it becomes Victorian Gardens, a child-friendly amusement park (*for info, T: 212 982 2229*).

CENTRAL PARK ZOO

East 64th St at Fifth Ave. Open April–Oct weekdays 10–5, weekends and holidays until 5:30; Nov–March seven days 10–4:30, last entrance a half hour before closing. Admission charge. Café and shop. T: 212 439 6500, centralparkzoo.com.

Although Olmsted and Vaux disapproved of caging animals and the Greensward Plan did not provide for a zoo, gifts of animals soon began to arrive, according to Olmsted many of them the pets of children who had died or left town. Some donations would have made poor pets: an alligator, a porcupine, a peacock, and a boa constrictor. In 1865 General William Tecumseh Sherman gave three African Cape buffaloes acquired on his historic march through Georgia. The park commissioners, deluged with donated animals, established a menagerie in the Arsenal that remained until 1934, with outdoor cages as well as animal exhibits in the basement, a situation said to be "insecure and dangerous," and certainly malodorous. The Central Park Zoo, which opened in 1935 during the Robert Moses era, originally exhibited both large and small animals, most confined to barred cages; a renovation in 1988 introduced naturalistic habitats and focused on smaller species appropriate to the zoo's urban scale; the popular sea lions, however, are still sporting in their pool.

Animal statuary nearby includes *Honey Bear* **(2)** and *Dancing Goat* **(3)** (c. 1935) by Brooklyn-born Frederick George Richard Roth, who trained in Berlin and Vienna and was hired in 1934 through the Works Progress Administration as chief sculptor for the city parks. *Tigress and Cubs* **(4)** (1866) by Auguste Cain, a prominent French sculptor, created a similar work for the Jardins des Tuileries in Paris.

At the north entrance to the Children's Zoo is the **Delacorte Clock** (1964–5; Andrea Spadini), commissioned by publisher George T. Delacorte, who admired the animated clocks of Europe. Every hour on the hour a parade of bronze animals marches around the clock, brandishing musical instruments and playing nursery tunes and such seasonal favorites as "Younger than Springtime," and "Winter Wonderland." A shorter performance takes place on the half-hour. At the Children's Zoo, young animal lovers can pet and feed sheep, and a pot-bellied pig. Paul Manship, most famous for his *Prometheus* at Rockefeller Center, sculpted the boys, goats, and tendrils of curling vegetation that decorate the gates.

THE ARSENAL

Beyond the zoo toward Fifth Ave is the Arsenal (1851; Martin E. Thompson), an eccentrically charming brick building surmounted by eight crenellated octagonal towers. The newel posts of the staircase represent cannons, while the cast-iron balusters supporting the railing look like muskets. The building has held the headquarters of the New York City Parks and Recreation Department since 1934.

It was constructed to store ammunition and weapons for the New York State National Guard, replacing an older ammunition depot downtown on Centre St whose decrepitude made it an easy mark for thieves. But its remoteness at the time rendered it dubiously effective for stockpiling arms and ammunition. One critic complained that the cannons in the Arsenal, four and a half miles from the previous depot, would be useless, since a mob could riot before the troops could drag the artillery into action. The building later housed the Eleventh Police Precinct, the Municipal Weather Bureau, the American Museum of Natural History, and the menagerie that morphed into the Central Park Zoo. On the third floor is the **Arsenal Gallery** (*open Mon–Fri 9–5, closed municipal holidays; free; T: 212 360 8163*), whose changing exhibitions focus on nature, urban space, New York City parks, and park history. The original Greensward Plan, Frederick Law Olmsted and Calvert Vaux's winning entry in the competition for the design of Central Park, is viewable by appointment.

THE DAIRY

North of Wollman Rink is the **Dairy** (1870; Calvert Vaux), built as a refreshment stand and resting place for mothers and children, now a visitor center. The Gothic Revival building is said to combine features of a country church (the pointed-arch windows), a mountain chalet (the steep pitched roof and open-air loggia), and a barn (the framing of the beams and gambrel ceilings). Inside are displays on park history, information about daily programs, and a shop with maps, books, and gift items (*open daily 10–5, earlier closing in winter; free; T: 212 794 6564*).

Olmsted and Vaux set aside for children the southern part of the park, most accessible to the streetcars at 59th St. At a time when milk—much of it produced on farms within the city—was unregulated and often contaminated, the Dairy was more than a romantic pastoral feature: its herd of cows grazed in a field between the Dairy and what is now Wollman Rink.

Also in the Children's District were the Children's Cottage (demolished), the Carousel, two rustic shelters, and a playground. One of the shelters, replaced by the **Chess and Checkers House** in 1952, stood on the Kinderberg ("Children's Mountain"), a nearby rocky outcrop. The other shelter, the **Cop Cot**, is a close replica (1984) of the original rustic summerhouse, built of tree limbs and trunks constructed where possible with traditional joinery techniques instead of nails and screws.

CALVERT VAUX

Born in England, Vaux (rhymes with "squawks;" 1824–95) co-designed the Greensward Plan (the winning entry in the competition to design Central Park) with Frederick Law Olmsted and is also responsible for most of the built environment in the park. In addition to his talents as an architect, Vaux was a skilled draftsman. An exhibition of his landscape watercolors in a London gallery attracted the attention of Andrew Jackson Downing—America's leading landscape architect, a proponent of the Gothic Revival style, and an influential editor. Downing invited Vaux to join his firm in Newburgh, New York, and later introduced him to Olmsted.

Vaux was quiet, perhaps shy, and though his personality was overshadowed by Olmsted's charisma, he was an equal partner in their ventures: Central Park and Morningside Park in Manhattan, Prospect Park and Fort Greene Park in Brooklyn, and many projects outside New York City. Among his other commissions, Vaux designed the American Museum of Natural History and the rear façade of the Metropolitan Museum. In Central Park he designed most of the original buildings and bridges.

THE CAROUSEL
Open April–Oct daily 10–6 weather permitting; Nov–March, call before you go. Admission charge, cash only. T: 212 439 6900, ext. 12.

According to legend, the park's first carousel (1870) was turned by a blind mule and a horse in the basement, who were trained to respond to one or two knocks on the floor over their heads. When the predecessor to the present carousel was destroyed by fire, the Parks Department found this one in a trolley warehouse in Coney Island. The 57 horses were hand-carved in 1908 by artists Sol Stein and Harry Goldstein for a carousel-manufacturing company in Williamsburg, Brooklyn.

HECKSCHER BALLFIELDS AND PLAYGROUND
The restored playground west of the Carousel occupies the site of a 19th-century play area—really just a meadow without slides, swings, or other hardware. Adults were not allowed, and to protect the landscape even children needed permits for all sports except sledding. Around 1866, baseball was permitted for boys under 16 who could provide a certificate of exemplary character and good attendance from their teachers. Girls were allowed to play croquet three afternoons a week on a field several blocks away.

In 1927, compelled by overwhelming pressure for adult sports, the park managers installed five permanent fields with backstops. The ballfields and playground to the south are named to honor August Heckscher (1913–97), an advocate for parks, and parks commissioner in 1967–72.

Between the ballfields and the playground is a large outcropping, **Umpire Rock**, a hunk of Manhattan schist, the bedrock that underlies much of Manhattan, grooved and striated by the Wisconsin glacier that covered the city some 30,000 years ago.

THE MALL AND LITERARY WALK
The Mall (1,212 ft long) is a formal *allée*, based on European precedents and bordered by a stand of mature American elm trees. Most American elms in the US were destroyed by Dutch elm disease, which struck first in the 1930s, and these trees have survived only because they are closely monitored. The Mall is the only area Olmsted and Vaux considered appropriate for statuary; most memorials elsewhere in the park result from the passion for commemorative objects that gripped the city during the last half of the 19th century. Germans, Danes, Scots, Italians, and Latin Americans honored their countries by donating statues of military heroes and prominent inventors, writers, musicians, and poets ranging from Shakespeare to **Fitz-Greene Halleck (6)**, a popular 19th-century versifier who has disappeared into the mists of time.

The park's animal sculpture is superior. *Indian Hunter* (5) (1866) by John Quincy Adams Ward is the fruit of months spent by the sculptor in the Dakotas sketching Native Americans. Beyond the Willowdell Arch on the right, *Balto (7)* (1925; Frederick George Richard Roth) memorializes the leader of a team of heroic huskies that carried diphtheria serum across 600 miles of Alaskan wasteland to relieve the city of Nome in 1925.

Further up the Mall to the west is Christophe Fratin's *Eagles and Prey* (8) (c. 1850), depicting two ferocious eagles sinking their claws into a goat trapped between rocks. Fratin belonged to a group of French sculptors, *animaliers*, whose renderings of wild animals often expressed a fascination with violence and terror; some 19th-century critics found this work too violent for the tranquil beauty of the park.

To the east are the **Naumburg Bandshell**, with its coffered interior vault, and the **Wisteria Pergola**, covered by Chinese wisteria. The **Rumsey Playfield** (1936) behind the bandshell replaced the Casino, an expensive night spot for adults, including former Mayor James J. ("Beau James") Walker, who entertained lavishly and is alleged to have occasionally skipped out on his bills. The statue of *Mother Goose* (9) (1938) at the eastern edge of the playfield is by Frederick George Richard Roth.

BETHESDA TERRACE AND FOUNTAIN

At the top of the Mall the Bethesda Terrace Arcade leads under the vehicular road to Bethesda Terrace, often considered the heart of the park, its second formal element after the Mall. The elaborate design of walls and ceiling is by Jacob Wrey Mould.

JACOB WREY MOULD

Responsible for much of the decorative stonework near the Bethesda Terrace and elsewhere, as well as many small structures in Central Park, Mould (1825–86) was recognized by his contemporaries as a man of many gifts. Born in England, he trained with Owen Jones, an architect known for his studies of the Alhambra in Spain. Mould apparently visited Spain and much of his decorative work suggests Moorish influences. He came to New York when he was 27, with a commission to design the All Souls Unitarian Church (no longer standing), whose striped color scheme earned it the nickname "Church of the Holy Zebra." Mould translated opera libretti, played the piano, and composed. He worked easily in stone, metal, and wood. He designed houses as well as churches, and earned the praise of his colleagues for his decorative skills. Likeability, however, was not among Mould's gifts. Diarist George Templeton Strong, a lawyer and vestryman of Trinity Church, called Mould "ugly and uncouth but very clever... [an] architect and universal genius." The architectural critic Montgomery Schuyler, while admiring Mould's way with color, called him "that strange genius" and an "irresponsible bohemian," apparently because Mould flouted convention by living openly with a woman. He also earned a reputation for dishonest business dealings. In 1875 he left his job as an assistant architect for Central Park and went to Lima, Peru, for five years. Biographical sources are unclear as to the motive for this sudden uprooting.

When he died in 1886 he had few friends, but an acquaintance noted that "a woman he called his wife stuck with him to the last." He is buried in Green-Wood Cemetery in Brooklyn (*see p. 498*).

Mould designed the 15,876 handcrafted Minton encaustic tiles (restored 2000) covering the ceiling of the underpass. (Encaustic tiles are made of individual colored clays pressed and fired into the tile to form the design.)

At the center of the terrace is the **Bethesda Fountain** and its statue, *Angel of the Waters* (1868), by Emma Stebbins, one of the few statues especially commissioned for the park. It depicts the Biblical angel who "troubled" the waters of the Bethesda pool in Jerusalem, conferring miraculous healing powers ; more specifically the Bethesda Fountain commemorates the opening of the Croton Aqueduct (1842). In an era when frequent cholera outbreaks were caused by a contaminated water supply, Stebbins equated pure Croton water with the curative waters of Bethesda. On the column beneath the angel, four plump cherubs represent the virtues of Temperance, Purity, Health, and Peace.

Bethesda Terrace is prime territory for people-watching. During the 19th century the well-to-do flaunted their stylish clothing, horses, and carriages along Terrace

Drive, now the 72nd St vehicular road. Today stylish clothing and equally stylish pets are still on display here, though the carriages are long gone.

EMMA STEBBINS

Born to a wealthy and influential New York family, Stebbins (1815–82) was the only woman hired to create a work of art for Central Park. (The fact that her brother headed the park commissioners surely helped.) Stebbins was a feminist, a bohemian, and a lesbian who had a long relationship with Charlotte Saunders Cushman, one of the great actresses of the day. Cushman underwent years of treatment for breast cancer, with Stebbins caring for her, and after Cushman died in 1876, Stebbins never created another sculpture. The *Angel of the Waters* is her most famous work, but she is also represented in New York by *Columbus* in front of the Building in Cadman Plaza, Brooklyn.

STRAWBERRY FIELDS

This 2.5-acre area (*near Central Park West and 72nd St*) honors John Lennon, the songwriter, singer, and peace activist, who rose to fame with The Beatles and was assassinated in the courtyard of the nearby Dakota Apartments in 1980. "Strawberry Fields Forever," one of Lennon's most popular songs, took its title from the name of a Salvation Army children's home in Liverpool where he had played as a child. The title of another famous song, **"Imagine,"** is inscribed in the center of a black and white pavement mosaic—a reproduction of a mosaic in Pompeii and a gift of Naples, Italy. The garden, landscaped and set aside as a meditative **Garden of Peace**, was donated by Lennon's widow, Yoko Ono, and designed in conjunction with landscape architect Bruce Kelly.

Strawberry Fields opened in 1985 after its planners overcame some unusual obstacles, beginning with the wish of conservative City Council members to name the area for Bing Crosby instead of the politically controversial Lennon. When Yoko Ono ran an advertisement in the *New York Times* requesting rocks and plants from nations around the world, many countries sent plants suitable to other climates or offered gifts inappropriate to the park—a totem pole, a tile bench, and a large amethyst. Eventually 150 nations sent plants to create the Peace Garden, now one of the park's most popular destinations, a shrine at which fans from all over the world leave flowers and tokens of remembrance.

TAVERN ON THE GREEN

West Drive runs south from Strawberry Fields to the Tavern on the Green (*West 66th St at Central Park West*), a restaurant long popular with visitors, at its peak feeding more than a half million people yearly. Built as a sheepfold (1870; Jacob Wrey Mould), until 1934 it sheltered the Dorsets and Southdowns who grazed in the Sheep Meadow. Commissioner Robert Moses re-assigned the sheep to Prospect Park in Brooklyn and converted the sheepfold to a restaurant, with doormen in top hats, riding boots, and hunting coats; cigarette girls in court costumes; and a twelve-piece orchestra dressed in uniforms of forest-green. (*Open daily 11am–1am, weekends 9am–1am; T: 212 877 8684, tavernonthegreen.com.*)

CENTRAL PARK: 72ND–84TH STREETS

Subway: 4, 5, 6 to 72nd St. Bus: M1, M2, M3, M4, M30, M72.

MODEL BOAT POND (CONSERVATORY WATER)

The Model Boat Pond, formally the Conservatory Water, gets its name from an unbuilt glass conservatory for tropical plants, included by Olmsted and Vaux but abandoned after money ran short. The area planned as a flower garden near the conservatory was reconfigured as a hard-edged (as opposed to naturalistic) pond. In its waters children (and others) sail radio-controlled and wind-driven model yachts, some luxurious enough for model moguls.

During the Robert Moses era, the vicinity became a new Children's District, with sculptures from children's literature. At the north end of the pond an 11-ft **bronze *Alice in Wonderland* (10)** (1959; José de Creeft) sits on a giant mushroom, surrounded by the *Mad Hatter*, the *Dormouse*, the *Cheshire Cat*, and the *March Hare* and (usually) a crowd of children, who scramble over the mushrooms. George T. Delacorte commissioned the statue to honor his wife, who read the classic story to their children.

On the west shore an eight-foot seated **bronze *Hans Christian Andersen* (11)** (1956; Georg Lober) reads to a two-foot, 60-lb *Ugly Duckling* waddling in front. In 1973 a thief sawed the duckling off its base and made off with it, but the duck was recovered undamaged several weeks later in a paper bag near a Queens junkyard.

THE LAKE, BOW BRIDGE, AND RAMBLE

From the boat pond a path leads west under the **Trefoil Arch**. The brownstone arch, trefoil on one side only, designed by Vaux, is part of the scheme to separate different modes of transportation within the park, an innovative notion, as were the sunken transverse roads across the park carrying city traffic.

In front of the **Loeb Boathouse** (1954), donated by philanthropists Carl and Adeline Loeb, a small bronze statue, ***The Rowers*** (1968; Irwin Glusker), commemorates the donors. The gondola that plies the waters was built in Venice and donated in 1986, replacing one given in 1862 by the city of Venice. The original New York gondolier, a former mail sorter, was trained by two Venetian gondoliers who traveled here to teach him the art.

A walkway follows the shore of the lake past the Bethesda Terrace (*see p. 316*) to the beautiful cast-iron **Bow Bridge** (1859; Calvert Vaux), which crosses the Lake to the **Ramble**, a heavily planted glen with intricately winding paths and carefully organized cascades in a meandering brook, the Gill. In designing the park, Vaux and Olmsted studiously avoided straight paths (the Mall is the only one in the park, except for a straight section in the running track around the Reservoir, which postdated Vaux and Olmsted), and in the Ramble they outdid themselves, so it is easy to get lost here. Its wilderness attracts birds and their watchers, nature lovers, and walkers. (NB: Though the Ramble's reputation as a place for drug deals and anonymous sex has declined, the woods can be deserted.)

East of the Ramble along East Drive is Edward Kemeys's site-specific **Still Hunt (12)** (1881–3), a bronze panther crouched on a natural rock as if to pounce on the runners who jog obliviously along the road. In the late 1860s Kemeys wielded an axe for the engineering corps clearing the grounds for Central Park, earning two dollars a day.

BELVEDERE CASTLE AND TURTLE POND

North of the Ramble is **Vista Rock** (elevation 135ft), site of Belvedere Castle (1869), used as a weather station since 1919, now a visitor center. Built as a Victorian folly, its three terraces offer views of the surrounding landscape. North of the castle is Turtle Pond with the **Delacorte Theater** on its western shore. Near the entrance are Milton Hebald's bronze statues **(13)** representing *The Tempest* (1966) and *Romeo and Juliet* (1977) dedicated to Joseph Papp, the theatrical producer who brought Shakespeare to the park. The **Shakespeare Garden** (east of West Drive, between the theater and the Swedish Cottage at the latitude of 80th St) contains plants mentioned in the Bard's works. The **Swedish Cottage**, a replica of a Swedish schoolhouse made for the 1876 Philadelphia Centennial Exposition, houses the Swedish Cottage Marionette Theater (*for info, T: 212 988 9093*).

Turtle Pond is the last trace of the old Croton Receiving Reservoir (drained 1931 and filled with rubble from the excavation for Rockefeller Center), which once occupied the site of the 55-acre **Great Lawn**. Over the years the lawn has been a venue for large-scale events, including a papal Mass with John Paul II that attracted 350,000 people and a concert by Paul Simon that attracted 600,000. Compacted by heavy use, the Great Lawn became a dustbowl until a two-year restoration by the Central Park Conservancy brought it back to its former health and beauty; today events are carefully selected and monitored, but the New York Philharmonic and the Metropolitan Opera do give summer performances here.

Near Turtle Pond, a bronze **statue of King Wladyslaw Jagiello (14)** (1939; Stanislaw Kazimierz Ostrowski) honors a warrior under whom Poland became a major power. The statue shows him holding above his head the crossed swords of his adversaries, whom he defeated in 1410. The statue stood in front of the Polish Pavilion at the 1939 World's Fair; when World War II broke out, the statue remained in the US and was given to the City in 1945 by the Polish government in exile.

North of this statue behind the Metropolitan Museum of Art is New York's oldest piece of outdoor sculpture, the 69-ft, 220-ton **Obelisk**, erected as one of a pair in the 15th century BC by Thutmose III at Heliopolis on the Nile. It stood there a thousand years until toppled by the Persians, and thereafter lay on the ground until the Romans set it up in Alexandria (16 BC) not far from a temple built by Cleopatra (who had died in 30 BC), thus giving it its nickname, "Cleopatra's Needle." The khedive of Egypt gave it to the US in exchange for funds to modernize his country a few years after the Suez

Canal opened (1869), but it didn't arrive until 1881, after William H. Vanderbilt paid the $100,000 shipping bill. Part of the expense went toward constructing a trestle to drag the pink granite statue across town from the Hudson, a journey that took 112 days. A cleaning and restoration in 2013–14 revealed hieroglyphs hidden for decades by pollution and dirt. The second obelisk of the pair, also called Cleopatra's Needle, was given to Britain in 1819 and today stands on the Thames embankment in London.

SENECA VILLAGE

Between about 81st and 89th Sts, bounded by the Great Lawn and Central Park West, an African-American community known as Seneca Village existed until the inhabitants were uprooted to make way for the park. The origin of the name is unknown. African Americans began buying land here in 1825, building houses, churches, and a school, and establishing burial grounds. In the 1850s they were joined by German and Irish immigrants, and by 1855 the population had reached 264 people. Most of the men were domestics, waiters, or unskilled laborers, while the women were domestics or laundresses. The natural surroundings made life a little easier: trees provided fuel, the nearby river still had fish, land was available for gardens. In 1853 the state legislature authorized the use of eminent domain to take land for Central Park and as ground was broken for the park, the media began characterizing the residents of the future parkland as squatters, "insects," and "bloodsuckers." Although many residents of Seneca Village resisted through the courts, their efforts were futile; they were told to leave in the summer of 1856. By 1857 Seneca Village had disappeared. An archaeological dig in 2011 unearthed stone foundations and recovered an iron tea kettle, a stoneware beer bottle, shards of Chinese export porcelain, and a small shoe.

THE JACQUELINE KENNEDY ONASSIS RESERVOIR

The Reservoir, 40ft deep and holding a billion gallons of water, occupies the midline of Central Park, from about 86th to 96th Sts. The main entrance at East 90th St is through the Engineers' Gate, familiarly known as the **Runners' Gate**, where runners enter the park during the New York Marathon. Near the gate a granite monument (dedicated 1928; Adolph A. Weinman) honors John Purroy Mitchel, a political reformer who served a term as mayor. Another monument (1994; Jesús Ygnacio Domínguez) honors Fred Lebow (1932–94), who organized the New York Marathon in 1970 and developed it from a race with 127 participants to one that attracts more than 50,000 entrants.

Thousands of pedestrians round the 1.58-mile track every day. The stretch of road along Fifth Ave between about East 86th and East 94th Sts is the longest straight section in the park.

From 1862 until 1993, the billion-gallon reservoir supplied drinking water as part of the Croton system, but nowadays its water fills the three bodies of water in the northern park: the Loch, the Pool, and the Harlem Meer. The perimeter fence (2003) recalls the original fence, a piece of which was discovered by scuba divers at the bottom of the reservoir. After Jacqueline Kennedy Onassis died (1994), the reservoir was renamed to honor her commitment to the city. Three ornamental bridges cross the bridle path, and two stone gatehouses (Calvert Vaux) contain equipment designed to treat the water and control its flow.

CENTRAL PARK: 96TH–110TH STREETS

Subway: 4, 5, 6 to 96th St; 6 to 103rd St. Bus: M1, M2, M3, M4.

Less studded with attractions than the southern part, the northern park offers the beautiful Conservatory Garden, the Harlem Meer, and several sites that played a role in the Revolutionary War.

The **Vanderbilt Gate** at Fifth Ave and 105th St formerly kept the riff-raff away from the Cornelius Vanderbilt II mansion, where Bergdorf Goodman now stands (*58th St at Fifth Ave*). Made in Paris (1894), the wrought-iron gates were donated to the city in 1939 by Gertrude Vanderbilt Whitney, daughter of Cornelius II and founder of the Whitney Museum.

CONSERVATORY GARDEN

The six-acre Conservatory Garden (*104th to 106th Sts along Fifth Ave*), considered by many the city's finest garden (*open 8am–dusk*), is named for elaborate glasshouses (1899) that supplied shrubs and plants for city parks until torn down in 1934 during the Depression to cut costs. The present garden (opened 1937) began as a Works Progress Administration project, providing employment during the Depression. By the early 1970s the garden had fallen into disrepair, its fountains running dry, its hedges and trees straggling. In 1982 Lynden B. Miller, a painter and garden designer, took over, and the following year the Central Park Conservancy began restoring the perennial beds and planting wildflowers and bulbs. Today the Conservatory Garden, with its magnificent displays of blooms and fine collections of perennials, draws people to admire the flora, contemplate nature, and even get married.

The garden is divided into three sections. The **Center Garden** is Italian in style with a thick lawn bordered with flowering quince, yew hedges, and symmetrical rows of crab apples. On the hillside a wrought-iron arbor supports a beautiful mature Chinese wisteria. The **South Garden**, intimate and English in style, contains the **Burnett Memorial Fountain (15)** (1936; Bessie Potter Vonnoh), whose statues are said to represent two of the children in Frances Hodgson Burnett's classic *The Secret Garden*. The Woodland Slope on the periphery offers shrubs and plants that thrive in the shade. The **North Garden**, formal and French in style, centers around the **Untermeyer Fountain (16)** with its bronze *Three Maidens Dancing* (1947; Walter Schott). Circular beds surround the fountain, the outer ones planted with spectacular seasonal displays of tulips and chrysanthemums.

THE HARLEM MEER

Between 106th and 110th Sts, the Harlem Meer (completed 1866), once a swamp, now an artificial lake, is the largest body of water in the northern park. The water has been stocked with fish, so that children (and others) may try their luck at catch-and-release fishing. On its northern shore stands the **Dana Discovery Center** (1993), offering exhibits, family programs, and seasonal events (*open daily 10–5; T: 212 860 1370*). At the southwest edge of the Meer is the shallow **Lasker Pool and Rink**, where thousands splash or glide in season. Park preservationists consider the pool an ill-chosen intrusion, and it has been derided as the "Lasker sitzbath" and "the park's most disastrous 'improvement'."

CENTRAL PARK IN TIME OF WAR

The Albany Post Road, built over an old Indian trail, once ran northward approximately along the course of East Drive from 103rd to 106th Sts, threading its way between two jutting hills. During the Revolutionary War the pass became an escape route for Colonel William Smallwood's Marylanders, covering the retreat of the colonial troops after the British invasion at Kip's Bay (about the level of East 35th St) on Sept 15, 1776; for the rest of the war British troops and German mercenaries were garrisoned there to protect the city from a northerly invasion. About 30 years later, during the War of 1812, the pass again gained strategic importance as New Yorkers realized, following the bombardment of Stonington, Connecticut, that their city was vulnerable to a land attack from the north. A volunteer force that included gentlemanly Columbia College students as well as butchers, Freemasons, and tallow chandlers, worked by day and night to strengthen the old line of Revolutionary forts from Third Avenue to the Hudson. In the McGowan's Pass area were Fort Clinton, named after Mayor DeWitt Clinton; Fort Fish, named after Nicholas Fish, chairman of the defense committee; and Nutter's Battery. In the far northwest of Central Park, not far from Warriors' Gate on a hill overlooking the Harlem plain to the north, the **Blockhouse** remains from many fortifications built for the War of 1812. (*Occasional tours; check the Conservancy website, centralparknyc.org.*)

The Frick Collection
& Silk Stocking District

The exclusive "Silk Stocking District"—or Upper East Side—is home to clubs, consulates, and townhouses, testimony to the taste and ambition of early 20th-century millionaires. Even in such elite company, the superb Frick Collection and its mansion stand out.

The Frick Collection, housed in one of the few remaining grand Fifth Avenue mansions (1914; Carrère & Hastings), is a monument to the passion for acquiring European art that gripped many wealthy men around the turn of the 20th century. The interplay between the superb paintings and sculpture, the opulent house itself, and the fine collection of decorative arts provides an experience unique in New York. The area north and south of the Frick (the East 60s and East 70s off Fifth Avenue) reveal much of the era of the 19th-century business moguls—from Millionaires' Row (descibed as an "architectural meal" by Edith Wharton) to the mansions of the Astors, the Vanderbilts, and their circle.

THE FRICK COLLECTION

Map p. 617, D1. 1 East 70th St (Fifth Ave). Subway: 6 to 68th St. Bus: M1, M2, M3, M4, M72. Open Tues–Sat 10–6, Sun 11–5. Closed Mon and major holidays; open Sunday hours on Lincoln's birthday (Feb 12), Election Day (first Tues in Nov), Veterans' Day (Nov 11). Admission charge, but by donation Sun 11–1. Free mobile app; audio guide with admission. Shop. Children under ten not admitted. T: 212 288 0700, frick.org.

HISTORY OF THE COLLECTION

Henry Clay Frick began collecting art seriously around 1895 and continued for the rest of his life, at first—like other American millionaire industrialists—indulging a penchant for French works by Daubigny, Bouguereau, and the painters of the Barbizon School. As his taste matured, he sold earlier acquisitions and began buying the Flemish, Dutch, Italian, and Spanish paintings for which the collection is famous. When J. Pierpont Morgan died in 1913, Frick purchased paintings (including Fragonard's *Progress of Love*), porcelains, and small bronze sculptures from Morgan's estate, aided by the English dealer Joseph Duveen, a fierce competitor of Michael Knoedler, the dealer from whom Frick bought many of his Old Masters.

When Frick died, he bequeathed the house and outstanding works of the collection for a public museum. Since his death the collection has been increased by about a third. The house remains much as it was when the Fricks lived there, so that a visit to this great small collection also gives insight into the lives of the industrialists and financiers around the turn of the 20th century. The museum offers high-quality changing exhibitions related to its holdings.

HENRY CLAY FRICK

Henry Clay Frick (1849–1919) rose from humble beginnings in rural Pennsylvania to wealth and power as a pioneer in the coke and steel industries. From childhood he made it clear that he did not intend to remain poor, leaving school to clerk in a grocery store, moving on to become a bookkeeper in several local businesses, including the whiskey distillery of his maternal grandfather. While Frick was still a young man, an appraiser of his prospects remarked that he worked industriously all day, did the bookkeeping in the evenings, and was "a little too enthusiastic about pictures but not enough to hurt." During his twenties Frick laid the foundations for his future industrial empire, founding the H. Frick Coke Company and taking advantage of the low prices during the depression that followed the Panic of 1873 to buy out competitors. Coke was essential to the blast furnaces of the nascent steel industry and Frick soon attracted the attention of steel baron Andrew Carnegie. The two merged their interests and profited handsomely, dominating steel manufacture in Pennsylvania.

As an industrialist, Frick was far-sighted, daring, and fiercely competitive, remembered for his role in the Homestead Steel Strike of 1892. For two years before the strike, the price of steel products had dropped more than 35 percent and Frick was determined to lower workers' wages and to crush the union, which in more prosperous times had negotiated a favorable contract. To do so he used harsh tactics— slashing wages, locking out workers, refusing to negotiate with the union but only with individuals, and ultimately hiring mercenaries from the Pinkerton detective agency to confront the strikers. In the battle that followed, nine strikers and seven Pinkertons were killed and many more on both sides were injured. The governor then intervened with 8,000 state militia. Strikebreakers were brought in on sealed trains. Public sympathy, which had swung toward the workers because of Frick's ruthless suppression of the strike, swung back when anarchist Alexander Berkman attempted to assassinate the industrialist in retaliation. Berkman attacked Frick in his office, shooting him twice and stabbing him four times in the leg before Frick's employees pulled him away.

Though in business Frick was intensely private, guarded in his relationships and capable of lasting anger, to his family he was affectionate and devoted.

THE BUILDING

In 1905 Frick abandoned plans for a new house and gallery in Pittsburgh and bought the only complete full block facing Fifth Avenue available as a single parcel; it contained the Lenox Library, whose collections now form part of the New York Public Library. He commissioned Thomas Hastings (of Carrère & Hastings) to design a home that would suitably display his collection and eventually become a museum. After several false starts, Hastings came up with the design for this limestone mansion with a front portico in the style of Louis XVI and a Beaux-Arts axial plan. Frick, by now estranged from his former business partner Andrew Carnegie, certainly knew about Carnegie's mansion at Fifth Ave and 90th St, and, according to legend, remarked that his own mansion would make Carnegie's look like a miner's shack.

Attilio Piccirilli, best known for the *Maine* monument at Columbus Circle (*see p. 400*), sculpted bas-reliefs on the pavilion at the north end of the building. Interior details were planned by Sir Charles Allom, the eminent London designer who had redecorated Buckingham Palace for George V. In his correspondence, Frick repeatedly advised Allom to "avoid anything elaborate" and to make sure "the ceilings are almost plain." Upstairs furnishings and accessories were chosen by Elsie de Wolfe, a tastemaker who parlayed her sense of style into a career as a decorator and an international hostess, eventually marrying into the English aristocracy. Wadley & Smythe, the landscape architects, carted tons of soil onto the property and planted chestnut trees along the avenue, which have since been replaced by three magnificent magnolias. In 2011 the Portico facing the front lawn was enclosed to form a new gallery for sculpture and decorative arts. In 2014 the museum proposed a six-story addition on the site of the garden, but a year later, in the face of vocal opposition, withdrew the plan.

HIGHLIGHTS OF THE COLLECTION

The works on view are rotated and not all works of art are on display all of the time; only the Living Hall remains as it was when Henry Clay Frick was alive. Works purchased by Frick himself are given in bold.

(1) South Hall: Two of the Frick's three Vermeers hang here: *Officer and Laughing Girl* (c. 1655–60) and *Girl Interrupted at Her Music* (c. 1660), both typically enigmatic scenes. Agnolo Bronzino's **portrait of Lodovico Capponi** (c. 1550–5) depicts a page at the court of Cosimo I de' Medici in Florence, where Bronzino worked as court painter for most of his career. In 2014 the Frick acquired a **self-portrait of Bartolomé Esteban Murillo** (c. 1650–5), which had long been in the Frick family.

(2) Boucher Room: In this small sitting room, *The Arts and Sciences* (c. 1750–2), panels by François Boucher, depict plump, rosy-cheeked children playing at adult occupations. Period furniture includes pieces by the preeminent cabinetmakers during the reign of Louis XV.

(3) Dining Room: If the Boucher Room shows Frick's taste for 18th-century France, the Dining Room demonstrates his affection for the same period in England. Adorning the walls is a gallery

THE FRICK COLLECTION

1	South Hall	7	North Hall
2	Boucher Room	8	West Gallery
3	Dining Room	9	Enamels Room
4	The Fragonard Room	10	East Gallery
5	Living Hall	11	Garden Court
6	Portico Gallery		

of 18th-century English portraits, most of them aristocratic women. Thomas Gainsborough's *The Mall in St. James's Park* (1783) shows London's fashionable set, the ladies in fluttering gowns strolling beneath feathery trees.

During the season Frick presided over dinner parties at the oval mahogany table, designed by Allom, with his guests—usually 26, usually all male—enjoying the gastronomic luxuries of the day including terrapin, caviar, and orchid salad.

(4) The Fragonard Room: Decorated with paintings by Jean-Honoré Fragonard, a master of Rococo art, this room demonstrates Frick's taste toward the end of his collecting career. The four largest panels (*The Pursuit*, *The*

Meeting, *The Lover Crowned*, and *Love Letters*) are known collectively as *The Progress of Love* and were commissioned by Madame du Barry, who succeeded Madame de Pompadour as chief mistress of Louis XV. Fragonard had the ill luck to outlive the taste for the style he had perfected; unable to adapt to the more severe Neoclassical style associated with the French Revolution, he died in poverty. Frick bought the panels in 1915 for $1.25 million from the estate of J. Pierpont Morgan, who had installed them in his London house.

Sculpture here may include Jean-Antoine Houdon's *Comtesse du Cayla* (1777) and a terra cotta group by Clodion, *Zephyrus and Flora* (1799).

Among the porcelains is a rare **Sèvres pot-pourris vase** (c. 1759) in the form of a ship: the "port-holes" along the side and the holes in the "rigging" allowed the aroma of dried petals to escape.

(5) Living Hall: In this wood-paneled room, the only one that remains exactly as Frick and Allom planned it, every painting is a masterpiece.

Flanking the fireplace are two portraits by Hans Holbein the Younger. To the left is *Sir Thomas More* (1527), the author and statesman who served as Lord Chancellor to Henry VIII, but resigned over Henry's divorce from Catherine of Aragon. His refusal to subscribe to the Act of Supremacy, which made the king head of the Church of England, cost him his life. To the right of the fireplace is *Thomas Cromwell* (c. 1532–3), an opportunist of obscure origins who rose to high office under Henry VIII. His brokering of Henry's marriage to Anne of Cleves led to his

downfall and eventual execution when the union failed. Over the mantel is El Greco's masterful *St. Jerome* (c. 1590–1600); other versions of this painting exist at the Metropolitan Museum of Art and the National Gallery in London.

Giovanni Bellini's *St. Francis in the Desert* (c. 1475–8) reveals the painter's mastery of perspective and color and facility for capturing everyday details, which nonetheless carried hidden significance to those who understood religious symbolism. Flanking the Bellini are two works by Titian, *Pietro Aretino* (c. 1537) and *Portrait of a Man in a Red Cap* (c. 1510).

Also in this room are examples of luxurious furniture by André-Charles Boulle and small Renaissance bronzes, which Frick began to collect toward the end of his life, purchasing many from the estate of J. Pierpont Morgan.

(6) The Portico Gallery: The first new gallery space to open (2011) at the Frick in 35 years has rotating exhibits of sculpture and decorative arts, which increasingly interested Frick toward the end of his life. Jean-Antoine Houdon's life-size terra cotta *Diana the Huntress* (1776–95) remains on permanent view.

(7) North Hall: Here you may see Jean-Auguste-Dominique Ingres's elegant *Comtesse d' Haussonville* (1845), granddaughter of Madame de Staël, painted over three years and requiring more known studies and sketches than any of his other portraits. Sculpture may include Francesco Laurana's bust of Beatrice of Aragon (1471–4), the daughter of the King of Naples. As queen to Matthias Corvinus of Hungary, she brought art, craftsmanship—and, it is reputed, fine cuisine and table-manners—to a hitherto barbarous land.

(8) West Gallery: The majority of paintings here are tranquil scenes or portraits: landscapes by Ruisdael, Hobbema, Constable and Corot; and superb portraits by Van Dyck and Frans Hals, a painter whose work was much in demand at the time Frick was gathering his collection. Also here is Gerard David's *The Deposition* (c. 1495–1500), one of the earliest known works painted in oil on canvas rather than tempera on wood, a technique thought to have been brought to Italy from the Low Countries.

Flanking the doorway at the west end of the gallery are Veronese's *The Choice between Virtue and Vice* and *Wisdom and Strength* (both c. 1580). On the northern long wall *The Polish Rider*, mysterious in its subject, its meaning, and even its attribution, today is generally considered to be by Rembrandt, though perhaps with the assistance of others. **Rembrandt's self-portrait** (1658), painted during a period of financial and personal difficulties, shows the artist's face scarred by time, his hands large and prominent. Velázquez's *King Philip IV of Spain* (1644) poses in an outfit decorated with lace and silver thread, which he wore on a military campaign against the French. Vermeer's *Mistress and Maid* (1666–7), the third Vermeer in the collection, was the last purchase (1919) of Frick's career.

(9) Enamels Room: The beautifully paneled cabinet gallery beyond the large arch was originally Frick's home office, rebuilt after he bought a collection of Limoges enamels from the estate of J.

Pierpont Morgan. Dominating the room is Piero della Francesca's magisterial *St. John the Evangelist* (1454–69).

(10) East Gallery: Often on view here are fine portraits by Goya, Hogarth, Van Dyck, Reynolds, and David. The portrait of *General John Burgoyne* painted (probably 1766) by Sir Joshua Reynolds shows the general posed dramatically before a stormy sky; Burgoyne is known best in this country for his efforts in the Revolutionary War and his defeat at the crucial battle of Saratoga in 1777; this romantic portrait probably celebrates earlier victories.

Goya's *The Forge* (c. 1815–20) was an unusual purchase for Frick, both in its proletarian subject and its depiction of raw physical power. El Greco's *Purification of the Temple* (c. 1600) depicts a theme much explored by the artist. The collection includes only one work by Édouard Manet, *The Bullfight* (1864), actually a section of a painting cut in two by the artist after being savagely criticized; the other half, *The Dead Toreador*, is in the National Gallery in Washington.

(11) Garden Court: This coolly pleasant space, filled with the sound of fountains, was designed by architect John Russell Pope on the site of the original Frick carriage court when the house was remodeled as a museum. With its colonnade, its greenery and its sculpture, the Court is one of the city's most pleasant spots to sit and think about art or anything else. Here is Jean Barbet's lovely bronze *Angel* (1460) and Johann Gottlieb Kirchner's three-foot Meissen *Great Bustard* (1732), a gift to the Frick in 2013, one of some 300 large animal figures commissioned by August II (1670–1733), Elector of Saxony and King of Poland, who had a "*maladie de porcelaine*."

THE FRICK ART REFERENCE LIBRARY

10 East 71st St. Open to researchers Mon–Fri 10–5; Sat and Sept–May 9:30 –1; closed holidays, holiday weekends, and Mon and Fri during Aug. Call or check website for additional information: T: 212 547 0641, frick.org/research/library.

The Frick Art Reference Library (1931–5; John Russell Pope), a memorial to Henry Clay Frick from Helen Clay Frick, his youngest child, is a leading site for research, especially in determining provenance and studying the history of collecting. Helen Clay Frick (1888–1984) never married. She and her father became increasingly close, as her mother, grief-stricken by the death of two of her children, retreated into depression. After Frick's death, Helen inherited the largest share of his fortune and became the caretaker of his legacy. She struggled against other trustees of the collection, notably John D. Rockefeller Jr., to keep the public rooms much as they had been during her father's lifetime.

Inspired to emulate Sir Robert Witt's photo archive in London, she took over the mansion's basement bowling alley and soon made the library her life's work. In less than a year the library had expanded beyond the bowling alley and soon needed a home of its own. The collection, which contains some 228,000 books, 3,000 periodicals, 90,000 auction catalogs, and more than a million photographic reproductions of works of art (as well as an increasing number of electronic resources), is a tribute to Miss Frick's energy, ingenuity, and devotion.

Facing the Frick on the park side of Fifth Ave at East 70th St is a **memorial to Richard Morris Hunt** (1898; Daniel Chester French), whose architectural achievements include the pedestal of the Statue of Liberty, part of the Metropolitan Museum of Art, and former mansions for Astors, Vanderbilts, and their ilk. The memorial originally faced the Lenox Library (1870), one of Hunt's finest buildings, bought by Frick and torn down for his mansion. (Frick did offer to have the library dismantled piece by piece and rebuilt in Central Park on the site of the Arsenal, but the City refused.) Architect Bruce Price, a student of Hunt's, planned the granite monument on which rests a bust of his mentor flanked by two classically draped women: *Sculpture and Painting* (left) with a mallet and palette, and *Architecture* (right). The figures, six feet tall and weighing in at 600 pounds apiece, were stolen in 1962 and almost melted down in a belt buckle factory before they were recognized and returned.

South of the Frick on Fifth Ave at East 67th St is the **One Hundred Seventh Infantry Memorial** (1927; Karl Illava), a memorial to the men of that regiment who died in World War I. The larger-than-life-sized bronze foot-soldiers are posed as if charging into battle from the wooded park. The sculptor, a sergeant in the regiment, modeled the soldiers' hands on his own.

THE SILK STOCKING DISTRICT

Map pp. 617, D2–615, E4. Subway: 6 to 68th St-Hunter College. Bus: M1, M2, M3, M4.

The nicknames "Gold Coast" and "Silk Stocking District" have at one time or another accrued to the neighborhood east of Fifth Avenue more or less to Lexington Avenue between 59th and 79th Streets, whose conservative display of wealth was assured with the creation of the Upper East Side Historic District in 1981. In the 19th century Carnegies, Fricks, and Dukes competed in building palatial homes on Fifth Avenue, but the side streets are figuratively paved in silver if not gold. Here are clubs, consulates, decorous houses of religion, charitable foundations, and even private houses in a city where private houses are a huge luxury. Postal zip code 10021, which embraces the area between 69th and 76th Streets, is considered elite, with the blocks close to Central Park and around Park Avenue being the *crème de la crème*. The streets and avenues east of Lexington Avenue are less patrician, with less distinguished high rise apartments and less luxurious shops.

MILLIONAIRES' ROW

As the moguls of the late-19th century, many of whom had made their fortunes during the post-Civil War boom, arrived on the New York social scene eager to build suitably impressive homes, they turned for advice to the city's influential architects. What these architects—notably Richard Morris Hunt, Charles Follen McKim and Stanford White—offered was a selection of styles from the established orders of the past. The new "classical" architecture depended on the availability of cheap, skilled labor, supplied by the influx of immigrants, many of whom were experienced in masonry, ironwork, stone carving, painting and gilding, and ornamental plasterwork. The novelist Edith Wharton, whose upper crust background and judicious eye made her a keen commentator on social developments, once described this wide-ranging selection of detail as a "complete architectural meal." Some of the mansions, like the Frick, have become museums; others have been taken over by charitable or educational institutions. The greatest concentration of these variously classical buildings arose in the vicinity of Fifth Avenue, though more modest dwellings were built on the side streets.

The classic revival died after the end of World War I, when changing economic patterns and new building technology dictated the end of costly masonry construction and ushered in the era of the skyscraper and the high-rise apartment.

FIFTH AVENUE AND THE EAST 60s

The **Union Club** (1932; Delano & Aldrich), at 101 East 69th St and Park Ave, is the city's oldest social club, dating back to 1836. The architects were best known for their red-brick Georgian-style designs (for example, the Knickerbocker Club (*see p. 334*), the Colony Club for women on Park Avenue at East 62nd St, and the former Willard

Straight house at 1130 Fifth Ave), so this imposing limestone-clad building with its big mansard roof departs from their usual fare. When the club chose not to expel its Confederate supporters during the Civil War, offended members resigned and formed the Union League Club, now on Park Avenue at East 38th St.

The **Permanent Mission of the Federal Republic of Serbia to the United Nations** (1905; Warren & Wetmore), at 854 Fifth Ave (*East 66th and East 67th Sts*), occupies the former townhouse of R. Livingston Beekman and Eleanor T. Beekman. Designed to reflect 18th-century French architecture of the Louis XV period, the house is crowned by a steep copper-covered mansard roof with two stories of dormers.

Ulysses S. Grant bought **no. 3 East 66th Street** in 1881 with money raised by J. Pierpont Morgan and others to ease his financial difficulties. He lost his military pension when he became president, a position without a pension, and invested heavily with a Wall Street firm in which his son was partner. The other partner defrauded the investors, and in 1884 the firm went bankrupt, as did Grant. In the same year he was diagnosed with throat cancer. Desperate to provide financial security for his wife and children, Grant penned his war memoirs, which were published by a firm partly owned by his friend Mark Twain. Grant died in 1885, shortly after finishing the memoirs, which were both critically and financially successful.

The **Lotos Club** at 5 East 66th St is one of the oldest literary clubs in the country, founded in 1870. Mark Twain, who joined in 1873, called it the "The Ace of Clubs." The house was built in 1900 (architect Richard Howland Hunt) in the French Renaissance style as a wedding present for a granddaughter of William H. Vanderbilt.

PARK AVENUE ARMORY

643 Park Ave (East 66th–East 67th Sts). Subway: 6 to 68th St, F to 63rd-Lexington Ave. Bus: M101, M102, M103. Open during events or for guided tours (usually 10am Tues and Thur). T: 212 616 3930, armoryonpark.org.

Filling the block with its machiolated bulk, the red-brick Seventh Regiment Armory (1880; Charles W. Clinton) was originally both a social club and headquarters for the volunteer militia known as the "silk-stocking" regiment for its mostly upper class members. Inside are a huge drill hall (187ft by 290ft) and private rooms decorated by Louis C. Tiffany and Stanford White, among others. The building was to have been financed by the City, but a depression meant that some $350,000 didn't materialize. Instead, the guardsmen used their social status to raise money through subscriptions, gaining donations from the likes of William H. Vanderbilt and John Jacob Astor. Now known as Park Avenue Armory, it has been a cultural center since 2007, used for recitals, dramas, and large scale art exhibits that take advantage of the drill hall's huge proportions.

TEMPLE EMANU-EL

1 East 65th St (Fifth Ave). Open daily 10–4:30 for meditation, emanuelnyc.org. Bernard Museum of Judaica open Sun–Thur 10–4:30; T: 212 744 1400, ext. 313 to arrange a tour.
Established in 1854, Temple Emanu-El is the oldest Reform Jewish congregation and one of the most prominent in New York. The building (1929; Robert D. Kohn, Charles Butler, and Clarence Stein) is the largest Jewish house of worship in the world.

Congregation Emanu-El was founded by 33 German Jews, who came during the second wave of Jewish immigration after the failure of the liberal revolutions in central Europe. They met initially in a rented room on the Lower East Side, and moved northward as they become more prosperous—first to a former Methodist church on Chrystie St (still on the Lower East Side), then to a former Baptist church on West 12th St, then north to Fifth Ave and 43rd St, where for the first time the congregation raised its own building. Services were conducted in German until 1873, when the congregation hired its first English-speaking rabbi.

Congregation Emanu-El merged with Temple Beth-El in 1927, and two years later built the present imposing synagogue. Architecturally, the building incorporates Romanesque, Byzantine, Moorish, Gothic, Art Nouveau, and Art Deco styles, drawing on the decorative motifs of synagogues of earlier eras and suggesting the mingling of Eastern and Western cultures. Symbols of the twelve tribes of Israel decorate the arch. The wheel window has at its center the six-pointed star or Star of David.

The sanctuary seats 2,500 people. In accordance with the Jewish restriction on visual images, sanctuary decorations are limited to a few traditional designs: the six-pointed Star of David seen in the mosaics and stained glass windows, the Lion of Judah, and the crown, a traditional Torah ornament. The mosaics are by Hildreth Meière.

In the Beth-El Chapel, set back from the avenue north of the main building, the stained-glass window (over the ark) by Louis Comfort Tiffany, originally illuminated Temple Emanu-El's earlier building at 43rd St and Fifth Ave. The museum offers a small collection of Judaica and objects related to the history of the congregation.

MRS. ASTOR'S MANSION

Temple Emanu-El replaced the mansion of Mrs. Caroline Webster Schermerhorn Astor (wife of William Astor), also known as *the* Mrs. Astor, who dominated New York society in the closing years of the 19th century. Her mansion, designed by Richard Morris Hunt to resemble a French Renaissance château, featured a two-ton bathtub cut from a single block of marble, and a ballroom, the capacity of which was said to correspond to the number of acceptable people in New York society, the "Four Hundred." Her previous mansion was replaced by the former Waldorf-Astoria (*see p. 234*).

SARA DELANO ROOSEVELT MEMORIAL HOUSE
Map p. 617, D1. 47–49 East 65th St (Park and Madison Aves). Open for tours with advance notice if guides are available. T: 212 650 3174, roosevelthouse.hunter.cuny.edu.
This double house was commissioned (1908; Charles A. Platt) by Sara Delano Roosevelt as a Christmas gift, one half for herself and the other half for her son Franklin and his bride Eleanor (an arrangement not mentioned to the young couple in the letter describing the gift). Not only do the two halves share a front entrance, but they are connected by interior doors, probably a design no bride would welcome, especially Eleanor, whose mother-in-law wanted to continue dominating her only child's life.

When FDR was struck by polio he recuperated here, close to the centers of political power, a decision Eleanor supported. Since Sara had wished her son to retire from politics and live the life of a country gentleman at the family estate in Hyde Park, Eleanor's support for Franklin's political career, and her rejection of Sara's wishes, started the couple on the political partnership they would long share. As president, Roosevelt broadcast several of his *Fireside Chats* from the second floor library. The house serves as a public policy institute for Hunter College, part of the City University of New York.

MUSEUM OF AMERICAN ILLUSTRATION
Map p. 617, E1. 128 East 63rd St (Park and Lexington Aves). Open Tues 10–8, Wed–Fri 10–5, Sat noon–4. Closed Sun, Mon, month of Aug, legal holidays. Attractive restaurant; shop. T: 212 838 2560, societyillustrators.org.
Located in an 1875 carriage house, the museum is the exhibition space for the Society of Illustrators and offers changing exhibitions designed to encourage interest in the art of illustration. The society dates back to 1901, when its monthly dinners attracted such famous artists as Maxfield Parrish, Frederic Remington, and N.C. Wyeth. The museum as an institution, however, dates from 1981 and now has a collection of about 2,000 works. Exhibitions include solo and group shows, historical and thematic exhibitions, and the Illustrators' Annual Exhibition, which showcases the best book, editorial, advertising, and institutional illustrations of the year. In 2012 the Museum of Comic and Cartoon Art (MoCCA), formerly in SoHo, transferred its assets to the museum, where they are on rotating display in a special gallery.

BRICK AND LIMESTONE MANSIONS
The 14-story apartment building at **834 Fifth Avenue** at East 64th St (1931; Rosario Candela and James Carpenter) is one of the city's finest addresses, architecturally and socially. Candela, a Sicilian-born immigrant, son of a plasterer, became the most sought-after architect of luxury apartments during the 1920s and '30s. He arrived when he was 19, barely speaking English, and graduated from the Columbia School of Architecture three years later, in 1915. Keenly aware of his talent, he is reputed to have roped off his drafting table at Columbia so that other students could not copy his work. This building, one of the last completed before the Depression, is clad in limestone, decorated with a few Art Deco touches, and topped off with a 20-room triplex that once belonged to Laurance Rockefeller, grandson of the paterfamilias. Laurance Rockefeller moved into the building and liked it so much that he bought it (1926), converting it to co-ops and retaining the prime penthouse for himself. The 1929 Multiple Dwelling Law, which replaced the Tenement House Law of 1901, allowed taller apartment buildings than previously permitted if the upper floors were set back, and so this building, like others of the same period, has setbacks concluding in an elaborate skyline presence. Residents include select billionaires (not every billionaire who applies gets in), but have also included such celebrities as Bing Crosby—not so rich, but more famous.

The **former Edward Berwind mansion** at 828 Fifth Avenue (1896; Nathan C. Mellen), a brick and limestone Italianate palazzo, has been converted to apartments. Berwind was at one time reputedly the largest owner of coal mines in the nation and for many years served as the chief executive officer of the IRT (Interborough Rapid Transit) subway line. Described as Prussian in appearance, and as dour, close-mouthed, and acquisitive in business dealings, he was apparently socially charming and belonged to about 40 clubs and societies.

At 3 East 64th St stands the **former Marshall Orme Wilson House** (1903; Warren & Wetmore), today the Consulate General of India, one of the few remaining buildings of modest scale designed by Warren & Wetmore, famous for Grand Central Station. Mrs. Marshall Orme Wilson, neé Caroline Schermerhorn Astor, was the socialite daughter of the dowager Mrs. Astor (also named Caroline Schermerhorn Astor; *see p. 332*), who lived just a stone's throw away. The mansion of molded limestone with a slate and copper roof, arched drawing-room windows, and small oval dormers, exemplifies the Beaux-Arts style.

The opulent **no. 2 East 63rd Street** was built for William Ziegler Jr. (1920; Sterner & Wolfe), heir to the Royal Baking Powder fortune. He lived there for only five years, perhaps because he and his first wife divorced. A proposal to convert it to a hospital for actors and actresses came to nothing (perhaps to the relief of the neighbors), and Norman B. Woolworth, a distant cousin of the founder of the five-and-dime chain, bought it in 1929, later donating it to the New York Academy of Science. (The Academy is now located at 7 World Trade Center and the house is privately owned.)

Although the majority of nearby buildings reflect French or Italian originals, the **Knickerbocker Club** at 2 East 62nd St (1915; Delano & Aldrich) recalls a townhouse of the Federal period, with fine brickwork, marble lintels, and wrought-iron window gratings. The club was founded downtown in 1871 by several members of the Union Club who felt that admission standards were becoming too lax.

At 1 East 60th St is the **Metropolitan Club**, in an imposing Italian Renaissance palazzo (1892–4; McKim, Mead & White). The club is another offshoot of the Union Club, founded in 1891 for reasons quite different from those that gave birth to the Knickerbocker Club. J. Pierpont Morgan and other disgruntled members of the Union Club bolted after the board of governors blackballed John King, president of the Erie Railroad, whom Morgan had proposed for membership. One of the club members allegedly remarked that King had been voted down because, figuratively at least, he ate with his knife. Morgan is said to have told Stanford White to "build a club fit for gentlemen. Damn the expense." The expense turned out to be about $2 million, spent on marble walls, stained-glass windows, a coffered ceiling and grand staircase leading to a second-story loggia. The club founders purchased the land from Lily Churchill, who had inherited a fortune from her first husband before marrying the eighth Duke of Marlborough; some of her money went toward maintaining Blenheim Palace.

BLOOMINGDALE'S

Bloomingdale's (*Lexington to Third Aves, East 59th to East 60th Sts; map p. 617, E2*), the upscale department store, now has branches across the United States but its New York flagship is *the* Bloomingdale's. It is known as "Bloomies" to its habitués, who can be seen toting its trademark "Small," "Medium," and "Big" brown bags around the city. Lyman Bloomingdale, who with his brother Joseph founded the store in 1872, learned the retail business as a clerk in Bettlebeck & Co. Dry Goods in Newark, NJ, a firm whose all-star sales staff included Benjamin Altman (later of B. Altman & Co.; *see p. 363*) and Abraham Abraham (later of Abraham and Straus). Unlike the other 19th-century department stores, which began downtown and migrated uptown, Bloomingdale's started at 938 Third Ave, only a few blocks from its present location. In both its arrival and its demise, the Third Avenue elevated railway was a blessing to Bloomingdale's, first bringing so many shoppers from downtown when it opened (1879) that within seven years the store had to move to larger quarters on the northwest corner of Third Ave and 59th St, a block it now occupies completely. When the El was torn down (1954), the neighborhood, its real estate formerly depressed by the dark and dirty railway, began a swift climb to respectability and affluence. Fortunately Bloomingdale's' management had already begun upgrading the inventory from its former "good quality but sensible" merchandise to more stylish gear. By the 1970s, Bloomingdale's had become such a destination that Queen Elizabeth II visited in 1976, and though its star may have since faded somewhat, it remains an iconic store, known worldwide.

SHOPPING IN THE NEIGHBORHOOD

The Upper East Side, one of Manhattan's wealthiest neighborhoods, was built up in the early decades of the 20th century by the well-to-do and has remained their territory for a century. In its most elite commercial precincts—Madison Avenue between about 57th and 86th Sts, the shopping opportunities are commensurate with the general economic scale.

Two of the city's illustrious department stores—Bloomingdale's and Barney's—reside here. Flagship boutiques of European and American designers, and shops glittering with all kinds of luxury goods, line Madison Avenue. Here you can buy French crystal, Italian shoes, Chinese export porcelains, American leather handbags, and Swiss watches. You can eat hand-made chocolates, buttery pastries, and perfectly ripened cheese. You can have your nails done, your shoes fixed, your clothes dry-cleaned, and your hair styled. You can resell your wedding dress, or buy a designer gown that belonged to someone else. You can also buy more ordinary things, but that is not what this patch of pavement is known for. Stores are usually open Monday–Saturday 10–6. Some stay open late on Thursdays and are open on Sundays.

There are art galleries on both Madison Ave and East 57th St, sometimes offering museum-quality shows. In general the uptown galleries are traditional rather than cutting-edge, though there are exceptions. Saturday is the conventional gallery-hopping day. Many art galleries are closed Mondays and have restricted summer hours.

THE ASIA SOCIETY AND MUSEUM

Map p. 617, D1. 725 Park Ave (East 70th St). Open Tues–Sun 11–6, Fri until 9 (except July 4 through Labor Day). Closed Mon, July 4, Thanksgiving, New Year's Day. Admission charge. T: 212 288 6400, asiasociety.org.

In 1951 John D. Rockefeller III traveled to Japan, a journey that awakened his interest in the Far East. Five years later he founded the Asia Society to enrich American understanding of Asian cultures—the arts, history, and contemporary affairs of a diverse group of peoples. Today the society has become a global institution, with centers elsewhere in the US and in Asia.

The New York branch of the society occupies a distinctive building (1981; Edward Larrabee Barnes Assocs, expanded 2001). On the original Park Avenue façade, incised in the red Oklahoma granite, the society's logo, adapted from an 18th-century bronze Nepalese guardian lion, "protects" the entrance, like the ferocious beasts that shielded traditional Asian Buddhist temples against evil forces.

The collection

The society's exhibitions of Asian art range from ancient to contemporary and include work from private collections as well as from the society's own permanent collection, the core of which was given by Mr. and Mrs. Rockefeller. The Rockefeller donation includes objects from Japan, Korea, China, India, and Southeast Asia; Chinese bronze ritual vessels dating from the early 10th century BC and Ming Dynasty (early 15th century) ceramics, including Ching-te-chen blue and white ware; Indian sculpture from the Kushan period (late 2nd–3rd centuries); manuscript pages from the Rajput School (16th–19th centuries, northern India); Buddhist sculptures from Thailand (7th–8th centuries), Indonesia (8th–12th centuries), and Burma (11th–15th centuries); and Japanese woodcuts and ceramics, ranging from the Jomon period (c. 10,500–300 BC), through 16th-century stoneware, to elegant porcelains of the Edo period (1615–1867). In 2007 the society began collecting contemporary Asian and Asian-American art, focusing on video, animation, and new media. Both the Rockefeller collection and the contemporary Asian collection are shown in rotating exhibits.

DOMESTIC ARCHITECTURE ON EAST 70TH STREET

The rich and/or famous began moving east of Fifth Avenue around the turn of the 20th century, building townhouses on this quiet side street (and others nearby).

The Explorers' Club (*46 East 70th St, near Park Ave*), founded in 1904, has included on its roster Sir Edmund Hillary, Tenzing Norgay, Neil Armstrong, and Thor Heyerdahl. The club (*not open to the public except for occasional lectures*) owns rare books, manuscripts, and paintings of historical value as well as memorabilia of famous explorers. The building (1912; Frederick J. Sterner) was originally the home of Stephen C. Clark, younger son of Singer Sewing Machine magnate Edward Clark, who built the Dakota Apartments.

The Visiting Nurse Service of New York (*107 East 70th St*) occupies the **former Thomas W. Lamont residence** (1921; Walker & Gillette), a grandiose Tudor Revival home with leaded-glass windows and a heavy, detailed wooden door. Lamont was chairman of the board of J.P. Morgan & Company and as a diplomat worked to protect American financial interests abroad during the 1920s and '30s. His widow bequeathed the house to the Visiting Nurses.

The neo-Georgian house at **118 East 70th St**, with its attractive fanlight and sidelights, was designed (1900) by Trowbridge & Livingston, who also built (1903) the Beaux-Arts townhouse across the street (*123 East 70th St*) for architect Samuel Trowbridge himself. The undistinguished modern house at **124 East 70th St** was built in 1941 for Edward A. Norman, an heir to the Sears, Roebuck fortune. Architect William Lescaze, who earlier had built his own townhouse on East 48th St, was one of the pioneers of the International Style in New York.

The **former Paul Mellon House** (*125 East 70th St*), built for the philanthropist, art collector, and horse breeder, is one of the few townhouses built after World War II (1965; H. Page Cross). It is remarkable for its 40-ft width (two townhouses were torn down to make way for it) and for having a garden.

FIFTH AVENUE AND THE EAST 70s

The **former Joseph Pulitzer house** at 11 East 73rd St (1903) was modeled by McKim, Mead & White on two Venetian palazzi, with a wide façade, arched windows, and colonnades. It stood empty much of the time Pulitzer owned it, because the publisher's illness, near-blindness, and extreme sensitivity to sound made the house unattractive to him, despite the fact that it had a special room with double walls to minimize noise.

The **Commonwealth Fund** (*1 East 75th St*) has its headquarters in the former Edward S. Harkness house (1909; Hale & Rogers), an example of the superb craftsmanship available at the turn of the 20th century to those who could pay for it. Protected by a spiked iron fence and a "moat," the building, with its beautifully carved marble, resembles an Italian palazzo, elegantly detailed from the elaborate cornice to the iron ground-floor gates. The fund was started by Anna Harkness, wife of one of the original partners of Standard Oil, who was charged by her husband to "do something for the welfare of mankind"; it supports improvements to the health-care system, especially for the elderly and society's most vulnerable.

A WELL-PRESERVED PATRICIAN BLOCK

The **former James B. Duke mansion** at 1 East 78th St (1912) is now preserved as the New York University Institute of Fine Arts. Built of white limestone so fine that it would pass for marble, the building was modeled after an 18th-century mansion in Bordeaux. James Buchanan ("Buck") Duke rose from rural beginnings to dominate the tobacco industry, becoming president of the American Tobacco Company in 1890 and maintaining his position of power even after the Supreme Court found his company in violation of the anti-trust laws. The architect, Horace Trumbauer, was already known in Philadelphia for his grand houses; this is his first New York work. Duke lived here until his death in 1925; his daughter, Doris Duke, and his widow donated the property to New York University in 1957.

The Cultural Services of the French Embassy, on Fifth Ave between 78th and 79th Sts (*972 Fifth Ave*), are located in the **former Payne Whitney house** (1906) by McKim, Mead & White, one of the earliest Italian Renaissance mansions north of 72nd St. It is notable for its curved and elaborately carved façade of light gray granite, a material not generally used because of its extreme hardness. The house belonged first to Payne Whitney, philanthropist, financier, and horse racing fan, who kept stables in Kentucky and on Long Island. His estate was calculated at a quarter of a billion dollars. His elder brother married Gertrude Vanderbilt (*see p. 203*); his wife, Helen Hay Whitney, was a daughter of John Hay, secretary of state under Presidents William McKinley and Theodore Roosevelt. Their daughter, Joan Whitney Payson, was the principal owner of the New York Mets baseball team from its beginnings in 1962 until her death in 1975, and their son, John Hay (Jock) Whitney, was publisher of the *New York Herald Tribune* and ambassador to Great Britain.

The **former Henry H. Cook** house next door at 973 Fifth Ave (1902–5) is also by McKim, Mead & White, designed to look visually continuous with the Payne Whitney house. Cook, a banker and railroad developer, at one time owned the entire block and formerly occupied a larger, more extravagant dwelling on the site of the James B. Duke mansion.

Looming up on the southeast corner of Fifth Ave and 79th St is the home of the **Ukrainian Institute of America**. The house (1899), designed by C.P.H. Gilbert for Isaac D. Fletcher, is a picturesque French Gothic mansion, with high slate roofs, pinnacled dormers, gargoyles, and a "moat" protected by an iron fence. The Institute maintains a collection of contemporary Ukrainian art and mounts exhibitions of painting, sculpture, and folk art (*open Tues–Sun 12–6; suggested donation; T: 212 288 8660, ukrainianinstitute.org*).

THE ISAAC D. FLETCHER HOUSE

Isaac D. Fletcher, a broker and banker, died in 1917, leaving his art collection and $3 million in stocks to the Metropolitan Museum. The collection included several Corots, Millet's *Autumn Landscape with a Flock of Turkeys*, a charming portrait by Marie Villiers, and a *Head of Christ* formerly attributed to Rembrandt, plus many minor works, including a picture of the Fletcher mansion and a portrait of Fletcher himself.

After Fletcher's death, the house was sold to Harry D. Sinclair, founder of the oil company that bore his name. Sinclair was implicated in the Teapot Dome scandal during the administration of President Warren G. Harding and was indicted for bribery and conspiracy to defraud the government of lucrative oil leases. Sinclair spent six months in jail for contempt of court (he had hired a detective agency to shadow each of the jurors) and sold the house when he got out of prison, his reputation, but not his fortune, in tatters.

The next owner was Augustus Van Horne Stuyvesant, who lived here with his sister Anne. The pair, both unmarried, had sold their townhouse on 57th St to move north ahead of the onslaught of commerce. Augustus, the last direct male descendant of Governor Peter Stuyvesant, was a successful real estate dealer, but after Anne's death in 1938, he spent his declining years in the house, eventually becoming a complete recluse, attended only by his butler and his footman.

THE FORMER WHITNEY MUSEUM BUILDING

Between 1966 and 2015, after which time it moved to the Meatpacking District, the Whitney Museum of American Art occupied the landmark building at 945 Madison Ave at East 75th St. The building itself is considered a work of art. The Metropolitan

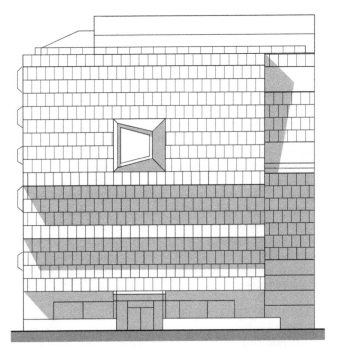

945 MADISON AVENUE

Museum will use it as an offshoot gallery—the Met Breuer—at least until 2023, while refurbishing its own galleries of modern art. Thomas Hart Benton's famous murals *America Today* (*see below*) are scheduled to be installed when the Whitney vacates.

The building (1966) was designed by Marcel Breuer, a pioneering Modernist. Born in Hungary, educated in part at the Bauhaus, Breuer joined the Harvard faculty in 1937 along with Walter Gropius, where the two of them influenced the next generation of American architects. Before the emergence first of SoHo and then Chelsea as important centers of contemporary art, the Whitney was squarely in the heart of the gallery district, a neighborhood mostly of low-rise buildings. Intended to stand out, perhaps brazenly, from its neighbors, the building's architectural power was recognized immediately. "At the top of the list of must-be-seen objects in New York," noted the architect-authors of the *AIA Guide to New York City* (American Institute of Architects); *New York Times* critic Ada Louise Huxtable found it harshly handsome, a "disconcertingly top-heavy inverted pyramidal mass [that] grows on one slowly, like a taste for olives or warm beer." Some critics objected to its Brutalism, but gradually the building won widespread if occasionally grudging admiration.

The building is sheathed in dark gray granite and overhangs a sunken sculpture court, spanned by a concrete bridge. The upper three floors are cantilevered outward, creating maximal gallery space and also throwing the sculpture court into shadow. The trapezoidal windows, irregularly spaced and sized, are angled so that light does not fall on the works of art within.

THOMAS HART BENTON'S *AMERICA TODAY*

Painted in 1930–1 for the boardroom in the New School of Social Research, these murals, donated to the Met in 2012, reflect one man's view of American life at a time when new technology seemed capable of propelling the nation toward a bright future; the murals express optimism about the prospect, but also a sense of nostalgia for a simpler past. Thomas Hart Benton was a populist, an admirer of small towns and rural expanses. A central panel of the murals shows the tools of technology—speeding locomotives, airplanes, oil wells. The life of working people includes tilling fields, building cities, mining coal, herding cattle; the sectors of the murals depicting urban scenes are more satirical, depicting dance halls, speakeasies, strippers, and subway riders. With historical hindsight, the optimism of the murals seems at odds with the realities of Depression America, but as Benton pointed out, the Depression hit hard only when he had almost completed the cycle; the final panel, however, "Outreaching Hands," painted after the others had been installed, depicts a breadline.

The success of the murals galvanized Benton's career and provided momentum for the Works Progress Administration mural programs instituted during the Depression. The murals will be on display at the former Whitney building while the Met's refurbishments take place.

ST. JEAN BAPTISTE CHURCH

The towered and domed silhouette of St. Jean Baptiste Church (1913; Nicholas Serracino) anchors the intersection of Lexington Ave at East 76th St (*map p. 615, E4*). It was built to serve a parish of French Canadian Catholics founded in 1882. Thomas Fortune Ryan, who made his money from streetcars, tobacco investments, and eventually insurance, paid for the building. According to legend, Ryan arrived late for Mass one Sunday in 1910 and had to stand throughout the service; afterwards he asked the priest the cost of a new, bigger church; without much reflection, the priest threw out the figure of $300,000, and Ryan immediately offered to foot the bill, which turned out to be at least twice as large as estimated.

This church has Italian Renaissance precedents, especially in its soaring dome, open towers, and Corinthian portico and in the decoration of the interior. Painted clouds float on the ceiling of the nave; gold-stenciled fleurs-de-lis adorn the wall behind the altar. The stained-glass windows were made in Chartres.

EATING AND DRINKING IN THE SILK STOCKING DISTRICT

While Fifth Avenue is strictly residential, except for its cultural and religious institutions, the nearby side streets and avenues offer upscale restaurants.

$$$$ **Café Boulud**. Possessor of a Michelin star, the café is the less formal relative of its more famous downtown counterpart. The food is French in inspiration and beautifully prepared. *Prix fixe* lunch. Lunch and dinner daily, Sun brunch. *20 East 76th St (Fifth and Madison Aves). T: 212 772 2600, cafeboulud.com. Map p. 615, D4.*

$$$$ **Daniel**. ▬ A Michelin two-star restaurant on a luxurious street, with elegant appointments and beautiful, perfectly prepared food. Has been criticized for uneven service. *Prix fixe* or tasting menu only, though the lounge has *à la carte* dining. Dinner Mon–Sat. *60 East 65th St (Madison and Park Aves). T: 212 288 0033, danielnyc.com. Map p. 617, D1.*

$$$ **Caravaggio**. Italian food in an elegant modern setting, with a more affordable *prix fixe* lunch. Lunch and dinner daily. *23 East 74th St (Fifth and Madison Aves). T: 212 288 1004, caravaggioristorante.com. Map p. 615, D4.*

$$$ **Il Riccio**. Upscale white-table-cloth Italian restaurant with food of the Amalfi Coast, many seafood choices. Tables are closely spaced. Dinner daily. *152 East 79th St (Lexington and Third Aves). T: 212 639 9111, eatilriccionyc.com. Map p. 615, E4.*

$$$ **Il Ristorante Rosi**. The East Side sister of a *salumeria* across town, offers small plates of Italian cured meats and cheeses as well as the usual Italian menu. Bar, abundant wine cellar, and some sake choices, since the chef finds sake a fine pairing with salumi. Lunch and dinner daily. *903 Madison Ave (72nd and 73rd Sts). T: 212 517 7700, salumeriarosi.com. Map p. 615, D4.*

$$ **Garden Court Café**. In the light and leafy Asia Society atrium, this quiet café serves pan-Asian cuisine: sushi, Vietnamese sandwiches, Malaysian curries. No need to pay the museum entrance fee. Lunch Tues–Sun. *725 Park Ave (70th St). T: 212 570 5202, http://asiasociety.org/new-york/garden-court-cafe. Map p. 617, D1.*

The Metropolitan Museum of Art

The Metropolitan Museum of Art, aka The Met, is the largest, most comprehensive art museum in the world.

Founded in 1870, today the Metropolitan Museum of Art draws more than six million visitors annually. The building occupies two million square feet (roughly 42 times the size of an American football field or 62.5 times the footprint of Westminster Abbey) and its collections include more than two million objects, whose range includes the entire world and 5,000 years of human civilization. The 400-plus galleries can be overwhelming, so you might test the waters with an hour-long guided Highlights Tour. Crowds can be overwhelming too, especially during the Christmas holiday season and on weekends, so try to go on weekdays or early on weekends.

Visiting the Met

Map p. 615, D3. Fifth Ave (West 79th–86th Sts). Open Sun–Thur 10–5:30, Fri and Sat 10–9. Closed Thanksgiving, Christmas, New Year's Day and the first Mon in May. Suggested donation: you are legally required to pay something, but while the museum suggests an admission fee, you may pay what you wish. Tickets also valid for Cloisters within a week of purchase. Tours and audio tours. Restaurant, cafés, and gift shops; app for mobile devices. T: 212 535 7710, metmuseum.org.

The Virtual Met

The Met website—metmuseum.org—is a virtual course in art history, suggesting itineraries, describing exhibitions, and offering some 400,000 images of works, many accompanied by written descriptions. You can search by artist, geographical location, date of composition, or material. A timeline of art history has links to thematic essays, and an interactive floor plan lets you click and zoom around galleries.

HISTORY OF THE MET

John Jay, grandson of the first chief justice of the US, first suggested what would become the Metropolitan Museum of Art while dining in Paris in 1866. Jay's fellow members of the Union League club, a group of sober and high-minded liberals, under-

THE METROPOLITAN MUSEUM
The central Beaux-Arts façade (1902) by Richard Morris Hunt.

took raising money for a noble institution, "not a mere cabinet of curiosities for the idle rich," but a democratic museum that would "educate and refine a practical and laborious people," as one of the trustees intoned at the building's opening ceremonies in 1880. The museum was originally closed on Sundays. The first open Sunday in 1891 drew a record 12,000 visitors. Sunday is still the most popular day.

The museum's first purchase was a collection of 174 paintings, mostly 17th-century Dutch and Flemish, bought for $116,180 by a trustee. Its first gift was a Roman sarcophagus (*see p. 348*). The museum's fortunes rose when trustee J. Pierpont Morgan became president. During his tenure (1904–13) the museum acquired important European art, began archaeological excavations in Egypt, and built wings for decorative arts and medieval works. After Morgan's death, the museum received between six and eight thousand objects from his collections many of which remain on display: paintings, sculpture, Gothic woodcarving, furniture, jewelry, Egyptian antiquities. Throughout the 20th century the Met continued to expand, building new wings and enlarging the collections, becoming a truly encyclopedic institution.

During the social upheavals of the late 1960s and '70s, under director Thomas P.F. Hoving, the museum sought to serve a broader population. Hoving broadened education programs, acquired the Temple of Dendur, opened the Islamic galleries, and developed the concept of the blockbuster exhibition (the Tutankhamen show attracted 1.3 million people in four months). He also provoked controversy by his de-accessioning paintings in order to buy others.

Philippe de Montebello followed Hoving and under his leadership the museum and its endowment nearly doubled in size. Refurbished galleries for Greek and Roman art opened; the Linsky, Annenberg, and Gelman collections arrived. Today under director Thomas Campbell, the museum is a major publisher of art books and a star in the city's cultural firmament, with 6.2 million visitors annually.

THE BUILDING

After some debate, the City allowed the young museum to locate in Central Park and taxed New Yorkers to raise half a million dollars for construction costs; the City still owns the building but the museum trustees own the art. Though the building has grown from modest Ruskinian Gothic beginnings to its present size and complexity, its additions reflecting reigning architectural styles, the original brick and limestone walls (1874–80; Calvert Vaux and Jacob Wrey Mould) are visible from the European Sculpture Court (Gallery 548) and the Lehman Wing.

Richard Morris Hunt designed the Beaux-Arts central Fifth Avenue façade (1902); the north and south wings (1911 and 1913) are by McKim, Mead & White. The uncarved blocks above the columns of Hunt's façade were intended to have allegorical groups representing major periods in the history of art, but funds never materialized.

During the 1970s and '80s Roche, Dinkeloo and Associates redesigned the Fifth Avenue stairs and added Modernist glass-walled wings on the other façades: the Lehman Wing (1975) on the west, the Sackler Wing for the Temple of Dendur (1979) to the north, and the Michael C. Rockefeller Wing (1982) to the south. Conservationists criticized the expansion, especially the Lehman Wing, echoing sentiments of Frederick

Law Olmsted, who regretted allowing the museum even a toehold in his territory. As a condition for the City's approval of the new wings, the museum agreed not to intrude further into the park; since then it has "built from within," reclaiming courtyards, offices, and the former restaurant for exhibition space. Recently renovated galleries include those for Oceanic art, arts of Native North America, French decorative arts, and the Roman sculpture court (all 2007), Byzantine art (2008), musical instruments (2010), art of the Arab Lands, Turkey, Iran, Central Asia, and Later South Asia (2011), the American wing (2007–12), and European paintings (2013). The Fifth Avenue plaza was redesigned (2014) with programmable fountains and shaded seating, but the monumental steps—a favorite meeting place—remain as they were.

THE COLLECTION

The steps from Fifth Ave lead into the Great Hall, with imposing floral displays and, often, equally imposing crowds. Highlights are given below. Numbering refers to numbering of the galleries in situ in the museum.

A: GREEK AND ROMAN ART

The collection of Greek and Roman art spans several millennia, several civilizations, and several thousand miles—from the Bronze Age cultures of the Aegean to the farthest-flung colonies of the Roman Empire. The earliest pieces come from the Cycladic civilizations of the 2nd and 3rd millennia BC and the most recent from the Roman Empire at the time of Constantine (emperor AD 306–337), whose conversion to Christianity marked a turning point in the history of the ancient world.

Prehistoric and Early Greek Art:
Galleries 150–2 contain Neolithic and Cycladic marble sculptures, monumental vases from the Geometric period, and small-scale bronzes. Notable pieces include a marble Cycladic statuette of a seated harp player (Gallery 151), a small bronze of a centaur confronting a man (Gallery 152), whose superior height indicates his victory, and a Mycenaean terracotta stirrup jar (Gallery 151), around whose swelling body a goggle-eyed octopus wraps its tentacles.

Greek Art, 6th–4th centuries BC:
Gallery 153, a barrel-vaulted and skylit corridor, is one of the city's great interior spaces. On view here are large-scale ceramics including Athenian prize amphorae—which were filled with olive oil and presented to victorious athletes. Except for temple decorations and grave reliefs, most Greek sculptures were executed in bronze; few have survived, but one superlative example is the museum's *Diskos Thrower*. Other Greek statues exist in Roman copies.

Greek Art, 6th century BC:
Dominating Gallery 154 is a large marble *kouros*, a nude male funerary figure, whose frontal pose, blocky form, and stylized wiglike hair derive from Egyptian art. Also here are grave steles, one showing a boy and girl guarded by a sphinx; it was erected by a father who lost his son, here shown as an athlete with an oil bottle strapped to his wrist.

METROPOLITAN MUSEUM
(FIRST FLOOR)

A   Greek and Roman Art
B   Arts of Africa, Oceania, and the
     Americas
C   Modern and Contemporary Art
D   European Sculpture and Decorative Arts

E   Medieval and Byzantine Art
F   Arms and Armor
G   Egyptian Art
H   American Art

Greek Vase Painting, 6th–4th centuries BC: The collection is set out in Galleries 155, 157 and 159. Greek vases of the 6th century BC include black-figure ware, an Athenian style that placed the human figure and narrative at the center of the decorative scheme. The figures are black (often decorated with red) against a natural, clay-colored ground. From about 530 BC, the red-figure style came into its own. Figures were drawn in black outline and the spaces between them filled with a black slurry. After firing, the figures showed

up red; details could be added with a paintbrush, a technique which offered more expressive possibilities than incision. Especially beautiful (Gallery 157) is an amphora attributed to the Berlin painter, depicting a rapt musician playing a lyre, swaying to his music.

Greek Art, 5th–4th centuries BC: On display in Galleries 156 and 158 are are grave markers from the time when Athens rose to artistic dominance. The most famous relief, *Girl with Doves* (Gallery 156), conveys the idealized

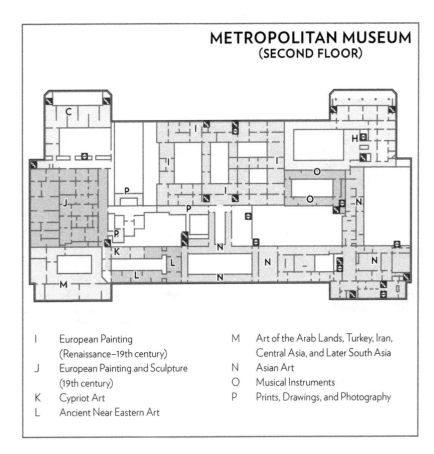

METROPOLITAN MUSEUM
(SECOND FLOOR)

I	European Painting (Renaissance–19th century)
J	European Painting and Sculpture (19th century)
K	Cypriot Art
L	Ancient Near Eastern Art

M	Art of the Arab Lands, Turkey, Iran, Central Asia, and Later South Asia
N	Asian Art
O	Musical Instruments
P	Prints, Drawings, and Photography

beauty and sweetness of the child, although the figure of the girl has been made more mature; actual children or old people do not appear in Greek sculpture until much later.

Hellenistic Sculpture and Architecture: The huge Sardis column in Gallery 160, a gracefully scrolled Ionic capital (here with only part of its deeply fluted shaft), stood in the Temple of Artemis in Sardis (capital of ancient Lydia, near modern Izmir in Turkey). Here also are marble and bronze

Hellenistic portraits and large painted vases from Southern Italy.

Roman Sculpture Court: Designed (1912–26) by McKim, Mead & White for Roman art but demoted to service as the museum's restaurant, the beautiful Gallery 162 has been restored as a two-story peristyle atrium, flooded with natural light. It provides an opulent setting for art based on Greek or Hellenistic models but created under Roman patronage. The marble *Statue of an Old Woman* is now thought to represent an aged courtesan on her way to a festival for the god Dionysos. That deity is portrayed in the *Hope Dionysos* and on the elaborate *Sarcophagus with the Triumph of Dionysos and the Seasons*. The marble *Garland Sarcophagus* was the first object offered to and accepted by the Met (1870).

The Hellenistic Treasury: The small Gallery 163 offers such luxurious objects as a pair of gold armbands decorated with male and female tritons, each holding a tiny figure of Eros; and a bronze statuette of a veiled and masked dancer, whose rhythmic movements are suggested by the drapery covering her body.

Roman Wall Paintings: The Met has the finest collection of Roman wall paintings outside Italy (Galleries 164–5). The three panels (c. 40–30 BC) from Boscoreale, a luxurious country villa north of Pompeii, probably created to celebrate a dynastic marriage, were preserved by the eruption of Vesuvius in AD 79. Bronze sculptures in the gallery include a statue of Eros as a plump baby and the powerful statuette of an artisan with silver eyes, evidence of Hellenistic artists' accurate depiction of youth and age. The wall paintings on the bedroom from Boscoreale show *trompe l'oeil* architectural vistas and garden scenes. The twisted mullions of the actual metal window frame, warped by the heat of the eruption, suggest the power of the cataclysmic event.

Art of Augustan Rome: Augustus became emperor in 26 BC, and during his long reign a style of imperial portraiture developed (Gallery 166) in which the emperor was depicted, whether in marble or on coins and gems, in idealized, ageless form; the larger-than-life marble head of Augustus, which exemplifies the idealizing style, was probably made after his death in AD 37. The wall paintings from Boscotrecase come from the bedroom of a villa built by Agrippa (friend of the Augustus and commander of the fleet that defeated Antony and Cleopatra), near the Bay of Naples.

The Black Room (Gallery 167) is reconstructed from the villa of Agrippa Postumus, with wall paintings in a later, more delicate style than those of Boscoreale.

Art of the Later Roman Empire: The larger-than-life nude bronze portrait statue of the emperor Trebonianus Gallus (Gallery 169), his brow lined with anxiety, his torso grotesquely thickened, dates from AD 251–253. A similarly anxious expression, typical of portraits from the 3rd century AD, strains the features of the irascible emperor Caracalla. Considering the rapid turnover of 3rd-century Roman emperors and the fates of these two, both murdered, the anxiety seems well-founded. The blocky, colossal head of Constantine with its uplifted eyes, possibly to indicate the spirituality of the emperor who first embraced Christianity, shows a further movement away from naturalism and back towards the idealization of the Augustan age.

Etruscan Art: The mezzanine overlooking the court (Galleries 170–2) contains the Study Collection and Etruscan art. Etruscan skill in metalwork is apparent in the most spectacular object, the reconstructed bronze ceremonial chariot found in a tomb near Spoleto. Dating from the late 6th century BC, the chariot is decorated with repoussé reliefs illustrating episodes from the life of the Greek hero Achilles. Also on view are gems, notably the Morgan amber, a five-inch chunk of amber carved to depict a reclining man and woman. One of the most important pieces of pre-Roman amber, it came from the bequest of J. Pierpont Morgan. Nearby are bronze mirrors, tripods, cauldrons, pails, and other utilitarian objects, as well as examples of Etruscan pottery and a fine display of jewelry.

B: ARTS OF AFRICA, OCEANIA, AND THE AMERICAS

The architecturally dramatic Michael C. Rockefeller Wing (1982; Roche, Dinkeloo and Associates) was given by former New York State governor Nelson A. Rockefeller in memory of his son Michael, who died in a rafting accident (1961) while on a collecting expedition in Papua New Guinea. It houses the collection of the former Museum of Primitive Art, privately founded by Rockefeller, as well as the governor's own personal collection, supplemented by gifts and museum acquisitions.

African art: Highlights of Galleries 350–2 include wooden sculptures from Western, Central, and Equatorial African cultures that signify power or authority, honor ancestors, or house spiritual forces. Near the entrance, an astonishing 19th-century *Kongo Power Figure* leans forward aggressively, the nails and metal objects driven into his body, and his headdress signifying the figure's authority. In the section devoted to the Guinea Coast are an extraordinary early 16th-century ivory pendant mask (Gallery 352) and collections of bronze and brass objects from the Court of Benin (Nigeria), as well as delicately carved Afro-Portuguese ivories.

Arts of Oceania and Native America: The glass-walled Melanesian gallery (Gallery 354) is one of the most spectacular spaces in the museum, in part because of the scale of the works exhibited and in part because of the subversive attraction of the pagan cultures they represent. On view are a seven-foot slit gong with vestigial hands and huge round eyes, originally part of a gong orchestra but also a means of long-distance communication. Overhead hang the ceiling panels of a ceremonial house composed of more than 270 separate paintings. Near the slanted glass wall stands a 49-foot Asmat canoe. Most impressive is the collection of towering ancestor poles, cut from single mangrove trees, turned upside down, the winglike projections carved from single roots. These monuments were used once, then discarded; the ceremonies at which they presided served as preludes to head hunting.

Native American art (Gallery 356) includes wood sculpture, prehistoric stone carvings, and a five-foot carved whale mask worn by a performer who moved the fins, flippers, and gaping mouth to imitate a whale in motion.

Arts of the Americas: The display of Mesoamerican, South American, and pre-Columbian artifacts in Galleries

357–9 includes ferocious Aztec and Toltec stone sculptures, ceramics from several cultures, and a roomful of luxurious gold and silver objects (Gallery 357). Among the Olmec artifacts are jade ornaments and a "baby" figure, possibly representing a god. The 6th-century *Mirror Bearer* (Gallery 358) is one of the few Maya wooden objects to have survived time, moisture, and insect infestation.

C: MODERN AND CONTEMPORARY ART

The Metropolitan awakened late to modernity, establishing a department of 20th-century art only in 1967, although earlier gifts, including Georgia O'Keeffe's bequest from the estate of Alfred Stieglitz, had nudged the museum toward the present. In recent decades the collection has benefited from donations of European Modernist art—the Gelman Collection (Galleries 904–7) and a generous gift from art dealer Klaus G. Perls, which included major works by Picasso. The collection has works on paper, paintings, and sculpture by such major European figures as Balthus, Braque, Matisse, Miró, Modigliani, and Picasso, but its strength lies in American Modernist art, particularly The Eight, the Alfred Stieglitz circle, and the Abstract Expressionists, all of whom had strong ties to New York City.

THE MADISON AVENUE BUILDING

In 2011, the Metropolitan Museum announced that it would lease the Whitney Museum of American Art's architecturally significant Madison Ave building when the Whitney moved downtown to its new home in the Meatpacking District in 2015. The Met will use the Madison Ave space to display modern and contemporary art while it renovates its present galleries. Thomas Hart Benton's Regionalist murals, *America Today* (1930–1) painted for the boardroom of the New School for Social Research in Greenwich Village and donated to the Met in 2012, will also be hung in the former Whitney (*see p. 340*).

Reimagining Modernism: Organized thematically, these U-shaped galleries (Galleries 900–3 and 908–13, with the Gelman collection as the crossbar) exhibit American and European Modernist works, arranged in interesting juxtaposition rather than chronologically. Leading into Galleries 900–1, whose paintings suggest a retreat from the stresses of modern life into nature or history, is Georgia O'Keeffe's famous *Cow's Skull* (1931) in patriotic red, white and blue. Elsewhere in the room are Balthus's enigmatic *The* *Mountain* (1936–7), Edward Hopper's melancholy *Lighthouse with Two Lights* (1929), and Grant Wood's *The Midnight Ride of Paul Revere* (1931), an overhead shot of the patriot galloping through an idealized village.

Direct Expression: Presented in Gallery 911 are works whose artists sought alternatives to what they saw as constricting European traditions. On view are Picasso's famous *Portrait of Gertrude Stein*, said to reflect his discovery of Iberian sculpture; Stein presented it to the Met because she wanted it here.

Also displayed in this gallery are works by the self-taught painter Horace Pippin; Jean Dubuffet's deliberately flat and unconventional *Woman Grinding Coffee* (1945); an elongated marble head by Amedeo Modigliani; and a surprising ebony carved head by Alexander Calder. Other artists represented here include Jacob Lawrence, George Grosz, Otto Dix, Charles Sheeler, and Marsden Hartley. Umberto Boccioni's bronze sculpture entitled *Unique Forms*

of Continuity in Space (1913) is an important exemplar of Italian Futurism.

The Gelman Collection: In 1998, the Met inherited the collection of Jacques and Natasha Gelman. Highlights (Galleries 904–7) include Matisse's *Young Sailor II* (1906), possibly the most famous Fauve portrait; Braque's Cubist *Still Life with Banderillas* (1911); de Chirico's *Jewish Angel* (1916); and Dalí's Surrealist *Accommodations of Desires* (1927) along with 14 works by Picasso, spanning his entire career.

D: EUROPEAN SCULPTURE AND DECORATIVE ARTS

The Metropolitan's collections, some 60,000 objects, contain sculpture from the Renaissance to 1900, and ceramics, glass, metalwork and jewelry, woodwork and furniture, tapestries, textiles, clocks, and mathematical instruments. The galleries are organized geographically and chronologically, but even so the exhibit can be overwhelming. Ceramics, clocks, goldsmiths' work, textiles, and light-sensitive works are usually shown in changing exhibitions. The department was established in 1907, during the presidency of J. Pierpont Morgan, with a gift of more than 1,600 French decorative objects. Highlights include French and English period rooms, Italian Renaissance sculpture, French and German porcelain, and Italian maiolica.

Italian Decorative Arts: Period rooms (Galleries 500–8) include the *studiolo* (c. 1479–82), a small room for study and reflection from the Ducal Palace in Gubbio and a bedroom from the 18th-century Venetian Palazzo Sagredo (Gallery 507).

English Decorative Arts and Period Rooms: Galleries 515 and 516 contain two Neoclassical rooms decorated by Robert Adam.

French Decorative Arts and Period Rooms: The spectacular French period rooms (Galleries 522–32 and 544–9) recreate the luxury and elegance of

the reigns of Louis XV and XVI. Among them are a carved oak Parisian shopfront (Gallery 545) from the reign of Louis XVI, and a reception room from the Hôtel de Cabris (Gallery 527) in Grasse, with magnificent painted and gilded paneling. Furniture includes Louis XV's red and gold lacquered writing table (Gallery 525) and examples of upholstered, lacquered, and gilded furniture by Martin Carlin and André-Charles Boulle. The collection also contains Savonnerie carpets, gold snuff boxes, silver, and Sèvres porcelains.

European Sculpture Court: This serene and formal court (Gallery 548) looks out into Central Park through large windows that bring changes of light into the galleries. Sculptures are arranged chronologically east to west (the Central Park side). Among the highlights are Jean-Louis Lemoyne's delicately erotic *Fear of Cupid's Darts* (1739–40), *Ugolino and his Sons* (1865–7) by Jean-Baptiste Carpeaux, and Auguste Rodin's *The Burghers of Calais* (1884–95), anatomically distorted and psychologically intense depictions of six citizens of Calais who volunteered for martyrdom to spare Calais from destruction. (Another casting of this work is in the Brooklyn Museum.)

The Jack and Belle Linsky Collection: The Linskys, Russian immigrants who had made their fortune manufacturing Swingline staplers, donated their collection of European paintings, sculpture, and decorative arts to the museum in 1982, stipulating that it be kept together and remain forever on display (Galleries 537–43); if the museum sold anything or put it into storage, the whole collection could go elsewhere. The Linskys first collected small precious objects—jewelry, French porcelain, bronzes—but their collection grew to include paintings by Carlo and Vittorio Crivelli, Giovanni di Paolo, and Andrea del Sarto.

The Robert Lehman Collection: This great bequest (Galleries 950–9) came to the museum with the condition that the collection remain permanently intact and that seven period rooms from Lehman's townhouse on West 54th St be recreated within the museum. The red-brick and gray granite east wall of the wing is the back wall of the original Metropolitan, designed by Calvert Vaux and Jacob Wrey Mould.

ROBERT LEHMAN, INVESTMENT BANKER AND COLLECTOR

In 1925 Robert Lehman succeeded his father as head of the Lehman Brothers investment bank. The younger Lehman, who invested early in such fledgling ventures as retail chains, airlines, and television, once remarked that the key to success in investment banking was to "put your money in the right place at the right time"—advice Lehman also applied to the art market, about which his knowledge was encyclopedic.

Lehman's father Philip had started collecting in 1911, purchasing Italian, Spanish, and French paintings, as well as decorative arts. As the available supply of Old Masters dried up, Robert began to buy Impressionist paintings, illuminated manuscripts, and exquisite drawings, but he also acquired a few Old Masters as they became available, including Rembrandt's *Gérard de Lairesse* and Ingres's *Princesse de Broglie*.

Among the artists of the Italian Middle Ages and Renaissance, painters of the Sienese School are represented with works by Ugolino da Siena, Simone Martini (c. 1326); the superbly dramatic *Creation of the World* and *Expulsion from Paradise* by Giovanni di Paolo (1445), and the Osservanza Master's mysterious *St. Anthony the Abbot in the Wilderness*. Outstanding among the Florentine paintings is a small Botticelli *Annunciation* with beautifully drawn figures of the Virgin and Angel curving toward one another. Among the northern Renaissance paintings are works by Hans Memling, Petrus Christus, and a well-known portrait of *Erasmus of Rotterdam* by

Hans Holbein. Dutch paintings include Rembrandt's portrait of *Gérard de Lairesse* (1665). Among the Spanish paintings are El Greco's *St Jerome as Cardinal* (c. 1610–14) as well as Goya's *Condesa de Altamira and her Daughter, María Agustina* (1787–8).

There are French masterworks of the 19th and 20th centuries: the glorious *Princesse de Broglie* (1851–3) by Ingres; the engaging *Two Young Girls at the Piano* (1892) by Renoir; paintings by the Post-Impressionists and the Fauves, and Balthus's *Nude Before a Mirror* (1955).

E: MEDIEVAL ART

NB: Medieval art is also on display at The Cloisters; see p. 461.

The collection contains Byzantine silver, enamels, glass, ivories, jewelry, metalwork, stained glass, sculpture, enamels, and tapestries—works created in Europe from the 4th to the early 16th centuries, roughly from the time of the fall of Rome to the beginning of the Renaissance. Although the first medieval object entered the museum in 1873, the department found its footing with a gift of two thousand objects collected by J. Pierpont Morgan, who died in 1913. (The accession numbers for objects in the Morgan bequest begin with 17.190.) The galleries are arranged more or less chronologically, with an introductory section on Byzantine art, two large galleries devoted to Romanesque and Gothic art, and a Medieval Treasury with small, richly decorated enamels, ivories, and examples of metalwork—jeweled or not.

Medieval Sculpture Hall: A 52- by 42-ft wrought iron Choir Screen from the Cathedral of Valladolid dominates Gallery 305. The beautifully carved alabaster mourners from the tomb of the Duc de Berry may represent relatives and allies of the duke, whose full-size effigy lay on top of the sarcophagus. Tapestries (rotated because of light sensitivity) may include *The Annunciation* (c. 1410–30) and the sumptuous *Rose Tapestries* (c. 1450), depicting courtiers and ladies, possibly woven for Charles VII of France.

Medieval Treasury: On display in Gallery 306 are stained glass panels, Gothic sculptures, and goldsmiths' work, as well as devotional objects, for example a small crib of the Infant Jesus decorated with scenes of the Nativity and the Adoration of the Magi; four angels stand watch on the bedposts.

F: ARMS AND ARMOR

The collection of arms and armor contains weapons that range from arrowheads to jewel-encrusted swords, revolvers and rifles, crossbows and halberds, powder horns and pistols, but the centerpiece is the Equestrian Court, whose armored men on horseback "parade" beneath colorful Arthurian banners. Among the finer pieces are suits of English armor made at the royal workshops in Greenwich, established by Henry VIII. Among the earliest pieces of European armor is a 6th-century gilded Germanic *spangenhelm* (Gallery 371); among the finest is a 16th-century *burgonet* (Gallery 374) signed on the brow piece by the Milanese master armorer Filippo Negroli.

The collection also contains astonishing examples of Japanese armor (Gallery 377). On view are ferocious face masks from the Edo period (1615–1868), armor from the Kamakura period (early 14th century), helmets in fantastic shapes (one represents a crouching rabbit), and Samurai swords.

G: EGYPTIAN ART

The Met owns the finest collection of Egyptian art in the United States; its 26,000 objects (almost all on display) date from 300,000 years ago to AD 400, i.e., from the time people settled in the Nile Valley until pharaonic hieroglyphics fell from use and the last Egyptian temple was closed. More than half of the collection comes from the museum's archaeological work in Egypt, during a series of important excavations that began in 1907 and continued for 35 years. J. Pierpont Morgan contributed significantly to the excavations, which he occasionally visited until his death.

The galleries are organized chronologically beginning with the prehistoric material just north of the Great Hall on the east side of the building; they continue in a U-shape, reaching the Temple of Dendur and then doubling back to the Great Hall.

Highlights of the collection, long a favorite with museum visitors, include tomb models illustrating aspects of everyday life, collections of royal jewelry, and superb funerary trappings—coffins, mummies. The Temple of Dendur and the Tomb of Perneb are notable architectural monuments.

The Tomb of Perneb: Built c. 2381–2323 BC, remarkable in its completeness, the tomb (Gallery 100) functioned both as a house for the departed court official Perneb and as a sacred place in which life-perpetuating rituals were eternalized through their depiction in the wall paintings. Paintings decorating the central offering room show Perneb at a table receiving food offerings from servants and relatives. On a far wall a false door allowed Perneb's spirit to emerge to enjoy goodies arranged on a slab in front of the door.

Models from the Tomb of Meketre: This marvelous set of wooden models (Gallery 105), buried with Meketre (c. 1990 BC; *see box opposite*), a powerful

administrator with a long career, assured him of a comfortable living in the world beyond; the bakery, granary, and brewery would eternally provide him with beer and bread. The exquisitely detailed statue of an offering bearer, a woman with a basket of meat on her head and a duck in her right hand, is the finest figure in the collection. The feather pattern on her dress was sometimes associated with the funerary goddesses Isis and Nephthys.

The Height of Middle Kingdom Art. In Gallery 111 is the red quartzite *Face of Senwosret III* (c. 1878–1841 BC), whose heavy-lidded eyes and lined cheeks create a somber, careworn expression, unusual in the portrayal of a ruler. The dark gray gneiss *Sphinx of Senwosret*

III, known for his military exploits, shows him as a stern, powerful figure. Also from this period is the blue faïence statuette of a hippopotamus, which has become a symbol for the Met's Egyptian collection. The figure may have been sculpted as a protective amulet since the ancient Egyptians, armed with first-hand experience, considered hippos threatening rather than cute; three of the legs have been restored, the originals were broken off to prevent the animal from wreaking havoc in the afterlife.

Other important artifacts include the jewelry of Princess Sithathoryunet. Her cloisonné pectoral of 372 precious stones precisely cut and set into metal cells depicts two falcons, representing the sun god Re; from the two cobras above the falcons hang two *ankhs* (symbols of life); the central cartouche encircles a hieroglyph with the throne name of Senwosret II.

THE DISCOVERY OF MEKETRE'S TOMB MODELS

By 1920, when museum archaeologists visited Meketre's tomb at Thebes, it had collapsed, leaving a dark, gaping cave. While having the rubble cleared, the museum's chief excavator, Herbert Winlock, discovered a small chamber dug into the floor. Although the rest of the tomb had been looted in antiquity, the hidden chamber and these beautifully preserved models had remained untouched for nearly 40 centuries. According to the agreement with the Egyptian government then in effect, the models were divided equally between the Egyptian Museum in Cairo and the Metropolitan, which received six boats, four models of food production, an enclosed garden, a procession of three offering bearers led by a priest, and the female offering figure holding the duck.

Sculptures of the Female Pharaoh Hatshepsut: Hatshepsut (c. 1473–1458 BC), the sister and wife of Thutmose II, produced no male heir; her successor, Thutmose III, a son of Thutmose II by a lesser wife, was therefore both her nephew and her stepson. When Thutmose II died young, Hatshepsut became regent for her stepson-nephew, a position that apparently gave her a taste for power. She consequently declared herself pharaoh and continued to rule using the authority of powerful advisors. It is uncertain whether Thutmose III killed Hatshepsut or simply waited for her to die, but on her death he saw to it that all her memorials were destroyed, including the 200 statues in her funerary temple in western Thebes.

The Metropolitan excavated thousands of fragments from the temple and pieced them together; twelve of the reconstructions now stand in Gallery 115. The most appealing is a limestone seated figure showing Hatshepsut in the traditional masculine garb of a ruler, but clearly a woman.

Art of the Amarna Period. Amenhotep IV declared that light was the only divine power in the universe; Aten, the sun disk, was the means by which divinity entered the world and Amenhotep himself, renamed Akhenaten, was the only prophet of the new deity. Running into resistance from the established priesthood, Akhenaten built a new capital downriver from Thebes near present-day Tell el-Amarna. Early depictions of the ruler, gaunt and long-jawed, are carved in a mannered style that approaches caricature. Akhenaten was married to Nefertiti, whose name means "the beautiful one is here." Tutankhamun, Akhenaten's son (or possibly nephew) and successor restored Amun as the state-supported god and renamed himself accordingly. On view in here (Gallery 121) is a limestone head of Tutankhamun (c. 1336–1327 BC) with the hand of the god Amun on the back of his crown as if in blessing. The woman represented by the beautifully carved yellow jasper fragment of a queen's face (c. 1353–1336 BC) cannot be surely identified, but may possibly be either Nefertiti or another wife of Akhenaten.

The Temple of Dendur: The temple (c. 23–10 BC) was built on the banks of the Nile by the Roman emperor Augustus in part as a public relations gesture to appease a conquered people; some 19 centuries later it came to the United States as a goodwill gesture for contributions to preserve Nubian monuments endangered by the Aswan Dam. The temple (Gallery 131) honors Osiris, a god associated with the Nile and its fertility, as well as two brothers who drowned in the sacred river during military campaigns.

Arts under the Ptolemies. Displayed in the claustrophobic Gallery 133 are mummies, decorated sarcaphagi, canopic chests (containers for mummified inner organs), and sculptures from the dynasty (332–30 BC) established by Ptolemy, a general of Alexander the Great. Also on view are a limestone head of Arsinoë II, sister and wife of Ptolemy II, and a long papyrus roll inscribed with the "Book of the Dead."

Egypt under Roman Rule: The faces in the Fayum Portraits, of people who lived 19 centuries ago, were found in 2nd-century Greco-Roman cemeteries in the Fayum district south of Cairo, where the customs of the large Greek community merged with traditional Egyptian ways. They are exhibited here (Gallery 138) together with the museum's most recent mummy, which dates to around AD 280.

H: THE AMERICAN WING

The American Wing holds a superb collection of American painting, sculpture, and decorative arts dating from the 17th- and 18th-century colonial settlements up to the early 20th century. The collection is organized chronologically in three broad areas: Architectural Elements, Sculpture, and Decorative Arts (Galleries 700–7); Historic Interiors and Decorative Arts (Galleries 708–46); and Paintings and Sculpture (Galleries 747–72). A study collection occupies Galleries 773–4.

Architectural Elements, Sculpture, and Decorative Arts: The Garden Court (Gallery 700) with fountains, greenery, and views of Central Park, provides a tranquil setting for 19th- and early 20th-century sculpture and architectural elements. On the north wall is the staid marble façade of the United States Branch Bank (1824), originally at 15½ Wall St. On the south wall Louis Comfort Tiffany's stained-glass window, *View of Oyster Bay* (c. 1905), with its subtle gradations of color, shows his technique at its most dazzling. Also in this gallery are two of Daniel Chester French's extraordinary marble funerary sculptures, "Mourning Victory" from the Melvin Memorial (1906–8) and the "Angel of Death and the Sculptor" from the Milmore Memorial (1889–93).

In the central open space are works in marble and bronze by 19th-century Neoclassical and Beaux-Arts sculptors: Anna Hyatt Huntington, Hiram Powers, Hermon Atkins MacNeil, and Frederick William MacMonnies. Augustus Saint-Gaudens's gilt bronze *Diana* (1892–3, cast 1928) is a half-size model of the shocking statue that stood on the second Madison Square Garden (*see p. 197*).

Above the Garden Court, on the balcony (Galleries 704–6), American decorative arts are arranged chronologically and by material, beginning in the northeast corner. The earliest pieces date from the colonial period (1660–1790) and the most recent from the middle of the 20th century. Displays of pewter, silver, glass, and ceramics range from simple utilitarian wares to opulent presentation pieces. On the west side is Tiffany's *Magnolia Vase*, whose opulent decoration includes plant motifs representing different geographic areas of the country (pine cones, magnolias, cacti). The *"Century Vase,"* created for Philadelphia's Centennial Exhibition of 1876, has handles modeled like bison heads, profiles of George Washington, and scenes from American history.

Historic Interiors and Decorative Arts: The museum's 20 historic interiors (period rooms) depict the sweep of American domestic architecture and decorative arts from the early colonial period to the opening decade of the 20th century, with the earliest room from Massachusetts (1680) and the most recent from Minnesota (1914). A core group (Galleries 708–30), donated together in 1924, is organized with the earliest rooms on the third floor and the more recent ones below. Highlights include the Hart Room (Gallery 709), from 1680, which demonstrates the architectural and craft practices of early British settlers; the early 19th-century Verplanck Room (Gallery 718), from a pre-Revolutionary house at 3 Wall Street, whose furnishings, including the portraits by John Singleton Copley, belonged to a single family; and the luxurious Richmond Room (Gallery 728) appointed with early 19th-century furniture by Duncan Phyfe and Charles-Honoré Lannuier, and printed French scenic wallpaper.

Later historic interiors, donated to the museum after this core group and installed elsewhere in the wing, include an austerely furnished Shaker Retiring Room (Gallery 734); parlors and a library in 19th-century Revival styles: Greek, Gothic, Rococo, and Renaissance (Galleries 736–40); and a stair hall by McKim, Mead & White. Highlighting the entire group is a living room from a "Prairie style" house by Frank Lloyd Wright (Gallery 745), built in 1912–14. Wright designed every piece of furniture and specified where each should be placed.

In Gallery 735, John Vanderlyn's *Panorama of the Palace and Gardens of Versailles* (1818–19), the largest painting in the museum, was painted to suggest the sensation of actually standing on the grounds of Versailles surrounded by its buildings and gardens. In an age when travel was arduous, panoramas of faraway places were popular, painted on great canvases, rolled up and carried from city to city. Vanderlyn hoped to make his fortune with this rendering of Versailles, but the painting failed to attract the public, possibly because of its formality and emptiness.

Paintings and Sculpture: The galleries of American Paintings unfold chronologically and thematically, beginning around 1730 and continuing up to about 1915. Interspersed among the pictures are examples from the museum's collection of small-scale sculpture, colonial silver, and folk art.

The earliest (Gallery 747) displays **Colonial portraiture** (1730–76), including the work of John Singleton Copley, the most gifted of American painters of his era, noted for his skill at characterization and his rendering of textures—not to mention his willingness to portray his subjects as they might wish to be seen. American heroes of the Revolution are portrayed (Galleries 753–5) by Charles Willson Peale, John Trumbull, and Gilbert Stuart, who had studied in London. Paintings in the **Folk Tradition** (Gallery 757),

include landscapes and portraits by painters who may or may not have been trained, but who chose to work within a stylistic framework of bright colors, flat or patterned surfaces, and altered perspective.

The landscape painters of the **Hudson River School** (Galleries 759–61) dominated the aesthetic landscape during much of the 19th century. Like Thomas Cole, generally considered the founder of the movement, they turned their attention to the natural beauty of the still-unspoiled continent. Cole's *View from Mount Holyoke, Northampton, Massachusetts, After a Thunderstorm—The Oxbow* (1836), with its foreground of untamed mountain wilderness and background of serenely pastoral fields, was seminal. Second-generation Hudson River School painters (Gallery 761) John Frederick Kensett, George Inness, and Martin Johnson Heade were influenced by trends in European art and preoccupied by the effects of light.

Emanuel Leutze's *Washington Crossing the Delaware* (1851; Gallery 760), a romantic reconstruction of history painted in 1851 and inaccurate in many details, is nonetheless deeply imprinted on the American consciousness. Also on view are large-scale canvases of distant and exotic landscapes: Albert Bierstadt's *The Rocky Mountains, Lander's Peak* (1863) and Frederic Edwin Church's *Heart of the Andes* (1859). Sculpture includes Hiram Powers's bust of a worn and toothless *Andrew Jackson*.

Among the works from the **Civil War Era** (Gallery 762) is Winslow Homer's *Prisoners from the Front* (1866), based on an event he witnessed as a correspondent-illustrator during the war. In the American West Gallery (Gallery 765) are the ever-popular paintings and bronzes by Frederic Remington, chronicler of cowboys, Indians, and army troopers.

The museum owns impressive work (Gallery 767) by Winslow Homer and Thomas Eakins, the outstanding painters of the late 19th and early 20th centuries. Eakins's *Max Schmitt in a Single Scull* (1871), with Eakins himself rowing in the middle distance, is as much a study of perspective and light as it is of the champion rower working out on the Skuylkill River. Also on view are Homer's late seascapes, depicting the turbulent north Atlantic off the coast of Maine.

In the 1870s and '80s, the **American Impressionists** (Galleries 769–70)—William Merritt Chase, Childe Hassam, Mary Cassatt, John Singer Sargent, John Henry Twachtman, and others—began using techniques that had flourished in France a decade earlier.

In Gallery 771, along with large-scale portraits by Eakins and James McNeill Whistler, is Sargent's *Madame X* (Mme Pierre Gautreau; 1883–4), scandalous in its day, both for the subject's real-life behavior and for her depiction, in a plunging gown with a wayward shoulder strap. Sargent later repainted the strap in its present, more modest location.

The early 20th-century Realist artists of the **Ashcan School** (Gallery 772) rejected both Impressionism and academic gentility, depicting the grittier aspects of urban life; included are Robert Henri, George Luks, William Glackens, John Sloan, and Everett Shinn.

I: EUROPEAN PAINTING 1250–1800

These rooms offer an overview of European painting from the Renaissance to the beginning of the 19th century. The galleries are divided into two suites leading off the doors in Gallery 601 (Baroque Painting in Italy). The southern suite presents the Northern schools: Netherlandish, German, Dutch, Flemish, and British painting, beginning with Jan van Eyck and continuing through Memling, Dürer, Cranach, Bruegel, Jacob van Ruisdael, Frans Hals, Rembrandt, Vermeer, Van Dyck, and Rubens, ending with the work of Sir Joshua Reynolds and Sir Thomas Lawrence. The northern row relates the history of Italian painting from Giotto and Duccio through Raphael and Titian, followed by the great 17th- and 18th-century figures from the Carracci and Caravaggio to Canaletto and Tiepolo.

ITALIAN PAINTING
Giotto and the Pictorial Revolution: Berlinghiero's Byzantine-influenced *Madonna and Child* (c. 1230) is one of only two paintings securely attributed to this seminal artist. Also here (Gallery 602) is a series of four Old Testament prophets by Lorenzo Monaco (c. 1408–10) and a *Crucifixion* (c. 1420–3) attributed to Fra Angelico.

Filippo Lippi to Botticelli: Highlights of Gallery 603 include Botticelli's *Last Communion of St. Jerome* (early 1490s) and his *Three Miracles of St. Zenobius* (c. 1500). Piero di Cosimo's *A Hunting Scene* (1507–8), depicts Man in his primitive, bestial state contending with satyrs and centaurs; its companion, *Return from the Hunt*, demonstrates the mollifying influence of civilization. Piero di Cosimo's *Young St. John the Baptist* depicts a patron saint of Florence.

Venice and North Italy in the 15th and 16th centuries: Fifteenth-century works (Galleries 606–7) include Giovanni Bellini's *Madonna and Child* (late 1480s), Andrea Mantegna's *The Adoration of the Shepherds* (c. 1450), painted when the artist was only about 20 years old, and Vittore Carpaccio's *Meditation on the Passion* (c. 1490), an important devotional image. Later works here include paintings by Titian, Lorenzo Lotto, Paolo Veronese, and Jacopo Tintoretto. Titian's renowned *Venus and the Lute Player* (1565–70) is one of several paintings by the master depicting Venus in a musical setting symbolizing love. Paolo Veronese's *Mars and Venus United by Love* (1570s), a work of the painter's maturity but of uncertain allegorical meaning, seems to show exhausted War collapsed at the feet of bounteous Love.

Central Italian Painting of the High Renaissance: During the 16th century, Rome became the center of Italian painting, with Michelangelo and Raphael its dominant figures. Raphael's *Madonna and Child Enthroned with Saints* (c. 1504; Gallery 609) is part of an altarpiece, painted when Raphael was about 20 years old. *The Agony in the Garden* belonged to the *predella* (small painting or paintings below the main panel) of the same altarpiece. Agnolo Bronzino's elegant *Portrait of a Young Man* (c. 1540) shows the arrogant, self-consciously posed subject in a fashionably slashed black doublet.

The Legacy of Duccio of Siena: Duccio di Buoninsegna, represented in Gallery 625 by a *Madonna and Child*, (1295–1300), is often considered the founder of the Sienese school and a father of European painting. Giovanni di Paolo's *Paradise* (c. 1445), a garden filled with saints and angels greeting and embracing one another, belonged to the same altarpiece as the *Creation and Expulsion from Paradise* (1445) in the Met's Robert Lehman Collection (*see p. 352*). Simone Martini, whose *St. Andrew* (1326) is on view here, probably trained with Duccio and followed the papal court to Avignon, widening Duccio's sphere of influence. This suite of galleries (Galleries 626–7) concludes with Gothic altarpieces, devotional and Northern Italian Gothic painting.

The chronological survey of Italian painting continues near the top of the Grand Staircase (Galleries 600–1 and 618–23) with **Italian Painting from Caravaggio to Tiepolo**, much of it by artists working in Rome. The 18th-century Venetian master Giovanni Battista Tiepolo is represented by three large canvases celebrating the victories of Roman generals.

In the following large gallery (Gallery 601) are examples of **Italian Baroque Painting**. In the 17th century Rome became the theological and artistic center of Italy as the Church during the Counter-Reformation underwrote heroically pious works, for example Guercino's dramatic *Samson Captured by the Philistines* (1619). Also here is Guido Reni's *Charity* (1767), allegorically represented as a nursing mother. John Ruskin considered "the divine

Guido" sentimental and insincere, thus scuttling Reni's reputation, which revived only a century later.

To the north of this large room, Galleries 623, 621, 618 have works by the influential and radical Annibale Carracci, Caravaggio, and Claude Lorrain. Gallery 619 offers **Venetian vedute** by Canaletto and Guardi, and three of Guardi's expressive Fantastic Landscapes, replete with Classical ruins, gnarled trees, and craggy rocks. The survey of Italian painting concludes with Gallery 620: **Rome and Naples in the Eighteenth Century**, dominated by Giovanni Paolo Panini's *Ancient Rome* and *Modern Rome* (1757).

SPANISH PAINTING
Spanish 17th-century Painting: One of the museum's most loved paintings is Velázquez's portrait of *Juan de Pareja* (1650; Gallery 610) the artist's mixed-race studio assistant, who performed menial work for the great painter and was, at the time he sat for this portrait, the painter's slave. Five years later Velázquez freed him and eventually Juan became a painter in his own right. The Met bought the painting in 1971 for $5.3 million (about $31 million in today's dollars), then the largest sum ever paid for a work of art at auction. Also in this gallery are portraits by Bartolomé Esteban Murillo and religious paintings by Jusepe de Ribera.

Spanish 16th- and 17th-century Painting: The Met has the finest holdings of El Greco outside Spain (Gallery 611), and of those paintings the eerie *View of Toledo* and his unsparing *Portrait of a Cardinal* (c. 1600) are

acknowledged masterpieces; both are from the Havemeyer bequest.

Goya: The Metropolitan has a fine collection of Goya portraits (Gallery 612), among them *Manuel Osorio Manrique de Zuñiga*, a tender picture of a young boy in a fancy red outfit, but with allegorical overtones. Other portraits include the *Condesa de Altamira and her Daughter, María Agustina* (1787–8), and Goya's friend *Sebastián Martínez y Pérez* (1792), a wealthy collector of books and paintings. Also on view is *The Afternoon Meal (La Merienda)* (c. 1771) by Luis Meléndez, often regarded as the finest still-life painter of the 18th century, his skill evident in the pebbly texture of the melon rind and the sheen on the grapes.

FRENCH PAINTING
The Salon on the Eve of the Revolution: In Gallery 613 are portraits, including J.-S. Duplessis's celebrated likeness of Benjamin Franklin (1778). There are also works by women painters, who were admitted to the Académie Royale although barred from life drawing classes featuring male nudes. Among the most important were Élisabeth Louise Vigée Le Brun and Adélaïde Labille-Guiard.

David and Neoclassicism: Jacques-Louis David's *The Death of Socrates* (1787; Gallery 614), painted just before the onset of the Revolution, depicts an idealized, heroically posed Socrates, stoically electing to drink hemlock rather than disavow his beliefs. Elegant portraits include David's depiction of the aristocratic *Antoine-Laurent Lavoisier and His Wife* (1788); Lavoisier, the father of modern chemistry, ended his life on the guillotine.

History, Portraits, and Genre in 18th-century France: During this period, when the Académie Royale controlled artistic training and exhibition in the Salons, historical, religious, and mythological subjects were in favor. In Gallery 615 are works by Greuze, Fragonard, and Chardin, who belonged to the Academy but was not trained there; *Soap Bubbles* (c. 1733–4) was influenced in subject and style by the 17th-century Dutch masters, for whom the delicate bubbles suggested the fragility of life.

Paris in the Early 18th century: The idyllic and pastoral works of François Boucher, Antoine Watteau, and their followers (Gallery 616) were painted to please a refined Parisian aristocracy who had abandoned Versailles as the reign of Louis XIV wound down. Watteau's fine *Mezzetin* (c. 1718–20) depicts a stock character in the *commedia dell'arte*, a sympathetic figure troubled by unrequited love, here wistfully depicted serenading an unseen lover.

French 17th-century Painting: Featured in Gallery 617 are Nicolas Poussin's canvases inspired by Classical mythological and literary themes: the haunting *The Blind Orion Searching for the Rising Sun*, painted late in his career, and *The Abduction of the Sabine Women*.

NORTHERN EUROPEAN PAINTING, 1420–1800
Jan van Eyck and his Influence: Although artists had been painting with oils as early as the 12th century in Northern Europe, it was the technical brilliance of such early 15th-century Netherlandish painters as Van Eyck and Van der Weyden (Gallery 641) that led to oils eventually becoming the major painting medium in Europe. Jan van Eyck's *The Crucifixion* and *The Last Judgment* (c. 1435–40) are remarkable not only for the acutely observed detail, but also for the masterful handling of paint to achieve effects of rippling waves and fleeting clouds. Also in this gallery is *Portrait of a Carthusian* (1446), a fine work by Petrus Christus, Van Eyck's chief follower.

Diverse Approaches to Early Portraiture: On view among the portraits (Gallery 644) is Rogier van der Weyden's arresting *Francesco d'Este* (c. 1460), a cool and aristocratic rendering of the illegitimate son of the Duke of Ferrara painted against an atypical white background.

Renaissance Painting in Germany: Hans Holbein the Younger's *Portrait of a Member of the Wedigh Family, Probably Hermann von Wedigh* (1532), is distinguished by its precise drawing and fine characterization. Also here (Gallery 643), Dürer's devotional *Virgin and Child with St. Anne* (1519) depicts the Virgin holding a sleeping Child, whose slumber in traditional iconography was said to foreshadow his death. Lucas Cranach the Elder's charming mythological *The Judgment of Paris* (c. 1528) was interpreted by contemporary German humanists as an allegory for three possible life paths: the contemplative (represented by Minerva), the active (Juno) and the voluptuous (Venus).

Patinir, Bruegel, and Landscape Painting: Gallery 642 has the three panels of Joachim Patinir's *The Penitence of St. Jerome* (after 1515), depicting St. Jerome, the Baptism of Christ, and the Temptation of St. Anthony. Patinir was known for his landscapes, which sometimes overwhelmed the religious subjects. Pieter Bruegel the Elder's *The Harvesters* (1565), suffused with the hot light of summer, was one of six paintings depicting the seasons commissioned by a wealthy Antwerp merchant.

Rembrandt and Hals: On view in Gallery 637 are portraits of prosperous Dutch burghers by Frans Hals, whose slashing brushwork impressed later painters including Van Gogh. The stunning collection of works by Rembrandt includes *Aristotle with a Bust of Homer* (1653), the philosopher resting his right hand on the poet's head, his left hand fingering a gold chain with a medallion of Alexander the Great, Aristotle's pupil. The museum bought this exceptional work in 1961 for the then-astronomical price of $2.3 million; back in 1907, Benjamin Altman wanted it, but Mrs. Collis P. Huntington got it instead. Other works by Rembrandt include: *Bellona* (1633), a plump and plain Dutch woman dressed as the Roman goddess of war; *Man in Oriental Costume ("The Noble Slav")* (1632), neither noble nor Slavic, but a friend whom Rembrandt supplied with props, the costume, and dramatic lighting.

BENJAMIN ALTMAN AS COLLECTOR

Benjamin Altman, founder of the now-defunct department store B. Altman & Company, which occupied a Renaissance-style palazzo on Fifth Avenue (*see p. 268*), never married, devoting himself totally to his work and his art collection. On his death in 1913, he left to the museum paintings and Chinese porcelains valued at $15 million (in 1913 dollars) on condition that the collection be maintained intact in two adjoining rooms.

Around 1900, Altman focused his zeal on porcelains from the Chinese Qing Dynasty (1644–1912). Soon he turned to painting, and like his wealthy contemporaries bought works by the Barbizon School. As his eye matured, he began purchasing works by Italian Renaissance and 17th-century Dutch painters among others—Botticelli and Memling, Vermeer, and, especially, Rembrandt. Unlike J. Pierpont Morgan, Altman was slow to decide on a painting, often vacillating for weeks. But once he made up his mind, he did not haggle.

Still-Life Painting in Northern Europe: In Gallery 635 are paintings of flowers, food including feathered and furred game, tableware, and expensive personal possessions—sometimes with implied moral messages (Pieter Claesz's *Still Life with a Skull and a Writing Quill*), sometimes chosen simply to display the artist's skill rendering light and texture (Jan Davidsz de Heem's *Still Life with a Glass and Oysters*).

Dutch Paintings in the Altman Collection: Benjamin Altman's landscapes (Gallery 634) include Aelbert Cuyp's *Young Herdsman with Cows* (c. 1800) and Jacob van Ruisdael's *Wheat Fields* (1670). He purchased genre scenes by Frans Hals, for example *Young Man and Woman in an Inn* (1623) and *Merrymakers at Shrovetide* (1616–17). But it was Rembrandt who captured Altman's imagination, and he bought more paintings by that master than any other American collector. Some of the works are superb; however, Altman was sometimes misled as to attribution and some of his purchases have been downgraded to "School of Rembrandt." Included among Altman's Rembrandts on view are a *Self-Portrait* (1660), *The Toilet of Bathsheba* (1643), *Portrait of a Man Holding Gloves* (1648), *Man with a Magnifying Glass* (early 1660s), and *Woman with a Pink* (early 1660s).

Vermeer and His Contemporaries: Of the 36 known paintings (according to the Met's tabulation) by Johannes Vermeer, the museum has five, four of them domestic interiors (Gallery 632). The serenely beautiful *Young Woman with a Water Pitcher* (c. 1662), a wonderful rendering of light and color, was the first work by that painter to enter an American museum. *Study of a Young Woman* (late 1660s) is one of Vermeer's few "portraits," though its intention was not so much to capture a likeness as to suggest character. *A Maid Asleep* (1656–7) is the earliest known Vermeer with the kind of domestic interior now recognized as his hallmark. Some commentators, influenced by the untidy table, suggested the painting was an allegory of sloth, but x-ray studies have revealed a man in the background, and the painting may depict a social encounter that has just ended. Also on view are *Woman With a Lute* (early 1660s) and, the least successful of the artist's extant works, the heavy-handed *Allegory of the Catholic Faith* (early 1670s), to which Vermeer converted when he married. Nevertheless, the rendering of the glass sphere, said to represent Heaven, is masterful.

Dutch History Painting: History painting was long esteemed the highest form of art. In Gallery 631 are works by painters from Utrecht and Amsterdam, including Hendrick ter Brugghen's altarpiece *Crucifixion with the Virgin and St John* (c. 1624–5), probably painted for a church in Utrecht, which had the largest Catholic population in predominantly Protestant Holland.

Rubens and Van Dyck: Peter Paul Rubens, the most celebrated northern European figure in Baroque art, lived primarily in Antwerp but absorbed influences from travels to Rome, Genoa, Paris, London, and Madrid. *Venus and Adonis* (Gallery 628) was influenced by Titian's painting of the same subject (in Gallery 607). *Rubens, his Wife Helena Fourment, and their Son, Peter Paul* (c. 1639) is a full-size portrait of Rubens and his second wife, whom he married (1630) when he was 53 and she was 16. Anthony van Dyck, who lived in England during the 1630s, was much in demand by the aristocracy and influenced several generations of English painters; *James Stuart, Duke of Richmond and Lennox* (c. 1633–5) is a flattering portrait of a cousin of Charles I.

British 18th-century Painting:
Pictures of well-to-do patrons and their families by Reynolds, Gainsborough, Raeburn, Romney, and Hoppner (Gallery 629). Especially appealing is Sir Thomas Lawrence's *Elizabeth Farren* (1790), the work of a young virtuoso; the sitter was a popular actress who retired from the stage and married the Earl of Derby.

J: NINETEENTH-CENTURY EUROPEAN PAINTINGS

The Met's 19th-century paintings—spanning Neoclassicism, Romanticism, the Barbizon School, Salon Painting, Impressionism, and Post-Impressionism—are beloved by visitors. There are extensive holdings of the work of Corot, Courbet, Manet, Monet, Degas, Cézanne, and Van Gogh; a renovation and internal expansion in 2007 opened up new gallery space that allowed the museum to broaden its definition of "19th-century European."

Puvis de Chavannes and Salon Painting: Pierre Puvis de Chavannes, best known for his murals, is represented in Gallery 800 by several classically inspired, dreamlike paintings. Nearby are sculptures by Auguste Rodin, an admirer of Puvis. French Salon paintings—large, formal works on traditional subjects, many exhibited in the ultra-conservative Paris Salon—fill the other end of the long gallery. Also on view are animal sculptures by Antoine-Louis Barye.

Neoclassicism and Romanticism:
Among the Neoclassical painters, Jean-Auguste-Dominique Ingres is represented (Gallery 801) by portraits of the industrialist Joseph-Antoine Moltedo (c. 1810) and of Jacques-Louis Leblanc (1823) and his wife (Françoise Poncelle). Major works by painters of the Romantic persuasion include Eugène Delacroix's turbulent *The Abduction of Rebecca* (1846), inspired by Sir Walter Scott's *Ivanhoe*.

19th-century British Painting:
In Gallery 808 are realistic rural scenes by John Constable and several early works by J.M.W. Turner, both of whom inspired their continental contemporaries. Constable's *Salisbury Cathedral from the Bishop's Grounds* (1825) is a study for a painting now in the Frick Collection. Turner's *Venice, from the Porch of Madonna della Salute* (c. 1835) is not an actual view of Venice, but a composite with buildings drawn from multiple perspectives.

Courbet: In Galleries 809 and 811–12 are character-capturing portraits: *Louis Gueymard as Robert le Diable* (1857), showing the tenor posing theatrically in a dashing red costume; *Woman in a Riding Habit (L'Amazone)* (1856), which Mary Cassatt greatly admired; and the demure *Madame Auguste Cuoq* (1852-7). Other works by Courbet include landscapes, seascapes, hunting scenes and provocative realistic nudes, which scandalized the bourgeoisie and the Academy. Also on view is Rosa Bonheur's tumultuous *Horse Fair* (1852–5), given by Cornelius Vanderbilt, scion of a family with a strong interest in horses.

Fin de Siècle Art and Design—Wisteria Room: The reconstructed dining room from the Paris apartment of Auguste Rateau (Gallery 813) is the only complete French Art Nouveau interior in an American museum.

IMPRESSIONISM AND POST-IMPRESSIONISM

The Annenberg Collection—19th- and 20th-century Masters: The Annenberg bequest (announced 1991) of more than 50 works by Manet, Degas, Monet, Renoir, Toulouse-Lautrec, Cézanne, Van Gogh, Seurat, Gauguin, Bonnard, Vuillard, Matisse, Picasso, and Braque, valued at the time at about $1 billion, stipulated that the works be kept together and remain forever on the premises (Galleries 821–3). Among them are Braque's *Studio* (1939), with the signature pink bird that flies through other *Studio* pictures; Cézanne's *Mont Sainte-Victoire*, one of the finer of the many versions Cézanne painted of that scene; Monet's *Path through the Irises,* painted when the artist's vision had begun to dim; and Van Gogh's *La Berceuse* (of Madame Roulin, wife of the postmaster, rocking an unseen cradle).

Manet, Impressionism, and Degas: Although Manet revered the great painters of the past, he was denounced for his modernity in his subject matter (immoral depictions of nudity) and his style (rejection of the smooth, slick, surfaces of academic painting). The Met owes its Manets (Gallery 810) largely to Mrs. H.O. (Louisine) Havemeyer, or rather to her friendship with Mary Cassatt, who advised the Havemeyers on their collection. Among them: *Young Lady in 1866; Mlle V... in the Costume of an Espada; The Spanish Singer; Young Man in the Costume of a Majo; Boy with a Sword; A Matador;* and *The Dead Christ with Angels.* Mrs. Havemeyer was especially captivated by the work of Degas (who had encouraged Cassatt). On view along with small-scale bronzes is his most famous sculpture, *The Little Fourteen-Year-Old Dancer* (1880; cast 1922), the only piece exhibited during the artist's lifetime (Gallery 815).

Monet: Works by Claude Monet here (Galleries 818–19) span his long career, including Impressionist works from the 1860s (*The Green Wave, Garden at Sainte-Adresse,* and *La Grenouillière*); and later works such as *Poplars* (1891), his "series paintings" (*Rouen Cathedral,* the *Houses of Parliament,* and haystacks in different conditions of light and weather), and paintings from his garden at Giverny.

Pissarro: Pissarro's work bridges the gap between Realists (such as Courbet, with whom he studied), Impressionists, and Post-Impressionists (for example Seurat and Cézanne, whom he inspired). In Gallery 820 are landscapes from the French countryside; still lifes and figures; and several later cityscapes.

Renoir and his Contemporaries: Renoir's luminous portraits of women and children include (Gallery 824) an elegant portrait of *Mme Charpentier and her Children* (1878), a society matron a world away socially from *A Waitress at Duval's Restaurant* (c. 1875). Also on view are still lifes and flowers by Henri Fantin-Latour and several scenes by the British painter Alfred Sisley, the quintessential *plein-air* painter, who spent most of his life in France.

Cézanne: The Metropolitan bought its first Cézanne, the first of his paintings to enter an American museum, from the groundbreaking Armory Show in 1913. Today the museum's holdings range from the early portraits with thickly applied paint to the still lifes of the mid-1870s, to his later landscapes that expressed his desire to "do Poussin again, from Nature" and to create "something solid and enduring, like the art of museums." Works on display (Gallery 825) include *The Gulf of Marseilles Seen from L'Estaque, Mont Sainte-Victoire and the Viaduct of the Arc River Valley, Mme Cézanne in a Red Dress, The Card Players*, and several still lifes in which the painter creates the shapes of the fruits, fabrics, and ceramic pots using subtle gradations of color.

Post-Impressionism: In the 1880s avant-garde painters, including some who had been associated with Impressionism, began seeking new directions. Georges Seurat, impressed by contemporary scientific treatises on color, sought a rational basis for achieving vibrant effects; his solution, using a myriad of tiny, precise dots of color, came to be called "Pointillism." On view in Gallery 826 are his *Study for A Sunday on La Grande Jatte* (1884), the final study for the masterpiece owned by the Art Institute of Chicago. Also here is the mysteriously illuminated *Circus Sideshow* (1887–8), as well as works by Paul Signac, his disciple and champion.

Between 1886 and 1888, Vincent van Gogh lived in Paris where he encountered the works of the Impressionists and the innovative paintings of Seurat and Signac that influenced his attitude toward color and the application of paint. His *Portrait with a Straw Hat* (1887) dates from this period; on the back of the panel is *The Potato Peeler* (1885), an earlier peasant study. Paintings made in the south of France include *Cypresses* (1889); *L'Arlésienne: Madame Joseph-Michel Ginoux* (1888–9); and *Irises* (1890).

Henri Rousseau, called Le Douanier, was self-taught but endowed with an imagination that allowed him to paint jungles when he had only seen botanical gardens; the dreamlike quality, naïve style, and flat colors of *The Repast of the Lion* (c. 1907) would later attract Picasso and influence the Surrealists.

Paul Gauguin departed France for Tahiti hoping to find a tropical paradise whose inhabitants lived harmoniously in nature, worshiping ancient gods. *Ia Orana Maria* ("Hail Mary") (1892), his first major Tahitian canvas, shows a brown-skinned, yellow-winged angel announcing Mary and the child Jesus to two Polynesian women.

Salon Paintings: Many of the Academic paintings in Gallery 827, by Alexandre Cabanel, Pierre-August Cot, Léon Bonnat, and other painters popular in the waning decades of the 19th century, came from a bequest by Catharine Lorillard Wolfe, philanthropic heiress to part of the Lorillard tobacco fortune.

Bonnard and Vuillard, *Fin de Siècle* Avant-Garde, Early Picasso and Matisse: Galleries 828–30 offer works from the turn of the 20th century by artists who laid the groundwork for modern and contemporary art. Included are paintings by Picasso from his "Blue Period."

K: CYPRIOT ART

The museum has the best collection of ancient Cypriot art outside of Cyprus, much of it gathered by Luigi Palma di Cesnola (1832–1904), the Metropolitan's first director. An immigrant from Italy with a military background, Cesnola fought in the American Civil War and was rewarded by being appointed consul on Cyprus. Once there, he devoted his considerable energy to excavating some 35,000 works, which he quickly shipped to New York. Although Cesnola was untrained in archaeology and his methods today are highly suspect, his collection when put on view at the Metropolitan greatly enhanced the reputation of the fledgling museum. Works range chronologically from the early Bronze Age to the end of antiquity, and since Cyprus came under the successive domination of Assyria, Persia, Egypt, and Greece, its art exhibits a range of influences. The collection is strong in limestone sculpture, which includes tall male and female votive figures, funerary steles and sarcophagi, and images of gods and goddesses. There are also vessels in gypsum, terra cotta, glass, and silver. A limestone sarcophagus (Gallery 175) from c. 475–460 BC displays hunting and banqueting scenes as well as images from Greek mythology. In Gallery 174 is a silver-gilt bowl with Egyptian, Assyrian, and Phoenician images. The most important piece in the collection (also Gallery 174) is the monumental Amathus sarcophagus, notable for its remaining polychromy and its decoration—a chariot procession (on the two long sides), fertility figures of Bes and Astarte (on the short sides), with sphinxes and palmettes on the lid.

L: ANCIENT NEAR EASTERN ART

The collection of Ancient Near Eastern Art reaches back to the 8th millennium BC and forward to the Arab conquest of the Near East in the mid-7th century AD. Geographically the collection extends from the Mediterranean to the valley of the Indus River, now in central Pakistan, and from the Arabian Sea to the Caucasus and Eurasian steppes. The heartland is Mesopotamia, the fertile valley between the Tigris and Euphrates Rivers.

The history of the Ancient Near East, unlike that of Egypt unified by the presence of the Nile, is fragmented into many political and cultural areas. In southern Mesopotamia alone the Sumerians, Akkadians, Babylonians, Seleucids, Parthians, and Sasanians built capital cities in succession through the centuries. Yet despite chronological and cultural remoteness, the objects from these cultures have an immediacy that often speaks across time and distance.

After the Introductory Gallery (400), the exhibit is arranged chronologically, beginning with the Neolithic period and continuing through the development of many of the underpinnings of modern civilization: writing, organized religion, permanent settlements, cities and territorial empires, and trade routes—the Silk Road—that linked far flung areas. On view are items as small as jadeite beads from the 8th millennium BC and as large as the monumental stone reliefs (Gallery 401) and carvings that decorated the palace of King Ashurnasirpal II (reigned 883–859 BC). There are cylinder seals with geometric symbols, human and animal shapes, and cuneiform inscriptions. Religious figures include a wide-eyed gypsum statue (Gallery 403) of a bearded Sumerian worshiper wearing a long sheepskin skirt with a tufted border. The glazed and molded brick wall panels (Gallery 404) were taken from the palace of Nebuchadnezzar II (r. 604–562 BC), known in biblical stories for his wickedness, but also a great builder of palaces, gateways, and roads.

M: ART OF THE ARAB LANDS, TURKEY, IRAN, CENTRAL ASIA, AND LATER SOUTH ASIA

The collection, one of the world's finest, traces the development of Islamic art over 13 centuries, starting with its beginnings in the Middle East and then ranging geographically from Morocco and Spain to Central and South Asia. The layout of the galleries suggests the connectedness of the (mostly secular) works on display, as well as the complex history that shaped them.

The Introductory Gallery (450) offers exceptional works that suggest the scope of the collection (ceramics, carpets, miniature paintings, architectural fragments, calligraphy, weapons, luxury items, metalwork): a 10th-century bowl from Iran, its elegant calligraphy warning, "planning before work protects you from regret"; a gold-encrusted sword (c. 1525) from the Court of Suleiman the Magnificent; a pair of carved, inlaid doors with geometric designs from 14th-century Cairo; pages from several Qur'ans; and a 16th-century illustration from a "Khamsa" (Quintet) of Amir Khusrau Dihlavi (India).

From here the galleries proceed counterclockwise, beginning (Gallery 451) with early Middle Eastern dynasties from the 7th–10th centuries and ending (Gallery 464) with South Asian art from the 16th–20th centuries. Among the early highlights are a folio from a Qur'an (Gallery 451) written in "new style" script with dramatic vertical strokes. Further along are a brass ewer lavishly decorated with repoussé and inlay, and a large 13th-century bronze incense burner shaped like a lion (Gallery 453). The blue-tiled prayer niche or *mihrab* (Gallery 455), c. 1354–5, decorated with geometric and calligraphic designs, is an extraordinary example of early mosaic tile work. Arts of the book include painted folios from the famous *Assembly of the Birds* or *Mantiq-al-Tair* (Gallery 455), illustrations from the Book of Kings or *Shahnama* (Gallery 462), and pages from the *Shah Jahan Album* (Galleries 463–4). Large and magnificent carpets (Gallery 459) may include the "Kuba" carpet, more than 21ft long, woven in the 18th century in the Caucasus. One of the most astonishing pieces of calligraphy (Gallery 460) is the *tughra* (official royal seal and signature) of the Ottoman sultan Suleiman the Magnificent (16th century). Islamic architecture is best represented in the collection by the opulent Damascus Room (Gallery 461) from an 18th-century home of the late Ottoman period.

N: ASIAN ART

The collection of Asian art is organized geographically, with separate sections devoted to ancient and modern China, Korea, Japan, South and Southeast Asia and the Himalayan kingdoms. The works—paintings, lacquer work, calligraphy, textiles, sculpture, and ceramics—date from the 2nd millennium BC to the present.

Chinese Art: Examples tracing the history of Chinese ceramics are displayed on the Great Hall balcony (Galleries 200–5). Beyond Gallery 206, with its monumental Chinese Buddhist sculptures from the 5th and 6th centuries, are galleries devoted to the arts of ancient China. The collection is rich in archaic bronzes, painting and calligraphy (shown in rotation), and decorative arts. Gallery 217, "Chinese Courtyard in the Style of the Ming Dynasty," is modeled on a 12th-century court from Suzhou, which was built by a public official as a retreat from the burdens of his job. Constructed in China, the court was assembled here (1980) according to traditional methods by a team of Chinese craftsmen. Against the south wall stands a fantastically shaped Taihu rock, one of several in the courtyard harvested from the bottom of Lake Tai, whose waters and sands give them their characteristic forms, savored by connoisseurs.

Japanese Art: The Japanese galleries (Galleries 223–32) contain paintings, sculpture, ceramics, lacquer, textiles, metalwork, and woodblock prints spanning more than 4,000 years, from the 3rd millennium BC up to the present. Installations of painting, sculpture and decorative arts change twice a year, with fragile works—hand scrolls with narrative paintings, folding screens, textiles—rotated more frequently. Among the works familiar to Met habitués are the mid-17th-century *Old*

Plum Tree by Kano Sansetsu; Ogata Korin's *Eight Plank Bridge*, also called *The Irises* (after 1709); and Katsushika Hokusai's *Great Wave at Kanagawa* (c. 1831). Sculptures in Gallery 224 on permanent display include a 12th-century Dainichi Buddha seated upon a lotus pedestal in a contemplative posture.

In Gallery 229 Isamu Noguchi's sculptural *Water Stone* evokes Japan's tradition of symbolic, spiritual gardens.

Korean Art: Gallery 233 offers changing displays of ceramics, painting, sculpture, metalwork, textiles, and lacquer work from the 4th century BC through the present.

South and Southeast Asian Art: Galleries 234–53 are arranged chronologically and geographically to trace the development of Hindu, Buddhist and Jain religious sculpture from the early centuries BC until the 16th century AD. Among its strengths are Buddhist sculpture in stone and bronze, fine bronze images from the Chola period, Javanese metalwork, and Khmer sculpture. Overhead in Gallery 242 rises a carved wooden dome and its supporting structure that belonged to a meeting hall in a 16th-century Jain temple in Gujarat.

On the mezzanine level (Galleries 251–3), rotating exhibits offer Nepali and Tibetan art including *tangkas* (paintings on cloth), sculpture, and ceremonial vessels.

O: MUSICAL INSTRUMENTS

Drawn from six continents and dating from about 300 BC to the present, the musical instrument collection includes the oldest of three extant pianos by Bartolommeo

Cristofori (Gallery 684), credited with creating the first hammer-action keyboard (c. 1700). At the opposite end of the design spectrum is a grand piano from Erard et Cie (c. 1840), its elaborate gilding and marquetry denoting its function as a status symbol. The inscription on a Venetian *spinettino* made (1540) for the Duchess of Urbino warns performers, "I am rich in gold and rich in tone; if you lack goodness, leave me alone."

Among the reed instruments are saxophones, sarrusophones (double-reeded saxophones), shawms, oboes, and bassoons. Bagpipes include folk versions made of fur, leather, and wood with goats' heads carved on them, as well as the familiar Scottish variety. Pre-eminent among the stringed instruments are three Baroque violins by Antonio Stradivari, one of them restored to its original appearance and tone.

In the galleries of the Americas, Asia, and Africa are instruments as simple as pottery whistles and as elaborate as an Indian *mayuri*, a fretted lute-like instrument with a tail of peacock feathers. One of the most visually beautiful of the percussion instruments is a *Goqing* or sonorous stone (Gallery 681) from 19th-century China, a large piece of jade carved and incised to resemble a drooping lotus leaf. Among the Tibetan instruments are drums made from human skulls, intended to ward off evil. Indian exhibits include sitars, drums, trumpets, and other bowed and plucked stringed instruments.

P: PRINTS, DRAWINGS, AND PHOTOGRAPHY

More than 17,000 **drawings**, 1.2 million **prints**, and 12,000 **illustrated books** reside at the Met, including works by Michelangelo, Leonardo, Picasso, Mary Cassatt, Jasper Johns, and Andy Warhol, along with ephemera such as 19th-century American wallpaper and 31,000 baseball cards. These light-sensitive works are shown in changing exhibitions.

The collection of more than 40,000 **European and American photographs** dates from the 1830s to the present. Strengths include 19th-century British photography; the Alfred Stieglitz Collection; American and European photography between the World Wars from the Ford Motor Car Collection; and the personal archives of Walker Evans and Diane Arbus. Contemporary holdings feature Bernd and Hilla Becher, Cindy Sherman, and Sigmar Polke. Photographs are shown in changing exhibitions.

THE COSTUME INSTITUTE

The Costume Institute (on the ground floor) contains a collection of more than 35,000 costumes and accessories from seven centuries and five continents, ranging from Central African tribal headgear to elegant European couturier clothing. The collection is shown in special exhibitions, mounted (not surprisingly) with great style.

MANHATTAN

To many people New York City is synonymous with the borough of Manhattan, a slender island 12.5 miles long and 2.5 miles wide. It is the third-largest borough in population (1.6 million in 2013), yet the smallest in size (22.6 square miles). Manhattan, the borough, is coextensive with New York County.

Topographically not much remains of Manhattan's appearance before the Dutch arrived. Strata of Manhattan schist provide the bedrock on which the skyscrapers of Lower Manhattan and Midtown stand; further north, the island's natural typography is more evident—for example, Central Park's outcroppings of Manhattan schist laced with granite intrusions and glacial scratches; the tall ridges of Morningside Heights; or the valley that slashes diagonally across West 125th St. The island—its highest altitude about 268ft and its lowest, sea level—is encircled by rivers: the Hudson (once called the North River) on the west; the East River—actually a tidal inlet from Long Island Sound—on the east; and the Harlem River on the northeast, part of which, the Harlem Ship Canal, was dug at the end of the 19th century to facilitate navigation.

Manhattan is the engine that drives the city's economy, with its many corporate headquarters, its powerful financial industry, and its cultural institutions that attract some 50 million tourists annually. Downtown has recovered from the economic (and literal) devastation that followed the 9/11 terrorist attacks of 2001 and is enjoying a boom; in fact, all over the city new construction shrouds many buildings with scaffolding.

Disparity in wealth is keenly felt across the borough. Many prominent buildings—the headquarters of J. Pierpont Morgan's former bank, the Plaza Hotel, and the Woolworth Building—are going residential, at least partly. Elsewhere super-tall, super-slender, super-expensive apartment towers are pushing the skyline ever upward. Most areas of the city have undergone some form of gentrification in recent years, and, as with any metropolis, this has had conflicting consequences: it has brought more shops, restaurants and cultural attractions, but smaller businesses are closing their doors and the individual characters of many neighborhoods are inevitably changing.

MANHATTAN NEIGHBORHOODS

If Parisians think of themselves as inhabiting such-and-such an *arrondissement*, Manhattanites think of themselves as living in a certain neighborhood—Greenwich Village, or the Meatpacking District, or the Upper East Side. As the demographics and economics of the island have changed, new names have accreted to old neighborhoods, usually to polish a tarnished image (Clinton, formerly Hell's Kitchen) or to establish a zippier identity for a formerly drab area (Tribeca).

The island was settled from south to north, with its oldest neighborhoods in Lower Manhattan. The Financial District, at first residential, had already begun to assume some public functions when the British took over in 1664. Battery Park City, built, from the late 1970s, on landfill largely excavated from the original World Trade Center, includes a financial center, parkland, and a planned residential community. North of it are the Civic Center, Chinatown, Little Italy, and the Lower East Side, the last three of which saw the influx of large immigrant populations toward the end of the 19th century. The East Village, once simply considered part of the Lower East Side, gained recognition (or notoriety) as the home of the counterculture during the 1960s, its far eastern reaches—Avenues A through D—renamed Alphabet City.

On the Lower West Side, north of Battery Park City, are Tribeca and SoHo—former industrial areas, now residential and expensive. Above Houston St are Greenwich Village, once a village outside of "New York," and the Meatpacking District, formerly the Gansevoort Market, where bloody butcher aprons have by and large given way to designer duds, and "gritty" has evolved into "gritty chic." Chelsea has developed along similar lines, but with the added fillip of high-powered art galleries on its far western edge. The garment industry has mostly left the Garment District, between 34th and 42nd Sts on the West Side (though some high-style showrooms remain), but the Theater District to its north still thrives, with a tourist-packed Times Square at its center. North of that, on the West Side, are Hell's Kitchen (politely known as Clinton); the Lincoln Center neighborhood; and the Upper West Side.

On Park and Madison Avenues in eastern Midtown stand glassy and masonry towers, both residential and commercial. The quiet districts of Murray Hill, Kips Bay, and Turtle Bay are named for geographical features that no longer exist. Fifty-seventh Street, formerly known for upscale shopping, is earning a reputation for upscale living, with very tall, very expensive new residential buildings giving some blocks the nickname "Billionaires' Row."

Central Park divides the East Side from the West Side above 59th St. The Upper East Side includes expensive residential real estate along Fifth Avenue and in other elite neighborhoods like Sutton Place and Beekman Place. Yorkville, once an uptown immigrant neighborhood for Germans, Czechs, and Hungarians, has lost its ethnicity and gone mainstream. Above 96th St lies East Harlem, also known as El Barrio or Spanish Harlem; formerly an Italian enclave, it now includes a growing Asian population.

On the West Side, the residential areas of Central Park West and Riverside Drive were established decades ago. The commercial avenues of Broadway, Amsterdam Avenue, and Columbus Avenue all offer restaurants, bars, and shops geared towards an affluent middle class. North of 96th St is Morningside Heights, dominated by Columbia University, the Cathedral of St. John the Divine, and other educational and religious institutions. To the east and below Morningside Heights lies the Harlem plain, home to the nation's most famous African-American community, though the area today is less black than formerly. Upper Manhattan consists of Washington Heights and Inwood, both residential and less affluent. The Cloisters in Fort Tryon Park is the major cultural institution in Upper Manhattan.

Liberty, Ellis, & Governors Islands

The Statue of Liberty on the island of the same name is probably New York's most famous and beloved landmark, a place of pilgrimage for Americans and foreigners alike, a marvel of 19th-century French engineering, and an emblem of freedom and democracy. Ellis Island remains a potent symbol of the hopes of the millions of immigrants who poured into this nation seeking a better life. Governors Island, for centuries a military reservation, has recently been opened to the public. All three islands belong politically to Manhattan.

The Statue of Liberty (1886; Frédéric-Auguste Bartholdi), officially called *Liberty Enlightening the World*, is the most famous piece of sculpture in the US, rising majestically on Liberty Island in direct view of ships entering the Upper Bay. A gift of the people of France, the figure stands on a pedestal donated by the American public. A radiant crown surrounds her head; broken shackles lie at her feet. Her uplifted right hand holds a torch; her left arm cradles a tablet representing the Declaration of Independence. The pedestal of pinkish Stony Creek granite stands above the star-shaped walls of Fort Wood, erected to defend the city against Great Britain in the War of 1812. (During that struggle, the British blockaded European ports, seized American ships, impressed American sailors into the British navy to prevent American shipping interests from supplying Napoleonic France, and burned Washington, D.C.)

Visiting the Statue of Liberty and Ellis Island

Map p. 610, C3. You can reach Liberty and Ellis Islands only by a Statue Cruise ferry. Since almost four million people visit yearly, waiting times for tickets, boarding, and security can be long (more than 90mins on peak days); book your ticket in advance (see below) and arrive early, preferably for the day's first departure. The round trip, about 1hr 15mins, includes stops at both islands; the last trip that allows enough time to visit both departs Battery Park at 3pm.

To reach the departure point by subway: 1 to South Ferry, 4 or 5 to Bowling Green, R to Whitehall St; by bus: M5, M15, M20. From the subway or bus walk to Castle Clinton in Battery Park, for the ticket kiosk. Better yet, purchase online (see below). Statue and Ellis Island open daily at least from 9:30–3:30; closed Dec 25. For information about the statue, T: 212 363 3200, nps.gov/stli.

UPPER BAY
View of the Statue of Liberty.

Tickets

Book online at statuecruises.com or in person at Castle Clinton in Battery Park (map p. 620, C4). A basic ticket admits you to the statue grounds and Ellis Island. To visit the Statue Museum and the top of the pedestal (215 steps up from the lobby), buy a "pedestal access" ticket (no additional charge). To ascend to the crown of the statue (up 377 steps from the lobby), buy a "crown ticket" (additional charge). All reserved tickets include priority ferry-boarding. For ferry and ticket information, T: 877 523 9849 (877 LADYTIX), statuecruises.com.

Security

You will be screened before you board the ferry and again before you enter the statue. Anything that could be used as a weapon will be confiscated and not returned. Food, drinks, backpacks, tripods, laptops, non-folding umbrellas, oversized bags, and strollers must be checked; lockers available (cash only).

THE STATUE OF LIBERTY MUSEUM

Exhibits in the museum at the pedestal level explore the conception, construction, and impact of the statue as its meaning has altered over time. Also on view is the original torch, altered by Gutzon Borglum in 1916 after an explosion damaged it (*see p. 41*). Also on view is a plaque with "The New Colossus," Emma Lazarus's sonnet (1883), whose lines, "Give me your tired your poor/Your huddled masses yearning to breathe free..." have come to symbolize the statue's promise of hope."

STATUE STATISTICS

Height of statue alone	151ft
Height of pedestal	89ft
Height of torch above sea	305ft
Weight	225 tons
Waist measurement	35ft
Width of mouth	3ft
Length of index finger	8ft
Size of fingernail	13 by 10 inches
Weight of fingernail	about 3 ½ pounds
Length of nose	4ft 6 inches
Approximate fabric in gown	4,000 square yards
Length of sandal	25ft
Approximate women's shoe size (US)	879

HISTORY OF THE STATUE OF LIBERTY

The inspiration for the Statue of Liberty came primarily from Édouard de Laboulaye (1811–83), a political philosopher, professor, anti-slavery activist, and admirer of the US Constitution, who proposed a joint Franco-American monument as a testament to liberty and to the friendship between the two countries. Laboulaye introduced the notion to his friend Bartholdi, a sculptor of monumental ambitions.

Alexandre-Gustave Eiffel (1832–1923), known for his iron trusswork railway bridges (the tower came later), engineered the statue's iron skeleton, devising an interior framework with a heavy central iron pylon supporting a lightweight system of trusswork that reached out toward the interior surface of the statue. The hammered copper "skin," only $3/32$ of an inch thick, is joined to the trusswork so that it "floats," accommodating wind and thermal changes.

The French were charged with funding the statue, while the Americans were to provide a site and pay for the pedestal. The French raised an estimated $250,000–$450,000 (scholars disagree) in a public campaign that began with a banquet at the Hôtel du Louvre (successful), followed by a concert for which Charles Gounod wrote a cantata (a financial failure), a painted diorama of New York harbor that visitors paid to view (successful), and the sale of signed and numbered clay models of the statue (also successful). The completed head of the statue was set up on the Champ de Mars, and for a price visitors could climb 36 steps and look out through the windows in the crown. In all, 100,000 people subscribed to the campaign.

The statue was constructed in Paris by the firm of Gaget, Gauthier et Cie, dismantled, and shipped to New York. The 214 crates sat unopened for more than a year as the Americans struggled to raise money for the pedestal (designed by French-trained architect Richard Morris Hunt). Donations trickled in so slowly that the committee was considering returning the statue to France, when *New York World* publisher Joseph Pulitzer promised to print the name of every donor in his newspaper, even if the gift were only a penny. The scheme raised the final $102,000 in three months from 121,000 donations. On October 28, 1886, as fireworks burst over the harbor, President Grover Cleveland dedicated the statue.

The centennial year saw the triumphant unveiling of a restored statue: the connection between the central pylon and the upraised right arm was strengthened and the wire mesh that had long enclosed the spiral staircase to the crown was stripped away making the interior of the statue itself, the great volumes of the body and the billowing folds of the robe, visible in their full glory.

For security reasons Liberty Island was closed for 100 days after 9/11. Visitors were allowed into pedestal again in 2004 and into the crown in 2009. Liberty Island closed again for more than eight months in 2012–13 after the storm surge of Hurricane Sandy covered it with eight feet of water, though the statue remained undamaged.

ELLIS ISLAND

Accessible from the Statue of Liberty ferry. Main Building and museum free with ferry ticket. Free ranger-led tours of Main Building; hard-hat tours (additional charge) to unrestored hospital and service buildings on south island (see statuecruises.com).

Originally a low-lying sandbar, Ellis Island lies about a mile southwest of Battery Park in Upper New York Bay. It is the site of the former United States Immigration Station, through which an estimated twelve million immigrants passed on their way to a new life in America. To the right of the ferry slip is the Main Building, the former immigration station, with a museum. To the left of the slip on filled land stand derelict hospitals and other onetime service buildings.

HISTORY OF ELLIS ISLAND

The Native Americans called Ellis Island "Kioshk" (Gull Island); the Dutch bought it from them in 1630 and named it Little Oyster Island. During the 18th century, the British called it Gibbet Island because a few pirates were hanged there in the 1760s. Samuel Ellis (d. 1794), who farmed in New Jersey and sold general merchandise in Manhattan, owned it during the Revolution; in 1808, after his death, the federal government spent $10,000 acquiring it for a fort. Like the other fortifications built at this time, it was intended to protect the city from a British naval invasion in the War of 1812, but saw no action. From 1835–90 it served as an ammunition dump, threatening nearby New Jersey residents with the possibility of accidental explosions.

In 1890, when the federal government took over the immigration service, Ellis Island became the site of the main receiving station, which opened in 1892, admitting the first immigrant, 13-year-old Annie Moore, who arrived from Cork, Ireland, in steerage on the SS *Nevada* with her two younger brothers. Five years later, the wooden station burned to the ground; no one died, but most of the immigration records from 1855–90 were destroyed. In 1898 construction began on the present building and the immigration service moved to Battery Park. The new fireproof station opened on December 17, 1900, when it received 2,251 immigrants.

At the station inspectors processed the arrivals, detaining those who would be unable to earn a living and weeding out paupers, criminals, prostitutes, the insane, proponents of beliefs such as anarchy or polygamy, or people suffering from contagious diseases. In 1907, the peak year of immigration, 1,004,756 people entered the US through Ellis Island, approximately twice the number the station was designed to handle.

The heavy influx continued until 1915, when World War I shut down transatlantic shipping. Under the National Origins Act (1924) immigrants were processed in their own countries and Ellis Island fell into disuse. In 1954, the last detainee, a Norwegian sailor who had jumped ship, was released; the station closed and the island was vacated. The buildings deteriorated rapidly, ravaged by the weather and stripped by vandals. In 1965, it became part of the Statue of Liberty National Monument, with the Main Building opening as a museum in 1990.

THE MAIN BUILDING

This building (1897–1900; Boring & Tilton) was formerly the Immigrant Receiving Station. To the right of it, the **American Immigrant Wall of Honor** bears the names of more than 700,000 immigrants who entered here. Among the famous: Russian-born composer Irving Berlin (who wrote "God Bless America") and the Sicilian-born gangster "Lucky" Luciano.

The building must have impressed new arrivals with its scale and splendor. Built in a French Renaissance style, of red brick with exuberant granite and limestone trim, its four corner towers rise 100 feet; arched entrances on each side reach above the second story. Even today the **Registry Room** (200ft by 100ft by 56ft) retains its visual impact. Until 1911, iron pipes divided it into a maze reminiscent of cattle pens, through which immigrants wound their way past the inspectors. Designed to handle 5,000 immigrants a day, on the peak day, April 17, 1907, the station processed 11,747. The barrel-vaulted ceiling of Guastavino tile replaced a plaster one destroyed by the Black Tom explosion of 1916 on a nearby New Jersey wharf. Despite the decades of neglect after the building was abandoned, only 17 of the 28,880 tiles needed to be replaced during the restoration of the 1990s. Throughout the building the photos, artifacts, and exhibits shed light on the immigrant experience and document the station's abandonment, decay, and restoration.

THE BLACK TOM EXPLOSION

On July 30, 1916, more than a thousand tons of munitions exploded on the Black Tom Wharf in Jersey City, rocking the harbor with the force of an earthquake estimated at 5.0–5.5 on the Richter scale. The explosives had been stored on the wharf en route to the Allies in World War I. Shrapnel from the blast hit the Statue of Liberty, and the shock waves—which knocked down the plaster ceiling of the Registry Room at Ellis Island—were felt as far as Philadelphia. The explosion is attributed to German agents, who sabotaged the munitions so they would not reach Britain and France.

GOVERNORS ISLAND

About 800 yards off the southern tip of Manhattan, 172-acre Governors Island was for centuries a military reservation, insulated from the commercial and political forces that shaped the rest of the city. The island still feels secluded and serene, offering wide-angle views of the downtown skyline and harbor, historic military buildings including two 19th-century forts, and parkland with bike trails, ball fields, gardens, and an artistically enhanced landscape. New York City owns 150 acres; the remaining 22 acres, the original island before it was enlarged by landfill, constitute the Governors Island National Monument, overseen by the National Park Service.

Visiting Governors Island

Map p. 610, C3. Open daily Memorial Day (end of May) until late Sept, weekdays 10–6, weekends 10–7. Information available from National Park Service: T: 212 825 3045, nps.gov/gois; or from the Trust for Governors Island: T: 212 440 2200, govisland.com.

Access by ferry from the Battery Maritime Building (next to the Staten Island Ferry Terminal; map p. 620, C4) or weekends from Brooklyn Bridge Park, Pier 6 (Atlantic Ave-Furman St in Brooklyn Heights; map p. 622, A3). Ferry is free on Sat and Sun mornings; tickets available online. The East River Ferry stops at Governors Island seasonally on weekends; T: 800 533 FERRY (800 533 3779), eastriverferry.com.

Free tours of Fort Jay and Castle Williams. Food carts and concessions.

HISTORY OF GOVERNORS ISLAND

The Native Americans called it "Pagganck," for its abundant nut trees; the Dutch, who landed there before they settled on Manhattan, called it "Nooten Eylandt" (Nut Island). The British changed the spelling to "Nutten Island" and set it aside (1698) for the "accommodation of His Majesty's governors"; during the colonial period, it served briefly as a quarantine station and a sanctuary for English pheasants.

The first fortifications were crude earthworks hastily thrown up during the Revolution by General Israel Putnam to protect against British warships. Before the next conflict, the War of 1812, three permanent fortifications arrived: Fort Jay, Castle Williams, and the South Battery. After c. 1820, advances in technology made the forts obsolete and the island became a military post, which it remained until 1996. By the turn of the 20th century, erosion had reduced Governors Island to about 70 acres and as the Army found itself cramped, an estimated four million cubic yards of the rubble excavated from subway construction were dumped (1901–11) south of the forts. In the 1930s Mayor La Guardia wanted an airfield on the level terrain and accused the army of building Liggett Hall across the midsection of the island to thwart his wishes.

In 1966, the Army left and the Coast Guard took over. Twenty years later the Coast Guard departed and Governors Island's long military history drew to a close. So much empty real estate so near Manhattan quickened the pulses of would-be developers, who proposed various schemes—a SpongeBob-SquarePants-themed hotel, a replica of the Globe Theater, an international peace park, and a casino—none of which came to fruition. Today the Trust for Governors Island administers 170 acres and is developing the park while seeking to attract commercial tenants to underwrite its estimated $12-million yearly upkeep.

WHAT TO SEE ON GOVERNORS ISLAND

The two most important structures on the island are Fort Jay and Castle Williams. Uphill from the ferry landings, the star-shaped **Fort Jay** (1798; rebuilt 1806–9) was the island's first permanent fortification named for John Jay, governor of New York State and first chief justice of the US. It sits surrounded by a dry moat on high ground where earthworks had been thrown up before the Revolution. By 1806 the fort was falling into ruin, its earthen walls degraded by rain, its wooden parapet a mass of rotten wood, or, as army engineer Col. Jonathan Williams called it, "a mass of ligneous putrification." Williams was chosen to expand and strengthen it. Today Fort Jay projects a show of strength with an earthen berm rising to masonry walls, a moat and drawbridge, and an imposing gateway.

South of Fort Jay is the **Parade Ground**, used at various times for training, ceremonies, as a prison, and for public executions. Nearby is **Nolan Park**, surrounded by yellow clapboarded Victorian houses (c. 1878–9) built for officers and their families. Facing Nolan Park west of Barry Rd is the **Commander's House** (1843; Martin E. Thompson), the work of a 19th-century celebrity architect and the site of a 1988 meeting of President Ronald Reagan and Mikhail Gorbachev. The Chapel of St. Cornelius the Centurion (1905; Charles C. Haight), on the corner of Barry Rd and Evans Rd, replaces a wooden church built by Trinity Parish when the army decided against appointing a post chaplain. The **South Battery** or Half Moon Battery (1812), the third component of the fortifications preceding the War of 1812, was intended to protect the city from invasion via Buttermilk Channel, the waterway separating the island from Brooklyn.

Castle Williams (1810–11; Jonathan Williams), constructed only a few years after the refurbished Fort Jay, served as a prototype for a new kind of seacoast fortification, the casemated fort. Built of red sandstone, it is three tiers high; its circular walls are eight feet thick at the bottom and seven at the top. Its fortified casemates (armored artillery compartments) protected both guns and gunners, while allowing cannon to be stacked several stories high and increasing the fort's firepower. Its 100-plus heavy guns facing those of the West Battery (now Castle Clinton) on Manhattan across the bay, could rake the harbor with heavy crossfire. Like Castle Clinton it originally stood offshore on submerged rocks, but landfill has joined it to the island.

Untested in the War of 1812, though probably a deterrent to invasion, the fort fell into disuse afterwards. During the Civil War both Fort Jay and Castle Williams deteriorated into makeshift prisons for Confederate soldiers. Officers housed in barracks at Fort Jay were more or less given "full sway of the island," as one noted. The enlisted men were confined to dank, claustrophobic Castle Williams, packed into cannon emplacements retrofitted with metal doors. Summer brought cholera, measles, and typhoid. Winter brought grinding cold. In 1895 Castle Williams, by then upgraded with running water, became a US Army disciplinary barracks, nicknamed the "Eastern Alcatraz," but considered cushy for a military prison on account of its view, decent guards, and, above all, lack of opportunities for back-breaking labor.

The handsome brick houses along Hay Rd, called **Colonels' Row** (1893–1917), faced the island's southwestern shoreline before landfill. South of the Row, **Liggett Hall** (1929; McKim, Mead & White), formerly a barracks, was the largest military building in the world when built. Liggett Arch gives onto an open courtyard with gardens, food concessions, and fountains. Paths lead to a Hammock Grove for resting, a Play Lawn, and landscaped paths to the water. The rest of the island is under development.

GUGGENHEIM MUSE

Museum Mile

*Fifth Avenue, between the Metropolitan Museum at 82nd St and the top
of Central Park at 110th St, has more museums than any other part of
the city—several in the retro-fitted homes of bygone bankers and industrialists.
The Neue Galerie, the Guggenheim, the National Academy, the Cooper Hewitt,
the Jewish Museum, El Museo del Barrio, and the Museum of the City of New
York form a vital part of the city's cultural life.*

A t the turn of the 20th century the blocks facing Fifth
Avenue between 81st and 83rd Sts were an enclave for
the very rich, a row of grandiose townhouses staring
proudly across the avenue toward the Metropolitan Museum.
Apartments were just beginning to encroach—for example
those at 998 Fifth Ave (1910; McKim, Mead & White) on the
northeast corner of 81st St. Their tasteful decor and spacious
layouts (typically 17 rooms), helped ease the wealthy into
the idea of sharing a building. Among the first tenants was
Elihu Root, secretary of state and Nobel Peace Prize winner,
to whom the rental agent reputedly offered a cut rate, hoping
(successfully) to lure his social peers into the building.

A few townhouses remain from this transitional period. No. 1009 Fifth Ave (*corner
of 82nd St*), a Beaux-Arts beauty built on speculation in 1901 by Welch, Smith & Provot,
is handsomely ornamented with wrought iron and limestone. It was first sold to
Benjamin N. Duke, brother of the tobacco king James B. Duke, and remained in the
Duke family until 2006, when a private buyer bought it for $40 million.

THE NEUE GALERIE

*Map p. 615, D3. Subway 4, 5, 6 to 86th St. Bus: M1, M2, M3, M4 to 86th St. Open Thur–
Mon 11–6; closed Tues, Wed, major holidays. Admission charge; but free first Fri of month
6–8pm. Children under 12 not admitted; children aged 12–16 must be accompanied by an
adult. Restaurant (reservations advised), café, and shop. T: 212 628 6200, neuegalerie.org.*

The small, elegant Neue Galerie focuses on early 20th-century Austrian and German
art and design. Its name recalls an earlier Viennese Neue Galerie (1923) devoted to
the work of Gustav Klimt, Egon Schiele, and other artists rebelling against 19th-cen-

tury academic art. Serge Sabarsky (1912–96), an art dealer and collector, and Ronald S. Lauder (b. 1944), philanthropist, collector, and heir to the Estée Lauder cosmetics fortune, conceived the museum, which opened in 2001.

THE BUILDING

William Starr Miller, an industrialist, real estate entrepreneur, and banker, commissioned the house in 1914 from Carrère & Hastings, the architects of the New York Public Library. Built of red brick, trimmed with limestone, and crowned with a slate mansard roof, the mansion is unusual on Fifth Avenue, where millionaires generally favored palazzo-inspired white marble and limestone. Instead the mansion recalls the 16th-century houses in the Place des Vosges in Paris—perhaps because the architects had studied at the École des Beaux-Arts. In 1944 Grace Wilson Vanderbilt, widow of Cornelius Vanderbilt III, bought the 28-room house, referring to it as the "Gardener's Cottage"—it was a comedown from the 58-room palazzo she had occupied further down Fifth Ave, but she entertained lavishly nonetheless. After her death in 1953, the YIVO Institute for Jewish Research occupied the building until Lauder and Sabarsky bought it. YIVO could not afford to remodel it, so the original architectural details remain. German-born architect Annabelle Selldorf oversaw the conversion.

THE COLLECTION

Second floor: These galleries explore the relationship between fine and decorative arts in early 20th-century Vienna. Painters include Gustav Klimt, Egon Schiele, and Oskar Kokoschka. Klimt's gold-flecked *Portrait of Adele Bloch-Bauer* (1907), the wife of a Jewish sugar magnate and a leader of salon society, is considered one of the artist's finest works and is the finest in the collection. The Nazis looted it when they invaded Austria; Lauder bought it at auction in 2006 from Bloch-Bauer's niece, who had successfully sued the Austrian government for its return; the price, $135 million, was the highest ever paid for a painting at the time. The work is the subject of the 2015 movie *Woman in Gold.*

Also on view are examples of furniture designed by Viennese architect Otto Wagner, one of the greatest exponents of *Jugendstil,* the German form of Art Nouveau, who later turned to Functionalism; and the Functionalist Adolf Loos, author of the famous essay "Ornament is Crime," as well as decorative pieces by Josef Hoffmann and Koloman Moser, co-founders of the Wiener Werkstätte.

Third floor: Unless filled by a special exhibition, these galleries exhibit early 20th-century German art from the Brücke (Ernst Ludwig Kirchner, Emil Nolde), the Neue Sachlichkeit (Otto Dix, Georg Grosz), and the Bauhaus. Paintings by Max Beckmann include *Self-portrait with Horn* (1938), painted just after he had fled Nazi Germany. Rational, functional Bauhaus design principles are visible in furniture and household objects by Mies van der Rohe (*see the Seagram Building, p. 262*) and Marcel Breuer (*see the former Whitney Museum building, p. 339*).

THE SOLOMON R. GUGGENHEIM MUSEUM

Map p. 615, D3. 1071 Fifth Ave (East 89th St). Subway: 4, 5, 6 to 86th St. Bus: M1, M2, M3, M4. Open Sun–Wed and Fri 10–5:45, Sat 10–7:45. Closed Thur, holidays. Admission charge (expensive), but pay what you wish Sat 5:45–7:45 (last ticket issued at 7:15). Café and restaurant. T: 212 423 3500, guggenheim.org.

The Solomon R. Guggenheim Museum (opened 1959) is Frank Lloyd Wright's masterpiece, a building so remarkable that it often overshadows the art inside—a collection that embraces works from the mid-19th century through the present. Crowds of visitors fill the Rotunda, photographing one another in front of the cantilevered ramps or aiming their cameras at the fractured geometric spaces of the great oculus.

HISTORY OF THE COLLECTION

Like other millionaires of his time, Solomon R. Guggenheim (1861–1949), whose fortune rested on mining and smelting, started out collecting traditional European paintings. This focus shifted in the late 1920s after he met Baroness Hilla Rebay von Ehrenwiesen, an intense, highly opinionated, and notably difficult woman, an artist who introduced him to her artist friends and to her almost fanatical passion for non-representational art. In 1939 the Solomon R. Guggenheim Collection of Non-Objective Painting was shown in rented quarters at 24 East 54th St, with the baroness in charge. To Rebay, Non-Objective art, unlike Abstract art, had no natural or biomorphic implications whatsoever and referred to nothing in the outside world. Her choices often reflected a future museum that would be a "temple of the spirit" and included the work of artists whom she befriended and sometimes supported (Robert Delaunay, Fernand Léger, Vassily Kandinsky).

James Johnson Sweeney followed Rebay as museum director in 1952, and under his guidance the collection became less narrowly ideological, acquiring Picassos and Cézannes, for example, which Rebay probably would have outlawed on the grounds that they were figurative. A gift of Impressionist and Post-Impressionist work from Justin K. Thannhauser, a dealer and collector, further enriched and broadened the holdings. The bequest of Peggy Guggenheim (Solomon's niece) put her entire collection of Cubist, Surrealist, and postwar painting and sculpture in the custody of the Guggenheim Foundation, though her collection remains physically in Venice and is shown in New York only occasionally. In 1990 the museum acquired (not without controversy) the Panza di Biumo collection of American Minimalist art from the 1960s and '70s, with such works as Carl Andre's *Alstadt Copper Square* (1967) and *Fall* (1968), a modular arrangement of 21 large pieces of rolled steel. The purchase disturbed some critics because the then-director sold off pieces from the core holdings to finance it.

In 1993, the Robert Mapplethorpe Foundation gave the Guggenheim nearly 200 photographs and other works, introducing photography into the collection.

THE BUILDING

The idea of building an architecturally remarkable museum and of hiring Frank Lloyd Wright to design it apparently came from Rebay; and since Solomon Guggenheim died long before plans came to fruition, the realization of the building fell to her and to Harry Guggenheim, Solomon's nephew and successor. The building is instantly recognizable: a spiral with a ramp cantilevered out from its interior walls sitting above a horizontal slab. The ramp, about a quarter of a mile long, rises 1.75 inches per 10ft to a domed skylight 92ft above the ground, 100ft in diameter at the bottom, 128ft at the top. Wright called it "organic" architecture, imitating the forms and colors of nature, while his critics called it a "bun," an "insult to art," and, with a nod to "organic," a "snail."

Between the time of Wright's original design and the completion of the building 16 years elapsed, many of them spent arguing with the Department of Buildings (whose ideas on construction were tamer than Wright's) and in quarrels with former museum director Sweeney, who argued that Wright's design would create serious problems in storing and hanging the collection (reservations that proved well-founded).

Today, however, the building is greatly admired—so much so that loyalists derided as an insult to Wright's masterpiece the rectilinear expansion (1992; Gwathmey Siegel & Assocs), which allows more of the permanent collection to be shown.

HIGHLIGHTS OF THE COLLECTION

Since works are rotated through the galleries or may be displaced by major exhibitions, you can never be sure what you will see on a given visit, so the following description outlines the general holdings of the collection.

Impressionist and Post-Impressionist painters are shown in the Thannhauser Gallery on the first level above the gift shop. Camille Pissarro's *The Hermitage at Pontoise* (c. 1867), painted before his Impressionist works, is the earliest picture in the collection. Also here are paintings by Van Gogh, Cézanne, Gauguin, and early works by Picasso.

Early 20th-century works and Pioneers of Modernism: Paintings from the first decades of the 20th century include Modigliani's *Reclining Nude* (1917) and *Jeanne Hébuterne with a Yellow Sweater* (1908–19); Matisse's *The Italian Woman* (1916), and Bonnard's *Dining Room on the Garden* (1934–5) as well as analytical

monochromatic studies by Braque and Picasso. Fernand Léger's *The Great Parade* (1954) is considered by many to be the definitive work of his career. Also represented: Albert Gleizes, Robert Delaunay, Ernst Ludwig Kirchner, Emil Nolde, Oskar Kokoschka, Egon Schiele, Gino Severini, Kazimir Malevich, Piet Mondrian, Theo van Doesburg, Joan Miró and Paul Klee. The Guggenheim owns a trove of paintings by Kandinsky, a particular favorite of Rebay's.

Postwar painters: Here are canvases by Willem de Kooning, Jackson Pollock, Mark Rothko, Franz Kline, and Richard Diebenkorn, as well as color field paintings by Morris Louis and Ellsworth Kelly. Andy Warhol is represented (among other works) by a silk screen with multiple images of an electric chair, *Orange Disaster* (1963); and Roy Lichtenstein by *Preparedness*, which he called "a muralesque painting about our military-industrialist complex."

Sculpture: Although Hilla Rebay envisioned a collection of painting only, the museum began purchasing sculpture after her departure. Represented here are sculptors including Alexander Archipenko, Constantin Brancusi, Alberto Giacometti, Henry Moore, Jacques Lipchitz, Isamu Noguchi, Louise Nevelson, and David Smith.

THE NATIONAL ACADEMY MUSEUM & SURROUNDINGS

Map p. 615, D3. 1083 Fifth Ave (89th–90th Sts). Subway: 4, 5, 6 to 86th St. Bus: M1, M2, M3, M4. Open Wed–Sun 11–6; closed Mon, Tues, some holidays. Admission by donation. Tours Sat and Sun at 1:30. T: 212 369 4880, nationalacademy.org.

The National Academy Museum occupies a staid townhouse, small in comparison with its Fifth Avenue neighbors. The museum is the exhibition space of the National Academy, an artists' honorary association and art school founded in 1825 by painters Samuel F.B. Morse, Rembrandt Peale, and others, to promote American painting and sculpture at a time when American artists were considered poor stepchildren of their European masters. The building (1914; Ogden Codman Jr.), was donated (1940) by Archer M. Huntington—art-bedazzled heir to a railroad fortune—whose second wife, the sculptor Anna Hyatt Huntington, had been voted into the academy the year before their marriage.

The academy, conservative by definition, embraces painters, sculptors, architects, and graphic artists drawn from the ranks of the establishment—some still famous, some whose reputations have faded to invisibility over the years. The collection of more than 7,000 works, donated by academicians when elected, epitomizes most of the established 19th- and 20th-century styles in American art: idealized landscapes from the Hudson River School, examples of American Impressionism, Fauvism, Abstraction, and Photo-Realism. Recent inductees include Maya Lin, Chuck Close, Renzo Piano, and Cindy Sherman. The exhibition program includes loans, works drawn from the collection, and an annual juried show.

Across the street in Central Park (*Fifth Ave at 91st St*) the **William T. Stead Memorial** (1913; George James Frampton), a bronze tablet, commemorates the British journalist who died on the *Titanic* after helping other passengers into lifeboats.

The **Protestant Episcopal Church of the Heavenly Rest** (*Fifth Ave at 2 East 90th St; open daily 10–6 for rest and meditation; the Heavenly Rest Stop open-air café on Fifth Ave open daily 8–6; T: 212 289 3400; heavenlyrest.org*) was founded by Civil War veterans in 1865. Today it occupies a site purchased from Andrew Carnegie's widow, who lived across 90th St. She sold the lot with a deed that restricted building to a Christian church no more than 75ft high not counting the steeple, thus preserving the view from her garden. Begun by Bertram Grosvenor Associates, the church was completed in a Gothic-Art Deco style by Goodhue's successor firm, Mayers, Murray & Phillip. The sculptural program with Lee Lawrie, Malvina Hoffman, and others was begun but never completed.

THE COOPER HEWITT, SMITHSONIAN DESIGN MUSEUM & ENVIRONS

Map p. 615, D2. 2 East 91st St (Fifth Ave). Subway: 4, 5, 6 to 86th, or 6 to 96th St. Bus: M1, M2, M3, M4. Open weekdays and Sun 10–6, Sat until 9. Closed Thanksgiving, Christmas New Year's Day. Admission charge; discount for online tickets. Café accessible from 90th St without museum entrance. Shop. T: 212 849 8400, cooperhewitt.org.

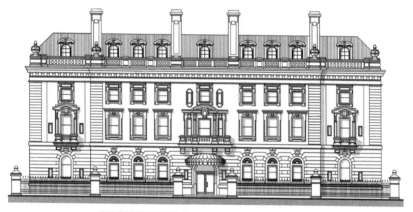

THE COOPER HEWITT, SMITHSONIAN DESIGN MUSEUM: 91ST STREET FAÇADE

The Cooper Hewitt is the nation's only museum devoted exclusively to historic and contemporary design, its exhibitions drawn from its stupendous collections that include everything from antique wallpaper to sand toys, bird cages, and Asian porcelains. The museum occupies a mansion constructed for steel baron and philanthropist Andrew Carnegie (*see opposite*). In 2014, after a three-year hiatus and a gut renovation (2014; Beyer Blinder Belle; Gluckman Mayer Architects; Diller Scofidio + Renfro, and others) the museum re-opened with newly conceived exhibits that explore the process of design and its impact on daily life. Several galleries offer interactive possibilities: design your own wallpaper and see it projected on the walls of a room, or re-design the contents of your pockets, or sit in an ergonomically devised wheelchair whose mechanical advantage becomes immediately obvious. Other exhibits explore the Hewitt sisters' collection (*see below*). Still others look at the components of design—color, form, line, and so on. One gallery is devoted to models and prototypes, for example beautifully crafted staircase models, for religious and secular buildings. A gallery on the third floor offers space for major exhibitions, the inaugural one on tools—from a Paleolithic chopper to a satellite-transmitted image of the sun—with an installation, *Controller of the Universe* (2007; Damián Ortega), serving as the artistic center of the room.

THE COLLECTION

Sarah, Eleanor, and Amy Hewitt, granddaughters of industrialist Peter Cooper, founded the museum in 1897 as part of the Cooper Union for the Advancement of Science and Art. During their travels, the three had been impressed by the South Kensington Museum (now the Victoria & Albert) in London and the Musée des Arts Décoratifs in Paris, and they began their own collection, intending it as a "practical working laboratory" where people could learn the "arts of decoration." Helped by their friends (for example J. Pierpont Morgan, who donated European textiles), they collected decorative objects, prints and drawings, napkins, gloves, cookie tins, and other items that appealed to them as good design.

ANDREW CARNEGIE AND HIS FIFTH AVENUE MANSION

Andrew Carnegie (1835–1919), an immigrant from Scotland, amassed a fortune in iron, coal, steel, and steamship and railroad lines. In 1898 he announced his intention to build "the most modest, plainest, and roomiest house in New York." For this plain and roomy house, he chose a rocky, semi-rural plot far north of the trophy houses of his more fashionable financial peers. His architects, Babb, Cook & Willard, finished the house in 1901.

The house was remarkably advanced for its time, well-suited to Carnegie's domestic needs and to the philanthropic projects he administered from his first-floor office. Sophisticated pumps and boilers filled the sub-basement, two of each major piece so that a spare was always available. If city water or electricity were interrupted, an artesian well and generator would spare the family and servants any inconvenience. Up in the attic great fans pulled air through cheesecloth filters over tanks of cool water, a primitive system of air-conditioning. The house was the first private residence in the city with a structural steel frame, an Otis passenger elevator, and central heating.

Over the main door on 91st St hangs an ornate copper and glass canopy. The marble vestibule leads to the Great Hall, paneled in Scottish oak, a token of Carnegie's affection for his homeland. At the east end of the hall an organ occupied the spot where the admissions desk now stands. The doorways to Carnegie's study and library, on the west end, are scaled to his height (he was 5ft 2in tall). Along the south side of the first floor, facing the garden, were public rooms—the music room on the west with musical motifs, including a Scottish bagpipe, in the ceiling moldings. In the garden vestibule, next to the music room, are leaded-glass windows by Louis Comfort Tiffany. The townhouse across the garden facing 90th St formerly belonged to Carnegie's daughter.

The Hewitt sisters admired both European culture and their grandfather's American industrial savvy (along with his other accomplishments, he had designed the first American locomotive), and their choices reflect these preferences. Among their first acquisitions were Italian architectural and decorative drawings that had belonged to the curator of the Borghese collection. Later came 1,500 drawings, sketches, and paintings by American landscapist Frederic Edwin Church and the contents of Winslow Homer's studio. The collection grew in size and quality over the years, until by 1963 Cooper Union could no longer maintain it financially, and supporters engineered its adoption by the Smithsonian Institution.

The collections today include more than 217,000 objects: industrial products, decorative arts, wallpaper, textiles, drawings, prints, and examples of graphic design. Occasional treasures have turned up: in 2002, Sir Timothy Clifford, then director of the National Galleries in Scotland, discovered in an old storage box a drawing of a candelabrum, which has since been attributed to Michelangelo. The museum had bought the drawing in 1942 from a London dealer along with other decorative designs, the whole batch for $60.

THREE RECYCLED MANSIONS

The **Convent of the Sacred Heart** (1918; C.P.H. Gilbert & J. Armstrong Stenhouse), a Roman Catholic girls' school (*1 East 91st St at Fifth Ave*), occupies the former mansion of Otto Kahn (1867–1934), financier, philanthropist, and patron of the arts. Alumnae of Sacred Heart include Caroline Kennedy and Lady Gaga. The building is neo-Italian Renaissance in style with unusual arched carriage entrances. Kahn, a member of the German-Jewish elite known as "Our Crowd," chaired the board of the Metropolitan Opera, which he saved from artistic mediocrity by hiring Giulio Gatti-Casazza (manager) and Toscanini (conductor), and from financial bankruptcy by personally donating an estimated $2.5 million. His generosity and acumen were such that he was known, probably behind his back, as "the Great Ottokahn."

The **former James A. Burden House** (*7 East 91st St*), now also part of the Convent of the Sacred Heart, was built in 1902 by W.D. Sloane (heir to the high-end furniture company; *see p. 187*) and his wife Emily Vanderbilt Sloane for their eldest daughter, Adele, a beautiful and spirited woman. Adele made a brilliant match, marrying James A. Burden, heir to the ironworks in Troy, New York, that produced most of the horseshoes for the Union Army during the Civil War (at a peak rate of 3,600 per hour).

The architects of the mansion, Warren & Wetmore, who stood in the good graces of the Vanderbilts (they built Grand Central Terminal), created a house that has been described as a modern French interpretation of an Italian palazzo: Italian in its massing and the simplicity of details, French in the inventive ornament and the presence of a service floor between the ground floor and what in a less imposing building would be called the parlor floor.

The nearby **John Henry Hammond House** (1909; Carrère & Hastings; *9 East 91st St*) was built for Adele Sloane's younger sister, named Emily Vanderbilt Sloane like her mother. Young Emily married John Henry Hammond, graduate of Yale and

Columbia Law School; when shown the plans for the magnificent house, Hammond is said to have declared: "I'm going to be considered a kept man." Their son, also named John Henry Hammond (1910–87), spent his lifetime discovering, nurturing, and promoting musical talent, shaping American popular music from the early years of the Depression until his death. Passionately committed both to music and to civil rights, Hammond promoted the careers of Billie Holiday and Count Basie among others. He fostered the young Benny Goodman and urged him to hire black musicians Teddy Wilson and Lionel Hampton. No fan of bebop, which hit the charts in the mid-1940s, Hammond faded from prominence until the 1960s and '70s, when he sparked the careers of Aretha Franklin, Bob Dylan, and Bruce Springsteen.

CARNEGIE HILL

Carnegie Hill, the neighborhood from Fifth Ave east to about Third Ave, from about East 86th to East 96th St, is quietly residential and upscale, with townhouses, occasional mansions, fine apartment buildings, and prestigious private schools. Geographically it is remarkable for actually having a hill, since many of New York's topographical features were sliced down or filled up as the street grid made its way inexorably northward.

92ND TO 110TH STREETS

Further uptown, the Jewish Museum, the Museum of the City of New York, and Museo del Barrio round off Museum Mile.

THE JEWISH MUSEUM

Map p. 615, D2. 1109 Fifth Ave (92nd St). Subway: 4, 5, 6 to 86th St, or 6 to 96th St. Bus: M1, M2, M3, or M4. Open Sun–Tues 11–5:45, Thur 11–8, Fri 11–5.45, Sat 11–5:45. Closed Wed, major Jewish holidays, New Year's Day, Martin Luther King Day (check website). Admission charge, but Thur 5–8 by donation. Shop, restaurant, children's exhibition, and interactive exhibits are closed on Sat but the galleries are open and free. Mobile apps for exhibitions. T: 212 423 3200, thejewishmuseum.org.

Founded in 1904, the Jewish Museum is considered to have the most important collection of Judaica in the Western Hemisphere: some 25,000 works of art, ceremonial objects, and antiquities. The permanent exhibition, "Culture and Continuity: The Jewish Journey," on the top two floors, explores around 4,000 years of Jewish culture, from its archaeological beginnings to the present, touching on major themes: the ability of Judaism to thrive for thousands of years across thousands of miles, and the essence of Jewish identity. Highlights include Torah arks and crowns, Kiddush cups, and other ceremonial objects; paintings by Édouard Vuillard, Larry Rivers, Raphael Soyer, Ben Shahn, and Ross Bleckner; photography by Weegee, Diane Arbus, and Bernice Abbott; and sculpture by Elie Nadelman. In addition to the permanent exhibition, well-reviewed changing shows are drawn from the museum's own holdings and elsewhere.

The museum occupies the former mansion of Felix Warburg a banker and philanthropist who admired the Isaac Fletcher House (*see p. 338*) and hired its architect, C.P.H. Gilbert, to design something in the same French Gothic style. The house remained in the family until 1944, when the financier's widow, Frieda Schiff Warburg, donated it to the Jewish Theological Seminary for a museum. From 1990–3 the museum restored and expanded the building, doubling the exhibition space and replicating along Fifth Ave its intricately carved limestone façade, using stone from the original quarry.

THE MUSEUM OF THE CITY OF NEW YORK

Map p. 615, D1. 1220 Fifth Ave (East 103rd St). Subway: 6 to 103rd St. Bus: M1, M2, M3, M4. Open seven days 10–6; closed Thanksgiving, Christmas, New Year's Day. Café and shop with excellent selection of New York books. T: 212 534 1672, mcny.org.

The Museum of the City of New York (founded 1923) is the best place to explore the city's history from its days as a Dutch colony to its present eminence. The collections contain more than a million and a half artifacts. Changing exhibitions have included a show of graffiti; gowns and baubles from the Gilded Age at the end of the 19th century; documentary photographs of Hurricane Sandy (2012), and an exploration of Rafael Guastavino's architectural tile. The museum's Colonial Revival building (1932; Joseph H. Freedlander) remained more or less unchanged until it was expanded and renovated (2006–15) by Ennead Architects.

The museum's holdings include real and toy fire engines, maps and prints, ship models, and even a section of wooden pipe from the city's first water supply system. Among the paintings are portraits of prominent New Yorkers and cityscapes by Childe Hassam, Asher B. Durand, and Reginald Marsh. The toy collection has more than 100,000 dolls, books, soldiers, trains, boats, and puppets from the colonial period to the present, including its undisputed star, on permanent display, the Stettheimer Dollhouse. Created (1916–35) by Carrie Stettheimer, sister of the painter Florine Stettheimer and the writer Ettie Stettheimer, the decorations include miniature versions of the work of their friends Alexander Archipenko, Marcel Duchamp, and Gaston Lachaise, contributed by the artists.

EL MUSEO DEL BARRIO

Map p. 615, D1. 1230 Fifth Ave (East 104th St). Subway: 6 to 103rd St. Bus: M1, M2, M3, M4. Open Tues–Sat 11–6; closed Sun, Mon, Thanksgiving, Christmas Eve and Day, New Year's Eve and Day, July 4. Suggested donation. Café and shop. T: 212 831 7272, elmuseo.org.
Small and sharply-focused, El Museo del Barrio is the city's leading institution of Latino culture. Located at the edge of Spanish Harlem or *El Barrio* (literally "the

neighborhood"), it was founded in 1969 by community activists, teachers, and artists, mainly Puerto Ricans, as part of the Nuyorican movement of the 1960s–70s, dedicated to furthering the art and culture of the city's Puerto Ricans. The museum operated first from a school classroom, moving to successive storefronts until it found a long-term home in this building, originally a settlement house for children. At first it focused on Puerto Rican culture, but as New York's Latino population has grown and diversified, it has broadened its scope—for example with its retrospective on Marisol Escobar; a survey of the Mexican cinematographer Gabriel Figueroa; and an exhibition on Brazilian architect Oscar Niemeyer. In 2009 the museum celebrated its 40th anniversary with a new glass façade, redesigned galleries and courtyard, and a café specializing in Latino food.

El Museo's permanent collection, some 7,000 objects, includes Taíno pre-Columbian artifacts and folk art, prints, and works on paper; traditional Latin American arts including musical instruments, miniature houses, dolls, and masks; and fine prints from the 20th and 21st centuries by Puerto Rican, Nuyorican, Mexican, and Chicano artists.

COMING TO THE MILE: THE AFRICA CENTER

When the former Museum for African Art, recast in 2013 as the Africa Center, moves into its new home on the northeast corner of 110th St and Fifth Ave, it will be the first addition to Museum Mile since the Guggenheim opened in 1959. Devoted to public policy and education as well as African art, it will occupy several floors of a building designed by Robert A.M. Stern, which has been under construction since 2008.

EATING AND DRINKING ON MUSEUM MILE

Since Fifth Avenue is zoned residential, there are no restaurants on the Mile itself, though all the museums have cafés, except for the National Academy. Nearby Madison Ave has cafés and delis; more formal restaurants are further east.

$$$ **Paola's.** ■ Classic Italian cuisine with Roman specialties in this Carnegie Hill favorite. Can be noisy. Lunch, dinner daily; weekend brunch. In the Wales Hotel. *1295 Madison Ave (92nd St). T: 212 794 1890; paolasrestaurant.com. Map p. 615, D2.*

$$ **Beyoglu.** ■ Popular Turkish restaurant serving *meze* and specials including kebabs of grilled lamb or beef over rice or pita. Lunch and dinner daily. *1431 Third Ave (81st St). T: 212 650 0850, no website. Map p. 615, E3.*

$$ **Café Sabarsky.** This neo-Viennese café in the Neue Galerie offers German and Austrian food several cuts above usual museum fare. Breakfast and lunch Wed–Mon, dinner Thur–Sun. *1048 Fifth Ave (86th St). T: 212 288 0665, kg-ny.com. Map p. 615, D3.*

Yorkville, The East River, & Roosevelt Island

Formerly a neighborhood of Germans, Hungarians, Czechs, and Slovaks, Yorkville today is similar to other middle-class locales that attract the young and well-to-do. It is home to the mayor's residence, which looks out over the East River toward Hell Gate—infamous for its tortuous tides. Residential Roosevelt Island, once a site of exile for society's outcasts, is an incongruously tranquil spot, just 300 yards off the eastern shore of frenetic Manhattan.

In the late 18th century Yorkville (*map p. 615; subway: 6 to 77th St; bus: M15, M18, or M72*) was a small hamlet between New York and the village of Harlem, a summer retreat for wealthy families of Germanic origin—Schermerhorns, Rhinelanders, and Astors. When the New York and Harlem Railroad arrived in 1834, Yorkville became a suburb drawing middle-class Germans, among them the Rupperts, who operated a brewery. (Less wealthy Germans usually settled first on the Lower East Side, notably around Tompkins Square in a neighborhood called "Kleindeutschland.") By 1900, as waves of eastern European and Italian immigrants poured into downtown Manhattan,  many downtown Germans began moving to Yorkville, a migration hastened in 1904, when the *General Slocum*, an excursion steamer packed with Kleindeutschland women and children, burned and sank in the East River (*see p. 178*).

Irish immigrants arrived during the construction of the Croton Reservoir (completed 1842), becoming the second largest ethnic group. Their presence remains visible in several parish churches—for example, St. Ignatius Loyola (originally St. Lawrence O'Toole)—and a smattering of Irish pubs.

Though Yorkville was never rich, it remained solid throughout the Depression, a place where people worked either in small businesses or for the breweries, and enjoyed themselves at local restaurants, beer gardens, or Viennese-styled cafés. Before World War II, Yorkville became a center of both Nazi and anti-Nazi activity, and after the war the area saw a last wave of German immigration. Thereafter ethnic newcomers were largely Hispanics filtering down from Spanish Harlem, on the northern edge of Yorkville.

As elsewhere, immigrant groups clustered together. Little Bohemia (Czechs and Slovaks) lay at the southern end of Yorkville around First Ave (upper 60s to the mid-70s). North of that was Little Hungary, around Second Avenue in the upper 70s and low 80s. The failed Hungarian Revolution (1848) touched off the first wave of immigrants, lasting until just before World War I, with Hungarians beginning the move uptown from the Lower East Side around 1905 and a second wave arriving after the Soviet Union invaded Hungary in 1956. Most of the Irish settled between 81st and 85th Sts.

SOTHEBY'S
Sotheby's (*map p. 617, F1; 1334 York Ave near 72nd St*) is the headquarters of the multinational auctioneers of fine arts, jewelry, wine, antiquities, and real estate (*open for viewing before some auctions; T: 212 606 7000, sothebys.com*). Founded in London in 1744 with an auction of rare books, Sotheby's opened its New York branch in 1954. Spectacular sales have included the Guennol Lioness, a tiny limestone figurine from ancient Mesopotamia, sold in 2008 for $57.2 million, the most ever paid for an antiquity at auction; the last privately owned copy of *Magna Carta*, for $21.3 million in 2007; and Edvard Munch's pastel of *The Scream*, which brought $119.9 million in 2012.

CHEROKEE APARTMENTS
Stretching across Cherokee Place (*map p. 615, F4; 507–23 East 77th St to 508–22 East 78th St*) are the Cherokee Apartments (1911), a six-story complex formerly known as the Shively Sanitary Tenements because they incorporated Dr. Henry Shively's notions for treating tuberculosis with fresh air and sunlight. Anne Harriman Vanderbilt, second wife of William Kissam Vanderbilt, largely funded the project. The architect, Henry Atterbury Smith, who had long wanted to build attractive and healthful low-income housing, designed an open-stair floor plan, balconies accessible through floor-to-ceiling windows, and Guastavino-tiled tunnels leading to central courtyards. Seats built into the stairwells served as places for people to rest as they climbed. Smith correctly assumed that the apartments would be attractive and healthful, but they proved to too expensive for the poor whom he had hoped to help. Today they are co-ops on the open market.

HENDERSON PLACE AND THE ASPHALT GREEN
The well-preserved **Henderson Place Historic District** (*along East End Ave and Henderson Place, East 86th and East 87th Sts; map p. 615, F3*) was once part of John Jacob Astor's country estate. John C. Henderson, who made his fortune in furs and fur hats, built the houses for people of moderate means, though they seem upscale today. Twenty-four of the original 32 two-story Queen Anne row houses (1882) remain. Built of brick and rough stone, they are glorified with the usual appurtenances of the Queen Anne style: bays, oriel windows, dormers, and gables.

The former Municipal Asphalt Plant (1944; Kahn & Jacobs; *555 East 90th St, east of York Ave*) was the first American steel-framed concrete parabolic arch. Abandoned by the City in 1968, it has been converted to a not-for-profit center for fitness and sports, the **Asphalt Green** (*map p. 615, F2*).

CARL SCHURZ PARK AND GRACIE MANSION

Map p. 615, F3. On the East River, East 84th to East 90th St.

Carl Schurz Park is named for the most prominent German American of the 19th century. Schurz (1829–1906), a hero of the German revolutionary movement of 1848, arrived in America in 1852, becoming in turn a brigadier general in the Civil War, a US senator, and secretary of the interior. He moved to New York in 1881 and lived in Yorkville. The park has beautiful trees and gardens, as well as dog runs and playgrounds. The bronze **statue of *Peter Pan*** (1928; Charles Andrew Hafner) near the middle of the park opposite East 83rd St was sculpted for the lobby of the old Paramount Theater in Times Square. The riverside promenade, **John Finley Walk**, honors John Huston Finley (1863–1940), president of the City College of New York, associate editor of the *New York Times*, state commissioner of education, and unflagging pedestrian, who several times walked the 32 miles around Manhattan Island. From the promenade Mill Rock, Hell Gate, the Triborough (RFK) Bridge, and the Hell Gate Arch are visible, as well as the lighthouse at the northern tip of Roosevelt Island (*see p. 390*).

The mayor's official residence, **Gracie Mansion** (*in Carl Schurz Park; 88th St and East End Ave; for info about tours, T: 311 in New York or 212 570 4773*), faces the East River. One of Manhattan's oldest residences (1799, later additions), its fine detailing—leaded glass sidelights and a semicircular fanlight above the main doorway, railings around the roof and above the main floor—exemplifies rural Federal-style domestic architecture for the well-to-do. Early on, Gracie Mansion served as the country retreat of wealthy merchant and ship owner Archibald Gracie, whose townhouse stood at the foot of Broadway near Battery Park. Gracie's business foundered during the War of 1812 and he sold the mansion in 1823. In 1896, the City seized it for unpaid taxes, but never seemed to know quite what to do with it; its nadir came when it housed the ice cream concession and toilets for Schurz Park. Robert Moses pushed to have it designated the mayor's residence, and Fiorello La Guardia, a man of modest tastes who had rejected a (now-demolished) 75-room neo-château on Riverside Drive, became the first mayor to live here.

MILL ROCK AND HELL GATE

Mill Rock (*map p. 615, F2*), 2.5 acres of undeveloped land about 1,000 feet offshore roughly opposite East 96th St, seems to have been the site of a tidal mill in the early 18th century. Before the War of 1812 a blockhouse there protected the eastern entrance to New York harbor. Today Mill Rock belongs to the Parks Department and harbors colonies of egrets and cormorants, but is not open to the public.

East of Mill Rock is **Hell Gate**, a channel between Queens and Wards Island, joining the East River to the protected waters of Long Island Sound. Navigated by explorer Adriaen Block in 1612, Hell Gate is 22.5 miles from the open sea via New York Bay but more than 100 miles via Long Island Sound, creating three hours' difference in the tides at the two ends of the East River. These conflicting tides along with reefs and rocks once made Hell Gate so tortuous that hundreds of ships are said to have sunk there. The most famous wreck, the Revolutionary frigate *Hussar*, went down in 1780, carrying a fortune in gold coins, the payroll for British troops. Neither the ship nor the coins have been found, though divers keep looking.

In the mid-19th century the Army Corps of Engineers blasted away navigational hazards, a process that culminated on October 10, 1885 in the detonation of 150 tons of explosives, reducing to rubble nine-acre Flood Rock in the largest intentional man-made explosion until the atomic bomb was dropped 60 years later. The name, Hell Gate, despite its infernal connotations, seems to be a corruption of the Dutch *hellegat*, usually translated as "bright channel."

THE ROBERT F. KENNEDY AND HELL GATE BRIDGES

The T-shaped, gray-green **Robert F. Kennedy Bridge** (*map p. 613, F3*), formerly the **Triborough Bridge** (1936; Othmar Ammann, chief engineer) and often still called that, links Randalls Island (now a single landmass joined to Wards Island by landfill) to the Bronx, Manhattan, and Queens. The Bronx arm, which crosses the Bronx Kill, was designed so it could be converted into a lift bridge if the kill, now a ditch, were made navigable, but the waterway has been partially filled to create parkland. The Queens arm between Randalls Island and Astoria is a 1,380-ft suspension bridge. The Manhattan arm, 310ft long, begins at East 125 St and crosses the Harlem River to Randalls Island.

The second bridge (faded red) is **Hell Gate Bridge** (1917; Gustav Lindenthal, engineer, and Henry Hornbostel, architect), a 1,017-ft span carrying four railroad tracks across the East River over Wards Island (at the time a separate island). Considered the peak of Lindenthal's brilliant career, this structurally beautiful and brilliantly engineered bridge is unusual in that the upper arc curves upward at the towers, providing overhead clearance for locomotives and allowing deeper stiffening trusses to increase the bridge's rigidity. The granite-faced towers with their arched openings reminded early observers of the portico to a mammoth temple. Lindenthal's engineers constructed the arch without supporting the unfinished span on scaffolding, which would have closed Hell Gate to navigation. When they hoisted the final central steel section into place, they needed to adjust it by only 5/16 of an inch to close the arch.

ROOSEVELT ISLAND

Map p. 609, B2. Accessible by subway (F train) and by aerial tram (Manhattan tram station on Second Ave at 60th St); fare payable by MetroCard. Bus from Queens: Q102. Visitor Center at the Roosevelt Island Tram Plaza (summer hours: open daily except Tues, noon–5; winter hours: open Thur–Sun, 11–4; closed in inclement weather). Self-guided internet-connected historical tours. The local Red Bus circles the island at frequent intervals.

Formerly Welfare Island (1921), Blackwell's Island (1686), Manning's Island (1665), Hog Island (1637; Dutch, *Varckens Eylandt*), and Minnahannock (before the Dutch arrived), Roosevelt Island (1973) is a two-mile slice of land long used for exiling madmen, criminals, and incurables. It emerged in the 1970s as a planned community for people of varying economic backgrounds. Only 300 yards off the shore of the East Side, it seems quiet and remote, untouched by the frantic energy of Manhattan, to which it belongs politically.

In the island's mid-section rise the towers of the original new town, whose housing, schools, transport, and even trash removal reflect a master plan by architects Philip Johnson and John Burgee. Down the midline runs a Main Street; girding the shoreline a promenade offers terrific views of Manhattan's high-rise skyline and more modestly scaled Queens. Near the ends of the island newer residential developments have arisen, some upscale, alongside monuments of the island's pathological past—to the south a ruined smallpox hospital designed by James Renwick (of St. Patrick's Cathedral fame) and, to the north, a lighthouse built by penitentiary inmates (or perhaps a lunatic).

SOUTH OF THE TRAM STATION

South of the sports complex, the construction site for Cornell University's NYC Tech obliterates the **former campus of Goldwater Memorial Hospital** (1939, demolished beginning 2014). A facility for chronic diseases, it was named for Dr. Sigismund Schultz Goldwater, commissioner of the city's Department of Hospitals. During World War II, conscientious objectors volunteered at Goldwater for secret experiments pertaining to synthetic anti-malarial drugs (quinine, the treatment of choice, was unavailable from Japanese-controlled territories) and research on the effects of starvation, exposure to extreme cold, and drinking saltwater.

The hospital replaced the Blackwell's Island Penitentiary (1832, demolished 1936), a great, gray, grim building constructed of gneiss quarried locally by convicts. Among its most famous inmates were "Boss" Tweed (1874) and Mae West (1927), both of whom enjoyed comfortable conditions, though West complained of the "fuzzy" texture of the standard-issue underwear. The penitentiary complex grew to include a workhouse (1852) for minor offenders, "drunks and disorderlies," who were compelled to perform hard labor.

Further south are the Gothic remains of James Renwick's **Smallpox Hospital** (1854–6), the only NYC landmark to be designated as a picturesque ruin. Declared a landmark in 1976, it has stood exposed to the weather and deteriorated with alarming speed. Partially stabilized in 2008, its future is doubtful.

FRANKLIN DELANO ROOSEVELT FOUR FREEDOMS PARK
Southern tip of Roosevelt Island. From the tram station, walk south about 15mins, or walk north to Main St and take the Red Bus to the park. Open April–Sept Wed–Mon 9–7; Oct–March Wed–Mon 9–5; closed Tues. Free. Tours (also free) Sat and Sun at 11am, meet at entrance gate to park, limited to 15 visitors, first-come, first-serve. Private tours (admission charge) also available: fdrfourfreedomspark.org.

At the island's southern end, where it narrows to a blunt point, the four-acre Franklin Delano Roosevelt Four Freedoms Park (2012) honors the 32nd president of the US. Simple and powerful, the memorial is the posthumous work of Louis Kahn, often considered America's greatest late-20th-century architect. When Kahn died of a heart attack in Penn Station in 1974, he was carrying the completed drawings for the project in his briefcase, but the plans gathered dust for more than 30 years as funding dried up during New York's fiscal crisis and supporters left town or lost their political clout. Nevertheless, park campaigners fought off opportunistic proposals for development including luxury condos. The film *My Architect* (2003), by Kahn's son Nathaniel, re-awakened interest in the work of the elder Kahn; William vanden Heuvel, lawyer, businessman, diplomat, and admirer of FDR, raised nearly $54 million to finance the project's construction.

The memorial today is considered, like much of Kahn's best work, a masterpiece of simplicity, a composition of powerful geometric forms created from austere materials. A broad staircase ascends to a triangular lawn bordered by linden trees; the lawn slopes down to a stone box—Kahn called it a "room," with 36-ton blocks of near-white granite for walls and the sky for a roof. The central granite block holds a bronze portrait head of FDR, enlarged from an original (1933) by Jo Davidson; on its southern face are inscribed Roosevelt's Four Freedoms, basic human rights that should be available to everyone, everywhere: freedom of speech and worship, freedom from want and fear.

STRECKER MEMORIAL LABORATORY
Along the Promenade on the east side of the island, just north of Four Freedoms Park, blocky Romanesque Revival Strecker Memorial Laboratory (1892; Withers and Dickson) was the gift of an otherwise unknown Mr. Strecker. It housed a pathology lab, an autopsy room, a morgue, and research facilities. Beginning in 1999 the Metropolitan Transit Authority restored the exterior and converted the building to a subway power substation.

NORTH OF THE TRAM STATION

Just south of the main residential area, the clapboard **Blackwell House** (1796–1804), serves as headquarters of the Roosevelt Island Historical Society (*rihs.us*). The Blackwell family came to the island through marriage. Captain John Manning, the British officer who botched the defense of the fort at the Battery and then formally surrendered New York to the Dutch in 1673, an interlude that lasted from 1673 to 1674, retired in humiliation to the privacy of this island, which he had bought five years earlier. His stepdaughter married Robert Blackwell and the house, built later, remained in the family until the City bought the island for the penitentiary and the house became the home of the warden.

The apartment complexes along **Main St**, constructed in 1975–6 in the then-reigning Brutalist style, reflect the original Johnson–Burgee master plan and were built, many of them subsidized through state and federal programs, for working- and middle-class tenants.

Tucked between the northernmost apartment buildings is the Victorian Gothic **Chapel of the Good Shepherd** (1899; Frederick Clarke Withers; restored 1976, Giorgio Cavaglieri), now an ecumenical community center. Banker George N. Bliss donated the money to the New York Protestant Episcopal Missionary Society for the church, which served the inmates of the nearby almshouse. The building recalls English parish churches, not surprising since Withers was born and trained in England; the original five-toned bell sits on the adjoining plaza.

Further north, the **AVAC Building** (1975, Kallmann & McKinnell) contains the computerized Automated Vacuum Collection System, which sucks household garbage from apartment chutes whence it arrives through underground tubes at 55mph, ready to be separated, shredded or compacted, packed into containers, and shipped off the island by the Department of Sanitation.

Two more landmarks and a hospital stand at the northern end of the island. The **Bird S. Coler Hospital** (1952) replaces Goldwater as a municipal hospital for the chronically ill. The **Octagon**, originally the rotunda of the New York City Lunatic Asylum (1839; Alexander Jackson Davis) is now the central pavilion of The Octagon apartment development. The asylum was founded to accommodate the mentally ill, who until then were housed in overcrowded wards at Bellevue Hospital. Their treatment at the asylum could hardly have been enlightened since they were supervised by inmates from the penitentiary. Since physical labor was considered therapeutic, able-bodied male patients were put to work in vegetable gardens or building sea walls; the women did housework or sewed. Charles Dickens, who visited in 1842, found it pervaded by a "lounging, listless, madhouse air." In 1887 Nellie Bly, the pen name of journalist Elizabeth Cochrane, feigned madness to report on conditions; the asylum's boredom, filth, and brutality were enough, she said, to make anyone go insane. Her exposé, *Ten Days in a Madhouse* (1887), became a bestseller and led to the transfer of patients to a better facility on Ward's Island.

At the very northern tip of the island, in a small park, stands a 50-ft **lighthouse** (1872) designed by James Renwick, architect of the Smallpox Hospital (*see above*) and built by inmates of the penitentiary with the gray local gneiss also used for the Octagon, the Penitentiary, and other older institutional buildings. Legends surround the old tower, especially about one John McCarthy, a patient at the Lunatic Asylum, who claimed to have built it. McCarthy, apparently paranoid, is said to have built a fort where the lighthouse now stands to protect the island from invasion, but was persuaded to dismantle it so that the lighthouse could rise in its place. A plaque at the foot, which disappeared in the 1960s, asserted:

This is the work
Was done by
John McCarthy
Who built the Light
House from the bottom to the
Top All ye who do pass by may
Pray for his soul when he dies.

Lincoln Center & its Neighborhood

The city's pre-eminent performance venues and several fine restaurants cluster around Lincoln Square, once the center of a tenement district. The neighborhood's 21st-century legacy may be the skinny towers of West 57th St, currently chiseling out a new skyline near Central Park.

L incoln Square, the name for the neighborhood from Columbus Circle to West 70th St along Broadway and Columbus Aves, and also the intersection of Broadway and Columbus Ave, is a thriving residential area, an educational hub, and a cultural center whose major institution is Lincoln Center for the Performing Arts. Before its construction the neighborhood was known as San Juan Hill, described by the NYC Housing Authority as the worst slum in the city. Its tenements, home to Puerto Rican, African American, and Afro-Caribbean communities, were used as background for the film of *West Side Story*, and then torn down for the urban renewal project that included Lincoln Center.

LINCOLN CENTER FOR THE PERFORMING ARTS

Map p. 616, B1–B2. West 62nd to West 66th Sts, Amsterdam to Columbus Aves. Subway: A, B, C, D, 1 to 59th St-Columbus Circle. Bus: M5, M7, M10, M66, M104. Visitor Center in the Atrium (Broadway between West 62nd and West 63rd Sts); open Mon–Fri 8am–10pm, Sat and Sun 9am–10pm. Atrium box office open Tues–Fri 2pm–7:45pm, Sat noon–2pm & 3pm–7:45pm. Tours of Lincoln Center, T: 212 875 5456. Cafés in Atrium, Alice Tully and David Geffen halls, Film Center. Restaurants at Metropolitan Opera House (ticket holders) and David Geffen Hall. Shop in Metropolitan Opera House. For event info, visit lincolncenter.org.

Lincoln Center for the Performing Arts is North America's pre-eminent cultural center, visited by more than five million people yearly. Occupying 16.3 acres, its eleven performing arts organizations present more than 5,000 events annually, while its travertine-clad, colonnaded buildings are widely recognizable. Architecturally Lincoln Center usually evokes an image of its three largest halls—the Metropolitan Opera House, David Geffen Hall (previously Avery Fisher Hall, originally Philharmonic Hall), and the David H. Koch Theater (formerly the New York State Theater)—which surround the central plaza. The three halls were designed to complement one another: all are classical in inspiration; all face the plaza with colonnades and large expanses of glass; and all are finished with travertine, a creamy white marble from ancient quarries near Rome (which has not fared well in New York's winter climate).

The plaza's well-known **fountain** (1964), with its pavement design of concentric circles and spokes, the work of Philip Johnson, is the visual center of the complex. In the summer music and dance events enliven the space, while at Christmas a ceremonial tree glitters. At any time of the year the plaza draws passers-by to sit by the fountain and people-watch.

HISTORY OF LINCOLN CENTER

Two major factors paved the way for the development of Lincoln Center. In 1955 Lincoln Square, the then-dingy neighborhood around Broadway and Amsterdam Ave at West 65th St, was targeted for urban renewal by Robert Moses. In addition, the Metropolitan Opera needed a modern venue to replace the "Old Met," which had opened on Broadway at 38th St in 1893. John D. Rockefeller III directed the fundraising, while Wallace K. Harrison (a Rockefeller family friend and associate) headed the board of architects.

In 1959 President Dwight D. Eisenhower turned over the first shovel of earth, beginning a period of construction that ended with the opening of the Juilliard School in 1969. Architects for the individual buildings and spaces included Harrison, Gordon Bunshaft (Skidmore, Owings and Merrill), Eero Saarinen, Pietro Belluschi, and Philip Johnson. In 1962 Philharmonic Hall opened, with a gala performance in which Leonard Bernstein conducted the New York Philharmonic, 200 black-robed choristers, and 13 big-name soloists. By 1987, however, most of the companies had outgrown their facilities and the trustees broke ground once again. The Rose Building (1991; Davis Brody Inc.) on West 65th St opened four years later.

Despite its obvious successes—or perhaps because of them—Lincoln Center has not escaped controversy. In particular, the complex to many seemed aloof, a forbidding bastion of classical music. Social critics initially decried the destruction of a lower-income neighborhood: 1,647 families had to find new homes when their buildings were demolished for the center. Acoustics in several buildings have been troublesome. Though time and familiarity have mellowed the glossy marble, architectural critics never liked Lincoln Center. At worst they have accused it of slick, mediocre Classicism or even "monumental Modernism," a term usually reserved for Fascist architecture. At best they have faintly praised buildings' scale and their relationships to plazas and open spaces. Others have sometimes found it too institutional, too rich, too powerful, too elitist. The undeniable fact remains, however, that Lincoln Center, despite its initial cost overruns, ongoing budgetary struggles, and perpetual attraction of criticism, is a vital cultural institution for both the city and the country, and one that has helped revitalize a neighborhood.

Beginning in 2006, after years of sub-par maintenance and changing artistic needs, the center underwent a $1.3-billion renewal (Diller Scofidio + Renfro, with FX Fowle) that addressed aging infrastructure and congestion while seeking to make public spaces more welcoming. West 66th Street lost its dark and grimy overpass; Alice Tully Hall gained a new entrance; roof gardens and small groves of trees sprouted; new restaurants opened. The plaza appears much as Philip Johnson designed it, though the fountain, re-designed by Mark Fuller, has been fitted out with more than 300 computer-controlled nozzles and some 272 lights that illuminate the columns of water as they rise and fall, froth and foam.

THE METROPOLITAN OPERA

Known for its lavish productions, the Metropolitan Opera House (*T: 212 362 6000, metopera.org*) is the nation's largest musical organization, fielding a virtuosic orchestra and star-studded casts. Facing Broadway from the west side of the plaza, the ten-story building (1966; Wallace K. Harrison) is the centerpiece of Lincoln Center.

The Metropolitan was founded in 1880 by a group of "new" capitalists—i.e., Goulds, Whitneys, J. Pierpont Morgan, and the occasional Vanderbilt—who couldn't get boxes at the Academy of Music on 14th Street because the "old nobility" held title to them all. The opera's first house (1883; J.C. Cady and Louis de Coppet Bergh), on Broadway at West 38th St, had an auditorium whose deep "diamond horseshoe" gave box holders an unrivaled opportunity to look at one another, but which made it more difficult to look at the stage—some 700 seats having a partial or obstructed view. The present house opened on September 16, 1966, with the premiere performance of Samuel Barber's *Antony and Cleopatra*, the title roles sung by Justino Diaz and Leontyne Price.

At night when the house is illuminated, two murals by Marc Chagall (*see below*) gleam through the windows between the five marble arches (curtains sometimes protect them by day). The long side walls of the house reach back the equivalent of 45 stories.

The interior

Finished in red plush, gold leaf, and marble, the lobby recalls the color scheme of the old Met, attempting to match the splendor of traditional opera houses with a more contemporary feel, an attempt that some critics felt erred on the side of over-decoration. The concrete forms for the sweeping curves of the Grand Staircase were executed by boat builders. Chagall's predominantly red mural on the south side, *Le Triomphe de la Musique*, contains visual references to opera, folk music, and jazz, as well as images of the New York skyline. Sir Rudolf Bing, the charismatic general manager at the time the house opened, appears in gypsy costume (the central figure in the group of three on the left). The yellow mural, *Les Sources de la Musique*, with a King David–Orpheus figure holding a lyre, and a Tree of Life afloat in the Hudson River, contains motifs drawn from Wagner, Verdi, Bach, Beethoven's *Fidelio*, and Mozart's *The Magic Flute*. The crystal sunburst chandeliers were donated by the Austrian government.

The auditorium, also decorated in red, has 3,788 seats arranged in the traditional manner, though with a widened horseshoe to improve sightlines. Large by European standards (c.f. Covent Garden's 2,268 seats), it offers only a single tier of boxes. Otherwise the seating is "democratic," in contrast to the old Met, where lower-paying customers rode in segregated elevators and sat in less comfortable seats. The free-form sculpture for the proscenium arch (1966) is by Mary Callery.

THE DAVID H. KOCH THEATER

On the south side of the plaza the former New York State Theater (1964; Philip Johnson & Richard Foster) was renamed for oil-and-gas billionaire David Koch after a $100-million gift (2008) for renovation of the hall. One-time home of the now-defunct New York City Opera, it is a prime venue for dance. Its resident company, the New York City Ballet, founded in 1948 by general manager Lincoln Kirstein and artistic director George Balanchine, has long been famous for its performances of Balanchine's abstract, Neoclassical ballets.

Art inside the hall includes work by Lee Bontecou and Jasper Johns, as well as two large, curvaceous statues at either end, one pair representing *Two Nudes*, the other, *Two Circus Women* (originals 1930 and 1931; Elie Nadelman), which were duplicated in Carrara marble at twice the original size. At the time of installation detractors called them "absolutely pneumatic," likening their polished whiteness to yogurt, while admirers have found them to combine "high style, sly levity, and swelling monumentality."

The auditorium (seats 2,586) is decorated with big jewel-like lights studding the tiers of balconies and a central chandelier that resembles a colossal, many-faceted diamond. The stage, engineered specifically to meet the demands of dancers, features a sprung floor with air spaces between its layers.

DAVID GEFFEN HALL

Facing the plaza from the north is David Geffen Hall (1962; Max Abramovitz), originally Philharmonic Hall, a glass box caged by 44 tapered travertine columns, with an auditorium seating 2,738. The hall is the home of the New York Philharmonic, the nation's oldest symphony orchestra. It was renamed first (1973) for Avery Fisher, inventor and manufacturer of hi-fi components and donor of $10.5 million to Lincoln Center; and again (2015) for David Geffen, who donated $100 million toward its modernization and renovation.

Ironically, Philharmonic Hall was planned as a miracle of modern acoustic science. Originally designed in a shoe box shape (like Boston's acoustically successful Symphony Hall), the auditorium was altered to accommodate more seats even before construction began. From its opening performance, the hall's acoustics have continued to disappoint both musicians and audiences. When small adjustments failed to improve the acoustics, engineers resorted to increasingly radical measures, changing wall contours, replacing heavily upholstered seats with thinly padded, wooden-backed chairs, and adding plywood to the ceiling. Even so, in 1974 the Boston and Philadelphia Orchestras, still dissatisfied, went back to Carnegie Hall for their New York appearances. In 1976, using half of Avery Fisher's gift, architects Philip

DAVID GEFFEN HALL

Johnson and John Burgee with acoustical guidance from Cyril Harris, consultant for the Metropolitan Opera House, had the auditorium completely rebuilt. Another gut renovation was in progress at the time of writing.

Between David Geffen Hall and the Lincoln Center Theater, a reflecting pool harbors Henry Moore's two-piece bronze *Lincoln Center Reclining Figure* (1965), which the sculptor described as "a leg part and a head and arms part." Near the library entrance is Alexander Calder's *Le Guichet* (1965), a stabile of blackened steel (22ft long, 14ft high). The name means "the ticket window."

LINCOLN CENTER THEATER
This theater complex (1965; Eero Saarinen) is situated west of the reflecting pool, its main façade a horizontal slab of travertine projecting over a glass wall. The principal performance space inside is the Vivian Beaumont Theater (the donor inherited a department store fortune), whose 1,080 seats make it the only venue outside the Times Square Theater District large enough to qualify as a "Broadway theater." The stage was conceived as a compromise between a traditional proscenium arch and a thrust stage. Also in the building is the Mitzi E. Newhouse Theater, a 299-seat house for Off-Broadway-style productions. The newest addition, the Claire Tow Theater, a 121-seat house perched on the roof of the building, features the work of young and experimental playwrights. Operated by the non-profit Lincoln Center Theater Inc. since 1985, the venue has enjoyed success presenting new dramas, classics, and revivals.

THE NEW YORK PUBLIC LIBRARY FOR THE PERFORMING ARTS
40 Lincoln Center Plaza. Open Mon and Thur 12–8; Tues, Wed, Fri, Sat 12–6; closed Sun. T: 917 275 6975, nypl.org/locations/lpa.
This 1965 building (Skidmore, Owings & Merrill) houses some 250,000 books, audio and video recordings, and music. Highlights include manuscripts of Mozart and Bach, diaries of Nijinsky, correspondence of John Barrymore and Tennessee Williams, and rare cylinders of Metropolitan Opera performances from the turn of the 20th century.

THE JUILLIARD SCHOOL AND ALICE TULLY HALL

60 Lincoln Center Plaza, on West 65th St between Amsterdam and Columbus Aves. T: 212 799 5000, juilliard.edu.

One of the country's premier performing arts conservatories, Juilliard was founded in 1905 as the Institute of Musical Arts by Frank Damrosch and James Loeb, and endowed in 1920 through a bequest from Augustus D. Juilliard, a textile merchant who worked his way up to banks and railroads. Of all the buildings at Lincoln Center, this (1969, Pietro Belluschi; remodeled 2009, Diller Scofidio + Renfro) is the most complex, housing Alice Tully Hall (seats 1,096), home of the Chamber Music Society of Lincoln Center, as well as the school itself, which offers performance training in music, dance, and drama. Also on site are the Juilliard Theater (seats 1,026); a small recital hall; a drama workshop theater; and 82 soundproof practice rooms, three organ studios, some 200 pianos, 35 teaching studios, and 16 two-story studios for dance, drama, or orchestral rehearsals.

ALICE TULLY, SOPRANO AND PHILANTHROPIST

Alice Tully (1902–93), born in upstate New York, enjoyed a modest career as a classical singer in the 1930s. When she inherited her grandfather's fortune—he had founded the Corning Glass Works—she turned to philanthropy, supporting the arts, often anonymously. Her cousin, one of the founders of Lincoln Center, convinced her to fund a hall for chamber music, and though she long resisted giving the hall her name, she was convinced when an acoustician whose work she admired was hired to design the hall. Miss Tully, as she was known, was also an enthusiastic amateur pilot and, during World War II, a Red Cross nurse's aide.

THE ROSE BUILDING

Visible above the Juilliard building is the Samuel and David Rose Building (1992; Davis Brody & Assoc. and Abramovitz Kingsland Schiff), with the Meredith Willson Residence Hall rising above it. The 28-story tower contains office space, living quarters for Juilliard and American Ballet School students, rehearsal studios, and the 300-seat Walter Reade Theater for the Film Society of Lincoln Center. On the tenth floor of the 28-story tower is the Kaplan Penthouse, a small venue with a big view, used for intimate concerts and recitals (*165 West 65th St at Broadway and Amsterdam Ave*).

LINCOLN CENTER TO COLUMBUS CIRCLE

Dante Park, the southern triangle created by the intersection of Broadway and Columbus Avenue at 63rd St (*map p. 616, B1*), contains a bronze statue of Dante Alighieri (1921; Ettore Ximenes), erected to commemorate the 600th anniversary of the poet's death. Originally the New York chapter of the Dante Alighieri Society had hoped for something larger in Times Square to celebrate the 50th anniversary of Italian unification, but fundraising fell short and the society settled for this compromise. *Time Sculpture* by Philip Johnson, made in 1999 when he was 93, a 28-ft bronze pylon with four clock faces, updates the traditional street clock.

In **Richard Tucker Park**, the northern of the two triangles, near West 66th St, a bronze portrait bust of Richard Tucker (1913–75), by Milton Hebald, sits on granite pedestal inscribed with the names of 31 operas in which the tenor performed. A native New Yorker, Tucker appeared in 499 performances in 21 seasons with the Metropolitan Opera, was one of the company's most popular singers, and the only person whose funeral took place in the present opera house.

AMERICAN FOLK ART MUSEUM
Map p. 616, B1. 2 Lincoln Square, Columbus Ave between West 65th and West 66th Sts. Open Tues–Thur 11:30–7, Fri 12–7:30, Sat 11:30–7, Sun 12–6, closed Mon. Free. Shop. T: 212 595 9533, folkartmuseum.org.
Founded in 1961, this is New York's only institution devoted solely to traditional and contemporary American folk art, including the work of modern self-taught "outsider" artists. Among the traditional works are paintings, trade signs, weather vanes, quilts, scrimshaw, and carvings. Ammi Phillips's *Girl in a Red Dress with Cat and Dog* (1830–5), the *St. Tammany Weathervane* (c. 1890), and the well-known *Flag Gate* (c. 1876) are iconic. The collection includes the nation's largest holdings of work by Henry Darger, a Chicago recluse who devoted much of his life to a fantastic 19,000-page epic illustrated with hundreds of watercolors. The collection is shown in rotating displays.

FORDHAM UNIVERSITY, LINCOLN CENTER CAMPUS
A Jesuit institution founded in 1841 in the west Bronx, Fordham University built this campus (*map p. 616, B2*) as part of the Lincoln Center urban renewal project. Facing Columbus Avenue at West 61st St in front of the Law School is Lila Katzen's **City Spirit** (1968), its curved forms, according to the sculptor, signifying the interlocking elements of the city. Closer to West 62nd St is **Circle World #2** (1969; Masami Kodama), a cube of black granite inserted in a broken circle of pink granite. In the elevated plaza of the Lowenstein Center, not easily visible from the street, is Frederick Shrady's 28-ft bronze statue, **Peter, Fisher of Men** (1965).

CHURCH OF ST. PAUL THE APOSTLE
Map p. 616, B2. 8 Columbus Ave (West 60th St). Open weekdays 7–end of 5:15 Mass, Sat 7–6:30 Mass, Sun 7am–9pm. T: 212 265 3495, stpaultheapostle.org.
This Roman Catholic church was inspired by Father Isaac Thomas Hecker, born to Protestant immigrant German parents. Father Hecker worked in his family's (still-extant) flour business as a child, converted to Roman Catholicism around 1844 and in 1858 founded the Missionary Society of St. Paul to spread Catholicism in the then-largely Protestant US and Canada. When built, this church (1885; Jeremiah O'Rourke) was the second largest in the city after St. Patrick's Cathedral; it so impressed viewers

with its fortress-like solidity that some referred to it as "Fort Deshon," after Father George Deshon, an engineer trained at West Point military academy who took over from O'Rourke. It incorporates stones from the decommissioned Croton Aqueduct and Distributing Reservoir as well as from a former theater. The bas-relief by Lumen Martin Winter (1958) on the neo-Gothic façade depicts the conversion of St. Paul on the road to Damascus and contains 50 tons of travertine fixed against a mosaic background of Venetian glass tiles in 15 shades of blue. Stanford White designed the baldachin over the high altar and the altars at the ends of the aisles. The *Angel of the Moon* mural (high on the south wall of the sanctuary), the Connemara marble altar of St. Patrick in the north aisle (second bay from the main entrance), the east window, and the two blue outer windows in the chancel were designed by John La Farge.

COLUMBUS CIRCLE

Map p. 616, C2. Subway: A, B, C, D, 1 to 59th St-Columbus Circle. Bus: M5, M7, M10.

In his original plan for Central Park, Frederick Law Olmsted included a nameless circle at its southwest corner. The area became Columbus Circle after a monument was placed here with funds donated by Italian-Americans to commemorate the 400th anniversary of the explorer's "discovery." From the top of a 77-ft granite column, a marble statue of the explorer (1892; Gaetano Russo) gazes down Broadway. At the base of the column a winged allegorical figure represents *Discovery*; two bronze tablets depict the explorer's departure from Spain and his arrival in the New World. The column itself sports three pairs of bronze rostra—the beaky prows of ancient warships, intended for ramming enemy vessels.

For years heavy traffic made crossing the street a hazardous undertaking, but in 2005 an enlarged central circle, pedestrian walkways, new plantings, seating, and bigger and better fountains (designed by Water Entertainment Technologies) made the intersection a safer, friendlier, and more attractive place.

TIME WARNER CENTER

Map p. 616, B2. 10 Columbus Circle (West 58th to 60th Sts).

The Time Warner Center (2003; Skidmore Owings & Merrill; David Childs, design partner), curves around Columbus Circle, its two towers rising 750ft. The lower floors house a shopping mall, with a large upscale grocery store below street level and three floors of stores above. On the fourth floor several even more upscale restaurants open from a large lobby, clad in gray Indian granite, green Australian marble, black Russian granite, and snowy Italian marble. Stacked above are offices, the headquarters of Time Warner, studios for CNN (the TV station owned by Time Warner), an ultra-luxury hotel, condominiums, and penthouses.

COLUMBUS CIRCLE
Time Warner Center's towers rising above the monument to Columbus.

In the street-level lobby stand two fat, anatomically correct, 12-ft nudes, **Adam** and **Eve**, by Fernando Botero. Adam in particular has proven irresistible as a photo op for passing shoppers.

JAZZ AT LINCOLN CENTER

In the Time Warner Center. T: 212 258 9800, jazz.org. For details of shows and tickets, see website, or call 212 721 6500.
The home of Lincoln Center's jazz programs occupies the fifth through seventh floors of the northern tower of the Time Warner Center (*accessed by elevator from the ground floor of the shops*). Designed by Rafael Viñoly, its three performance spaces comprise the 1,233-seat Rose Theater, the first auditorium acoustically designed for jazz; the 483-seat Allen Room, with its 50-ft plate-glass window overlooking Central Park; and Dizzy's Club Coca-Cola, seating about 140 people in a cabaret setting.

THE MAINE MEMORIAL

The Maine Memorial (*Central Park West at Central Park South and West 59th St*) commemorates the sinking of the US battleship *Maine* (February 15, 1898), an incident that helped trigger the Spanish-American War. The memorial (1913; architect H. van Buren Magonigle) consists of a blocky granite stele (43½ ft) with bronze and marble allegorical sculptures by Attilio Piccirilli (*see below*). The group on the top, with *Columbia Triumphant* standing in a shell pulled by three sea horses, is made of bronze recovered from the guns of the *Maine*. At the base facing the circle, a boatload of marble figures includes *Victory* (a youth kneeling in the prow), accompanied by *Courage* (a male nude), and *Fortitude* (a mother comforting a weeping child). Behind them stands a robed figure representing *Peace*. Another group, facing the park, includes *Justice*, *History*, and a *Warrior*, whose upraised hand once clenched a bronze sword. The reclining youth on the side of the stele facing downtown represents the *Atlantic*, while the *Pacific*, facing uptown, appears as an aged man. The symbolic conception of the memorial suggests America's perception of itself in 1898 as a dominant world power.

ATTILIO PICCIRILLI

Attilio Piccirilli (1866–1945) was born in Massa Carrara in Tuscany, near the veins of white Carrara marble used for Trajan's Column in Rome, Michelangelo's *David*, and Marble Arch in London. The family immigrated to New York when Attilio was eleven years old, eventually opening a studio in the Mott Haven section of the Bronx. Attilio and his five brothers all followed in their father's footsteps and became stonecutters; Attilio and Furio also became sculptors. Attilio developed a close friendship with Fiorello La Guardia, who called him Uncle Peach. The Piccirillis' most famous work is Daniel Chester French's statue of Abraham Lincoln in the Lincoln Memorial in Washington, D.C., but they also contributed to the streetscape of New York City.

Among their works are the Maine Memorial (*see opposite*); the lions by Edward Clark Potter and pediment statues at the New York Public Library (*Fifth Ave near 42nd St*); *The Four Continents* by Daniel Chester French and the pediment statues by various artists at the Alexander Hamilton Custom House (near Bowling Green Park); the pediment figures by John Quincy Adams Ward and Paul Wayland Bartlett at the New York Stock Exchange; the two figures of George Washington by Alexander Stirling Calder and Hermon A. MacNeil on the arch at Washington Square; more than 600 sculptures at Riverside Church (*Riverside Drive and West 122nd St*); the Fireman's Memorial by H. van Buren Magonigle (*Riverside Drive and West 100th St*); *Youth Leading Industry* (1935) at Rockefeller Center; the figures of *Manhattan* and *Brooklyn* by Daniel Chester French and pediment statues at the Brooklyn Museum; and the simple monument in the Bronx's Woodlawn Cemetery for Fiorello La Guardia's wife and infant daughter, who died in 1921.

THE MUSEUM OF ARTS AND DESIGN (MAD)

2 Columbus Circle (59th St and Broadway). Open Tues–Sun 10–6, Thur and Fri 10–9, closed Mon and major holidays. Admission charge, but by donation Thur and Fri after 6pm. Guided gallery tours. Restaurant and shop. T: 212 299 7777, madmuseum.org.

A & P Supermarket heir Huntington Hartford commissioned the original building (1965; Edward Durell Stone) to house his Gallery of Modern Art, a very personal collection of figurative painting and sculpture, his riposte not only to the abstract art on display at MoMA nearby, but to the glass and steel skyscrapers of the then-ascendant International Style. Stone, who had designed an early wing of MoMA, obliged Hartford with a romantic ten-story marble-clad tower, curved on the north to follow the arc of Columbus Circle, pierced with more than a thousand portholes, topped off with a loggia, and raised above the ground on curved "legs" also perforated with round holes. Critics hated it. The influential critic Ada Louise Huxtable called it a "die-cut Venetian palazzo on lollipops," a nickname that stuck, but the "Lollipop Building" eventually found a place in the hearts and memories of New Yorkers.

Hartford's museum lasted five years, and thereafter the building declined, a rotating roster of tenants alternating with periods of vacancy. In 2002 the Museum of Arts and Design bought it and three years later got permission to alter it. Loud objections followed. Efforts to have the building landmarked were unsuccessful, and amidst demonstrations, accusations, and lawsuits, the museum went ahead with the alterations.

The replacement by Brad Cloepfil has fared almost as poorly, critically speaking, as the original, both because it changed Stone's building and because it retained some of its elements. A skin of iridescent terra cotta tiles replaces the white marble façade; instead of the portholes that punctuated the corners of Stone's building, horizontal slits admit light to the galleries. The "lollipops," load-bearing and structurally essential, remain.

The museum
Founded (1956) as the Museum of Contemporary Crafts, the museum has worked over the years to broaden the definition of "craft" and to assign it a place in the artistic pantheon equal to painting and sculpture. The museum offers changing, often fascinating, exhibits of contemporary and traditional hand-made works of glass, ceramics, fiber, paper, wood, and metal. The permanent collection includes art from all over the world, most of it created since 1950, and embraces architecture, fashion, interior design, and technology. Almost a half century after her original condemnation of the building, Huxtable remarked on the vitality of the museum as "an oasis of enchantment, a kind of Camelot on Columbus Circle."

ALONG WEST 57TH STREET

Just two blocks south of Central Park, West 57th Street is becoming a nouveau "Billionaires' Row," hosting a string of über-tall skinny towers stacked to penthouse level with luxury condominiums. Several of these are in progress; at the time of writing the residential skyscraper rising at **225 West 57th St** was projected to reach 1,522 ft with an added spire bringing it to 1,775 ft—a foot shorter than One World Trade Center. A Nordstrom department store will anchor the base and the building will cantilever over the Art Students League.

ART STUDENTS LEAGUE OF NEW YORK
The Art Students League of New York at 215 West 57th St (*Seventh and Eighth Aves*) enjoys a dignified French Renaissance building (1892) by the architect of the Plaza Hotel (Henry J. Hardenbergh). The League was founded in 1875 as an alternative to the more rigid and formal National Academy, though the curriculum required "painting from the antique"—copying plaster models of Greek and Roman statues—before students progressed to drawing from life. Long known for its outstanding teachers the League was fortunate to have many outstandingly talented (though not necessarily like-minded) students: William Merritt Chase taught Georgia O'Keeffe; Thomas Hart Benton taught Jackson Pollock; George Grosz and Hans Hofmann taught Louise Nevelson.

One57 (2014; Christian de Portzamparc) at 157 West 57th St (*near Seventh Ave*) is the first of the new skinny towers to be occupied. Rising 1,004 ft, it is New York's second-tallest residential building, its condos sitting atop a hotel. Many of the owners—Russian oligarchs, Chinese buyers of unknown identity, Canadian backers of big-name fashion houses, and entrepreneurial Americans—bought their units as investments and will live in them part-time, if at all. Amenities include a swimming pool with piped-in underwater music. Although architectural critics have praised it—if faintly—a vocal contingent of New Yorkers continues to express concern about the shadows that this building and those that follow it will cast over Central Park.

At **111 West 57th St** (1924–5; Warren & Wetmore), another skinny residential tower will replace **Steinway Hall**; this one, only 60ft wide, scheduled for completion 2018, is projected at 1,428 ft. It will rise from Steinway's former courtyard and maintain the Hall's landmarked façade and legendary decorated showroom (without the Steinways). The piano manufacturer will open a new sales center at 1133 Sixth Ave at West 43rd St, until recently the home of the International Center for Photography.

CARNEGIE HALL

Map p. 616, C2. 154 West 57th St (Seventh Ave). Depending on rehearsal schedule, tours Oct–June Mon–Fri 11:30, 12:30, 2, 3; Sat 11:30 and 12:30; Sun 12:30. Tickets at the box office before tour. Tours last approx. 1hr and depart from the main lobby. T: 212 903 9765, carnegiehall.org. Box office for event tickets, T: 212 247 7800.

Carnegie Hall (1891) was financed by Andrew Carnegie partly as a venue for the Oratorio Society, whose board he headed, and partly as a $2-million investment. Designed by architect (and cellist) William B. Tuthill, the bulky brownish neo-Italian Renaissance building with a high square corner tower is a musical landmark. The **Rose Museum** (1991) on the first tier level offers exhibits on the history of the hall (*museum open 11–4:30 daily during concert season; closed July 1–Oct 1*).

The acoustics of the original auditorium were famous, delighting audiences and performers beginning with Tchaikovsky, who appeared as guest conductor during opening week. Even so, the hall came close to demolition in the early 1960s when its owners began yearning for larger profits (Andrew Carnegie didn't make much money on his investment, either); but preservationists headed by violinist Isaac Stern saved it. Although the New York Philharmonic, which first made Carnegie Hall its home and appeared here under the batons of Toscanini and Leopold Stokowski, now resides at Lincoln Center, major orchestras and soloists as well as stars of pop and jazz are still booked here. The hall houses three performance spaces: the Main Hall (2,804 seats), Zankel Hall (599 seats), and Weill Recital Hall (268 seats).

NEW YORK CITY CENTER

At 135 West 55th St (*Sixth and Seventh Aves*) is the elaborate, neo-Moorish **City Center for Music and Drama** (1924), built as a temple for the Shriners (Ancient Order of Nobles of the Mystic Shrine) when they outgrew their clubhouse on West 45th St. The hall, originally the Mecca Temple, never succeeded financially, and the City took it over in 1943, converting it to a theater. It is a major venue for dance and drama, also known for its *Encores!* series of classic American musicals in concert (*T: 212 581 1212, nycitycenter.org*).

EATING AND DRINKING AROUND LINCOLN CENTER

Columbus Circle is notable for its upscale restaurants; of the city's six three-Michelin-star restaurants, two—Per Se and Masa—are here. But the Time Warner Center also offers more affordable restaurants, bars, and a Whole Foods supermarket with a café. For other less luxurious restaurants, walk up Broadway toward Lincoln Center.

$$$$ Lincoln Ristorante. Lincoln Center's own fine-dining option, owner of a Michelin star, offers modern Italian cuisine in a glass-walled space right next to the reflecting pool. Open kitchen, interesting cocktails. Lunch Wed–Sun, dinner nightly. *142 West 65th St (Amsterdam Ave and Broadway). T: 212 359 6500, lincolnristorante.com. Map p. 616, B1.*

$$$$ Marea. ■ The seafood restaurant (*marea* in Italian is "tide") in the Museum of Arts and Design exemplifies the care that some museums are taking offer feasts for the body as well as for the eye. The Michelin Guide, which awards it two stars, calls it "swanky" and "high-spirited," unusual qualities in restaurants where serious foodies think deeply about what they are eating. On the menu are extravagant dishes (for example stuffed with caviar) but more ordinary ones as well. It has been voted the city's best Italian restaurant. Lunch and dinner daily. *240 Central Park South (Broadway and Seventh Ave). T: 212 582 5100, marea-nyc.com. Map p. 616, C2.*

$$$$ Masa. A shrine to sushi, Masa is the inspiration for pilgrimages from afar, and many liken the meal there to a religious experience. The room is austere and beautiful, the hinoki wood sushi counter is sanded daily; the staff is solicitous, though there have been reports that the attentiveness of the staff fluctuates with the familiarity of the diner or the size of the tab. There is no menu; you simply put yourself into the hands of the master, Masa Takayama, and know that everything will be fine. Lunch Tues–Fri, dinner Mon–Sat. *Fourth floor, Time Warner Center (10 Columbus Circle). T: 212 823 9807, masanyc.com. Map p. 616, B2.*

$$$$ Per Se. Next door to Masa are the blue doors of the building's second culinary temple, the dominion of chef Thomas Keller. The restaurant offers beautiful seasonal meals in a luxurious setting, with two nine-course *prix fixe* menus and some *à la carte* options in the dining salon. The views, the setting, and the wine all contribute to the experience. Jacket required. Lunch Fri–Sun, dinner nightly. *Fourth floor, Time Warner Center (10 Columbus Circle). T: 212 823 9335, thomaskeller.com/per-se. Map p. 616, B2.*

$$$ Bar Boulud. Daniel Boulud's least formal restaurant, with

charcuterie, burgers, classic brasserie food. Slightly lower prices than the other Boulud restaurants, but very crowded around show time. Lunch and dinner daily. *1900 Broadway (63rd and 64th Sts). T: 212 595 0303, barboulud.com. Map p. 616, B1.*

$$$ Bar Masa. The (somewhat) downmarket relative of the famous sushi restaurant serves a less refined, more Westernized version of Japanese cuisine, understandably popular with tourists and local shoppers alike. Lunch Tues–Fri, dinner Mon–Sat. *Fourth floor, Time Warner Center (10 Columbus Circle). No reservations. T: 212 923 9800, barmasanyc.com. Map p. 616, B2.*

$$$ Boulud Sud. Mediterranean specialties from Sicily to North Africa and back. Airy décor. Usually crowded. Also has a bar and lounge. Lunch and dinner daily. *20 West 64th St (Broadway and Central Park West). T: 212 595 1313, bouludsud.com. Map p. 616, B1.*

$$$ Café Fiorello. Right across Broadway from Lincoln Center. Good for the pizzas and better for the antipasto bar. Crowded, verging on frenetic around show time, so go early or late. Outdoor seating seasonally. Lunch and dinner seven days, breakfast weekends. *1900 Broadway (63rd St). T: 212 595 5330, cafefiorello. com. Map p. 616, B2.*

$$$ Telepan. ■ A fine choice for dining in the Lincoln Center area, but leave time for a leisurely meal. The logo, a cross between cutlery and garden tools, suggests the emphasis on farm-to-table ingredients in its updated American food. Michelin-starred. Dinner nightly, weekend brunch. *72 West 69th St (Central Park West and Columbus Ave). T: 212 580 4300, telepan-ny.com. Map p. 616, B1.*

$$ Café Luxembourg. This Lincoln Center standby has pleased concert-goers for decades with its bistro cooking. It's loud and the tables are close, but the atmosphere is festive and the crowd good-looking. Breakfast, lunch and dinner daily. *200 West 70th St (Amsterdam and West End Aves). T: 212 873 7411, cafeluxembourg.com. Map p. 616, B1.*

AMERICAN MUSEUM OF NATURAL HISTORY
Skeleton of a woolly mammoth in the museum's Milstein Hall.

Central Park West

Central Park West, with its historic apartment buildings and its religious and cultural institutions—the American Museum of Natural History and the New-York Historical Society—exemplifies traditional New York and its historic intellectual pursuits.

The extension of Eighth Avenue from 59th to 110th Sts was rechristened Central Park West in 1883 to boost real estate values already enhanced by the presence of the park. A few older buildings date back to the end of the 19th century when the arrival of the Ninth Ave elevated railroad in 1879 made the Upper West Side accessible to the middle class. Apartment-hotels rose along the park: the Park Royal, the Kenilworth, the Majestic. Considered suitable for bachelors and newly-married couples, they had living quarters and servants' rooms but no kitchens, since bachelors and young brides were presumed not to cook. Long blocks of 19th-century brownstone row houses arose and still line some of the side streets, many with imposing stoops and exuberant ornamentation.

In 1929 the City passed the Multiple Dwelling Act, which permitted tall residential buildings on building lots larger then 30,000 square ft, so long as they had courtyards to provide light and air. Soon the stately masonry apartments that give Central Park West its character began replacing the older apartment-hotels. Making their mark on the skyline are three twin-towered apartment buildings, which have attracted celebrities as well as the anonymously wealthy. (The triple-towered Beresford at West 81st St, built in 1929, is considered one of the masterpieces of architect Emery Roth; *see overleaf.*)

COLUMBUS CIRCLE TO WEST 76TH STREET

Map p. 616, C2. Subway: 1, A, B, C, D to Columbus Circle. Bus: M5, M7, M10, M20, M30.

Adjacent to Columbus Circle, Central Park West remains commercial. The **Trump International Hotel and Tower** (*1 Central Park West*) rises 44 stories, occupying the former Gulf + Western office building (1969; Thomas E. Stanley). Real estate developer Donald Trump bought the building and had architect Philip Johnson and others redesign it during the 1990s, cladding it with bronze-tinted glass and promoting it with characteristic bluster as "the most important new address in the world." Trump also commissioned the 40-ft stainless steel *Unisphere* (1997; Kim Brandell), a scaled-down replica of the one in Queens.

15 Central Park West (2007; Robert A.M. Stern) looks architecturally for inspiration to the staid and spacious pre-World War I apartments of Rosario Candela (*see p. 333*). Its apartments have drawn celebrities (Sting, Denzel Washington), hedge-fund managers, and assorted moguls; among the amenities are a lap pool, a private screening room, and a waiting room for chauffeurs.

EMERY ROTH

The firm of Emery Roth & Sons built more than 100 glass and steel skyscrapers after World War II (few of them distinguished), but between 1903 and the late 1930s, Emery Roth père produced many fine masonry apartment buildings and hotels ornamented with Neoclassical detail. Among them were three twin-towered stars of Central Park West: the San Remo, the Beresford, and the El Dorado. Roth (1871–1908), of Hungarian parentage, came to the US from what is now Slovakia in 1886 at the age of 13, and four years later began working as a draftsman on the Chicago World's Columbian Exposition. Like other conservative architects, he was deeply impressed by the dignity of the Beaux-Arts buildings that dominated the exhibition, a style later reflected in his own work. He came to New York on the invitation of Richard Morris Hunt, who had been impressed by the young man's skill at draftsmanship.

The twin-towered Art Deco **Century Apartments** (1931, Jacques Delamarre and the Irwin S. Chanin Construction Co.; *25 Central Park West between West 62nd and West 63rd Sts*) take their name from the Century Theater (1909), a grandiose undertaking with national ambitions that turned out to be too big and too far uptown to make a profit, even when Florenz Ziegfeld staged spectaculars here.

The **New York Society for Ethical Culture** (*West 63rd and West 64th Sts*) was founded in 1876 by Felix Adler to further morality independently of organized religion. The Ethical Culture school system began with the city's first free kindergarten (1878), early establishing itself as a force in experimental education. Today the society operates the prestigious Fieldston Schools in the Bronx as well as the Ethical Culture School here, all known for their progressive outlook. The southern building (1902; Robert D. Kohn and Carrère & Hastings) houses the school; the limestone Art Nouveau northern building at 2 West 64th St (1910; Robert D. Kohn with Estelle Rumbold Kohn, sculptor) houses the meeting hall.

The **Prasada** (*50 Central Park West*) was built on speculation in 1907 (Charles W. Romeyn & Henry R. Wynne), its name of uncertain origin retained from the former apartment-hotel. Oscar J. Gude, said to have introduced electric advertising signs to Times Square, once lived here; so did novelist Edna Ferber. **55 Central Park West** (*between 65th and 66th Sts*; 1940, Schwartz & Gross), Art Deco-inspired with an ironwork marquee over the entrance, is faced with brickwork shaded from red at the bottom to tan at the top—giving the impression to some of a ray of sunshine perpetually shining on the façade. Radio singer Rudy Vallee lived here.

The **Hotel des Artistes** (1915; George Mort Pollard) at 1 West 67th St, was constructed for working artists, with large two-story windows and fanciful neo-Gothic statuary above the second story. Among its tenants were Noel Coward, Isadora Duncan, Norman Rockwell, and Howard Chandler Christy, whose risqué murals of cavorting nymphs still adorn the upscale ground-floor restaurant.

BROWNSTONES

Both West 70th and West 71st Sts retain rows of houses faced with brownstone, a Triassic sandstone whose characteristic color comes from iron ore. A "brownstone" in the local dialect is a single-family row house, usually dating from the late 19th century, usually four or five stories high and two or three windows wide, usually featuring a tall stoop and a cornice at the top, and faced with brownstone. Masons or builders constructed most of these houses, but the one at 20 West 71st St enjoyed the talents of an architect (1889; Gilbert A. Schellenger), who designed a row of four here.

Brownstones were usually constructed in small groups, and their widths were fractions of the standard city building lot (25ft by 100ft). The most spacious are 25ft wide, while smaller varieties are 20ft (a fifth of four lots), 18¾ ft (a quarter of three lots) or 162/3 ft (a third of two lots). Because these houses were built for prosperous middle-class families, the interiors were executed in fine materials and the façades were often elaborately ornamented; note, for example, the cupids at the cornice of no. 24 West 71st St; the cartouches on nos. 26, 28, and 30; and the lions' heads on nos. 33–39.

As a child, the novelist Edith Wharton lived in a brownstone on West 23rd St, but, never sentimental about her childhood home, she opined in *A Backward Glance* that brownstone rendered New York "hide-bound in its deadly uniformity of mean ugliness." And in *The Age of Mirth*, she speaks of brownstone as the uniform hue that "coated New York like a cold chocolate sauce."

SHEARITH ISRAEL SYNAGOGUE
Map p. 616, C1. 2 West 70th St. Open during services. T: 212 873 0300, shearithisrael.org.
Also known as the Spanish and Portuguese Synagogue, this is the newest home (1897; Brunner & Tryon) of the nation's oldest Jewish congregation, Congregation Shearith Israel (*see p. 54*). Earlier synagogue builders in America often chose styles that pointed toward the Moorish heritage of Sephardic Jews, but this building's classical style

reflects the archaeological discovery of the ruins of the Second Temple in Jerusalem, built during the Roman occupation.

Under Dutch rule Jews had to worship in secret, but in 1682 under the British the immigrants founded Congregation Shearith Israel ("Remnant of Israel") and held organized services, first in a rented room on Beaver St, then in the upper story of a flour mill on Mill Lane and South William St. The first synagogue building (1730) is gone, but some of its artifacts and two large millstones from the Dutch mill are preserved in the synagogue here, which reconstructs the original sanctuary. Prominent members of the congregation have included US Supreme Court justice Benjamin Cardozo and Emma Lazarus, author of "The New Colossus," the poem inscribed on the base of the Statue of Liberty.

The Majestic (*115 Central Park West between West 71st and West 72nd Sts*) is one of four double-towered apartment buildings that give the Central Park skyline its distinction. Stylistically related to the Century downtown (*see p. 408*), the Majestic was also built (1931; Jacques Delamarre) by the Irwin S. Chanin Company. René Chambellan, known for the fountains at Rockefeller Center, designed the brickwork. Art Deco architects often favored corner windows because steel cage construction allowed open corners (unlike masonry construction, where corners were load-bearing), widening the view.

The Langham (1905, Clinton & Russell; *135 Central Park West between West 73rd and West 74th Sts*) stands on land bought (but later sold) by the Clark family at the time they developed the Dakota. According to a 1904 account in the *New York Times,* it was intended as the finest apartment building in the city. As well as floorspace (only four residences per story), it offered such luxuries as a central refrigeration plant and a conveyor system for delivering mail to individual apartments. Famous residents have included Edward Albee (grandfather of the playwright and head of a chain of theaters), Isadore Saks, who founded Saks 34th Street, and Lee Strasberg, director and acting teacher.

The twin-towered **San Remo Apartments** (1930, Emery Roth; *145–146 Central Park West between West 74th and West 75th Sts*) are finished in Neoclassical garb with cartouches over the entrances and finialed temples on top. Celebrities have also gravitated to the San Remo: Stephen Spielberg, Steve Jobs, and Donna Karan, among others. Rita Hayworth spent her declining years here; Eddie Cantor, who was making about a half million dollars a year in the early 1930s, was also a tenant.

The Gothic **Fourth Universalist Society of New York** (1898; William A. Potter), originally the Church of the Divine Paternity, is one of the few non-Neoclassical buildings on Central Park West (*160 Central Park West at West 76th St; visitors welcome during the day, except when special events are in progress; T: 212 595 1658, 4thu.org*). It has decorative work by Louis Comfort Tiffany and Augustus Saint-Gaudens, as well as an exceptional Skinner organ. *New York Tribune* editor Horace Greeley, showman Phineas T. Barnum, and baseball immortal Lou Gehrig worshiped here.

THE DAKOTA APARTMENTS
The Dakota Apartments (*1 West 72nd St; map p. 614, B4*; 1884, Henry J. Hardenbergh) are architecturally and socially pre-eminent.

In 1884 apartments were beginning to find favor with the well-to-do, so when the Singer Sewing Machine heir Edward S. Clark undertook a magnificent apartment house on West 72nd St, he was doing nothing startling. His choice of location, however, was daring: uptown, surrounded by shanties and vacant land—so far north and west of civilization that detractors called it Clark's Folly, one of them allegedly remarking that the building might as well be in the Dakota territory. Whether this story is true or not, the architect garnished the building with ears of corn, arrowheads, and a bas-relief of an Indian's head above the main gateway.

Hardenbergh is outstanding for his sense of composition, and the Dakota is acknowledged to be his masterpiece. Built around an open central courtyard, it is finished in buff-colored brick with terra cotta and stone trim, and embellished with balconies, oriel windows, turrets, gables, finials, and flagpoles. The fence railings are decorated with griffins and heads of Zeus (others see them as sea monsters and heads of Poseidon), fabricated by the Hecla Ironworks, also responsible for decorative work at Grand Central Terminal, the St. Regis Hotel, and the interior of the New York Stock Exchange.

Not surprisingly the building has attracted a striking clientele, notably people involved in the arts. Among them have been Boris Karloff, Zachary Scott, Leonard Bernstein, Lauren Bacall, Roberta Flack, and scientist Michael Idvorsky Pupin. Most famous of all was John Lennon, who was shot and killed in the courtyard by a deranged admirer on December 8, 1980.

THE NEW-YORK HISTORICAL SOCIETY

Map p. 614, B4. 170 Central Park West (West 76th and West 77th Sts). Open Tues–Thur and Sat 10–6; Fri 10–8; Sun 11–5. Closed Mon and holidays. Admission charge. Restaurant and excellent shop. T: 212 873 3400, nyhistory.org. Children's historical museum on the ground floor.

The New-York Historical Society is the city's oldest museum, founded in 1804 (70 years before the Metropolitan) by the city's elite—Bleeckers, Stuyvesants, and important political figures. The society originally operated as an exclusive private club and library, its goal to preserve historical documents and artifacts (including those of New York's "first" families) and perhaps to dispel the notion that New York (unlike Boston, for example) was a cultural wasteland. The fact that the organization keeps the old hyphenated spelling of New-York suggests both its historical roots and the conservatism of which it was so long a bastion. Today its exhibits present the nation's history through the lens of the city's.

In 1868 the Society turned down the City's offer of land in Central Park, preferring to accept support only from private individuals. (The Metropolitan Museum of Art occupies the rejected land.) After surviving multiple crises in the 20th century, the society seems on a surer footing. Its collections remain outstanding and its changing exhibitions have attracted major attention.

The building and introductory gallery

Designed by a firm (1908, York & Sawyer; north and south wings 1938, Walker & Gillette) later renowned for bank architecture, the building is a paragon of Neoclassical severity, faced in hard gray granite and barely ornamented. In 2004 the façade was altered to make it more welcoming, and in 2011 the interior was redesigned, admitting more light, making the lobby seem more open and spacious.

In the airy gallery inside the main entrance, artifacts related to key themes of New York and national history are shown on the walls, in cases, in digital displays, and under the floor. Portholes underfoot contain small archaeological discoveries (for example, slices of shoddy wooden pipe from Manhattan's first water supply system and a 7½-inch oyster shell harvested during colonial times). Rotating exhibits have explored the connections between the American, French, and Haitian revolutions; showcased the museum's fine paintings; and examined New York's contribution to the founding of the US. Over the Admissions Desk hangs a section of the painted ceiling from Keith Haring's former "Pop Shop" at 292 Lafayette St, where he sold T-shirts, inflatable babies, posters, and other souvenirs bearing his instantly recognizable designs.

The collection

The collection boasts works by Hudson River School landscapists, portraits from the colonial period, and every one of John James Audubon's 435 hand-colored prints from *The Birds of America* (1827–38), one of the great achievements of American art. Portraits of early New Yorkers include an arresting depiction of a woman once thought to be a man—Edward Hyde, Viscount Cornbury, governor of New York and New Jersey (1702–8); now known to be simply an unidentified, somewhat heavy-featured woman. Also in the collection is an anonymous portrait of the freed slave Peter Williams (*see p. 92*) from c. 1815. Thomas Cole is represented not only by landscapes but also his five-part allegory *The Course of Empire*, a romantic rendering of the rise and fall of a mythical civilization from its savage beginnings to its ruinous ending. Sculpture includes work by John Quincy Adams Ward, Augustus Saint-Gaudens, and Frederick MacMonnies.

Among the many artifacts relating to New York's participation in local and global events are those relating to the slave trade, the American Revolution, and the terrorist attack on the World Trade Center. Decorative objects include fine furniture and a large collection of American silver, much of which belonged to prominent old New York families including Roosevelts, Schuylers and De Peysters, or was made by such outstanding silversmiths as Cornelius Kierstede and Myer Myers. There are examples of practically every type of lamp created by Louis Comfort Tiffany.

The Research Library, open to researchers, has half a million books, 10,000 newspapers, and every New York City directory printed since 1768. There is a rich trove of letters, manuscripts, and other documents pertaining to the founding of the Republic, as well as a collection of 10,000 dining menus.

The Henry Luce III Center for the Study of American Culture (*being renovated at the time of writing; due to open Dec 2016*) on the fourth floor is to include permanent displays of Audubon's *Birds of America* and Tiffany glass shades, and a center for the study of women's history at the turn of the 20th century.

THE AMERICAN MUSEUM OF NATURAL HISTORY

Map p. 614, B4. Central Park West at 79th St. Subway: B train weekdays or C 81st St; 1 to Broadway/79th St, walk two blocks east to museum. Bus: M7, M10, M11, M79, M86, M104. Open daily 10–5:45 except Thanksgiving and Christmas. Suggested admission, plus mandatory fee for movies, space shows, special exhibitions. Tours. For recorded information, T: 212 769 5100. Café, food court. Shop. Free app for mobile devices. amnh.org.

The American Museum of Natural History (AMNH) was founded in 1869 by Albert S. Bickmore, one of the country's first major naturalists, and supported financially by influential figures of the day including J. Pierpont Morgan and Theodore Roosevelt Sr. It opened in Central Park's Arsenal, which it quickly outgrew, and moved to Central Park West in 1877. Few visitors ventured so far uptown, and the museum soon fell into debt. Morris K. Jessup, the museum's third president and a successful securities broker, boosted attendance by keeping it open on Sunday (two years before the Metropolitan Museum) and encouraged programs in paleontology, anthropology, and zoology. His successor, the wealthy and aristocratic Henry Fairfield Osborn, a paleontologist hired to update the fossil collection, captured attention by sponsoring trips to Mongolia and Africa to search for human ancestors. In 1935, the Hayden Planetarium opened.

The museum has pioneered new exhibit techniques and is generally credited with being the first to mount animal skeletons in natural poses and to create habitat exhibits. While most other institutions collected whatever specimens came to hand, the museum sent scientists into the field to gather specific items.

Through the years the museum itself has evolved, adding new exhibit halls and updating the displays to reflect new discoveries and changes in scientific thinking. In 2014 it announced plans to construct an addition along Columbus Ave, which will be devoted to enhancing the museum's role in scientific research and education.

The building
The museum occupies the equivalent of four city blocks, an area formerly called Manhattan Square and intended by the designers of Central Park as a park annex. The first building (1877) is now almost walled in by the wings and additions that have made the present complex an architectural hodge-podge of some 22 buildings.

Facing West 77th St, the oldest visible part of the façade (1892; J. Cleveland Cady & Co.) is also the most attractive. Romanesque in style, it is faced with pink granite and flanked by two round towers. The façade facing Central Park West (1924; Trowbridge & Livingston) was built the same year that Governor Alfred E. Smith appointed a commission to build a Theodore Roosevelt Memorial, honoring the former governor and US president who had long supported the museum. John Russell Pope won the architectural competition, proposing a grand Classical façade with a 350-ft-wide terrace, and a triumphal arch. The frieze on the low walls depicts animals that had interested Roosevelt and were suitably dignified. According to a contemporary account, the museum staff supervised the carving, even going so far as to chain a grizzly bear near the sculptor Edward Sanford, so that he could study the animal's head formation. The arch frames a 16-ft equestrian **statue of Roosevelt** (1940; James Earle Fraser), depicted as an explorer, flanked by African and Native American guides, a representation today sometimes criticized as paternalistic. Above the huge Ionic columns are representations of Daniel Boone, John James Audubon, William Clark, and Meriwether Lewis.

The collection

The collection comprises some 32 million specimens (a mere one percent of which are on display) ranging from the famous dioramas of animal habitat groups and dinosaur exhibits to the world's largest cut gem. There is far too much to see in one, two, or even three visits; for a sampling you might try a guided tour. Highlights are given below.

Fossil halls: The Dinosaurs: On the fourth floor are the fossil halls (13–17), with about five percent of the museum's collection—the world's largest and finest—of fossil bones: the ferocious carnivores, sluggish but gigantic plant eaters, mammal-like reptiles, and fossil fish that have instilled a love of "dinosaurs" in generations of children. Unlike most fossil exhibitions, which are arranged chronologically, these exhibits are organized in pathways that show evolutionary relationships, each animal grouped with its closest relatives. Taken together, the groups form a giant evolutionary diagram, or cladogram. Black stripes down the center of the gallery floors represent the "trunk" of the dinosaur family tree; many of the most spectacular specimens are shown along this midline, with offshoots leading to alcoves showing related groups of dinosaurs. To follow this evolutionary path in the correct sequence, you should enter from the Hall of Vertebrate Origins (Room 13).

As part of a reinstallation of the fossil halls in the 1990s the museum restored the famous murals by Charles R. Knight, one of the first artists to use fossil remains in painting prehistoric animals and to show dinosaurs interacting in dramatic ways. Four murals from Knight's series, the *Age of Mammals in North America* (1930s), based on discoveries in Wyoming, are on display. Painted in an Impressionistic style and influenced by Japanese artists Knight's work remains a magnificent example of early recreations of past life.

Highlights of the halls include a 65-million-year-old ***Tyrannosaurus rex* (Room 14)** with a four-foot jaw, six-inch teeth, and massive thigh bones. Its stalking pose reflects modern scientific thinking; the injuries to the neck and lower back indicate the traumas of fighting. Also on view are an immense *Apatosaurus* (formerly called *Brontosaurus*), dinosaur eggs, *Stegosaurus* and *Triceratops*, and the "mummified" skeleton of *Edmontosaurus* , one of the great discoveries of paleontology, remarkable in having evidence of skin and soft tissues. Among the fossil mammals are mammoths, mastodons, saber-toothed cats, and giant ground sloths—and the Warren mastodon, found in a bog in Newburgh, NY, standing upright as it died, legs pushing forward, its head tilted upward as if gasping for air.

Animal Habitat Dioramas: The dioramas are world-famous for their beauty, workmanship, and accuracy; their creator, Carl Akeley, is considered the father of modern taxidermy. When his **Hall of African Mammals (9)** opened in 1936, the *New York Times* devoted a full page to its wonders, reporting that visitors could imagine themselves in Africa, even feeling the wind sweeping over the plains. Dominating the exhibit are eight East African elephants led by a ten-foot bull, his trunk raised menacingly. Settings were recreated from photographs and sketches made on site: local vegetation was carefully simulated (a blackberry bush in the gorilla diorama, with 75,000 artificial leaves and flowers, took eight months to make); and the animals were presented in characteristic poses—vultures and hyenas devouring a dead zebra, giraffes grazing.

The **Hall of Asian Mammals (10)** is considered the best such collection of animals in the world, with Indian elephants, tigers, wild boar, rhinoceros, water buffalo, and lions.

The background paintings in the **Hall of North American Mammals (2)** are by masters of the genre, including James Perry Wilson and Charles Shepard Chapman.

Other habitat groups include **Birds of the World (11)** and **Ocean Life (5)**, with a 94-ft female blue whale (polyurethane, steel, and fiberglass) hanging overhead.

CARL AKELEY

Earlier taxidermists usually simply skinned their specimens and stuffed them, but Akeley (1864–1926) pioneered a technique of mounting that began with observing the living animal in its habitat and photographing it in motion. Akeley then copied the skeleton of the specimen and filled out the muscles and tissues with clay; from this he made a plaster cast and from that a *papier mâché* mould onto which the skin was glued. The hall was completed in 1936, ten years after Akeley died of a fever during an expedition in the Belgian Congo, where he was buried, near Mount Mikeno—the volcano seen furthest to the right in the gorilla diorama.

Ecology and Biodiversity: The exhibits in the **Hall of Biodiversity (3)** are one expression of the museum's efforts to alert the public to ecological issues. The walk-through Dzanga-Sangha diorama reconstructs a rainforest in the Central African Republic; the Spectrum of Life displays some 2,500 models and specimens: bacteria, fungi, plants, and animals. The extraordinary blown-glass protozoa were created as educational models, by Herman O. Mueller, whose family had been glass-blowers in Germany for generations. Mueller spent 40 years working on the models, completing the series in 1943. Other ecology halls include **North American Forests (4)** with a display, 24 times larger than life, of the earthworms, millipedes, and weevils of the forest floor.

Human Origins and Human Culture: The **Hall of Human Origins (6)** was the first exhibit anywhere (2007) to com-

AMERICAN MUSEUM OF NATURAL HISTORY

FIRST FLOOR

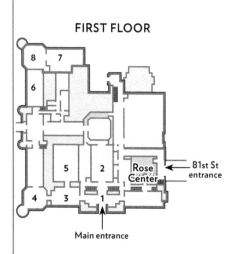

81st St entrance

Main entrance

SECOND FLOOR

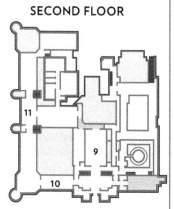

1	Theodore Roosevelt Memorial Hall	**8**	Hall of Meteorites
2	Hall of North American Mammals	**9**	Hall of African Mammals
3	Hall of Biodiversity	**10**	Hall of Asian Mammals
4	Hall of North American Forests	**11**	Birds of the World
5	Hall of Ocean Life	**12**	Hall of Pacific Peoples
6	Hall of Human Origins	**13–17**	Fossil Halls: Dinosaurs
7	Hall of Minerals and Gems		

THIRD FLOOR

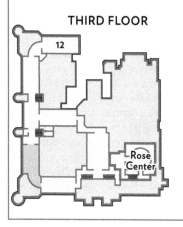

FOURTH FLOOR

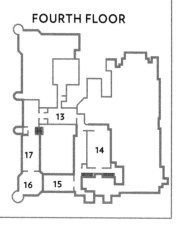

bine DNA research with the study of fossils in explaining evolution. Fossil evidence includes some 200 casts of human and pre-human fossils showing evolving physical characteristics. Life-size dioramas depict possible scenes in the lives of human predecessors: *Homo ergaster, Neanderthal, Cro-Magnon* and *Homo erectus* (the latter depicted just before falling prey to a hyena). In a freestanding case is a lifelike reconstruction of "Lucy," a three-million-year-old fossil found in Ethiopia in 1974, whose skeletal development showed that she walked upright. Other exhibits show human developments in language, music, art, and the use of tools. The DNA exhibits, including a sample of Neanderthal DNA, 38,000 years old, explore the genetic similarities between humans and their nearest non-human relatives. Exhibits on human culture explore the art and traditions of peoples of Central and South America, Africa, Asia, and North America (Eastern Woodland Indians, Plains Indians, and Northwest Coast Indians).

The **Margaret Mead Hall of Pacific Peoples (12)**, named after the anthropologist who spent 53 years as a curator of ethnology here, is the only hall of its kind in the world, reflecting cultures that include Polynesia, Australia, Indonesia, and the Philippines.

Earth and Planetary Sciences: The **Halls of Minerals and Gems (7)** displays some 6,000 of the museum's 120,000 specimens, including a half-ton copper block with malachite and azurite crystals, a giant topaz crystal (597lbs or 1,330,040 carats), the Star of India sapphire, and the Patricia emerald. In 1900 J. Pierpont Morgan bought the 12,300-specimen collection of a Philadelphia industrialist that contained 580 meteorites and had it shipped in two boxcars to the AMNH.

The centerpiece of the **Hall of Meteorites (8)** is a 34-ton fragment of Ahnighito (the name means "the tent"), the Cape York meteorite discovered in 1897 in northern Greenland by explorer Robert Peary, who spent four Arctic summers digging it out of the frozen ground. The exhibit of moon rocks includes the three major lunar types. Newer additions include meteorites from Mars and nano-diamonds.

The Theodore Roosevelt Memorial Hall: In the barrel-vaulted lobby (1), bright murals (1935) depict scenes celebrating TR's life. Crowded with figures—the sons of Noah, boy and girl scouts, zebras, Christopher Columbus, a Mayan, the emperor of Japan, and two American girls representing Justice and Mercy—the murals were painted by William Andrew Mackay, chosen by competition.

In the center of the hall a 55-ft skeleton of a *Barosaurus* defends its young; the 150-million-year-old fossilized skeleton was found in the southwestern US, but since the actual bones are too fragile to be mounted vertically, the exhibit is a resin-and-foam replica. On the hoof the *Barosaurus* weighed about 25 tons.

On the lower level, below the memorial, a bronze statue of Roosevelt in camping gear poses for photo ops. A floor medallion shows American bison grazing in Theodore Roosevelt National Park in the North Dakota Badlands; other exhibits explore TR as a young naturalist, an explorer, and a conservationist.

THE ROSE CENTER FOR EARTH AND SPACE

The $210-million Rose Center for Earth and Space, a visually stunning aluminum-clad sphere (87ft in diameter) within a cube of super-transparent water-white glass on a gray granite base (2000; Polshek Partnership), dramatically updates the former Hayden Planetarium (opened 1935). In the **Space Theater** the custom-built Zeiss Mark IX Star Projector virtually recreates the night sky and throws other dazzling simulations on the inner surface of the dome. Other exhibit areas include a walkway that conveys the relative sizes of objects in the cosmos, from the astronomically large to the sub-atomically small. A descending circular ramp shows how the universe has changed over the last 13 billion years, with all of recorded human history appearing as the thickness of a hair at the very end. On the lower level, exhibits explore the discoveries of modern astrophysics.

The **Hall of Planet Earth** uses spectacular geological specimens to address basic questions about the Earth's evolution and its habitability.

THE WILLAMETTE METEORITE

Formed more than four billion years ago, this mass of iron and nickel is the largest meteorite found in the US. It was discovered in Oregon, where it had been carried by glaciers during the last ice age, probably from an impact site in Idaho. It was acquired by the museum in 1906. To the Clackamas, Native Americans of the Willamette Valley, Oregon, the meteorite is known as Tomanowos ("Heavenly Visitor") and is greatly revered. It is said that warriors would dip their arrowheads in rainwater that collected in pits in the meteorite's surface, believing that this would endow them with special power. In June 2000, the museum signed an agreement with the tribe that ensures members an annual ceremonial visit. As part of the pact, the tribe dropped its claim for return of the meteorite and the museum agreed to place a description of the meteorite's spiritual significance to the Clackamas alongside the description of its scientific importance.

EATING AND DRINKING AROUND CENTRAL PARK WEST

$$$$ Jean-Georges. ■ A culinary cathedral serving Asian-influenced French cuisine with great wines, beautiful presentation, and an attentive but not overbearing staff. **$$ Nougatine** ■, in the same space, also provides sterling food and a pleasant atmosphere. Both open daily. *1 Central Park West, in the Trump International Hotel. T (for both): 212 299 3900, jean-georgesrestaurant. com. Map p. 616, C2.*

$$$ 'Cesca. Stylish, chic *ristorante* with farm-to-table vegetables, homemade sausage, and a pleasant noise level. Dinner nightly; happy hour daily from 5–7. *164 West 75th St (Amsterdam Ave). T: 212 787 6300, cescanyc.com. Map p. 614, B4.*

$$$ Dovetail. Michelin-starred restaurant, close to the Museum of Natural History and the park, run by a well-pedigreed chef-owner who offers creative American food. The four-course *prix fixe* is a relative bargain, as is the three-course Sunday "suppa." Dinner nightly, lunch Sun. *103 West 77th St (Columbus Ave). T: 212 362 3800, dovetailnyc.com. Map p. 614, B4.*

$$ Café Frida. Authentic Mexican food in a colorful rustic café with highly reputed margaritas, and guacamole in a traditional *molcajete*. Happy hour in the bar with specials on beer and sangria. Lunch and dinner daily. *368 Columbus Ave (77th and 78th Sts). T: 212 712 2929, cafefrida.com. Map p. 614, B4.*

$$ Caffe Storico. In the New-York Historical Society, this light and airy eatery enjoys a prime location in a building whose recent remodeling has made its beauties evident. On the walls are antique dishes from the Society's collection; on the menu are Italian dishes with a Venetian accent, and Italian wines. Dinner Tues–Sun, lunch Tues–Fri, brunch weekends. *170 Central Park West (77th St). T: 212 485 9211, nyhistory.org/dine. Map p. 614, B4.*

$$ Gazala's. A small, informal Lebanese restaurant with Druze specialties, including hummus, falafel, and Gazala's platter, a big plate with nine hot and cold mezes. Lunch and dinner daily. *380 Columbus Ave (78th St). T: 212 873 8880, gazalasplace.com. Map p. 614, B4.*

$$ Nice Matin. A neighborhood favorite, with Mediterranean food and a major wine list. Breakfast, lunch and dinner daily. *201 West 79th St (Amsterdam Ave). T: 212 873 6423, nicematinnyc.com. Map p. 614, B4.*

$ Gray's Papaya. A hot dog stand with attitude (open 24/7), and such an icon that news of the demise of a downtown branch evoked mournful howls on the blogs. The "papaya" part refers to a fruit drink. *2090 Broadway, corner of 72nd St. T: 212 799 0243, grayspapayanyc.com/. Map p. 614, B4.*

$ Zabar's. A family business since 1934; Kosher purveyor of lox, bagels, knishes, and other goodies (take out or eat in). Open daily, regular store hours. *2245 Broadway at 80th St. T: 212 787 2000, zabars.com. Map p. 614, B4.*

MORNINGSIDE HEIGHTS
Christ in Glory, detail of the "Portal of Paradise," the main
entrance to the Cathedral Church of St. John the Divine.

Morningside Heights

Bounded by Cathedral Parkway and the deep valley of West 125th St, Morningside Heights sits on the rocky ridge that runs the length of Manhattan. Among its institutions are Columbia University, Riverside Church, and the Cathedral of St. John the Divine.

Before the Revolutionary War much of Morningside Heights (*map p. 612, A4*) was rural. The Battle of Harlem Heights, fought in a field near Broadway and 117th St, was Washington's only significant victory in the campaign for Manhattan, his other efforts resulting in a series of lost battles and spectacular retreats.

Until the Ninth (Columbus) Avenue El opened in 1879, Morningside Heights was isolated. In its pastoral serenity dwelt the owners of small farms and the squires of country estates, as well as the orphans of the Leake & Watts Asylum and inmates of the Bloomingdale Insane Asylum. Riverside Drive opened in 1880, touted as a new Fifth Avenue, a prophecy that was never quite realized, though by the end of the 19th century it seemed that the Heights would become a cultural, intellectual, and spiritual center with the Cathedral Church of St. John the Divine, Columbia University, and St. Luke's Hospital ministering to the needs of spirit, mind, and body. These major institutions not only dominated the social and economic tone of the area but owned much of its real estate too. Surrounding neighborhoods suffered during the Depression, and by the mid-20th century had deteriorated economically and socially.

The disparity between the wealth of the institutions and the struggles of local communities created hostility, especially apparent during the 1960s. Columbia University's attempt (1968) to build a gymnasium in Morningside Park provoked protests from students as well as locals. Tensions still exist as these institutions continue to expand.

THE NICHOLAS ROERICH MUSEUM

Map p. 614, A1. 319 West 107th St (Riverside Drive). Subway: 1 to 110th St. Bus: M4, M5, M104. Open Tues–Sun 12–5, weekends 2–5; closed Mon, holidays. Requested donation. Shop. T: 212 864 7752, roerich.org.

On a quiet street in a beautifully restored townhouse, the Nicholas Roerich Museum (1923) celebrates the life and work of Roerich (1874–1947), a Russian-born artist, mystic, archaeologist, writer, and humanitarian. As an artist, he created stage sets for Russian ballets, establishing an international reputation working with Sergei

Diaghilev. His humanitarian efforts led to the Roerich Pact, a treaty designed to protect cultural, scientific, and religious institutions and works of art during times of war.

Despite all this, Roerich is virtually unknown today. The museum aims to promote awareness of his ideas, which are embodied by the institution's symbol—three red circles enclosed in a red ring—and its motto Pax Cultura ("Peace through Culture").

The permanent collection contains about 200 paintings, many celebrating the Himalayas and the people of the Tibetan highlands; there are also displays of Roerich's writings and a small collection of Indian and Asian artifacts.

THE CATHEDRAL CHURCH OF ST. JOHN THE DIVINE

Map p. 612, B4. Amsterdam Ave at 112th St. Subway: 1, B, or C to 110th St-Cathedral Pkwy. Bus: M4, M11, M 60, M104. Open daily 7:30–6. Free, but admission charge for guided tours; ask at the Visitor Center inside the entrance. Highlights Tour Mon 11am and 2pm, Tues–Sat 11am and 1pm, select Sundays 1pm. Vertical Tours ascend spiral staircases to the cathedral roof Wed at 12 and Sat at 12 and 2. Spotlight Tours feature architecture, history, art; reserve online or T: 866 811 4111 for Vertical and Spotlight Tours. For other information, T: 212 316 7540, or visit stjohndivine.org.

The Cathedral Church of St. John the Divine stands in uncompleted splendor on the heights above Morningside Park. The enormous stone arches intended to support the never-built dome and tower of the crossing stand exposed to the sky and to the eyes of passers-by, who have a rare opportunity to see the bones of a masonry cathedral. St. John the Divine, sometimes irreverently called "St. John the Unfinished," is known also for its many social and cultural programs.

Building the cathedral

Although the city's powerful Episcopalian community had been contemplating the construction of a great cathedral as early as 1828, developments in the later years of the 19th century made the idea seem more urgent. New York's rise after the Civil War had spurred powerful men to erect buildings that proclaimed the eminence of their city: the Metropolitan Museum on Fifth Ave (1894), the Metropolitan Opera House (1881–4), and the American Museum of Natural History (1888) among them. New York's wealthy and powerful Episcopalian community also watched as the city's only cathedral and largest church—St. Patrick's Roman Catholic Cathedral—rose on prime Fifth Avenue real estate under the leadership of Archbishop John Hughes, an Irish immigrant. The Episcopalians wanted something at least as grand.

In 1873 the Cathedral of St. John the Divine was incorporated and in 1887 the diocese purchased a 13-acre wooded plot from the Leake & Watts Orphan Asylum for a then-momentous $885,000. The next year 68 entrants submitted designs in an architectural contest, from which the firm of Heins & LaFarge emerged victorious. Like many of the other entries, the winning Heins & LaFarge Romanesque design placed the long axis of the building along the spine of Morningside Heights. This would have given the church a spectacular flight of entrance stairs down to 110th St, but the tradition of building cathedrals with the nave running east–west eventually prevailed. In 1892 the cornerstone was laid.

Excavations for the heavy building proved difficult, and J. Pierpont Morgan poured half a million dollars into an ever deeper hole before workers struck bedrock some 70ft down. George Heins died in 1907. In 1911, almost 20 years after the digging had begun, only the choir and the four stone arches to support the central tower were in place. Five years later Ralph Adams Cram (of Cram & Ferguson) redesigned the church on Gothic principles, discarding Heins & LaFarge's Romanesque plan. Ground was broken for the nave foundations in 1916, but the nave and west front were not dedicated until 1941. During World War II major construction halted again.

In the 1960s a plan for completing the crossing in a contemporary style with a stand-alone campanile was submitted but not approved. Then in 1967, during an era of intense national social awareness, the bishop announced that the building might never be completed; instead the church would devote its energies to relieving poverty in the surrounding community. After a decade of social involvement, the trustees in 1978 announced a fundraising campaign for completion of the crossing and the west façade, including the two towers.

Master masons from England arrived to teach apprentice stonecutters, some from the local neighborhood, who cut enough limestone blocks for the southwest tower. The first stone was mortared into place in 1981. High-wire artist Philippe Petit, famous for walking between the towers of the World Trade Center, opened the ceremonies, crossing Amsterdam Avenue 15 stories above the road carrying a ceremonial trowel for the bishop, who awaited him on the cathedral roof.

Construction halted again in 1993, with about 50ft added to the south tower, although the stone carving on the "Portal of Paradise" continued to completion (1997). To commemorate its centennial, the cathedral instituted another architectural competition for completion of the south transept, won by Spanish architect Santiago Calatrava, whose proposed glass-enclosed biosphere was never built.

In 2001 a fire devastated the unfinished north transept, filling the cathedral with smoke and damaging the 17th-century Barberini Tapestries, two of them irreparably. The cathedral re-opened in 2008 after a $16.5 million restoration, with the interior, cleaned of smoke and the grime of decades, shining as it hadn't done for many years.

The exterior

Because towers on the west façade were never completed, the cathedral squats rather than soars, but impresses by its sheer mass. The central doorway is known as the "Portal of Paradise" **(1)**, its bronze doors (sculptor Henry Wilson) cast in Paris by Barbedienne, the foundry that cast the Statue of Liberty. Their 60 panels depict scenes from the Old Testament (left-hand doors) and the New Testament (right-hand doors). The frieze above the doors shows the peoples of all nations standing before the Lamb. The figure on the central post, his eyes raised heavenward, is St. John the Divine, author of the Book of Revelation, with the Four Horsemen of the Apocalypse beneath this feet. Directly above him in the tympanum, a *Majestas* shows Christ in Glory surrounded by the seven lamps and the seven stars of St. John's revelation.

The biblical statues surrounding the doors were carved (1988–97) by British master sculptor Simon Verity and others. Some are based on local people, for example Noah (upper rank figure furthest north), who was modeled on the seventh dean of the cathedral. He holds the unfinished Ark and looks back toward the unfinished cathedral, his Welsh corgi at his feet. Some of the decorative sculpture on the column capitals offers wry contemporary interpretations of conventional iconography. The prophet Jeremiah (third figure to the right of the portal), who foretold the destruction of Jerusalem, stands on a column whose capital depicts a mushroom cloud over a New York with its skyscrapers (including the Twin Towers) tilting wildly; another apocalyptic scene shows a Brooklyn Bridge broken in two, a bus plummeting into the river below.

THE CATHEDRAL TAPESTRIES

The cathedral owns two remarkable sets of tapestries. The Mortlake Tapestries, woven in England and based on cartoons by Raphael, depict *The Acts of the Apostles*. Commissioned by Pope Leo X (c. 1513), the cartoons, from which several sets of tapestries were woven, were dispersed throughout Europe. Sir Francis Crane, founder of the Mortlake tapestry works, rediscovered them in Genoa in 1623 and sent them to England where a set was woven for Prince Charles (later Charles I) and others.

Twelve Barberini Tapestries were woven during the first half of the 17th century on the papal looms founded by Cardinal Francesco Barberini. Eleven depict scenes from the life of Christ; the other is a map of the Holy Land. The cartoons, by Giovanni Francesco Romanelli, are now in the Vatican. The two tapestries irreparably damaged in the 2001 fire showed *The Last Supper* and *The Resurrection*.

Interior of St. John the Divine

The nave (2): The piers of the nave are alternately massive and slender (16ft by 6ft), an arrangement reflected both in the exterior buttressing and in the vaulting. The thick piers have an inner core of granite and are faced with limestone; the slender piers are solid granite. Each outer aisle is divided into seven bays, illuminated by stained-glass windows. The bays refer to the religious aspect of various professions and human activities: law, education, fatherhood and motherhood, the armed services, medicine, and so on. Some of them contain memorials, for example to firefighters, to victims of AIDS.

The largest of the cathedral's six organs (1910, Ernest M. Skinner; rebuilt 1954) has 151 ranks and 8,514 pipes, including a State Trumpet, whose 61 silver pipes are directly under the rose window in the west front.

The rose window itself, designed by Charles Connick, contains more than

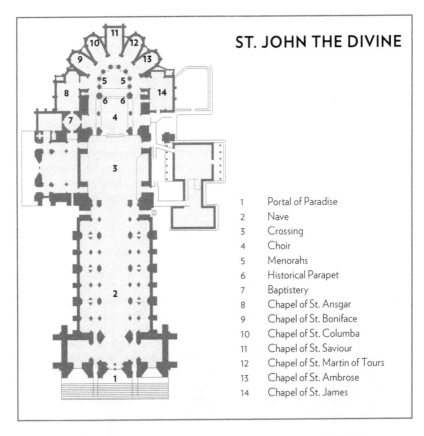

ST. JOHN THE DIVINE

1	Portal of Paradise
2	Nave
3	Crossing
4	Choir
5	Menorahs
6	Historical Parapet
7	Baptistery
8	Chapel of St. Ansgar
9	Chapel of St. Boniface
10	Chapel of St. Columba
11	Chapel of St. Saviour
12	Chapel of St. Martin of Tours
13	Chapel of St. Ambrose
14	Chapel of St. James

10,000 pieces of glass. Symbols radiating from the life-size central figure of Christ represent the gifts of the Holy Spirit, the Beatitudes, and the heavenly choir. The lesser rose window below it, also by Connick, develops the symbolism of the number seven, which figures prominently in St. John's vision: seven fountains, seven growing vine forms, seven pairs of doves, and seven stars.

The crossing (3): Visible here are the imposing "bones" of the cathedral, the great granite piers, the uncompleted arches, and the remarkable "temporary" dome of Guastavino tile hastily installed in the summer of 1909 as an inexpensive way to cover the opening until a central tower could be built. The self-supporting tile served as its own scaffolding, and masons worked from above, standing on the previous day's work to add a few more rows of tiles each day.

The choir (4): The lower part (from the ground to the balustrade below the clerestory windows) remains from Heins & LaFarge's original Romanesque plan (completed 1911); above (altered 1939–41) is Cram's Gothic remodeling.

The eight 52-ft granite columns from Vinalhaven, Maine, were quarried as monoliths but cut in two after the first two cracked while being turned and polished. Because the land slopes sharply downhill at this end of the church, the column foundations go down 135ft. Although the choir is relatively short (145ft), a kind of false perspective makes it seem longer: the arcades at the east end are closer together and the floor slopes upward in that direction.

In the choir the two **menorahs (5)** near the altar, designed after those in the Temple of Jerusalem depicted on the 1st-century AD Arch of Titus in Rome, were donated (1930) by former *New York Times* publisher Adolph Ochs.

Carved on the **Historical Parapet (6)** at the ascent to the sanctuary (in two sections at either side) are figures of notable men (and one woman) from the first 20 centuries of the Christian era, including St. Augustine of Hippo, St. Francis of Assisi, Shakespeare, and Abraham Lincoln. The statue of George Washington was decapitated by vandals in 2006, but a new head has been carved. The most recent figures (*left end of the northern section of the parapet*) represent Martin Luther King Jr., Albert Einstein, Susan B. Anthony, and Mohandas Gandhi.

The baptistery (7): This octagonal chamber (1928; Frank Cleveland of Cram & Ferguson) was donated by August Van Horne Stuyvesant and his sister (*see p. 338*), their Dutch origins symbolized by the tulips and windmills in the decoration. The marble font derives from the one in the cathedral of Siena.

The **Chapels of the Tongues**, listed below, celebrate national or ethnic groups, in keeping with the international ideal of the cathedral. Each is associated with a relevant saint and most are constructed in styles appropriate to the groups they honor.

Chapel of St. Ansgar (8) (1918), named after a 9th-century Frankish missionary to Denmark, Sweden, and Germany, suggestive of 14th-century English Gothic architecture, honors Scandinavian immigrants.

Chapel of St. Boniface (9) (1916), honors immigrants from Germany. St. Boniface, an English monk (c. 680–755), was sent by Pope Gregory II to convert the Germanic tribes. The 11-ft stiff-winged bronze statue of St. Michael the Archangel was made and donated (1963) by Eleanor M. Mellon.

Chapel of St. Columba (10) (1911), dedicated to immigrants from the British Isles, commemorates the Irish saint (521–97) who founded the monastery of Iona and worked at converting the Celts. Gutzon Borglum, of Mount Rushmore fame, sculpted the figures flanking the doorways, which represent influential figures in English church history. Heins & LaFarge designed this chapel in their favored Romanesque style. Keith Haring's *Life of Christ* triptych, said to be based on a traditional Russian icon, was his last work before his death from AIDS in 1990, and his only religious work.

Chapel of St. Saviour (11): The central chapel and the first one built (1904; Heins & LaFarge) is dedicated to the

Eastern Church, though its style is Gothic, not Byzantine. The 20 figures flanking the entrance represent the Heavenly Choir, and were designed by Gutzon Borglum, as were the figures of scholars, bishops, and saints of the Eastern Church on either side of the window. The Heavenly Choir stirred up controversy when installed, since all the figures are female. In the ambulatory directly opposite the entrance to the chapel is the tomb of Bishop Horatio Potter (1802–87), designed after the tomb of Edward the Confessor in Westminster Abbey and occupying the spot behind the high altar traditionally reserved for a cathedral's founder.

Chapel of St. Martin of Tours (12), a 4th-century Gallic bishop, was designed by Ralph Cram (1918) in a style reminiscent of 13th-century French Gothic, and honors French immigrants. It is noteworthy for its beautiful windows

(Charles Connick) depicting scenes from the lives of (*left to right*): St. Louis, St. Martin, and St. Joan of Arc. The statue of Joan of Arc (donated 1922) on the left wall is by Anna Hyatt Huntington and stands above a stone taken from the saint's cell in Rouen. A small chip of Reims Cathedral blasted away during World War I is embedded in the trefoil above the altar cross.

Chapel of St. Ambrose (13), named after the 4th-century bishop of Milan and patron saint of lawyers, was designed (1914; Carrère & Hastings) in a style Cram called "purely Renaissance." Dedicated to Italian immigrants, it is decorated with Italian marble.

Chapel of St. James (14) (1916) is dedicated to the people of Spain. The decoration is reminiscent of 14th-century English Gothic.

THE GROUNDS

The cathedral grounds cover about eleven acres. Near the sidewalk at West 111th St, the bronze **Peace Fountain** (1985; Greg Wyatt), variously described as fascinating, repugnant, and "gnarly," depicts the battle between Good and Evil represented by the figures of Satan and the archangel Michael. The pedestal, formed like a double helix, suggests DNA, carrier of the genetic code.

In the center of the **Pulpit Lawn**, where resident peacocks sometimes stroll and shriek, is a tall open-work Gothic spire. **Cathedral House** further east once housed the bishop; J. Pierpont Morgan, who donated money for its construction, defended its elegance by opining that bishops should live "like everyone else," though he must have had a rarefied view of how "everyone else" lived. Adjoining it is **Ogilvie House**, once the deanery, now the bishop's home. Beyond is the Cathedral School, formerly a day school for choirboys, and now a co-educational elementary and middle school. The **Biblical Garden** is planted with flora mentioned in the Bible. Ithiel Town, one of the nation's first professional architects, designed the **Town Building** (1843) for the Leake & Watts Orphan Asylum; it houses social outreach programs and the Textile Conservation Laboratory.

In the former stone yard (*corner of Amsterdam Ave and 113th St*) a 14-story apartment is rising, the land leased for 99 years to provide income for the cathedral.

IN THE NEIGHBORHOOD

Opposite the cathedral, the **Hungarian Pastry Shop** (*1030 Amsterdam Ave near 111th St*), a student hangout, serves traditional Central European and other sweets. Further up Amsterdam Ave, the square stone building (*West 113th St*), now an adult day care center, was built as a gatehouse (begun 1870) to control water flowing from the Croton watershed into the city. In the early 19th century an aqueduct ran down Amsterdam Ave above street level, but when the neighborhood was developed, the aqueduct was removed and iron pipes were laid below the street. A second gatehouse stands at West 119th St.

The Roman Catholic **Église de Notre Dame** (*Morningside Drive and West 114th St*; apse 1909–10, Daus & Otto; remainder 1914, Cross & Cross), originally built as a mission church of the Church of St. Vincent de Paul (*on West 24th St*), once ministered to a congregation of French-speaking immigrants. The building, with its portico of Corinthian columns, was modeled after the Invalides in Paris, but a planned dome was never built. The interior is remarkable for its exposed Guastavino tiles and replica of the grotto at Lourdes, the money for which was donated by Geraldyn Redmond, whose son was cured there.

Along Morningside Drive at West 116th St, is the **Carl Schurz Memorial** (1913; sculptor Karl Bitter, architect Henry Bacon). Forced to flee Germany because of his revolutionary political sentiments, Schurz (1829–1906) emigrated to the US where he became a leader of the Republican party, a friend of Abraham Lincoln, a major general in the Union Army during the Civil War, a senator, and an editor. Bitter's bronze statue depicts Schurz as strong and idealistic; the low relief panels on the monument portray the liberation of oppressed peoples: Native Americans, Asians, and blacks. From the overlook to Morningside Park there is a sidelong view across the rockface of Jacob Wrey Mould's massive retaining wall.

MORNINGSIDE PARK

Morningside Park occupies about 30 acres, including a rocky cliff of Manhattan schist, which plunges down to the Harlem Plain. In the mid-19th century the Parks Department took over these precipitous slopes, which were unsuitable for real estate development, and hired Frederick Law Olmsted and Calvert Vaux, already famous for their work in Central and Prospect Parks, to design a park. Realizing that the most attractive feature of the area was the view to the east, Vaux and Olmsted planned a walkway on top of the cliff, and studded it with balconies facing the Harlem Plain below. When their original design (1887) was rejected, Jacob Wrey Mould, who had worked with them on Central Park, planned the massive, buttressed masonry wall that supports the overlooks.

The park had a reputation for danger as early as the 1930s, but in 1981 some Columbia undergraduates founded the Friends of Morningside Park, which advocated returning the then overgrown and neglected park to its original design, and reclaiming its wilderness. Since that time crime has significantly decreased.

COLUMBIA UNIVERSITY

Map p. 612, B4–B3. Morningside Campus: Morningside Drive to Riverside Drive, West 111th–West 122nd Sts. Subway: 1 to 116th St-Columbia University. Bus: M4, M5, M11, M60, M104. For free campus tours, T: 212 854 4900. Free podcast walking tour by architectural historian Andrew Dolkart available at columbia.edu/node/59.html.

Columbia University, one of the oldest, wealthiest, and most respected of all North American universities, is known for its professional schools—medicine, law, business, education, journalism, and architecture—and for the School of General Studies, where adults of any age can work toward degrees. Undergraduate Columbia College is co-educational; affiliated with the university are Barnard College (women), Teachers College, the Jewish Theological Seminary, and Union Theological Seminary.

HISTORY OF THE UNIVERSITY

Columbia was founded as a gentlemen's college to "instruct youth in the learned languages and in the liberal arts and sciences." By the mid-18th century it became apparent to observers that while New York outstripped its American rivals commercially, it lagged behind culturally, its populace (according to citizens of Boston and Philadelphia) afflicted by ignorance, their lives dominated by a sordid thirst for money. Consequently a group of prominent men set out to establish a center of learning that would lighten the intellectual gloom, in the process outshining Harvard, Yale, and the College of New Jersey (later Princeton). Among them were several vestrymen of Trinity Church, who arranged a transfer of five acres of church property to the proposed college—a plot near the present World Trade Center site. It was Columbia's first piece of valuable real estate.

The college was chartered by King George II in 1754 and named King's College, the fifth such institution in the colonies. The first president was Dr. Samuel Johnson, an Anglican pastor from Stratford, Connecticut; the first class of eight men bore such resoundingly old New York names as Verplanck, Van Cortlandt, and Bayard.

Among the early students were Alexander Hamilton (enrolled 1775), who became the first secretary of the US Treasury; and John Jay, first chief justice of the US Supreme Court. After the Revolution the college, renamed Columbia, entered a period of intellectual dormancy that lasted into the 19th century. In 1814 the trustees appealed for financial aid, instead of which they received a plot of land between 47th and 51st Sts, rocky, overgrown, and remote from the city. The trustees thought the state appraisal at $75,000 wildly inflated. But it turned out well in the long run: Rockefeller Center now stands on that 11.5-acre parcel, sold by the university in 1985 for $400 million.

In 1856 the college moved uptown to buildings between Madison and Fourth (now Park) Aves, remaining there until its relocation to Morningside Heights in 1897. In 1902 Nicholas Murray Butler became president; under his guidance Columbia achieved its high reputation.

MORNINGSIDE HEIGHTS CAMPUS

The university purchased the land from the Bloomingdale Insane Asylum (1892 and 1903) for $3.9 million. The original campus, built on the earlier parcel north of West 116th St, contains Columbia's finest buildings, Low Library and St. Paul's Chapel. McKim, Mead & White designed the campus (1893), but it is principally the work of Charles Follen McKim, who envisioned a densely developed area with small side courtyards and a narrow central quadrangle. The only side courtyard actually built is the one bounded by Schermerhorn, Avery, and Fayerweather Halls, and St. Paul's Chapel (and it has been altered by the Avery Library extension). After McKim's death (1909) the university elected to retain the central open space and expand instead into surrounding city streets, a policy that has expanded the campus but caused local conflict. The building anchoring the Lower (South) Quadrangle is Butler Library (1934; James Gamble Rogers), named after Nicholas Murray Butler, housing the main collection, about 11.9 million volumes.

LOW MEMORIAL LIBRARY

Dominating the upper quadrangle, Low Memorial Library (1895–7; McKim, Mead & White) was donated to the University by Seth Low, president of Columbia from 1890–1901, to honor his father, Abiel Abbot Low (1811–93), a wealthy tea-merchant and China-trade pioneer, whose warehouses remain in the South Street Seaport area (*see pp. 56 and 479*). The younger Low resigned his office to become mayor of New York (1901–3), a position he won not because of political acuity but because his opponents were flagrantly corrupt. Low Library remained the main university library until 1934, when Butler Library superseded it. Today it houses the Visitor Center and offices.

On its broad steps sits ***Alma Mater*** (1903; Daniel Chester French), originally covered with gold leaf and occasionally re-gilded. In 1970 *Alma Mater* survived a bomb set off during student uprisings and continues to sit graciously on her throne flanked by torches symbolizing enlightenment. Her right hand holds a scepter topped with a crown, an emblem referring to Columbia's beginnings as King's College. Architecturally Low Library looks back to the Roman Pantheon, its general plan a Greek cross with an octagonal transition to a saucer dome. The former Main Reading Room, with its 16 polished granite columns topped by gilt bronze capitals and a domed ceiling, is an elegant example of McKim, Mead & White's work. The sub-basement formerly contained a large canvas tank and a stationary rowing rack for the Columbia crew.

Three-story, brick **Buell Hall** (1885), east of Low Library, is the only remaining structure from the Bloomingdale Asylum, built as a residence for wealthy male patients so they would not have to live in an institutional setting. In front of Philosophy Hall is a cast of Rodin's ***The Thinker*** (modeled 1880, cast 1930).

ST. PAUL'S CHAPEL

One of the campus's most beautiful buildings, St. Paul's Chapel (1904–7; Howells & Stokes) was donated by Olivia Egleston Phelps Stokes and Caroline Phelps Stokes as a memorial to their parents, with the stipulation that it be designed by their nephew Isaac Newton Phelps Stokes, at the time a young and relatively untried architect. It was the first building at Columbia not designed by McKim, Mead & White, though as a compromise that firm acted as consulting architect. Stokes is also remembered for his six-volume history, *The Iconography of Manhattan Island* (1915–28), the *sine qua non* of scholarly books about the borough.

St. Paul's is shaped like a short Latin cross with a portico on the west and a semicircular apse on the east, and a dome over the crossing. Gutzon Borglum sculpted the small cherub heads on the column capitals flanking the entrance.

The interior is the best part. Above its tan brick walls rises a vault tiled with salmon-colored Guastavino tile. The three apse windows (John La Farge) show St. Paul preaching to the Athenians on the Areopagus (the hill west of the Acropolis where the city philosophers had invited "the babbler" to explain his strange conduct and even stranger god). The windows in the transepts show teachers of the Old Testament (north transept) and the New Testament (south transept). The chapel, originally affiliated with the Episcopal Church, as was Columbia, offers ecumenical religious services, concerts, and other events.

SCULPTURE ON THE OVERPASS

East of the chapel, an overpass crosses Amsterdam Ave. Towering above the entrance to the Law School is Jacques Lipchitz's ***Bellerophon Taming Pegasus*** (installed 1977), which according to the sculptor symbolizes the control by law over the forces of disorder. On the overpass are: ***Three-Way Piece: Points*** (1967; Henry Moore), a swelling bronze abstraction resting on three points (which has been compared to a tooth); David Bakalar's ***Life Force*** (1988), another biomorphic form; and ***Tightrope Walker*** (1979; Kees Verkade), a 14-ft bronze elongated aerialist with a second figure balanced on his shoulders, donated as a monument to William "Wild Bill" Donovan, a Columbia alumnus and head of the Office of Strategic Services during World War II. In the courtyard behind the Law School is ***Flight*** (1981) by Gertrude Schweitzer.

AVERY AND SCHERMERHORN HALLS

Back on the main campus north of St. Paul's Chapel, **Avery Hall** (1912: McKim, Mead & White) houses the School of Architecture and the nation's largest architectural library. In front of it stands a three-ton, hollow, black-painted steel sculpture: *Curl* (installed 1968) by Clement Meadmore. The Australian sculptor, known for his monumentally-scaled metal works, was especially proud of this one and visited it shortly before his death in 2005.

Schermerhorn Hall (1897), a gift of William Schermerhorn (class of 1840), housed the natural sciences. On the eighth floor the **Wallach Art Gallery** hosted exhibitions, curated by faculty members, graduate students, and independent scholars, covering a wide range of art-historical periods and including works from university and private collections. *NB: At the time of writing, the gallery was expected to move to the Lenfest Center for the Arts on 125th Street, just west of Broadway, in the university's new Manhattanville campus; for updates, see columbia.edu/cu/wallach.*

Between Low Library and Lewisohn Hall, on the west side of the campus, reclines the bronze **Great God Pan** (1898) by George Grey Barnard, originally intended for the Dakota Apartments (*see p. 410*). Barnard spent years in Paris where, though he denied it, he was influenced by Rodin; he also collected medieval architectural fragments and sculpture, some of which later formed the core of The Cloisters.

The **School of Journalism** (1912–13; McKim, Mead & White), on the southwest corner of Broadway and College Walk, was founded by the publisher Joseph Pulitzer in 1912. Considered the most prestigious journalism school in the nation, it comes into the public eye each spring when it announces the Pulitzer Prizes. South of the Journalism Building is **Lerner Hall** (1999; Bernard Tschumi/Gruzen Samton), the student center, designed by a former dean of the Architecture School.

THE BATTLE OF HARLEM HEIGHTS

Outside the campus rectangle, on the Broadway wall of the Mathematics Building at about 117th St, a large plaque depicts the Battle of Harlem Heights. On September 15, 1776, the British Army landed at Kip's Bay (near East 35th St), routing the defenders, and trapping the main body of the American forces in Lower Manhattan. The following day a force of American troops, encamped on Harlem Heights, moved south to encounter a British force in a field in this vicinity. The Americans hoped to lure some of the British down into the valley where 125th St now runs, to outflank and cut them off. The plan failed since the flanking party fired prematurely, revealing their whereabouts. Nevertheless, the Americans did hold off the British for several hours and forced them to retreat. While the battle had little significance in the course of the war, it bolstered sagging American morale and demonstrated to Washington that his soldiers, despite disastrous recent performances, were capable of standing up to the British.

BARNARD COLLEGE
The campus of Barnard College (*facing Broadway between West 116th and West 120th Sts*) was founded to provide women's education equal to that of the elite private men's undergraduate colleges, most of which until the 1960s admitted only men.

Frederick A.P. Barnard became president of Columbia in 1864, following a string of men distinguished more for piety than administrative abilities. Among his liberal innovations was a women's course, which the trustees grudgingly accepted in 1883. But since women were not allowed to enter the classrooms, and faculty members were not allowed to counsel or advise women beyond handing out reading lists, the enterprise was not notably successful. Nevertheless, through Barnard's efforts the women's college was founded in 1889. Columbia College (the undergraduate college of the university) began admitting women in 1983 after a decade of failed negotiations to merge with Barnard, which still admits only women.

WEST 120TH STREET AND TEACHERS COLLEGE

Columbia's **Pupin Physics Laboratories** (*on the east side of Broadway at West 120th St*) were built in 1925 but named ten years later for Michael Idvorsky Pupin (1858–1935), a Serbian immigrant who became one of America's foremost inventors and a revered professor of electrical engineering. In this building in the late 1930s and early 1940s, Harold C. Urey, Enrico Fermi, and I.I. Rabi did the work in nuclear fission that won them the Nobel Prize.

The row of red brick buildings on the east side of Broadway between West 120th and 121st Streets houses **Teachers College**, an affiliate of Columbia University. Founded in 1889 by Nicholas Murray Butler, the college began life as the Kitchen Garden Association, dedicated to teaching girls, primarily immigrants, housekeeping and gardening. The skills and discipline involved were not only essential for future domestic servants, but were felt to improve the students' moral fiber too. Butler and Grace Hoadley Dodge, philanthropist and heiress to part of the Phelps, Dodge & Co. mining and metals fortune, were instrumental in forming the college.

Since the days when John Dewey belonged to the faculty, Teachers College has earned a reputation for spearheading progressive education. Most of the buildings date from around the turn of the 20th century. Halfway down the block on 120th St is **Main Hall** (1892; William A. Potter), the campus's earliest building, an elaborate composition of dormers, gables, pointed-arch windows, porches, and turrets.

TWO SEMINARIES AND THE MANHATTAN SCHOOL OF MUSIC

Union Theological Seminary (*Broadway, West 120th–West 122nd Sts*), founded in 1836 as a graduate school for Protestant ministers, has long enjoyed a reputation for social activism and liberal religious thought. Its library is said to be second only to the Vatican in the breadth of its holdings. Among its faculty and graduates have been such luminaries as Reinhold Niebuhr, the socialist Norman Thomas, and James H. Cone, founder of black liberation theology. The classroom and residential buildings (1910; Allen & Collens) are organized in a quadrangle around a central courtyard dominated by the Brown Memorial Tower on Broadway and the James Memorial Tower on Claremont Ave. Constructed of rough-faced Manhattan schist quarried during excavations for the foundations, the buildings belong to an era when American universities imitated the Gothicism of Oxford and Cambridge.

The **Jewish Theological Seminary** (*Broadway, West 122nd–West 123rd Sts*) is a center of Conservative Judaism and an important rabbinical seminary. The building (1930; Gehron, Ross, Alley) is a large and prosaic example of neo-Colonial architecture. Founded in 1886, the seminary has become a major center of Jewish education and is affiliated with Columbia University. Its library has the most comprehensive collection of Judaica and Hebraica in the western hemisphere.

Across Broadway stands the **Manhattan School of Music** (*West 122nd St between Broadway and Claremont Ave*), a leading conservatory (1917) for classical music and jazz. The building (1910; Donn Barber) was constructed for the Institute of Musical Art, which merged with the Juilliard School of Music. Famous alumni include soprano Dawn Upshaw, composer Tobias Picker, and drummer Max Roach.

RIVERSIDE CHURCH

Map p. 612, A3. 490 Riverside Drive (West 120th St). Subway: 1 to 116th St; walk north to 120th St and west to Claremont Ave. Bus: M104, M4, M5. Claremont Ave entrance open daily 7am–10pm. Guided tour Sun at 12:30 after worship. T: 212 870 6700, theriversidechurchny.org.

High on a bluff overlooking the Hudson River, the Riverside Church is interdenominational, interracial, and international, affiliated with the United Church of Christ and the American Baptist Churches. Long known for its political liberalism and community service, the church has invited Martin Luther King Jr., Nelson Mandela, César Chávez, Desmond Tutu, Fidel Castro, and Reinhold Niebuhr to speak. Its first senior minister was liberal theologian Harry Emerson Fosdick.

The church began as a small Baptist congregation meeting on the Lower East Side, moving uptown as demographics changed. The present church was built largely with money from John D. Rockefeller Jr., originally a Baptist and later a leader in the ecumenical church movement.

The exterior

The Riverside Church (1930, Allen & Collens and Henry C. Pelton; south wing 1960, Collens, Willis & Beckonert) may resemble a European masonry cathedral, Chartres for example, but unlike the still-uncompleted St. John the Divine it is a modern, steel-framed, limestone-faced building, constructed in only three years. Originally criticized for its disproportionately tall tower (392ft), its aesthetic servitude to Europe, and its eclecticism, the church is distinguished for its fine stained glass, stone carving, and woodwork, which represent the finest materials and craftsmanship available.

The long axis runs north–south parallel to Riverside Drive. The 22-story tower at the south end contains classrooms and offices as well as the carillon. The elaborately carved principal entrance on the west is clearly intended to recall the portals at Chartres. The tympanum depicts a seated Christ surrounded by the symbols of the Evangelists. Above the tympanum are five archivolts, the first and fifth depicting angels, the others portraying scientists, philosophers, and religious leaders drawn from the sweep of human history. The chapel door, just south of the West Portal, is thematically devoted to the Nativity. Near the cloister entrance on Claremont Ave is a bronze *Madonna and Child* (1927) by Jacob Epstein.

The interior

Narthex: The two windows of 16th-century Flemish glass are the only ones not made specifically for the church. The small **Gethsemane Chapel** contains Heinrich Hofmann's painting of *Christ in Gethsemane*, donated by Rockefeller. Also accessible from the narthex is **Christ Chapel**, inspired by the 11th-century nave of the Church of St-Nazaire at Carcassone, France.

Nave: The magnificent nave, 215ft long, is finished in Indiana limestone and divided into three aisles. The clerestory windows are copies of the famous 12th–13th-century windows at Chartres, while those in the aisles have modern motifs as well as historical ones. The 51 colored stained-glass windows in the church were made by firms in Boston, Chartres, and Reims. On the rear wall of the nave at the gallery level is Sir Jacob Epstein's imposing *Christ in Majesty*, the original clay model, now gilded, for the aluminum statue at Llandaff Cathedral in Cardiff, Wales.

Chancel: The nine-ton pulpit is carved from three blocks of limestone; its niches contain figures of prophets; ten of the figures on the upper level stand beneath canopies representing cathedrals of France. In the center of the chancel floor a marble maze has been adapted from the labyrinth at Chartres, whose route medieval penitents traced on their knees. The chancel screen portrays seven aspects of the life of Christ, shown surrounded by people who have fulfilled the divine ideal, including Pasteur, Savonarola, Florence Nightingale, and J.S. Bach. The panels represent (*left to right*) physicians, teachers, prophets, humanitarians, missionaries, reformers, and lovers of beauty.

Tower: The 74 bells of the Laura Spelman Rockefeller Carillon, given in memory of Rockefeller's mother, range from the 20-ton Bourdon (the largest tuned bell ever cast) to a 10-lb treble bell. Cast (1925, 1930, and 1956) in England and Holland, it is the largest, heaviest carillon ever made. (*At the time of writing, the tower was closed to the public.*)

North of Riverside Church and east of Grant's Tomb are the two-plus acres of **Sakura Park**, formerly owned by John D. Rockefeller Jr. Hundreds of cherry trees, donated by Japan in 1912, bloom in spring. Also in the park are Gutzon Borglum's statue (1918) of General Daniel Butterfield and a traditional stone lantern donated by the city of Tokyo in 1960. North of the park **International House**, a residence for international students, was also funded by Rockefeller.

GENERAL GRANT NATIONAL MEMORIAL

Map p. 612, A3. Riverside Drive at 122nd St. Subway: 1 to 116th St. Bus: M5. Open Wed–Sun 10–11, 12–1, 2–3 & 4–5. Free. Visitor Center (across Riverside Drive) open Wed–Sun, 9–5. Monument and Visitor Center closed Mon, Tues, Thanksgiving, Christmas Day, and during severe snowstorms (call ahead); T: 212 666 1640, nps.gov/gegr.

The General Grant National Memorial, familiarly known as **Grant's Tomb**, is the imposing resting place of the victorious commander of the Union forces in the Civil War. The massive granite sepulcher (1891–7; John H. Duncan) contains the remains of Ulysses S. Grant (1822–85) and his wife, Julia Dent Grant. It was intended to be unmistakably tomblike, despite objections that it would give the area a funereal tone.

HISTORY OF THE TOMB

After an illustrious career as commander-in-chief of the Union Armies in the Civil War and a less glorious period as president (1868–76), Ulysses S. Grant died in 1885. He had requested burial in New York City, or at the US Military Academy at West Point, or in Galena, Illinois, his home before the Civil War. Because Galena seemed too remote and Mrs. Grant, a civilian, could not be buried at West Point, New York won by default. John H. Duncan's design is based largely on the tombs of Mausolus at Halicarnassus (4th century BC), Hadrian in Rome (2nd century AD), and Napoleon in Paris.

Ground was broken in 1891, and the general's remains were quietly brought to the finished tomb in 1897. Despite the scandals that marred his administration, Grant himself remained a revered figure, and even while the tomb was under construction two attempts were made to claim his remains for other locales.

In the early years of the 20th century, Grant's Tomb was more a popular site even than the Statue of Liberty, with 607,484 people visiting in 1906, the peak year (about 100,000 come yearly now). In the 1970s and '80s the monument fell on hard times, despoiled by vandalism and neglect, until in the 1990s Frank Scaturro, a history major at Columbia, mobilized public opinion to restore it.

Grant's Tomb has a cube-like base topped by a drum supporting a stepped conical dome, patterned after the tomb of Mausolus. A broad flight of steps flanked by two large eagles (rescued from a demolished downtown post office) leads to the Doric portico and entrance. The stone blocks above the portico were intended to support equestrian statues of Union generals and the stepped cone was to have been crowned by a statue of Grant in a triumphal chariot. Above the cornice a tablet contains Grant's words, "Let us have peace," spoken upon accepting the presidential nomination of 1868.

The austere interior was inspired by Napoleon's tomb in Paris, with a sunken crypt containing the red granite sarcophaghi of General and Mrs. Grant. Beneath the dome, sculptured women (by J. Massey Rhind) symbolize phases of Grant's life. Niches in the wall at the crypt level contain bronze busts of Grant's generals Sherman and Sheridan (by William Mues), and Thomas, Ord, and McPherson (by Jeno Juszko); all were installed in 1938 as part of a Work Progress Administration (WPA) endeavor.

THE GRAVE OF AN AMIABLE CHILD

The rather forlorn park surrounding the monument, Grant Centennial Plaza, commemorates Grant's establishment in 1872 of Yellowstone, the first national park in North America. Directly behind the tomb a fence encloses the Commemoration Tree, a ginkgo given by China in 1897 to honor Grant. The free-form mosaic benches (1972–4; Phillip Danzig and Pedro Silva), now a bit dilapidated, were created as part of a community project.

Across Riverside Drive to the west (*roughly opposite the public restrooms in the park*), a fence near the footpath encloses a small stone urn "Erected to the Memory of an Amiable Child," St. Claire Pollock, age five, who died in a fall from the rocks on July 15, 1797. His uncle, George Pollock, a wealthy Irish linen merchant, had built his home at what is now Riverside Park and 123rd St, on high land commanding a view of the river. The house (c. 1783), called Strawberry Hill, stood at the north end of the landscaped oval behind Grant's Tomb. After the child's death, Pollock sold the house to Joseph Alston, husband of Aaron Burr's daughter Theodosia, and returned to Ireland, requesting that the child's grave remain untouched. In the mid-19th century the house became the Claremont Inn, popular with travelers and numbering among its illustrious guests Morgans and Whitneys. It was damaged by fire and was demolished by the City in 1952.

COLUMBIA'S MANHATTANVILLE CAMPUS

Columbia is expanding northward with a 17-acre satellite campus west of Broadway from West 125th St to West 133rd St. The first phase will include four buildings the Jerome L. Greene Science Center, the Lenfest Center for the Arts, the Forum, and the School of International and Public Affairs.

EATING AND DRINKING IN MORNINGSIDE HEIGHTS

$$ **Pisticci.** ■ A local favorite for highly regarded Italian food, named for a town in Basilicata. Free jazz on Sun. No reservations. Lunch and dinner daily, but closed week of July 4. *125 La Salle St (Broadway and Claremont Ave. T: 212 932 3500, pisticcinyc.com. Map p. 612, A3.*

$ **Miss Mamie's Spoonbread Too.** Near St. John the Divine, Miss Mamie's serves up big portions of Southern comfort food, including possibly the world's best short ribs. Friendly service. Lunch and dinner daily. *366 West 110th St (Columbus and Manhattan Aves). T: 212 865 6744, spoonbreadinc.com/miss_mamies.htm. Map p. 612, B4.*

$ **Xi'an Famous Foods**. On the southern border of Morningside Heights, this no-frills Chinese restaurant features highly rated hand-pulled noodles and much more. Surprisingly good. Lunch and dinner daily. Other locations. *2675 Broadway (101st and 102nd Sts). T: 212 786 2068, xianfoods.com. Map p. 614, A1.*

Harlem

*Harlem is world-famous as the center of African-American
culture and the neighborhood's pride in its heritage is evident.
Major sites include the Studio Museum in Harlem, the Schomburg
Center, the Apollo Theater, Hamilton Grange, and the Abyssinian
Baptist Church with its renowned gospel choir.*

Bounded by the East and Harlem Rivers, the cliffs of
Morningside Heights and St. Nicholas Terrace, and
by 110th and 168th Sts, Harlem (*map pp. 612–3*) is
the nation's most famous center of African-American life
and culture. Until recently African Americans have made up
most of the population of central and western Harlem, with
the area east of Park Avenue and north of 96th St known as El
Barrio or Spanish Harlem.

HISTORY OF HARLEM

In 1658 Dutch farmers founded Nieuw Haarlem ten miles north of New Amsterdam,
attracted by the fertile soil of the Harlem plain. Increasingly in the 18th and early
19th centuries this beautiful outlying land attracted gentlemen farmers and wealthy
merchants, who developed country estates here.

In 1837 the New York and Harlem Railroad along Park Avenue opened the area for
development, but simultaneously raised a barrier between the east and west sides
of Harlem, creating a strip of blight where factories, squatters' shacks, and tenements sprang up. Eastern Harlem attracted immigrants from Russia, Germany, Italy,
Ireland, Hungary, Scandinavia, England, and Spain, as well as Eastern European Jews,
while western Harlem drew middle-class German-Americans, both Jew and gentile.
Speculators, anticipating the full-blown arrival of the middle class from downtown,
put up substantial apartment buildings and handsome row houses in western Harlem,
and established cultural institutions, for example Oscar Hammerstein's Harlem
Opera House (1889) at 205 West 125th St. When an affluent middle class did not show
up, the real estate market collapsed, leaving landlords with unrentable buildings. In
1904, black realtor Philip A. Payton stepped into the gap, taking over building man-

agement and guaranteeing high rents to landlords who would accept black tenants, thereby making decent housing available to blacks for the first time in New York.

At the close of the Civil War, New York's black population, estimated at 15,000, had been concentrated in ghettos in Lower Manhattan, notably around Thompson St in Greenwich Village. By the end of the 19th century the black population was centered around the Tenderloin (*west of Broadway between 32nd and 42nd Sts*) and Hell's Kitchen (*the 40s and 50s west of Seventh Ave*). As demolition for the construction of the old Penn Station displaced them, blacks moved up into the San Juan Hill neighborhood, north and west of Columbus Circle. The next move was to Harlem, and during the 1920s its black population increased from 83,248 to 203,894 with a density of 236 people per acre, twice that of the rest of the city. White business and property owners fought bitterly to keep Harlem white, but failed simply because landlords found it too profitable to rent to blacks, although the arriving blacks were barred from holding jobs in white-owned businesses.

Nevertheless, the 1920s were years of optimism and great artistic activity, as writers, artists, and intellectuals made the pilgrimage to Harlem, by then the capital of black America. The **"Harlem Renaissance,"** usually considered as the years from 1924 until the stock market crash of 1929, saw the flowering of black literature, art, music, and political thinking. Black authors—Zora Neale Hurston, Countee Cullen, James Weldon Johnson, Langston Hughes—were published with greater frequency than ever before. Marcus Garvey awakened black self-respect and militancy with his back-to-Africa movement, while black and white intellectuals enjoyed cordial relations. Harlem also became famous for its music. Whites flocked uptown to enjoy the ballrooms and cabarets, and the jazz at famous nightclubs—the Cotton Club, Connie's, and Smalls' Paradise—many white-owned with white-only audiences.

The Depression devastated Harlem, revealing the poverty behind the glittering exterior. Throughout the city, the marginally employed were the hardest hit, and blacks, excluded from virtually all but menial jobs, were among the first to suffer. The 1930s were the years of "rent parties," where guests paid a fee to hear the music, drink the bathtub gin, and help pay the month's rent. Literary output dried up, housing deteriorated, and racial tensions heightened.

During the civil rights era of the 1950s and '60s, Harlem became a focus of activism. Black Muslims founded the Temple of Islam at 116th St and Lenox Ave. Civil rights leader Malcolm X worked there until he founded his own Organization of Afro-American Unity in 1964. After riots in 1964 and 1968, federal, state, and local money was channeled into Harlem to improve housing and education.

In the 1970s, as the city at large fell into fiscal difficulties, Harlem suffered acutely: businesses closed; vacant buildings pocked the streets. For some landlords it was cheaper to walk away than pay delinquent taxes; arson began to look like an attractive alternative for many as a way to collect the insurance. During these years the City became the unwilling owner of 65 percent of Harlem's real estate, collected for delinquent taxes, and it subsequently demolished many empty buildings.

Since the late 1990s, gentrification has reached Harlem, though pockets of poverty remain. Middle-class families have moved in; there are brownstone renovations in

Mount Morris Park, Striver's Row, Hamilton Heights, and other enclaves with fine housing stock. Today Harlem is less uniformly African-American, with an increasing white, Latino, and Asian population. The 1990 census counted only 672 whites in central Harlem; ten years later the number had increased to 2,200, and in 2008 to 13,800. The city, state, and federal governments as well as private developers have invested hundreds of millions of dollars in Harlem, the offices of former President Bill Clinton at 55 West 125th St being a notable example. Restaurants and cafés have arrived as well as more services, but, as with other gentrifying areas, long-term residents may be priced out.

GATEWAYS TO HARLEM

The northern edge of Central Park marks the southern boundary of Harlem. Anchoring Museum Mile, **Duke Ellington Circle** (*Fifth Ave at 110th St*) honors the jazz giant, who died in 1974. The monument (unveiled 1997; Robert Graham) consists of an eight-foot figure of Ellington standing by a grand piano, which rests on three ten-foot columns, each topped by three nude female caryatids representing the Graces. When it was unveiled, some viewers found it sexist, others found it ugly. Most of the money was raised from private donations solicited by the cabaret singer-pianist Bobby Short.

At the opposite corner, **Frederick Douglass Circle** (*Central Park West at West 110th St*) honors the great abolitionist, statesman, and orator. Gabriel Koren's bronze statue of Douglass (2010) stands in the center, surrounded by paving patterns based on traditional African-American quilt designs; the bronze fence symbolizes wagon wheels, suggesting escape, according to site designer Algernon Miller.

AROUND MARCUS GARVEY PARK:
FIFTH AVENUE, 120TH–124TH STREETS

Map p. 613, D3. Subway: 2, 3 to 125th St. Bus: M1, M101. The Mount Morris Park Community Improvement Association offers historic house tours on the second Sun in June; T: 212 369 4241, mmpcia.org.

The **Mount Morris Park Historic District** (*West 118th to West 124th Sts from Fifth Ave to Seventh Ave/Powell Blvd*) has a rich architectural heritage. In the late 19th century when Harlem saw its future as an upscale residential area, the streets around Mount Morris filled up with brownstone row houses and churches constructed for upper-middle class families arriving from downtown, most of them American-born white Protestants, a few of them wealthy. After the turn of the 20th century, many of these original residents moved on, replaced by poorer families including Jews from the Lower East Side, and then later by African Americans. While some buildings remained single-family homes, others were divided into apartments or rooming houses. Today as houses are being restored, the neighborhood is becoming increasingly desirable.

The well-preserved row of four-story, high-stooped houses flanking the west side of

Marcus Garvey Park, built in several late 19th-century architectural styles, suggests the affluence of their original owners. The mansion at the corner of West 123rd St was for many years a sanitarium and later a synagogue for a congregation of West Indians who saw the people of Africa as one of the lost tribes of Israel. The house was built (1889–90) for John Dwight, founder of the Arm & Hammer Baking Soda company.

HARLEM STREET NAMES

The major avenues take on different names as they pass through Central Harlem. Eighth Avenue is Frederick Douglass Boulevard. Seventh Avenue became Adam Clayton Powell Jr. Boulevard shortly after the black congressman (*see p. 446*) died in 1972. Sixth Avenue north of Central Park was renamed twice—first Lenox Avenue, after James Lenox, a wealthy white landowner and book collector and later Malcolm X Boulevard, after the assassinated civil rights leader. Many people still call it Lenox Avenue. Officially, 125th St is Martin Luther King Jr. Boulevard, but it remains generally known as 125th St.

MARCUS GARVEY PARK

Originally Mount Morris Park, Marcus Garvey Park straddles Fifth Ave between 120th and 124th Sts. Established in 1839, it is the neighborhood's centerpiece—mainly because its steep, rocky terrain and high central hill (called Snake Hill by the Dutch) made it unsuitable for building. The cast-iron watchtower (1855; Julius Kroehl), based on designs by James Bogardus (*see p. 99*), is today the sole survivor of many similar such fire lookouts. (*NB: At the time of writing the tower was slated to be dismantled and renovated.*)

The park was renamed in 1973 to honor Marcus Garvey, a charismatic black leader who arrived in Harlem from the West Indies in 1914, dedicated to advancing his race. Garvey encouraged blacks to work toward establishing their own social and political institutions, but his major interest was in leading his people back to Africa. To this end he formed two steamship companies, whose vessels (along with many others of the period) attempted to subvert Prohibition by carrying some $3 million worth of liquor from New York to Cuba, a voyage that ended with government confiscation of the cargo. Later Garvey was convicted of mail fraud, imprisoned and deported to Jamaica; he died an exile in London in 1940.

At 201 Lenox Ave (*northwest corner of West 120th St*) is the **Mount Olivet Baptist Church** (1907), built for an affluent German-Jewish congregation by Arnold W. Brunner, who also designed Shearith Israel's home on Central Park West (*see p. 409*). Architectural features include Stars of David above the column capitals and in the stained glass. Brunner, a second-generation "uptown" Jew educated at MIT and the École des Beaux-Arts, chose classicism over traditional Moorish Revival synagogue architecture. The Mount Olivet Baptist Church moved here in 1924 from West 53rd St, where there was at the time a large African-American population.

THE 125TH STREET CORRIDOR

Harlem's main commercial street, 125th St, runs from river to river (with accommodations for bridge and highway ramps). Once the glittering center of an uptown entertainment district, later drab and depressed, it is undergoing a renaissance with stores, offices, and residential buildings arriving at a quickening pace. There is a geologic fault that crosses Manhattan around 125th St. The Manhattan Valley (sometimes called the Harlem Valley) lies inside it and Riverside Drive crosses it on the **Riverside Drive Viaduct** (1900; F. Stuart Williamson; *map p. 612, A2*).

Harlem Hybrid (1976, restored 2008), the 5,500-lb welded bronze sculpture in Roosevelt Triangle (*West 125th St at Morningside Ave and Hancock Place; map p. 612, B3*), may look like a jagged rock outcropping, but its maker, Richard Howe Hunt, says it was also inspired by the forms of nearby buildings. It stands across from the Roman Catholic **Church of St. Joseph of the Holy Family** (1860), which predates the Civil War and is the borough's oldest church north of 44th Street. Built for a German congregation, today it offers Masses in English and Spanish.

In the triangle where Frederick Douglass Blvd intersects West 122nd St and St. Nicholas Ave, Alison Saar's powerful statue (2008) *Swing Low* shows the anti-slavery campaigner Harriet Tubman striding forward, pulling up the roots of slavery behind her. Saar explained at the dedication that she had depicted Tubman "not as the conductor of the Underground Railroad but as the train itself, an unstoppable locomotive." Frederick Douglass said of Tubman that except for John Brown he knew of "no one who has willingly encountered more perils and hardships to serve our enslaved people."

APOLLO THEATER

Map p. 612, C3. 253 West 125th St (Powell and Douglass Blvds). For group tours, T: 212 531 5337, apollotheater.org. Tours for groups of 20 or more by appointment, but individuals may join tour groups depending on availability; call for information.

The Apollo Theater (1913; George Keister) has been a major force shaping American entertainment and especially the careers of black performers. The theater was built when Harlem's population was largely German-Jewish: originally the Hurtig & Seamon's New Theatre, it was a burlesque and vaudeville house for whites only. As the neighborhood evolved, so did the Apollo. In 1934 Leo Brecher and Frank Schiffman, white businessmen who had previously run several Harlem clubs and theaters, took over the theater, opened it to black audiences, and began showcasing black performers. The same year the theater offered its first Amateur Nights, which over the years launched Sarah Vaughan and Ella Fitzgerald, Billie Holiday, Diana Ross, Sammy Davis Jr., and James Brown, among others.

The Apollo, like many theaters, fell on hard times during the 1970s, becoming a movie house, but was rescued in 1991 by the State of New York. Today it draws more than a million annual visitors to its jazz, funk, rock, R&B, and pop, world music, dance, new musicals, poetry-music events, and Amateur Nights. The building has been extensively restored inside and out, and garnished with an LED marquee.

THE INTERSECTION WITH POWELL BOULEVARD

The **Theresa Towers**, formerly the Hotel Theresa (1912–13; George and Edward Blum; *2090 Adam Clayton Powell Jr. Blvd at West 125th St; map p. 612, C3*), was built by Gustavus Sidenberg, a German-Jewish immigrant from Breslau, who named it after his two (successive) wives, both called Theresa. Only whites were welcome until 1940, but when that policy changed the Theresa drew so many black celebrities that it became known as the "Waldorf of Harlem." Fidel Castro famously stayed while visiting the UN in 1960, meeting with Soviet leader Nikita Khrushchev at the hotel. Castro had angrily departed the Shelburne Towers in midtown because the management demanded a hefty cash payment upfront; or because he thought the people of Harlem would be more amenable to his politics (they were, gathering nightly on 125th Street to applaud him); or because he and his entourage were asked to leave after dropping lighted cigars onto the carpets and bringing live chickens into the hotel—the rumors remain conflicted. Malcolm X's Organization of Afro-American Unity was also headquartered here.

The **Adam Clayton Powell Jr. State Office Building** (*163 West 125th St at Powell Blvd*) built as a consequence of the racial unrest of the 1960s in the then-popular Brutalist style (1973; Ifill Johnson Hanchard) became the tallest building in Harlem, displacing the Hotel Theresa. Originally called the Harlem State Office Building, it was renamed after Powell (*see p. 446*) in 1983, the year after his death.

THE STUDIO MUSEUM IN HARLEM

Map p. 612, C3. 144 West 125th St (Lenox Ave and Powell Blvd). Subway: 2, 3, A, B, C, D. Bus: M2, M7, M10, M100, M101, M102 or BX 15. Open Thur–Fri 12–9, Sat 10–6, Sun 12–6; closed Mon–Wed, major holidays. Admission charge but free on Sun. T: 212 864 4500, studiomuseum.org.

Founded in 1968 to collect and exhibit the work of artists of African descent and those influenced by black culture, the museum mounts exhibitions that feature traditional and contemporary African art. The permanent collection embraces 19th- and 20th-century African-American art, 20th-century Caribbean and African art, and traditional African art, but the emphasis is on contemporary artists. The museum also owns the archive of photographer James Van Der Zee, whose work constitutes the best visual record of Harlem during the 1930s and '40s. The museum's Artist-in-Residence program, the fruit of its original purpose of providing artists with studio space, has enhanced the careers of some 100 emerging artists, many of whom have gone on to substantial careers.

NATIONAL JAZZ MUSEUM IN HARLEM

Map p. 613, E3. 104 East 126th St (Park and Lexington Aves), Suite 2D. Open Mon–Fri 10–4, Sat 11–4. Requested donation. T: 212 348 8300, jazzmuseuminharlem.org.

This small venue offers performances, educational events, and exhibits on jazz and its place in American culture. Founded in 1997 by Leonard Garment, a lawyer, advisor to Richard Nixon during the Watergate scandal and a jazz saxophonist of no mean ability, the museum acquired (2010) an archive of more than a thousand radio broadcasts from the 1930s recorded by Bill Savory, an eccentric but gifted studio engineer. The museum also has thousands of books, periodicals, and an ongoing oral history archive.

Nearby, the **former Mount Morris Bank Building** (*81 East 125th St, at Park Ave*), once a symbol of Harlem's affluence, is now one of its resurgence. Constructed (1883; Lamb & Rich) with fine apartments above an arcaded second-floor banking hall, it was taken over by the Corn Exchange in 1913; when that bank left, the building spiraled downward. By the end of the 1990s it stood derelict hard by the tracks of the MetroNorth commuter railroad, where tens of thousands of tourists daily watched its decay. The City, who had claimed it for unpaid taxes, cut off the upper floors. Today, happily, it is being restored as office and retail space, perhaps reclaiming some of its former glory.

NORTH OF 125TH STREET

Harlem Renaissance poet Langston Hughes lived on the top floor of the brownstone at **20 East 127th St** (*Park and Madison Aves*) from 1948 until his death in 1967. The ivy on the house had withered, and the upper floors appeared vacant at the time of writing.

Keith Haring's ***Crack Is Wack*** (1986, restored 2007) fills both sides of the wall in the handball court at East 128th St and Second Ave with the artist's familiar cartoon figures (the more elaborate side is visible from the southbound Harlem River Drive, near exit 19). Haring painted the wall illegally at the height of the drug epidemic, was arrested for disorderly conduct and fined; the mural was painted over. When parks commissioner Henry Stern discovered this, he apologized, offering the artist other blank walls and free paint; Haring, however, repainted the mural on the original site.

COLLYER BROTHERS PARK

Although most New York parks honor statesmen, soldiers, reformers, or civil leaders, tiny Collyer Brothers Park (*map p. 613, D2*) perpetuates the memory of two men remembered, sadly, for mental illness. Between 1909 and 1947 they lived in a brownstone on the site at the intersection of West 128th St and Fifth Ave. For the last couple of decades they went without electricity or gas, becoming increasingly reclusive, and accumulating the more than 15 tons of trash that would eventually kill them both. Homer, the elder, went blind and his brother Langley cared for him. As the brothers grew more fearful of burglars, Langley packed the house with stacks of newspapers, honeycombed the piles with tunnels, and booby-trapped the tunnels with trip wires. On March 20, 1947, perhaps on his daily expedition for food, he set off a trap and was crushed or suffocated beneath the falling newspapers. The police, responding to a tip, used ladders to get into the house because the doors were barricaded. They found Homer's emaciated body on the third floor dressed in a shabby gray bathrobe, but failed to find Langley. His body was discovered almost three weeks later, when the debris had been excavated, close to where his brother's had been. The trash included several grand pianos, an old car chassis, thousands of books, cans and bottles, an old stove, a gas mask, and newspapers that dated back to 1918.

THE SCHOMBURG CENTER FOR RESEARCH IN BLACK CULTURE

Map p. 612, C2. 515 Malcolm X Blvd at West 135th St. Open Mon, Fri, Sat 10–6; Tues–Thur 12–8. Closed Sun. T: 917 275 6975, nypl.org/locations/schomburg.

A branch of the New York Public Library, the Schomburg Center (1969–80, Bond Ryder Assocs; redesigned 2007, Richard Dattner) is one of the world's finest facilities for studying the experience and history of peoples of African descent. The nucleus of the collection was gathered by Arturo Alfonso Schomburg (1874–1938), of Puerto Rican and African heritage, motivated to undertake his life's work by a schoolteacher's remark that blacks had no history and no accomplishments. In 1926 the Carnegie Corporation bought the collection and merged it with the New York Public Library's holdings. Schomburg was curator from 1932 until his death; the center was named for him in 1940. Today there are works by authors of the Harlem Renaissance; a recording of a speech by Marcus Garvey; a first edition of slave Phyllis Wheatley's poetry; paintings by Horace Pippin, Faith Ringgold, Elizabeth Catlett, and Romare Bearden; films of early jazz and tap dance; sheet music; and artifacts, including some from Africa. In the atrium, the ashes of poet, writer, and activist Langston Hughes (1902–67) lie beneath the terrazzo installation *Rivers* (1991). The artwork was inspired by Hughes's poem "The Negro Speaks of Rivers," and created by Houston Conwill, Estella Conwill Majozo, and Joseph DePace. In the reading room are Aaron Douglas's murals (1934), *Aspects of Negro Life.*

The Schomburg Center has previously occupied the former 135th Street Branch of the NY Public Library (1903–5; McKim, Mead & White) at 103 West 135th St (*Lenox Ave and Powell Blvd*) and the **Countee Cullen Branch of the New York Public Library** (*104 West 136th St at Lenox Ave*). Cullen was a poet, editor, and social critic, and an important figure of the Harlem Renaissance. The building (1941; Louis Allen Abramson; restored 1988) stands on the site of the 1913 mansion of Mme C.J. Walker. Born Sarah Breedlove (1869–1917) to former slaves in Louisiana, Walker married young and was widowed young when her husband Charles J. Walker disappeared in Mississippi and was presumed dead. Beginning as a laundress, she built an empire of hair-care products for black women and reaped a fortune. She arrived in Harlem already wealthy and built a townhouse and a country estate on the Hudson near railroad baron Jay Gould's. When she died, she left money to civil rights and religious organizations and a million dollars plus the hair-care empire to her daughter, A'Lelia Walker Robinson. A'Lelia became Harlem's outstanding hostess during the 1920s, and for a time established one floor of the mansion as a café and gathering place for black poets and intellectuals.

THE HARLEM HOSPITAL MURALS

On the block-long, five-story façade of the Patient Pavilion of **Harlem Hospital** (2010; HOK), at 506 Lenox Ave (*West 136th and 137th Sts*), three panels from Vertis Hayes's WPA mural *Pursuit of Happiness* (1937) have been digitized, enlarged, and printed on 429 panes of glass. Part of a series showing African-American history beginning with its roots in Africa, the panels depict modern urban life. Inside are Georgette Seabrooke's *Recreation in Harlem* (1937); Charles Alston's *Modern Medicine* and *Magic in Medicine* (both 1940); and Alfred D. Crimi's *Modern Surgery and Anesthesia* (1936).

THE ABYSSINIAN BAPTIST CHURCH

Map p. 612, C1. 132 West 138th St (Powell and Malcolm X Blvds). Subway: 2, 3, B, C to 135th St. Bus: M2. T: 212 862 7474, abyssinian.org. The church is popular with tourists who want to experience its famous gospel choir; see the website for details.

One of Harlem's most influential religious institutions, the Abyssinian Baptist Church is built of New York bluestone and was designed (1923) by Charles W. Bolton & Son, a Philadelphia firm of architects that specialized in Protestant church design.

The church was founded downtown on Worth St (then called Anthony St) in 1808, when a group of free black parishioners, including some Ethiopian (i.e. Abyssinian) merchants, broke off from the First Baptist Church because they were unwilling to sit in the "slave balcony". Thereafter the congregation moved uptown in stages, following the black centers of population. Pastor Adam Clayton Powell Sr. took over in 1908 and moved his flock to Harlem. In 1920 he instituted a tithing campaign during which two thousand church members pledged ten percent of their income to the building fund. The present church, with its European stained-glass windows and Italian marble pulpit, was dedicated three years later.

ADAM CLAYTON POWELL JR.

Adam Clayton Powell Jr. succeeded his pastor father in 1938. The younger Powell, a charismatic preacher, became the first black city councilman; four years later he was elected to the US House of Representatives, where he sponsored legislation focusing on civil rights and education, the minimum wage, and segregation in the armed forces. He became powerful both in Harlem and in Congress, where he was the first black to chair major committees (education and labor). Always controversial, Powell was censured by the House for financial irregularities in 1967 and stripped of his office, but reinstated by the Supreme Court in 1969.

THE ST. NICHOLAS HISTORIC DISTRICT

Also known as the King Model Houses or **Striver's Row**, the two-square-block area of West 139th and 138th Sts, between Frederick Douglass and Adam Clayton Powell Jr. Boulevards (*map p. 612, C1*) is today known as the St. Nicholas Historic District.

The houses were built in 1891 to offer good design to the middle class. David H. King Jr., the builder of Stanford White's original Madison Square Garden, put up four sets of row houses (146 in all) on speculation, hiring several architects for the project. On the north side of 139th St are White's Italian Renaissance buildings of dark brick with terra cotta trim. On the south side of 139th St and the north side of 138th St are Georgian-inspired rows in yellow brick with terra cotta and limestone trim, by Bruce Price and Clarence Luce. On the south side of 138th St, also Georgian in style, are James Brown Lord's red-brick houses with brownstone trim.

The project succeeded architecturally but not financially; only nine houses sold. After the crash of 1893 the unsold houses reverted to the Equitable Life Assurance

Company, which foreclosed, rented some (to whites) and kept the others. In the 1920s and '30s, the rented houses were sold to black families, some of them successful professionals, most of them working people who had to "strive" to maintain the style of living implied by the architecture. Among the well-to-do buyers were W.C. Handy, often called "Father of the Blues"; bandleader Fletcher Henderson; surgeon Louis T. Wright; and songwriter-pianist Eubie Blake. Among the less affluent, some of whom converted their homes into rooming houses, was one Anna Hames, who in 1925 housed 15 lodgers—railroad workers, elevator operators, dressmakers, and domestic servants.

SPANISH HARLEM

Map pp. 613 and 615. East 96th to 125th Sts, Fifth Ave to the East River.

Eastern Harlem was once Italian Harlem, though few traces of the southern Italian population remain. The area became Spanish Harlem—El Barrio ("the neighborhood")—with immigrants arriving first in the 1920s and *en masse* between 1945 and 1965, when about two-thirds of the nearly one million Puerto Ricans moving to the US settled in New York. While the neighborhood has struggled with poverty and drugs, it has also nurtured Latino culture and became a center of art during the 1970s when El Museo del Barrio and Taller Boricua established roots here. Today the population remains mostly Puerto Rican, though there are other Latinos, a few Italians, and a growing Chinese population around Pleasant Avenue.

On East 104th St at Lexington Ave (*southeast corner*), Hank Prussing's mural *The Spirit of East Harlem* (1978; restored 1998; Manuel Vega) depicts El Barrio back in the 1970s. Prussing, an art student from Maryland, photographed local people and included them in the mural. Today Hope Community Inc., an organization that works for affordable housing, owns the building and the copyright to the mural.

Taller Boricua (*1674 Lexington Ave at East 105th–106th Sts; map p. 615, E1; galleries open Tues–Sat noon–6, Thur 1–7; free; T: 212 831 4333, tallerboricua.org*), a community workshop (the name means "Puerto Rican workshop") and art collective (1970), offers small-scale changing exhibitions in the Julia de Burgos Latino Cultural Center. Julia de Burgos was a Puerto Rican poet, nationalist, and civil rights activist, whose mosaic mural by Manuel Vega (2006) appears (at eye level) at 151 East 106th St and Lexington Ave.

HAMILTON HEIGHTS & SUGAR HILL

Named for Alexander Hamilton, who built a country home here, Hamilton Heights lies on high ground roughly between West 125th and West 155th Sts, from St. Nicholas Ave to the Hudson River. Within its boundaries are the City College of New York, several parks, and an enclave known as Sugar Hill.

CITY COLLEGE OF THE CITY UNIVERSITY OF NEW YORK

Map p. 612, B1. West 138th to West 141st Sts, St. Nicholas Terrace to Amsterdam Ave.
Known as City College or CCNY, the university was long the stepping stone for immigrant children into the middle class. Founded as the Free Academy of New York, the school was experimental in that it offered admission on academic grounds alone, testing "whether the children of the people, the children of the whole people, can be educated," as the college president remarked at the school's opening ceremony. Known sometimes as "the poor man's Harvard," the school long offered free tuition. Among its alumni are George Washington Goethals, who directed construction of the Panama Canal; film director Stanley Kubrick; and ten Nobel laureates.

The original Gothic Revival campus (1902–7), designed by George B. Post, is clad with Manhattan schist dug up during construction of the first subway (the Broadway IRT line, now trains 1, 2, and 3) and decorated with terra cotta. The main building is **Shepard Hall** (*160 Convent Ave at West 138th St*). The **Harlem State Gatehouse Theater** (1884–90; converted in 2006; Ohlhausen Dubois), at West 135th St and Convent Ave, marks the end of the masonry aqueduct that crossed High Bridge.

Convent Avenue itself takes its name from the Convent of the Sacred Heart, a girls' convent and academy, whose campus originally reached from West 126th to West 135th Sts. In 1952 it moved to suburban Westchester County, selling its land to City College.

HAMILTON GRANGE NATIONAL MEMORIAL

Map p. 612, B1. 414 West 141st St (Convent and St. Nicholas Aves). Subway: 1 to 136th St or A,B, C, D to 145th St. Bus: M100 or M101. Open Wed–Sun 9–4.30 except Thanksgiving and Christmas. T: 646 548 2310, nps.gov/hagr.
Hamilton Grange sits at the north end of St. Nicholas Park, rolled to the site (2008) down the steep slope of Convent Ave from its previous location where it was wedged between a church and an apartment building. (It had been relocated to the second site in 1899, because it blocked the north-creeping street grid.) Designed (1801) by John McComb Jr., best known for his work on City Hall, it was one of the finest Federal houses of its day. Hamilton lived there only at the end of his life, which ended tragically (1804) when he was fatally wounded in a duel by Aaron Burr, his political enemy. During this brief residency, however, Hamilton and his family enjoyed a spectacular river-to-river view, rolling fields, and a carefully planned garden.

The house has been consummately restored down to the last egg and dart of the moldings and furnished with reproduction and period furniture. Well-designed exhibits and videos focus on Hamilton's life and career—as a soldier in the Revolution, as the nation's first Secretary of the Treasury, as an opponent of slavery, as an opinionated politician—making evident his many abilities and liabilities.

Hamilton Terrace, a street that runs from St. Nicholas Park to West 144th St, is a protected enclave with fine row houses built for well-to-do families at the end of the 19th century. Today it is the Gold Coast of Hamilton Heights.

OUR LADY OF LOURDES AND *LA GRANDE JATTE IN HARLEM*

Our Lady of Lourdes Church (*map p. 612, B1; 467 West 142nd St*) is an astonishing exercise in early architectural recycling. The Rev. Joseph MacMahon, charged with constructing the church, had ambitions bigger than his budget, but thanks to demolitions elsewhere he was able to piece together this remarkable building (1904; O'Reilly Brothers), re-purposing salvaged windows and beams from the Catholic Orphan Asylum (*50th St and Madison Ave*), the gray and white marble Ruskinian-Gothic façade from the National Academy of Design (1865; *Park Ave South at East 23rd St*), and the apse and parts of the east wall from St. Patrick's Cathedral. The pedestals flanking the main entrance were rescued from department store millionaire A.T. Stewart's mansion (1867; John Kellum) on the northwest corner of 34th St and Fifth Ave.

On the side wall of a building further west along West 142nd St, between Amsterdam Ave and Hamilton Place, **Homage to Seurat: La Grande Jatte in Harlem** (1986; restored 2009, Eva Cockcroft) reproduces Seurat's famous painting of a Sunday afternoon in a Parisian park, except that the people enjoying the park are Harlemites. Using the textured blobs of stucco on the wall, Cockcroft created something akin to Seurat's pointillist dots.

SUGAR HILL

In the 1920s and 1930s, as Harlem increasingly attracted black residents, Sugar Hill (*roughly between West 145th and West 155th Sts, Amsterdam and Edgecome Aves*), with rows of houses originally built for the white upper middle class, became a symbol of "the sweet life." Well-to-do African-Americans moved in—musicians, artists, writers, and professional people. Among them were the muralist Aaron Douglas; W.E.B. DuBois, activist and editor of *Crisis*; Thurgood Marshall, the first African-American Supreme Court Justice; Paul Robeson, singer, actor and civil rights activist; and jazz pianist and bandleader Count Basie.

EATING AND DRINKING IN HARLEM

$$$ The Cecil. Refreshingly different Afro-Asian-American fare, the comfort food of the African diaspora. Menu choices range from Afro-Asian-American oxtail dumplings to grilled Wagyu rib burger, to macaroni-and-cheese casserole. Dinner nightly, weekend brunch. *210 West 118th St (St. Nicholas Ave). T: 212 866 1262, thececilharlem.com. Map p. 612, C3.*

$$–$$$ Red Rooster. World-renowned chef-cookbook-author Marcus Samuelsson's wildly popular first restaurant. The eclectic menu ranges from hot wings with blue cheese dressing to seared bass. Downstairs is **Ginny's Supper Club** with live music; up front is the **Nook** with sweets and sandwiches to go. Lunch weekdays, brunch weekends, dinner nightly. *310 Lenox Ave (125th and 126th Sts). T: 212 792 9001, redroosterharlem.com. Map p. 612, C3.*

$$ Covo Trattoria. In West Harlem (Hamilton Heights), solid Italian pastas and pizzas in a roomy setting, with caring servers, rustic Tuscan decor. Night owls tout the upstairs lounge. Can be noisy; outdoor seating. Lunch and dinner daily, weekend brunch. *701 West 135th St (Hamilton Heights). T: 212 234 9573, covony.com. Map p. 612, A2.*

$$ Dinosaur Bar-B-Que. Under the Riverside Drive near the Hudson. Delicious barbecue in a large, family-friendly restaurant. Can be loud and there are often long lines. Children's menu. Lunch and dinner daily. *700 West 125th St (12th Ave). T: 212 694 1777, dinosaurbarbque.com. Map p. 612, A2.*

$ Amy Ruth's. Classic Harlem menu: fried chicken with waffles or not, ribs, catfish, pork chops, and other specialties. Family friendly. Lunch and dinner Mon; breakfast, lunch and dinner other days; open 24 hrs Fri and Sat. *113 West 116 St (Lenox and 7th Aves). T: 212 280 8779, amyruths.com. Map p. 612, C4.*

STATE STREET
The Seton Shrine dwarfed by newer towers.

Lower Manhattan:
Around Battery Park

*New York owes its historic supremacy among American cities to its closeness to
the sea—and nowhere are these ties more evident than at the southern tip of Manhattan,
where the East and Hudson Rivers converge and empty into New York Bay.*

Manhattan Island's seaward tip—encompassing
South Ferry, Battery Park, and the South Street
corridor—harbored New York's first European
settlers and witnessed its earliest commercial enterprises.
Bounded by the Hudson and East rivers and the towers of the
Financial District, Lower Manhattan, perhaps more than any
other neighborhood, juxtaposes the city's past and its present.

PETER MINUIT PLAZA

Map p. 620, C4. Subway: 1 to South Ferry, 4 or 5 to Bowling Green, R to Whitehall St. Bus:
M1, M6, M15.

Just outside the Staten Island ferry terminal, **Peter Minuit Plaza**, usually crowded
with commuters and tourists, commemorates the Dutch governor who, in 1626,
made the city's most famous real-estate deal, allegedly "purchasing" Manhattan from
Native Americans for 60 guilders, a sum traditionally valued at $24. The white four-
lobed pavilion, with an information booth and café, is officially the New Amsterdam
Plein and Pavilion, a gift of the Netherlands in 2009 on the 400th anniversary of
Henry Hudson's journey. The plaza also contains a flagpole/monument to New York's
first Jewish immigrants, Sephardic refugees fleeing persecution in Brazil. Pirates
seized their Holland-bound ship, only to be overtaken a few days later by a French
frigate whose captain charged the refugees for a voyage to Amsterdam but dropped
them off in New Amsterdam instead. The Jews arrived in September 1654, and despite
the opposition of Peter Stuyvesant, the last Dutch director-general (1647–64) of the

colony of New Netherland, were allowed to remain. Peter Stuyvesant's townhouse (c. 1657) stood near the present intersection of State and Whitehall Sts, renamed Whitehall by the first English governor of New York.

The free **Staten Island Ferry**, which docks at the Whitehall Terminal (2005; Schwartz Architects) offers Staten Islanders a half-hour commute and visitors an unbeatable sightseeing bargain. Adjacent to the terminal, the restored **Battery Maritime Building** (1909; Walker & Morris) at 11 South St, repainted in its original colors, was being redeveloped at the time of writing, with a boutique hotel on top. Constructed of cast iron, rolled steel, and stamped zinc and copper, and elaborately decorated with rivets, latticework, rosettes, and marine designs, the terminal serves the Governors Island Ferry (*see p. 42*).

THE SETON SHRINE

Holding its own in a row of big shiny office buildings, the red-brick **Shrine of Saint Elizabeth Ann Seton** at the Church of Our Lady of the Rosary (*7 State St, facing Battery Park*) commemorates the first American-born saint, canonized in 1975.Originally the James Watson House, it is the sole survivor of an early 19th-century residential row. It was designed in two sections (east wing 1793, west wing 1806) and has been attributed to John McComb Jr. The details of the façade reflect its Georgian and Federal heritage: the marble plaques in the brickwork, the oval windows on the west wall, the splayed lintels above the rectangular windows. Its most distinctive feature, however, is the curved wooden portico that follows the street line, its tapered Ionic columns said to be made from ships' masts. After the Civil War an Irish immigrant, Charlotte Grace O'Brien, inspired the Roman Catholic Church to buy the house and establish the Mission of Our Lady of the Rosary, a haven for immigrant Irish girls.

BATTERY PARK

Map p. 620, C4. Subway: 1 to South Ferry, 4 or 5 to Bowling Green, R to Whitehall. Bus: M5, M15, M20 to South Ferry. For information (Battery Conservancy), T: 212 344 3491, thebattery.org. Restaurant, café, and food kiosks. Battery Gardens, T: 212 809 5508.

Battery Park, at Manhattan's southern tip, offers spectacular views of the harbor, as well as bike paths, an urban farm, a carousel, fountains, and other pleasures for children and adults. The place can be frenetically busy, crowded with tourists and office workers, but it offers pockets of serenity—a labyrinth of walking paths and beautiful gardens designed by Piet Oudolf. The name recalls a row of cannons on the shoreline (present site of State St) that protected New Amsterdam.

MONUMENTS IN THE PARK

NB: At the time of writing, parts of the park were under construction; some monuments were being relocated for better visibility.

BATTERY PARK
Detail of the Netherlands Memorial, commemorating the "sale" of Manhattan to Peter Minuit.

Monuments in the park, most of them donated by ethnic, religious, and professional groups, range from simple plaques and inscribed stones to large sculptures and multi-part memorials elaborated with plinths, steles, and statuary. The honorees include explorers, inventors, soldiers, immigrants, and those who have perished in the Atlantic; their common theme (if any) is the sea.

The flagpole near the park entrance at the foot of Broadway is the **Netherlands Memorial**, given to the city in 1926 by the Dutch; the flagpole base bears a map of Manhattan in Dutch times and a representation of Peter Minuit handing over to the legendary Native American goods worth the fabled $24 in exchange for the island.

On the State St side, beginning at the Netherlands Memorial, are a **marble tablet** (1818) marking the location of the southwest bastion of Fort George (*see p. 51*) as observed by British army engineer Captain John Montresor and American scientist/surveyor David Rittenhouse in 1769; a **pre-Revolutionary cannon** that once protected the fort; a statue of **John Ericsson** (1902, replacing an earlier statue of 1893; Jonathan Scott Hartley), the Swedish-American designer of the ironclad *Monitor*, whose clash with the Confederate frigate *Merrimac* in 1862 marked the beginning of the end for wooden warships; and the **Wireless Operators Memorial** (1815; architects Edward S. Hewitt and Will L. Bottomley), a tribute to radio men who lost their lives at sea in the line of duty. Best known is Jack Phillips, senior operator of the *Titanic*. The bust of **John Ambrose** (reconstruction of the original, 1936; Andrew O'Connor) depicts the Irish immigrant who designed the Ambrose ship channel (1899), which made the harbor safer and more accessible, heralding the arrival of the great luxury liners of subsequent decades.

On the Battery Place side are monuments to the **Salvation Army**, marking its arrival in New York (1880); the **Walloon Settlers** (1924; Henry Bacon), honoring 32 Huguenot families who joined the original Dutch settlers in 1624; **Pieter Caesar Alberti**, the first Italian settler (1635); and **Giovanni da Verrazzano**, the first European known to have sailed into the harbor (1524)—the latter a larger-than-life bronze, donated by the Italian community (1909; Ettore Ximenes), depicting the explorer boldly scanning the distant horizon; the allegorical figure represents Discovery. Also on this side of the park is the **Korean War Veterans Memorial** (1991; Mac Adams), a 15-ft granite stele with the silhouette of an infantryman excised from the center. Toward Battery Place stands Fritz Koenig's *Sphere* (originally dedicated 1971), moved here temporarily in 2002 from the plaza of the World Trade Center, where it had been buried by debris on 9/11. Conceived as a symbol of world peace through trade, today the 45,000-lb brass sculpture honors those who perished in the tragedy. Koenig, who at first did not want his work re-installed, but later oversaw the reconstruction, remarked: "It was a sculpture, now it's a monument... It has its own life—different from the one I gave to it."

CASTLE CLINTON
Open every day except Christmas, 7:45–5. Ticket booth for Statue of Liberty cruises. Guided tours 10am, noon, 2pm. T: 212 344 7220, nps.gov/cacl.
The squat red sandstone walls of Castle Clinton were raised (1808–11) to protect the city against naval invasion. Beyond the main gate, the passageway opens into a circular parade field.

Nearby stands Luis Sanguino's bronze *The Immigrants* (1973, dedicated 1983), a sculptural group paying homage to the eight million who passed through Castle Clinton during its 35 years as the Immigrant Depot Station. The 3.75-acre wooded Bosque garden features a circular stone fountain with illuminated jets of water.

THE ESPLANADE
Along the Esplanade the **Gardens of Remembrance**, planted with native grasses and flowers, honor those touched by September 11, 2001. The decorative railing of the sea wall, "The River That Runs Both Ways," visually translates the Native American name describing the Hudson's estuarial nature. Artist Wopo Holup's 37 cast-iron panels (2000), divided by wavy bronze bands representing the river, evoke the history of the Battery: the images above the water-line suggest human history, while those below refer to the ecological story of the river from the glacial era to the present.

South of Castle Clinton along the Esplanade, the great bronze eagle of the **East Coast War Memorial** (1961; Albino Manca) faces out to sea, its eight marble pylons bearing the names of more than 4,000 Americans who died in Atlantic coastal waters during World War II.

At the north end of the Esplanade, dramatically sited in the water, the **American Merchant Mariners' Memorial** (1991; Marisol Escobar) depicts three men on a sinking lifeboat, a fourth in the water. The scene was reconstructed from a photograph taken by a German sailor whose U-boat torpedoed the SS *Muskogee* in 1942, leaving the men to drown. The watery setting heightens the work's impact as the figure of the drowning man alternately emerges from and recedes into the river with the ebb and flow of the tide.

Jutting 300ft into the river, Pier A (1884–6) is the oldest city pier in the Hudson. The pier house has done turns as headquarters for the Harbor Police, the Department of Docks (later renamed the Department of Marine and Aviation), and the Marine Division of the fire department. The tower, originally a lookout, holds a clock donated (1919) by Daniel Gray Reid, a financier and industrialist who rose from Midwestern messenger boy to become the "tin plate king" and one of Wall Street's "big insiders." The clock, which tells time in ships' bells, honors servicemen who gave their lives in World War I. After a $42-million redevelopment and a delay caused by Hurricane Sandy, the building re-opened (2014) as **Pier A Harbor House**, with a bar, restaurant, and event space.

CASTLE CLINTON: TWO CENTURIES OF ADAPTIVE RE-USE

Before the days of landfill, the original fort, the Southwest Battery, sat on an island connected to the mainland by a wooden causeway with a drawbridge. In the early years of the 19th century, as rising hostilities increased the likelihood of another war with England, New York constructed four harbor forts: Fort Wood on Bedloe's (now Liberty) Island, Fort Gibson on Ellis Island, Castle Williams on Governors Island, and the Southwest Battery here.

Built from plans by John McComb Jr., one of New York's earliest native architects, the fort's seaward walls were pierced by a row of 28 black 32-pounders, which commanded the harbor shore to shore; the landward walls housed powder magazines and officers' quarters. The fort was untested during the War of 1812 and was renamed (1817) Castle Clinton to honor DeWitt Clinton, mayor of the city and later state governor. In 1824 it opened as Castle Garden, a center for entertainments (balloon ascents, fireworks), scientific demonstrations (Samuel F.B. Morse's "wireless telegraph"), political speeches (Daniel Webster, Henry Clay), and receptions for heroes (the Marquis de Lafayette, Andrew Jackson). Roofed over in 1845, Castle Garden attracted more serious cultural fare, reaching its apogee on September 11, 1850, when P.T. Barnum staged the American début of Jenny Lind, the "Swedish Nightingale," before a sellout crowd of over 6,000.

After more than a quarter of a century, Castle Garden closed its doors to theatergoers and reopened them (1855) to immigrants streaming in from abroad. Because landfill had joined Castle Garden to Manhattan, immigration officials fenced off the depot to protect the bewildered new arrivals from swindlers who lurked nearby. In 1890 the Immigration Service became a function of the federal government and two years later Ellis Island opened.

In 1896 Castle Garden was recast as the New York Aquarium, a popular attraction that lasted until 1941 when Robert Moses, Commissioner of Parks and head of the Triborough Bridge Authority, shut it down. Seeking revenge for the defeat of his proposed bridge to Brooklyn, whose ramps and overhead roadways would have destroyed Battery Park, Moses determined to raze the fort. Activists protested and in 1946 Congress declared Castle Clinton a National Monument.

THE CUSTOM HOUSE
& MUSEUM OF THE AMERICAN INDIAN

The former Alexander Hamilton Custom House (*map p. 620, C4*) stands on the probable site of New York's first permanent settlement. Today it houses a Federal Bankruptcy Court and a branch of the National Museum of the American Indian.

THE CUSTOM HOUSE

In 1892 the US Treasury announced an architectural competition for a custom house—an important building since, before the institution of the income tax, customs revenue contributed significantly to the federal budget. Architect Cass Gilbert won with a plan that symbolized the commercial greatness of the nation and of the city.

The building (1907) is a triumph of Beaux-Arts exuberance, the façade adorned with emblems of commerce and the sea. In the window arches are heads of the eight "races" of mankind. Above the cornice statues representing twelve great commercial nations of history stare down on Broadway, while the head of Mercury, Roman god of commerce, crowns the capital of each of the 44 Corinthian columns encircling the building. Gilbert commissioned Daniel Chester French, best known for his statue of Abraham Lincoln in the Lincoln Memorial (Washington, D.C.), to design heroic lime-stone statues of the four continents (left to right): Asia, America, Europe, and Africa. The sculptures reflect early 20th-century cultural attitudes: Asia and Africa, meditative and somnolent at the periphery; Europe, robed in a Grecian gown, enthroned among the achievements of the past; America, with a sheaf of maize on her lap, looking dynamically forward while Labor turns the wheel of progress on her right, and on her left a Native American kneels, eyes downcast.

The main entrance leads into a hallway finished in opulent marbles. In the center of the main floor is the great rotunda (135ft by 85ft by 48ft high). The ceiling, constructed of 140 tons of tile and plaster (no steel), was engineered by Spanish architect Rafael Guastavino. Below the dome, frescoes (1937) by Reginald Marsh, a painter who specialized in New York City life, mostly low but sometimes high, depict early explorers, an ocean liner entering New York harbor, and movie star Greta Garbo surrounded by the press. The murals were financed by the Treasury Relief Art Project, which supported artists with government commissions during the Depression.

NATIONAL MUSEUM OF THE AMERICAN INDIAN (HEYE CENTER)

1 Bowling Green (Broadway). Subway: 2 or 3 to Wall St, 4 or 5 to Bowling Green, 1 to Rector St or South Ferry, R to Whitehall St. Bus: M5, M15, M20. Open daily 10–5, Thur until 8; closed Dec 25. Free. Tours. Gift shop. T: 212 514 3700, nmai.si.edu.

In 1994 the Custom House opened as the George Gustav Heye Center, a branch of the Smithsonian's larger National Museum of the American Indian in Washington, D.C. George Gustav Heye (1874–1957), the son of a wealthy German oil baron, gathered the core collection and previously displayed it as the Museum of the American Indian (opened 1922) on Audubon Terrace.

On view are Native American artifacts and images, both historic and contemporary, from a collection (825,000 objects and more than 325,000 photographs) ranging geographically from the Arctic to Tierra del Fuego, and chronologically from prehistoric times to the present. Highlights include feathered headdresses and buffalo-hide robes from the Plains Indians; masks and ceremonial wood carvings from the Northwest Coast tribes; feather-work from the Amazon; and Peruvian and Navajo fabrics. The ongoing exhibit "Infinity of Nations: Art and History in the Collections of the National Museum of the American Indian" is supplemented with changing displays, some of which showcase the work of contemporary Native Americans; music and dance performances; films, and symposia that explore the native cultures of the Americas.

NEW AMSTERDAM'S FIRST FORT

In 1624 the Dutch ship *Nieuw Nederlandt* deposited eight men on what is now Governors Island, and sailed up the Hudson to settle others at the present site of Albany. The men, sponsored by the Dutch West India Company, and the families who followed them, moved to the southern shore of Manhattan, where they built shelters and a fort. Fort Amsterdam (1626), approximately where the Custom House stands today, consisted of a crude blockhouse protected by a cedar palisade. As the town alternately fell under the jurisdiction of the Dutch, the British, the Dutch again, and the British once more, the fort was strengthened and serially renamed. The final version, called Fort George after the reigning British monarch, remained until after the Revolution, when it was torn down (in 1789) to make way for Government House, the intended residence for the new nation's president.

LOWER BROADWAY

The small fenced plot of lawn just north of the Custom House façade is **Bowling Green Park**, the city's first park. During the Dutch colonial period, this open place at the south end of de Heere Wegh ("the Gentleman's Street," now Broadway) hosted a cattle market; hence the name of Marketfield St, a block east. Later the area became a parade ground and still later a bowling green, leased in 1733 for the fee of one peppercorn per year. The Bowling Green Fence (1771), built to keep the park from collecting "all the filth and dirt in the neighborhood," failed to protect a gilded lead equestrian statue of George III, which was torn down on July 9, 1776 by a crowd of patriots incited by a reading of the Declaration of Independence. The original fence survived, though the statue did not: it was carted off to Connecticut and melted down for ammunition. Just beyond the park, a flagpole commemorates the evacuation of the British troops on November 25, 1783 (*see overleaf*). Though Lower Broadway no longer harbors the offices of the great transatlantic steamship lines, it still maintains fragile ties to its maritime past. The façade of **No. 1 Broadway** (1884), once the United States Lines Building (on the west side of Bowling Green), is decorated with tridents, shells, and fish, and the doorways are labeled for first- and cabin-class passengers.

EVACUATION DAY

New York, a vital port city, was a crucial battleground during the Revolutionary War. In September 1776, George Washington and his men retreated from Manhattan and fled south along the New Jersey Coast. Under the seven years of British occupation, life in New York was harsh. On November 25, 1783, Washington made his triumphal return to Manhattan with state governor George Clinton, who declared a public holiday— Evacuation Day—and repaired to nearby Fraunces Tavern to celebrate. As a parting defiant gesture, the British nailed a Union Jack to the flagpole at Fort George in Battery Park and greased the pole. A sailor, John Van Arsdale, climbed the pole using cleats and replaced the flag with the Stars and Stripes. For many years, the city commemorated Evacuation Day with a ceremony at Battery Park, in which one of Van Arsdale's descendants raised the flag (without having to climb a greased pole).

Behind the Renaissance Revival façade of the **former Cunard Building** at 25 Broadway (1921; Benjamin Wistar Morris) lies one of the city's great interiors (now an event space). With its ornate domed ceiling, wall paintings of steamship routes, and frescoes of historic ships, it illustrates the bygone romance of steamship travel in a manner suitable to the company that launched the *Queen Mary* and *Queen Elizabeth*.

On an island near 25 Broadway, Arturo Di Modica's bronze ***Charging Bull*** (1989) symbolizes the city's financial district while providing myriads of tourists with photo ops. Di Modica created the bull at his own expense, trucked it at night to the front of the New York Stock Exchange, and left it there on December 15, 1989. The Stock Exchange had it hauled away, but the Department of Parks and Recreation, responding to public protest, relocated it here. In 2010 guerilla needlewoman Agata Olek dressed the bull in a crocheted pink and purple outfit, which the authorities removed two hours later.

Across the street at 26 Broadway is the **former Standard Oil Building** (1922; Carrère & Hastings). The façade curves to follow Broadway but the tower, best seen from Battery Park, is aligned with the north–south street grid, a concession to the uptown skyline. Decorated with huge Ionic columns at its base and crown, it epitomizes the Neoclassical skyscraper, New York's special contribution to early 20th-century urban architecture. On top, a structure resembling an oil lamp conceals a chimney. Reliefs of oil lamps flank the main entrance, and the names of former company executives, including John D. Rockefeller, adorn the marble walls of the vestibule.

Near the intersection of State St, Bowling Green, and Battery Pl., just outside the fence of Battery Park, the **Battery Park Control House** (1904–5) is the original entrance to the Bowling Green station of the city's first subway, designed by Heins & LaFarge, better known for their work on the Cathedral of St. John the Divine.

MANHATTAN'S OLDEST STREETS

The curved and irregular streets south of Wall Street, landmarked in 1983 when part of Stone Street was demapped, preserve the roads of colonial New Amsterdam and New York, dictated by the shoreline, Native American pathways, and the necessities of geography and economics. **Pearl Street** was named for the opalescent shells that dotted its beaches when it stood at the water's edge. Herman Melville (1819–91), author of *Moby-Dick*, was born at 6 Pearl St, now the site of the 42-story office building 17 State St, a wedge-shaped tower with a curved wall of mirrored glass. **Stone Street**, probably the city's first paved road, was formerly Brouwers Straet, named for its breweries. At noon and night, it is the center of a busy social scene, with tables set up in the alley, drawing local professionals. During the Dutch colonial period **Broad Street** was a canal (de Heere Gracht, "the Gentleman's Canal") for drainage and shipping. It became polluted and the British filled it about 100 years before the Revolution, but the street's extra width remains as evidence of the former waterway (at **Bridge Street**, the city's first bridge crossed it). Further north, the old streets, which approximate the street plan of New Amsterdam, have fared better. This district, built with wood during the 17th and early 18th centuries, burned "to an indistinguishable mass of ruins" during the Great Fire of 1835 (*see p. 55*), according to a contemporary observer. Within a year, brick Greek Revival buildings, with ground-floor shops and warehouses above, rose from the rubble of this then-vital waterfront neighborhood. Many survive on Stone, South William, and Pearl Sts, some with picturesque early 20th-century alterations in a mishmash of styles. Details include granite lintels and star-shaped tie-rod plates, as well as later whimsical neo-Dutch, neo-Tudor, and neo-Gothic façades.

The small brick plaza between Water St and South St is **Vietnam Veterans Plaza**, its greenish glass-brick wall (1985; William Britt Fellows and Peter Wormser), 70ft long and 14ft high, etched with words written home by American soldiers in Vietnam. Once called Jeannette Park, after a ship that took part in the tragic polar expedition of 1879–81, the plaza reflects the shape of Coenties Slip. As the coastline was pushed out by landfill, breakwaters were built and the East River slips between the wharves were dredged to provide adequate draft. Eventually they were filled in to create new land, but the old names and street configurations remain.

FRAUNCES TAVERN MUSEUM

Map p. 620, C4. 54 Pearl St (Broad St), 2nd floor. Subway: R to Whitehall St–South Ferry, 4 or 5 to Bowling Green, 1 to South Ferry, J or Z to Broad St. Bus: M5, M15, M20. Open Mon–Sun 12–5. Closed New Year's Day, Thanksgiving, and Christmas. Admission charge. Tours. T: 212 425 1778, frauncestavernmuseum.org.

Fraunces Tavern is the centerpiece of one of the few full blocks of 18th- and early 19th-century buildings to have escaped both the Great Fire of 1835 (*see p. 55*) and successive downtown building booms. The present Colonial Revival tavern (1907; William Mersereau) conjecturally reconstructs a mansion built (c. 1719) for Stephen (or Étienne) De Lancey and is probably not historically accurate.

Above the ground floor restaurant the Fraunces Tavern Museum offers two period rooms and changing historical exhibits that focus on New York in the 18th century. George Washington and Governor George Clinton celebrated Evacuation Day in the tavern, an event commemorated in the Clinton Room, notable for its historic hand-printed wallpaper. Washington bade farewell to his troops on December 4, 1783 in the Long Room, now furnished as a late 18th-century tavern.

TRACES OF OLD NEW YORK

Occupying the block between Pearl and South William Sts and Coenties Alley is the austere brown stone **No. 85 Broad Street** (1983; Skidmore, Owings & Merrill). Its 30 stories were made possible by the purchase of the air rights from the small-scale Fraunces Tavern block across the street. Near the corner of Coenties Alley and Pearl St (displayed under the arcade below sidewalk level) are parts of walls unearthed during the city's first archaeological dig (1979–80), including those of the Dutch colonial **Stadt Huys** or City Hall. The *Stadt Huys* began as a waterside tavern in about 1641 and became the city hall when New Amsterdam was granted its municipal charter in 1653. It served not only as a meeting place, but as a jail, debtors' prison, courthouse, and public warehouse. A windmill built by the Dutch in 1626 once stood approximately at the intersection of Mill Lane and South William St (formerly Mill St). During the 1680s it was rented by the city's first Jewish congregation, **Shearith Israel**, many of whose members were descendants of the refugees from Brazil who had arrived in 1654 (*see p. 45*). In 1729 they bought land south of the mill for 100 pounds sterling plus a loaf of sugar and a pound of tea, and built their first synagogue (site of 26 South William St). Two millstones can be seen at Shearith Israel's current synagogue on Central Park West.

Delmonico's Restaurant (1891) at 56 Beaver St, a decorative pile of brownstone, terra cotta, and orange iron-spot brick, is the most recent incarnation of one of New York's historic eateries. The columns flanking the door, salvaged from an earlier Delmonico's, were (mistakenly) believed to have been excavated at Pompeii. In the 19th century its chef is said to have invented Baked Alaska and Lobster Newburg. Today it is a high-end steakhouse; you can still get Baked Alaska and Lobster Newburg.

HANOVER SQUARE

Hanover Square—which is actually a triangle bounded by Pearl St, Stone St, and a street also called Hanover Square—was once a public common at the center of a fine residential district. Its most notorious early resident was sea captain William Kidd, who was hanged in England in 1701 for piracy. At the end of the 17th century the area became the city's first Printing House Square, home of New York's first newspaper (1725), the *New-York Gazette*, published weekly by William Bradford. At 1 Hanover Square is **India House** (1851–4), one of the city's finest surviving Italianate brown-stones. Originally built for the Hanover Bank, this palazzo exemplified a new direction in New York commercial architecture as grander buildings based on European models began to replace modest brick counting-houses. The New York Cotton Exchange (1870–86) and the Haitian consulate later occupied the building, but in 1914 it became India House, a social center for shipping executives and merchants involved in international commerce. In the middle of the square, the **Queen Elizabeth II September 11 Garden** (*queenelizabethgarden.org*) commemorates the 67 British subjects who died on 9/11. The abstract map of the counties of England in the paving stones is by Simon Verity, who also worked on the stone carving at the Cathedral of St. John the Divine in Morningside Heights.

THE GREAT FIRE OF 1835

Early New York, constructed mostly of wood, suffered many fires. One of the worst, in 1835, was at Hanover Square. On the night of December 17, a gas explosion ignited stockpiles of dry goods and chemicals; whipped by winds, the fire raged out of control. Sub-zero temperatures froze the fire hoses, and by noon the square had been incinerated. When the blaze finally burnt itself out, it had destroyed 20 acres and more than 650 buildings, including all the Dutch colonial structures in downtown New York.

The "fortified" Italianate Renaissance palazzo in the middle of **Old Slip** (*map p. 620, C4*) originated as the **First Precinct Police Station** (1909–11), designed by architects William Howland Hunt and Richard Howland Hunt, sons of the more famous Richard Morris Hunt. The Hunts, father and sons, were known for designing swank residences, but this building, reminiscent of Florence's Palazzo Medici Riccardi, manages to suggest grandeur despite its diminutive size. The New York City Police Museum was located here from 2002 until Hurricane Sandy flooded the building in 2012. (*At the time of writing the museum was closed; for information, see nycpm.org.*)

THE SOUTH STREET SEAPORT

Map p. 621, D3. Subway: 2, 3, 4, 5, A, C, J, or Z to Fulton St. Bus: M15 to Fulton St. New York Water Taxi to seaport.

This gathering of modest Federal and Greek Revival commercial buildings around Fulton St and the East River piers evokes South Street's glory days as a center of world trade. The masts and spars of the *Wavertree* still rise above the historic buildings and the streets are still cobblestone; but today the seaport attracts shoppers, tourists, and Wall Streeters on lunch break to its eateries, bars, and shopping opportunities. In the summer people bask in the sun on the Fulton St mall; in the winter an ice rink (with a tree at Christmas) attracts skaters of all levels. The TKTS booth (*see p. 577*) at the corner of John and Front Sts is a handy alternative to the one in Times Square. The South Street Seaport Museum maintains galleries on Water St and ships on the piers.

At the corner of Fulton and Water Sts is the **Titanic Memorial Lighthouse** (1913; moved here 1976). It commemorates the sinking of the liner in 1912, with a plaque on the base inscribed with the ship's longitude and latitude at the moment she struck the fatal iceberg. Originally surmounting the long-gone Seamen's Church Institute (*South St at Coenties Slip*), the lighthouse was visible by night for miles; during the day a mechanical ball dropped on the stroke of twelve, signaling noon to the ships in the harbor.

THE SOUTH STREET SEAPORT MUSEUM

Visitor Center at 12 Fulton St open Thur–Sat 12–7. Galleries on Water St open 7 days, 11–7. Street of Ships on Pier 16 open Thur–Sat, noon–dusk. Galleries at 12 Fulton St are currently open for research by appointment only. Restaurants and cafés nearby. T: 212 748 8600, southstseaport.org.

Schermerhorn Row (1812), on the south side of Fulton St between South and Water Sts, is the seaport's architectural centerpiece, a treasured block of Georgian-Federal buildings. In 1793 Peter Schermerhorn, a ship chandler, bought water lots, filled them in, and constructed twelve red-brick buildings with counting houses and warehouse space; the storefronts came later. The building on the corner of South St (*2 Fulton St*) became a hotel, first McKinley's, later the Fulton Ferry Hotel, catering to steamboat travelers, the mansard roof added in 1868. Joseph Mitchell immortalized it in 1952 in "Up in the Old Hotel," published in *The New Yorker*. Around the corner at 92 South St stood Sloppie Louie's, founded in 1930 by Louis Morino, an immigrant from Genoa. Morino died in 1976; the restaurant, a favorite with seamen and other locals, lasted until 1998.

SOUTH STREET: A WORLD TRADE CENTER

Before the Civil War, the city's maritime activity focused on the East River, less affected than the Hudson by ice, flooding, and the prevailing westerlies. Fulton St became a major thoroughfare to the waterfront and to the Fulton Ferry to Brooklyn (1814), and a market developed around the ferry landing. In 1822 the Fulton Fish Market, long the most important wholesale seafood distribution point on the eastern seaboard, settled on the north side of Fulton St. The opening of the Erie Canal (1825) flooded New York with Midwestern industrial and farm products, and 500 new shipping firms sprang up around South St to handle the new business. By the 1840s trade to California and China was burgeoning, spearheaded by the firm of A.A. Low on Burling Slip (now John St). But after 1880, when steamships superseded the great sailing vessels and trade moved to the Hudson's deep-water docks, South St declined.

After a century of neglect, preservationists stepped in, chartering the South Street Seaport Museum (1967) and acquiring historic buildings and ships. In the mid-1970s, under financial pressures, the museum entered an uneasy alliance with the City; a developer built a "festival market place" on Pier 17. In 1983 much of the restoration opened, including a restored Schermerhorn Row, but commercial development stalled—along with the developer's promise to support the museum. Today the fragile equilibrium between preservation and profit seems to be tilting toward the latter.

THE SHIPS, PIER 16

You can take a self-guided tour around two ships at Pier 16. The *Ambrose Lightship* (1908), officially *US Lightship LV-87*, marked the entrance to the deep-water Ambrose

Channel until 1932 when a tower and beacon replaced her. The *Peking* (1911), a four-master from Hamburg, was one of the last commercial sailing vessels. The *Wavertree* (1885), an English square-rigged iron-hulled ship, is not currently open to visitors.

WATER LOTS AND LANDFILL

To raise money, the City sold water lots—land between the extremes of high and low tide and therefore underwater half the time—to merchants with the provision that they fill and build on them. The owners constructed wooden cribbing, usually timber but sometimes including the hulls of derelict ships, and dumped cartloads of dirt and refuse into them—often old bottles, and broken crockery—pushing the shoreline of Lower Manhattan riverward by several blocks. Landfill has yielded important archaeological discoveries, including an 18th-century merchant ship on Water Street in 1982. In 2010 the remains of an 18th-century oak ship were unearthed at the World Trade Center site.

WATER STREET, BEEKMAN STREET, AND PECK SLIP

The three Greek Revival warehouses (1835–6) at **207–11 Water St** are among the finest remaining in New York city, their granite steps, lintels, piers, and cornices all still intact. At 211 Water St, the recreated 19th-century printing shop of **Bowne & Co. Stationers** turns out business cards and stationery instead of the broadsides and handbills of the past.

One of the most charming houses in the district is **No. 142 Beekman St** (1885; George B. Post), on the corner of Front St, built for a Schermerhorn descendant and originally occupied by a fish dealer. The marine motifs on the façade—starfish on the tie-rod ends, cockleshells on the cornice, and fish wriggling on the terra cotta keystones—identify his trade. **146–8 Beekman St** (1885; George B. Post) still sports a faded advertisement for "Fresh, Salt and Smoked Fish" and "Myers Brand Finnan Haddie."

The **Captain Joseph Rose House and Shop** (*273 Water St near Peck Slip and Dover St*), one of the oldest buildings in Manhattan (either 1773 or 1781), was built for Joseph Rose, an importer of mahogany and later a distiller. The house became notorious a century later when Christopher Keyburn, aka Kit Burns, ran Sportsmen's Hall there. One of the sports in question was rat baiting, conducted in a first-floor amphitheater with purses beginning at $125; a good terrier could finish off a hundred rats in an hour and three quarters. Burns died in 1870; according to his obituary in the *New York Times*, his "tastefully attired" remains were conveyed to the cemetery by a hearse drawn by six white horses.

A *trompe l'oeil* mural (1978) by Richard Haas fills the windowless south-facing wall of an electrical substation at **Peck Slip** and Front St with an imaginary 19th-century building façade and a vista of Brooklyn Bridge.

For Eating and Drinking in Lower Manhattan, see p. 73.

Upper Manhattan

Upper Manhattan, largely unknown to visitors except for The Cloisters, has some of the city's best scenery, two of its oldest houses, and the remarkable Hispanic Society of America on Audubon Terrace. The area from 155th St to Dyckman St is known as Washington Heights; north of that is Inwood.

Situated on two spines of Manhattan schist, Washington Heights (*map p. 609*) was fiercely—but futilely—defended during the Revolutionary War. Later a hinterland where the wealthy built estates, John James Audubon among the landowners, it was developed in the early 20th century when the subway arrived. Thereafter it attracted successive waves of immigrants, with one ethnic group quickly replacing another. The Irish came in the early years of the 20th century, followed by European Jews escaping the Nazis in the 1930s and '40s, when the Heights were known as "Frankfurt on the Hudson." Along with the Jews came well-to-do African Americans, migrating uptown from Harlem, among them Count Basie and other successful musicians. During the next two decades, a large population of Greeks arrived, and the Heights became "the Astoria of Manhattan," after the Greek enclave in Queens (*see p. 521*). At the same time Cubans and Puerto Ricans were beginning to come, only to be superseded in the 1980s and '90s by Dominicans, who are now being replaced by more affluent whites. For the past three decades Washington Heights has had the largest Dominican community outside the Dominican Republic.

THE CHURCH OF THE INTERCESSION
AND TRINITY CEMETERY

550 West 155th St (Broadway). Subway: 1 to 157th St; C to 155th St. Bus: M4, M5. Church open during services, Thurs 12pm, Sun 10am, and by appointment. T: 212 283 6200, intercessionnyc.org. Cemetery open 9–4:30 daily; entrance to the western parcel on 155th St near Riverside Drive; entrance to the eastern parcel from 155th St east of Broadway.

The Church of the Intercession (1911–14; Cram, Goodhue & Ferguson), formerly a chapel of Trinity Parish, recalls the neighborhood's rural past; its bell-tower, cloister, parish house, and vicarage evoke the Gothic Revival ideal of the country church.

Trinity Cemetery, established in 1842 to relieve the near-full churchyard at Trinity Church Wall St, is Manhattan's last remaining active cemetery. The section around the church includes the burial plot of John James Audubon (1785–1851), who after years of struggle achieved fame and financial security with *The Birds of America* (*see p. 412*) His gravestone, a tall brown Celtic cross with reliefs of animals and birds, rests on a pedestal whose sculpted rifles and powder horn, palette and paintbrushes summarize his life's work. In the southeast corner (*near Amsterdam Ave and 153rd St*) lies Edward I. Koch, mayor 1978–89. Koch, who was Jewish, chose the site five years before his death, telling the press, "I don't want to leave Manhattan, even when I'm gone. This is my home."

The western parcel between Broadway and Riverside Drive, West 153rd and West 155th Sts, slopes toward the Hudson River suggesting landscape before developers exercised their leveling powers over northern Manhattan. Here lies Clement Clarke Moore, alleged writer of "'Twas the night before Christmas..." (*lower slope, near the Riverside Drive retaining wall and 155th St*). Eliza Bowen Jumel (*see p. 454*) lies near a pathway closer to the center of the western section.

AUDUBON TERRACE

Subway: 1 to 157th St; C to 155th St. Bus: M4 or M5 to 155th St.

Between West 155th and West 156th Sts along the west side of Broadway stand the imposing classical buildings of Audubon Terrace, home of the Hispanic Society of America and the American Academy of Arts and Letters.

HISTORY OF AUDUBON TERRACE

Archer Milton Huntington (1870–1955), stepson and heir of railroad builder Collis P. Huntington, gravitated to poetry, archaeology, and scholarship, and is remembered more for the money he gave away than for the money he made. Huntington intended to build an American acropolis on Washington Heights, and in 1904, thinking that Manhattan's cultural center would continue moving uptown, he started buying up the former estate of ornithologist-painter John James Audubon. Huntington hired architects including his cousin, Charles Pratt Huntington, to build a quadrangle of buildings (1908–30) for cultural institutions. At one time the Terrace included the American Geographical Society, the American Numismatic Society, and the Museum of the American Indian, which have moved elsewhere. The newest institution is Boricua College, whose curriculum is oriented toward its Latino and Puerto Rican student body.

Statues by Anna Hyatt Huntington, already well known as a sculptor when she married Archer Huntington, dominate the plaza. The largest, a bronze equestrian statue of *El Cid Campeador* (1927), celebrates the legendary medieval hero who defended Spain against the Moors. She also contributed several animal groups and the equestrian reliefs *Don Quixote* (1942) and *Boabdil* (1944), the last Muslim ruler of Granada; the inscriptions beneath them are taken from her husband's poetry.

THE HISPANIC SOCIETY OF AMERICA

Audubon Terrace, 613 West 155th St (Broadway). Open Tues–Sat 10–4:30, Sun 1–4. Free. Tours 2pm Sat. T: 212 926 2234, hispanicsociety.org.

For anyone interested in Spanish painting, decorative arts, and architecture, the Hispanic Society is a hidden treasure, its remarkable collection gathered mainly by Archer Milton Huntington, whose fascination with Spanish and Portuguese culture dated from a youthful visit to Spain.

The **Main Court**, two stories high, painted dark burgundy and illuminated by skylights, its terra cotta archways ornately worked in Spanish Renaissance style, is one of the city's most remarkable interiors. On the ground level are decorative arts, tomb effigies, and several polychrome terra cotta groups by Luisa Roldán (1652–1702), Spain's first recorded female sculptor. Pedro de Mena's *Bust of St. Asisclus* (c. 1680) shows the martyred patron saint of Cordoba as a handsome young man, his harried expression and the bloody line encircling his neck foreshadowing his martyrdom. In the ground-floor **Sorolla Room**, some 230 linear feet of murals by Joaquín Sorolla y Bastida depict light-filled street scenes, festivals, church processions, bullfighters and fishermen. Archer Huntington commissioned the set, entitled *Vision of Spain* (1912–19), for this room; when it traveled to Spain in 2009, two million people flocked to see it.

Upstairs are examples of Spanish painting from the Middle Ages to the 20th century, including works from the Spanish Golden Age (1550–1700). Here are paintings by El Greco (*St. Jerome*; c. 1600) and Velázquez; and Goya's *The Duchess of Alba* (1797), shown dressed as a Spanish *maja*, the most famous work in the collection. Also on view are works by Francisco de Zurbarán, Jusepe de Ribera, and Bartolomé Esteban Murillo. Two rooms devoted to ceramics include examples of Hispano-Moresque lusterware, a specifically Spanish style that combines Islamic and Western traditions.

THE AMERICAN ACADEMY OF ARTS AND LETTERS

In Audubon Terrace. Gallery entrance from Audubon Terrace between West 155 and West 156 Sts. Open only during exhibitions, mid-March to mid-April, and mid-May to mid-June, Thur–Sun 1–4. T: 212 368 5900, artsandletters.org.

The honorary organization for 250 of the nation's most eminent artists, writers, architects, and musicians is housed in two of Huntington's Beaux-Arts buildings, connected (2009; James Vincent Czajka) by a glass link (the Annex used to be the home of the American Numismatic Society). The membership roster includes Chuck Close, Tony Kushner, John McPhee, Marilynne Robinson, and Richard Serra.

ALSO IN WASHINGTON HEIGHTS

THE MORRIS-JUMEL MANSION

Map p. 609, B2. 65 Jumel Terrace (in Roger Morris Park, West 160th–West 162nd Sts, near Edgecombe Ave). Subway: C to 160th St. Bus: M2, M3, M101. Open Tues–Sun 10–4. Admission charge. Shop. T: 212 923 8008, morrisjumel.org.

Though George Washington is reputed to have slept in many places, he really did sleep in this pre-Revolutionary Georgian mansion (1765; remodeled 1810), the oldest house in Manhattan. Built as the summer retreat of Roger Morris, a retired British colonel, and his American wife Mary Philipse, the house once stood on 130 acres, with river-to-river views. It still retains its original Georgian hipped roof, wooden corner quoins, and wide-board façade, as well as the unusual two-story portico and octagonal room. George Washington may have used the office on the second floor.

During his northward retreat through Manhattan, Washington used the house as his headquarters (September 14–October 21, 1776), evacuating as his army was forced off the island. Morris remained loyal to the king, and after the war the house was confiscated and sold, with the Morrises returning to England. Stephen Jumel, a wealthy French wine merchant, later bought it for his wife, Eliza Bowen Jumel. On view are rooms with period furnishings, some of them Jumel family pieces, including a mahogany sleigh bed that Mme Jumel asserted had belonged to Napoleon.

West of Jumel Terrace, between West 160th and West 162nd Sts is **Sylvan Terrace**, once the mansion's carriage drive. Two rows of modest wooden houses, built (c. 1882) for workers, face one another across this quiet street.

ELIZA JUMEL

What is known of Eliza Bowen Jumel is hazy and full of contradictions, but sources agree on her beauty and forceful personality. Her fortunes soared when she married (1804) Stephen Jumel, a wealthy French wine merchant, though wagging tongues said that Eliza, already Jumel's mistress, feigned a deathbed crisis to lure him into wedlock. In 1810 the Jumels bought the house and restored it, adding the portico and enlarging the doorway in the Federal style.

Mme Jumel had an imperious tongue and boundless social ambition, which remained unfulfilled in New York because of her dubious past. In 1815 the Jumels went to Paris, where they did find acceptance; she became an outspoken Bonapartiste, unwise in the first years after Napoleon's exile, and was asked to leave France. She brought back Empire furniture, an extensive wardrobe, and Francophilic tastes.

In 1832 Jumel died after a carriage (or wagon) accident. It was whispered that Eliza let him bleed to death. A year later, now one of the city's richest women, she married 77-year-old Aaron Burr. He was apparently fortune hunting, and the marriage was stormy and brief; Burr only lived in the house for about a month before they separated. A divorce was granted in 1836, ironically on the day of Burr's death. Eliza remained in the mansion, growing eccentric and reclusive, and died there at the age of 90.

THE SHABAZZ CENTER IN THE AUDUBON BALLROOM

3940 Broadway (West 165th St). Subway: 1, A, C to 168th St. Bus: M2, M3, M5. Open Tues–Fri 10–6. Free. T: 212 568 1341, theshabazzcenter.net.

In 1965 civil rights leader Malcolm X, who took the name Malik el-Shabazz, was assassinated at the Audubon Ballroom by members of the Nation of Islam, which Malcolm had embraced and then rejected. After his death, the ballroom (1912; Thomas Lamb), originally a vaudeville and movie theater, closed (1967) and was taken over for unpaid taxes by the City. Columbia-Presbyterian Medical Center bought it (1983), intending to replace it with a research facility. Public pressure forced a compromise and part

SYLVAN TERRACE
Wooden row houses on the historic mews leading to the Morris-Jumel Mansion.

of the building has been restored as the Malcolm X and Dr. Betty Shabazz Memorial and Education Center, dedicated to advancement of human rights and social justice. Inside are a life-size **statue of Malcolm X** (1995; Gabriel Koren) and exhibits on his life and teachings.

Highbridge Park (*West 155th St to Dyckman St, Edgecombe Ave to Amsterdam Ave*) is best known for the High Bridge Water Tower (1872) and the High Bridge, a former aqueduct that brought water from the Croton Reservoir into the city.

THE GEORGE WASHINGTON BRIDGE

Spanning the Hudson River from 178th St to Fort Lee, New Jersey, the George Washington Bridge (1931; Othmar H. Ammann and Cass Gilbert) links Manhattan to the outer world. Like the Brooklyn Bridge, it embodied cutting-edge technology while becoming an object of beauty and inspiration. Its 3,500-ft span doubled the record for suspension bridges, while its soaring steel towers and curving cables inspired Le Corbusier to call it "the only seat of grace in the disordered city."

A trans-Hudson railroad bridge had been contemplated as early as 1868, when the state of New Jersey authorized one further south. Conflicting interests and difficulties in financing and engineering halted progress until the Port of New York Authority, formed in 1921, brought the project to fruition. Chief engineer Othmar H. Ammann, who had emigrated from Switzerland in 1904 expressly to participate in American bridge projects, studied the political, financial, and structural problems surrounding previous attempts at a Hudson River crossing and proposed an automobile crossing, not a railroad bridge, thus cutting costs and anticipating America's romance with the internal combustion engine. The Port Authority funded the bridge ($59 million) by selling bonds, difficult in the years before 1929 when stock prices were booming.

The original plans called for sheathing the towers in masonry, for which Cass Gilbert produced designs, but by 1931 the Port Authority, having spent $48.5 million to buy the recently completed Holland Tunnel, was unwilling to pay for cosmetic improvements in the midst of a Depression. Between 1958 and 1962 a lower deck was constructed without disturbing traffic on the existing bridge, a feat accomplished by raising 76 steel sections from the shores or from barges. Snidely nicknamed the Martha Washington Bridge, the new deck brought the total cost to $215.8 million and took longer to build than the original bridge—but increased its capacity by 75 percent. In 2013 the Port Authority reported eastbound traffic (the direction in which tolls are taken) of 49.4 million vehicles.

Just under the tower of the George Washington Bridge in Fort Washington Park stands the **Little Red Lighthouse**, whose light and foghorn warned ships of the shoals off Jeffrey's Hook until 1947. Because the navigational lights on the bridge made it obsolete, the lighthouse went up for auction (1951) but was saved by the pleas of admirers, many of whom had read Hildegarde Hoyt Swift's children's tale *The Little Red Lighthouse and the Great Gray Bridge* (1942). (*You can visit the interior only during Urban Park Ranger tours; T: 212 628 2345, nyc.gov/parks/rangers.*)

WASHINGTON HEIGHTS
The George Washington Bridge (1931).

THE BATTLE OF FORT WASHINGTON

After defeats on Long Island and in Manhattan, General George Washington led his troops north, leaving a garrison at Fort Washington, a crudely fortified earthwork, under the command of Colonel Robert Magaw. On November 16, 1776, Hessian mercenaries fighting for the British scaled the outworks on Long Hill (the ridge in what is now Fort Tryon Park) from the north and east and attacked the Americans. General Cornwallis invaded Manhattan across the Harlem River at the present site of 201st St; the 42nd Highlanders crossed the Harlem River more or less where High Bridge now stands, and British troops led by Lord Percy marched up from downtown Manhattan, while warships bombarded the fort from the Hudson. The defenders of the outworks were killed or pushed back into the fort, which quickly surrendered after it became clear that the American troops were outnumbered. The loss of 54 lives and the capture of 2,634 of Washington's best-equipped troops were severe blows to the ragged, inexperienced American army.

INWOOD

Inwood (*map p. 609*) is two-fifths greenbelt with the rest largely residential. Fort Tryon Park contributes to the open space (as does Inwood Hill Park, further north), 196 acres stretching west to the Hudson and north to the Harlem River. The park is Manhattan's only true wilderness, with steep rock slopes and caves where Native Americans once sought shelter. Inwood's most important institution is The Cloisters, a branch of the Metropolitan Museum of Art.

FORT TRYON PARK

Map p. 609, B1. Subway: A to 190th St-Overlook Terrace. Exit by elevator and take bus M4 or walk up Margaret Corbin Drive (about 10mins). Bus: M4. By car: Henry Hudson Pkwy north to first exit after the George Washington Bridge (Fort Tryon Park). Some free parking around The Cloisters. New Leaf Restaurant & Bar in the park; a portion of gross sales goes toward park maintenance; reservations advised on weekends (see p. 465 for contact information).

The roadway into Fort Tryon Park from 190th St, **Margaret Corbin Drive**, is named after Margaret Cochran Corbin, a 26-year-old Revolutionary War heroine who fought beside her husband John in the Battle of Fort Washington (*see box above*). When he was killed, she continued firing his gun until she herself was severely wounded. After the war Corbin, known familiarly as Captain Molly, became a domestic servant. A woman known to have an unbridled tongue and an indifference to the niceties of dress, she died in 1800 and was buried in modest circumstances until the Daughters of the American Revolution had her body exhumed and re-interred at West Point.

THE BILLINGS ESTATE

The contours of Fort Tryon Park bear traces of the former estate of Cornelius K.G. Billings, a millionaire horseman, yachtsman, and aficionado of automobiles. He retired from a Chicago utilities company in 1901 and devoted himself to his hobbies, eventually becoming known as the American Horse King.

In 1903, Billings, who lived on Fifth Ave at 53rd St, bought land here and built a 25,000-square-ft stable (near the site of the New Leaf restaurant) and a country lodge to go with it. To celebrate their completion, he threw a dinner for 36 friends at Sherry's restaurant, an affair known in the annals of New York society as the Horseback Dinner. Billings's companions were seated on horses, which had been brought upstairs in the freight elevators; the meals were served on little tables attached to the saddles. Lest anyone snigger at the incongruity of it all, the walls of the restaurant were masked with painted woodland scenery and the floor was covered with grasses.

Billings expanded his lodge into a turreted and towered French-style mansion complete with a swimming pool, bowling alley, formal gardens, and a yacht-landing in the Hudson River. The original entrance was on 190th St, but when Riverside Drive was paved in 1908, the millionaire wanted a roadway up the hill from the river. The hill was so steep that one of the switchbacks would have had to swing out into mid-air, so the architects built an arched structure to support the road (still visible from the northbound lanes of the Henry Hudson Parkway). By 1916 Billings had tired of his hilltop home and sold it to John D. Rockefeller Jr. Nine years later, the house burned to the ground in a fire that attracted thousands of onlookers.

The park today encompasses 66 acres of hills and rocks, landscaped gardens, wooded slopes, and several miles of paths, some overlooking the Hudson River. The fort for which it was named (its site marked by a plaque) was intended to protect Fort Washington to the south during the Revolutionary War. When the American troops were forced to retreat, the British renamed the outpost after the governor, Major General Sir William Tryon (1729–88); as it turned out, he was the last British governor of colonial New York.

John D. Rockefeller Jr. bought the land for the park from C.J. Billings (*see above*) in 1916 and in the early 1930s hired the Olmsted brothers, John and Frederick, sons of the famous co-designer of Central Park (*see p. 309*), to transform Fort Tryon's rocky topography into a park that would maintain the area's magnificent vistas. Frederick Law Olmsted Jr. worked for four years creating promenades and gardens, including the Heather Garden, still one of the park's most beautiful features. In 1935 Rockefeller donated the park to the City.

THE CLOISTERS

Map p. 609, B1. 99 Margaret Corbin Drive in Fort Tryon Park (directions as for Fort Tryon Park, see p. 458). Open daily March–Oct 10–5:15, Nov–Feb 10–4:45. Closed New Year's Day, Thanksgiving, Christmas. Recommended donation (ticket from Metropolitan Museum also valid for Cloisters the same day). Seasonal open-air café. Shop. T: 212 923 3700, metmuseum.org/visit/visit-the-cloisters.

Standing on a rocky hill, The Cloisters was long the only branch of the Metropolitan Museum (*the Met Breuer is the latest branch; see p. 338*), remote from the rest of the city both in its surroundings and in the contemplative atmosphere created by its art and architecture. It takes its name from the colonnaded medieval courtyards that form its architectural core. On view along with medieval architectural elements are manuscripts and tapestries, and works—mostly 11th–14th-century—of metal, stone, wood and glass. The beautiful views of the Hudson from both inside and outside the building and the three gardens, recreated where possible from medieval sources, are added pleasures.

HISTORY OF THE COLLECTION

The sculptor George Grey Barnard (1863–1938) gathered the nucleus of the collection. A self-taught medievalist, Barnard lived in France for years while laboring over a commission for the Pennsylvania State Capitol. When money ran low, he began dealing in medieval art, becoming a knowledgeable collector. He claimed that he found unrecognized architectural treasures stowed away in barns, farmhouses, cellars, and, on one occasion, a pigsty, though it is now thought that he bought many of the works from dealers. Among the nearly 700 pieces Barnard brought to New York were large sections of the cloisters of four medieval monasteries—one Romanesque, three Gothic—and such treasures as the tomb effigy of Jean d'Alluye, which he said he had discovered lying face down, serving as a bridge over a stream. Barnard was fortunate in his timing, sending his collection to New York in 1913, just as France was growing concerned about the dispersal of its national treasures. As a placating gesture Barnard donated a fine set of arches from the cloister at Cuxa to France, which perhaps ensured the safe departure of the rest of his collection.

In 1914 Barnard put the works on display in a building he designed and named The Cloisters, located on Fort Washington Ave. He then turned his attention to building a peace memorial showcasing the achievements of world architecture, a project that ate up so much of his capital that he had to sell his museum. In 1925, with money from John D. Rockefeller Jr., the Metropolitan Museum purchased Barnard's collection. Five years later Rockefeller gave the City the land for Fort Tryon Park in exchange for the East Side acreage where Rockefeller University now stands. Rockefeller reserved space at the north end of the park for the present museum and then, to ensure a perpetually unspoiled view, prudently bought land across the river along the palisades and gave it to New Jersey for a park. In this he followed the lead of J. Pierpont Morgan, who had in 1901 financed the purchase of twelve miles of shoreline and cliff face along the Palisades to which Rockefeller added land to the west of the edge of the plateau.

The building

The Cloisters (1934–8; Charles Collens of Allen, Collens & Willis) was not copied from any single medieval original, but was built around medieval architectural elements so as to make modern additions as unobtrusive as possible. The exterior granite was quarried by hand near New London, Connecticut, matching the dimensions of building blocks in Romanesque churches, especially the church at Corneille-de-Conflent near Cuxa. The Italian limestone of the interior was hand-sawn to suggest weathering. The courtyards and ramparts were paved with Belgian blocks taken from New York streets and the grounds landscaped with trees intended to recall those surrounding Europe's medieval monasteries (with allowances for New York's harsher climate).

The collection

While the Metropolitan's medieval collections span the period from the barbarian invasions (from c. AD 370) to the close of the 14th century, works in The Cloisters focus on two principal medieval styles: Romanesque and Gothic. The display is organized more or less chronologically, beginning with the Romanesque Hall and ending with the Late Gothic Hall and the Froville Arcade. (The accession numbers beginning 25.120 on the labels indicate works purchased from the original Barnard collection.)

Main Level: Reconstructed around medieval architectural elements, rooms here include the **Romanesque Hall (001)**, the earliest, whose three portals illustrate the evolution of sculptured church doorways in the 12th–13th centuries, from a round-arched Romanesque French doorway (c. 1150) to a magnificently decorated 13th-century door from Burgundy.

The **Fuentidueña Chapel (002)**, with a mid-12th century frescoed apse, is from a church near Madrid that was probably part of a castle built by Christians struggling to regain the Iberian peninsula from its Islamic conquerors. The large 12th-century Spanish Crucifix of carved, painted oak is one of the finest surviving Romanesque examples.

The small **Saint-Guilhem Cloister (003)** has remarkable columns, their capitals carved with plants and motifs including Daniel in the Lions' Den and a "Mouth of Hell," with cloven-hoofed demons forcing sinners into the flames

of Hell—terrifying to medieval believers.

Other medieval rooms include the **Pontaut Chapter House (006)**, a meeting room from a 12th-century abbey where the monks met to discuss business or to hear readings or sermons.

The Romanesque **Cuxa Cloister (007)** comes from a Benedictine monastery founded in 878 and left to fall into ruins after the French Revolution. In the center is an enclosed garden with quadrants of lawn, crab apple trees, and borders of herbs and flowers. In winter the arcades are glassed in and filled with pots of acanthus, olive, and bay.

Other rooms contain fine examples of stained-glass windows from French and German churches notably **Boppard** on the Rhine **(016)**; paintings, among them **Robert Campin's** *Annunciation* **triptych (019)**; and tapestries, including the 14th-century French series of **Nine Heroes**, three Classical, three Biblical and three Christian **(018)** and the much loved **Unicorn Tapestries (017)**.

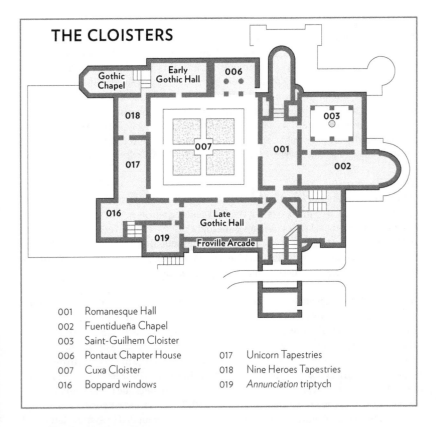

THE CLOISTERS

001 Romanesque Hall
002 Fuentidueña Chapel
003 Saint-Guilhem Cloister
006 Pontaut Chapter House   017 Unicorn Tapestries
007 Cuxa Cloister   018 Nine Heroes Tapestries
016 Boppard windows   019 *Annunciation* triptych

THE UNICORN TAPESTRIES

These seven late medieval tapestries depicting the Hunt of the Unicorn were probably designed in Paris and woven in Brussels (c. 1495–1505), but no one knows who commissioned them or the occasion they celebrated, though it was probably a marriage. The tapestries were seized during the French Revolution and later damaged when they served to protect a potato garden from frost. During the 1850s they were rediscovered lying in a barn.

According to medieval legend a unicorn could be caught only by a virgin, whose presence tamed the normally wild creature. This story was interpreted both as an allegory of human love and an allegory of the Incarnation (with the unicorn a symbol of Christ). *The Unicorn in Captivity*—one of the most cherished works in the collection—shows the wounded Unicorn, subdued and docile, inside a small corral, surrounded by flowers and fruiting plants. The image is said to symbolize both the Resurrection and the consummation of a marriage. John D. Rockefeller Jr. bought them in 1923 from the Comte de la Rochefoucauld, whose family had owned them since the 17th century, and donated them to the museum.

Lower Level: In the Gothic Chapel are stained-glass windows from the 14th century and tomb effigies. The figure of Jean d'Alluye (d. 1248), a young man fully armed, his feet resting against a crouching lion (a frequently-used foot rest, symbolizing knightly courage), was one of George Grey Barnard's major acquisitions. Other galleries on this level display a rotating selection of small objects—manuscripts, carved ivories, enamels, glass, textiles, and metalwork. Among the more astonishing are the *Belles Heures* of the Duc de Berry, a private devotional book illuminated by the most gifted artists of the period; and the ivory *Cloisters Cross*, intricately carved with more than 100 figures illustrating stories from the Old and New Testaments.

INWOOD HILL PARK

Inwood Hill Park, stretching over 196 acres bounded by the Hudson and Harlem Rivers on the west and north, Dyckman St on the south, and various city streets along its eastern border, is *old* old Manhattan, with the island's only remaining natural forest and salt marsh, walking trails, and a nature center (*walks and nature events led by Urban Park Rangers, check schedule at nycgovparks.org/events*). Like the rest of Washington Heights, Inwood consists of two ridges with a valley between, and geologically the park is a textbook of the larger city: there are outcroppings of Manhattan schist, exposures of Inwood marble, and boulders of Fordham gneiss, as well as glacial striations and potholes scoured out of the bedrock by the gravel-bearing water of the melting glacier.

The park became the last refuge for the Native Americans as white settlers pushed them back and it contains caves where native artifacts—pottery shards and arrowheads—have been found. After the Native Americans were driven out, the arable lowlands were given to Dutch settlers, notably Jan Dyckman and Jan Nagel. During the Revolution, a five-sided earthen fort stood on high ground, known as Cock Hill (or Cox Hill), perhaps a corruption of the Native American "Shorakapock." Pewter buttons, musket shot, regimental insignias, and blue-patterned earthenware have been found.

Until the 1930s, the park remained untouched, but the Henry Hudson Parkway, pushed through by Robert Moses, has intruded on its solitude. The **Henry Hudson Bridge** (1936; David Steinman) spans the Harlem River with a fixed steel arch 2,000 ft long, at its highest point 142.5 ft above the river. The bridge (span 800ft), a Robert Moses project, was constructed with a single deck and only four lanes because bankers underwriting the project would authorize no more than $3.1 million in bonds, unable to believe that commuters would choose a toll bridge over the free nearby Broadway Bridge. When the bridge proved itself financially viable, the second deck was added.

North of the park flows the **Harlem River**, not navigable to the Hudson until a channel was cut through the bulbous promontory that formerly extended north of where Columbia University's stadium and Ninth Ave are now located. Before then, narrow Spuyten Duyvil Creek flowed in a looping curve, today marked by the present northern boundary of Manhattan. In 1895 the Harlem River Ship Canal was cut (400ft wide, 15ft deep), straightening the shipping route from Long Island Sound to the Hudson. When the project was finished, the creek was filled, making the area now known as Marble Hill physically part of the Bronx, though politically it is still part of Manhattan.

SPUYTEN DUYVIL

The origin of the creek's strange name is unknown. Washington Irving suggested one in *Knickerbocker's History of New York*: Anthony Van Corlaer, sent to warn the settlers north of the creek of an imminent British attack, reached the waterway during such a storm that no one would ferry him across. Emboldened by a few swigs from his flask, Van Corlaer swore he would swim across "en spijt den Duyvil" ("in spite of the devil"), threw himself into the wild waters, and drowned. A more recent explanation is that "spuyten duyvil" ("spitting devil") described the roiling waters of the creek, whose violent and irregular tides according to some unnamed colonist could only be the Devil's handiwork.

DYCKMAN FARMHOUSE MUSEUM

Map p. 609, B1. 4881 Broadway (West 204th St). Subway: 1 or A to 207th St. Bus: M100. Open Thur–Sat 11–4, Sun 11–3. T: 212 304 9422, dyckmanfarmhouse.org.

Built c. 1784, this modest farmhouse survived the ambitions of developers through the determination of two Dyckman descendants, who bought it in 1915, restored it, and donated it to the City. Once the center of the 300-acre Dyckman farm, whose meadows reached to the Harlem River, the present house replaces an earlier Dyckman homestead destroyed by the British during the Revolutionary War. It has the overhanging eaves and gambrel roof typical of the Dutch Colonial style. Inside are period rooms with early American furnishings, a winter kitchen, and a staircase built around an outcrop of Inwood marble. Behind the house is a garden with a military hut built to resemble those used during the Revolutionary War, when both British and Hessian soldiers camped on the farm.

EATING AND DRINKING IN UPPER MANHATTAN

$$$ New Leaf. Restaurant and bar in Fort Tryon Park, near The Cloisters. Seasonal American farm-to-table menu in one of the city's most beautiful settings. Terrace seating, too. Lunch and dinner daily, weekend brunch. *1 Margaret Corbin Drive. T: 212 568 5323, newleafrestaurant.com.*

$-$$ Garden Café. New American menu at this Inwood restaurant, created by an Inwood native, serving straightforward American food. The pleasant garden, sometimes with live music, is a bonus. Lunch and dinner daily. *4961 Broadway (Isham St and 207th St). T: 212 544 9480, gardencafeny.com.*

THE OUTER BOROUGHS

To many, Manhattan is synonymous with "New York," but of the city's
five boroughs, it is neither the largest (Queens is) nor the most
populous (Brooklyn takes that title). In 1683, thirteen years after the British
came into power, they divided the colony of New York into twelve "shires," or
counties, the basic units of government. Among them were New York County
(now Manhattan), Kings County (now Brooklyn), Bronx County, Queens
County, and Richmond County (now Staten Island). In 1898, when New York
was consolidated, the counties became boroughs, the present administrative
divisions of the City. Thus Manhattan, the borough, is co-extensive with
New York County of the State of New York, and so on.

From the time the Dutch first set foot in New Amsterdam, Manhattan
was central, the seat of government and the focus of economic activity.
The surrounding counties developed as their geography and proximity to
Manhattan—and the ease of getting there—dictated. Thus the Dutch village
Breuckelen, close to the Manhattan waterfront, became the town and then
the City of Brooklyn, the dominant urban area of the future borough. The
Bronx, which embraced country estates, farming communities, and waterfront
industrial zones, became more urban as New York (i.e., Manhattan) undertook
major construction projects—railroads, the Croton Aqueduct, even the Bronx
Zoo, which attracted immigrant labor and swelled the population.
What were formerly individual settlements and towns in the outer boroughs
became today's neighborhoods, named for early landowners or for geographical
features—Flatbush, Bensonhurst, Morrisania, Todt Hill, Bayside, Astoria.
Although the arrival of public transportation encouraged Manhattanites
to settle beyond the borough limits, the far reaches of Queens and
Staten Island remained relatively undeveloped into the 20th century.
After World War II, the large, open tracts in those boroughs led to the
creation of dense suburban communities.

Today, as Manhattan is experiencing intense pressures of development
in a confined space, the outer boroughs are drawing people beyond the rivers,
once again changing the demographics of the city.

Brooklyn

Brooklyn, once sleepy and agricultural, later a solid borough of working- and middle-class families, and still later a victim of urban blight, is today, at least in part, a magnet for the young, the affluent, and the artistic. It is world-famous for its bridge, its brownstones, and its seaside playground, Coney Island.

Brooklyn, the largest of the five boroughs by population (2.6 million) is also growing the fastest. Its 71 square miles make it the second-largest in size. Lying on the western tip of Long Island, it is bounded on the west and north by the East River, the Narrows, and Upper New York Bay; by the Atlantic Ocean on the south; and the borough of Queens on the east. Rocky ridges created by the Wisconsin glacier run east and west through its central and western portions, while its southern and eastern parts are largely coastal plain created by the glacial outwash. Many neighborhood names describe local geography: Brooklyn Heights, Park Slope, Crown Heights, Bay Ridge, Flatbush, Flatlands, and Midwood. Even the name "Brooklyn," first applied to the 17th-century village near the present intersection of Fulton and Smith Sts, refers to a topographically similar Dutch town, Breuckelen ("Broken Land").

Its geography determined its history. The waterfront attracted industry and shipping; the downtown area around Fulton St developed because of proximity to the ferries; the rest of Brooklyn remained first agricultural and then became residential, the pattern of its settlement influenced by transit lines—first horse cars, then elevated railways, and eventually subways—fanning outward.

Bridges link Brooklyn to the rest of the city. The Brooklyn Bridge, the Manhattan Bridge, and the Williamsburg Bridge span the East River to Manhattan. Othmar H. Ammann's beautiful Verrazano-Narrows Bridge (1964) soars above the Lower Bay, joining the Bay Ridge section of Brooklyn to Staten Island and to the national interstate system.

HISTORY OF BROOKLYN

The Dutch first settled Brooklyn in the 17th century, buying land from the Canarsie Indians and chartering five of its six original villages: Breuckelen (1657); 't Vlacke Bos, now Flatbush (1652); Nieuw Utrecht (1662); Nieuw Amersfoort, now Flatlands (1666); and Boswijck, now Bushwick (1660). The sixth charter, for s'Gravensande, now Gravesend, went in 1643 to Lady Deborah Moody, an Englishwoman. Dutch culture, agrarian and conservative, endured in Brooklyn long after the Revolution, especially inland, although New Yorkers (from Manhattan), many of them of British origin, were

THE BROOKLYN BRIDGE (1883)
View from the central walkway.

drawn for residential and commercial reasons to the waterfront and northern districts. Steam ferries to Manhattan began in 1814, linking this rural area to the big city, making it a desirable place to live and do business. From 1820–60, Brooklyn's population nearly doubled every decade. In 1834 the town of Brooklyn, which had developed near the ferry landing, became an independent city. As the century progressed, it gradually absorbed outlying towns: New Lots, Flatbush, Gravesend, New Utrecht, and Flatlands.

In 1898, responding to fiscal needs and geography, Brooklyn voted by a slim majority to join Greater New York. The later decades of the 19th century were a golden age: cultural institutions (the Brooklyn Museum, the Academy of Music, the Botanic Garden, the Historical Society) found fertile soil and industries (oil and sugar refining, brewing and distilling, publishing, glass and ceramics, cast iron) provided jobs for a growing population. Major public works projects (Prospect Park, the Brooklyn Bridge, the development of the Atlantic Basin in Red Hook) as well as the construction of good housing along the rapid transit lines testified to its economic health.

By the turn of the 20th century, Brooklyn's demography was changing as immigrants poured in from Europe and, after the 1930s, from the American South, all seeking jobs in the manufacturing and port center that Brooklyn had become. By 1930 half of Brooklyn's adults were foreign-born, most gravitating to ethnic neighborhoods: Brownsville, Bensonhurst, and Greenpoint. The Depression hit hard, and by the mid-1930s some of these areas had become slums. Established middle-class families moved out to suburban neighborhoods. The borough's population kept growing—between 1890 and 1940, it soared from 1.2 million to 2.7 million.

Despite the setbacks of the Depression, Brooklyn remained economically sound through the end of World War II, when the exodus to the suburbs of much of the remaining middle class, as well as government policies favoring other parts of the country, eroded its economic base. The port withered, the breweries of Bushwick shut down, the Defense Department abandoned the Navy Yard, and large neighborhoods became derelict. In 1955 the *Brooklyn Eagle* folded, and two years later the Brooklyn Dodgers left for Los Angeles, both losses potent symbols of the borough's decline. For the next three decades Brooklyn, sometimes along with the rest of the city, struggled with drugs, crime, infrastructure decay, and other urban problems.

Then the balance shifted. Young professionals and families, priced out of Manhattan or seeking a less harried atmosphere, moved to neighborhoods such as Park Slope and Cobble Hill, and elsewhere, attracting new restaurants, shops, galleries, and other upscale businesse. Artists colonized former industrial buildings in Williamsburg, Dumbo, and Red Hook. In 2001 the minor league Brooklyn Cyclones took the field at a new park in Coney Island, bringing professional baseball back to Brooklyn for the first time since the Dodgers departed. In 2012 the first sections of Brooklyn Bridge Park opened on the waterfront, replacing abandoned piers and car sheds with open space.

Today gentrification continues apace, spreading inland from the shoreline and along transportation lines just as the original population did. Though pockets of poverty remain, many neighborhoods are becoming too pricey for the artists, hipsters, and young families to whom they owe their regeneration.

THE BROOKLYN BRIDGE

Map p. 622, B1. Pedestrian access from Manhattan just east of City Hall Park at the corner of Centre St and Park Row. From Brooklyn, you reach the bridge via a long ramp beginning at the corner of Adams and Tillary Sts or via a walkway and staircase from the north end of Cadman Plaza Park.

The Brooklyn Bridge is the best-known and most-loved bridge in the city. The pedestrian walkway draws runners, cyclists, and walkers to enjoy spectacular views, day or night, up to the cables or down to the river, to Manhattan or to Brooklyn.

HISTORY OF THE BRIDGE

When the Brooklyn Bridge opened on May 25, 1883, it was justly considered one of the world's greatest wonders. It was the largest suspension bridge in existence, with a single span arching 1,595 ft across the East River, and massive granite towers that stretched 276ft above the water. Only the thin spire of Trinity Church stood taller, at 281ft. The bridge was also a public works project of a scale never before seen in New York, employing approximately 4,000 people, taking 14 years, and ultimately costing $15 million dollars.

Before the Brooklyn Bridge, the only way across the East River was by ferry. Limited to small loads and idle in poor weather, the ferry system could not keep pace with the mid-19th-century expansion of industry and as the Civil War ended, a push began for a bridge. The New York Bridge Company, chartered by the state, chose the brilliant John A. Roebling to head the project. An inventor, manufacturer, and engineer, he had hit on the idea of making wire rope for industrial use and become the nation's most successful producer.

Roebling had already sketched out plans for a bridge over the East River in 1856, and he returned to the project convinced that his suspension bridge would be the greatest in the world. Aided by his son, Colonel Washington Roebling, a surveyor and engineer in the Union Army, Roebling put forth a daring plan. Two mammoth granite towers would be built offshore on underwater foundations. Four huge cables would be hung over the towers and secured by massive anchorages at either end of the bridge. A single arching span would hang from the cables, supported by a web of stays and a truss system for an extra measure of safety. In short, the great towers would support the weight of the cables and roadway, and the anchorages would offset their pull. The entire bridge would be over a mile long and could accommodate 18,700 tons. Roebling also planned a promenade on the upper level, tracks for a special steam-powered train system, and cavernous storage houses within the massive anchorages.

Important aspects of Roebling's design, such as the giant steel suspension cables and underwater foundations, had never been tested on such a grand scale. The work would prove dangerous, and dozens of men died during the construction. Roebling himself would not live to see a single stone of his great bridge laid, for he contracted tetanus in a freak accident while surveying the site in 1869 and suffered an excruciating death two weeks later. The task then fell to Washington Roebling to build his father's great bridge.

At the bottom of the riverbed lie the two gigantic caissons employed by Roebling to sink the foundations of the bridge. Like mammoth diving bells, these huge, inverted boxes of timber, iron, and cement (each roughly 170ft by 100ft) were built on the shores, "inflated" with compressed air and floated into position. Once in place, heavy stones were piled on top of each box until it came to rest on the riverbed. Then, through a system of airlocks, men descended into the caissons to excavate the muddy riverbed until they hit solid rock. Inside they toiled away by dim light, removing boulders that appeared in the muck and hauling river mud and gravel to large buckets, which hoisted the debris out of the caisson. After ten months of digging the Brooklyn caisson touched bedrock. The New York caisson was sunk in eight and a half months. Both caissons were then filled with cement to form the foundations on which the towers would rest.

Caissons had previously been tried only on a much smaller scale, and the hazards of working with compressed air were not understood. A phenomenon called "caisson disease" began to plague workers as they went deeper. The symptoms, which included temporary paralysis, vomiting, nose bleeds, joint pain, and sometimes death, resulted from the formation of nitrogen bubbles in the body during the rapid drops in pressure which the men experienced as they ascended after their shifts. Washington Roebling himself fell victim to caisson disease and developed a nervous disorder, which for several years left him unable to visit the work site or communicate with anyone but his wife Emily. As the towers rose and the cables were spun across the river, Roebling watched with binoculars from his home in Brooklyn Heights, delivering detailed instructions to his engineers through his highly numerate wife.

The bridge remains an important link in the city's transportation network, carrying approximately 100,000 cars daily. Twice in recent years the bridge has played a crucial role in evacuations of Manhattan: on September 11, 2001, and on August 14, 2003, during a severe blackout. On the second occasion, vibrations from shoulder-to-shoulder pedestrian traffic caused the bridge to sway so much that some felt seasick, while the huge cables jerked and groaned. Still the bridge remained stable: Roebling's tripartite system of supports had been designed for such emergencies. Although the Brooklyn Bridge has slipped to 88th place among the world's suspension bridges, it remains a testament to the optimism and determination of a great city.

THE CIVIC CENTER & BROOKLYN HEIGHTS

At the foot of the bridge ramps is the **Civic Center**, whose municipal and state buildings surround Cadman Plaza, developed in the 1950s. On the east side is the **Kings County Supreme Court** (1957; Shreve, Lamb & Harmon) by the architects of the Empire State Building. In front stands Emma Stebbins's statue of *Christopher Columbus* (1867), brought here in 1971 from Central Park. On the west side of Cadman Plaza, opposite Montague St, is John Quincy Adams Ward's 8-ft bronze figure of *Henry*

Ward Beecher (1891), the face modeled from a death mask, the preacher's powerful personality (*see overleaf*) apparent in both his face and his posture.

Brooklyn's **Borough Hall**, originally City Hall (1845–8; Gamaliel King, cupola added 1898), at the southwest corner of the park (*209 Joralemon St at Cadman Plaza West*), was designed to be a smaller version of City Hall in Manhattan, built 40 years earlier.

THE NEW YORK TRANSIT MUSEUM

Map p. 622, C3. Corner of Boerum Place and Schermerhorn St. Subway: A, C, or G to Hoyt-Schermerhorn; A, C, F, R to Jay St-MetroTech; 2, 3, 4, 5 to Borough Hall; R to Court St. Open Tues–Fri 10–4, Sat–Sun 11–5. Admission charge, but seniors free on Wed. Gift and book shop. T: 718 694 1600, mta.info/museum.

This museum, located in the unused Court St subway station, was inaugurated in 1976 for the bicentennial celebrations and proved too popular to close afterward. Run by the Metropolitan Transit Authority, it includes exhibits on buses and trolleys, but emphasizes the history and construction of the subway system. On view are historic photographs, maps, models and drawings, but the real draw is the lineup of vintage subway cars, including the fondly remembered Lo-V model with rattan seats and ceiling fans. Other exhibits offer fare collection devices, from an early wooden ticket chopper to a full-body turnstile known as the "iron maiden"; and mosaics from early stations (intended partly as decoration but also to assist riders who could not read English). The museum organizes popular tours and special events, including trips to the city's first subway station, locked away under City Hall Park (*see p. 87*).

BROOKLYN HEIGHTS

Map p. 622. Subway: 2, 3 to Clark St; A, C to High St; 4, 5 to Borough Hall.

Bounded by the East River, Old Fulton St, Atlantic Ave, and Court St, Brooklyn Heights is sometimes called New York's first suburb. It became the city's first designated Historic District in 1965.

Part of the larger village of Brooklyn, Brooklyn Heights started thriving after 1814, when Robert Fulton's steam ferry began scheduled crossings to and from New York (Manhattan) across the river. Local landowners soon began dividing their farms into standard 25-ft by 100-ft building lots, and as the area was developed, one architectural style followed another, summarizing the whole history of domestic architecture in 19th-century New York. Row houses were built in the Federal style (1820s and '30s), in the Greek Revival style (1830s and '40s), Gothic Revival style (1840s), and the Italianate (1860s), followed by a few picturesque Queen Anne and Romanesque Revival houses in the 1880s and '90s.

Victorian Brooklyn Heights was known for its fine families, its churches, and its clergymen. When the bridge (1883) and the subway (1908) arrived, the Heights lost its patrician edge. By the early 20th century, many private homes had been converted to rooming houses; a few had become seamen's clubs, missions, and even brothels. The Heights remained in social limbo until the late 1950s and early '60s, when young couples willing to invest labor and money began redeeming the old houses, awakening the spirit of preservation. Today Brooklyn Heights is one of the city's most expensive and desirable neighborhoods.

PLYMOUTH CHURCH OF THE PILGRIMS

75 Hicks St (Orange St). Tours Mon–Fri 10–4 (by appointment), and most Sundays after 11am worship. T: 718 624 4743, plymouthchurch.org.

This red-brick Italianate barn of a church (1849) is best known for its first minister, Henry Ward Beecher, who thundered forth from its pulpit for 40 years, expounding on the great issues of the day: temperance, woman suffrage, and slavery. (Beecher's sister, Harriet Beecher Stowe, wrote the anti-slavery novel *Uncle Tom's Cabin*.) In the garden a statue by Gutzon Borglum, sculptor of Mount Rushmore, depicts Beecher and two slave children. Borglum also executed the nearby bas-relief of Lincoln, who, as a presidential aspirant in 1860, trekked to Brooklyn to hear the eloquent preacher.

The sanctuary, intended as a setting for Beecher's oratorical skills, is arranged like a theater auditorium without a central aisle. The opalescent stained-glass windows (c. 1915) designed by the Lamb Studios—the oldest known American stained glass studio (founded 1857)—are unusual in depicting historical rather than biblical events. The church's Hillis Hall, given by coffee merchant John Arbuckle, has windows from the Tiffany Studios, originally in the Church of the Pilgrims on Remsen St (*see p. 478*), which merged with Plymouth Church in 1934.

HENRY WARD BEECHER

Called by the founders of the Plymouth Church of the Pilgrims— many of them New England abolitionists—Henry Ward Beecher (1813–87) came to Brooklyn in 1847. When fire damaged the original building, the present one, large enough to hold Beecher's growing congregation, replaced it. Beecher was especially popular with the middle-class women in his congregation, and—perhaps through their influence— took an interest in women's rights. At the height of his popularity "Beecher boats" ferried throngs of New Yorkers across the river to hear him, while policemen reined in the crowds that gathered hours before services. Abraham Lincoln commented on Beecher's productive mind, but Mark Twain, a skeptic in religious matters, described him as "sawing his arms in the air, howling sarcasms this way and that, discharging rockets of poetry and exploding mines of eloquence."

Always theatrical, Beecher staged mock auctions at which he would "sell" slaves to the highest bidder; when he took bids on nine-year-old Sally Maria Diggs, called "Pinky," the congregation, outraged by Beecher's imitation of a slave auctioneer, purchased her freedom. One congregant threw her fire-opal ring into the plate; Beecher placed it on the child's hand, saying "With this ring I wed thee to freedom." The church became a stop on the Underground Railway, offering aid to runaway slaves, and it sent rifles, known as "Beecher's Bibles," to anti-slavery settlers in Kansas. A sensational trial for adultery, of which he was acquitted, damaged Beecher's later career, but when he died, Brooklyn declared a day of mourning.

A WALK THROUGH BROOKLYN HEIGHTS

Quiet, leafy Brooklyn Heights offers a respite from hectic Manhattan. Here you will find well-preserved 19th-century houses in all the reigning architectural styles; stunning views across the East River to the Manhattan skyline; and the Brooklyn Historical Society, whose exhibits examine the borough's past.

FROM PLYMOUTH CHURCH OF THE Pilgrims, walk east to Henry St and turn north. Continue on Henry St to **Middagh St**, where the former Mason, Au & Magenheimer Confectionery Company building (1885) still stands. There's a recently repainted advertisement—"Peaks Mason Mints"—at the top of the building, which nowadays contains condos instead of candies. Turn left at Middagh St and walk west to Willow St. The house on the southeast corner, no. 24 Middagh St, is a well-preserved clapboarded house (1824) with fine carved Federal detailing around the door, dormer windows, and quarter-round attic windows visible from **Willow St**. Joined to it by a wall is the former carriage house.

While many Brooklyn Heights place names recall prominent 19th-century families, five streets—Pineapple, Orange, Cranberry, Poplar, and Willow—have botanical names. Legend (probably apocryphal) attributes them to the ire of one Miss Middagh, who allegedly tore down street markers bearing the names of neighbors she disliked and substituted the present ones.

Walk south on Willow St to no. 57 Willow St on the northeast corner of Orange St, a Federal-style house (c. 1824) with dormers, pitched roofs, Flemish bond brickwork, tooled stone lintels, and a parapet between the chimneys concealing the roof gable.

Turn right on Orange St and walk a block to **Columbia Heights**. At the site of no. 124 (formerly 110 Columbia Heights) Washington Roebling oversaw construction of the Brooklyn Bridge with a telescope, crippled by the "bends" and unable to leave his house (*see p. 472*).

Turn left on Clark St. The **former Leverich Towers Hotel** (1928; Starrett & Van Vleck) at no. 21 once glittered as one of Brooklyn's brightest social spots, its four corner towers spotlighted at night. It was long one of many residence halls belonging to the Jehovah's Witnesses, a religious group that moved their headquarters to Brooklyn Heights in 1909 and were for many years the Heights's largest landholder; since 2013 the Witnesses have been selling off their real estate empire as they relocate.

On the next block, between Hicks and Henry Sts, the **former Hotel St. George**, eight buildings of it (1885–1930), reigned for a while the city's largest (2,632 rooms), famous for its Art Deco ballroom and mirrored indoor pool.

Double back and walk south down **Willow St**. Nos. 108–12 (c. 1880) exemplify the offbeat Queen Anne style, which flourished in New York 1880–1900. Introduced from England at the Philadelphia Centennial Exposition (1876), the style picturesquely combines medieval and Renaissance elements. These houses form one visual unit, displaying a satisfying variety of forms (gables, bay windows, chimneys, dormers; round, square, and elliptical

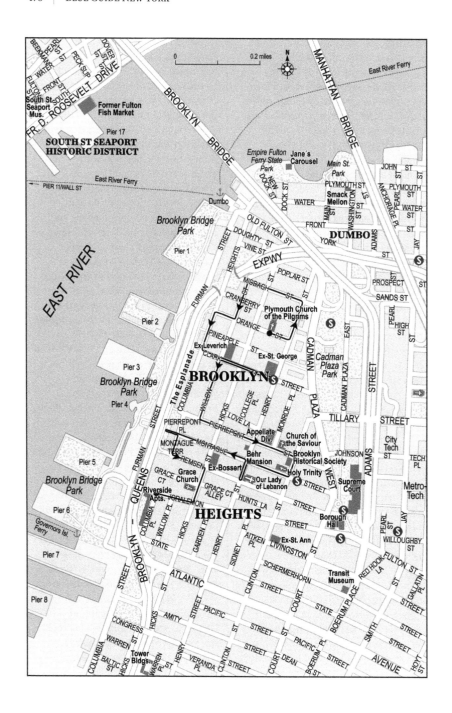

openings) and materials (brick, stone, terra cotta, ironwork, shingles).

Continue south to no. 151 Willow St, a red-brick carriage house set back from the street. Nearby is a towering dawn redwood (*Metasequoia glyptostroboides*), planted here in the 1950s. Until the 1940s, when it was discovered in a remote area of China, the species was thought extinct, but today it is planted as a street tree thanks to its resistance to the Asian long-horned beetle. Nos. 155–159 Willow St are a trio of pristine small Federal row houses (c. 1829) with sidelights, leaded transoms, and paneled front doors flanked by colonnettes.

Turn left at **Pierrepont St**, named for Hezekiah Beers Pierpont, landowner and gin distiller, who early saw the advantages of opening Brooklyn Heights for development. He backed the Fulton Ferry (1814) and by 1823 was offering 25-ft by 100-ft lots to "gentlemen whose duties require their daily attendance in the city." Hezekiah's children reverted to the earlier, fancier spelling of Pierrepont.

Continue east to no. 82 (*southwest corner of Henry St*), the **former Herman Behr mansion** (1890), a handsome Romanesque Revival building by Frank Freeman, Brooklyn's best architect. Behr was a manufacturer of abrasives; one son survived the *Titanic* and became a tennis star; another designed golf courses. With an addition in 1919, the house became the Palm Hotel; it lost its luster, became a brothel, and was redeemed by the friars of nearby St. Francis College, who made it a residence for novitiates.

No. 104 Pierrepont St (c. 1857) is a four-story brownstone with elaborately carved console brackets on the first and second stories. No. 108–14 Pierrepont St (1840) was once a Greek Revival double

house with a central cupola; drastic remodeling has made it a strange hybrid, half Greek Revival, half Romanesque Revival. The doorway pediment and corner quoins on one half remain from the original façade. The other half was given its present Romanesque form for publisher Alfred Barnes by adding brownstone facing, terra cotta ornament, a turret, and a rounded bay.

Walk east to Monroe Place, named after James Monroe, the nation's fifth president, who finished his life in straitened circumstances in New York. On the northwest corner of Monroe Place and Pierrepont St is the **Appellate Division of the Kings County Supreme Court** (1938), stately but incongruous in this residential neighborhood. On the northeast corner, at 50 Monroe Place, stands Minard Lafever's Gothic Revival (1844) **Church of the Saviour**, also called the First Unitarian Church. Some windows (the Low, Woodward, Farley, and Frothingham memorials and possibly the other opalescent windows) are by the Tiffany Studios. No. 46 Monroe Place has Brooklyn Heights's only remaining ironwork basket urn, topped with the traditional pineapple for hospitality.

At the corner of Pierrepont and Clinton Sts is the **Brooklyn Historical Society** (*Subway: 2, 3, 4, 5 to Borough Hall; A, C, F to Jay St-Borough Hall; R to Court St open Wed–Sun 12–5; closed Mon, Tues, July 4, Thanksgiving, Christmas, New Year's Day. Interesting book and gift shop. T: 718 222 4111, brooklynhistory. org*). Founded as the Long Island Historical Society in 1863 when Brooklyn was an independent city, the society changed its name in 1985 to reflect political reality. In the building are a library, museum, and an education center dedicated to Brooklyn history and culture. The permanent collection has photographs and paintings (of Brooklyn people and places), as well as newspapers, books, manuscripts, and other materials. A long-term exhibit documents Brooklyn's significant role in the anti-slavery movement; rotating shows explore aspects of borough history—ferries, sugar refining, historic maps. On the building façade (1878; George B. Post), are terra cotta heads of a Native American and a Norseman and busts of Johann Gutenberg, Benjamin Franklin, Michelangelo, Christopher Columbus, Shakespeare, and Beethoven, sculpted by Olin Levi Warner, who studied at the École des Beaux-Arts and returned to New York in 1872. Warner later reused the Norseman and Native American on the doors of the Library of Congress.

Turn right on Clinton St and walk one block to the neighborhood's main street, Montague St, named after English writer Lady Mary Wortley Montagu, née Pierrepont. The final "e" in "Montague" is a misspelling. **Eateries** here, some with outdoor seating, include: Caffe Buon Gusto, 151 Montague St (*lunch and dinner daily; T: 718 624 3838, caffebuongusto. net*); Armando's Ristorante, 143 Montague St (*lunch and dinner daily; T: 718 624 7167, armandos143.com*); Gallito's Kitchen, 140 Montague St (*lunch and dinner daily; T: 718 855 4791, gallitoskitchenbrooklyn.com*); and Heights Café, 84 Montague St (*open until midnight daily, brunch weekends; T: 718 625 5555, heightscafeny.com*).

Walk west on Montague St. At Henry St turn left and walk south to the church on the corner of Remsen St (named after landowner Henry Remsen). Originally the Church of the Pilgrims (1846; Richard Upjohn; addition 1869, Leopold Eidlitz) and the first Congregational church in Brooklyn, this historic building has served Middle Eastern Catholics of the Maronite rite as **Our Lady of Lebanon Church** since 1944. The nation's first round-arched, early Romanesque Revival church, it represents a brief departure from Upjohn's opulent Gothic Revival style, which he lavished on buildings for High Church Episcopalians. The doors in the west and south portals originated as the dining room doors of the luxury liner *Normandie*, which burned in 1942 and sank at its Hudson River berth. Purchased at auction by the pastor of the church in 1945, the medallions depict Norman castles, Norman churches, and the SS *Ile de France*.

Return to Montague St. The **former Hotel Bossert** at no. 98 on the southeast corner of Hicks St (1909) got its name from founder Louis Bossert, a millwork manufacturer. In the 1920s and '30s the Marine Roof, decorated by theatrical designer Joseph Urban, afforded visitors a vista of the Manhattan skyline while they dined and danced.

Continue to the foot of Montague St and the waterfront. **The Esplanade**, known locally as the Promenade (1951), a five-block walkway from Remsen to Orange Sts, provides spectacular views of the Manhattan skyline, the Statue of Liberty, and Ellis Island. It cantilevers over the Brooklyn–Queens Expressway, which accounts for the constant whooshing of traffic sounds. A plaque at the entrance recalls the site of "Four Chimneys," the mansion where George Washington planned his army's retreat from Brooklyn (*see box overleaf*). Hezekiah Pierpont later bought it.

BROOKLYN HISTORICAL SOCIETY
Terra cotta head of a Native American (1878).

Exit the promenade and look left to **nos. 2–3 Pierrepont Place**, two superb Renaissance Revival brownstones (1857) by Frederick A. Peterson, the architect of Cooper Union. An 1858 city directory lists the owners as Abiel Abbot Low (teas) and Alexander M. White (furs), though White's obituary later describes him as a banker; he was also the father of Alfred Tredway White (*see p. 489*). Low, a Yankee from Salem, Massachusetts, got into the China trade early, made a fortune, and settled here; his son Seth became mayor of Brooklyn and of New York City. From his opulent home—four stories, elaborated with quoins, a heavy cornice, Corinthian pilasters, and a conservatory on the south end—Low could watch his ships setting sail.

To the right of the Promenade entrance is Montague Terrace; follow it and turn left onto Remsen St, and then right onto Hicks St. Walk a short block to **Grace Court Alley** (*on the left*), once

a mews for the carriages of the Remsen and Joralemon St gentry. The converted stables today house the modern gentry.

Across the street at 254 Hicks St is **Grace Church** (1847); Upjohn here reverted to his usual Gothic Revival manner a year after his experiment with the Church of the Pilgrims. Three Tiffany windows adorn the sanctuary.

Walk south a block to Joralemon St and west to Columbia Place. At 4–30 Columbia Place, the **Riverside Apartments** (1890; William Field & Son, remodeled 1988) are one of Alfred Tredway White's experiments (*see p. 489*) in moderate-price, limited-profit housing. Construction for the BQE obliterated a former central garden.

The nearest subways are the 2, 3, 4, 5, at Borough Hall and the R at Court St, but you can also continue west to the water along Joralemon St and walk back north through Brooklyn Bridge Park.

BROOKLYN BRIDGE PARK & DUMBO

Map p. 622, B1–B2. Brooklyn waterfront and piers from Adams St near the Manhattan Bridge south to Atlantic Ave. Subway: A, C to High St; 2, 3 to Clark St; R to Court St. New York Water Taxi (nywatertaxi.com) and East River Ferry (eastriverferry.com) also provide access from Manhattan. Open 6am–1am. Restrooms at Pier 1, Pier 2, Pier 6, Squibb Park, and Empire Fulton Ferry. Walking tours April–end Oct, Sun 11. Food concessions (seasonal). For info, brooklynbridgepark.org.

Brooklyn Bridge Park, landscaped beginning in 2010 by Michael Van Valkenburg, has returned 85 acres including 1.3 miles of waterfront to the public, lining the rivers with a strip of green and reclaiming the warehouses and piers that once energized Brooklyn's economy. Still under construction at the time of writing, the park offers playing fields, paths for running and cycling, lawns, a roller rink, a rip-rapped sandy beach (not for swimming), changing art installations, and spectacular views of the Manhattan skyline and the historic East River bridges. The park's seven ecosystems include ornamental gardens, woodland gardens, meadows, and salt marshes.

A branch of the Brooklyn Ice Cream Factory in the **former fireboat station** (1926) draws big crowds in hot weather (*T: 718 246 3963, brooklynicecreamfactory.com*). **Bargemusic** (*bargemusic.org*), at the foot of Old Fulton St (not part of the park), founded by violinist Olga Bloom aboard a former coffee barge, has presented chamber music since 1977; north of the ferry landing is the luxury River Café restaurant (*see p. 505*).

BROOKLYN HEIGHTS IN THE REVOLUTION

After the disastrous Battle of Brooklyn on August 27, 1776, in which the American forces were surrounded and slaughtered, the remaining colonial army retreated to Brooklyn Heights. In a half-day of fighting, some 1,200 Americans had been killed and 1,500 wounded or captured; the British lost only 60, with 300 wounded. Had General Howe pressed his advantage, he might well have been able to push the ragtag and demoralized American troops into the East River. Instead, he waited, for two days. After dark on August 29, Washington silently brought his troops down from the Heights to the ferry landing (near present Fulton St). Waiting there with commandeered boats was a regiment of fishermen from Massachusetts. The fishermen rowed back and forth all night, hidden by fog, evacuating Washington's entire force of 9,500 men by daybreak.

DUMBO

Until about 20 years ago Dumbo (or DUMBO), instantly recognizable as a gentrified neighborhood by its acronymic nickname (Down Under the Manhattan Bridge Overpass), was an anonymous industrial district (albeit with glorious views of the Manhattan waterfront), whose factories turned out cardboard boxes and tin cans,

Brillo, soap, shoes, and other useful things. The Belgian block streets and the occasional railroad spur remain, as do warehouses and factory buildings, but the residential population has gone upscale and the old foundries and engine works have given way to tech companies, restaurants and cafes, and art galleries. In 2007 the City designated parts of Dumbo as a historic district, bounded roughly by the Manhattan and Brooklyn bridges, and the Brooklyn–Queens Expressway. As of 2015 the arts scene is in transition; some galleries are moving to new space in the neighborhood, while soaring real estate prices are forcing others to seek greener pastures elsewhere. **Smack Mellon** (*map. 622, C1; 92 Plymouth St at Washington St; open Wed–Sun 12–6, smackmellon. org*), a not-for-profit gallery that nurtures emerging artists, remains.

Between the Manhattan and Brooklyn Bridges is the Empire Fulton Ferry district, where the **Fulton Ferry Landing** (formerly part of a small state park) marks the location of the first steam ferry service (1814) to Manhattan. Here too stand the remains of the 19th-century brick warehouses that once stored coffee, sugar, tobacco, cotton, and jute from all over the world. The hulking **Empire Stores** (1869 and 1885), once the center of the Arbuckle brothers' far-flung coffee operations and the roofless ruin of the **former Tobacco Inspection Warehouse** (c. 1860) evoke Brooklyn's commercial past and are slated for renewal as commercial and exhibition spaces. Near them on the lawn **Jane's Carousel** (1922) enjoys an all-year pavilion (2011) designed by Jean Nouvel (*open May–Sept daily 11–7 except Tues; Sept–May Thur–Sun 11–6; admission charge; T: 718 222 2502, janescarousel.com*).

VINEGAR HILL

The little neighborhood of Vinegar Hill is located along the East River between Dumbo and the Brooklyn Navy Yard. John Jackson, a shipbuilder turned developer, sold 40 acres to the federal government for a navy yard, held on to the rest, and erected housing for the workers whom the yard would employ. He dubbed his development Vinegar Hill to attract Irish refugees who had emigrated after the last stand (1798) of an abortive rebellion against the British at Vinegar Hill in Co. Wexford. Today the modest Federal and Greek Revival row houses, Belgian block streets, and some early 20th-century industrial architecture give the neighborhood its pleasantly gritty character.

THE NAVY YARD & FORT GREENE

Map p. 623, E2. 63 Flushing Ave (Carlton Ave). Visitor Center, Building 92. Open Wed–Sun 12–6. Free. Gift shop. The yard itself is accessible only by tour (admission charge): Turnstile Tours (see p. 578). Subway: F to York St. Turn right when you exit the station; turn right again at the corner onto York St. Walk along York St for three blocks until the street curves to the right (mural on Navy Yard wall on your left); follow York St to end; turn right into Navy St; continue on Navy St, past Sands St and the Sands Street Gate; turn left into Flushing Ave, and continue for five blocks until you arrive at Flushing Ave and Carlton Ave; Navy Yard Center will be on your left. You may also take the B69 bus from near the York St station, which departs from Sands St and Pearl St, two blocks south of the station.

HISTORY OF THE NAVY YARD

In 1781 John Jackson and his brothers founded a shipyard on the shores of Wallabout Bay whose facilities included a sawmill and a pond for seasoning ships' timbers. The US Navy paid Jackson $40,000 for his 40 acres in 1801 and five years later established the Brooklyn Navy Yard. During the War of 1812, the yard fitted out vessels to raid British merchant ships; thereafter it launched the steam warship *Fulton* (1815); the ship-of-the-line *Ohio* (1820); schooners for the China trade; packets for transport, mail, and freight; slavers; and many steamboats. During the Civil War the yard, whose workforce had grown to about 6,000, converted more than 400 merchant vessels and private ships to military service. Among the distinguished vessels built later were the battleship *Maine*, blown up in Havana harbor (1898); the *Arizona*, sunk at Pearl Harbor (1941); and the battleship *Missouri*, on whose decks Japan signed the surrender ending World War II.

Activity in the Yard peaked during World War II, when 70,000 workers on continuous shifts turned out battleships and destroyers, and repaired or overhauled some 5,000 vessels. By then, the yard had grown to include six dry docks, two building ways, eight piers, 270 buildings, and 30 miles of railroad tracks for moving equipment and supplies. After the war the Yard fell victim to Defense Department cutbacks and was decommissioned in 1966. In 1969 the City bought it for $24 million; it became the non-profit Brooklyn Navy Yard Development Corporation in 1981.

Today it is an eco-industrial park, its 300 acres housing 330 businesses employing 5,800 people—including artists, designers, and producers of camouflage, countertops, movies, and modular homes. Because the BNYDC is committed to sustainability, the Yard has wind and solar street lights, a rooftop farm, and facilities for recycling water.

NAVY YARD LANDMARKS

Dry Dock No. 1 (1840–51; William J. McAlpine, engineer; Thornton MacNess Niven, architect and master of masonry), acknowledged as a masterwork of 19th-century engineering, took more than ten years to build, partly because underground springs and quicksand repeatedly flooded the excavation. By the time the foundation was laid, 6,539 piles had been driven into the ground. The granite walls, quarried in Maine and Connecticut, are still beautiful to behold, worth every bit of the dry dock's cost of more than $2 million.

The **Commandant's House** (1805–?6), behind a high brick wall and gated iron fence (*visible from Little St off Water St*), formerly known as Quarters A, is a large clapboarded building with narrow dormers, imposing porches, and leaded glass windows. Commandant Matthew Perry lived here for two years before setting off for Japan. It is now privately owned.

The austere **former US Naval Hospital** (1830; Martin E. Thompson) is slated for adaptive re-use. Thompson, an outstanding architect of the Greek Revival period, is probably best known for the façade of his Assay Bank, now in the Metropolitan Museum. This hospital, with its fine granite stonework, two-story square-columned colonnade and wide flight of steps, set the standard for other institutional buildings that followed.

Admirals' Row (c. 1850–1900), along Flushing Ave near Navy St, is slated for demolition. Formerly housing for high-ranking officers, the buildings are girdled by invasive vines and in danger of collapse. The *WPA Guide* described them in 1934 as "scrupulously neat...and bordered by gardens, tennis courts, and carefully kept walks."

Here Goes Something, A 3,000-sq-ft mural on the Navy Yard wall (*along Navy St near Sands St*), depicts the history of the area through its workers: from Native American fishermen to the modern workforce seeking jobs. The painting (2012) was sponsored by Groundswell, an organization that creates public art as a tool for social change.

WALLABOUT BAY AND THE PRISON SHIPS

Wallabout Bay, a cove in the East River between the Williamsburg and Manhattan bridges, was settled by Dutch (1637) who called the bay "Waal-bogt" ("bend in the inner harbor" or possibly "Walloons' bay"). The bay became infamous during the Revolution when the British anchored derelict warships and transports in its shallow waters; stripped the hulks of their guns, masts, rigging, sails, and rudders; and imprisoned thousands of American soldiers, sailors, and civilians in the holds. The notorious *Jersey*, which lay about 100 yards offshore with as many as 1,100 men confined aboard, became a visible reminder to New Yorkers of the war's brutality. Shipboard conditions were appalling—darkness, stench, starvation, putrid food, sadistic guards, disease, dysentery, and despair. A daily work party buried the dead on the shore in shallow graves, and for years whitening bones littered the sandy beach, the skulls, according to a contemporary observer "as common as pumpkins in an autumn cornfield." An estimated 11,500 men died on the prison ships around Manhattan, twice the number of those who died in battle during the Revolutionary War.

In 1902 Navy Yard workers uncovered timbers from the *Jersey* under 14–16 feet of silt, reawakening interest in those who had died on the ships. Six years later the Prison Ship Martyrs Monument was dedicated. The 149-ft Doric column designed by McKim, Mead and White, topped with a brazier by A.A. Weinman, stands in Fort Greene Park (*DeKalb Ave to Myrtle Ave, Washington Park St to Edwards St*).

FORT GREENE
South of the Navy Yard at the foot of the Manhattan Bridge, Fort Greene is named for Nathanael Greene, a hero of the Revolutionary War, who supervised the construction of a hilltop fort overlooking Wallabout Bay. Originally it was named for General Rufus Putnam and was later renamed to honor Greene.

BROOKLYN ARTS DISTRICT

Anchored by the venerable Brooklyn Academy of Music, an arts district is transforming the area around the commercial axes of Flatbush Ave and Fulton St into New York's Left Bank. The population is ethnically mixed, mirroring the city at large.

The former Williamsburgh Savings Bank Tower, now the residential **One Hanson Place** (at Ashland Place; *map p. 623, D4*) was long Brooklyn's tallest (1927–9; Halsey, McCormack & Heine), famous also for its four-faced clock and the number of dentists' offices it housed. The interior relief carvings of thrifty squirrels, bees, and pelicans recall the building's origins.

Home turf of the Brooklyn Nets (basketball) and the New York Islanders (ice hockey), the rust-red, hunchbacked **Barclays Center** (Ellerbe Becket/AECOM, and SHoP architects) opened in 2012 after years of controversy and multiple design revisions (*map p. 623, D4; Atlantic Ave at Flatbush Ave; subway: B, D, N, Q, R, 2, 3, 4, or 5 to Atlantic Ave-BarclaysCenter; T: 917 618 6700, barclayscenter.com*). Conceived as the centerpiece of a mega-development called Atlantic Yards, it also hosts college basketball, boxing, and concerts, and can seat up to 19,000 people. The building has drastically changed the neighborhood and has elicited mixed opinions: some have remarked on its hard-core industrial glamour, while others have compared it to a pile of rusting crankcases. The mega-development was renamed Pacific Park in 2014, and is rising east of the Barclays Center.

MoCADA (Museum of Contemporary African Diasporan Arts) is a small attractive museum offering changing exhibitions, educational programs, and community events that focus on black artists (*map p. 623, E4; 80 Hanson Pl. at South Portland Ave; subway: 2, 3, 4, 5, B, G to Atlantic Ave; C to Lafayette Ave; G to Fulton St; N, R, D, to Pacific St; open Wed, Fri, Sat 12–7, Thur 12–8, Sun 12–6; suggested admission; book and gift shop; T: 718 230 0492, mocada.org*). It is situated in a borough whose population reflects the diversity of the African diaspora—its geography suggested graphically in the latticed walls of the museum reception area.

Across the intersection the landmarked former Hanson Place Baptist Church (1857–60), now the **Hanson Place Seventh Day Adventist Church**, predates the Civil War.

THE BROOKLYN ACADEMY OF MUSIC (BAM)

Map p. 623, D4. Subway: B, Q, 2, 3, 4, 5 to Atlantic Ave; C to Lafayette Ave; D, M, N, R to Pacific St. Peter Jay Sharp Building, 30 Lafayette Ave (Ashland Pl. and St. Felix St); Harvey Lichtenstein Theater, 651 Fulton St (Ashland Pl. and Rockwell Pl.). Open Mon– Fri 10–6, weekends 12–6. T: 718 636 4100, bam.org.

The Brooklyn Academy of Music, the borough's most important performing arts venue, was founded in 1861 as the home of the Brooklyn Philharmonic, whose first building burned in 1902, replaced by the present neo-Italianate hall (1908), designed by Herts & Tallant, prominent theater architects. In its glory days, famous performers appeared here: Enrico Caruso and Geraldine Farrar inaugurated the Academy with the Metropolitan Opera's production of *Faust*; in 1920 Caruso suffered a throat hemorrhage on stage during the first act of *L'Elisir d'Amore*; he gave only three more performances and died within the year.

Brooklyn's decline after World War II took its toll on the academy, which found itself reduced to renting out studios for language and martial arts classes. Beginning in 1967 Harvey Lichtenstein, a dancer-turned-arts administrator, resuscitated it by dint of daring programming, broadening its offerings to include theater, opera, dance, and world music. He established the Next Wave Festival (1983), which drew crowds from across the river, breaking BAM's parochial isolation.

The main building houses a performance hall (2,109 seats) and movie theater, as well as the popular **BAMcafé** (*see p. 505*). In 1987 BAM expanded into the former Majestic Theater (*651 Fulton St*), its innards revitalized (1987; Hardy Holzman Pfeiffer) but not restored—the cracks and wrinkles of its auditorium carefully preserved. Now called the **BAM Harvey Theater** (874 seats), it opened with Peter Brook's marathon *Mahabharata*. In 2012 BAM opened a reclaimed Salvation Army building as the **Fisher Building** (*321 Ashland Pl.*) with a 250-seat auditorium, rehearsal space, and classrooms.

At 262 Ashland Place (*Fulton St and Lafayette Ave*), the long-itinerant Theatre for a New Audience (TAFNA) has found a home in the **Polonsky Shakespeare Center** (2013; Hugh Hardy), architecturally reminiscent of the Dorfman Theatre of the National Theatre in London. The company presents Shakespearean and classic plays. Nearby is the **Mark Morris Dance Center** (*3 Lafayette Ave at Flatbush Ave*), in a formerly derelict building (rehabilitated 2001; Beyer Blinder Belle) with a 97-ft by 67-ft mural (facing the parking lot) by street artist Barry McGee.

WILLIAMSBURG & GREENPOINT

Map p. 623, E1 and p. 609. To get to Southside (south of Grand St) by subway: J, M, or Z to Marcy Ave; East River Ferry to Schaefer Landing-South Williamsburg. To Northside by subway: L to Bedford Ave; East River Ferry to North 6th St-North Williamsburg.

The neighborhood of Williamsburg fans out from the foot of the eponymous bridge to Greenpoint on the north and Flushing Ave on the south. Close to the waterfront and sundered by the Brooklyn–Queens Expressway, it was long a modest residential and heavily industrial area, but recent decades have seen a remarkable rise in its fortunes.

In the 19th century its waterfront drew shipbuilders, and oil and sugar refineries, among them Astral Oil (later part of Standard Oil), the Pfizer Pharmaceutical Company, the Havemeyers and Elder sugar refinery (eventually Domino Sugar), and the F & M Schaefer Brewing Company.

The completion of the Williamsburg Bridge (1903) opened the neighborhood to an influx of immigrants escaping the Lower East Side, many of them Eastern European Jews. In the 1940s, Williamsburg became the first American home of the Satmar Hasidic Community, an ultra-Orthodox Jewish sect (*Hasidim* means "pious ones") whose presence remains highly visible. Puerto Ricans and other Latin Americans arrived after the 1950s, attracted by manufacturing jobs.

Beginning in the early 1970s, and increasingly from the early '90s, impecunious artists, musicians, and students began moving in, particularly to the Northside. Galleries opened, as well as bars, restaurants, and shops. By the early 2000s the neighborhood had become the very cynosure of hipness. Zoning changes in 2005 led to the waterfront area and former industrial zones being redeveloped and built up, dramatically changing the low-rise flavor of the area; shopping, music venues, and nightspots now dominate. The Southside remains primarily Hasidic and Latino, with a large group of Domincans.

POINTS OF INTEREST IN WILLIAMSBURG

The **Williamsburg Bridge** (chief engineer Leffert L. Buck with architect Henry Hornbostel) was originally designed for horse-and-carriage and rail traffic. It opened in 1903, and with its 1,600-ft free span and overall length of 7,308 ft was then the world's longest suspension bridge. It now accommodates vehicles, mass transit, bicyclists, and pedestrians; the footpath and bike route are accessible to people with disabilities.

Near the foot of the bridge, at 175 Broadway, is the **former Williamsburgh Savings Bank** (1875; George B. Post; additions 1906, 1925; Helmle, Huberty & Hudswell). One of the Neoclassical building's two large domes, with its clerestory base, is visible from the street; the form of the second dome, with an oculus, is visible only from the interior. The building has recently undergone an extensive and meticulous restoration on the way to becoming an event space; the original bird-cage elevator and a mural by the bank's interior architect Peter B. Wight are among many details preserved.

Across Broadway, at no. 178, the venerable **Peter Luger Steak House** was established in 1887 as "Carl Luger's Café, Billiards and Bowling Alley." The bowling alley is gone but the dry-aged porterhouse steaks are still famous.

The erstwhile **Domino Factory** on the East River waterfront (*at Kent Ave between South 5th and South 3rd Sts*) was at the time of writing greenlit for redevelopment as luxury housing and office space. The familiar "Domino Sugar" sign has been removed from the factory's refinery tower but will be re-erected once construction is complete.

The **Brooklyn Art Library** (*103A North 3rd St at Wythe Ave and Berry St*) is the physical home of The Sketchbook Project (*open daily 11–7; T: 718 388 7941, sketchbookproject.com*). Thousands of sketchbooks, submitted by artists from all over the world, line the walls of the library. Visitors can browse or register (via smartphone) and search for works by subject, place, type, artist, and more.

The Russian Orthodox **Cathedral of the Transfiguration** (1916–21; Louis Allmendinger), at the corner of Driggs Ave and North 12th St near the southern border of Greenpoint stands out for its five copper-clad onion domes, the original cladding (since replaced) installed by parishioners to save money.

McCARREN PARK

Bounded by North 12th St, Lorimer St and Manhattan Ave, Bayard St and Berry St-Nassau Ave, McCarren Park draws visitors from the whole of North Brooklyn to its 35 acres of ballfields, running track, and gardens. In 2012, the McCarren Park Pool and Play Center—a Robert Moses-era public works project—re-opened after a $50-million restoration. The original project, opened in the summer of 1936, had a 6,800-swimmer capacity. Over the decades it became run-down and dangerous, and in 1984 it closed, leaving its 55,440-square-foot expanse available for trysting couples, drug users, and at least one family of ducks that lived on an undrained bathhouse roof. Rogers Marvel Architects' renovation includes new changing room pavilions, a concrete "beach," and the original bathhouses repurposed as a recreation and fitness center.

GREENPOINT

Map p. 609, A3. Subway: G to Nassau Ave or Greenpoint Ave; East River Ferry to India St-Greenpoint. From Williamsburg you can walk to Greenpoint along Bedford Ave or Driggs Ave across McCarren Park.

Greenpoint, the neck of land on the East River bounded by Newtown Creek and the Brooklyn–Queens Expressway, has long been a quiet residential area with a significant Polish population. Like Williamsburg, its history is tied to the waterfront and to heavy industry; its recent growth and gentrification have also paralleled Williamsburg's. Manhattan Avenue, the main north–south thoroughfare, is now a mix of longtime Polish businesses and newer concerns, while once-industrial Franklin St is the primary locus of the recent hipster influx, with many restaurants, bars, and boutique stores. Among them is **Word** (*126 Franklin St; T: 718 383 0096, wordbookstores.com*), an independent bookstore that hosts readings and events.

ALONG DRIGGS AVENUE
Monsignor McGolrick Park, bounded by Nassau and Driggs Aves and Russell and Monitor Sts, was once Winthrop (pronounced "winthrow") Park, after Winthrop Jones, a lumberyard owner and politician. In 1941 it was renamed for Monsignor Edward J. McGolrick, an Irish immigrant who served the parish of St. Cecelia and the neighborhood for 50 years. Allées of plane trees lead to the central shelter building (1910; Helmle & Huberty) inspired by the Grand Trianon at Versailles. The **Monitor memorial** (1938; Antonio de Filippo), a monumental bronze sailor pulling at a hawser, celebrates the local origin of the ironclad USS *Monitor*, built at the Continental Ironworks, then on West St at Calyer St, and outfitted at the Brooklyn Navy Yard.

The Roman Catholic **St. Stanislaus Kostka Church** (c. 1878), imposing and ornate (*607 Humboldt St, corner of Driggs Ave*), serves the borough's largest Polish congregation. St. Stanislaus Kostka, beatified in 1605 and canonized in 1726, was a Jesuit novice who walked to Rome from Vienna to follow his vocation, and to escape from the harsh treatment of his elder brother, who was alarmed by his sibling's exuberant piety. Young Stanislaus died shortly after arriving, having predicted his own death. He was not quite 18. A section of Driggs Ave is signposted "Walesa-Solidarity Square," and a street sign reading "Saint John Paul II Square" is affixed to the church itself—testament to the affection of many long-time residents for the former pope.

ON THE WATERFRONT

Transmitter Park and Pier, off West St at the western end of Greenpoint Ave and Kent St, formerly housed the local radio station's transmission towers. The park (opened 2012; WXY Architecture + Urban Design and landscape architect Donna Walcavage) is small but offers panoramic views of the East River and Manhattan.

Newtown Creek, a three-and-a-half mile long estuary that forms the northern Brooklyn-Queens boundary, has historically been the site of glue factories, coal yards, lumber yards, and oil refineries. It is estimated that between 17 and 30 million gallons of petroleum products have leaked or been spilled over the past hundred-plus years, contaminating soil and groundwater. But there is a bright side to the story. The **Newtown Creek Wastewater Treatment Plant**, with its eight digester eggs that glow blue at night (courtesy of lighting designer Hervé Descottes), turns sewage into fertilizer. There is also a **Nature Walk** (environmental sculptor George Trakas with landscape architects Quennell Rothschild & Partners; *Visitor Center open Fri and Sat noon–4; T: 311, nyc.gov/dep*). Beginning at the end of Paidge Ave, the trail passes through industrial territory to the water, providing great views along the way, and incorporates displays about the area's native plants, ecology, and industrial history.

SOUTH BROOKLYN

The residential neighborhoods of Boerum Hill, Cobble Hill, Carroll Gardens, and Red Hook (the first three sometimes known collectively as BoCoCa) once were called South Brooklyn, not because they stood at the southern edge of the borough but because they were south of the former village of Brooklyn—before Brooklyn was absorbed into Greater New York. All were renamed in the 20th century during the "brownstone revolution" to heighten both their appeal and the prices of the brownstones (*see p. 409*) that give these neighborhoods their character.

COBBLE HILL

The name of Cobble Hill dates back to the Revolutionary War when Washington's Continental army fortified "cobbleshill" at the intersection of Court St and Atlantic Ave (*map p. 622, B4*). After the British took Long Island, they destroyed the fort and cut down the hill so it wouldn't overlook their headquarters in Brooklyn Heights. Today the **Cobble Hill Historic District**, from Atlantic Ave to Degraw St, has rows of

19th-century brick and brownstone houses in Greek and Romanesque styles, many built on speculation for an upper middle class that arrived after the ferry service from Manhattan was established. These restored row houses now make Cobble Hill a desirable and expensive neighborhood. The main commercial district is Smith Street.

An exception among the houses built for a prosperous middle class are Alfred Tredway White's low-rent working-class dwellings, all built (or designed) by William Field & Son: the **Tower Buildings** (*417–435 Hicks St, 136–142 Warren St, and 129–135 Baltic St*), **Workingmen's Cottages** (*Warren Place off Warren St between Henry and Hicks Sts*) and **Home Buildings** (*439–445 Hicks St and 134–140 Baltic St*). White, a successful businessman, engineer, and devout Unitarian, based his buildings on Sir Sydney Waterlow's model tenements in London; the apartments provided space and sunlight, outdoor stairways, indoor toilets, and basement bathtubs. White expected to make a five percent profit on these investments in human dignity, espousing a philosophy of "philanthropy plus five percent" to encourage other developers to follow his example. When he died, leaving a fortune estimated by his *New York Times* obituary at $15 million, he was hailed as "Brooklyn's foremost citizen."

BOERUM HILL AND CARROLL GARDENS

South of Cobble Hill is Boerum Hill, renamed to disassociate it from Red Hook to the south. Carroll Gardens, southeast of Boerum Hill, also residential but less affluent, is named for Charles Carroll, a signer of the Declaration of Independence. The "garden" part of the name comes from the deep yards fronting many of the brownstones, especially on the "place" streets—First through Fourth. The neighborhood was for years Italian-American, focused on the waterfront and still retains some of its small town atmosphere.

Al Capone was married at **St. Mary's Star of the Sea Church** (*467 Court St between Nelson and Luquer Sts*).

RED HOOK

Map p. 609, A4. The nearest subways are the F and G trains at Smith-9th Sts, perhaps a mile away. Bus B61 runs from the subway stop to Red Hook, or you can take it from Boerum Place-Joralemon St. An easier option from Manhattan is the New York Water Taxi shuttle to IKEA from Pier 11 at Wall St on the East River; free on weekends.

The fortunes of Red Hook, south of the Gowanus Expressway and along the waterfront, rose and fell with the maritime economy. The Dutch who settled there in 1636 called it "Roode Hoek," (*roode* for the soil color and *hoek*—"point, corner"—for the geographical shape). For two hundred years the marshy, low-lying area remained sparsely populated. The Dutch farmers filled in wetlands, built tidal mills, and cut a canal from Buttermilk Channel to Gowanus Creek, thus shortcutting the trip around the point. During the Revolution Fort Defiance, part of a chain of primitive fortifications, stood on present day Beard Street, and fired its guns at the British fleet entering the Upper Bay.

Not until after 1825, when the opening of the Erie Canal brought tons of agricultural products from the Midwest into the Port of New York, did Red Hook begin turning away from its agrarian roots. In 1839 Daniel Richards began constructing the Atlantic Basin, dredging the swamp and building docks that could berth 150 ships. Its 20 acres of wharves, warehouses, and shipbuilding facilities attracted Irish, German, and Scandinavian workers as did the later Erie Basin (1850s), built by the entrepreneur and railroad man William Beard. Beard, himself an Irish immigrant, charged ship owners 50 cents a cubic yard to dump their rock ballast into the harbor, creating the long breakwater that hooks into the bay. By the beginning of the 20th century, Red Hook had become one of the busiest shipping centers in the country, especially for transporting and storing grain.

Sometimes called the Hell's Kitchen of Brooklyn, the neighborhood was tough, populated largely by Irish, Italian, and, later, Puerto Rican immigrant dock workers. Al "Scarface" Capone got his start here, along with the eponymous injury. Elia Kazan's *On the Waterfront* (1954) chronicled Red Hook's corrupt waterfront politics (though the film was shot in Hoboken, NJ). The simultaneous grit and beauty of the place inspired Arthur Miller's *View from the Bridge* (1955) in which one of the characters called Red Hook "the slum that faces the bay on the seaward side of the Brooklyn Bridge...the gullet of New York swallowing the tonnage of the world."

The construction of the Brooklyn–Battery Tunnel (1950), the Gowanus Expressway (1964), the Brooklyn–Queens Expressway (1957) severed Red Hook's main commercial thoroughfare from the waterfront and all of Red Hook from the rest of the borough. As containerization replaced break-bulk shipping, jobs disappeared and the neighborhood slumped. Red Hook hit bottom around 1988, when *Life* magazine voted it one of the ten worst neighborhoods in the country, "the crack capital of America." Then, in the 1990s, former police officer Gregory O'Connell began buying waterfront properties, including some of the old 19th-century brick warehouses, and leasing them to small businesses and artists. By 1994, a writer for the *New York Times* was wondering whether Red Hook would become the next SoHo, or in his words, "RedHo."

Since the turn of the 21st century the waterfront has continued to enjoy a renaissance. In 2006 a Fairway supermarket opened in a pre-Civil War coffee warehouse, and a cruise ship terminal arrived on the Red Hook Piers. Two years later the Swedish furniture designer IKEA opened the doors of a blue-and-yellow big-box store on the grounds of the former Todd Shipyards, formerly a symbol of Red Hook's maritime prowess. (The parking lot covers the shipyard's dry dock.) Though badly hit by Hurricane Sandy in 2012, Red Hook has recovered thanks, in part, to the do-it-yourself pioneering spirit of its residents.

VAN BRUNT STREET

The neighborhood's main axis, Van Brunt Street runs north-south to the waterfront. Along it are shops, small restaurants, and cafés. The **Kentler International Drawing Space** exhibits works on paper in a storefront gallery; the building was constructed (1877) by the Kentler family as a haberdashery (*353 Van Brunt St near Wolcott St; open Thur–Sun 12–5; T: 718 875 2098, kentlergallery.org*). The granite warehouse originally

Brooklyn Clay Retort & Firebrick Works (*76–86 Van Dyke St at Van Brunt and Richards Sts*) was built (c. 1860) to store firebricks, used for lining furnaces, kilns, and fireplaces. A remnant of Brooklyn's industrial past, it was Red Hook's first designated landmark.

THE WATERFRONT

Nineteenth-century warehouses (called "stores," as in "storehouses") line the waterfront. The **Waterfront Museum and Showboat Barge** (*290 Conover St at Pier 44 near Reed St; open all year Sat 1–5, spring–fall Thur 4–8; by donation; T: 718 624 4719, waterfrontmuseum.org*) dates back to 1914 when it belonged to the Lehigh Valley Railroad and ferried freight across the Hudson. The museum houses historic photos of the harbor and marine artifacts. **Erie Basin Park** (2006; Lee Weintraub, landscape architect), adjacent to the IKEA store (*intersection of Halleck and Columbia Sts*), takes advantage of bits and pieces of maritime detritus from the Todd Shipyards (closed 1985) to recall the history it displaced. Arrayed around the park are nautical objects small and large: bollards, winches, rope, and gantry cranes. The park exists as a trade-off for IKEA's permission to build a retail store in an area zoned for heavy industry. From the end of Columbia St there is a dramatic view of the **former Port of New York Grain Elevator Terminal** (1922), its huge concrete silos rising into the sky.

The 70-acre **Red Hook Recreational Area**—once a marshy shantytown called Tinkerville—was established in 1934. Today Mexican, Central American, South American, and Caribbean food trucks make the fields a destination for street-food fans as well as for ball players (*Sat and Sun afternoons, May through Oct*).

PROSPECT PARK & ENVIRONS

Map p. 609, A4. Subway: 2, 3 to Grand Army Plaza. Park open 5am–1am; woodlands, Parade Ground, and playgrounds close at sunset; attractions have various hours. Admission charge for skating. Café and snack bar. T: 718 965 8951, prospectpark.org.

With its 526 acres of meadows, woods, and lakes, Prospect Park is the largest in Brooklyn. Laid out (1866–7) by Frederick Law Olmsted and Calvert Vaux after they had cut their teeth on Central Park, the park is thought by many to be their masterpiece. In addition to Olmsted's romantically enhanced landscape, there are picnic grounds, a small zoo, nature trails, a carousel, a water playground, and a skating rink. The Brooklyn Museum and Botanic Garden are located adjacent to the park.

GRAND ARMY PLAZA

Grand Army Plaza (1867) lies at the intersection of Flatbush Ave, Eastern Parkway, Prospect Park West, and Union St. Designers Olmsted and Vaux conceived of the plaza as a formal entrance to the park, inspired by Baron Georges Haussmann's modernization of Paris, which emphasized grandeur and urban planning on a Roman scale. The wide boulevards, patterned after Haussmann's Place de l'Étoile-Place Charles de Gaulle, are a welcome departure from the utilitarian street grid, allowing a panoramic view of the surrounding architecture, sculpture, and greenery.

The addition of the **Soldiers' and Sailors' Arch**, designed by John H. Duncan (later of Grant's Tomb fame) memorializes defenders of the Union in the Civil War. Despite its heroic subject and grand proportions (80ft wide by 80ft high, with the arch reaching 50ft), the unadorned monument was considered artistically negligible when dedicated in 1892, so the firm of McKim, Mead and White was hired to oversee its ornamentation. Frederick MacMonnies (1863–1937), a Brooklynite who had previously worked with Stanford White, was hired to design the sculpture. His flanking groups representing the *Spirit of the Army* and *Spirit of the Navy* are considered masterpieces. On top a figure of Columbia, symbolizing the United States, appears in the company of angels, riding in a Roman quadriga, bearing a sword and flag. In 1976, she fell out of the chariot, but was set up again. Bas-reliefs on the inner sides of the arch depict Lincoln and Ulysses S. Grant astride their horses; William O'Donovan sculpted the men; Thomas Eakins the horses (both 1894).

To the east and west of the central ellipse earthen berms designed by Olmsted and Vaux isolate the Plaza from traffic noise. Near the ends of the berms stand statues of Civil War figures Gouverneur Kemble Warren (1896; Henry Baerer) and General Henry Warner Slocum (1905; Frederick W. MacMonnies), both of whom led troops at Gettysburg. Near the center of the ellipse is the cheerfully eclectic **Mary Louise Bailey Fountain** (1932; Eugene Savage, sculptor; Egerton Swartwout; pedestal), whose Art Deco allegories of Felicity and Wisdom stand above a neo-Baroque pedestal shaped like a ship's prow. Neptune and sportive tritons splash and blow their conch-shell horns in a rocky basin reminiscent of Italian Renaissance grottoes (Frank Bailey, a Brooklyn-based financier and philanthropist, and his wife donated the fountain).

Stanford White completed the plaza's Beaux-Arts design in the late 1890s, installing four Doric columns, decorated at the base with axes and rams' heads and topped with soaring eagles; he also designed the pedestrian shelters resembling Chinese pagodas. Inside the park entrance stands a **statue of James Stranahan**, the "Father of Prospect Park" (1891; Frederick MacMonnies), whose tireless advocacy for public gardens in Brooklyn is largely responsible for the park we enjoy today.

THE BROOKLYN BOTANIC GARDEN

Subway: 2, 3 to Eastern Pkwy-Brooklyn Museum; 4, 5 to Botanic Garden. Entrances at 990 Washington Ave (Eastern Pkwy), from parking lot behind the Brooklyn Museum, and near the subway stop at Eastern Pkwy. Open March–Oct Tues–Fri 8–6, weekends and holidays 10–6; Nov–Feb Tues–Fri 8–4:30, weekends 10–4:30. Closed Mon (except Mon holidays), Thanksgiving, Christmas Day, New Year's Day. Admission charge but free Nov–Feb weekdays. Café, restaurant, gift shop. T: 718 623 7200, bbg.org.

Hedged around with asphalt and apartment houses, the Brooklyn Botanic Garden is a 52-acre urban oasis of verdant beauty. Within the garden are lawns with fountains, ornamental trees, magnificent specimens of oak and pine, and perennial borders. The Japanese Hill-and-Pond Garden (1914), considered the masterpiece of Japanese-born designer Takeo Shiota, reveals changing scenes and views as you stroll its winding path. The Cherry Esplanade is spectacular in late April or early May. Small specialized gardens include an herb garden, a fragrance garden, a rock garden with a bubbling waterfall, a Shakespeare garden, and the Cranford Rose Garden with nearly 1,200 varieties. The rock garden grows around glacial boulders stranded in Brooklyn, one of them said to have been dragged from the Adirondacks 250 miles away.

In the conservatories are displays of tropical forests, deserts, and temperate zones. Nearby is a hothouse full of aquatic plants and orchids. The Bonsai Museum has one of the largest collections outside Japan.

THE BROOKLYN MUSEUM

Map p. 609, A4. 200 Eastern Pkwy (Washington Ave). Subway: 2, 3 to Eastern Pkwy-Brooklyn Museum. Parking lot accessible from Washington Ave. Open Wed 11–6, Thur 11–10, weekends 11–6; first Sat of each month open until 11pm. Closed Mon, Tues, Thanksgiving, Christmas, and New Year's Day. Suggested donation (except first Sat, free 5–11). Excellent book and gift shop. T: 718 638 5000, brooklynmuseum.org.

Situated between Prospect Park and Grand Army Plaza, two of the borough's grandest landmarks, the Brooklyn Museum (founded 1823) harks back to the days when Brooklyn was a separate city, fired with ambition to rival New York across the river. Today its rich collections (1.5 million objects), displayed in a grand 19th-century building, make it one of the nation's finest art museums. Foremost among the reasons to visit is the superb Egyptian collection, recently re-installed, which includes many objects dug up during the museum's own program of excavations. The museum has a large collection of American painting and decorative arts, from the colonial period through the years after World War II. The African and South American collections are also remarkable.

THE BUILDING
The massive Beaux-Arts building (1897; McKim, Mead & White; later additions), complete with Ionic portico and imposing pediment, represents only a quarter of the architects' original plan for a truly encyclopedic museum whose four wings would encompass all spheres of human knowledge. Brooklyn's change in status from independent city to borough of Greater New York in 1898 curtailed this grandiose vision, and most construction halted in 1927. In 1934–5 the original grand staircase was torn down, possibly to make the museum more welcoming, though the result was unfortunate. Today the welcoming entrance pavilion (2004; James Stewart Polshek Assocs) is filled with light (and some sculpture).

The heroic sculptures on the frieze above the cornice include Mohammed, Praxiteles, Pindar, and Plato, personifying religion, art, poetry, and philosophy. On the pediment eight heroic figures by Adolph A. Weinman and Daniel Chester French represent the Arts and Sciences.

Daniel Chester French's statues of *Manhattan* and *Brooklyn* (1916) flanking the main entrance on Eastern Parkway originally stood near the Brooklyn approach to the Manhattan Bridge. In the 1960s Robert Moses proposed an expressway through Lower Manhattan that would necessitate demolition of the bridge approaches. Since Moses usually got what he wanted, the Municipal Art Commission gave permission for the demolition under the condition that some of the sculpture be salvaged. The Brooklyn Museum volunteered to take these two sculptures, which arrived in 1963. The roadway was defeated in 1969 but the statues have remained here. Left of the entrance, *Manhattan* sits surrounded with symbols of wealth, culture, pride, and power (a strongbox, a headless Greek statue, a peacock). A small child reading a book leans against the more modest domestic figure of *Brooklyn*, with a church (Brooklyn was once called "the borough of churches") and a lyre on her left.

FIRST FLOOR

Pavilion: Inside the steel and glass pavilion are sculptures from one of Auguste Rodin's greatest works, *The Burghers of Calais*. The Metropolitan Museum also has a casting (*see p. 352*).
Great Hall: "Connecting Cultures: A World in Brooklyn," a long-term exhibition, offers a sample of the collection's riches. The objects, grouped into categories, include Gaston Lachaise's bronze *Standing Woman* (1955–6), radiating sexual power and vitality; ancestral figures from different cultures; Picasso's fractured *Portrait of a Woman in Gray*; and a Victorian "century" vase, sporting a dizzying array of patriotic motifs, made in Brooklyn's Union Porcelain Works.
Williamsburg Murals: In the glass corridor near the restaurant are displayed the Williamsburg Murals,

executed by pioneer American Abstract artists Ilya Bolotowsky and Balcomb Greene among others, commissioned in 1936 by the Works Progress Administration, a bold choice at a time when murals generally depicted American regional life or Socialist Realist subjects.
Sculpture Garden: The outdoor Sculpture Garden contains architectural ornaments and statuary salvaged from demolished buildings, ranging from Pennsylvania Station to obscure tenements. Adolph A. Weinman's *Night* (c. 1910) was commissioned for the former Pennsylvania Station (destroyed 1963) and rediscovered buried in the New Jersey Meadowlands. The 47-ft replica of the Statue of Liberty formerly crowned the Liberty Storage Warehouse on West 64th St near Lincoln Center.

SECOND FLOOR

Arts of Islam and Asia: *NB: At the time of writing the galleries on this floor were closed for renovation.* The collection is wide in its scope, including art from the Islamic world, from Iran, Arabia,

Pakistan and Mughal India; Buddhist and Hindu art from India, Tibet and Cambodia; and the arts of Japan, Korea and China.

THIRD FLOOR

European art (1): Selections from the European painting collection are arranged thematically around the Beaux-Arts court. Three of the sections—"Art and Devotion," "Painting Land and Sea," and "Tracing the Figure"—offer religious works by Maso di Banco, Carlo Crivelli, Jusepe de Ribera, and others; landscapes by Monet and Cézanne from the museum's collection of French paintings; and portraits by Goya, Rembrandt, and Berthe Morisot. On the fourth wall, "Russian Modern," explores the influence of Russian and former Soviet artists on modern European painting.

Ancient Near Eastern Art (2): Twelve spectacular Assyrian reliefs from the palace of King Ashurnasirpal II (9th century BC) dominate this gallery, each panel incised with lines of cuneiform

script that relate the story of the king's lineage and his empire.

Egyptian art (3): The museum's collection, one of the finest in the nation, spans the 5,000 years from the Pre-dynastic era through the age of Roman domination. The museum began acquiring Egyptian antiquities at the beginning of the 20th century, buying works and sponsoring archaeological excavations, also obtaining the important collection of pioneer American Egyptologist Charles Edwin Wilbour (1833–96).

Three large galleries house antiquities from all major periods of Egyptian civilization. The central gallery introduces ancient Egypt through such topics as farming and culture, and the importance of the River Nile. Two

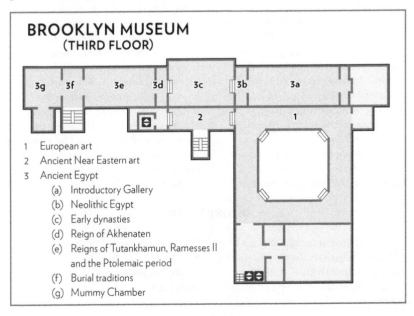

BROOKLYN MUSEUM
(THIRD FLOOR)

1 European art
2 Ancient Near Eastern art
3 Ancient Egypt
   (a) Introductory Gallery
   (b) Neolithic Egypt
   (c) Early dynasties
   (d) Reign of Akhenaten
   (e) Reigns of Tutankhamun, Ramesses II and the Ptolemaic period
   (f) Burial traditions
   (g) Mummy Chamber

galleries on the right contain works from Pre-dynastic Egypt (6th–3rd centuries BC) through the early New Kingdom (2nd century BC). Galleries to the left contain artifacts from the early New Kingdom through the Roman Period (1st century BC and 1st century AD).

The **Introductory Gallery (3a)** offers an overview of Egyptian society. Varied portraiture styles show the assimilation of the cultures that either subjugated, or submitted to, Egypt's rule. Near the door to the right stands one of the museum's oldest treasures, a terra cotta female figurine, nicknamed the "Bird Lady" (3500–3400 BC), with extended arms and a beaklike face, excavated during the first of the museum's many archaeological expeditions.

A small chamber **(3b)** displays objects from the **Neolithic period**, when farming communities dotted the shores of the Nile, and Egypt had yet to be unified under one ruler. Here are carved stone vessels, crude ceramics, and jewelry.

In the large chamber beyond **(3c)** are objects from the **earliest dynasties** (2972–1540 BC), including alabaster vases from the burial site of Djoser, the king who raised the first pyramid, and a huge stone sarcophagus from Giza, site of the Great Sphinx. Old Kingdom sculptures in stone and painted wood depict early kings and court officials. Among the goods produced throughout the Aegean and Mediterranean region is a spectacular Minoan jug decorated with octopi, aquatic plants, and fishermen's nets (c. 1575–1500 BC). The gallery ends with the **early 18th Dynasty** of the New Kingdom, the beginning of Egypt's great cultural flowering, including an elegant relief of Amunhotep I bearing the White Crown of Upper Egypt (New Kingdom, c. 1514–1493 BC) and a colorful tomb painting of a woman with offerings (New Kingdom, c. 1539–1425).

On the other side of the introductory gallery, a small chamber **(3d)** exhibits treasures from the **reign of Akhenaten** (14th century BC), the pharaoh who established a monotheistic religion centered on the worship of Aten, a sun god of his own devising. The beautiful Wilbour plaque is thought to depict Akhenaten and his queen Nefertiti.

Just inside the larger second gallery **(3e)** are works from the **reigns of Tutankhamun** (r. c. 1336–1327 BC) and **Ramesses II** (r. 1279–1223 BC), including luxurious objects, tomb reliefs, statuettes and papyri. The center of the gallery contains material from the Third Intermediate Period (c. 1075–656 BC). The most spectacular object is a mummy case with almost perfectly preserved decoration. The gallery ends with the **Ptolemaic period**. Sculpture here shows the reigning influence of Hellenism, best seen in the head of a reigning official, also called the *Brooklyn Black Head* (50 BC), a colossal head of a man whose strong features and curly hair combine Egyptian artistic traditions with Greek influences in a style that would disappear with conquest by the Romans.

The last galleries, devoted to religion and burial traditions, display funerary objects, sarcophagi, and depictions of major gods and goddesses. In the always-popular **Mummy Chamber (3g)** are human and animal mummies, canopic jars for preserving vital organs, and objects intended to ensure a comfortable afterlife. The 26-ft-long papyrus *Book of the Dead of Sobekmose*, contains spells to ease the journey to the underworld.

FOURTH FLOOR

On this floor are the **Center for Feminist Art** and selections from the decorative arts collection, including period rooms.

Feminist art: Judy Chicago's mixed-media installation *The Dinner Party* (1974–9) occupies center stage. Installed in a triangular exhibition hall, the work honors 39 women—from the Primordial Goddess to Georgia O'Keeffe, symbolized by place settings at a ceremonial table.

Period rooms: The museum's 23 period rooms, ranging from a 17th-century Dutch farmhouse in the Flatlands

section of Brooklyn to a ritzy Park Avenue apartment during Prohibition, are worth a visit. A discreet door in the Park Avenue apartment concealed a small walk-in bar.

In 1865 John D. Rockefeller bought the house at 4 West 54th St from Arabella Worsham, who later married railroad magnate Collis P. Huntington. The opulent Near Eastern appearance of the Moorish smoking room reflects Worsham's taste, not Rockefeller's.

FIFTH FLOOR

The museum's collection of American painting, sculpture, and decorative arts is one of the best in the country. Themed galleries on this floor place the art in its historical and social contexts. Also here are changing exhibitions of contemporary art.

American Art: The galleries begin with the Colonial period and proceed through rooms that depict the American landscape (with Albert Bierstadt's enormous *A Storm in the Rocky Mountains—Mt. Rosalie*); everyday life; paintings and decorative objects that illustrate the awakening of interest in exotic locales; naïve and folk traditions; and modern life, the last with paintings by John Sloan, Mark Rothko, Edward Hopper, and Charles Sheeler that explore the urban landscape. Of special interest is the gallery devoted to the Civil War, with Augustus Saint-Gaudens's bust of Lincoln and his figure of *Victory* from the memorial to Robert Gould Shaw, commander of the first black regiment in the Union Army. Eastman Johnson's *Ride for Liberty: The Fugitive Slaves* depicts a slave family racing towards freedom on horseback.

Art of the Americas: "Life, Death, and Transformation in the Americas" presents about 100 pre-Columbian and historical artworks exploring themes of life, death, fertility, regeneration, and spiritual transformation. Among the reminders of mortality on view is the famous Huastec *Life-Death Figure* (900–1250), a carved stone statue with a healthy muscular male on one side and a grinning skeleton on the other. A replica of a death cart (1890–1910), pulled by penitents during Holy Week, carries a figure of the Angel of Death. Also on view are examples from the Hopi and Zuni *kachina* collection; masks from all over the Americas; Aztec and Maya sculptures; pre-Columbian gold ornaments; and ancient Andean textiles including the 2,000-year-old *Paracas Textile*, the most famous piece in the Andean collection.

OTHER BROOKLYN NEIGHBORHOODS

PARK SLOPE

West of Prospect Park (*map p. 609, A4*), the area from Flatbush Ave down to the Prospect Expressway has traditionally had two distinct neighborhoods. West of Seventh Avenue is housing built for working people, mostly Irish employed by factories (including the Ansonia Watch Company) or on the docks. The **North Slope** alongside the park, with fine 19th-century architecture and many churches, has been called "Brooklyn's Gold Coast." **Montgomery Place** just off the park is especially attractive. Seventh Avenue and Fifth Avenue are the main commercial streets, with stylish restaurants and cafés as well as shops. Park slope today, especially near the park, is affluent and family-friendly, its brownstones handsomely maintained and its sidewalks dense with baby strollers.

GREEN-WOOD CEMETERY

Map p. 609, A4. Fifth to McDonald Aves, 20th–37th Sts. Subway: R to main entrance at 25th St; walk one block east. Main entrance open 7:45–5 daily, extended hours in summer. Check website for other entrances. Free. Guided trolley tours Wed and Sun at 1pm; free map at entrance; self-guided tour booklets for sale. T: 718 768 7300, green-wood.com.

Almost rivalling Prospect Park in size, this 478-acre cemetery rises to Brooklyn's highest point (216ft). It was the chosen burial place of so many late 19th-century New Yorkers that the *Times* reported in 1866 that "it is the ambition of the New Yorker to live upon the Fifth Avenue, to take his airings in the [Central] Park, and to sleep with his fathers in Green-Wood." The first burial took place in 1840.

The landscape of the cemetery takes advantage of the hills and valleys left by the glaciers. The Gothic Revival gates are by Richard Upjohn. Architects Warren & Wetmore (Grand Central Terminal), Griffith Thomas (cast-iron buildings in SoHo), and Stanford White (Washington Square Arch, among many other buildings) all designed memorials here. Among those sleeping with their fathers are the politician William M. "Boss" Tweed (*see p. 89*), composer Leonard Bernstein, designer Louis Comfort Tiffany, artists William Merritt Chase and Jean Michel Basquiat, architect Jacob Wrey Mould, and newspaper editor Horace Greeley.

A more recent arrival is Frederick MacMonnies's enormous (57 ton) marble statue **Civic Virtue**. When originally placed in front of Manhattan's City Hall (1922), it offended onlookers in part for the near-nudity of its central figure, a muscular male (*Virtue*) whose modesty is protected by wisps of seaweed and bubbles of foam, and in part because of the two writhing female forms (*Vice*) on whom the hero appears to be trampling. Women had achieved suffrage two years earlier and many booed the unveiling. MacMonnies defended his work by pointing out that Virtue's foot does not actually tread upon the women, but feminist groups, the Women's Christian Temperance Union, and the president of Harvard continued to object. In 1941 the statue was exiled to a plaza in Queens; in 2012 it was invited here and stands at the intersection of Garland and Jasmine Aves.

CROWN HEIGHTS

South of Atlantic Ave between Ralph Ave and Empire Boulevard, Crown Heights is largely residential with a mixed population, including a large group of Hasidim, whose ultra-Orthodox branch of Judaism was founded in 18th-century Poland. They migrated to New York mostly after World War II, settling here, in Williamsburg, and in Borough Park. They are instantly recognizable by their dress: men are bearded and wear long dark frock coats and black hats; women dress in modest clothing that covers their knees, elbows and collarbones. Married women do not show their hair in public, covering it with a wig or a scarf. Since Hasidim have large families, usually seven or so children, their number is increasing; they are politically effective, since they vote *en bloc*.

The main thoroughfare in Crown Heights is Eastern Parkway, a six-lane boulevard that runs from Grand Army Plaza to Ralph Ave, designed by Frederick Law Olmsted and Calvert Vaux with multiple roadways for carriages, pedestrians, and horseback riders. The West Indian American Parade held annually on the parkway on Labor Day draws huge crowds to its carnival of music, spectacular costumes, food, and floats.

WEEKSVILLE

On the far eastern border of Crown Heights are the four small houses that remain from a once-thriving, free, landowning African-American community, now preserved as a historic site. The community was named for James Weeks, a former dockworker from Maryland, who bought property from a Dutch farming family and settled here in 1838, a little more than a decade after the state abolished slavery. The small community sheltered blacks fleeing Manhattan's Draft Riots in 1863 and possibly slaves fleeing north on the Underground Railroad. It was the home of Susan McKinney Steward, the state's first black woman doctor, and boasted the office of an early black newspaper, *The Freedman's Torchlight*. Engulfed in the 1930s by surrounding neighborhoods, it was almost forgotten until 1968, when it was "rediscovered" by James Hurley, then director of the Long Island (now Brooklyn) Historical Society, who had read about it in a turn-of-the-20th century account. He found no traces of Weeksville on foot, but hired a pilot and saw the four houses from the air, hidden from the street grid but lined up parallel to a colonial road (by then an alley) formerly known as Hunterfly Avene.

The **Weeksville Heritage Center**, housed in a handsome building, offers tours, exhibits, and events. (*158 Buffalo Ave. Subway: A, C to Utica Ave. Walk four short blocks south on Utica Ave to Bergen St; turn left onto Bergen St, continue to Heritage Center on Buffalo Ave between Bergen St and St. Marks Ave. Open Tues–Fri 9–5. Public tours Wed and Fri 3pm. Admission charge. T: 718 756 5250, weeksvillesociety.org.*)

BEDFORD-STUYVESANT

Also known as Bed-Stuy, this neighborhood is an amalgam of Bedford to the north and Stuyvesant Heights toward the south. It has one of the nation's largest African-American populations and is known for its rows of handsome brownstones. Like other outlying Brooklyn areas, it developed first as farmland, later as a suburb, then a middle-class urban neighborhood and latterly a ghetto. Its black population was present even during the colonial period, with slave laborers on Dutch farms making up

25 percent of the populace in 1790. During the years of the Great Migration (beginning c. 1910) blacks arrived from the South. In the 1930s others took the A train and resettled here from Harlem as that neighborhood became overcrowded. During World War II, when the Navy Yard was running round-the-clock shifts, Bedford-Stuyvesant attracted many black workers, beginning another cycle of overcrowding. During the 1940s, whites began moving out and by 1950 Bed-Stuy's population was more than 80 percent black. As the city fell on hard times, the neighborhood was hit hard. By 1977, an estimated 1,400 buildings stood empty and abandoned. Now, however, real estate prices have soared, new restaurants and shops have appeared, and Bed-Stuy is being seen once again as an opportunity.

BAY RIDGE

Map p. 609, A4. Subway: R to Bay Ridge Ave. Express bus B27 runs from Madison Ave-57th St in Manhattan.
The Dutch called it Yellow Hook for the color of its clay, but it was renamed in 1853 following a yellow fever epidemic. Until the end of World War II, this quiet residential neighborhood had a significant population of Scandinavians, along with Irish and Italian immigrants, but today its largest ethnic group is Chinese. Tall apartments along Shore Road overlook the bay, though Bay Ridge's most picturesque residence at 8220 Narrows Ave is a pseudo-thatched fieldstone Arts-and-Crafts house (1916).

Fort Hamilton, built 1825–31, faces Fort Wadsworth on Staten Island across the Narrows. On the grounds is the **Harbor Defense Museum** (*entrance from Fort Hamilton Pkwy at 101st St; open Mon–Fri 10–4, but phone ahead; closed weekends and holidays; free; visitors over 18 must show a state or federally issued photo ID, or a valid passport and visa if from overseas; T: 718 630 4349, harbordefensemuseum.com*), which chronicle the history of the fort, the battle of Brooklyn in the Revolution, and the system of harbor defense fortifications.

THE VERRAZANO-NARROWS BRIDGE

Its eastern anchorage sitting solidly in Bay Ridge, the Verrazano-Narrows Bridge is often considered the crowning achievement of bridge designer Othmar Ammann, the last of his six New York City spans. When it opened on November 12, 1964 it was the world's longest suspension bridge, a title it lost when the Humber Bridge in England (main span 4,626 ft) was completed in 1981. The 38,290 tons of galvanized steel wire in its cables could girdle the earth about six times; the towers reach some 70 stories above the sea. Its location at the entrance to New York harbor confers upon it a special prominence and has also restricted the height of the ships that must pass under it.

The bridge fulfilled a dream of road builder Robert Moses, connecting Brooklyn to Staten Island and thereafter to the mainland network of highways. It was named after the Tuscan explorer Giovanni da Verrazzano to placate Bay Ridge's Italian-American community, since more than 8,000 people were displaced by its construction. Although about 193 thousand cars cross daily and the runners of the New York Marathon cross once yearly, the bridge has no path for pedestrians or cyclists—a raw spot that continues to chafe.

CONEY ISLAND

Map p. 611, D4. Subway: D, F, Q, and N train to Coney Island-Stillwell Ave. Rides and attractions open weekends from about mid-Apr through May, and then daily until early Sept; from Sept until the end of Oct, open weekends. Boardwalk open all year. Rides and attractions run from around noon until late evening, with extended weekend hours. Many attractions have no websites or phone numbers.

Joined by landfill to the rest of Brooklyn in the early 20th century, this peninsula encompasses the neighborhoods of Coney Island (where the amusements are), Manhattan Beach, and Brighton Beach to the east, and at the west end, Sea Gate.

Like its fabled roller coasters, Coney Island has had its ups and downs. Once, it was the empire of the nickel, the great populist playground where anyone who could afford the subway could bathe in the Atlantic, gawk at freaks, and drift earthward from the Parachute Jump. In the popular imagination it survives as the archetype of American honky-tonk—the birthplace of the hot dog and home of the world's most terrifying roller coaster—remarkable for high energy and dubious taste. In the 1990s it almost went under, but today the frayed amusement strip along the boardwalk has come to life again.

HISTORY OF CONEY ISLAND

Coney Island was settled by the Dutch, who named it *Konijn Eiland* after the rabbits they found there. Its history as a resort started with the Coney Island Hotel (1829), but its golden age began around the turn of the 20th century when three spectacular amusement parks opened: Steeplechase Park (1897), with a horserace ride, funhouse mirrors, jets of air that lifted women's skirts, and its trademark grinning Funny Face; Luna Park (1903), tricked out with a million electric light bulbs; and Dreamland (1904), more sedate and less financially successful. Dreamland burned in 1911; Luna Park burned in 1944 and did not reopen; Steeplechase lasted until 1964 and was bulldozed in 1966.

During the 1920s and '30s crowds thronged the boardwalk (opened 1923) and lay thigh to thigh on the sand. But the hordes were thinning by the 1940s thanks to the rise of the automobile, the development of air-conditioning, and Robert Moses's efforts to lure people to less raucous forms of entertainment. In the decades after the closure of Steeplechase Park in 1964, urban renewal programs filled housing projects with the elderly and the poor. Three classic rides have now been landmarked and cannot be destroyed: the Parachute Jump (built 1939; *not operative but illuminated at night in season*), the Cyclone roller coaster (1927), and the Wonder Wheel (1920).

And the crowds are returning. In 2001 a new baseball venue welcomed the Brooklyn Cyclones; in 2005 the Stillwell Ave subway station, transformed with a train shed reminiscent of the great European railway terminals, enhanced the trip to Coney Island. New attractions have opened; old ones have been restored or repainted; new restaurants and bars have arrived. In 2014 around 1.5 million people visited, of whom more than 182,000 were brave enough to ride the new Thunderbolt (*see below*).

Across Surf Ave from the subway station, glowing with neon, is **Nathan's Famous hot dog stand**, founded in 1916 by Nathan Handwerker (1890–1974), a Polish-Jewish immigrant who worked slicing rolls at then-famous Feltman's German Garden. According to legend, Jimmy Durante and Eddie Cantor, working as singing waiters at Feltman's, encouraged him to start up on his own and to undercut Feltman's ten-cent hot dogs by charging a nickel. Today Nathan's sponsors the egregious hot-dog eating contest every July 4, an event that seems to have begun in the 1970s; at the time of going to press the world record holder was Joey "Jaws" Chestnut, who gulped down 69 hot dogs (with buns) in 10mins in 2013. Inundated by six feet of water by Hurricane Sandy, Nathan's re-opened in May 2013, refurbished and upgraded with a raw bar.

THE BOARDWALK, EAST TO WEST

The Boardwalk (officially the Edward J. Riegelmann Boardwalk, after a Brooklyn politician) was constructed 1921–3 and has been reconstructed many times. It is about 2.7 miles long, from West 37th St to Corbin Place; according to the NYC Parks Department it contains 1.3 million boards and 15.6 million screws and nails (about twelve to a board). At the time of writing, the Parks Department was replacing five blocks of boards with more weather-resistant concrete and wood-effect plastic; preservationists have strongly objected, but their efforts to get the Boardwalk landmarked have so far failed. (*Beach and Boardwalk, NYC Department of Parks and Recreation: T: 311 or 212 NEW-YORK.*)

The **New York Aquarium** (*602 Surf Ave at West 8th St; subway: F, Q to West 8th St station on Coney Island or N, D to Coney Island-Stillwell Ave; open daily 10–4:30, last entry 1hr before closing; admission charge; gift shop; T: 718 265 3574, nyaquarium.com*) first opened in 1896 in Battery Park but has been at Coney Island since 1957, when it was moved here by Robert Moses. Operated by the Wildlife Conservation Society, which also runs the Bronx Zoo, it was still recovering from Hurricane Sandy at the time of writing, with a major expansion and reconstruction underway.

West of the Aquarium between West 8th and West 10th Sts, the **Cyclone**, an irre-placeable wooden roller coaster (1927), thrills with its very creakiness. The track is 2,640 ft long; the steepest drop plunges at a 58.1-degree angle; the highest point is 85ft above the ground. According to a 1948 story in the *New York Times*, the Cyclone cured a World War II veteran, mute since 1943 despite seeking hospital treatment; after the second dip he began to scream and at the end of the ride uttered his first words in five years, "I feel sick." The day it opened for the 2015 season the train got stuck near the top, and the passengers had to walk down the track to safety, a thrill they had not antic-ipated. Many, however, returned the next day for a complete ride.

Between West 10th and West 12th Sts is **Luna Park** (opened 2010), owned by Zamperla, the international amusement company, operator of the Cyclone and, fur-ther west, the Thunderbolt. Other attractions include bumper cars, and new-style rides that spin and lurch (*T: 718 373 5862, lunaparknyc.com*).

Just to the west is the **Wonder Wheel**, a 150-ft Ferris wheel (1920) with some cars that slide back and forth on tracks as the wheel rotates. Invented by Charles Hermann,

CONEY ISLAND
The Parachute Jump.

it operated for years as Deno's Wonder Wheel, owned by Denos Vourderis, whose family bought and restored it in the 1980s (*Deno's Wonder Wheel Amusement Park; T: 718 372 2592, wonderwheel.com*).

At the foot of the Wonder Wheel is the exhibition center of the not-for-profit **Coney Island History Project**, founded in 2004, with walking tours, an oral history archive, and exhibits with photos, films, and artifacts documenting Coney Island's storied past: for example, Woody Guthrie's years in Coney Island; bathhouses; and the Dreamland fire (*open weekends from Memorial Day to Labor Day, end of May to early September 12–6; exhibits free but admission charge for walking tours; coneyislandhistory.org*).

Another not-for-profit arts organization, **Coney Island USA** (mission: "to defend the honor of American popular culture") sponsors the Coney Island Museum and offers the modern equivalent of the historic freak show at the Coney Island Circus Sideshow (*1208 Surf Ave, corner of West 12th St; T: 718 372 5159, coneyisland.com*). The organization, founded 1980, has been an important factor in Coney Island's revitalization; it also sponsors the Mermaid Parade, held on the Saturday in June closest to the solstice, a joyously garish procession with sea-themed costumes and considerable visible flesh.

Near West 15th St the new **Thunderbolt** (2014)—steel not wood—offers hair-raising drops and loops. Fifteen stories tall, with a track 2,233 ft long, a 100-ft vertical loop, and an 80-ft roll, it is not for the faint-hearted. The original Thunderbolt roller coaster (memorialized in Woody Allen's film *Annie Hall*) closed in 1982 and was dismantled in 2000 (*T: 718 373 5862, lunaparknyc.com*).

The **B&B Carousell** (the two L's keep the original manufacturer's spelling), a historic merry-go-round bought by the City as it was about to be sold at auction, has been restored (re-opened 2013) and housed in an all-weather pavilion. Among the beautifully carved and painted horses, is one by master carver Marcus C. Illions (1872 –1949), created to celebrate the centennial of Abraham Lincoln's birthday, not originally on the Carousell; it stands out from the herd for its spangled and jeweled trappings.

Inland from the Carousell (*1904 Surf Ave, West 17th–West 19th Sts*), **MCU Park**, formerly KeySpan Park (2001) is the home field of the Brooklyn Cyclones, a minor league team of the NY Mets. Along the sidewalk leading to Surf Ave is the Brooklyn 9/11 Memorial; near Surf Ave a statue (2005; Will Behrend, sculptor) of Jackie Robinson and Pee Wee Reese commemorates a historic moment (though possibly apocryphal), when Reese, a white Southerner, walked over to Robinson and put his arm around the second baseman's shoulder in a gesture of support and friendship.

The **Parachute Jump** (James H. Strong; 1939, moved here 1940–1), constructed for the first New York World's Fair, where it was said to give it riders "all the thrills of 'bailing out' without hazard or discomfort," the Parachute Jump imitated those built to teach the military the proper jumping technique. After the fair closed George C. Tilyou bought it and moved it to Steeplechase Park. Steeplechase closed in 1964 and with it, the Parachute Jump. The jump was landmarked in 1989. It has since been stabilized, painted red, and furnished with thousands of LED lights that are programmed to flicker and flash in seasonal scenarios.

EATING AND DRINKING IN BROOKLYN

BROOKLYN ARTS DISTRICT
$$ BAMcafé. Pre- and post-show dining at the Brooklyn Academy of Music, open two hours before most major performances. Bar open Fri and Sat nights during BAMcafé Live events for small plates and drinks. Happy hour on select evenings, 6–8pm. *In the Peter Jay Sharp Building, 30 Lafayette Ave (Ashland Pl. and St. Felix St). T: 718 636 4100.* The website also lists other nearby venues: *bam.org/dining. Map p. 623, D4.*

BROOKLYN HEIGHTS
$$ Colonie. ■ Contemporary American food, many vegetarian choices, sustainable when possible. Eco-chic decor. Lunch weekends, dinner nightly, snack menu weekend afternoons. *127 Atlantic Ave (Clinton and Henry Sts). T: 718 855 7500, colonienyc.com. Map p. 622, B3.*
$$ Henry's End. Contemporary regional American: Ozark barbecue, Louisiana *andouille*, New England lobster. Plenty of craft beers. Dinner nightly. *44 Henry St (Cranberry and Middagh Sts). T: 718 834 1776, henrysend.com. Map p. 622, B2.*
$$ Noodle Pudding. Excellent, well priced Italian food, convivial setting; service can be variable. Dinner every night except Mon. *38 Henry St (Middagh St). T: 718 625 3737, no website. Map p. 622, B2.*

CONEY ISLAND
Nathan's Famous, the mother house of a nationwide hot dog realm,
re-opened in 2013 after being flooded during Hurricane Sandy. *1310 Surf Ave at Stillwell Ave. T: 718 333 2202, nathansfamous.com.* Two restaurants remain from the era when Coney Island had a large Italian population; **Totonno's** ■ classic pizzeria opened in 1924 (*1524 Neptune Ave between West 15th and West 16th Sts; T: 718 372 8606, totonnosconeyisland.com*); and **Gargiulo's** (1907), a large restaurant offering large servings of southern Italian food (*2911 West 15th St between Mermaid and Surf Aves; closed Tues; T: 718 266 4891, www.gargiulos.com*). Further away in Sheepshead Bay is **Randazzo's Clam Bar**, an Italian restaurant known for its raw bar, seafood, and red sauce dishes (*2017 Emmons Ave, near 21st St; T: 718 615 0010, randazzosclambar.com*). Bars, very casual, include **Freak Bar** (*in the Coney Island USA building, 1208 Surf Ave at West 12th St; T: 718 372 5159, coneyisland.com*) and **Ruby's Bar & Grill** (*Boardwalk between West 12th St and Stillwell Ave; T: 718 975 7829, rubysbar.com*).

DUMBO, NAVY YARD, FORT GREENE
$$$ The River Café. ■ Hurricane survivor with a post-Sandy Michelin star, serving excellent food since 1977. Luxurious neighborhood stalwart with panoramic views of Manhattan. Prix fixe only. Dinner nightly, weekend brunch. *1 Water St (Furman and Old Fulton Sts). T: 718 522 5200, therivercafe.com. Map p. 622, B1.*

$$ **Caffe e Vino**. Steps away from BAM, a small rustic *trattoria*, with friendly service, pre-theater menu, outdoor tables in season. Lunch and dinner daily. *112 Dekalb Ave (Ashland Pl. and St. Felix St). T: 718 855 6222, caffeevino.com. Map p. 623, D3.*

$$ **Gran Eléctrica**. Street-style Mexican, but with tip-top ingredients. Applause-winning margaritas, tequila, mescal, Mexican beers. Dinner nightly, brunch weekends. *5 Front St (Old Fulton St). T: 718 852 2700, granelectrica.com. Map p. 622, B1.*

$$ **Junior's**. Legendary for the cheesecake; also has sandwiches, burgers, and specials. Breakfast, lunch, and dinner daily. *386 Flatbush Ave Extension (Dekalb Ave). T: 718 852 5257, juniorscheesecake.com. Map p. 623, D3.*

$$ **Roman's**. Intimate Italian with carefully prepared dishes. Italian-based wine list. Dinner nightly, lunch weekends. *243 Dekalb Ave (Clermont and Vanderbilt Aves). T: 718 622 5300, romansnyc.com. Map p. 623, E3.*

$$ **Vinegar Hill House**. Both the décor and the clientele are classic mod-urban Brooklyn; the carefully crafted American bistro menu does comfort food with style. Dinner nightly, brunch weekends. *72 Hudson Ave (Front and Water Sts). T: 718 522 1018, vinegarhillhouse.com. Map p. 623, D1.*

RED HOOK

$$ **Defonte's Sandwich Shop**. Serving longshoremen (and others of sturdy appetite), its heroically sized sandwiches since the 1920s. Breakfast and lunch. *379 Columbia St (Luquer and Coles Sts) T: 718 625 8052, defontesofbrooklyn.com.*

$$ **Grindhaus**. Small, eccentric, friendly, contemporary; probably NY's only restaurant with a stuffed horse head on the wall. Dinner only, closed Tues, Wed. *275 Van Brunt St, (Visitation Pl.). T: 718 909 2881, grindhausnyc.com.*

$$ **Fort Defiance**. A Red Hook anchor since 2009; well prepared food, cocktails. Breakfast weekdays after 10am, lunch daily, dinner nightly except Tues, weekend brunch. *365 Van Brunt St (Dikeman St). T: 347 453 6672, fortdefiancebrooklyn.com.*

$$ **The Good Fork**. ◼ A pioneer, owned and run by locals; loved by regulars and the press; worldly, eclectic food.Weekend brunch, dinner Tues–Sun. *391 Van Brunt St (Coffey and Van Dyke Sts). T: 718 643 6636, goodfork.com.*

$$ **Kao Soy**. Attractive brick-walled Northern Thai, with some unusual specialties including the namesake noodle dish. Lunch and dinner. *283 Van Brunt St (Pioneer St) T: 718 875 1155, no website.*

$$ **Pok Pok Ny**. Slightly north of Red Hook proper; authentic Thai, no frills, but so popular the website features a live feed of the wait line. Dinner nightly, lunch weekends. *117 Columbia St (Degraw and Kane Sts). T: 718 923 9322, pokpokny.com.*

$$ **Red Hook Lobster Pound**. Lobster fresh from Maine in rolls, in soup, with mac. Re-opened 2015 after renovation. Other locations and trucks. Lunch and dinner Tues–Sun.

284 Van Brunt St (Visitation St). T: 718 858 7650, redhooklobster.com.

$$ Steve's Authentic Key Lime Pies. Authentic is the key word; much loved bakery with takeout. Hours roughly Fri–Sun, 11–6. *185 Van Dyke St (at the very end of the street) T: 718 858 5333, stevesauthentic.com. Phone for weekday hours: T: 888 450 5463.*

$ Sunny's Bar. Century-old waterfront place, cluttered, homey. Cash only (but there's an ATM). Folk, bluegrass, and jazz. *253 Conover St (Beard and Reed Sts). T: 718 625 8211, sunnysredhook.com.*

WILLIAMSBURG, GREENPOINT

$$$$ Luksus. ■ With its *prix fixe* tasting menu, this Scandinavian-inflected New American restaurant in the back of a beer bar has zoomed to popularity, earning a Michelin star. Beer only, no wine. Reservations essential. The bar, **Tørst**, offers snacks and craft beers. Bar: open daily. Restaurant: dinner Tues–Sun, closed Mon. *615 Manhattan Ave (Nassau Ave). T: 718 389 6034, luksusnyc.com.*

$$$$ Peter Luger Steak House. At this most venerable of steakhouses at the foot of the Williamsburg Bridge, order your porterhouse by number of eaters. Lunch and dinner daily. Cash only (or a Peter Luger credit card). *178 Broadway (Driggs Ave). T: 718 387 7400, peterluger.com.*

$$$ Delaware and Hudson. Named for a 19th-century canal system, this 38-seat gem serves homey yet urbane food from the Mid-Atlantic states— funnel cakes, Amish chicken pot pie. Lunch Tues–Fri, dinner Tues–Sun,

brunch weekends. *135 North Fifth St (near Bedford Ave). T: 718 218 8191, delawareandhudson.com.*

$$ Fette Sau. Very Williamsburg, and not for vegetarians, a foodie barbeque with dry-rubbed meat, "gallons of craft beer" and a whiskey list. Outdoor tables and communal seating. Dinner daily, lunch weekends. *354 Metropolitan Ave (Havemeyer and Roebling Sts). T: 718 963 3404, fettesaubbq.com.*

$$ Five Leaves. Burgers and pancakes, shepherds' pie and duck breast in this hip Greenpoint bistro; long lines for weekend brunch. Breakfast, lunch, and dinner daily. *18 Bedford Ave (Lorimer St). T: 718 383 5345, fiveleavesny.com.*

$ Saltie. Nautically themed, delicious sandwiches: the Captain's Daughter (sardine, pickled egg, salsa verde), the Spanish Armada (potato tortilla with pimentón aioli). Cash only. Open daily 10–6. *378 Metropolitan Ave (Havemeyer St and Marcy Ave). T: 718 387 4777, saltieny.com.*

$–$$ Smorgasburg. Founded in 2011, this has grown into a major attraction, rotating between Williamsburg and Fort Greene as part of the huge Brooklyn Flea market. Up to 100 food vendors sell plenty you can take home; but more important are the tacos, doughnuts, barbecue, and Asian hot dogs that you can eat right there. *176 Lafayette Ave (Clermont and Vanderbilt Aves), Sat 11–6. Williamsburg: 50 Kent Ave (10th And 11th Sts), Sun 11–6.* Other locations at Prospect Park, Coney Island, Queens, and South St Seaport. *Brooklynflea.com.*

The Bronx

H ome of the Bronx cheer (i.e. a raspberry) and the Bronx Bombers (or New York Yankees), the Bronx (*map p. 609*) is the only borough attached to mainland North America, and even so it is surrounded on three sides by water: the Hudson River on the west, the Harlem and East Rivers on the south, and Long Island Sound on the east. Part of Bronx County, its area of 43.1 square miles and population of approximately 1.42 million make it the second-smallest borough in both categories.

The eastern Bronx is largely flatland, some of it originally salt marsh, sliced into long peninsulas by inlets and tidal rivers. Tons of garbage, euphemistically known as landfill, have been dumped onto the marshes since World War II, and the filled areas along Eastchester Bay are now densely populated. West of the flatlands, three north-south ridges give the middle and western sections of the borough their hilly terrain. The westernmost ridge runs through Riverdale near the Hudson and west of Broadway, with Broadway following the lowland valley. The second ridge crosses Van Cortlandt Park and runs south to the Macombs Dam Bridge area with the Grand Concourse laid out along its spine. The third and lowest proceeds through the Bronx River Park and Crotona Park, falling away to the flatlands along the East River.

Most of the Bronx is residential, developed with apartment houses that range from the onetime luxury Art Deco buildings along the Grand Concourse and the finely kept high-rises overlooking the Hudson to the institutional towers of Co-Op City and the urban-renewal housing projects of the southern Bronx. The strip along the East River has seen the rise and fall of various industries. Today an immense food distribution center, which includes the relocated Fulton Fish Market, dominates Hunts Point.

Writers Sholem Aleichem, Theodore Dreiser, and Edgar Allan Poe lived for a while in the Bronx, and E.L. Doctorow and Herman Wouk grew up there, but the art form most closely associated with the borough is hip hop.

Visiting the Bronx
The Bronx is the smallest of the Outer Boroughs, but still almost twice the size of Manhattan. Its main attractions—the Bronx Zoo, the New York Botanical Garden, and Yankee Stadium—are accessible by public transportation. Van Cortlandt Park and Woodlawn Cemetery lie at the far ends of northward-reaching subway lines. The Art Deco architecture and the Bronx Museum of the Arts along the Grand Concourse are an easy subway ride from Manhattan. Though accessible by public transportation, Riverdale, Wave Hill, and City Island are easiest reached by car.

HISTORY OF THE BRONX

In 1639 the Dutch West India Company purchased from Native Americans the land that is now the Bronx, and in 1641 Jonas Bronck, a Dane who arrived in the New World by way of Amsterdam, purchased 500 acres along the river, which soon was known as the Broncks' River. Among those arriving later was Anne Hutchinson, who had earlier been expelled from the Massachusetts Bay Colony for her dissenting theological views. She settled at what is now Pelham Bay in the early 1640s. Around the same time, John Throgmorton, an Anabaptist, arrived with 35 families. Soon after, Native Americans attacked both colonies, and though some of Throgmorton's followers escaped, Anne Hutchinson's colony was annihilated except for one of her daughters, Susannah, who was taken hostage. After two years with her captors, Susannah was returned, unwillingly, when the Dutch and Native Americans made a treaty to settle their differences. The place names "Throgs Neck" and "Hutchinson River" remain as evidence of these early sojourners. The British took over the territory in 1664 and the Bronx remained quietly rural, its land divided between modest farmers and large landowners whose style of life imitated that of the English landed gentry. Villages evolved along the post roads to Albany and Boston and later along the railroads.

After 1840, however, advances in transportation resulted in a population influx. The first newcomers were the Irish, who came to labor on the railroads and on the Croton Aqueduct. After 1848 Germans followed, mostly farmers. In 1888 the Third Avenue elevated railway reached the hinterland of 169th St and a flood of newcomers began settling near it. Politically the Bronx joined New York in two sections: first the western towns in 1874, then, 20 years later, the eastern towns. The two areas officially became the Borough of the Bronx in 1898.

The golden age of the Bronx lasted from about 1920 to the early 1950s, when it was a patchwork of tightly-knit neighborhoods, most dominated by one ethnic group. City services—education, transportation, parks—made life comfortable and attractive. In the later 20th century, as job opportunities shriveled and the middle class decamped for the suburbs or to government-subsidized developments, the Bronx fell on hard times. Although it no longer has acres of burned, abandoned buildings and rubble-filled lots, the problems that plagued it since the 1970s and '80s are only in part resolved. But the streets are cleaner, crime is down, real estate values and the population are rising, and the borough's future looks more promising.

THE SOUTH BRONX & GRAND CONCOURSE

The Grand Concourse, once called the "Park Avenue" and the "Champs Élysées" of the Bronx, runs from 138th St past Bronx Borough Hall at 161st Street and continues north to Van Cortlandt Park, about 4.5 miles. Louis Aloys Risse, who came to the Bronx from Alsace as a teenager and quickly rose to prominence as a civil engineer, conceived of a broad avenue running along the Bronx's central rocky ridge. It would connect Manhattan's parks with the 4,000 acres of undeveloped parkland in the Bronx and also serve as a speedway for horse racing. It was completed in 1909, but by then the carriage roads had to be paved over for the emerging automobile.

In the late 1920s and '30s the Grand Concourse became the borough's finest residential boulevard, its residents mostly well-to-do Jewish families. Still today it is a showcase of Art Deco architecture. The Concourse Plaza Hotel (*900 Grand Concourse*) attracted celebrities—Yankee stars from Babe Ruth to Mickey Mantle—and aspiring politicians. Like the rest of the borough it deteriorated in the 1970s, served as a welfare hotel for a while, and in 1983 was converted to subsidized housing for the elderly. Today the Concourse is home to working- and middle-class residents.

At the southern end of Joyce Kilmer Park the **Lorelei Fountain** (*Grand Concourse at 161st St*), honors the poet Heinrich Heine, whose poem of the same name assured the Lorelei's fame. A gleaming white marble maiden stands on a pedestal surrounded by mermaids and sea shells, but there is also a skull beneath her feet suggesting her fatal attraction. According to legend she was spurned in love and transformed into a siren whose singing lured sailors to their death in the waters of the Rhine. The sculpture (1899; Ernst Herter) was intended for the German city of Düsseldorf, but the rising tide of nationalism and anti-semitism in the German Reich (Heine was Jewish) led to its rejection. A German singing group brought the statue to New York, hoping to put it at the southeast entrance to Central Park, but it was judged too mediocre an artwork for so prominent a spot. Eventually it was installed here, in an area that had a large population of German Jews. Repeatedly vandalized, it has equally repeatedly been restored. The park is named for Kilmer, the poet of "Trees," who was killed in World War I.

Across the street (*851 Grand Concourse at 161st St, facing Lou Gehrig Plaza*) is the severe Art Deco **Mario Merola Bronx County Building** (1934; Joseph Freedlander & Max Hausle), formerly the Bronx County Courthouse, named for a Bronx district attorney. The frieze by Charles Keck above the base takes themes of agriculture, industry, religion and the arts. The large groups of figures at the entrance, supervised by Adolph A. Weinman, depict illustrate themes appropriate for a government building: *Civic Government*, the *Majesty of Law, Victory and Peace, Loyalty, Valor, Sacrifice*, and so on.

YANKEE STADIUM

Map p. 609, B2. East 161st St and River Ave. Subway: B, D, or 4 to 161st St-Yankee Stadium. This is the home turf of the New York Yankees, major league baseball's most successful team. Founded in 1901, the team has chalked up victories thanks to the talents of Babe Ruth, Lou Gehrig, Joe DiMaggio, Mickey Mantle, and many more.

The present stadium (2009; HOK Sport) is sometimes called "the House that Steinbrenner Built," for the free-spending and free-speaking George Steinbrenner, who owned a majority share in the team from 1973 until his death in 2010. The building cost at least $1.5 billion, an all-time record for a baseball stadium.

BRONX MUSEUM OF THE ARTS

Map p. 609, B2. 1040 Grand Concourse at 165th St. Subway: B (anytime) or D (not during rush hours) to 167th St-Grand Concourse; exit at rear of station, walk two blocks south along Grand Concourse. Open Thur–Sun 11–6, Fri until 8; closed Mon–Wed, Thanksgiving, Christmas, New Year's Day. Free. T: 718 681 6000, bronxmuseum.org.

The small, highly reputed Bronx Museum of the Arts was founded (1971) to serve the borough's ethnically diverse population. The shining aluminum surfaces of today's admired, updated building (2006; Arquitectonica) symbolize, to some, the revitalization of this part of the Bronx. The permanent collection numbers about 1,000 works in all media by African-American and Latin-American artists and those of Asian descent, as well as artists with a personal connection to the Bronx, including Willie Cole, David Hammons, Glenn Ligon, and Kara Walker.

EDGAR ALLAN POE COTTAGE

Map p. 609, B1. 2640 Grand Concourse (Kingsbridge Rd). Subway: 4 to Kingsbridge Rd (walk three blocks east to Grand Concourse); D to East Kingsbridge Rd. Open Thur, Fri 10–3; Sat 10–4; Sun 1–5; closed mid-Dec through mid-Jan and major holidays. Admission charge; smartphone audio tour. T: 718 881 8900, bronxhistoricalsociety.org/poecottage.html.

Edgar Allan Poe lived in more than half a dozen places in New York, stalked by poverty and his own bleak outlook; he came to this little house in 1846 when the Bronx was rural, hoping the country air would cure his wife Virginia's tuberculosis. She died during the first winter, but the poet stayed on to write "Ulalume" and "The Bells," and perhaps part of "Annabel Lee," a eulogy to his bride, whom he had married when she was just 13 years old. Poe rented out the cottage in 1849 and went south, dying in October of that year in Baltimore. The house has been converted to a simple museum, with a few period furnishings and memorabilia. The Bronx must have agreed with Poe, since he remained here after his wife's death, longer than he stayed anywhere else in New York, his isolation broken by walks to Fordham village where the Jesuits of St. John's College (now Fordham University) loaned him books and allowed him use of the library.

HALL OF FAME FOR GREAT AMERICANS

Bronx Community College. 2155 University Ave. Subway: 4 to Burnside Ave; B or D to Tremont Ave. T: 718 289 5170, www.bcc.cuny.edu/halloffame.

On the campus of Bronx Community College, formerly a campus of New York University, the honorees of the country's first Hall of Fame look down from the heights to the Harlem River. In 1901 Henry Mitchell MacCracken, chancellor of NYU, established the outdoor monument to honor men and women whose energy, commitment, and intellect contributed to the development of the nation and the good of humanity.

Lined up on a majestic 630-foot colonnade (1901; Stanford White), 98 bronze busts commemorate artists, educators, humanitarians, statesmen, theologians, and others. Some of the honorees are as famous as George Washington; others are as obscure as Charlotte Cushman (1816–76), an actress known for her role as Lady Macbeth. Her partner was the sculptor Emma Stebbins (*see p. 317*). Many of the statues were created by leading sculptors of the era: Daniel Chester French, Hermon A. MacNeil, Augustus Saint-Gaudens; others were sculpted by people whose names have faded from memory. The most recent bust is Franklin Delano Roosevelt, sculpted in 1973 (from a model by Jo Davidson) and installed in 1992.

At one time the unveilings of the statues were reported in the press, attended by crowds, and accompanied by parades. Today the Hall of Fame, restored in 1999, is sparsely attended. Nevertheless, the faces of the long-dead and their heroic words inscribed in bronze remain inspirational and evocative.

BELMONT

Bounded by East Fordham Rd, the Bronx Zoo, East 187th St, and Arthur Ave, Belmont is the remnant of an Italian-American community that began in the 19th century as workers arrived to construct the Bronx Zoo. Today Belmont's population includes Albanians and Latin Americans, but retains its core Italian population. Along Arthur Ave, an area sometimes called "The Real Little Italy of New York," especially between 184th and 187th Sts, are enticing Italian food shops, plus the indoor Arthur Avenue Retail Market (*2344 Arthur Ave; open Mon–Sat 8–5*), established by Mayor La Guardia.

THE NORTH BRONX

BRONX ZOO

Map p. 609, B1. Bronx River Pkwy at Fordham Rd. Most convenient public transportation from Manhattan: BxM11 express bus, which stops along Madison Ave; for schedule, T: 718 445 3100 or visit the zoo website. Open daily Nov–March 10–4:30, until 5pm in summer and 5:30 on summer weekends and holidays. Admission charge (expensive), except Wed, pay what you wish. Guided tours. Cafés. Shop. T: 718 367 1010, bronxzoo.com.

The Bronx Zoo, founded (1899) as the New York Zoological Society, was one of the first great urban zoos; today it offers modern outdoor and indoor habitat exhibits with more than 6,000 animals of 650 species on a 265-acre preserve. A monorail and shuttle (*extra fees*) cut down walking distances, but the zoo offers too much to see in a single day. Among the popular exhibits are the Congo Gorilla Forest, a small-scale walk-through rain forest; Tiger Mountain; World of Reptiles; and Wild Asia (*visible only from the monorail*). In 2008 "Madagascar!" opened in the restored Lion House, with leaping lemurs, huge Nile crocodiles, and thousands upon thousands of Madagascar hissing cockroaches. The zoo has active ecology and wildlife conservation programs throughout the world.

THE NEW YORK BOTANICAL GARDEN

Map p. 609, B1. 200th St and Southern Blvd. Metro-North Harlem local trains from Grand Central stop at the Botanical Garden station. Subway: 4, B, D to Bedford Park; transfer to Bx26 bus. Open Tues–Sun 10–6, Mon federal holidays; closes at 5pm mid-Jan–Feb and for some events; admission charge except free admission to grounds Wed and from 9–10am Sat; closed Thanksgiving, Christmas, and Mon except federal holidays. Narrated tram tour; self-guided tours for mobile phone; art exhibitions. Café. T: 718 817 8700, nybg.org.

As well as being a leader in research, the New York Botanical Garden is the site of a world-famous botanical library, a force for ecological education, and one of the city's great retreats. On its 250 acres grow a million plants; gardens include a 50-acre uncut woodland; a rose garden reconstructed after the designs of Beatrice Farrand; stands of magnolias, lilacs, and other flowering trees; conifer displays; seasonal bedding plants; and thousands of naturalized daffodils. The spectacular Conservatory, which recalls the Victorian glasshouses of the Royal Botanical Gardens in Kew, London, has been completely renovated, each of its 17,000 panes of glass replaced. Inside are towering palms, as well as habitat exhibits of tropical and desert flora, aquatic and insectivorous plants, extravagant seasonal displays, as well as special exhibitions, including the Holiday Train Show (*late Nov to Jan*) and the annual Orchid Show (*early spring*).

WAVE HILL

Map p. 609, B1. Independence Ave at West 249th St. Metro-North Hudson line local train from Grand Central to Riverdale; free Wave Hill shuttle meets trains 9:45am–3:45pm, at 45mins past the hour. Return shuttles leave Wave Hill's front gate 12:20–5:20, at 20mins past the hour. Subway: 1 to West 242nd St; free Wave Hill shuttle van meets passengers on west side of Broadway in front of Burger King 9:10am–10pm, at 10mins past the hour. Van returns visitors to same location, leaving Wave Hill front gate on the hour, from noon until 5pm. For additional travel directions, see website. Gardens open March 15–Oct 31 Tues–Sun 9–5:30; Nov 1–March 14 Tues–Sun 9–4:30; greenhouses open all year 10–noon & 1–4; closed New Year's Day, Thanksgiving, Christmas, and Mon holidays except Memorial Day, Labor Day, Columbus Day and Veterans Day. Admission charge, but free Tues and Sat 9–noon. Café. T: 718 549 3200, wavehill.org.

Wave Hill, formerly a country estate, has hosted Charles Darwin, Thomas Henry Huxley, Mark Twain, and Arturo Toscanini in its historic gray fieldstone house (1843; restored 2013, Beyer Blinder Belle) surrounded by landscaped grounds and gardens. Theodore Roosevelt lived here for a while as a child, and the beauty of the place surely contributed to his love of nature. Mark Twain wrote that the roaring blasts of wind through the treetops thrilled him and made him want to live always. Wave Hill's gardens today are justly famous, established by master gardener Marco Polo Stufano, who served as head horticulturist for 34 years. The views across the Hudson River to the palisades in New Jersey are beautiful at any time, but spectacular during the autumn leaf season and also in winter when the trees are bare. You can visit an aquatic garden; wander beneath mature specimen trees; and visit greenhouses with tender plants, cacti, and palms. Glyndor (1927), the second house on the estate, hosts art exhibitions.

EASTERN BRONX

CITY ISLAND

Map p. 609, C1. Subway: 6 to Pelham Bay Park (last stop); transfer to bus Bx29 marked "City Island."

Linked to the Bronx by a bridge from Pelham Bay Park, City Island was named by its pre-Revolutionary developer who hoped to make it a major port. It never happened.

Today City Island is a small community with a long maritime history. During the 19th century the yachts of J. Pierpont Morgan and his fellow financiers were built here. Later the Minneford Boat Yard turned out America's Cup defenders, for which Ratsey & Lapthorn made sails, and during World War II its shipyards manufactured landing craft and minesweepers. Though several yacht clubs remain, the boat-building industry has largely gone elsewhere. Along City Island Ave, seafood restaurants, shops, and a few galleries attract a summer crowd. Charming Victorian houses stand on the side streets (along with some new condos and houses). The **City Island Nautical Museum** (*190 Fordham St; open Sat and Sun 1–5 and by appointment; call before going in winter; T: 718 885 0008, cityislandmuseum.org*), in a former public school, preserves photos and other artifacts of the island's history.

From the foot of Fordham St a ferry departs for **Hart Island** (*not open to the public*), the city's potter's field since 1869, when Louisa Van Slyke, an orphan who died in the city's Charity Hospital, was the first of more than a million unclaimed or unknown people interred here. Prisoners from Rikers Island bury the dead.

PELHAM BAY PARK & THE BARTOW-PELL MANSION

Map p. 609, C1. Subway: 6 to Pelham Bay Park stop and then Westchester Bee-line bus 45 into the park itself. Bus leaves subway station at 11.20, 12.20, 1.20, and 2.20; ask to get off at the Pelham Bay-Bartow-Pell Mansion Museum stop. Bus returns to the subway station 12–5, just after the hour. For Bee-line bus information, T: 914 813 7777.

Pelham Bay Park, the city's largest, embraces 2,118 acres of salt marsh, lagoon, forest, meadow, and shoreline. The Hutchinson River, emptying into Eastchester Bay, divides the park into two sections. In the northern sector are golf courses, Orchard Beach, and the Bartow-Pell Mansion Museum, the only survivor of several fine country estates that once stood in the neighborhood. Anne Hutchinson and her followers (*see p. 509*) are believed to have settled near the park site.

THE BARTOW-PELL MANSION MUSEUM

895 Shore Rd, Pelham Bay Park. Subway and bus as above. Mansion and Carriage House open Wed, Sat, Sun 12–4. Admission charge. Visits to the mansion by guided tour only; tours begin at quarter past the hour. Gardens open daily 8.30–dusk. Free. T: 718 885 1461, bartowpellmansionmuseum.org.

In 1654 Thomas Pell, an English doctor from Connecticut, bought more than 9,000 acres from the Siwanoy Indians, including the present park land, but had to swear allegiance to the Dutch to keep it. When the British took over the colony he was granted (1666) a royal patent for the land. He constructed the original homestead, where four generations of Pells lived. That house was burned during the Revolutionary War and the estate was divided. In 1836 Pell's descendant, Robert Bartow, a successful printer and editor, husband of Maria Lorillard of the tobacco dynasty, bought the land and built the present gray stone Greek Revival mansion, moving in with his family in 1842. Outside were pastures, orchards, and lawns sloping down to the water.

The Bartows lived in the house until 1888 when encroaching industry was diminishing the neighborhood's charm, and their heirs sold the estate to the City of New York. The mansion sat more or less vacant until the International Garden Club bought it in 1914 to use as a club house. They hired the firm of Delano & Aldrich to enlarge and restore it, and established terraced gardens. In the sizzling summer of 1936, Mayor Fiorello La Guardia moved his staff into the mansion, conducting municipal business from a phone bank in the basement. Ten years later, the Garden Club opened the mansion as a museum.

The house is furnished with period furniture, much of it in the Empire style, and the interiors have been repainted the original colors. A free-standing elliptical stairway and a 19th-century parlor stove are noteworthy. The pastures and orchards are gone, but the sloping lawns, several modest gardens, and the basic structure of the 1914 terraces remain, as does a small Pell family graveyard, along with nearby walking trails.

VAN CORTLANDT PARK & WOODLAWN CEMETERY

Van Cortlandt Park (*map p. 609, B1*) occupies about two square miles along the ridges and valleys of the northern Bronx. Fragmented by several major roadways, it offers hiking and cross-country trails, as well as the nation's first public golf course. Established in 2013, the park's ten cricket fields, heavily used on weekends and holidays, are said to make up the largest site for the sport in the US.

Also in the park is the **Van Cortlandt House Museum** (*Broadway at 246th St; Subway: 1 to 242nd St-Broadway; open Tues–Fri 10–3, Sat and Sun 11–4; closed Mon, holidays, and the day after Thanksgiving; admission charge but free on Wed; T: 718 543 3344, vchm.org*). Frederick Van Cortlandt (1699–1749) built the fieldstone and brick mansion (c. 1748) in the Georgian style; inside, the fine paneling and woodwork attest to the family's wealth, as does the elegant wallpaper, recreated from period originals. The house is furnished with English, Dutch, and colonial furniture, including pieces that belonged to the Van Cortlandts. On the second floor is a bedroom where George Washington slept.

WOODLAWN CEMETERY
Map p. 609, B1. Main entrance on Webster Ave at East 233rd St; another entrance on Jerome Ave at Bainbridge Ave. Metro-North Harlem Line local train from Grand Central to Woodlawn station. Subway: 4 to Woodlawn; from station, walk about half a block. Jerome Ave entrance is on the right. Or, take the 2 or 5 train to 233rd St and walk three blocks along 233rd, downhill. Cross over Webster Ave; the cemetery entrance is on the left. Open daily 8.30–4.30. Free. Maps at Webster Ave administration office or from security guards at the main entrance. Audio tour available (rental charge) at administrative office (Mon–Sat 8.30–4.30). T: 718 920 0500 or toll-free 877 496 6352; thewoodlawncemetery.org.
Woodlawn Cemetery was founded in 1863, its location chosen in part for its proximity to the railroad: 35mins from Manhattan by train. Woodlawn is pleasantly landscaped and has its share of monumental funerary architecture, but is most famous for the notable people buried here. Among them: F.W. Woolworth, Herman Melville,

Robert Moses, and Fiorello La Guardia. Financier Oliver Hazard Perry Belmont, founder of Belmont Racecourse, hired Richard Morris Hunt to model his mausoleum after the Chapel of St. Hubert at the Château d'Amboise in France. He is buried here with his wife Alva Smith Vanderbilt Belmont (mother of Consuelo Vanderbilt; *see p. 298*). The earthly remains of meatpacker Herman Armour rest in a mausoleum by James Renwick (architect of St. Patrick's Cathedral), whose pinkish marble walls have reminded some observers of ham or liverwurst. Duke Ellington and Miles Davis are buried here, as are drummer Max Roach, sax players "Illinois" Jacquet and Coleman Hawkins, and vibraphonist Lionel Hampton. Perhaps the strangest epitaph in the cemetery belongs to one George Spenser (1894–1909): "Lost life by stab in falling on ink eraser, evading six young women trying to give him birthday kisses in office of Metropolitan Life Building."

EATING AND DRINKING IN THE BRONX

BETWEEN THE CONCOURSE AND BRONX ZOO

$$ Roberto's. ■ Chef Roberto Paciullo's first restaurant (followed by Zero Otto Nove) offers a superior version of Southern Italian cooking, with local products, fresh pasta, and "nothing from a can," according to the website. Lunch and dinner Mon–Sat. *603 Crescent Ave (Hughes Ave). T: 718 733 9503, robertos.roberto089.com.*

$$ Trattoria Zero Otto Nove. Named for the telephone area code of Salerno, Italy, this *trattoria* serves authentic Neapolitan pizza baked in an imported oven, generous portions of *antipasto*, and other southern Italian dishes. Lunch and dinner, Tues–Sun. *2357 Arthur Ave (186th St). T: 718 220 1027, roberto089.com.*

$$ Tra di Noi. A favorite family-run *trattoria*, with a chef who learned to cook in the kitchens of Italian noble families. Lunch and dinner Tues–Sun. *622 East 187th St (Belmont and Hughes Aves). T: 718 295 1784, tradinoi.com.*

CITY ISLAND

With its seafaring village atmosphere, City Island Avenue has some small, pleasant seafood restaurants.

$$ Bistro SK. This attractive place, owned by a native of Alsace, advertises itself as the only French restaurant in the Bronx. On the menu are classics including *moules marinières* and *frites*. Dinner Tues–Sun, brunch weekends (cash only for brunch). *273 City Island Ave (Carroll and Hawkins Sts). T: 718 885 1670, bistrosk.com.*

$$ Crab Shanty. Seafood Italian style, lobsters, surf and turf. Lunch and dinner daily. Closed Thanksgiving. *361 City Island Ave (Tier St). T: 718 885 1810, originalcrabshantycom.*

$$ Sammy's Shrimp Box. Casual restaurant that draws big crowds in summer to its generous servings of seafood. *64 City Island Ave (Horton St). T: 718 885 3200, shrimpboxrestaurant.com.*

Queens

Queens (*map pp. 609 and 611*), the largest borough in the city, covers 112.2 square miles (about 35 percent of the city's total area) and is bounded by Brooklyn on the west, the East River on the north, the Atlantic Ocean on the south, and Nassau County on the east. Topographically it resembles the rest of Long Island, with a chain of hills created by glacial deposits running across the north and a low outwash plain in the south. The north shore is indented by Flushing and Little Neck bays, while the Rockaway peninsula juts across the mouth of Jamaica Bay in the south to form an eleven-mile oceanfront.

Queens is the second most populous borough (pop. 2.3 million) after Brooklyn. About 48 percent of the population is foreign-born, making Queens by far the nation's most diverse county, with more than 130 languages spoken. In fact the 7 train, which runs from Times Square to Flushing, has been dubbed the "International Express."

Queens is largely residential, with one- and two-family homes and apartment buildings of various heights, but it lacks the concentration of 19th-century brownstones and tenements that characterize Manhattan, Brooklyn, and the Bronx. While Queens has earned its reputation as a bedroom community in the second half of the 20th century, areas that developed earlier became industrial, with concentrations of factories in Long Island City, Maspeth and College Point, and along the right-of-way of the Long Island Rail Road. Commercial centers throughout the borough are often located at the crossroads of earlier towns, established independently before the creation of Greater New York in 1898: the most important ones are Jamaica, Flushing, and Elmhurst.

Because of its former spaciousness and an 1851 law prohibiting further burials in Manhattan, Queens became the resting place of uncounted souls. A belt of cemeteries begins on the Brooklyn-Queens border and stretches eastward along the Jackie Robinson Parkway, an area known by the waggish as the "terminal moraine."

More than any other borough, Queens bears the stamp of Robert Moses, who as parks commissioner preserved acres of forests, meadow, beaches, and marshes, while as master road builder he blighted equally large areas by lacing the borough with highways: the Grand Central Parkway, Interborough (now Jackie Robinson) Parkway, Clearview Expressway, Cross Island Parkway, Laurelton Parkway, Long Island Expressway, Brooklyn–Queens Expressway, and the Whitestone Expressway.

The presence of two major airports, John F. Kennedy and LaGuardia, make transportation-related industries critical to the borough's economy. Some manufacturing jobs remain, as well as service jobs in business and healthcare. TV and motion picture production studios have returned to Long Island City, which now has a flourishing art district. Two major sports venues are Citi Field, home of the New York Mets baseball team, and the USTA Billie Jean King National Tennis Center in Flushing Meadows-Corona Park, where the US Open is played.

Visiting Queens

Glance at a road map and you'll see that Queens is laid out in a simple rectilinear pattern, but it is deceptively hard to navigate. Numbered avenues generally run east–west (with the lower numbers on the north), but they are sometimes interspersed with Roads, Drives, and even an occasional Court bearing the same number. Streets generally run north–south, with lower numbers on the west. The pattern is further complicated by the vestiges of old roads dating from the colonial period, which in turn followed Native American paths that conformed to topographical features, now erased by landfill or leveling. Modern highways have disrupted the continuity of street layouts (as well as the social fabric of the neighborhoods they cross).

HISTORY OF QUEENS

The first inhabitants of Queens were the Rockaway Indians, whose name lives on in the peninsula stretching across Jamaica Bay (whose name in turn recalls the Jameco Indians). The first settlers were Dutch, who arrived c. 1635, staking out their claims to the western part of Long Island, followed by the English, who some 20 years later colonized the eastern part. In 1683, 19 years after the British took title to the former Dutch colony of New Amsterdam, the towns of Newtown, Flushing, and Jamaica were organized as Queens County, one of twelve making up the British province of New York. The name honors Catherine of Braganza, queen of Charles II. During the Revolution most residents of Queens were British sympathizers, and after the war many loyalists emigrated to Newfoundland.

Although a few industries, notably Steinway & Sons, established manufacturing plants in Queens during the 19th century, the borough long remained rural and agricultural. As the railroads began pushing east across Long Island, the beaches began attracting summer residents: at the turn of the 20th century the land now occupied by LaGuardia Airport held an amusement park, and the Rockaways with their ten-mile shoreline attracted the well-to-do to grand hotels or private estates.

In 1898 most of Queens joined Greater New York, although several of the eastern towns chose to remain independent. The population of 152,999 tripled in the next 20 years and doubled again between 1920 and 1930, as transit links opened Queens to development. In 1910 the Queensboro Bridge and the East River tunnel of the Pennsylvania Railroad allowed direct access to Manhattan; during the next decades the subways reached the outer areas. The Triborough Bridge (1936), now the Robert F. Kennedy Bridge, the Bronx–Whitestone Bridge (1939), the Queens–Midtown Tunnel (1939), and the Throgs Neck Bridge (1961) made Queens readily accessible by car.

Several of these public works projects, along with the creation of LaGuardia Airport, were undertaken to coincide with the opening of the 1939–40 World's Fair, the first of two held in Flushing Meadows. After World War II, Queens experienced its second great boom—suburban development—as builders filled open space with tract housing, small homes on small lots, repeated row upon row, block upon block. Despite the blandness of much of Queens's suburban housing, its very newness has saved the borough from some of the urban problems that afflict Manhattan, Brooklyn, and the Bronx.

LONG ISLAND CITY'S ART DISTRICT

The free LIC Art Bus (begun 2014) travels to Socrates Sculpture Park, the Noguchi Museum, Sculpture Center, and MoMA PS1, May–Sept, weekends 1–6. For info visit socratesculpturepark.org.

Long Island City (*map p. 609, B3*), which encompasses the smaller neighborhoods of Astoria, Steinway, Hunters Point and others, grew around the mid-19th century as an industrial center, influenced by its proximity to midtown Manhattan across the river. Its factories churned out chemicals, glass, chewing gum, cookies, batteries, and pianos. Huge advertising signs along the riverfront continue touting Pepsi-Cola (sign 1936) and Silvercup bread (1939), though the latter factory is now a TV and movie studio, and the Pepsi sign will be installed in front of an apartment.

In recent decades Long Island City has become a center for contemporary art, particularly sculpture, since its industrial architecture lends itself to the installation of large works. MoMA PS1 and SculptureCenter are within walking distance of one another; also near one another are the Noguchi Museum and Socrates Sculpture Park; the Fisher Landau Center is in between but accessible by subway. (*Check the website of the Long Island City Cultural Alliance, licca.org, for events and additional venues.*)

MoMA PS1
Map p. 609, B3. 22–25 Jackson Ave (46th Ave). Subway: 7 to 45th Rd-Courthouse Sq; exit onto Jackson Ave and walk right one block. See museum website for alternative travel directions. Open Thur–Mon 12–6; closed Tues–Wed, Thanksgiving, Christmas, New Year's Day. Admission charge. Restaurant and shop. T: 718 784 2084, momaps1.org.
MoMA PS1 is one of the best places in the city to see new and adventurous art, its high-ceilinged galleries friendly to site-specific and large-scale works. The former school building dates back to 1890–1900 and its cavernous basement, institutional stairways, and long corridors add atmosphere. Although the center has no permanent collection, it offers several long-term installations, for example Saul Melman's *Central Governor*, the old basement boiler covered with gold leaf. Others are tucked away so you have to hunt them down. (James Turrell's *Meeting* was not on view at the time of writing.)

P.S.1 was founded (1971) by Alanna Heiss as the Institute of Art and Urban Resources, which converted abandoned or underutilized buildings into art spaces. Renamed P.S.1 Contemporary Art Center (1988), it became an affiliate of MoMA (2000), giving MoMA a 21st-century presence. In 2010 the two institutions merged and P.S.1 became MoMA PS1.

SCULPTURECENTER

Map p. 609, B3. 44–19 Purves St (near Jackson Ave). Subway: 7 to 45th Rd-Courthouse Sq; the park is one block north of the Noguchi Museum. Open Thur–Mon 11–6. Suggested donation. T: 718 361 1750, sculpture-center.org.

Founded by a group of artists as The Clay Club in 1928, SculptureCenter moved into a Manhattan townhouse in 1948 and to Queens in 2002, taking over a former trolley repair shop (redesigned 2002, Maya Lin and David Hotson). Though distinguished artists (Isamu Noguchi, Louise Nevelson) have exhibited here, the focus remains on less established names. The 40-ft ceiling and outdoor courtyard allow for the exhibition of large-scale pieces and the dark, pipe-filled basement level has its own ambiance.

FISHER LANDAU CENTER FOR ART

38–27 30th St (38th and 39th Aves). Subway: N or Q to 39th Ave. Go through turnstiles and take the right-hand staircase. At the corner of 31st St and 39th Ave, turn right and walk one block west on 39th Ave, then turn right onto 30th St. NB: Occasionally the N train does not run on weekends, in which case take the Q train. Open Thur–Mon 12–5. Free. T: 718 937 0727, flcart.org.

Housed in a factory building that turned out parachute harnesses, the Fisher Landau Center (1993) offers rotating exhibitions from the personal collection built up by Emily Fisher Landau from the 1960s. Mrs. Landau, now in her nineties, was inspired to collect art when burglars made off with a jewelry-filled safe from her Upper East Side apartment. She decided to replace the (insured) jewelry with Dubuffets instead of diamonds, Picassos instead of pearls. She also supported young artists, many of whom have since become household names. The collection includes works by Robert Rauschenberg, Ellsworth Kelly, Andy Warhol, Anselm Kiefer, Jasper Johns, Glenn Ligon, and Jenny Holzer. In 2010 Mrs. Landau pledged 417 works by nearly 100 artists to the Whitney Museum of American Art.

NOGUCHI MUSEUM

Map p. 609, B2. 9–01 33rd Rd (between Vernon Blvd and 10th St). Subway: N to Broadway in Queens. From there you can take the Q104 bus toward the river or walk ten blocks west on Broadway towards the East River. Turn left onto Vernon Blvd and walk two blocks to 33rd Rd. Turn left. Check website for additional travel directions. Open Wed–Fri 10–5, Sat–Sun 11–6; closed Mon, Tues, Thanksgiving, Christmas, New Year's Day. Admission charge; pay what you wish on first Fri of month. Gallery talks at 2pm. Café, small shop. T: 718 204 7088, noguchi.org.

In the early 1960s Isamu Noguchi moved his studio from Manhattan to Queens near his marble suppliers on Vernon Blvd and in 1975 bought a former photo engraving plant, now part of the museum. Over the years Noguchi nurtured the idea of creating a space to display works that he had kept for himself; the museum opened in 1985 and now houses more than 250 works by the Japanese-born sculptor, whose sensibility blends Japanese aesthetics with Modernism. The collection spans Noguchi's career, from his brass sculpture of the 1920s showing the influence of Brancusi (for whom he acted as a studio assistant) to mature, austere pieces sculpted from basalt and granite.

The rocks in the garden have been chiseled and worked, in contrast to those in a classical Japanese garden, which remain in their natural forms. The well (1982) is a variant on the Japanese *tsukubai*, a hollowed stone into which water trickles, though in Noguchi's rendering the water rises to the surface and slides down the outside.

SOCRATES SCULPTURE PARK

Vernon Blvd (Broadway). Subway: N to Broadway in Queens; walk eight blocks along Broadway toward the East River. Follow directions for the Noguchi Museum above. Open all year 10–dusk. T: 718 956 1819, socratessculpturepark.org.

Socrates Sculpture Park is the only place in the greater Metropolitan area where artists can create and exhibit large-scale outdoor sculpture and installations. It is also a pleasant four-acre windswept riverside park, reclaimed from its former status as a dumping ground (1986) through the efforts of activists and artists including sculptor Mark Di Suvero. Changing exhibitions are mounted in the spring and fall. Much of the work is created onsite, so you can sometimes watch art in process.

ASTORIA & STEINWAY

One of New York's more diverse neighborhoods, Astoria has been known for its Greek population, now joined by Brazilians, Colombians, Bangladeshis, Chinese, Guyanese, Koreans, Ecuadorians, Romanians, Indians, Filipinos, Albanians, Bosnians, and Arabs from Lebanon, Egypt, Tunisia, Yemen and Morocco. It is named for John Jacob Astor, who invested $500 in local real estate.

THE MUSEUM OF THE MOVING IMAGE

Map p. 609, B3. 36–01 35th Ave (37th St). Subway: M (weekdays only) or R to Steinway St; use the 34 Ave exit near the end of train; walk south along Steinway St; turn right on 35th Ave; walk three blocks to museum entrance just past 37th St. See website for more travel info. Open Wed and Thur 10:30–5, Fri 10:30–8, Sat and Sun 11:30–7. Admission charge but free Fri after 4. Screenings, exhibitions. Café and shop. T: 718 777 6888, movingimage.us.

Gloria Swanson, Paul Robeson, the Marx Brothers, and Rudolf Valentino all once worked in the Astoria Studio Complex (buildings 1919–21)—part of which has been transformed into the Museum of the Moving Image (opened 1988; expanded and renovated 2008–11). Before World War II, Astoria was a center of the movie-making industry, when the Famous Players-Lasky Corporation (later Paramount Pictures) turned out hundreds of silent films and early talkies. During World War II the US army took over the property, turning out training films and propaganda. After the government departed in 1971, the Astoria Motion Picture and Television Foundation was formed. It is now the most successful film-making property on the East Coast.

The Museum of the Moving Image is one of the city's premier attractions, with a shiny new lobby and a curated video installation. The futuristic theater has state-of-the-art technical facilities and a stunning auditorium in Yves Klein blue. The expanded core exhibit, "Behind the Screen," examines the technical aspects of producing, promoting, and presenting movies, TV, and digital entertainment. It has been updated but you can still enjoy Red Grooms's installation, "Tut's Fever Movie Palace," a tongue-in-check rendering of a 1920s movie house with Egyptoid figures of movie greats (Mae West standing behind the candy counter, James Dean laid out in a mummy case). Also on view: historic movie cameras and TV sets; licensed merchandise including super-hero lunch boxes and a large number of action figures; a video arcade with console games; posters and fan magazines; and (a favorite) the mechanical doll with a 360-degree-rotatable head that shocked audiences of *The Exorcist*.

STEINWAY & SONS

Map p. 609, B2. 19th Ave and Steinway Pl. Free factory tours Tues 9:30am, not in July or Aug; reservations essential several months ahead. T: 708 721 2600, steinway.com.

Since 1872, when it moved from Manhattan's Park Ave (then Fourth Ave) where the Seagram Building stands, the factory of **Steinway & Sons** has been a major presence in Queens. Heinrich Steinweg, a woodworker-turned-piano-maker, arrived as an immigrant in 1850 with eight of his nine children. His business thrived in a society where the prosperous middle class was seeking cultural improvement, of which a piano was a potent symbol. After a series of labor disputes the factory moved to rural Queens, allowing the firm to expand and removing Manhattan workers from "the machinations of the anarchists and socialists," who incited rebellion. The Astoria Steinway factory was a giant undertaking, with its own foundry and sawmill, and an enclosed dock and basin on Bowery Bay for receiving raw materials and seasoning timber. When the business passed to Heinrich's sons, William (formerly Wilhelm) built a company town with tidy red brick workers' houses, a church, a library, a school, and a trolley line to the East River. (Workers' housing remains in the area of 20th Ave and 41st St; plaques on the corner houses bear the names of Steinway family members for whom the streets were formerly named.) William, in partnership with George Ehret, founder of the Hell Gate Brewery, transformed the part of the shoreline now occupied by LaGuardia Airport into Bowery Bay Beach (later called North Beach), a picnic ground whose beer halls flowed with Ehret's Hell Gate Beer. Steinway promoted the construction of a trolley tunnel to Manhattan, not completed in his lifetime, but now the Steinway Tunnel (opened 1915) carries the 7 subway train to Flushing.

William Steinway's dour granite mansion remains at **18–33 41st St** (*Berrian Blvd and 19th Ave*) overlooking Long Island Sound, though today a water treatment plant spoils the view the Steinway family once enjoyed.

HISTORIC FLUSHING

Flushing, with its large Chinese, Korean, Indian, and African-American population, is a destination for lovers of Asian food. The Friends' Meeting House and Bowne House remain from the pre-Revolutionary period: both played a role in the history of religious freedom in the US. As befits a town with such a history, Flushing has Catholic and Protestant churches, Buddhist temples, a Greek Orthodox church, a Muslim Center, synagogues, the Quaker Meeting House, and—most spectacularly—a Hindu temple.

FRIENDS' MEETING HOUSE

Map p. 609, C3. 137–16 Northern Blvd (Linden Pl). Subway: 7 to Main St, Flushing; walk north to Northern Blvd (four short blocks); turn right and walk half a block. The meeting house is on the right. Open for worship Sun at 11, tours at 12 or other times by appointment two weeks in advance. T: 929 251 4301, flushingfriends.org.

The Friends' Meeting House (1694), a simple wooden building with a steep hipped roof and small windows, has changed little in the past three centuries. The back faces busy Northern Boulevard while the front opens onto a garden and small graveyard whose stones were unmarked until 1848 in accordance with the Quaker belief that death equalizes everyone. Except for a period during the British occupation (1776–83) when it served as a prison, hay barn, and hospital, the Meeting House has been used continuously for religious services since its construction. Worship must have been uncomfortable during its first 50 winters, as iron stoves were not installed until 1760; central heating followed two centuries later (1965).

BOWNE HOUSE

Map p. 609, C3. 37–01 Bowne St at 37th Ave. Visits by appointment: office@bownehouse. org, T: 718 359 0528, bownehouse.org.

Bowne House is the oldest dwelling in Queens, built in 1661 by John Bowne, a Quaker convert born in England. The Quakers' heretical beliefs and ecstatic form of worship (hence their name) drew the wrath of conforming Christians, notably Governor Peter Stuyvesant, who particularly abhorred the sect and even arrested those who allowed Quakers to meet in their homes. In 1657 he issued an edict declaring the Dutch Reformed Church the only permitted denomination in the colony. Thirty Flushing citizens responded with the Flushing Remonstrance, which rebuked Stuyvesant for curbing the religious freedoms promised to them by the original town charter. Stuyvesant arrested and fined several of the signers. John Bowne subsequently let the Quakers meet in his kitchen and in 1662 Stuyvesant fined Bowne and banished him to Holland. Bowne pleaded his cause with the Dutch West India Company and its business-minded directors advised Stuyvesant to moderate his antagonism, stressing that increased immigration to the under-populated colony was more important than religious conformity.

The **Hindu Temple Society of North America** or Šri Mahã Vallabha Ganapati Devasthãnam (*45–57 Bowne St, between Holly Ave and 45th Ave*), also known as the Ganesh Temple, was founded in 1970 and occupies a site formerly owned by a Russian Orthodox church. The building (1977) was constructed by artisans from India according to the rules of temple-building scripture. It is crowned with ornate sculpture, including images of the elephant-headed god. The basement canteen serves good, inexpensive Indian food (*see p. 530*).

FLUSHING MEADOWS–CORONA PARK

Map p. 609, C3. Van Wyck Expressway and Grand Central Parkway east of 111th St. Subway: 7 to Mets-Willets Point. Walk south past the tennis stadium to the park.

Flushing Meadows-Corona Park, girded by the Grand Central Parkway and the Van Wyck Expressway, occupies 897 acres running north–south along what was once the Flushing River, a navigable waterway to the old town of Flushing. In the park are artifacts left from two World's Fairs, a pool, a skating rink, a carousel, the New York Hall of Science, the Queens Museum, a small zoo, a marina, sports' stadiums, and a theater.

FROM DUMP TO PARK

The Flushing Meadows were once salt marshes, inundated by tides and therefore useless for housing. Saved thus from development, the marsh became the Corona Dump and the river an open sewer. By the 1920s trainloads of trash and garbage that arrived daily from Brooklyn smoldered nightly, giving the place a Dantesque aura and inspiring F. Scott Fitzgerald to immortalize it as the "Valley of Ashes" in *The Great Gatsby*. The swamp disappeared beneath tons of filth, one mound rising high enough to earn the name Mt. Corona. During the 1930s, Robert Moses converted the marshland into the grounds for the 1939–40 World's Fair, a project that involved channeling part of the Flushing River into a conduit as large as a tube of the Holland Tunnel, building sewage plants to decontaminate Flushing Bay, and removing hundreds of thousands of tons of garbage. In 1964 a second and less successful fair occupied the grounds, which were returned to the city in 1967. Remaining from the 1939 fair are the lake and the New York City Building (now the Queens Museum); from the 1964 fair are the Unisphere, Space Park (now the New York Hall of Science), and the Singer Bowl (now Louis Armstrong Stadium in the Tennis Center).

CITI FIELD AND THE NATIONAL TENNIS CENTER

Completed in 2009 (HOK Sport), **Citi Field** (*123-01 Roosevelt Ave; subway: 7 to Mets-Willetts Point*) is the home of the New York Mets National League baseball team and is named for Citigroup, the financial services giant, which bought the naming rights for $400 million, evoking loud protests. In style the stadium, which seats 45,000 recalls classic baseball stadiums, especially Ebbets Field, home of the departed Brooklyn Dodgers, as does the Jackie Robinson Rotunda, which honors the baseball immortal who broke the color line. It replaces Shea Stadium (1974), which in turn replaced the Singer Bowl, an 18,000-seat stadium built for the 1964–5 world's fair.

The **USTA Billie Jean King National Tennis Center** (*Flushing Meadows-Corona Park*) is home to the US Open tennis tournament, played in late-Aug–early Sept. Its three stadiums—Arthur Ashe Stadium, the largest, named for the tennis star; Louis Armstrong, named for the jazz great and Queens resident; and the Grandstand, so far not named for anyone—accommodate some 700,000 fans during the Open.

FLUSHING MEADOWS-CORONA PARK
Detail of the *Unisphere*, built for the 1964 New York World's Fair.

MONUMENTS IN THE PARK

Also surviving from the 1964–5 World's Fair, one of whose central themes was space exploration, is Donald de Lue's 43-ft statue *The Rocket Thrower*, a modestly draped, heavily muscular bronze athlete hurling a missile through a circle of stars. The *New York Times* critic John Canaday unkindly called it a "lamentable monster," adding that it made "Walt Disney look like Leonardo da Vinci." Robert Moses, trying to console de Lue, was quoted as saying "this is the greatest compliment you could have...[Canaday] hates everything that is good." Straight down the mall is the steel *Unisphere* (1963–4; Gilmore D. Clarke), 700,000 lbs, twelve stories high and 120ft in diameter, covered with steel shapes depicting the continents. Its theme was originally "Man's Achievements on a Shrinking Globe in an Expanding Universe," but it has since come to symbolize the borough. The sphere was planned to rotate at the fair, but that proved too costly and it was outfitted with fountains and lights to give the sense of motion. The supporting cables and the country of Sri Lanka were repaired in 2010 and 2012 after storm damage.

Not a monument in the usual sense, but monumental, the former **New York State Pavilion** (1964; Philip Johnson and Richard Foster) stands in decrepit splendor, an eyesore to some, an icon to others. A circle of tubular columns of concrete, it originally had a roof of translucent colored plastic. Though it has been declared a National Treasure by the National Trust for Historic Preservation, its future is uncertain.

THE QUEENS MUSEUM

In the park. Subway: 7 to Willets Point-Shea Stadium. Walk south past Citi Field and the tennis center (10–15mins). Open Wed–Fri 10–5, Sat and Sun 12–5; closed Mon, Tues, and major holidays. Suggested admission. Shop. T: 718 592 9700, queensmuseum.org.

The Queens Museum occupies the former New York City Building (1939; Aymar Embury II; renovated 1994, Rafael Viñoly, and 2011, Grimshaw Architects), built for the 1939–40 World's Fair and later used by the United Nations General Assembly before its permanent headquarters was built. The museum has three long-term exhibitions: a display on New York City's water supply; the Neustadt Collection of Tiffany Lamps; and the **New York Panorama**, an unforgettable architectural model of the city, commissioned by Robert Moses for the 1964 fair and last updated in 1992, though a few other features have been added, including Citi Field. Altogether there are some 895,000 buildings.

THE NEW YORK HALL OF SCIENCE

47–01 111th St at 46th Ave. Subway: 7 to 111th St. Open April–Aug Mon–Fri 9:30–5, weekends 10–6; Sept–March closed Mon but same hours; closed Labor Day, Thanksgiving, Christmas. Admission charge, but free Fri 2–5 and Sun 10–11. Café and shop. T: 718 699 0005, nysci.org.

Geared primarily to children, the Hall of Science has hundreds of interactive exhibits. It opened (1964) in the New York City science pavilion at the fair, a 100-ft undulating wall of poured-in-place concrete containing myriad pieces of blue glass. The visually astonishing interior has a precedent in architect Wallace K. Harrison's "Fish" Church (1958) in Stamford, CT, constructed using similar technology. The addition (1999; Polshek Partnership and Beyer Blinder Belle) compensates for the drawbacks of the original building as an exhibition space.

LOUIS ARMSTRONG HOUSE MUSEUM
Map p. 609, C3. 34–56 107th St (34th and 37th Aves), Corona. Subway: 7 to 103rd St-Corona Plaza. Walk two blocks north on 103rd St; turn right onto 37th Ave. Walk four short blocks, then turn left onto 107th St. The house is a half-block north of 37th Ave. Open Tues–Fri 10–5, Sat and Sun 12–5. Admission charge. Guided 40-min tours leave every hour on the hour; last tour at 4pm. T: 718 478 8274, louisarmstronghouse.org.
The great jazz trumpeter (1901–71) and his fourth wife, Lucille, moved into this house in 1943 and stayed for the rest of their lives. When Lucille died in 1983, she left the house to the City to be made into a museum (opened 2003). The building and its furnishings remain much as they were during Armstrong's lifetime, and while the home is modest, it has occasional flamboyant touches: the turquoise kitchen and the mirrored bathroom with gold fixtures, and plenty of wallpaper, a passion of Lucille's. Armstrong described his pleasure in living there in words as distinctive as his musical style: "The house may not be the nicest looking front... But when one visit the Interior of the Armstrongs' home they see a whole lot of comfort, happiness & the nicest things. Such as that Wall to Wall Bed." The tour includes clips from his home-recorded tapes.

JAMAICA BAY & ROCKAWAY PENINSULA

Jamaica Bay (*map p. 609, B4–C4*), about 32 square miles off the south coast of Long Island between Queens and Brooklyn, sheltered from the Atlantic by the long arm of the Rockaway Peninsula, is dotted with small islands, only one of which, Broad Channel (sometimes called Rulers Bar Hassock) is inhabited. The Jamaica Bay Wildlife Refuge, with its two freshwater pools, is a bird watcher's paradise, especially during the spring and fall Atlantic Flyway migrations. The Rockaway Peninsula is home to the Gateway National Recreation Area, whose main draw is its expanse of public beaches.

Getting there
Wildlife refuge: *By car: Belt Parkway to Exit 17 S, Cross Bay Boulevard. Proceed south on Cross Bay Boulevard across the Joseph Addabbo-North Channel Bridge. The Visitor Center is approximately 1.5 miles past the bridge on the right. Turn right at traffic light for parking. Subway: Rockaway bound A train (make sure you get one that says "Rockaway") to Broad Channel; walk along Noel Rd to Cross Bay Boulevard. Turn right and walk about three quarters of a mile to the Refuge Visitor Center. Bus: Q21 from Liberty Ave (Queens) or Q53 bus from 61st St and Roosevelt Ave (Queens) to the Refuge.*

Rockaway peninsula: *Subway: A train marked "Rockaway Park-Beach 116th St" or A to Broad Channel and transfer to the S (Rockaway Shuttle) to Rockaway Park-Beach 116th St.*
Gateway National Recreation Area: *Subway and Bus: 2 to Flatbush Ave; change to bus Q35 to the park. Or A train to Rockaway Park, then bus Q35 or Q22. After the bridge, ask driver to let you off at either Fort Tilden or Riis Park. Ferry: Ferries run on summer weekends and holidays to Riis Landing from Pier 11, Wall St. Service begins Memorial Day weekend and continues until Labor Day. For fares and schedules, see New York Beach Ferry (newyorkbeachferry.com) or T: 718 474 0593. For weekend bicycle and beach equipment rental, see wheelfunrentals.com.*

THE JAMAICA BAY WILDLIFE REFUGE

Open all year sunrise to sunset. Visitor Center (open daily 8.30am–5pm) off Cross Bay Blvd on Broad Channel. T: 718 318 4340, nps.gov/gate.
The refuge encompasses about 14.3 square miles of salt marsh, dunes, brackish ponds, woodland and fields, and an expanse of open bay. It has harbored more than 325 species of birds, and large populations of butterflies and horseshoe crabs. Walking trails circle the shelter's two ponds, though the West Pond trail is discontinuous since the dike was breached by Hurricane Sandy in 2012. Activities include ranger-led nature walks, birding, exhibitions, and cruises.

In 1880 the Long Island Railroad built a five-mile wooden trestle across the bay to join the Rockaway peninsula and its seaside resorts to the rest of Queens. As industry arrived and polluted the water, the resorts floundered and closed. Fishing and swimming were banned in 1916. A spectacular fire in 1950 damaged the trestle so severely that the City bought the rail line and rebuilt the trestle with concrete. Enter Robert Moses, who hankered for public beaches and parks. He engineered a transfer of the bay to the jurisdiction of the Parks Department, and negotiated with the Transit Authority for dikes to create two freshwater ponds, which became the core of the refuge. In 1951 the Jamaica Bay Wildlife Refuge was created. Today it is part of the Gateway National Recreation Area (*see below*).

ROCKAWAY PENINSULA

An eleven-mile neck of sandy land, the Rockaway Peninsula reaches westward from Nassau County in Long Island across the mouth of Jamaica Bay. Part of the western stretch of the peninsula belongs to the Gateway National Recreation Area, which includes **Jacob Riis Park**—considered New York's finest beach—and the hikable former army base of **Fort Tilden** (1917). **Rockaway Beach**, which runs from Beach 3rd St to Beach 153rd St, made famous by a song with the same name by the Ramones (1977), has the city's only legal surfing beach. Millions of visitors descend between Memorial Day weekend and Labor Day weekend (roughly late May to early Sept), enjoying the water, tanning, and noshing at the concessions. Further west, beyond the gated cottage colony of Breezy Point (established in the 1960s but damaged by Hurricane Sandy in 2012) is **Breezy Point Tip**, a remote 200-acre plot of ocean-facing beach, sand dunes and marshland, popular with bird watchers (*accessible on foot from Jacob Riis Park*).

EATING AND DRINKING IN QUEENS

ASTORIA

An ethnic conglomerate, Astoria offers Greek, Brazilian, Italian, and other ethnic restaurants; even an Eastern European beer hall that dates back about a century.

$$$ Trattoria L'incontro. Family-run restaurant with exceptional cooking from Abruzzi, huge menu, friendly, relaxed. Stuffed pasta dishes, seafood, pizzas. And homemade gelato. Closed Mon, lunch and dinner other days. *21–76 31st St (Dtmars Blvd). T: 718 721 3532, trattorialincontro.com.*

$$ Malagueta. Small, simple corner restaurant serving delicious home-cooked Brazilian specialties—not just grilled meats—and other continental dishes. Easy on the wallet. Close to Noguchi Museum. Lunch and dinner seven days. *25–35 36th Ave (28th St), T: 718 937 4821, malaguetany.com.*

$ Agnanti. ■ Small plates with Greek and Turkish dishes, brick-walled simple restaurant near Astoria Park, with fireplace in winter, sidewalk seating in warm weather. Meatballs, seafood, salads. Lunch and dinner seven days. *19–06 Ditmars Blvd (19th St). T: 718 545 4554, agnantimeze.com*

$ Bohemian Hall and Beer Garden. Founded and operated by the Bohemian Citizens' Benevolent Society, an immigrant support group, to help newcomers flocking to the neighborhood during the closing decades of the 19th century. Authentic Eastern European food, and many pilsners. Outdoor picnic tables in shaded garden; special events with music. Dinner every day, lunch weekends. *29–19 24th Ave (29th St). T: 718 274 4925, bohemianhall.com.*

$ Butcher Bar. Organic barbecue restaurant and market, take out or eat in. Beef, pork, steak, ribs, and a few vegetarian options. *37–10 30th Ave (37th St). Lunch and dinner seven days. T: 718 606 8140, butcherbar.com.*

$ Taverna Kyclades. Friendly, casual Greek restaurant with seafood specialties, calamari, souvlaki, Greek sausage. Understandably popular, so can be crowded. No reservations, go early. Lunch and dinner seven days. *33–07 Ditmars Blvd (33rd St). T: 718 545 8666, tavernakyclades.com.*

FLUSHING

Flushing has Queens's largest population of Asians, and Asian restaurants—Chinese, Malaysian, Korean, Indian. Most are modest, authentic places that won't empty your pockets while they fill your stomach. Go for the food, not the décor. Expect crowds on Sundays. Most have beer and wine; some let you BYO—with or without a corkage fee.

$ Biang! As the website explains, the name suggests the sound of handmade noodles being pulled and slammed against the work surface. Xi'an street foods offered in attractive sit-down restaurant. Noodles, skewers, dumplings based on remembered family recipes. Offshoot of Xi'an Famous Foods stall nearby. Lunch and dinner seven days, cash only. *41–10 Main St (41st Ave), T: 718 888 7713, biang-nyc.com.*

$ Dumpling Galaxy. Famous dumpling house, attractive red and gold décor with private tables and more than 100 kinds of dumplings, with stuffings including seafood, vegetarian, pork, lamb, tofu. Breakfast, lunch and dinner daily. No alcohol. *42–35 Main St (inside Arcadia Mall, Maple & Franklin Aves). T: 212 518 3265, dumplinggalaxy.com.*

$ Ganesh Temple Canteen. Vegetarian south Indian food, some of it fiery. Lentil dosas, and *uttappam*, somewhere between a crepe and a pizza. Served cafeteria style in the basement by temple volunteers. Open daily, morning through evening. *45–57 Bowne St (Holly Ave). T: 718 460 8484, nyganeshtemplecanteen.com.*

$ Spicy & Tasty. ■ Shrine to the Szechuan pepper draws Asian families and others from all over the city; well-prepared Szechuan classics. Beer and wine. Lunch and dinner, cash only. *39–07 Prince St. T: 718 359 1601, spicyandtasty.com.*

LONG ISLAND CITY

$$$ M. Wells Dinette (at MoMA PS1). ■ More than a standard museum restaurant, re-incarnates a former diner as a school cafeteria, but with far better food, served up by a French-Canadian chef. Lunch only,

but open until 6pm; closed Tues, Wed. Museum entry not required. *MoMA PS1, 22–25 Jackson Ave (46th Ave). T: 718 786 1800, magasinwells.com.*

$$ Bear. Highly rated restaurant with sophisticated Russian-influenced cuisine (ditto for the cocktails). Located on quiet residential street. Borscht, smoked whitefish, kasha, small plates. Not far from Noguchi Museum and Socrates Sculpture Park. Dinner Tues–Sun, brunch weekends. *Cash only. 12–41 31st Ave (12th St). T: 917 396 4939, bearnyc.com.*

$$ Casa Enrique. Outstanding Mexican food by French-trained Mexican chef; stylish, bright, and cheerful. Lunch weekends, dinner seven days. *5–48 49th Ave (Vernon Blvd), T: 347-448-6040, henrinyc.com.*

$$ Shi. ■ Pan-Asian upscale, with excellent views of the Manhattan skyline; sushi, Chinese and American-Asian dishes; sleek lounge; reserve ahead. Lunch and dinner seven days. *47–20 Center Blvd (Vernon Blvd); T: 347 242 2450, eatdrinkshi.com.*

$$ Tournesol. Pleasant, cheerful neighborhood French eatery with bistro favorites. No lunch Mon, dinner nightly. AmEx only. *50–12 Vernon Blvd (50th St); T: 718 472 4355, tournesolnyc.com.*

$ Dutch Kills Bar. Wooden booths, hand-carved ice, well-designed cocktails. Open daily 5pm–2am. *27–24 Jackson Ave. T: 718 383 2724, dutchkillsbar.com.*

Staten Island

To the world at large Staten Island (*map p. 610*) is simply the end point of one of the greatest free rides in the domain of tourism, the Staten Island ferry (*see p. 549*), which runs across Upper New York Bay. The island is 13.9 miles long and 7.3 miles wide in its largest dimensions, and is separated from Manhattan by Upper New York Bay; from Brooklyn by Lower New York Bay and the Narrows; and from New Jersey by the Kill Van Kull and the Arthur Kill (the word "kill" is a Dutch term for channel). It is the third-largest of New York's boroughs in area (60.9 square miles), but the smallest in population (c. 472,600). It is the only borough without a subway.

Down the center of the island runs a spine of rocky hills whose highest point, Todt Hill (409.2 ft), is also the highest point on the Atlantic seaboard south of Maine. Around the turn of the 20th century, the wealthy built mansions along the crest of these hills, and today many still survive, though some have been adapted as schools or charitable institutions and others have surrendered part of their land to newer homes. East of the central ridge lie low coastal plains, densely developed with back-to-back rows of tract housing and continuous commercial strips. The southern tip of Staten Island, once dominated by the sea, retains some of its former charm, though the fishing villages and oystering communities no longer exist.

Staten Island was long infamous for its vast dump, the Fresh Kills Landfill, which is currently being recycled as a park.

Visiting Staten Island

You can reach the sights by local buses from the St. George ferry terminal (though it is more convenient by car). Except for Historic Richmond Town and the Snug Harbor Cultural Center, the island's offerings are small in scale, but worth the ferry ride.

HISTORY OF STATEN ISLAND

Both Giovanni da Verrazzano (1524) and Henry Hudson (1609) made note of Staten Island during their explorations of the New World. Verrazzano stopped off at a spring to refill his water casks and Hudson gave the borough its name, Staaten Eylandt, after the States General, the governing body of the Netherlands. When the British took over New Amsterdam, Staten Island (i.e. Richmond County) was renamed after the Duke of Richmond, illegitimate son of Charles II. During the British colonial period, Staten Island continued to develop as an agricultural community, with its less fertile areas devoted to raising stock while its long coastline and protected waters harbored fishing, oystering, and shipbuilding. Along the kills, the waterways north and west of the island, several tidal mills were built for grinding grist and sawing lumber. In the early summer of 1776, the arrival of some 30,000 British soldiers and Hessian mercenaries disrupted the agrarian quiet of the island, which soon became a vast military camp from which the British would stage operations on Long Island. Although the population was largely loyalist and welcomed the arrival of the British forces, the billeting of so many soldiers strained resources and tensions inevitably developed. At the end of August the British attacked what is now Brooklyn and took the western end of Long Island, using barges built on Staten Island. After the war Staten Islanders continued their way of life, largely unaffected by the heady changes across the bay.

In 1829 teenaged Cornelius Vanderbilt, born in northern Staten Island, started a regular ferry service to Manhattan, the first step in a business empire that would eventually make him the borough's wealthiest and most famous son. Staten Island burgeoned as a seaside resort, especially New Brighton, where hotels attracted prominent New Yorkers and a large clientele from the South.

Garibaldi sojourned here for three years during his exile from Italy. Herman Melville frequently visited his brother Tom, governor of Sailors' Snug Harbor from 1867–84. And Frederick Law Olmsted tried his hand at farming in the southern part of the island before finding his life's work as a landscape architect.

Toward the end of the 19th century, Staten Island became less rural, but again changed more slowly than the other boroughs. Industries began to dot the northern and western shoreline. South Beach on the Lower Bay and Midland Beach, just south of it, became popular resort areas. The first railroad (1860) was extended along both sides of the island and charitable institutions, aware of the growing shortage of land in Manhattan, began buying sites for hospitals, orphanages, and schools. Nevertheless, in 1898, when Staten Island became part of Greater New York, it had only about 67,000 inhabitants, a population slightly larger than that of Manhattan in 1800.

Today the island is struggling to balance growth with the preservation of its heritage and remaining natural beauty. The opening of the **Verrazano–Narrows Bridge** (1964) brought the growth spurt long desired by some, but increases in crime and poverty too. (For reasons that remain obscure, when the bridge was named for Giovanni Verrazzano the Port Authority decided on one "z," though it is generally thought the explorer came from Castello di Verrazzano, near Florence.) Rural and small-town Staten Island have been mostly replaced by suburban sprawl. The waterfront areas are also dangerously flood prone; in 2012 Hurricane Sandy inundated roughly 16 percent of the island.

AROUND ST. GEORGE

St. George (*map p. 610, C3*) is Staten Island's downtown, its transportation hub, and the seat of borough government. Up the steep hill beyond the ferry terminal stands the monumental, French-influenced **Borough Hall** (*2–10 Richmond Terrace; open*

Mon–Fri 9–5), designed by the white-glove firm of Carrère and Hastings (1906) and intended as part of a grand civic center that never materialized. In the lobby is a set of WPA murals (1940; Frederick Charles Stahr) depicting scenes of local history, beginning with the arrival of Giovanni da Verrazzano and ending with the construction of the Bayonne Bridge.

STATEN ISLAND MUSEUM
75 Stuyvesant Place (Wall St). Open Mon–Fri 11–5, Sat 10–5, Sun 12–5. Closed national holidays. Recommended admission charge. Shop. T: 718 727 1135, statenislandmuseum.org. See also p. 536.
The small Staten Island Museum (opened in 1909), which evolved from the Staten Island Institute of Arts and Sciences (1881), still reflects the interests of its founders, a handful of Staten Islanders deeply interested in natural science, and to a lesser extent the arts. Permanent exhibits include the Hall of Natural Science—the best examples culled from a collection of more than a million insects, stuffed birds and mammals, shells, eggs, and minerals displayed as in a Victorian cabinet of curiosities. Among the insects are more than 35,000 cicadas, the specialty of William T. Davis, one of the founders. An exhibit on the ferry recounts its first 100 years of municipal service, and one on the Lenape examines the Native American inhabitants of the island.

NATIONAL LIGHTHOUSE MUSEUM
5 Bay St. From the ferry, exit the terminal to the left and follow the signs to the museum. Museum only partially open at the time of writing; call or check website for updates: T: 718 390 0040 or 855 NLM SINY, lighthousemuseum.org.
South and east of the ferry terminal, in what used to be Building 11 of the US Lighthouse General Service Depot, the National Lighthouse Museum occupies a former foundry. It will offer exhibits on the history of the site, a timeline of lighthouses from ancient Alexandria to the present, stories of lighthouse keepers and their families, lighthouse models, and an interactive exhibit on the light sources and reflectors that once warned ships of coastal dangers.

WEST OF THE FERRY TERMINAL

The Esplanade along the Kill van Kull leads past the **Richmond County Bank Ballpark**, home turf of the Staten Island Yankees, a farm club of the major league Yankees. Huge container ships glide along the kill, their scale dwarfing everything on land. Across the kill in New Jersey are the storage tanks of Bayonne's industrial waterfront, lined up on the shoreline.

Along the Esplanade past the ballpark, the **September 11 Memorial** honors the 270 Staten Islanders who died in the fall of the World Trade Center towers. Designed by architect Masayuki Sono and called "Postcards" (2004), two white resin wings reach skyward and frame the point on the Manhattan skyline where the original World Trade Center stood. Granite plaques bear the names, birthdates, and facial profiles of the victims.

THE NEW YORK WHEEL

At the time of writing plans were under way for what was originally slated (in 2012) to be the world's tallest observation wheel (630ft; the London Eye is 443ft), on the St. George waterfront offering spectacular views across the harbor. When the New York Wheel does open, it won't be the world's tallest, however, since the Dubai Eye, projected at 689ft, is currently under construction.

SNUG HARBOR CULTURAL CENTER & BOTANICAL GARDEN

Map p. 610, C3. 1000 Richmond Terrace (Tysen St). Bus: From the ferry terminal, take bus S40 (bus stop in front of the ballpark) to Snug Harbor (a 10-min ride). Tell the driver that you want to get off at Snug Harbor. Grounds and Botanical Garden open daily dawn to dusk. Visitor Center open Tues–Sun 10–5. Admission to grounds free, but charge for Chinese Scholar's Garden and the Newhouse Center for Contemporary Art. (For the John A. Noble Center, see below.) Seasonal café. T: 718 425 3504, snug-harbor.org.

Snug Harbor Cultural Center, formerly Sailors' Snug Harbor, a haven for "aged, decrepit, and worn out sailors," is set in 83 acres of landscaped grounds. Beautiful Greek Revival buildings, as well as less imposing dormitories, laundries, and cottages, have been recycled as exhibition and performance spaces, and artists' studios. Within the grounds are a botanical garden, a Chinese Scholar's Garden, the Staten Island Children's Museum, a music hall, the Heritage Farm, a composting project, and the Staten Island Conservatory of Music.

HISTORY OF SAILORS' SNUG HARBOR

Sailors' Snug Harbor was established by the will of a well-to-do merchant, Robert Richard Randall. When he died in 1801, he stipulated that his assets be used to construct a home and hospital for retired sailors on his Manhattan farm. During two decades of family litigation, New York grew northward and the Randall farmland became valuable residential property, too valuable for a seamen's retirement home. Therefore Snug Harbor's trustees leased the farm (near present Washington Square) and bought land on Staten Island (1831). The first building was completed in 1833.

Many older sailors were ill or injured, without families, or suffering from alcoholism. Of the original 37 who came to Snug Harbor, seven were one-legged, two were blind, others had "rheumatism," probably arthritis. In 1900 Snug Harbor housed more than 1,000 sailors, but after social security took effect and sailors had other retirement options, the population dwindled; by the 1970s, fewer than 100 remained. The trustees of Snug Harbor wanted to demolish most of the buildings, but preservationists succeeded in getting them landmarked and eventually convinced the City to buy the land and its 28 buildings. Snug Harbor Cultural Center opened in 1976.

Among the original Snug Harbor trustees were the rector of Trinity Church and the minister of the First Presbyterian Church. They were concerned with the spiritual welfare and social decorum of the "Snugs," whose lives had been spent under the authoritarian structure of shipboard rules, and who, in many cases, were not equipped emotionally for independence. Drunkenness and disorderly behavior were significant problems, reflected in the by-laws of the organization: "Any member...who shall bring in...ardent spirits or intoxicating liquors shall be forthwith expelled; Any member who shall be convicted of getting drunk, either on or off the premises of the Sailors' Snug Harbor, of quarrelling with or assaulting any of his fellow-inmates, or of using profane or obscene language, or of leaving the premises without permission from the Superintendent...shall be expelled; No person shall commence eating at the table before the blessing shall have been asked; Every member shall attend all the religious services of the Institution..."

Theodore Dreiser stayed near Snug Harbor for about a year and observed the sailors in local bars and on the waterfront. In *The Color of the Great City*, he wrote of the banality of the place, its insistence on conformity, "a monotonous system which wears as the drifting of water." Yes, he continued, Snug Harbor was a material benefaction. "But where," he asked, was there a "peaceful haven of the heart—on what shore, by what sea—a Snug Harbor for the soul?"

WHAT TO SEE IN SNUG HARBOR

The **five Greek Revival buildings** (1833) facing the kill, used as dormitories, are the architectural centerpiece of Snug Harbor. The three middle ones were designed by Minard Lafever, an influential architect whose work and publications helped disseminate the Greek Revival style in America. The **north gatehouse**, Italianate in style, was built in 1873 to keep the sailors from smuggling liquor into the complex. The **perimeter fence** (original portion 1842), according to the Landmarks Designation Report was likewise intended to discourage "too frequent visits to neighboring purveyors of unauthorized forms of refreshment."

The **Visitor Center** occupies the central building (1833), Lafever's earliest documented work, and the first building erected at Snug Harbor. The rotunda ceiling was decorated 50 years later with Victorian-style murals depicting nautical motifs. In the Visitor Center is the **Newhouse Center for Contemporary Art** (*open Tues–Sun 10–5; admission charge, but ask about combination ticket with Chinese Scholar's Garden; T: 718 425 3524, snug-harbor.org/visual-arts/newhouse-center-for-contemporary-art*). Founded in 1977 as an alternative art space that showed emerging Staten Island artists, the Center now offers as many as ten group exhibitions yearly, featuring local and international figures, some of them cutting-edge.

Veterans' Memorial Hall, now a theater, was originally the chapel. The Music Hall (1892) is the city's second oldest theater behind Carnegie Hall. Offerings include drama and musical comedy, music, dance, and film (*for events, check the Snug Harbor website*).

THE STATEN ISLAND MUSEUM AT SNUG HARBOR

1000 Richmond Terrace, Building A. Open Mon–Fri 11–5, Sat 10–5, Sun 12–5. Recommended admission charge, but free Tues 12–2. Shop. T: 718 727 1135, statenislandmuseum.org.

Long a fixture of St. George, the Staten Island Museum opened more facilities at Snug Harbor in 2015, allowing objects that have long languished in storage to be put on display. Long-term exhibits explore the island's natural history, diversity, and ecology—potent issues today. A life-sized model based on a skeleton unearthed on Staten Island introduces "Remember the Mastodon," which explores extinct and surviving species and documents efforts to preserve bio-diversity. Paintings, drawings, and photographs document Staten Island's landscape, from its pristine hills and wetlands to its parking lots and strip malls. Also on view are selections from the wide-ranging permanent collection: an Egyptian statuette, a Congo mask, Native American beaded moccasins. "From Farm to City" uses primary sources to document people and historical themes in the island's human history as it developed over the centuries.

THE BOTANICAL GARDEN

Grounds open daily dawn to dusk. Free, but admission charge to Chinese Scholar's Garden. Maps available at the Visitor Center or online. T: 718 273 8200, snug-harbor.org.

Barely sprouted as New York's botanical gardens go, the Botanical Garden (opened 1977), has grown to include several "international" gardens. The most famous is the **Chinese Scholar's Garden** (*open April–Oct Tues–Sun 10–5, Nov–April Tues–Sun 10–4*), whose serene courtyards and pavilions, sparsely planted with plum, pine, and bamboo, are modeled after precursors from the Ming Dynasty (1368–1644). Forty Chinese artists and artisans (and a chef) from Suzhou came to Staten Island to build the garden (opened 1999), constructing it in the traditional manner without nails or glue.

The **Tuscan Garden** (2010), based on the one at the Villa Gamberaia outside Florence, grows authenticated Renaissance plants. The central Tuscan-style villa served as a nurses' dormitory back in the days when the old salts roamed the grounds. Other features of the Botanical Garden are the **Pond Garden** (the pond dug by the sailors who sailed their model boats in it), **Glass House**, **Rose Garden**, **White Garden** (modeled after Sissinghurst in England), and the **Healing Garden**—planted to commemorate Staten Islanders who died on 9/11. Between Cottage Row and the World Trade Center Educational Tribute, an allée of 120 hornbeams arches overhead: a living tunnel.

THE NOBLE MARITIME COLLECTION

1000 Richmond Terrace, Building D next to the Visitor Center. Open Thur–Sun 1–5. Closed New Year's Day, Easter, July 4, Thanksgiving, Christmas. Call for winter hours. Admission by donation. T: 718 447 6490, noblemaritime.org. (NB: The Noble Collection is on Snug Harbor's grounds, but is administratively independent of the Cultural Center.)

Housed in a Minard Lafever building (stunningly restored, mostly by volunteers), the Noble Maritime Collection is one of the gems of Snug Harbor. The museum pays homage to John A. Noble (1913–83), one of Staten Island's finest maritime artists and a passionate activist whose work helped save Snug Harbor from commercial development. In 1928, while working on a schooner in the Kill Van Kull, Noble "discovered" the former Port Johnston coal docks, by then a graveyard for wooden ships. The sight changed his life. In the following decades he committed himself to documenting the history of the harbor, working from a floating studio on a houseboat which he had built "out of the small bones of larger vessels." Changing exhibitions focus on Noble's work, the history of New York waterways, and Snug Harbor. Also on view are re-creations of the ingenious floating studio, a dormitory room, and the French atelier of Noble's father, the American romantic painter, John "Wichita Bill" Noble (1874–1910).

OTHER SIGHTS ON THE ISLAND

THE ALICE AUSTEN HOUSE
Map p. 610, C4. 2 Hylan Blvd (Edgewater St). Bus: S51 from the ferry terminal to Hylan Blvd and Bay St (15mins). Walk one block east toward the water. Open March–Dec Tues–Sun 1–5. Closed Jan, Feb, and major holidays. Grounds open daily until dusk. Suggested donation. T: 718 816 4506, aliceausten.org.
This charming Gothic Revival cottage (1691–1710, later alterations) is the former home of photographer Alice Austen (1866–1952), whose pioneering work depicts New York life at the turn of the 20th century. Alice's grandfather John Austen bought the house in 1844 and modernized it. When Alice's father deserted his wife and daughter, she and her mother moved into the cottage with the financially comfortable elder Austens. Alice started taking photos in childhood and grew up to become one of the first female photographers in the nation to work outside the studio, her interests taking her beyond the boundaries of Staten Island and the restrictions of her cosseted upbringing. Her photos document the social customs of her generation but also the influx of immigrants to New York City and the workings of the former Staten Island Quarantine Station. She lived in "Clear Comfort" as the house was called, until illness and poverty forced her out at age 70. The house, furnished with Victorian period pieces, has a magnificent view of New York Harbor and a pretty garden replanted following Austen's photographs with weeping mulberry, flowering quince, and other shrubs.

THE GARIBALDI-MEUCCI MUSEUM
Map p. 610, C4. 420 Tompkins Ave (near Chestnut Ave). Bus S52 or S78 from ferry terminal to the corner of Chestnut and Tompkins Aves. Open Wed–Sat 1–5. Closed Sun–Tues and all major holidays, Christmas Eve, and New Year's Eve. Admission charge. T: 718 442 1608, garibaldimeuccimuseum.org.
This small, bare-bones house-museum memorializes the Italian freedom fighter Giuseppe Garibaldi, who lived here with his friend Antonio Meucci from 1850–3. Exiled from Italy after the fall of the Roman Republic in 1849, the impoverished Garibaldi sought refuge in the US and was taken in by Meucci and his wife. The two men just barely managed to support themselves hunting and making candles (there is

a big kettle in the back yard where they melted tallow). The museum contains photos, military artifacts, and other memorabilia of Garibaldi's life, as well as models of a prototype for Meucci's telephone (*see below*).

ANTONIO MEUCCI

Born near Florence, Antonio Meucci (1808–89) came to Staten Island in 1850 after a stint as a set designer and stage technician in Havana. While in Cuba, Meucci, an inveterate tinkerer and an avid reader of scientific literature, became curious about the therapeutic uses of electric shock, and one day while experimenting on a friend, heard the friend's exclamation (presumably of pain) transmitted over a copper wire from the next room. Realizing that he had discovered something significant, he spent the next ten years bringing his observation to a practical stage.

Meucci's lack of entrepreneurial skill, his inability to speak English, and his increasing poverty worked against him. Although he filed a notice of intent to take out a patent on his invention in 1871, six years before Alexander Graham Bell filed for his patent, Meucci could not come up with the $250 necessary to register it officially. Thanks to a series of Kafkaesque bureaucratic blunders (including the loss of his prototypes), it was Bell who received credit for the invention of the telephone and the rights to the financial rewards that went with it. Although Meucci sued to regain his commercial rights, he was at a disadvantage in court, which not unexpectedly ruled in Bell's favor. Investigations eventually uncovered collusion between employees of the Patent Office and officials of Bell's company, and although the government in 1886 upheld Meucci's claim and initiated prosecution for fraud against Bell's patent, Meucci died in 1889 and the case was eventually dropped.

FORT WADSWORTH
Map p. 610, C4. 210 New York Ave (the extension of Bay St). Bus: S51 from the ferry terminal. On weekdays some buses stop inside the fort; check with the driver. Overlook open daily dawn to dusk. Free. Ranger-guided tours in summer, special events. T: 718 354 4655, nps.gov/gate/index.htm.
Just north of the Verrazano Bridge, Fort Wadsworth overlooks the Narrows from a high cliff. Today part of the Gateway National Recreation area, the fort protected the entrance to New York harbor for more than two centuries, raking the Narrows with guns that were upgraded over the years. The site, fortified first by the Dutch, remained in use through the Cold War, when the military post served as the control center for New York City's Nike missile defense system. There are walking trails and spectacular views of the harbor and the imposing masonry forts on the hillside.

JACQUES MARCHAIS MUSEUM OF TIBETAN ART
Map p. 610, B4. 338 Lighthouse Ave (past St. George Rd). Bus: S74 or S54 from the ferry terminal to Lighthouse Ave (about 30mins). Walk up the (steep) hill (5–10mins) to the museum. Or take the Staten Island Railway from the ferry terminal to Great Kills, then bus S54. Open Wed–Sun 1–5. Closed holidays (call ahead, or check the website, especially around Christmas). Admission charge. T: 718 987 3500, tibetanmuseum.org.

Sitting high on the rocky spine of Staten Island, the Jacques Marchais Museum of Tibetan Art (founded 1947) is the creation of a Midwestern woman enamored of the East. The museum's architecture recalls Tibetan monasteries: sturdy buildings whose thick stone walls are pierced with small windows and overhung by cedar roofs. On permanent view are some 125 beautiful artifacts from Tibet and nearby countries, including fine bronze sculptures dating from the 12th–20th centuries.

Jacques Marchais (1887–1948) was born Edna Coblentz in Illinois. A child actor, she grew up to become a successful Asian art dealer. Using the professional name Jacques Marchais (her married name was Jacqueline Klauber), she ran a gallery on Madison Ave while building her personal collection. Despite never visiting the Far East, Marchais enlarged her holdings buying pieces at private sales or auctions, and working closely with dealers.

HISTORIC RICHMOND TOWN

Map p. 610, B4. 441 Clarke Ave (Richmond Rd and Arthur Kill Rd). Bus S74 from the ferry terminal to Richmond Rd and St. Patrick's Place (about 30mins). Open July and Aug Wed–Sat 10–5, Sun 1–5; Oct–June Wed–Sun 1–5. Closed Thanksgiving, Christmas, and New Year's Day. Admission charge but free on Fri. Tours Wed–Fri at 2:30, and on weekends at 2 and 3:30. T: 718 351 1611, historicrichmondtown.org.

An outdoor museum on the site of the island's early government center, the buildings of Historic Richmond Town trace the evolution of village life on Staten Island between the 17th and 19th centuries. There are homes, shops, taverns, and courthouses, some restored, some relocated from other parts of Staten Island. A small museum (in the Visitor Center) explores the island's development from its agricultural and maritime past, through the growth of industries (beer, terra cotta, linoleum), to suburbanization. Most impressive are a Staten Island skiff, once used for tonging oysters in the shallow waters of the bays, and an array of oystering tools.

One of the most important buildings on the 100-acre site is Voorlezer's House (c. 1695), the oldest surviving elementary school building in the nation, built by the Dutch Reformed congregation for its *voorlezer* (lay reader), who lived and taught there.

CONFERENCE HOUSE

Beyond map p. 610, B4. 7445 Hylan Blvd (Satterlee St). Bus: S78 from the ferry terminal to the last stop on Craig Ave (1hr or more); buses run less frequently on weekends. Staten Island Railway to Tottenville; exit near intersection of Main St and Utah St. Walk south on Main St. Turn right onto Craig Ave. Turn right onto Hylan Blvd. Turn left onto Satterlee St for the Visitor Center or right towards the Conference House (about 15mins). Grounds open dawn to dusk. House open April–mid-Dec Fri–Sun 1–4. Suggested donation. Visitor Center on grounds with exhibition gallery, restrooms, gift shop. T: 718 984 6046, conferencehouse.org.

Also known as the Billop House, this manor house (c. 1680) overlooking Raritan Bay once hosted an abortive peace conference during the Revolution. On Sept 11, 1776, American delegates including Benjamin Franklin and John Adams met here with Admiral Lord Richard Howe. Howe offered to pardon those who had taken up arms against the Crown if the colonies would rescind the Declaration of Independence; the Americans replied that independence was not negotiable and the talks broke off.

The house is built of local stone with ground seashells mixed into the mortar. Inside are parlors, a large basement kitchen, and a vaulted root cellar. An aged white mulberry survives on the front lawn, wired together, its branches drooping to the ground.

The surrounding 267-acre park, leafy and serene, slopes down to the bay, hinting at how Staten Island looked centuries ago, even with the industrial plants of New Jersey visible in the distance. Trails lead to the beach and to the southernmost point in the state of New York, marked by a red pole, the South Pole.

FRESHKILLS PARK

Map p. 610, B4. You may visit the park by joining a tour or a hike, or taking part in a special event. For information, freshkillspark.org/tour-information.

A 2,200-acre park is coming into being on what was once the world's largest garbage dump, whose mountains of decaying trash reached higher than the upstretched arm of the Statue of Liberty. Before 1948, Fresh Kills was mostly salt marsh. To Robert Moses it provided a perfect opportunity for dumping garbage, filling in land that could later be developed. A 20-year lifespan was intended, but it remained in use until 2001, rising higher and higher, attracting rats, feral dogs, and flocks of ravenous seagulls. Legally slated to close on December 31, 2001, it reopened temporarily to receive rubble from Ground Zero; over a million tons of material were sorted and sieved for human remains.

In 2006 James Corner Field Operations (the High Line) won the competition for Fresh Kills' master plan. When completed, perhaps in 2035, Freshkills Park will be three times the size of Central Park and will be "green" in all senses: methane from the former dump is already being recycled and sold; buildings will have passive heating and cooling systems; the soil will support native plants. As the mountains of garbage slowly subside, a few areas are now open.

EATING AND DRINKING ON STATEN ISLAND

CHARLESTON
In southwestern Staten Island, away from the usual tourist haunts, though near Clay Pit Ponds Park.

$$ Killmeyer's Old Bavaria Inn.
Since 1859, this restaurant-cum-beer-garden has served German fare: *schnitzels* and *sauerbraten*, salads, soups and sandwiches. Long list of international beers. Lunch and dinner daily, open late. *4254 Arthur Kill Rd*

(Sharrotts Rd). T: 718 984 1202, killmeyers.com.

IN OR NEAR ST. GEORGE
$$$ Enoteca Maria. ■ Italian grandmas in the kitchen in this intimate restaurant; menu varies according to the grandma of the day. Good wine list. Cash only (ATM nearby). Open Wed–Sun from 3pm. *27 Hyatt St (Central Ave). T: 718 447 2777, enotecamaria.com.*

$$ Ruddy & Dean Steakhouse. Traditional steakhouse, seafood, and comfort food. Terrace dining. Lunch daily; dinner daily except Mon. *44 Richmond Terrace (Wall St). T: 718 816 4400; ruddyanddean.com.*

$ Dosa Garden. Outstanding Sri Lankan, with many vegetarian choices but also lamb, chicken; superb dosas and naan. Lunch and dinner six days, dinner only Mon. *323 Victory Blvd (Cebra St). From the ferry, bus S46, S61, or S66. T: 718 420 0919; dosagardenny.com.*

$ New Asha. Small and frill-free, with delicious chicken and vegetarian dishes, curry and rice, rotis. Locals prefer takeout; either way the food is good and the prices are low. Open daily 9–9. *322 Victory Blvd (Cebra Ave). From the ferry bus S46, S61 or S66. T: 718 420 0649, no website.*

$ Pier 76. Pizzeria with burgers, pasta, seafood, and sandwiches. Convivial bar/dining room with red checkered tablecloths. Lunch and dinner daily. *76 Bay St (Slosson Terrace). T: 718 447 7437; pier76si. com.*

NEAR SNUG HARBOR

$$ Blue. Waterfront terrace; American and Mediterranean food; seafood and vegetarian specialties. Reservations for groups of four or more. Brunch, lunch, and dinner daily. *1115 Richmond Terrace (Kissel Ave). T: 718 273 7777, bluerestaurantnyc.com.*

$ Adobe Blues. Homey cantina-style Tex-Mex, with bar snacks, standout beers, and margaritas. Live jazz and blues weekends. Lunch and dinner. *63 Lafayette Ave (Fillmore St). T: 718 720 2583, no website.*

$ Crispy Pizza. Handy corner pizzeria adjacent to Snug Harbor. Lunch and dinner seven days. *782 Richmond Terrace (Clinton Ave). T: 718 420 6050, crispypizzany.com.*

TWO STATEN ISLAND LEGENDS

Staten Island has a large Italian American population and many pizzerias. It's debatable which is best: Denino's pizza is much loved. As is Ralph's ice cream.

$ Denino's Pizzeria and Tavern. A historic family business, serving thin-crust pizza and casual Italian food since 1937. Lunch and dinner daily. Cash only. *524 Port Richmond Ave (Hooker Pl and Walker St). T: 718 442 9401, deninossi.com.*

Ralph's Famous Italian Ices. Ralph Silvestro began by selling ices from a truck in 1928 and opened his first store in 1945. Today it's a franchise, with more than 70 locations selling more than 100 flavors. Open daily 11am until late. *501 Port Richmond Ave (Catherine St). T: 718 273 3675, ralphsices.com.*

PRACTICAL INFORMATION

Getting Around

GETTING TO AND FROM THE AIRPORTS

Three airports serve New York City: John F. Kennedy International Airport (JFK), LaGuardia Airport (LGA), and Newark Liberty International Airport (EWR). Getting to Manhattan from the airports is not as easy as it might be, but there are several options with convenience directly proportional to price. Fares are always subject to change. Consult the relevant airport websites.

Taxis: Taxis are the easiest option. They depart from outside the baggage claim at all three airports; lines may be long but usually move quickly when dispatchers are on duty. Ignore offers of transportation from people who approach you in or outside of the terminal; ignore non-uniformed people offering to help with baggage. Taxi drivers are legally required to stay inside their cabs except to help with luggage; they can pick you up only at taxi stands. They will expect a 15–20 percent tip. The passenger pays the tolls.

Private car services: More expensive than taxis, these services (which offer SUVs and vans as well as sedans) can be economical for groups. They must be booked in advance, preferably at least 24hrs. Coming from the airport, parking fees and waiting time for the driver may increase the cost. Some services require you to telephone the dispatcher when you arrive at the airport. The nearest available car will come and pick you up. Port Authority authorized car services include:

Carmel Super Saver: *T: 866 666 6666/800 924 9954, carmellimo.com*
Dial 7 Car & Limousine: *T: 212 777 8888/800 222 9888, dial7.com.*

Shared shuttles (vans or buses): Cheaper than taxis or cars but they may stop to pick up or drop off multiple other passengers, or they may wait to fill up before departing, making the trip longer than you expected. Shuttles run from the airports to Grand Central, the Port Authority Bus Terminal, and Penn Station. Some drop off at Midtown hotels in Manhattan. Shuttle information from all three airports available at the Ground Transportation desks. Port Authority authorized services include SuperShuttle (*T: 212 258 3826 or 800 258 3826, supershuttle.com*) and AirLink (*T: 212 812 9000 or 877 599 8200, goairlinkshuttle.com*).

Public transportation: The least expensive option, good if you are not in a hurry and don't have much luggage. The Port Authority of New York and New Jersey (*panynj.*

gov), which operates the airports, has detailed information about ground transportation to Manhattan and the suburbs, available online and by telephone hotline (*T: 800 AIR RIDE (800 247 7433); live operator available Mon–Fri 8–6; recorded information other times*).

JOHN F. KENNEDY AIRPORT (JFK)
Map p. 611, F3. T: 718 244 4444, jfkairport.com or panynj.gov/airports.
Most international and many domestic flights arrive at Kennedy, about 15 miles from midtown Manhattan (35–60mins, longer by public transportation).
Private car service fares from JFK to Midtown Manhattan depend on the size of the car, plus tolls plus tip; from Midtown to JFK expect to pay about $10 less. **Taxis** from JFK to Manhattan (and vice versa) charge a flat fare, plus tax plus tolls plus tip (15–20 percent). They carry up to four passengers but the fare applies only to the first destination. **Shuttles** will take you from JFK to Midtown and elsewhere. You should book your return trip to the airport 24hrs in advance. **Public transportation** from JFK is by AirTrain plus either a subway or the Long Island Railroad, depending on where in Manhattan or Brooklyn you are going (*for complete info, see the Port Authority website: panynj.gov/airports/jfk-airtrain.html*). To Midtown: AirTrain to Jamaica Station, then subway (E train) to Penn Station (34th St and Eighth Ave). To Lower Manhattan: AirTrain to Howard Beach Station, then subway (A train) to Manhattan.

LAGUARDIA AIRPORT (LGA)
Map p. 611, E2. T: 718 533 3400, airport-laguardia.com or panynj.gov/airports.
About 8 miles (30–45mins) from Midtown, LaGuardia serves domestic flights.**Taxis** are metered, plus tolls and tip. There is also a **shuttle service**. Public transportation is not recommended (no subway).

NEWARK LIBERTY INTERNATIONAL AIRPORT (EWR)
Map p. 610, B3. T: 973 961 6000, airport-ewr.com or panynj.gov/airports.
About 16 miles (45–60 mins) from Midtown, serving international and domestic flights. Newark Airport is convenient to Manhattan's West Side. Reservations for shared-ride van and for private car services can be made at the Port Authority Welcome Center located on the Arrivals level of each terminal. If the center is closed, you can contact authorized services from the self-service kiosk nearby. Because Newark Liberty is in New Jersey, not New York state, the options are slightly different. **Taxis** to and from Newark are metered. There are surcharges for large pieces of luggage, for all destinations in NY state except Staten Island, and for travel during rush hours and on weekends. You pay the metered amount, plus tolls and tip. From the airport, you can organize a shared group rate for up to four passengers from 8am–midnight; make arrangements with the taxi dispatcher. **Shuttles** are available. **AirTrain Newark**, a light public rail service, will take you without charge around the airport (to terminals and parking lots) and to Newark Liberty International Airport Station. From Airport Station to Midtown, you can take either NJ Transit (30mins) or Amtrak (15mins but twice as expensive) to New York Penn Station. From Airport Station to Lower Manhattan, take

NJ Transit to Newark Penn Station, then transfer to the PATH train to the World Trade Center (about 40mins). Trains run 24hrs, frequently during the day, less so from midnight to 5am (*for information, T: 888 397 4636; panynj.gov/airports/ewr-airtrain.html*).

TOURIST INFORMATION

NYC & Company is the motherlode of official New York City information. It maintains information centers at **Macy's** (*151 West 34th St between Seventh Ave and Broadway; map p. 618, C1*); the southern tip of **City Hall Park** (*Broadway sidewalk at Park Row; map p. 620, C3*); the **South Street Seaport** (*East River Waterfront Esplanade at Pier 15; map p. 621, D3*), and **Chinatown** (*traffic triangle at Canal, Walker and Baxter Sts; map p. 620, C1*). Phone number for all these centers: T: 212 484 1222. The centers carry brochures with info about attractions, discounted theater tickets, subway and bus maps, lists of hotels and restaurants. You can download the **Official NYC Guide and Map** from the website (*nycgo.com*), which also has a list of useful apps for getting around, dining, shopping, and events (search "smartphone apps").

BARGAIN MULTI-ATTRACTION PASSES

New York CityPass allows you to skip the lines when visiting six top attractions (including the Empire State Building, Statue of Liberty, and 9/11 Memorial Museum) at a 42 percent discount from list prices (*T: 888 330 5008, citypass.com*). With the **New York Explorer Pass** you choose three, five, seven or ten attractions from 50 sites and tours including the Hop-on/Hop-off double-decker bus, and visit them any time you want within 30 days (*T: 866 629 4335, smartdestinations.com*). The **New York Pass**, available in increments of three, five, or seven days allows you to visit as many of the 80 selected attractions as you can squeeze in during the allotted time; the faster you go, the more you save (*T: 877 714 1999, newyorkpass.com*). The **Downtown Culture Pass** offers similar discounts over a three-day period for attractions south of Chambers St (*downtownculturepass.org*).

GETTING AROUND IN THE CITY

An atlas of Manhattan and the outer boroughs appears on pp. 609–23.

WALKING
This is the best way to see New York. In Lower Manhattan the street plan is irregular; you will probably need a map or an app to get your bearings. North of about 14th St a grid system makes navigation easy.

Avenues run north–south and are either named (e.g. Park, Lexington, West End), numbered (First, Fifth), or lettered (Avenue A, B, C, and D on the Lower East Side). Sixth Avenue, officially The Avenue of the Americas, is still Sixth Avenue to New Yorkers. Traffic on most avenues flows in one direction, with alternate avenues running north and south, though there are exceptions.

Streets run east–west and are numbered east or west of Fifth Avenue, with the smallest numbers closest to it; thus 12 East 72nd St lies east of Fifth Avenue but fairly near to it. Broadway, originally an Indian trail and the major exception to the grid, runs diagonally northwest–southeast.

Traffic generally flows east on even-numbered streets and west on odd-numbered ones, though again there are exceptions. Some major crosstown streets with two-way traffic are 14th, 23rd, 34th, 42nd, 57th, and 72nd Sts. Transverses cross Central Park at 65th/66th Sts, 79th/80th Sts, and 96th/97th Sts.

There are 20 north–south blocks to a mile (crosstown blocks, except between Lexington and Madison Aves, are about three times as long).

CYCLING

New York has miles of bike paths: car-free bike trails include routes in Central Park, Riverside Park, and Hudson River Park, and on Governors Island. In Brooklyn, Prospect Park and Brooklyn Bridge Park also have good paths.

Bicycle rental

Bike and Roll has locations in Central Park, Battery Park, Brooklyn Bridge Park, and Riverside Park on weekends (*T: 212 260 0400, bikenewyorkcity.com*).

Blazing Saddles rents regular and tandem bikes, with locations at the South Street Seaport, Hudson River Park, and Governors Island (*T: 917 440 9094, blazingsaddles. com/new-york*). Both organizations offer group bike tours.

Citi Bike, a municipal bike-sharing program begun in 2013 and slated to expand, has more than 300 stations in Manhattan and in the Brooklyn and Queens neighborhoods close to Manhattan. The blue, three-speed, unisex bikes have adjustable seats, reflectors, and a carrying rack. Helmets are suggested but not mandatory. Bikes are available 24/7, 365 days a year. You can buy a Citi Bike pass for a day, a week, or a year. You may keep a bike for 30mins before incurring extra charges, but as soon as you put the bike into a docking station, you may take another, even from the same station. A free app shows the location of docking stations, availability of bikes, and empty bays for returns (*T: 855 2453 311, citibikenyc.com*).

PUBLIC TRANSPORTATION: BUSES AND SUBWAYS

Official bus and subway maps, including bus maps of the outer boroughs, are available at the information booth on the Main Concourse in Grand Central Terminal. Subway maps are available at the token booths of subway stations and are posted inside the stations and in the trains. Popular transit apps for mobile devices are listed at nycgo. com. Some give real-time locations of trains and buses; some work underground.

MetroCards

If you plan to use public transportation even minimally, buy a MetroCard, a prepaid fare card that can be read by subway turnstiles and fare boxes on buses. There is a very small charge ($1 at the time of writing) to buy a new MetroCard, but no fee to refill one. The **Unlimited Ride MetroCard** comes with 7-day or 30-day expiration dates, and you can add time to your card if needed. The **Pay-Per-Ride MetroCard** comes in various denominations. You can share your Pay-Per-Ride MetroCard with others, but **Unlimited Ride** cards will work only once during an 18-min period in the same subway station or on the same bus route. The **EasyPayXpress** card refills automatically from your credit or debit card. There is also a **single-ride MetroCard**. Reduced-fare cards (half price) are available for travelers with disabilities and the elderly (65 and older); for info about reduced-fare cards, *T: 718 243 4999*.

MetroCards allow you one free transfer from bus to subway or vice versa, and from one bus to another one crossing its route. When your card is swiped, the scanner automatically records a transfer, good for the next 2hrs. You can check your MetroCard balance at bus fare boxes or in subway stations at a MetroCard reader.

The easiest place to buy a MetroCard is in a subway station, although there are also participating neighborhood merchants (news centers, pharmacies, delicatessens and grocery stores, check-cashing centers, etc.). The larger MetroCard vending machines accept cash, credit cards or debit cards. The small MetroCard vending machines are for credit cards or debit cards only. Single-ride tickets are available only at the larger MetroCard vending machines and must be purchased with cash and used within 2hrs of purchase.

Buses

Buses are a good way to travel east–west in Manhattan (subways run primarily north–south) and to see the city if you are not in a hurry. Pay the fare with exact change (no bills) or a MetroCard (the easiest way). If you pay with cash and want to transfer to an intersecting bus line (free), ask the driver when you board; the paper transfer will enable you to change within 2hrs to a second bus on an intersecting route. If you pay with a MetroCard, the card will automatically enable you to transfer to another intersecting bus or a subway.

Most buses stop on demand about every two blocks going uptown and downtown, and every block crosstown. Buses marked "Limited" make fewer stops. Buses marked "Select" are like Limited buses except that they can be boarded from the middle as well as the front; before boarding you must buy a paper ticket at the kiosk on the sidewalk.

Most buses run on a 24-hr schedule with reduced service at night. Press the yellow or black tape on the wall, or pull the cord to signal that you want to stop.

For late-night safety, the **Request-A-Stop** bus service (daily 10pm–5am) allows you to get off along the route between regular stops. Tell the driver where you want to get off and he or she will stop there or at the closest corner where it is safe to stop the bus.

Subways

Subways are the fastest but not always the most pleasant way to get around, since certain lines can be very crowded. Avoid rush hours (7:30–9:30am and 5–6:30pm). You must pay the subway fare with a MetroCard.

The cars are heated and air-conditioned, but the platforms are not, so they can swelter in the summer and freeze in winter. Fewer trains run on weekends when track work takes place, so you may have to wait or take alternate routes.

The trains run 24hrs a day in four boroughs (excluding Staten Island), serving around five million riders on an average weekday. Express trains make only certain stops; local trains stop at every station. Trains to widely different destinations often travel on the same track, so check the number/destination on the front of the train before you board. Announcements over the public address system are sometimes difficult to understand.

The subway's reputation for crime is exaggerated, but use common sense: stay with other people; avoid going down empty stairwells or riding in empty cars; don't lean over the edge of the platform. Panhandlers, pickpockets, and purse snatchers work the subways as well as the street. If you take the subway late at night alone, ride in the car with the transit policeman, if there is one, or the conductor, who has a telephone, and use the Off-Hours Waiting Area.

TAXIS

The city fleet contains about 13,000 cabs, a statistic difficult to believe during a rainy rush hour. Yellow and apple-green Boro cabs are licensed and regulated by the City; they have the same fee schedules, but Boro cabs cannot pick up passengers from the street south of 96th St on the East Side or 110th St on the West Side. They can drop off anywhere. Rates, which cover up to four passengers, are posted on the door. Fares to destinations outside the city should be negotiated before you start. Passengers must pay for bridge or tunnel tolls. Cab drivers will expect a tip of 15–20 percent. Credit-card readers have been installed in all taxis, though drivers sometimes resist accepting cards, claiming a broken card reader. If so, the driver is obliged to take you to an ATM machine, but it is a good idea to carry small bills to avoid hassle. Keep your receipt.

If a cab is available, the center panel of the roof light is illuminated and the side panels are not. Taxi drivers do not always speak or understand English perfectly. Have an idea of your destination's cross street; ask to go to Madison Ave at 61st St rather than 660 Madison Ave.

To inquire about lost property or to register complaints: *T: 212 NYC TAXI (212 692 8294)*. You must know either the taxi identification number or the driver's identification number, posted inside the cab. Your receipt has the taxi ID number printed on it, another reason for keeping it.

"Gypsy" cabs (not recommended) operate in the outer boroughs and in Manhattan outside the central districts. They are painted colors other than yellow and apple green, and may have "livery" license plates.

DRIVING

Unless you plan excursions out of town, a car is no advantage in New York. Traffic can approach gridlock. Street parking is hard to find; parking garages are expensive; parking tickets even more so. Cars parked illegally may be towed and impounded. It is expensive in time, emotional energy, and money to retrieve your vehicle. If you park on the street, do not leave valuables in your car.

FERRIES

The free municipal **Staten Island Ferry** runs daily. Journey time is approx. 25mins. For schedules, see the website (*www.siferry.com*). Terminals are in Lower Manhattan (*map p. 620, C4*) and at St. George on Staten Island (*map p. 610, C3*).

Privately-run ferries travel across the Hudson and East Rivers, to the harbor islands, and to the Rockaways:

NY Waterway (*T: 800 533 3779, nywaterway.com*) departs from Pier 11 at the eastern end of Wall St or the landing at East 35th St near the FDR Drive. Boats travel to Dumbo and Brooklyn Bridge Park, Williamsburg, Greenpoint, and Long Island City. From Pier 11 there is also seasonal service to Governors Island. From Pier 79 at West 39th St boats go to New Jersey and up and down the Hudson.

NY Water Taxi (*T: 212 742 1969; nywatertaxi.com*) offers express service from Pier 11 at Wall St to the IKEA store in Red Hook, Brooklyn. In addition to direct service, its All-Day Access pass lets you get on and off at locations in Dumbo, Battery Park, Christopher St, and West 39th St. The Port Authority website (*panynj.gov*) has a map showing ferry routes.

On weekends and holidays from Memorial Day (end of May) to Labor Day (early Sept), the **NY Beach Ferry** goes from Pier 11 on Wall St to Riis Landing on the Rockaway Peninsula (*T: 718 474 0593, newyorkbeachferry.com*).

TRAVELERS WITH DISABILITIES

New York is not totally accessible to disabled visitors, but it is manageable. The airports have accessible restrooms, telephones, and restaurants, as well as parking spaces. The website of the Port Authority of New York and New Jersey has detailed information about airport facilities (*panynj.gov; search "accessible services"*).

Public transit buses are wheelchair friendly. The subways are not, though some stations have elevators and other facilities. For information about a particular station or for help routing a journey, call New York City Transit (*T: 718 596 8585*). The Mayor's Office for People with Disabilities (MOPD) also has information on accessible transportation (*T: 212 788 2830, TTY: 212 788 2838*).

Some taxis are equipped to accommodate wheelchairs (*for info, T: 311, the New York City information line; dispatch center, T: 646 599 9999, mobile app: WOW Taxi*).

Some Broadway theaters have induction loops for hearing-impaired people. Restaurants vary in accessibility and hotels vary widely. Call ahead.

Big Apple Greeters offers free neighborhood visits guided by volunteers. Visitors with disabilities are especially welcome. Book at least 3–4 weeks before arriving. The website has useful reference guides (*T: 212 669 8159, bigapplegreeter.org*).

Accommodation

New York hotels are the most expensive in the country, with the average nightly rate well over $300. That sum will buy a very pleasant room in a four- or-five-star hotel elsewhere in the country; in New York it will get you something small, perhaps with an airshaft or brick-wall view. Although 25 percent more rooms have been added in the past five years, the average occupancy rate is about 88 percent, so you should book early. (Probably the most expensive place to stay is the penthouse at the Four Seasons, which at the time of writing was listed at $50,000 a night. It has a Bösendorfer piano and comes with a chauffeured Rolls Royce.)

To the already high tariff, the city and state add a 13.25 percent sales tax (8.375 percent for the state, and 5 percent for the city) plus an occupancy fee. Prices soar in the early autumn, in the pre-Christmas shopping rush, and for special events like the New York marathon. Booking online may ease the pain, even using the hotels' own websites. If online rooms are sold out, you can sometimes find space by calling the hotel directly—the New York number, not the 800 toll-free one.

Most major hotel groups have hotels in New York, and the budget chains— Econolodge, Super 8, Red Roof Inn, Comfort Inn, etc.—provide predictable lodging at more reasonable rates. There are also B&Bs, most of which require minimum stays. **City Lights Bed and Breakfast** (*T: 212 737 7049, citylightsbedandbreakfast.com*) and **City Sonnet** (*T: 212 614 3034, citysonnet.com*) are two agencies that offer listings. The **West Side YMCA** near Lincoln Center (*T: 212 912 2600, ymcanyc.org*) and the **Vanderbilt YMCA** near the United Nations (*T: 212 912 2500, ymcanyc.org*) offer basic accommodations and must be booked well in advance.

NB: Although many people use airbnb.com, it was illegal in New York at the time of writing to rent out your apartment for less than 30 days unless you are still present. The person who owns or leases the apartment can be fined, and some have been, though apparently there are no penalties for guests. The issue is contentious and may be resolved in the future.

BLUE GUIDES RECOMMENDED

Hotels and restaurants that are particularly good choices in their category—in terms of excellence, location, charm, value for money or the quality of the experience they provide—carry the Blue Guides Recommended sign: ■. All these establishments have been visited and selected by our authors, editors, or contributors as places they have particularly enjoyed and would be happy to recommend to others. To keep our entries up-to-date, reader feedback is essential: please do not hesitate to email us (editorial@ blueguides.com) with any views, corrections, or suggestions.

The listing below, which reflects prices at the time of writing, includes hotels from all categories and is intended to reflect the variety of choice on offer. Prices are as follows:

$$$$ Over $600 per room per night
$$$ $450–600
$$ $250–450
$ Under $250.

FINANCIAL DISTRICT

$$$$ Ritz-Carlton Battery Park. Wonderful views of New York Harbor (or Downtown skyline) and a high comfort level. Large rooms by New York standards, luxurious appointments, and windows that actually open. Telescopes in the harbor-view rooms let you view the comings and goings in the river; club-level rooms have a separate, private entrance. 298 rooms, 39 suites. *2 West St (Battery Place). T: 212 344 0800, ritzcarlton.com. Map p. 620, B4.*

$$ Andaz Wall Street. Part of the Hyatt chain, this hotel offers spacious rooms with sleek modern décor, free Wi-Fi and minibar, large windows and bathrooms, big flat-screen TVs. Restaurant not open for dinner Sun. *253 rooms. 75 Wall St (Pearl St). T: 212 590 1234, newyork.wallstreet.andaz.hyatt.com. Map p. 620, C3.*

$$ Wall Street Inn. This landmarked stone-cobbled structure is only seven stories high, which suits its location next to the Stone Street Historic District, a low-profile enclave tucked amidst the area's skyscrapers. The compact rooms are well-appointed with attractive furnishings and marble-tiled bathrooms. Rates here are higher during the week, but on the weekends can be more reasonable. 46 rooms. *9 South William St (Broad and William Sts). T: 212 747 1500, thewallstreetinn.com. Map p. 620, C4.*

TRIBECA

$$$ The Greenwich Hotel. The rooms have distinctive designer touches such as Tibetan silk rugs or English leather settees. Also HD TV, iPod docking stations, and free Wi-Fi. The hotel has the city's most stylish swimming pool, a destination restaurant (Locanda Verde), and an outstanding spa and fitness area. 88 rooms and suites. *377 Greenwich St (North Moore and Franklin Sts). T: 212 941 8900, thegreenwichhotel.com. Map p. 620, B2.*

$$$ Tribeca Grand. One of the first downtown hotels on the scene, tucked quietly behind a brick façade. Good dining and a lively bar. Bring your dog. Phones and TV in the bathrooms. 187 rooms, 14 suites. *2 Sixth Ave (White and Walker Sts). T: 212 519 6600, tribecagrand.com. Map p. 620, C2.*

$$ Conrad. Eco-friendly hotel in Battery Park City with a rooftop bar. Large rooms with sliding privacy partitions; big walk-in showers with rainfall showerheads. Pros include the cinema in the building, fitness center, and barber shop. Cons include a charge for Wi-Fi. 463 suites. *102 North End Ave (Vesey St and Murray Sts). T: 212 945 0100, conradnewyork.com. Map p. 620, B3.*

$$ Smyth. Handy to the subway and recently re-designed with a new ground-floor restaurant, the Little Park. Artfully décorated with a downtown, faintly mid-century look. Great service. 84 rooms and 16 suites. *85 West Broadway (Chambers and Warren Sts). T: 212 587*

7000, thompsonhotels.com/hotels/ smyth-tribeca. Map p. 620, B2.

$ The Cosmopolitan. Popular budget hotel, in business since 1853 (*see p. 100*). Few amenities, but simple, clean rooms. Some rooms are small and some, facing busy Chambers St, are noisy. Close to the World Trade Center site and conveniently near two subway lines. No restaurant, but a Starbucks in the building. 150 rooms. *95 West Broadway (Chambers St). T: 212 566 1900, cosmohotel.com. Map p. 620, B2.*

SOHO

$$$$ Crosby Street Hotel. Opened 2009, boutique hotel offers huge bathrooms, high style, a good bar, and attractive public spaces. Small fitness room, but free passes to a very good nearby gym. Romantic and luxurious, LEED certified. 86 rooms. *79 Crosby St (Prince and Spring Sts). T: 212 226 6400, firmdalehotels.com. Map p. 620, C1.*

$$$$ The Mercer. Opened in 1997 in a Romanesque Revival loft building (1892) constructed as an Astor family invest-ment. Large windows, high ceilings, thick walls, and spacious bathrooms. In the basement is Jean-Georges Vongerichten's stylish Mercer Kitchen. 67 rooms and 8 suites. *147 Mercer St (Prince St). T: 212 966 6060, mercerhotel. com. Map p. 620, C1.*

$$$ The James. An artful boutique hotel with a local vibe. Bedrooms are small but carefully designed. Free Wi-Fi, rooftop pool and bar, close to public transportation. David Burke restaurant. 114 rooms. *27 Grand St (Thompson*

St). T: 212 465 2000 or 888 526 3778, jameshotels.com. Map p. 620, B1.

$$ Hotel Hugo. Stylish newcomer to the up-and-coming Hudson Square neighborhood, opened in 2014. Designed by Marcello Pozzi in Italo-downtown industrial style. Maritime décor in the rooms, rooftop bar and club, easy walk to central SoHo and the river. 122 rooms. *525 Greenwich St (Spring and Vandam Sts). T: 212 608 4848, hotelhugony.com. Map p. 620, B1.*

$$ SoHo Grand Hotel. The first new luxury opening (1996) in SoHo since the 1870s, the Grand is owned by Hartz Mountain Industries, which made its name marketing pet products. Pet perks include chew toys and kitty litter boxes. Perks for humans include free bicycles in season and in-room goldfish. Chic bar with outdoor patio in warm weather. 369 rooms. *310 West Broadway (Grand and Canal Sts). T: 212 965 3000, sohogrand.com. Map p. 620, B1.*

LOWER EAST SIDE

$$$ The Ludlow. Opened in 2014, this hotel is the essence of downtown industrial: hip, edgy and nostalgic at the same time. In a brick high-rise, with lofty city views and full service bathrooms—soaking tubs, rainforest showers—the hotel has already attracted the young and the beautiful. Busy bar in the lobby, well-reviewed Dirty French restaurant. 184 rooms. *180 Ludlow St (Houston and Stanton Sts). T: 212 432 1818, ludlowhotel.com. Map p. 619, E4.*

$$ Hotel on Rivington. A sleek high-rise, hi-tech pioneer in the low-rise Lower East Side. Many, but not all, rooms offer jaw-dropping views of the city below. Bathroom showers have glass walls facing out (privacy screens available), service can be uneven. Complimentary continental breakfast. 90 rooms and 20 suites. *107 Rivington St (Ludlow and Essex Sts). T: 212 475 2600, hotelonrivington.com. Map p. 621, D1.*

EAST VILLAGE

$$$ The Bowery Hotel. Downtown chic with an interior that recalls English country lodges (carpets, dark wood ceilings, velvet armchairs, leather club chairs) except for the floor-to-ceiling industrial windows. Many amenities, including 24-hr room service and complimentary bikes. Good bar scene, even for night owls. 135 rooms. *335 Bowery (3rd St). T: 212 505 9100, theboweryhotel.com. Map p. 619, E4.*

$$$ Standard East Village. Hip location close to nightlife and Cooper Union in a 21-story high-rise (i.e., good views). Stylish rooms. Pretty garden for cocktails; the upscale Narcissa Restaurant, named for an upstate dairy cow, features farm-fresh produce. 145 rooms and eight suites. *25 Cooper Square (Fifth St and the Bowery). T: 212 475 5700, standardhotels.com/ eastvillage Map p. 619, E4.*

GREENWICH VILLAGE

$$ The Marlton. A venerable building in an excellent location near Washington Square in a block once known for shoe stores. Jack Kerouac lived here once, as did Julie Andrews; it has served terms as an SRO and a dorm for the New School. Of late under the guiding hand of Sean McPherson (of The Jane and the Bowery Hotel). The restaurant, the Margaux, has been a darling of the fashion forward. Small rooms, no room service. *105 rooms. 5 West 8th St. T: 212 321 0100,*

marltonhotel.com. Map p. 618, C3.

$$ Washington Square Hotel. At the northwest corner of Washington Square, long favored by writers, musicians, budget-minded visitors, and NYU students' parents. Small, clean rooms; those in front overlook the square; those in back can be dark. Art Deco lobby with Wi-Fi, free continental breakfast, and fitness room. 160 rooms. *103 Waverly Place (MacDougal St). T: 212 777 9515, washingtonsquarehotel.com. Map p. 618, C3.*

$ The Jane. In the Far West Village near the Hudson, The Jane is a hotel with a history, designed by the architect of the immigration station at Ellis Island as a seamen's hotel (hence the cabin-like rooms) and restored a century later. In 1912 the *Titanic* survivors stayed here during the investigation of the sinking. Some of the rooms have bunk beds; some have shared bathrooms. 171 rooms. *113 Jane St (West St). T: 212 924 6700, thejanenyc.com. Map p. 618, B3.*

CHELSEA

$$$ High Line Hotel. Opened in 2013 in the western wing of the General Theological Seminary close to the High Line and the Chelsea art galleries, the hotel opens onto 10th Ave with a terrace restaurant and bar, Champagne Charlie's. Also a coffee bar. The rooms have windows that open, wood floors, and antique furnishings including retro dial phones. The Gothic Revival refectory, where once seminarians dined, now hosts weddings and fashion shows. 60 rooms. *180 Tenth Ave (20th St). T: 212 929 3888, thehighlinehotel. com. Map p. 618, A2.*

$$$ Maritime Hotel. The portholes date back to the building's original mission as the headquarters of the National Maritime Union. Rooms are small, nautically themed, like ships' cabins. Fitness center, pet-friendly, can be noisy. 121 rooms. *363 West 16th St (Ninth Ave). T: 212 242 4300, themaritimehotel.com. Map p. 618, B2.*

$$ Hilton New York Fashion District. This new hotel (built 2010) in the former Garment District, now rebranded the Fashion District, celebrates the clothing industry in its décor and artwork. Rooms are straightforward and comfortable, prices are fair. The location is between the Times Square tourist hub and arty Chelsea. 240 rooms. *152 West 26th St (Sixth and Seventh Aves). T: 212 858 5888, hilton.com. Map p. 618, C1.*

$ Chelsea Lodge. A budget hotel frequented by European visitors. On a pretty block and well located for Chelsea sights. Shared bathrooms for most rooms, no restaurant or bar. 22 rooms and four suites. *318 West 20th St (Eighth and Ninth Aves). T: 212 243 4499, chelsealodge.com. Map p. 618, B2.*

NB: The famous **Chelsea Hotel** *(see p. 210), which has provided rest for the night to many famous names, was undergoing renovation at the time of writing. For updates, see chelseahotels.com.*

THE MEATPACKING DISTRICT

$$ The Standard. A Modernist statement hotel (2009, Polshek Partnership) overlooking the High Line, with a good restaurant, panoramic views, and several hip bars including one on the rooftop. Excellent service. 338 rooms. *848 Washington St (Little West 12th and 13th Sts). T: 212 645 4646, standardhotels.com/high-line. Map p. 618, B3.*

GRAMERCY PARK

$$$$ Gramercy Park Hotel. A hotel for arty types since the 1920s, now completely done over in an eclectic style. Super-sized paintings fill the lobby; giant chandeliers hang from the ceiling; walls are saturated with color. Guests have access to Gramercy Park, otherwise open only to neighborhood residents. In addition to the Rose Bar, the hotel has a Danny Meyer restaurant, Maialino. 184 rooms. *2 Lexington Ave (21st St). T: 212 920 3300, gramercyparkhotel.com. Map p. 619, D2.*

$$$ The Inn at Irving Place. An intimate and gracious inn (marked only by its address) in a genteel neighborhood. Charming and romantic with individually décorated rooms, some with (non-working) fireplaces; outstanding tea service in the afternoon and cocktail lounge in the evening; no full restaurant, but several nearby. There are stairs but no elevator. 12 rooms. *56 Irving Place (17th and 18th St). T: 212 533 4600, innatirving.com. Map p. 619, D2.*

FLATIRON DISTRICT

$$$ Hotel Giraffe. A themed boutique hotel; the eponymous giraffe appears in the hotel's graphics and as a statue in the roof garden. Art Deco, with an attractive lobby (piano music in the early evening). Pleasantly furnished rooms, some with balconies. Quiet and relaxing neighborhood, but not adjacent to any major tourist sites. Complimentary continental breakfast, daytime snacks, and wine reception. 73 rooms and 21 suites. *365 Park Ave South (26th St). T: 212 685 7700, hotelgiraffe.com. Map p. 619, D1.*

$$$ The NoMad Hotel. Opened in 2012 to great publicity, draws a bohemian crowd. Beautifully appointed and trendy.

Both room service and the fitness room are open 24hrs; rooftop terrace, location has easy access to transportation. 154 rooms and 14 suites. *1170 Broadway (28th St). T: 212 796 1500, thenomadhotel.com. Map p. 618, C1.*

$$$–$$ The Ace Hotel. Solid service and fair prices at this hip hotel in a turn-of-the-20th-century office building. Funky décor, art on the walls; rooms are small, but clean and comfy. Shop with gear for "traveling creative professionals and adventurers." Destination Breslin restaurant; lively happy hour at Breslin Bar. 280 rooms and suites. *20 West 29th St (Broadway). T: 212 679 2222, acehotel. com/newyork. Map p. 618, C1.*

MIDTOWN EAST

$$$$ Four Seasons New York. Designed by I.M. Pei, the luxurious Four Seasons New York is executed on a grand scale, from the monumental lobby décorated with severe granite columns

and a lighted onyx ceiling panel 33ft above the floor to the guestrooms, large by New York standards. Rooms above the 25th floor have views either of the skyline or Central Park. State-of-the-art spa and exercise facilities. 368 rooms and suites. *57 East 57th St (Madison and Park Aves. T: 212 758 5700, fourseasons. com/newyork. Map p. 617, D2.*

$$$$ The St. Regis. Built in 1904 by John Jacob Astor IV and designed by the architects of J. Pierpont Morgan's bank on Wall St, the St. Regis has long been known for its Gilded Age trappings—high ceilings, silk wall coverings, chandeliers, and lots of gilding. Recently the look has been updated and the hotel outfitted with a new fitness center and spa, though the impeccable service remains. Maxfield Parrish's famous mural overlooks the King Cole Bar & Salon. 182 rooms and 74 suites (some former rooms have been reconfigured as private apartments). *2 East 55th St (Fifth and Madison Aves). T: 212 753 4500, starwoodhotels.com/ stregis. Map p. 617, D2.*

$$$ The Waldorf-Astoria. One of New York's most famous hotels, occupying a niche in the city's social history. On the 50th St side is the more expensive and exclusive Waldorf Towers, a hotel-within-a-hotel. Famous Art Deco lobby, built on stilts to absorb the vibrations from the Metro North trains running below. Classic furniture and marble bathrooms; several restaurants including Peacock Alley (American casual). 1,235 rooms. *301 Park Ave (49th and 50th Sts). T: 212 355 3000, waldorfastoria3.hilton.com. Map p. 617, E3.*

$$ DoubleTree Metropolitan Hotel. A 1960s Modernist building by Morris Lapidus, best known for his curvilinear Miami Beach hotels. The recently renovated lobby is sleek and spare, as are the tastefully décorated rooms. On-site Met Grill and full business services. 755 rooms. *569 Lexington Ave (51st St). T: 212 752 7000, doubletree3. hilton.com. Map p. 617, E3.*

$$ Library Hotel. All the rooms in this boutique hotel are stocked with books organized according to the Dewey Decimal System, with each devoted to a category—religion, history, general knowledge, literature, and so on. Room 800.001, Erotic Literature, is reputedly a favorite. The public spaces include the glass-enclosed wraparound Poetry Terrace and the Writer's Den. Continental breakfast, complimentary passes to a nearby sports club, free wine-and-cheese event on weekdays. Close to Times Square (but far enough away to be restful) and a block from Grand Central. 60 rooms. *299 Madison Avenue (41st St). T: 212 983 4500 libraryhotel.com. Map p. 617, D4.*

$$ One UN New York. Upstairs (28th floor) in a tall building across from the UN, recently renovated. The attentive multilingual staff caters to diplomats and foreign visitors. 439 rooms. *One United Nations Plaza (44th St and First Ave). T: 212 758 1234 or 866 866 8086, millenniumhotels.com. Map p. 617, E3.*

$ The Pod Hotel. For the budget-minded, but not the claustrophobic. Good prices, good design, bright colors, and few frills, though there is Wi-Fi. About half of the rooms have shared bathrooms. (There is a second location on East 39th St.) 345 rooms. *230 East 51st St (Second and Third Aves). T: 212 355 0300, or 800 742 5945, thepodhotel. com. Map p. 617, E3.*

MIDTOWN WEST

Several major chains have hotels around Times Square including Hilton, Sheraton, Marriott, Westin, Best Western, Holiday Inn, Comfort Inn, EconoLodge.

$$$$ The Chatwal New York. A Stanford White building that housed the Lambs Club (*see p. 230*) for 70 years, its name enshrined in the ground floor restaurant (a popular lunch spot for fashion and publishing types). Lively bar scene, all the little luxuries. 76 rooms and suites. *130 West 44th St (Fifth and Sixth Aves). T: 212 764 6200, thechatwalny.com. Map p. 617, D3.*

$$$$ The Plaza. One of the city's most famous hotels, the Plaza was upscale when it opened in 1907; a hundred years later it reopened after a $400-million makeover in which the storied public spaces—the Palm Court, the Oak Room and Bar, and the Plaza Grand Ballroom—were returned to their former splendor, but many rooms were converted to private residences. Luxury in every detail, from white-gloved butlers to gold-plated bathroom fixtures. Prime location, facing Grand Army Plaza at the southeast corner of Central Park. *282 rooms and suites. 768 Fifth Ave (Central Park South). T: 212 759 3000 or 866 940 9361, fairmont.com/theplaza. Map p. 617, D2.*

$$$ JW Marriott Essex House. Famous 44-story Art Deco hotel opulently refurbished to evoke the "golden age of travel" (the 1920s and '30s). Some rooms have views of Central Park, some are smallish. The electronics and other amenities are cutting-edge The hotel's South Gate restaurant, featuring contemporary American cuisine, overlooks the park. 509 rooms. *160 Central Park South (Sixth and Seventh Aves). T: 212 247 0300, marriott.com. Map p. 616, C2.*

$$$ The Knickerbocker. Gazing down at the push and rush of Times Square, this historic hotel (*see p. 225*) reopened in 2015 after languishing for decades as an office building. Completely renovated with a lot of marble and bespoke furniture, it offers contemporary and sophisticated luxury, fine dining, a rooftop lounge, and all the amenities. 330 rooms. *6 Times Square (42nd St and Broadway). T: 212 204 4980, theknickerbocker.com. Map p. 616, C4.*

$$$ W Times Square. In the thick of the Theater District, this W Hotel picks up Times Square's neon vibe with its urban lobby and bar. The hotel reaches 52 stories into the sky, so try for a room with a view. Can be noisy and Times Square is always packed with tourists. Right downstairs, the Blue Fin offers glamorous dining. 509 rooms. *1567 Broadway (West 47th St). T: 212 930 7400, wnewyorktimessquare.com. Map p. 616, C3.*

$$ The Algonquin. This landmarked hotel has literary associations dating back to the 1920s when the editors and writers of the Round Table lunched here (*see p. 272*). The lobby, paneled in dark wood, is comfortably furnished with upholstered chairs. The guest rooms are on the small side, but pleasantly décorated, most recently in 2012. Close to Times Square and the Theater District, Fifth Avenue, and Grand Central. 181 rooms. *59 West 44th St (Fifth and Sixth Aves). T: 212 840 6800, algonquinhotel.com. Map p. 617, D3.*

$$ **City Club Hotel**. This block of West 44th St hosts the New York Yacht Club, the Harvard Club, and since 2001, the City Club Hotel, formerly a gentlemen's political club. The "petite" rooms were originally for gentlemen's servants; the duplex suites were carved out of the two-story ballroom. Furnishings combine tradition with innovation, the elaborately plastered ceilings and other original architectural details still intact. The onsite restaurant is

db Bistro Moderne, Daniel Boulud's upscale bistro, where you can lunch on the signature db burger, chopped sirloin stuffed with foie gras and truffles. 65 rooms. *55 West 44th St (Fifth and Sixth Aves). T: 212 921 5500, cityclubhotel.com. Map p. 617, D3.*

$ **Amsterdam Court**. This no-frills hotel is conveniently near Times Square, the Theater District, and public transportation. The price is right; the amenities beyond free coffee in the lobby are modest. Extra charge for in-room refrigerator and Wi-Fi. 136 rooms. *226 W 50th St (Broadway and Eighth Ave). T: 212 459 1000, amsterdamcourthotelnewyork.com. Map p. 616, C3.*

UPPER EAST SIDE, NORTH OF 59TH STREET

$$$$ **The Carlyle**. The luxurious Carlyle, with its familiar Art Deco tower, has long been a favorite of the rich and famous—presidents, foreign dignitaries, and celebrities—either seeking the limelight or trying to stay out of it. The rooms are furnished elegantly but conservatively. For a fee, pets (under 50lb) can enjoy spring water and suitable snacks. The Café Carlyle has a famous cabaret; the Bemelmans Bar retains its noted mural by Ludwig Bemelmans, the creator of the Madeline children's books (he was also a gourmet). 187 rooms and suites. *35 East 76th St (Madison Ave). T: 212 744 1600, rosewoodhotels.com. Map p. 615, D4.*

$$$$ **The Lowell**. A long-standing reputation (since 1926) among people who expect to be pampered and treated with discretion. Beautifully appointed

public spaces and rooms, some with working fireplaces, some with terraces. The Pembroke Room offers afternoon tea, as well as meals. On a quiet side street close to Central Park. 70 rooms and suites. *28 East 63rd St (Park and Madison Aves). T: 212 838 1400, lowellhotel.com. Map p. 617, D1.*

$$$ **The Mark**. ■ Luxurious Upper East Side hotel (opened 1927; reopened 2009), one of the city's best modern luxury hotels. The Mark Restaurant and bar are local favorites. Close to Central Park and the Guggenheim. High style, hi-tech, gracious. 118 rooms 25 suites. *25 East 77th St (Madison Ave). T: 212 744 4300, themarkhotel.com. Map p. 615, D4.*

$$ **Hotel Wales**. Small hotel at the edge of Carnegie Hill, a quiet, upscale residential neighborhood. Rooms are

simply décorated but comfortable; the beds have down comforters; the deluxe suites offer views of the Reservoir in Central Park. 46 rooms and 41 suites. *1295 Madison Ave (92nd St). T: 212 876 6000, hotelwalesnyc.com. Map p. 615, D2.*

UPPER WEST SIDE, NORTH OF 59TH STREET

$$$$ The Mandarin Oriental New York. Located on the 35th–54th floors of the Time Warner Center's north tower, this is a serious contender for the city's most luxurious hotel, with views of Central Park and/or the Hudson River. Asian-influenced décor, high-tech luxuries (surround-sound stereos, face-to-face video conferencing), impeccable service, a spa with steam room, soaking tubs, 75-ft lap pool, and floor-to-ceiling windows. Within the hotel are Asiate, a Japanese-French fusion restaurant; the Lobby Lounge, and the MObar, with Asian-influenced cocktails. 251 rooms. *80 Columbus Circle, (60th St). T: 212 805 8800, mandarinoriental.com/newyork. Map p. 616, B2.*

$$ The Empire Hotel. ■ Just across Broadway from Lincoln Center and not far from Central Park, with a rooftop lounge and small pool. Rooms are attractive but not spacious, and can be noisy. 376 rooms. *44 West 63rd St (Columbus Ave). T: 212 265 7400, empirehotelnyc.com. Map p. 616, B2.*

$$ Excelsior. In a quiet West Side residential neighborhood, half a block from Central Park West and across the street from the American Museum of Natural History; close to transportation. The public rooms and elevators sport wood paneling; the décor of the guest rooms is old-fashioned and the rooms are smallish but clean. Nuevo Latino restaurant, Calle Ocho. 200 rooms. *45 West 81st St (Central Park West). T: 212 362 9200; excelsiorhotelny.com. Map p. 614, C3.*

HARLEM

$$ Aloft Harlem. The Aloft hotels, part of the Starwood group, were developed to appeal to the hip, budget-conscious traveler. This one, a block away from the Apollo Theater, arrived in 2010, the first new hotel in Harlem since the 1960s. Hi tech amenities, colorful (though not large) rooms with a contemporary look, a 24/7 snack bar, business center, and flat-screen TVs complete the menu. 126 rooms. *2296 Frederick Douglass Blvd (Eighth Ave, between 123rd and 124th Sts). T: 212 749 4000, aloftharlem.com. Map p. 612, C3.*

BROOKLYN

$$ Aloft Brooklyn. The second boutique Aloft Hotel shares the ambience of the first: hip design, moderate amenities. Rooftop bar, walking distance to subways. Construction underway behind the hotel means noise during the day. 170 rooms and suites. *216 Duffield St*

(Willoughby St and Fulton Mall).
T: 718 256 3833,
aloftnewyorkbrooklyn.com.
Map p. 622, C3.

$$ Marriott at Brooklyn Bridge. Just over the bridge, this full-service hotel on a busy street offers reliable service, business amenities, a spa and fitness center with a pool, large rooms, and a parking garage. Subway is nearby, but the hotel offers a daily shuttle to Times Square. *666 rooms and suites. 333 Adams St (Johnson and Willoughby Sts). T: 718 246 7000, marriott.com. Map p. 622, C3.*

$$ Wythe Hotel. Opened in 2012 to great fanfare. Wonderful views of the Manhattan skyline from this refurbished barrel factory. Hip restaurant draws a clientele of knowledgeable diners. At the top of the building there's a popular rooftop bar.

Local Brooklyn-based design. No room service and a hike to the subway. 70 rooms and suites. *80 Wythe Ave (North 11th St). T: 718 460 8000, wythehotel. com.*

$ Hotel Le Jolie. Convenient, comfortable, and close to culture. No frills but all the basics. Can be loud because close to the Brooklyn–Queens Expressway, but also near the subway. Some parking. 52 rooms. *235 Meeker Ave (Jackson and Withers Sts). T: 718 625 2100, hotellejolie.com.*

$ Nu Hotel. Eco-friendly, wallet friendly (especially compared to Manhattan), and pet-friendly boutique hotel. Rooms are clean, comfortable, and attractive. Some have bunk beds. Loaner bikes, bar with seasonal outdoor seating and small plates menu. *85 Smith St (Atlantic Ave and State St). T: 718 852 8585, nuhotelbrooklyn.com. Map p. 622, C3.*

New York Food & Drink

The New York restaurant scene is perhaps the finest in the world (though Parisians or Londoners may dispute that). In 2015 more than 70 New York restaurants were awarded Michelin stars, including six three-star winners; most of the stars stayed in Manhattan but several were scattered about Brooklyn and Queens. New York's historic diversity is reflected in its eateries. If you want pizza or a hot dog with kraut, knishes or *pierogi*, you can find them in New York. If you want elegance, culinary sophistication, and fine dining bordering on the reverent, you can find that too, though for a price. Twice a year during **Restaurant Week**, usually in midsummer and again in the dead of winter, many restaurants offer *prix fixe* lunches and sometimes dinners at bargain rates (*for dates and participants, see nycgo.com*).

Reservations are absolutely necessary at the most popular restaurants, some of which start booking two months in advance. Eating early (before 6pm) or late (10pm) can improve your chances of getting a reservation. If your plans are flexible, you can ask to be put on a waiting list for cancellations. **Open Table** (*opentable.com*) is an online service for booking at many restaurants.

Many restaurants will call the day before to ask you to confirm that you plan to honor your reservation. If the restaurant doesn't call you, call them. If you change your plans, be sure to cancel. A much-told tale recounts André Soltner, owner of the late great Lutèce, calling a no-show at 3am and saying, "My staff and myself are still waiting for you, should we continue?"

A few high-end restaurants are beginning to include service with the price of the meal, and it is often included for groups of more than six people. When service is not included, a tip of 16–20 percent is appropriate. The easiest way to calculate the amount is to double the sales tax of 8.875 percent and add a little more if you're pleased. Tip the bartender at least dollar a drink, and the coat check person at least a dollar a coat.

Almost all restaurants accept major credit cards, though a few small places (for example in Chinatown) do not. Some high-end restaurants require jackets for men. There is no smoking in New York restaurants.

Zagat's New York City Restaurants (*zagat.com*), updated yearly, summarizes and tabulates comments from diners. *New York Magazine, The New Yorker,* and the *New York Times* also offer reviews, available online. Food blogs, up-to-the-minute and opinionated, include New York Serious Eats (*newyork.seriouseats.com*), EaterNY.com, GrubStreet.com (news about openings, closings, and the restaurant industry, as well as recommendations), MidtownLunch.com, and Immaculate Infatuation (*theinfatuation.com*).

Restaurants listed in the guide are categorized as follows: Price for a three-course meal excluding alcohol, tax, and tip. Lunch is usually 25 percent less.

$ under $25
$$ $25–50
$$$ $50–75
$$$$ over $75

MARKETS AND GREENMARKETS

Among New York's indoor markets is **Eataly**, a gigantic and enormously popular food emporium opposite Madison Square (*see p. 200*). In Brooklyn, **Smorgasburg** (*see p. 507*) is to food as Brooklyn Flea is to vintage paraphernalia. The **Chelsea Market** (*see p. 206*) has been around since 1997; the **Gotham West Market** opened in Hell's Kitchen in 2013 (*600 11th Ave at 44th St; T: 212 582 7940, gothamwestmarket.com*).

More than 50 **greenmarkets** provide retail outlets for some 230 small farmers, fishers, and producers providing fresh, seasonal food. Most are open from about 8am until around 6pm, though the daily schedule changes. In addition to produce, meat, and fish, you can buy ethnic breads and other baked goods, smoked and dried meat, flowers including orchids, jams, pickles, and farmstead cheeses. In Manhattan there are markets—and this is a small sampling—at Union Square, City Hall, Bowling Green, and Dag Hammarskjöld Plaza (*for a full listing see grownyc.org*).

FOOD TRUCKS

Street food is nothing new in New York. For generations pushcarts have been parked on corners, vending hot dogs forked out of warm water, roasted chestnuts, and thick pretzels coated with salt. Over the past decade they have been joined by food trucks, most offering ethnic specialties—Greek, Italian, Asian, and Latin American—but there are also cupcake trucks, vegan trucks, ice cream trucks and trucks dispensing American comfort food. Like the pushcarts before them, many offer immigrants a foothold in the economy. In September the annual Vendy Awards, a sellout competitive cook-off featuring the most popular sidewalk chefs, are held on Governors Island (*vendyawards.streetvendor.org/newyorkcity*). Many of these businesses have websites. You can track their location on Twitter and find them on sites such as nyctruckfood.com, roaming hunger.com or midtown lunch.com. The scene constantly shifts: some businesses switch from trucks to brick-and-mortar restaurants; others shut down; new entrepreneurs arrive. Some trucks accept cash only. Here are a few choices.

Biàn Dang. Blue be-flowered truck dishes up chicken or beef stew over rice, steamed pork dumplings, pork buns. *53rd St between Park and Lexington, biandangnyc.com. Map p. 617, E3.*

Calexico. Cal-Mex specialties including chipotle pulled pork or *carne asada* (grilled marinated beef) in burritos and tacos. Calexico now has restaurants in Park Slope, on the Lower East Side, and Red Hook as well as carts. *Wooster St near Prince St in SoHo and at 1030 Broadway in the Flatiron District, calexico.net.*

Eddie's Pizza Truck. An import from Hyde Park up the river, Eddie has been baking vegetarian bar pizzas for a couple of generations. They come in white and whole wheat with many vegetarian toppings. *Many lunch time locations; check the website, eddiespizzany.com/truck.*

Hallo Berlin. Founded by Berliner Rolf Babiel and still family-fun. The wursts—*bratwurst, alpenwurst, wienerwurst*—at this cart have been named for German vehicles, from the least expensive Trabant to the (slightly) pricier Porsche. *54th St near Fifth Ave, halloberlinrestaurant.com. Map p. 617, D2.*

Korilla BBQ. New York's first Korean barbecue truck, also a restaurant at 23 Third Ave near St. Marks Place. The tiger-striped truck offers burritos stuffed with your choice of protein (pork, chicken, tofu, beef), kimchi, and sauces that range from mild to blistering. *47th St and Park Ave, Front St and Gouverneur La, and other locations, korillabbq.com.*

NY Dosas. Since 2001, Thiru Kumar, aka the Dosa Man, has parked his cart near Washington Square, offering Sri Lankan vegetarian delights: lentil and rice pancakes, fried on a griddle and stuffed with potatoes and spicy vegetables. *Washington Square South near Sullivan St, no website. Map p. 618, C4.*

El Olomega. The original Red Hook Salvadoran *pupusa* truck, in business since 1988. Corn flour tortillas stuffed with pork or chicken, cheese and beans, not easy to make but easy to eat. *Sat and Sun lunch at the Red Hook ball fields, Brooklyn, elolomega.com.*

Wafels & Dinges. Belgian waffle trucks with sweet and savory toppings. Sweets include chocolate, maple syrup, nutella, spekuloos crumble. Savory toppings include pulled pork, chili con carne, and bacon. *Several locations, check website, wafelsanddinges.com.*

BARS

New York offers a wealth of places to imbibe, from historic taverns where famous writers overindulged to chic wine bars in trendy neighborhoods. Some of the establishments mentioned below are stand-alone bars, while others are in hotels or restaurants. Bars are permitted to stay open until 4am. The legal drinking age is 21.

LOWER MANHATTAN, FINANCIAL DISTRICT

Dead Rabbit. *See p. 73.*

Pier A Harbor House. In the newly renovated Pier A former fire station. Oyster bar and beer hall downstairs, and the Harrison Room, an upscale bar and restaurant on the second floor, and the Commissioners' Bar on the third. *22 Battery Place. T: 212 785 0153, piera.com. Map p. 620, B4.*

Ulysses. Irish-style pub (the eponymous Ulysses is Joyce's) in the Stone Street Historic District; popular after-work hangout for Financial District types; beer and pub food. *95 Pearl St (Hanover Sq.). T: 212 482 0400, ulyssesnyc.com. Map p. 620, C4.*

TRIBECA

Brandy Library. A clubby wood-paneled "library," with bottles on the shelves instead of books; *hors d'oeuvres*, cocktails, whiskeys, brandies. Expensive. *25 North Moore St (Hudson and Varick Sts). T: 212 226 5545, brandylibrary.com. Map p. 620, B2.*

City Hall. Historic photos on the walls at this comfortable, traditional restaurant with pleasant bar area; broad selection of American wines. *131 Duane St (Church St and West Broadway). T: 212 227 7777, cityhallnewyork.com. Map p. 620, C2.*

Terroir. This award-winning wine bar with good snacks offers hundreds of wines by the glass; discounted prices at happy hour (4–6pm); also beer; other locations. *24 Harrison St (Greenwich St). T: 212 625 9463, wineisterroir.com. Map p. 620, B2.*

SOHO, NOLITA, LITTLE ITALY, CHINATOWN

City Winery. Food, wine, and music. *155 Varick St (Vandam St). T: 212 608 0555, citywinery.com. Map p. 620, B1.*

Ear Inn. On the far West Side, at the edge of the West Village, a contender for oldest surviving New York bar; comfortable with good basic food. *326 Spring St (Washington and Greenwich Sts). T: 212 226 9060, earinn.com. Map p. 620, B1.*

Mulberry Street Bar. A Little Italy bar with gangster ambience (tile floor and a pressed-tin ceiling, c. 1908), popular with tourists, locals, and movie location scouts. Italian food. *176 Mulberry St (Kenmare St). T: 212 226 9345, mulberrystreetbar.com. Map p. 620, C1.*

Pegu Club. Named after a British officers' club in Burma, where the Pegu cocktail (gin, bitters, orange curaçao, and lime juice) was invented, this attractive bar emphasizes finely crafted cocktails. *77 West Houston St (West Broadway and Wooster St), 2nd floor. T: 212 473 7348, peguclub.com. Map p. 619, D4.*

Pravda. Snacks, small plates, large plates, caviar, and champagne along with 70 vodka drinks. *281 Lafayette St (Prince and Jersey Sts). T: 212 226 4944, pravdany.com. Map p. 619, D4.*

Toad Hall. Billiards, beer, brick walls; neighborly and a little divey. No restaurant, but you can order take-out or bring your own food. *57 Grand St (West Broadway and Wooster St). T: 212 431 8145, no website. Map p. 620, C1.*

LOWER EAST SIDE, EAST VILLAGE, ASTOR PLACE

Booker & Dax. At Momofuku Ssam. As part of the Momofuku enterprise, you would expect this hip bar to serve inventive and delicious cocktails involving new and old technologies including hot pokers and liquid nitrogen. It does. *207 Second Ave (East 13th St). T: 212 254 3500, momofuku. com/new-york. Map p. 619, E3.*

Death & Company. One among several East Village pseudo-speakeasies. Well-crafted cocktails, good bar food, and a clandestine atmosphere. The same team runs Mayahuel and Bourgeois Pig (*see below*). *433 East 6th St (First Ave and Ave A). T: 212 388 0882, deathandcompanyny.com. Map p. 619, E4.*

Joe's Pub. Small club in the East Village's Public Theater, with good cabaret; some say "uptown prices with a downtown feel." *425 Lafayette St (Astor Pl. and East 4th St). T: 212 539 8770, publictheater.org. Map p. 619, D3.*

bby Bar. In the Bowery Hotel. Aficionados praise the velvet couches, Oriental rugs, relaxed atmosphere, and strong cocktails. *335 Bowery (East 3rd St). T: 212 505 9100, theboweryhotel.com. Map p. 619, E4.*

Mayahuel. Mexican bar with top-notch tequila and mescal cocktails and highly praised Mexican bar food. *304 East 6th St (Second Ave). T: 212 253 5888, mayahuelny.com. Map p. 619, E4.*

McSorley's Old Ale House. Historic pub in East Village, with sawdusty floor, its own brews on tap. NYU students have replaced the working-class drinkers of yore. No credit cards. *15 East 7th St (Second and Third Aves). T: 212 473 9148, no website. Map p. 619, E3.*

GREENWICH VILLAGE, WEST VILLAGE

124 Old Rabbit Club. A neo-speakeasy with many craft beers; walk downstairs and press the buzzer to get in. Cash only. *124 MacDougal St (Minetta Lane). T: 212 254 0575, no website. Map p. 618, C4.*

Blue Note. A great old jazz club (founded 1981) where such legends as Dizzy Gillespie and Sarah Vaughan once came. Full bar and American food, cover charge for some shows. *131 West 3rd St (Sixth Ave). T: 212 475 8592, bluenote. net. Map p. 618, C4.*

The Bourgeois Pig. Cocktails at this Frenchified wine bar formerly in the East village include a Marie Antoinette, a Bourgeois royale, and an E.V. Swill. Beer, wine, and champagne. Charcuterie, fondue. *127 MacDougal St (West 3rd and West 4th St). T: 212 475 2246, bourgeoispigny.com. Map p. 618, C4.*

Employees Only. Another neo-speakeasy, with bartenders in white chefs' jackets (connoting mastery of their craft) serving up admirable cocktails in a bar considered by some to be the quintessential New York nightspot. *510 Hudson St (West 10th and Christopher Sts). T: 212 242 3021, employeesonlynyc.com. Map p. 618, B4.*

(Le) Poisson Rouge. One of the city's best venues for all kinds of music, founded by two grads of the Manhattan School of Music. Performers have ranged from Anna Netrebko to Iggy Pop & the Stooges. The parenthesis marks surrounding (Le) remain unclear, at least to all but the inner circle. *158 Bleecker St (Thompson St). T: 212 505 3474, lepoissonrouge.com. Map p. 618, C4.*

Orient Express. A train-themed cocktail bar, old fashioned, with updated drinks. The Agatha V has gin and lemon plus house-made grapefruit-thyme soda. *325 West 11th St (Greenwich and Washington Sts). T: 212 691 8845, orientexpressnyc.com. Map p. 618, B3.*

Smalls. Jazz club founded in 1993, where many present jazz greats got their starts. Full bar. Music begins at 7pm. *183 West 10th St at Seventh Ave South. T: 212 252 5091, smallsjazzclub.com. Map p. 618, C3.*

Village Vanguard. Now celebrating its 80th anniversary, this jazz club is where Thelonious Monk, Bill Evans, and John Coltrane once played. Monday evenings the Village Vanguard Orchestra holds forth. *178 Seventh Ave South (11th and Perry Sts). T: 212 255 4037, villagevanguard.com. Map p. 618, C3.*

White Horse Tavern. A poets' bar, once favored by Dylan Thomas (*see p. 156*) and others, now by literary pilgrims; atmospherically run-down. No credit cards. *567 Hudson St (West 11th St). T: 212 243 9260, no website. Map p. 618, B3.*

UNION SQUARE, GRAMERCY PARK, FLATIRON DISTRICT

The Ace Hotel. A trendy hotel with a busy lobby bar for workers from nearby Silicon Alley, other hipsters, and ordinary folk. DJ, beer, and battered wood tables. Also in the hotel is the Breslin bar and restaurant. *20 West 29th St (Broadway). T: 212 679 2222, acehotel.com. Map p. 618, C1.*

Molly's. An authentic Irish bar down to the sawdust on the floor. Burgers and brew, pints of Guinness, good old-fashioned bar food. *287 Third Ave (22nd and 23rd Sts). T: 212 889 3361, mollysshebeen.com. Map p. 619, D2.*

Pete's Tavern. Since 1864 a neighborhood fixture; cheerful, historic, and anything but fancy. Sidewalk café in season. *129 East 18th St (Irving Pl.). T: 212 473 7676, petestavern.com. Map p. 619, D2.*

MIDTOWN

Algonquin Hotel. This famous hotel has two bars: the Lobby Lounge, with upholstered chairs and wood paneling, and the Blue Bar, for cocktails and bar food. *59 West 44th St (Fifth and Sixth Aves). T: 212 840 6800; algonquinhotel. com. Map p. 617, D3.*

Ardesia. A casual Hell's Kitchen wine bar with unusual small plates (New York-style pretzels, homemade ice cream sandwiches) and Old and New World wines; also beer, spirits. *510 West 52nd St (Tenth and Eleventh Aves). T: 212 247 9191, ardesia-ny.com. Map p. 616, B3.*

Campbell Apartment. Occupying the former luxurious office of railroad magnate John Campbell. Vintage cocktails with vintage names: Gin-Berry Fizz, Vanderbilt Punch, and the Oxford Swizzle. *In Grand Central Terminal, 42nd St at Park Ave. T: 212 953 0409, hospitalityholdings.com. Map p. 617, D4.*

The Modern Bar. Bar adjoining MoMA's main restaurant; streamlined, cool; modern Alsatian small plates to accompany your drinks. *9 West 53rd St (Fifth and Sixth Aves) in MoMA. T: 212 333 1220, themodernnyc.com. Map p. 617, D2.*

UPPER EAST SIDE

Bar Pleiades. In the Surrey Hotel. A Daniel Boulud enterprise; Art Deco, subdued, deluxe and elegant, draws an upscale crowd. *20 East 76th St (Fifth and Madison Ave). T: 212 772 2600, barpleiades.com. Map p. 615, D4.*

Bemelmans Bar. Upper East Side through and through, elegant, expensive, good service, piano music, and Ludwig Bemelmans's Madeline murals. *35 East 76th St (Madison Ave). T: 212 744 1600,*

rosewoodhotels.com. Map p. 615, D4.

Metropolitan Museum of Art, Balcony Bar and Roof Garden Café. Cocktails and appetizers served with live classical music on the balcony overlooking the Great Hall; April through Oct, weather permitting, the Roof Garden offers drinks and light meals with a view of Central Park. *1000 Fifth Ave at 82nd St. T: 212 535 7710, metmuseum.org. Map p. 615, D3.*

UPPER WEST SIDE

Dizzy's Club Coca-Cola. Jazz at Lincoln Center's venue for live music in a club setting; great players, great views, but expensive—tickets plus minimums for food and drink. *In the Time Warner Center (5th floor), 10 Columbus Circle. T: 212 258 9595; jazz.org/dizzys. Map p. 616, B2.*

MO Bar. In the elegant Mandarin Oriental Hotel. Great views in outer lounge; caters to businessmen, out-of-towners; everything cool and very pricey. 35th floor. *80 Columbus Circle, Time Warner Center (60th St). T: 212 805 8800, mandarinoriental.com. Map p. 616, B2.*

HARLEM

Bier International. Harlem's first beer garden. Many beers, on draft and bottled, bar food, and outdoor tables for enjoying them. *2099 Frederick Douglass Blvd (West 113th St). T: 212 280 0944, bierinternational.com. Map p. 612, C4.*

Ginny's Supper Club. In the basement of the Red Rooster, a lounge that recalls an uptown speakeasy. Great live music, communal tables. *310 Malcolm X Boulevard, i.e. Lenox Ave (125th and 126th Sts). T: 212 421 3821, redroosterharlem.com. Map p. 612, C3.*

Events, Festivals, & Parades

This is a modest sampling of the city's hundreds of annual events. For dates, times, locations, call the NYC information line at 311, or visit nycgo.com; *Time Out New York* has comprehensive listings, and the Friday Weekend Arts section of the *New York Times* has a weekly calendar.

JANUARY

New Year's Day begins at midnight with the annual Ball Drop in Times Square. After dawn breaks, you can get a bracing start to the New Year by joining the Coney Island Polar Bear Club's annual New Year's Day Swim, some of whose proceeds go to charity (*T: 917 533 3568, polarbearclub.org*). The oldest winter swimming organization in the US, the club was founded in 1903 by physical culturist Bernarr Macfadden (1868–1955), who held that cold-water dips improved stamina, virility, and immunity.

Martin Luther King Day (third Mon in Jan). Citywide celebrations pay tribute to Dr. King's legacy as a leader in the civil rights' movement and an advocate for non-violence: arts events, readings, walking tours, and museum exhibitions.

National Boat Show (first week in Jan at the Javits Center). For more than 100 years this trade show has exhibited the newest yachts, cruisers, canoes, and kayaks—anything that floats, short of battleships—as well as fishing gear and marine electronics.

FEBRUARY

Chinese New Year (end of Jan or early Feb, in Chinatown around Canal and Mott Sts; *betterchinatown.com*). The Lunar New Year is celebrated with traditional lion and dragon dances, costumes, floats and confetti, and food vendors. Other events have included a Firecracker Ceremony in Sarah Delano Roosevelt Park.

Westminster Kennel Club Dog Show. The second oldest sporting event in the US after the Kentucky Derby. During the show the Empire State Building lights glow purple and gold (Westminster colors); the NY Stock Exchange has recently allowed the winner to ring the opening bell. Finals at Madison Square Garden (*westminsterkennelclub.org*).

MARCH

St. Patrick's Day Parade (March 17, unless March 17 falls on a Sun, then the day before; Fifth Ave, from about 44th–86th Sts; *nycstpatricksparade.org*). This event dates to 1762 and has become the city's largest parade with more than 150,000 marchers, plus bands, bagpipes, costumes, and green everywhere.

Greek Independence Day Parade (around March 25 at 1pm, but shifted according to Orthodox Lent; Fifth Ave from about 60th to 79th Sts; *greekparade. org*). Not as big (or excessive) as the St. Patrick's Day Parade, but patriotic with political overtones; floats, bands, costumed marchers, and Greek flags.

APRIL

Events include floral displays in Rockefeller Center, the Brooklyn Botanic Garden, the New York Botanical Garden, and elsewhere.

Easter Parade (Easter Sun 10–4, Fifth Ave, 49th–57th Sts). Not a parade in the organized sense, though Fifth Ave is closed to traffic, rather a promenade of spring finery

Macy's Flower Show (late March and

early April at the Herald Square store): tens of thousands of flowers, plants, and exotic trees from around the world fill the store's ground floor.

Tribeca Film Festival (late April to early May; *tribecafilmfestival.com*). A two-week extravaganza of new and independent films, lectures, and events; draws more than 100,000 viewers from 38 countries.

MAY

Cherry Blossom Festival (early May at the Brooklyn Botanic Garden; *bbg.org*), with drumming, dancing, sword-

fighting, and bonsai and ikebana tours as the BBG's 200 cherry trees burst into bloom. Rain or shine.

JUNE

Museum Mile Festival (Fifth Ave, 82nd–105th Sts, usually second Tues of the month 6–9pm). Fifth Ave is closed to traffic; museums are free and open late. Special events, street performances. (*museummilefestival.org*).

Mermaid Parade (Coney Island, Sat in June, 1pm, Surf Ave and West 21st St; *coneyisland.com*). King Neptune leads

fantastical marchers along the streets. Lots of glitter, lots of flesh.

Shakespeare in the Park (Delacorte Theater, Central Park at 81st St, through Aug; *publictheater.org*). Tickets on sale at noon on the day of performance, but lines form early and wind through the park; up to two tickets per person. For other ways to get tickets, see website. A tradition since 1962, the festival is the brainchild of Joe Papp (*see p. 168*), who fought with Robert Moses to keep it free.

NYC Pride March (June 28 parade, 36th St and Fifth Ave to the West Village, noon, but events through the month; *nycpride.org*). The march honors the gay rights movement sparked by the Stonewall Riots (*see p. 153*).

River to River Festival (late June, various downtown venues including Battery Park City, the South Street Seaport, and Governors Island; *lmcc. net*). Founded in 2002 to help revitalize Lower Manhattan after 9/11, the festival has developed into a major summer event. Free performances and exhibits, dance, music, discussions, and visual arts.

National Puerto Rican Day Parade (second Sun, on Fifth Ave from 44th to 86th St; *nprdpinc.org*). A huge parade, with bands, salsa, dancers, floats, even politicians among the estimated two million viewers.

JULY

Independence Day (July 4). Events at Battery Park, in the rivers around Lower Manhattan, fireworks from river barges sponsored by Macy's. Check nycgo.com or macys.com for location (usually they're in the East River). The fireworks start around 9pm, but plan to arrive at your viewing spot (if it's a public place) by 5pm. At Coney Island **Nathan's Famous Fourth of July International Hot Dog Eating Contest** (*see p. 502*) draws as many as 40,000 observers and in recent years has been televised. **St. Paulinus Festival** (Williamsburg,

Brooklyn; Italian street festival, early-mid July; *olmcfeast.com*). A procession with towering monument passes through the neighborhood; special masses and a street fair. Since 1903, the Southern Italian immigrant community has celebrated the feast of St. Paulinus of Nola (bishop 409–31), who offered himself in exchange for prisoners taken into slavery by pirates. The townsfolk of Nola celebrated Paolino's return with displays of lilies; since then the *giglio* (lily) has evolved into a wooden steeple, 82ft high, décorated with flowers.

AUGUST

Harlem Week (actually late July and much of Aug; *harlemweek.com*). Honors past, present, and future Harlem with shows, conferences, a 5km run, lectures, and special events at the Apollo.

New York International Fringe Festival (two weeks in Aug). Around 200 companies perform for over 75,000 spectators across downtown. Some of the shows sell out fast, but may be reprised in the FringeNYC Encore Series in Sept (*fringenyc.org*).

US Open Tennis Tournament (two weeks end of Aug–early Sept, at the Billie Jean King Tennis Center in Queens; *usopen.org*). The final grand slam of the international tennis tour.

SEPTEMBER

Labor Day (first Mon in Sept). The parade proceeds up Fifth Ave from 44th–72nd Sts.

West Indian-American Day Carnival (in Brooklyn, Labor Day weekend, with parade on Mon, along Eastern Pkwy from Utica Ave to the Brooklyn Museum; *wiadcacarnival.org*). Extravagant, colorful costumes, calypso music, steel-drum bands, food, and dancing in the streets.

Feast of San Gennaro (in Little Italy on Mulberry St, about ten days in mid-Sept; *sangennaro.org*). Garlands of red, green, and white lights illuminate the food stands and other vendors; there are doo wop bands, Italian folk songs, pizza-eating competitions. On the last Sat of Sept, a procession with saint's image winds its way from the Church of the Most Holy Blood through the streets.

New York Film Festival (Lincoln Center, late Sept–early Oct). The city's leading festival with films chosen by the Film Society of Lincoln Center and screened in Alice Tully Hall or the Walter Reade Theater. Emphasis is on avant-garde work, but also offers retrospectives and revivals. Attended by major critics (*filmlinc.org*).

OCTOBER

Pulaski Day Parade (first Sun, on Fifth Ave from 29th St to 53rd St; *pulaskiparade.org*). Celebrates the Polish heritage of the city and nearby communities and honors General Casimir Pulaski who fought in the American Revolution. Bands, costumes, floats, and display of the national colors, red and white.

Open House New York Weekend (first or second weekend, five boroughs). This increasingly popular event, sponsored by the not-for-profit organization of the same name (*ohny.org*), gives access to hundreds of sites normally off-limits to the public. Venues focus on the built environment and have included private apartments on Strivers' Row, the caves of Murrays' Cheese shop, the Little Red Lighthouse, and the digester eggs at the Newton Creek Water Treatment Plant.

Columbus Day Parade (second Mon, on Fifth Ave from 49th to 79th St; *columbuscitizensfd.org*). The parade, which celebrates the city's significant Italian heritage with 35,000 participants including more than 100 groups and their followers, draws about a million viewers along the avenue.

Halloween. The Halloween parade in Greenwich Village is a major city event, proceeding up Sixth Ave from Spring to 16th St, 7–11pm (*halloween-nyc.com*). You must wear a costume to march, but anyone can watch. The parade, founded by a maker of puppets and masks, grew from his involvement with his own family and is now unusual for the giant puppets that appear every year, as well as for the inventiveness and artistry of the costumes.

NOVEMBER

Thanksgiving (fourth Thur). Parade down Central Park West from 77th–59th Sts, then down Broadway to Macy's at 34th St. Floats, bands, but especially giant helium-filled balloons held down by more than 1,000 attendants. You can see the balloons being inflated the night before, on the side streets off Central Park West, between 77th and 81st Sts.

New York City Marathon. This 26.2-mile race through the five boroughs (Sun in late Oct/early Nov, begins at Verrazano Bridge 10:30am and finishes at Tavern-on-the-Green in Central Park; *tcsnycmarathon.org*). One of the world's most popular marathons, with 50,530 finishers in 2014, and one of the World Marathon Majors, it has been run every year since 1970, except for 2012, when

Hurricane Sandy devastated the city.

Veterans Day Parade (morning of Nov 11, Fifth Ave, 26th–52nd Sts, *americasparade.org*). Celebrating the end of World War I and honoring all US service personnel, the parade begins with a wreath-laying ceremony in Madison Square Park. Some 25,000 people—veterans, bands, supporters— participate, making it the nation's largest such event.

Holiday preparations for Christmas, Hanukkah, and Kwanzaa (late Nov). Décorating begins right after Thanksgiving, with store windows along Fifth Ave, Christmas trees, and menorahs in public and private spaces throughout the city.

DECEMBER

Christmas events include the famous tree and illuminated angels in the Channel Gardens at Rockefeller Center and the Radio City Music Hall Christmas Spectacular with a Christmas pageant and the high-kicking Rockettes. At the Planetarium (American Museum of Natural History), the Christmas star show draws crowds. Christmas tree lightings at Manhattan's City Hall, other borough halls, a large Christmas tree with 18th-century Neapolitan carved angels and crèche figures in the Medieval Sculpture Hall (Metropolitan

Museum); an origami tree at the American Museum of Natural History. For **Hanukkah**: candle lighting at City Hall, Hanukkah Menorah, Grand Army Plaza, 5th Ave at 59th St. **Kwanzaa** celebrations take place at the American Museum of Natural History, in Harlem at the Apollo Theater and other sites throughout the city.

On **New Year's Eve**, the midnight ball-drop in Times Square is recommended only for those undaunted by celebratory crowds.

General Information

ALCOHOLIC BEVERAGES

Liquor stores are open daily; on Sun they open at noon. Beer is also sold in grocery stores and delicatessens, except on Sun mornings. Wine is available only in liquor stores. The legal drinking age is 21; many bars will request photo ID. Bars are permitted to remain open until 4am and can open again at 8am.

BANKING AND BUSINESS HOURS

Most New York banks are open Mon–Fri 9am–4pm; some have extended hours; some are open Sat morning. Business hours for most offices are Mon–Fri 9am–5pm. Department stores and many specialty shops open at 10am; groceries, pharmacies, and other service shops usually open earlier.

CHOOSING A SEASON

You can enjoy New York at any time of the year, but the most predictably pleasant seasons are spring and fall. Winter can be invigorating, but it can also be bleak, gray, and bitterly cold as the wind whips down the canyons between skyscrapers. January is the coldest month, with daytime averages of 38–25°F (3–4°C). Summer can be warm and pleasant, but also stiflingly hot and humid. Buildings can be overheated in winter and over-cooled in summer; dress in layers. The cultural calendar is most interesting Sept–May. Christmas, when the city is brilliantly décorated, draws huge crowds, which in turn cause higher hotel rates.

CRIME AND PERSONAL SECURITY

Since 9/11, security in New York has been tightened and is highly visible in public places (for example, Grand Central). Do not leave bags unattended. You and your bag will probably be subjected to security inspections in the airports, some museums, government buildings, and large arenas or venues.

Although New York is safer than most other American cities, it is still a large metropolis. Common-sense advice includes being alert to your surroundings and looking confident about where you are going. (No statistics exist, however, as to the effectiveness of this posture.) If your instincts tell you the neighborhood is unsafe, leave. Don't flash cash, electronics, or jewelry on the street.

Walking is generally safe in New York. During the day you can go almost anywhere, and at night you can certainly walk on busy streets. Do not wander in the parks after dark; when attending a concert or other activity, stay with the crowds.

Hang on to your handbag. Shoulder bags are safer than backpacks. Put your wallet in a front pocket. Tourists are targets because they often carry a lot of cash. Use ATMs for small amounts and be alert when using one. Look both ways before stepping into the street; bicycle riders can be hazardous as can vehicles racing through red lights.

ELECTRICAL CURRENT
Electricity in the US is 110–120V, 60-cycle AC current.

EMERGENCIES
For fire, police, ambulance: call 911.

INTERNET AND INTERNET ACCESS
Most hotels offer Wi-Fi connections as do some commercial locations such as Starbucks and Kinko's copy centers. Public libraries have computer terminals, but you may have to wait and access time may be limited. There are Wi-Fi hot spots in some parks (*see nycgovparks.org; search "Wi-Fi hot spots"*). NYCwireless (*nycwireless.net*) has a map of hot spots in public places.

LEGAL HOLIDAYS

Jan 1	New Year's Day
Third Mon in Jan	Martin Luther King Day
Third Mon in Feb	Presidents' Day
Last Mon in May	Memorial Day
July 4	Independence Day
First Mon in Sept	Labor Day
Second Mon in Oct	Columbus Day
Nov 11	Veterans Day
Fourth Thur in Nov	Thanksgiving
December 25	Christmas Day

Schools and some businesses are closed on major Jewish holidays: Passover (March or April), Rosh Hashanah (Sept or Oct) and Yom Kippur (Sept or Oct).

NEWSPAPERS AND MAGAZINES
The *New York Times* is the doyen of daily papers, in print since 1851 and offering, as the front page states, "all the news that's fit to print." Three other major dailies are the *New York Post* and the *Daily News*, both tabloids, and the *Wall Street Journal*.

Among the weekly magazines, *New York Magazine* carries news about city life and politics as well as extensive theater, music, and event listings. *The New Yorker* has long been known for fine writing, reviews of cultural events, and urbane humor (including cartoons). *Time Out New York*, which arrived from London in 1995, is an excellent source for listings of art galleries, restaurants, clubs, concert halls, and movie theaters.

POST OFFICES

Most post offices are open weekdays from about 9am–5pm and Sat until noon or 1pm. Retail hours at the main post office on Eighth Ave at 33rd St are Mon–Fri 7:am–10pm, Sat 9am–9pm and Sun 11am–7pm.

PHARMACIES

Pharmacies in the US will not fill foreign prescriptions; many drugs available over the counter elsewhere are not available without a prescription in the US. The **Duane Reade** at 250 West 57th St and Broadway has a pharmacist on duty 24hrs (*T: 212 265 2101; duanereade.com*). Others are listed on the internet.

SHOPPING

Shopping is a major tourist attraction. Most department stores open at 10am and remain open until 6pm or later; some are open in the evening one day a week; some are open Sun 11–5 or 12–6. Specialty shops and boutiques may open and close later.

In former days, Midtown was the focus of fashionable shopping, with outlying neighborhoods known for specialized products sold in stores clustered together. Thus there were districts for lighting, kitchen supplies, flowers, musical instruments, and sewing and millinery supplies including feathers. Traces of this older economy remain, though most shopping areas now reflect the general economic level of the neighborhood rather than a specific trade or product. Shops with notions, trimmings, millinery supplies, and similar paraphernalia still exist in the Garment District (mid- to high 30s around Seventh Ave). West 47th St just off Fifth Ave is "Diamond Street," with upscale jewelers located nearby on Fifth Ave.

Lower East Side and East Village: The Lower East Side, once home to a large Jewish immigrant population, has traditionally been the center of bargain shopping, with Orchard St known for discounted clothing and lingerie stores (girdles in the old days), and the Bowery between Grand and Delancey Sts for lighting fixtures. Some stores on the Lower East Side are closed on Sat. In the East Village are shops selling books, used records and CDs, vintage clothing, and other paraphernalia.

SoHo: Now too expensive to be home turf for any but the most successful artists, SoHo still has an eye for style— fashions for men and women, home furnishings, cosmetics, even food.

The Meatpacking District: Like SoHo a stylish and expensive area, a good hunting ground for clothing, accessories, and home furnishings.

Chelsea and the Flatiron District: Both have large chain stores as well as clothing boutiques (to the west of the district near Eleventh Ave). Art galleries have moved to the western fringes of the district near 10th Ave.

Fifth Avenue: From Central Park South down to about 50th St there is a mix of expensive shops, department stores, and the kind of chain stores familiar from malls across the country. In addition to the classic department stores are the jewelers Cartier, Tiffany, Harry

Winston, and Bulgari. Trump Tower and Rockefeller Center have shops at various price levels. On Fifth Ave further south Lord & Taylor still anchors the block between 38th and 39th Sts.

57th St and environs: A center for luxury shopping, with clothing by internationally known designers. Madison Ave north of 57th St is a center of couture boutiques and art galleries.

New York's grand old department stores: Department stores are known for their wide range of goods and services, and many of the country's most famous have their flagship locations in New York. They offer convenience and comfort but not bargain prices. The most notable are Bergdorf Goodman (*Fifth Ave at 58th St*), Bloomingdale's

(*59th St and Lexington Ave*), Henri Bendel (*Fifth Ave between 55th and 56th Sts*), Lord & Taylor (*Fifth Ave at 39th St*), Macy's (*Herald Square, Sixth Ave at 34th St*) and Saks Fifth Avenue (*Fifth Ave at 50th St*).

Museum shops: Museum shops are a great source for high-quality items related to their collections. The New-York Historical Society, for example, has an exemplary selection of New York books and memorabilia. The New Museum has books on contemporary art and artfully designed gifts. If you want mathematical puzzles and games, try MoMath (*see p. 195*). The shops in the largest museums—the Met, MoMA, the Museum of Natural History—are veritable department stores of art and science.

TELEPHONES

The US phone system is run by private corporations: rates for long-distance calls vary from carrier to carrier. Hotels add surcharges for both local and long-distance calls; it is cheaper to use your cell (mobile) phone. Pay phones are disappearing from the streets and will continue to do so since the City plans gradually to replace them with hi-speed internet kiosks. Some phones will accept credit cards instead of coins. You can buy prepaid calling cards in various denominations at chain pharmacies (Duane Reade and Rite Aid), convenience stores, or newsstands. For directory assistance, dial 411.

All telephone numbers in the US consist of a three-digit area code, a three-digit exchange plus a four-digit number. To make a local call from a land line, you must dial 1 plus the area code plus the three-digit exchange plus the four-digit number (eleven digits).

THEATER AND PERFORMING ARTS TICKETS

You can purchase tickets to **Broadway and Off-Broadway** shows at the box office, online, or over the phone through Ticketmaster (*T: 877 250 2929, ticketmaster. com*) or Telecharge (*T: 212 239 6200, telecharge.com*). Both services add surcharges. Newspaper ads and websites tell you which service handles tickets for a particular event. The tickets can be mailed to you or held at the box office.

Buying tickets at the box office avoids extra fees. Most box offices no longer have direct phone lines; box office opening hours are 10am until curtain time.

Be prepared for sticker shock for Broadway musicals. Producers (like airlines) use dynamic pricing, charging more for desirable seats and discounting others. The average ticket for a Broadway show surpassed $100 in 2014, and premium center-orchestra seats at a hit musical can cost as much as $450. Dramas and comedies without music, Off-Broadway, and Off-Off-Broadway prices are proportionally lower. Metropolitan Opera tickets begin at $88 for the Family Circle (far away and high up) and top out at more than $572 for premium orchestra seats on premium days, though special offers and rush tickets are also available (visit *metopera.org*). **Discounted Tickets for Broadway Shows** can be accessed in the following ways:

Discount codes: Used as marketing tools, these codes are valid online, at the box office, or over the phone. To get them, you must register for a small fee with NYTix (*nytix.com*).

Rush tickets are offered on a first-come, first-serve basis the day of performance and are often for less desirable seats. Cash only. To see what is available, check *nytix.com* or go to the box office.

TKTS booths: Discounted theater tickets for the day of performance are available from TKTS booths. Cash or travelers checks only. Booths are located at Broadway and 47th St; Front and John Sts in the South Street Seaport; and 1 MetroTech Center, corner of Jay St and Myrtle Ave Promenade in Downtown Brooklyn. For opening hours and details, check the Theater Development Fund website (*tdf.org*); there is also a TKTS app.

Lincoln Center tickets are available through Telecharge (*T: 212 239 6200; telecharge.com*), online, or at the venue's box office (*for additional information, visit lincolncenter.org*). Discounted tickets are available at the Rubenstein Atrium on Broadway (*62nd and 63rd Sts; box office open Tues–Fri 2pm–7:45pm, and Sat 12–2pm, 3–7:45pm*).

TIPPING
In restaurants the usual tip is 15–20 percent; many people double the 8.875 percent sales tax. Coat-check attendants will expect at least $1 per coat. Room service waiters and taxi drivers should also receive at least 15 percent. Bellhops expect about $1 per suitcase, $2 in luxury hotels. Porters in airports expect at least $1 per bag. Others to tip include doormen who help with packages or summon a taxi ($1–2), hotel chambermaids ($2 per day), and concierges, with the tip commensurate with the level of service.

TOILETS
Public toilets are not easy to find in New York. Restaurants are usually unwilling to let non-customers use their facilities, though you can always walk in boldly and impersonate a customer. Other options are department stores, free museums, libraries, hotel lobbies (ask at the desk if necessary), buildings with public atriums (Trump Tower, CitiGroup Building), mega-stores with cafés, and Starbucks cafés. Both *nyrestroom.com* and *sitorsquat.com* offer apps that locate and/or rate restrooms.

TOURS

Although you may prefer to explore on your own, guided tours can take you places far from the beaten path. They range from drive-by bus trips with commentary to private guided visits; specialized group walking tours emphasize such themes as history, architecture, food, gardens, urban planning, and sustainability or geology. Many museums and not-for-profit organizations offer excellent tours, for example Green-Wood Cemetery, the Central Park Conservancy, or the Brooklyn Historical Society.

Gray Line New York Sightseeing bus tours provide an overview and take you to or past popular sites. There are hop-on-hop-off tours on double-decker buses as well as longer narrated tours. *777 Eighth Ave (46th and 47th Sts). T: 800 669 0051, graylineny.com.*

Circle Line boat tours circumnavigate Manhattan on a three-hour journey, offering fine views of the waterfront, the undersides of bridges, and the skyline, a good way to get the big picture. *Pier 83 at West 42nd St and 12th Ave. T: 212 563 3200, circleline42.com.*

Big Onion Walking Tours, on the go since 1991, are led by university graduate students in history, art history, and related fields. They focus on ethnic neighborhoods, museums, architecture, food, and history; some have seasonal themes—Christmas, the summer solstice, Passover; some have historic ones—e.g., Satan's Seat, the Prohibition era. *T: 888 606 9255, bigonion.com.*

The Municipal Art Society of New York offers tours of architecture and history. In addition to the daily walking tour of Grand Central Terminal, it offers visits to Midtown skyscrapers, Bronx street art, traditional store fronts, Chelsea art galleries, and bridges with sunset views. Guides are experts in their fields. *T: 212 935 3960, mas.org.*

Turnstile Tours, based in Brooklyn, has a lineup of fascinating and carefully researched tours that focus on ecology and sustainability, the built environment, and the city's ethnic history. You can visit the Brooklyn Navy Yard and the Brooklyn Army Terminal, sample food carts, or cruise the harbor; tours are conducted on foot, by bike, boat, or bus. Five percent of ticket receipts are donated to related non-profit community and economic development organizations. *T: 347 903 8687, turnstiletours.com.*

Glossary

Adirondack chair, sturdy wooden outdoor chair with arms and a slatted back

Ambulatory, typically the section of a church beside and round the high altar

Amphora, antique vase, usually of large dimensions, for oil and other liquids

Annunciation, the appearance of the Angel Gabriel to Mary to tell her that she will bear the Son of God; an image of the "Virgin Annunciate" shows her receiving the news

Anthemion, type of decoration originating in ancient Greece resembling leaf or honeysuckle fronds fanning out from a central stem

Apostles, the name for those sent out by Jesus to spread the Word

Archaic, period in Greek civilization preceding the Classical era: c. 750–480 BC. Art pertaining thereto

Architrave, the horizontal beam placed above supporting columns; the lowest part of an entablature (*qv*); the horizontal frame above a door

Archivolt, molded architrave carried round an arch

Areaway, a sunken space in front of a row house providing light and access to the basement

Ashlar, neatly cut square blocks of stone set smoothly together and used as facing on housefronts (c.f. Fieldstone)

Back house, a house with no street frontage

Baldachin, canopy supported by columns

Balusters, the upright, vertical elements of a balustrade

Baptistery, separate room or building used for baptisms in a Christian church

Bas-relief, sculpture in low relief

Beaux-Arts, academic, largely eclectic style of architecture taught at the École des Beaux-Arts in Paris, and hugely influential in America in the late 19th century

Belgian block, cube-shaped cobble of hard-wearing stone, used as street paving

Bracket, a supporting strut

Broadway theater, theater, a large, major commercial theater with 500 or more seats. Producers of shows in these venues are required to abide by certain contractual obligations. Employees are better paid and tickets cost more than at smaller houses. Thirty-nine of the forty Broadway houses are in the Theater District around Broadway from 41st to 53rd St. Off-Broadway theaters have 100–499 seats; tickets cost less; and many are known for presenting certain kinds of plays. Off-Off-Broadway theaters seat fewer than 100, are even less expensive but more experimental, and are scattered all over the city

Broken pediment, a pediment with a gap in the horizontal part, and/or where the cornices do not meet

Brownstone, brown-colored Triassic sandstone, a favored building material in mid-19th-century New York (*see p. 409*)

Bull's eye window, elliptical (not circular) window, often appearing in mansard roofs

Cabochon, an uncut, unfaceted gemstone in a fixed setting

Campanile, bell tower, often detached from the building to which it belongs

Canopic jar (or chest), ancient Egyptian urn used to preserve the internal organs of the deceased, and placed in the tomb beside the mummy

Cantoria, singing gallery in a church

Capital, the top part or "head" of a column

Carolingian, pertaining to Charlemagne and the dynasty he founded in the 9th century

Cartouche, tablet with a scrolled frame, usually round or oval, typically inscribed with initials or a coat of arms

Caryatid, sculpted female figure used as a supporting column

Chamfer, a cut-off corner (in appearance like a triangle with the top removed). Four chamfered corners at a street intersection form an octagon

Chancel, part of a church to the liturgical east of the crossing (*qv*), where the clergy officiate

Choir, part of a church reserved for the singers, usually with stalls; often synonymous with the raised easternmost end of a church where the clergy officiate

Ciborium, casket or tabernacle containing the Communion bread

Classical, in ancient Greece, the period from 480–323 BC; in general, when spelled with a capital C, denotes art etc. from the ancient world as opposed to classical ("classicizing") modern works

Clerestory, upper part of the nave wall of a church, above the side aisles, with windows

Coffered, of a ceiling or vault, having regularly spaced recessed panels, often (but not necessarily) square or rectangular in shape

Colonnette, small column with a decorative, not load-bearing, function

Console bracket, masonry structure, S-shaped with scrolls at top and bottom, placed vertically against a wall to support a projecting horizontal element (c.f. modillion)

Corinthian, ancient Greek and Roman order of architecture, a characteristic of which is a capital decorated with acanthus leaves

Cornice, any projecting ornamental molding at the top of a building beneath the roof (exterior) or ceiling (interior)

Crenellations, battlements

Crossing, the part of a church where the nave (central aisle) and transepts (side arms) meet

Cruciform, cross-shaped, from the Latin *crux, crucis*, a cross

Cupola, dome

Curtain wall, a non-load-bearing wall, essentially an infill or a screen between supporting piers or partitions

Dentiled, having a series of small blocks, projecting or hanging down like teeth

Dinette, small alcove or nook, designed, as the name suggests, for (informal) dining

Diptych, painting or tablet in two sections

Doric, ancient Greek order of architecture characterized by fluted columns with no base, and a plain capital

Drip moldings, molding over a hood, arch, or aperture designed to divert rainwater

Egg and dart, molding design consisting of ovoid shapes placed between arrow-like shapes

El, short form for elevated railway

Engaged, of a column, not freestanding, in other words, partly embedded in the wall

Entablature, upper part of a temple above the columns, made up of an architrave, frieze and cornice

Etruscans, influential ancient civilization that dominated central Italy from the 9th–4th centuries BC

Evangelists, the authors of the gospels, Matthew, Mark, Luke, and John. In Christian art they are often represented by their symbols: man or angel (Matthew); lion (Mark); bull (Luke); eagle (John)

Expressionist, art where the forms and/or colors of nature are exaggerated, distorted, or rendered unnatural to produce an emotional response in the viewer

Faïence, glazed decorative earthenware or terra cotta, named for the town of Faenza in Italy, where it originated

Fanlight, semicircular glazed aperture above a door, where the glazing bars are often arranged in a fan-like pattern

Federal style, architectural style that developed in America following creation of the new republic in 1789

Fieldstone, type of masonry consisting of irregular blocks of different sizes, held together with mortar

Flatware, cutlery

Flemish bond, style of brickwork where the bricks in each row (course) are placed alternately long (stretcher)-short (header)

Fluted, of a column shaft, having vertical grooves down its length

Foliate, decorated with a leaf pattern

Fresco, painting executed on wet plaster, beneath which the artist had usually made a working sketch

Gambrel, a "Dutch barn" roof, pitched in two stages, the upper stage less steeply inclined than the lower (c.f. mansard)

Geometric, in an antique context, refers to a pottery style with complex abstract decoration (900–700 BC)

Gesso, a chalk-based (or, nowadays, acrylic) primer applied to a surface before painting

Gold-ground, medieval Italian devotional painting style where the figures appear against a gold background

Gothic, medieval style of architecture originating in northern Europe, characterized by pointed arches, vaulted interiors and traceried (*qv*) windows

Greek cross, a cross with arms of equal length

Groin vault, type of vaulting where two barrel vaults cross each other at right-angles

Guastavino, a type of terra cotta tile, used by architect Rafael Guastavino in a self-supporting vaulting system. Layered with quick-drying cement and usually set in a herring-bone pattern, Guastavino tiles can span considerable distances without scaffolding

Hellenistic, art and sculpture of the period from 323 BC (death of Alexander the Great) to 30 BC (defeat of Antony and Cleopatra)

Hipped roof, a sloping roof, differing from a simple pitched roof in that it has four sloping sides, meeting not in a ridge at the top, but in "hips" up the sides

I-beam, load-bearing beam with an I-shaped cross-section, used in modern construction

Incunabulum (pl. incunabula) any

book printed in the same century as the invention of movable type (i.e. between 1450 and 1500)

International Style, 20th-century style of architecture characterized by blocklike shapes, flat roofs, a lack of ornament, and the use of materials such as glass, steel, and reinforced concrete as opposed to old-fashioned masonry

Ionic, an order of Classical architecture identified by its capitals with two volutes (scrolls). Columns are fluted, stand on a base, and have a shaft more slender than in the Doric order

Iron-spot brick, brick flecked with spots of black, from the iron deposits in the clay

Keystone, wedge-shaped strengthening block at the center point of the curve of an arch

Kouroi, from the Greek word for young man (*kouros*), the standing, nude male statues of the Greek Archaic (*qv*) period

Krater, a large ancient Greek bowl for mixing wine and water

Lady Chapel, chapel devoted to the worship of the Virgin Mary

Lancet window, slender, blade-shaped Gothic window aperture with a pointed arched head

Latin cross, a cross where the vertical arm is longer than the transverse arm

Louvered, with horizontal overlapping slats to admit air but not light

Lunette, semicircular space in a vault or ceiling, or above a door or window, often decorated with a painting or relief

Machicolated, of a parapet: having holes in the floor through which stones, boiling oil etc. could be dropped on attackers

Maenad, female participant in the orgiastic rites of Dionysus, god of wine

Mansard roof, typical roof type of the hôtels of Paris: pitched in two stages like a gambrel roof (*qv*), differing from it in that it is hipped, i.e. it has four, not two, sloped sides

Mayor's lamp, any survivor of the days when it was the custom to erect two lamps outside a mayor's residence

Meneely bell, a bell cast in the Meneely Bell Foundry in Troy, N.Y., which operated between 1826 and 1952

Minton, English firm from Stoke on Trent, the "potteries," known for its blue-printed ware. In the late 19th century its tiles were fashionable, and the company produced tiles for the US Capitol

Modillion, supporting bracket or block placed horizontally under a larger, heavier horizontal structure

Mortise and tenon, type of timber joint resembling the interlocking system of a jigsaw puzzle: a projecting tongue fits into a corresponding notch

Neo-Grec, an eclectic branch of Neoclassicism originating in mid-19th-century France, characterized by a profusion of Greco-Roman classical motifs, Egyptian Revival forms and the austerity of line of the Louis Seize style

Nereid, in Greek mythology, a water nymph

Newel post, upright post or column at the top, bottom, or turning-point of a flight of stairs, usually connected to a banister

Oculus (pl. oculi), round window or aperture

Oriel window, window projecting from an upper story

Palladian window, a window in three parts: a central round-arched aperture is flanked by two flat-topped apertures of lesser height. It derives its name from the Italian architect Andrea Palladio

Paschal, in the Christian church, pertaining to Easter

Pediment, triangular gable above a portico

Pendant, a painting or work which forms a companion or complement to another

Peristyle, court or garden surrounded by a columned portico

Pietà, representation of the Virgin mourning the dead Christ, usually spread on her lap

Pilaster, a shallow pier or rectangular column projecting only slightly from the wall

Pitched roof, a roof made of two sloping sides, meeting in a ridge at the top

Polychrome, from the Greek, meaning many colors

Porphyry, dark blue, purple or red-colored igneous rock

Potlatch, from a Chinook word meaning "gift," a ceremonial present-giving, as practiced by indigenous American peoples

Potter's field, a burial ground, especially for the indigent or unidentified

Putto (pl. putti), sculpted or painted figure, usually nude, of a male child

Quadriga, a two-wheeled chariot drawn by four horses abreast

Quatrefoil, four-lobed design

Queen Anne, picturesque, asymmetrical, late 19th-century architectural style characterized by turrets, steeply pitched roofs and gingerbread ornamentation

Quoin, from the French coin (corner), stones placed in courses at the outer corners of buildings, projecting from the wall

Raked, of a cornice, meaning sloping.

Thus a cornice that follows the line of a triangular pediment is necessarily raked

Repoussé, relief-work in metal achieved by hammering from the back, thus punching out the design

Reredos, panel or screen behind an altar, which may stand alone or be part of a larger retable (*qv*)

Retable, screen behind an altar, often a frame or setting for the reredos (*qv*)

Romanesque, architecture of the early Western (i.e. not Byzantine) Christian empire, from the 7th–12th centuries, preceding the Gothic style. A revival of this style, characterized by rounded arches, achieved great popularity in New York in the later 19th century

Rubblestone (*see Fieldstone*)

Rus in urbe, from the Latin meaning "country in the city," referring to the creation of a rural atmosphere in an urban environment

Rusticated, masonry surface where the blocks of stone are not flush with each other as in ashlar (*qv*), but are separated by deep joints or grooves, making the stone appear more massive

Trefoil, decorated or molded with three leaf- or lobe-shapes

Sanctuary, the part of a church around the high altar. It may be identical to the chancel or choir, depending on the size of the church and the position of the singers' stalls

Scrimshaw, carved or etched ivory or bone, typically whalebone

Second Empire, eclectic, opulent architecture from the reign of Napoleon III in France (1852–70), historicist in that it borrowed elements from many styles of the past

Segmental arch, arch where the curved part is formed of a simple arc, i.e. a segment of a circle

Setback, the extent to which a building leaves free space around it in its lot, both on the ground and as it rises into the air (*see p. 71*)

Sgraffito, design formed by scratchwork on plaster down to a layer of different-colored plaster beneath

Sidelights, fixed glass panes on either side of a door

Six-over-six, of a sash window, where both panels are divided into six panes

Spandrel, the area between two arches in an arcade or the triangular space on either side of an arch

Splayed, having vertical sides that rise obliquely rather than straight up

Stabile, an abstract sculpture that has no moving parts, a term coined by Alexander Calder to distinguish the artform from a mobile

Stations of the Cross, small paintings, panels, or carvings placed around the walls of a church or chapel depicting scenes from Christ's journey to Calvary

Stele, upright stone bearing a commemorative inscription

Stoop, narrow porch reached by steps in front of a house, typically a row house. New York's first Dutch settlers elevated the first floors of their houses with high stoops (from the Dutch *stoep*) just as they had in Amsterdam, where flooding was a threat

Stucco, plaster-work, usually molded

Swag, carved or painted design made to resemble bunched drapery

Tempera, a painting medium of powdered pigment bound together, in its simplest form, by a mixture of egg yolk and water

Terra cotta, from the Italian meaning "cooked earth," fired earthenware used in architecture or sculpture

Terrazzo floor, paving made up of small fragments of marble embedded in mortar, smoothed and polished

Tessera (pl. tesserae), small cube of marble, stone or glass used in mosaic work

Tie-rod, transverse truss to prevent walls sagging outward, passed through the wall and fixed with a plate, in the manner of a nut and bolt

Tracery, system of carved and molded ribs within a window aperture dividing it into patterned sections. Particularly associated with Gothic architecture

Transom, horizontal beam across a window; a fixed window above a doorway. When semicircular, this is called a fanlight

Transept, "side arm" of a church, leading to right and/or left off the nave or aisles

Triforium, upper-level arcaded aisle in a Romanesque or Gothic-style church, below the clerestory (*qv*)

Triple-hung window, tall sash window in three sections

Triptych, painting or tablet in three sections

Triton, sea god

Trompe l'œil, literally, a deception of the eye; used to describe illusionist decoration and painted architectural perspective

Tuscan, plain order of architecture, with an unfluted column rising from a base to a simple, unornamented capital

Tympanum (pl. tympana), the area between the top of a doorway and the arch above it; also the triangular space enclosed by the moldings of a pediment

Vermiform, "wormlike" decoration; a wriggling pattern

Zoomorphic, from the Greek *zoön* (animal), having an animal form

Index

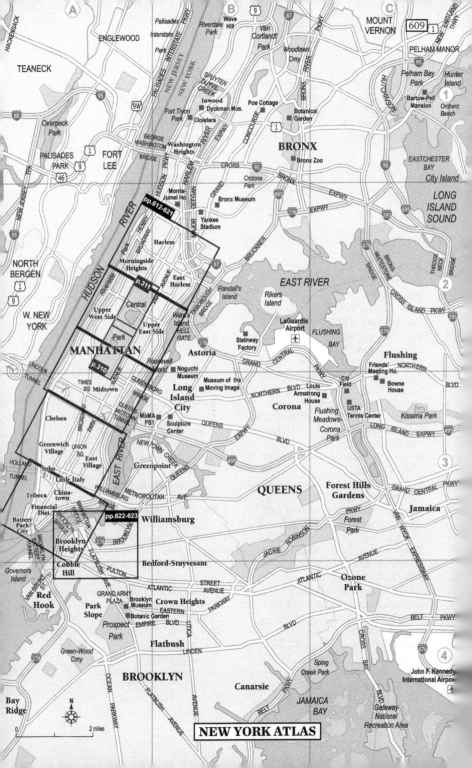

NEW YORK ATLAS

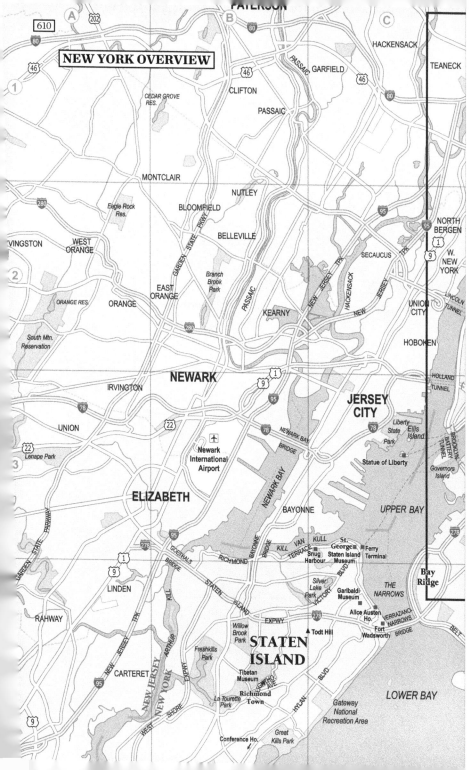

NEW YORK OVERVIEW

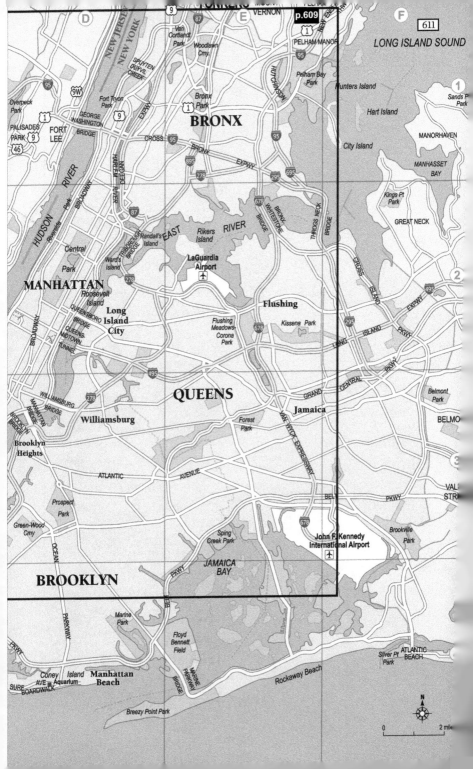

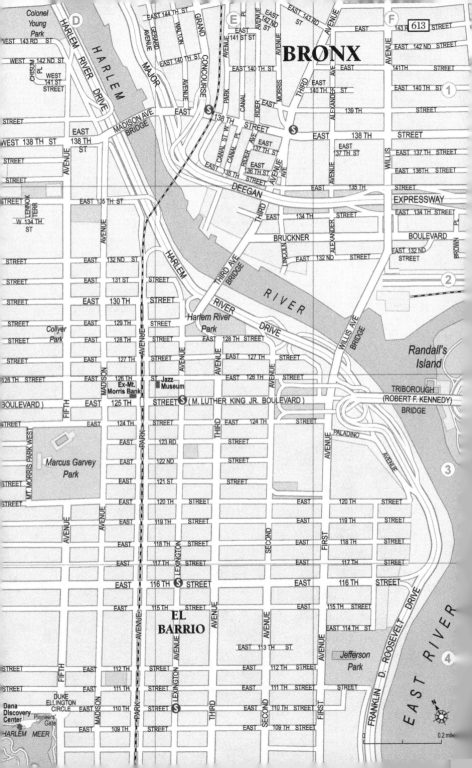

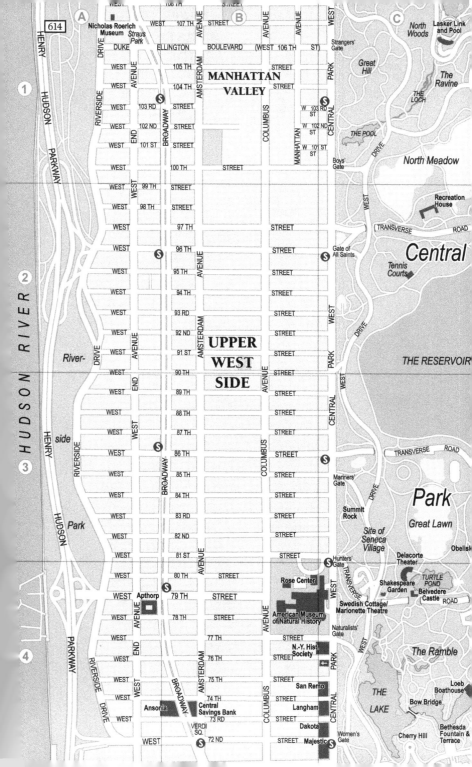

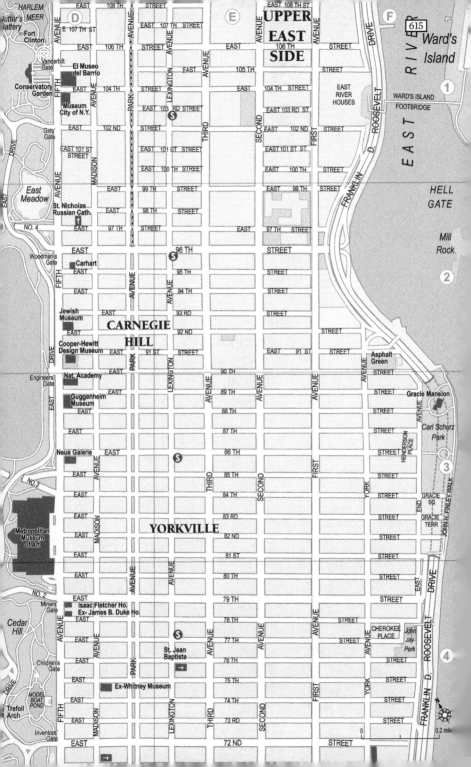

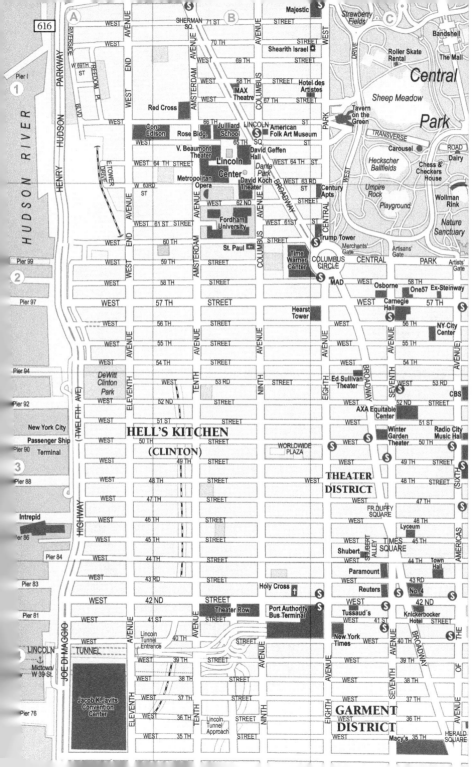

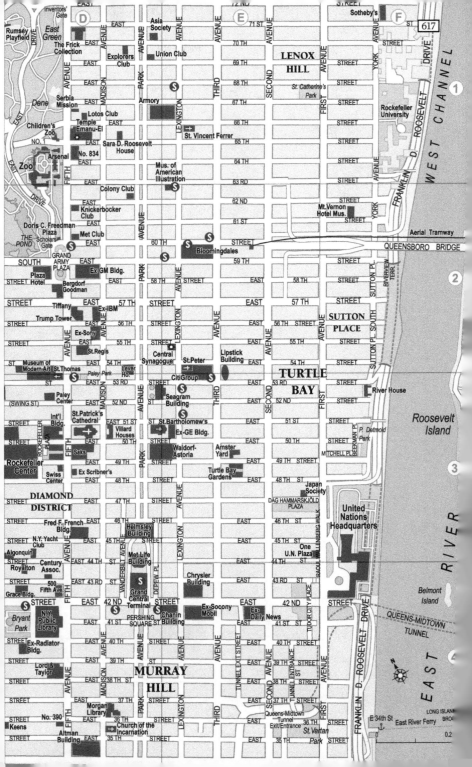

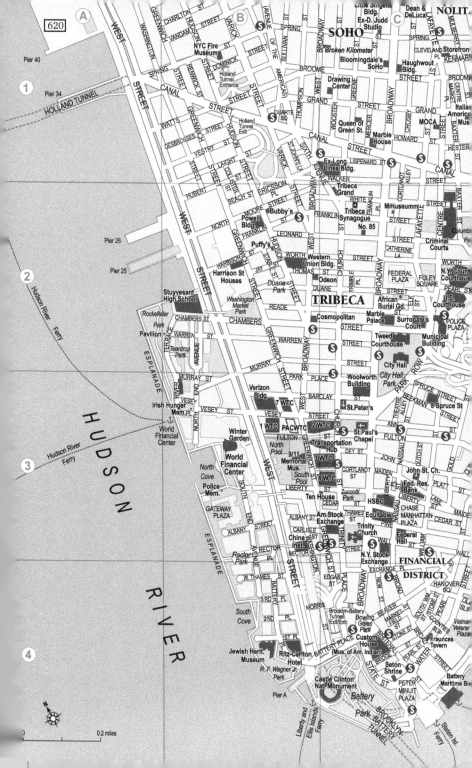

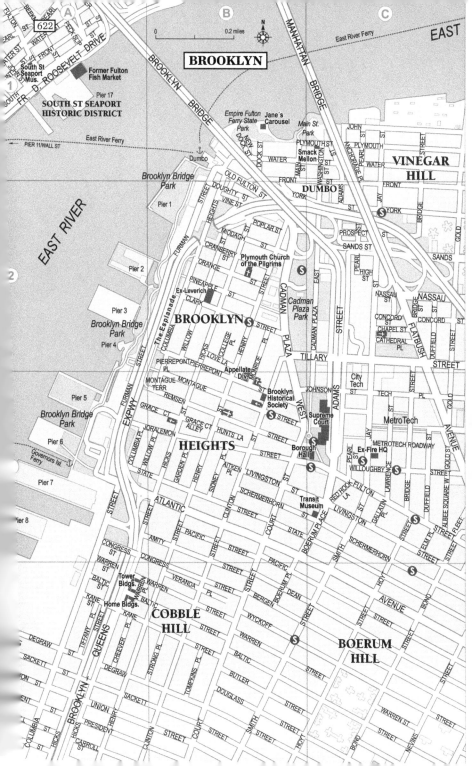

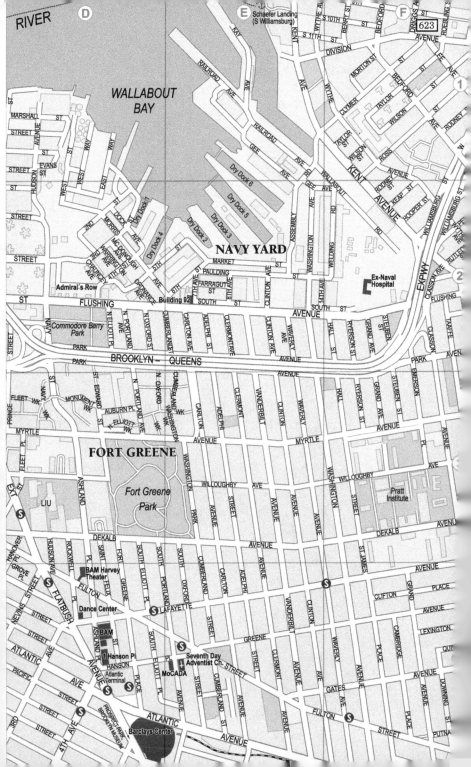

A WALK THROUGH BATTERY PARK CITY

This walk, from south to north along the Hudson River Esplanade in Battery Park City, will take you through gardens, past public art, and offer side trips to a couple of museums. (*Parks open 6am–1am daily; bpcparks.org.*)

To reach the starting point by subway: 4 or 5 to Bowling Green, 1 to Rector St, R to Whitehall St. Bus: M1 (weekdays), M6, M9, M15.

BATTERY PARK CITY, THE FRUIT OF thoughtful urban planning, sits on 92 man-made acres (completed 1976) along the Hudson River. In the mid-1960s, as commerce fled uptown and the unused Hudson River piers rotted in the water, Governor Nelson Rockefeller conceived of Battery Park City as a way to revitalize downtown Manhattan and its decaying waterfront, providing housing and off-loading the rock and earth excavated from the World Trade Center site. In 1968 the state, which by riparian rights owns all filled land in the river, created the Battery Park City Authority to develop the area. For a decade the project stagnated. Then, in 1979, architects Alexander Cooper and Stanton Eckstut created the master plan, which extended the Manhattan street grid into the landfill and called for an esplanade joining a commercial central area with residential neighborhoods abutting it. The design guidelines emphasized the human scale and variety of New York's successful older neighborhoods.

The small **Skyscraper Museum** (*39 Battery Pl near First Pl; open Wed–Sun 12–6; admission charge; bookshop; T: 212 968 1961, skyscraper. org*) explores tall buildings as real estate investments, construction sites, architectural artifacts, places to work

or live, and symbols of ego. The core exhibits include handmade models of a mini-Midtown and a Lilliputian Lower Manhattan, a history of tall buildings, and a chronicle of the rise and fall of the World Trade Center.

The 3.5 acres of **Robert F. Wagner Jr. Park** (1996), just upstream from Battery Park, are named for a lifelong public servant. Landscape architects Hanna/Olin laid out the park; Lynden B. Miller planned the gardens. Near the entrance on Battery Place are Tony Cragg's tuba- and lute-like bronze *Resonating Bodies* (1996). Toward the river two brick pavilions offer a café and viewing platforms with panoramas of the harbor and Statue of Liberty. Beyond, a green, flat lawn attracts sunbathers and Frisbee players; near the water are Louise Bourgeois's three-foot granite *Eyes* (1995) and further north toward the Museum of Jewish Heritage is Jim Dine's *Ape & Cat (At the Dance)* (1993).

The **Museum of Jewish Heritage** (*36 Battery Pl at First Pl; open Sun–Tues and Thur 10–5:45, Wed 10–8, Fri 10–3, extended Fri hours during Daylight Saving Time except on the eve of Jewish holidays; closed Sat, Jewish holidays, and Thanksgiving; admission charge except free Wed 4–8; café and shop; T: 646 437 4200, mjhnyc.org*), a "Living Memorial to the Holocaust" (1997), explores Jewish

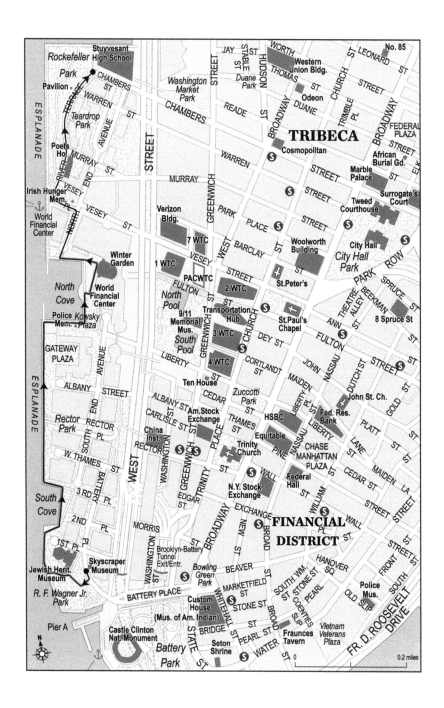

life and culture from the late 19th century, through the Holocaust, to the present. The hexagonal form of the building (Roche, Dinkeloo and Assocs.) suggests a Star of David without the points, and the six tiers of the ziggurat roof are said to symbolize the six million Jews killed in the Holocaust. The core exhibit depicts traditions of Jewish life, with artifacts and photos detailing ceremonies of birth, marriage, and the seasons of the Jewish year. On the second floor, "The War Against the Jews" documents the Holocaust, from the rise of Hitler to the liberation of the death camps. On the third floor a memorial Garden of Stones stands as a metaphor for the tenacity and fragility of life.

South Cove Park, north of the museum, represents the collaborative effort of architect Stanton Eckstut, landscape architect Susan Child, and environmental artist Mary Miss. With its meditative landscape of artfully sited rocks, pilings, grasses, and flowers, the three-acre park re-imagines the river's edge as it may have looked a couple of centuries ago. Competed in 1987, South Cove was one of the first New York landscapes to combine native plant life and industrial archaeology. The metal viewing tower evokes the Statue of Liberty's crown.

Rector Park, a residential square, intentionally recalls the civilized scale of Gramercy Park. *Rector Gate* (1988; R.M. Fischer), a 43-ft skeletal gateway of fanciful metal shapes, marks the park entrance. At the intersection of Albany St is Ned Smyth's *The Upper Room* (1987), an elevated plaza surrounded by columns of pinkish concrete with colorful, pebbly aggregate. The columns closest to the river have been

interpreted variously as papyrus plants, palm trees, or chess pieces.

The apartments of **Gateway Plaza** (1982), dour and reminiscent of post-war Soviet blocks, predate the Cooper-Eckstut master plan. Slightly inland, past the Sirius dogrun, Stuart Crawford's **New York City Police Memorial** (1997) commemorates NYPD officers killed in the line of duty; a stream of water rises from a fountain, flows through a narrow channel, and falls into a still pool surrounded by a granite wall inscribed with the officers' names.

Named for NYPD chaplain Monsignor John J. Kowsky (d. 1988), **Kowsky Plaza** (east of the intersection of Liberty and West Sts), formerly Pumphouse Park, occupies the roof of a subterranean pumping station that supplied water to the cooling towers of the first World Trade Center. East of the Police Memorial a 2.75-ton chunk of the Berlin Wall bears a green, fat-lipped cartoon face by artist Thierry Noir. The German government donated it (2004) to commemorate the fall of the Wall.

At the midpoint of the promenade, in front of the former World Financial Center, is **North Cove**, its marina for mega- and regular yachts notched into the shoreline. Scott Burton designed the seating above the stone steps; welded on the railing are lines by Walt Whitman ("City of the Sea!...City of wharves and stores—city of tall facades of marble and iron! Proud and passionate city!") and Frank O'Hara ("One need never leave the confines of New York to get all the greenery one wishes—I can't even enjoy a blade of grass unless I know there's a subway handy, or a radio store or some other sign that people do not totally regret life").

The hub of Battery Park City is **Brookfield Place**, better known as the former World Financial Center. Its four office towers (1985–8; Cesar Pelli) are distinctively topped with a pyramid, a truncated pyramid, ziggurat, and dome.

The **Winter Garden** (1988; Cesar Pelli), with its towering atrium, suggests a 19th-century crystal palace. Debris from the collapsing Twin Towers shattered the huge windows, but the atrium became an escape route for thousands of workers who fled west toward the river. In the ensuing months, the sixteen 43-ft *Washingtonia robusta* palm trees, imported from California when the building opened, succumbed to the rain sluicing in through the cracked dome. The building reopened in Sept 2002, after only a year of reconstruction. The floor and the palm trees have been replaced; marble steps lead up to a wall (110ft wide and 60ft tall) of German industrial glass overlooking the new World Trade Center. Art installations, concerts, and other free events take place in the atrium. Luxury shops surround it and an upscale food court (second floor) faces the river. (*NB: An underground passageway crosses West St from the Winter Garden to the World Trade Center and the 9/11 Memorial.*)

Further north in the park between Vesey and Barclay Sts, the **Irish Hunger Memorial** (2002; Brian Tolle), on a half-acre cantilevered platform, commemorates the potato famine, which killed millions and drove hundreds of thousands across the Atlantic beginning in the 1840s. The memorial's centerpiece, a ruined stone cottage (c. 1838), was brought from Ireland, reconstructed stone by stone, and placed on an artificial hillside planted with Irish grasses, heather, and wild flowers.

Founded by Stanley Kunitz in 1985, **Poets House** (*10 River Terrace near Murray St; open Tues–Fri 11–7, Sat 11–6; free; T: 212 431 7920, poetshouse.org*) moved into this glassy building (2009; Louise Braverman) after sojourns in a public school and a SoHo loft. The library and archive, now more than 60,000 volumes strong, seeks to hold all the books of poetry published in the US since 1990, plus a wide range of poetry published during the last century in English, and representative volumes of the poetry of all times and places. In addition to exhibits and lectures, Poets House also provides a quiet place for reading or composing your own verse.

Surrounded by tall apartments, **Teardrop Park** (2004; Michael Van Valkenburgh Associates), between Murray and Warren Sts, was inspired by Frederick Law Olmsted. Its most dramatic feature is a 27-ft-high, 168-ft-long wall of randomly coursed bluestone slabs.

Demetri Porphyrios's picturesque **Pavilion** (1992) at the foot of Warren St offers shelter from the sun or rain, its square wooden roof supported by stout brick Doric columns and thin wooden pillars. Near the foot of Chambers St, the small bronze cartoonish figures of Tom Otterness's **The Real World** (1992) evoke a comic but sinister realm in which money and power dominate. Little workers push giant pennies; a dog tied to a water-fountain eyes a cat, which eyes a bird, which eyes a worm.

At 345 Chambers St, **Stuyvesant High School**, open by competitive exam and free to NYC students, is renowned for its science and math programs, which have nurtured several Nobel laureates.

The Financial District

*The area around Wall Street, a name synonymous with high finance,
is home to Trinity Church and historic Federal Hall, along with the New York
Stock Exchange and other architectural expressions of fiscal might.*

Before visiting this area, you might be forgiven for visualizing only glassy skyscrapers as far as the eye can see (and the neck can bend). But strolling in the Financial District does give a sense of an earlier, more humanly scaled New York, whether discerned in the topography of the streets or glimpsed through the lobby doors of older buildings. Security has necessarily tightened up since 9/11, especially around the New York Stock Exchange, and some of the buildings whose interiors were formerly open to visitors are no longer accessible. The past decade has also seen the character of the area shift, as corporations have moved elsewhere and residential developers have moved in. The Financial District today remains popular with visitors, who throng the intersection of Wall and Nassau Sts, and climb the steps of Federal Hall to snap "selfies" beside the statue of George Washington.

TRINITY CHURCH & CHURCHYARD

Map p. 620, C3. Subway: 2, 3, 4, 5, J, Z to Wall St; 1 or R to Rector St. Bus: M5. Church open weekdays 7–6, Sat 8–4, Sun 7–4. Churchyard open (weather permitting) weekdays 7–4, Sat and holidays 8–3, Sun 7–3. Church tours Mon–Fri at 2pm and Sun after the 11:15 service. Free concerts Mon, Wed, Thur at 1pm and Sun at 8pm; check website for updates. Museum closed at the time of writing but usually open Mon–Fri 9:30–noon & 1–5, Sat 9:30–3, Sun 1–3. Free app available. T: 212 602 0800, trinitywallstreet.org.

At the head of Wall St on Broadway stands Trinity Church (1846), the tallest building in town until relegated to second place by the towers of the Brooklyn Bridge (1883), and now entirely dwarfed by office buildings. Despite its modest size, its dramatic setting makes Trinity one of New York's most famous houses of worship. As befits a parish situated in a district unabashedly devoted to Mammon, it is also the wealthiest:

THE NEW YORK STOCK EXCHANGE
"Integrity Protecting the Works of Man," tympanum sculpture by
John Quincy Adams Ward and Paul W. Bartlett.

its 14-acre holdings, including 5.5 million square feet of commercial real estate, were valued in 2013 at about $3 billion.

HISTORY OF TRINITY CHURCH

Established by royal charter in 1697 (with an annual rent of a single peppercorn), Trinity parish owes its immense wealth to a land grant made in 1705 by Queen Anne. This included the land west of Broadway between Fulton and Christopher Sts—an impressive chunk of lower Manhattan embracing parts of modern Tribeca and the West Village. (The queen also granted the church rights to all unclaimed shipwrecks and beached whales.) The first church (1698), a stone building facing the river, was paid for by all citizens, who were taxed for the construction regardless of religious denomination. It was burned in 1776 and remained in ruins until long after the Revolution. A second church (completed 1790) was demolished in 1839 after a heavy snowfall damaged the roof. The present church is the third on the site.

The building

The church is 79ft wide and 166ft long; its tower including the spire stands 280ft 5in above the ground. Richard Upjohn, the architect, was one of the principal exponents of the Gothic Revival in the US, and Trinity was the first Gothic Revival church in the city and one of the first in the nation. Its flying buttresses, stained-glass windows, Gothic tracery, and medievally inspired sculpture impressed and pleased 19th-century New Yorkers, though Upjohn's choice of brownstone for the façade drew criticism, since brownstone was generally used as a cheaper substitute for marble, granite, or limestone. Since Trinity parish could well have afforded marble, Upjohn probably chose it for aesthetic reasons. The Romantic movement, making itself felt in architecture as well as the other arts, favored the use of dark building materials, which were considered "picturesque" and "natural"—that is, close to the colors of the landscape.

The **church doors**, modeled after Lorenzo Ghiberti's famous bronze doors of the baptistery of the cathedral in Florence, were designed by Richard Morris Hunt and donated by William Waldorf Astor. Karl Bitter, who won the competition for the construction, executed the main west doors, whose panels illustrate biblical scenes: right door (top) *The Four Horsemen of the Apocalypse*; (center) *The Annunciation*; (bottom) *Jacob's Dream*. Left door (top) *The Throne of Heaven*; (center) *The Empty Tomb*; (bottom) *The Expulsion from Eden*. J. Massey Rhind and Charles H. Niehaus designed the doors on the north and south sides.

Architect Upjohn controlled all the interior details, including the **chancel window**, one of the earliest American examples of stained glass (though the glass itself is German-made since no American craftsman at the time possessed the requisite skills). Upjohn also decided that no memorials should disfigure the nave (untrue to the Gothic spirit in his opinion), so he planned a Monument Room on the south side of the church. The **Astor Memorial**, the altar screen behind the main altar, was given (later) by John Jacob and William Astor in memory of their father. Made of Caen stone and marble, it was designed by Frederick Clarke Withers.

Trinity churchyard

Some of the gravestones in the two-acre churchyard are old and striking, their incised frizzle-haired angels and grinning death's heads reminding onlookers of inevitable mortality. Near the Broadway sidewalk Steve Tobin's *Trinity Root* (2005) recreates in bronze the stump and roots of a mature sycamore that grew in the churchyard of St. Paul's Chapel (*see p. 81*) until killed by debris from the falling Twin Towers.

The oldest gravestone (north of the church) belongs to Richard Churcher, who died at the age of five in 1681. More elaborate monuments mark the burial places of Robert Fulton, whose *Clermont* proved the economic viability of steamboat travel; Alexander Hamilton; William Bradford, the publisher of the *New-York Gazette*; and Captain James Lawrence, whose nautical tombstone brings to mind his famous remark about not giving up the ship. The impressive Cross in the center of the northern portion of the graveyard commemorates Caroline Webster Schermerhorn Astor, queen of New York society in the later decades of the 19th century (*see p. 332*). At the northeast corner of the plot is a large tribute to the Martyrs of the American Revolution, who died while imprisoned by the British in a sugar house (*see below*).

THE "SUGARHOUSE" MARTYRS

During the 18th century sugar refining was big business in New York, attracting the city's merchant families—Bayards, Roosevelts, Rhinelanders, Van Cortlandts, and others—who profited from dealing with Caribbean plantation owners. After New York fell to the British during the Revolution several sugar houses (warehouses), including those of the Van Cortlandts (near the northwest corner of Trinity churchyard), the Livingstons (on Liberty St), and the Rhinelanders (Rose and Duane Sts), were converted to prisons by the occupying army. Conditions were foul and the common soldiers, crowded and underfed, suffered from successive outbreaks of smallpox, cholera, and yellow fever; many starved or froze to death.

WEST OF TRINITY

THE CHINA INSTITUTE GALLERY

Map p. 620, B3. 100 Washington St (Rector St). Subway: 1 or R to Rector St, 4 or 5 to Wall St, J or Z to Broad St, A or C to Fulton St, E to WTC. Bus: M5, M9. Shop. Café. T: 212 744 8181, chinainstitute.org.

The non-political, non-profit **China Institute in America** was founded (1926) by American educational philosopher John Dewey among others to promote the understanding of Chinese culture. The gallery, created in 1966, was the first non-profit venue in the US to showcase Chinese exhibits on a regular basis. With their scholarly catalogues, its small, high-quality shows, usually two a year, have commanded critical attention.

THE FORMER AMERICAN STOCK EXCHANGE

The former American Stock Exchange building (not to be confused with the New York Stock Exchange; *see below*) at 86 Trinity Place (*Thames St*) was first known as the New York Curb Market or simply The Curb. Many of its brokers were from Jewish or Irish immigrant backgrounds, excluded from the New York Stock Exchange for social or financial reasons. They brokered securities often of small, upstart companies and the curb market became something of a training ground, "a motley, agitated mass of struggling, yelling, finger-wriggling humanity," as the *New York Evening Post* described the scene in 1920. In 1921 the market moved to this handsome Art Deco building (1921, expanded 1930; Starrett & Van Vleck), reflecting its increasing prestige and influence. The Curb was renamed the American Stock Exchange in 1953, when it was the nation's second largest exchange. In 2008 the AMEX became part of NYSE-Euronext and closed a year later. The building is under consideration for adaptive re-use.

WALL STREET

Wall Street, sometimes simply called "The Street," runs from Broadway to the East River. The eponymous wall, erected around 1653, stretched river to river at the northern edge of the settlement protecting the Dutch town from its British neighbors, but was never needed for defense. Though the original plan called for a palisade of tree trunks sharpened and driven into the ground, the wall was actually constructed of 15-ft planks and oak posts. These proved overpoweringly attractive to homeowners as sources of firewood or lumber for household repairs, and in 1699, as the city sprawled northward, the British had the remnants of the wall torn down.

Wall St became synonymous with the financial district after the New York Stock Exchange moved to the neighborhood in 1903. Since the 1990s, however, many of the early 20th-century commercial buildings constructed for big banks and major corporations have gone residential, with restaurants, and shops to support an upscale community that stays on after working hours. Major financial corporations that moved away after the World Trade Center attacks did not return to Wall St: its buildings are now too old, too small, and technologically obsolete.

One Wall Street, originally the Irving Trust Company and now the Bank of New York Mellon, at the corner of Broadway, is one of New York's finest Art Deco skyscrapers, the masterpiece of Ralph Walker of Voorhees, Gmelin & Walker, completed in 1932. Clad entirely in limestone, it rises 654ft to a chamfered crown, its exterior detail emphasizing its verticality, its setbacks conforming to the provisions of the Zoning Resolution of 1916, and its ground-floor pointed-arch windows echoing the forms of Trinity Church across Broadway. To some observers the building seems chiseled out of a single block of stone; to others its curtain wall shimmers like undulating drapery.

The interiors are spectacular (*unfortunately closed to the public, though you can get a glimpse through the doors*). The original reception hall, where wealthy and corpo-

WALL STREET

rate clients awaited their private bankers, is decorated with glass mosaics by Hildreth Meière that shade from a dark burgundy at the bottom to a flaming orange at the top. The irregularly shaped tesserae are embedded in a mesh of gold lines that suggest a web, or perhaps the fault lines in minerals.

The office tower at **14 Wall Street**, originally the Bankers Trust Building (1912; Trowbridge & Livingston) is notable for its stepped pyramidal roof, later adopted by the firm as its logo: "A Tower of Strength." Inspired by the campanile of St. Mark's in Venice, the building was the first of several in the Financial District to display a recognizable skyline profile. The windowless, seven-story pyramid contained storage rooms and mechanical apparatus including a smokestack, which vented at the top, sometimes suggesting a volcano about to erupt. J. Pierpont Morgan was to have occupied the 31st floor as an apartment, but he never did: the *New York Times* ran a headline in 1912 that said, "No Morgan Bower Atop Bankers Trust: The $250,000 Wonderland Where He Was to Rest Is Really Empty and for Rent." Fifteen floors lower, in a restroom for female employees, a matron stood ready to dispense hair pins, powder and rouge.

THE NEW YORK STOCK EXCHANGE
The New York Stock Exchange (*8 Broad St; not open to the public*) is the world's largest in terms of the market capitalization of its listed companies. Its building (1903; George B. Post, addition 1923; Trowbridge & Livingston) is a "temple" of capitalism, constructed during an era when Classicist architecture was *de rigueur* for important public buildings. The pediment sculpture by John Quincy Adams Ward and Paul

W. Bartlett depicts *Integrity Protecting the Works of Man*, those "works" being the mechanical arts, electricity, surveying, and building (to Integrity's left); and mining and agriculture (to her right).

Shortly after the end of the Revolution, the Congress sitting in Federal Hall issued some $80 million in bonds to pay for the war debt. A central marketplace became necessary for these securities, and after a few years of informal trading outdoors and in coffee houses a group of 24 brokers drew up the "Buttonwood Agreement" (May 17, 1792). The document's name commemorated a buttonwood (sycamore) tree on the north side of Wall St, between William and Pearl Sts, near which the brokers used to meet. The stock exchange was formally organized in 1817, and moved to the present site in 1865.

JOHN QUINCY ADAMS WARD

Ward (1830–1910), one of the nation's most important 19th-century sculptors, classically trained and apprenticed to Henry Kirke Browne in Brooklyn, opened his own studio in New York in 1861, achieving his first major success with *The Indian Hunter*, now in Central Park (*see p. 305*). He has been praised for combining the grace of Classical sculpture with psychological intensity, especially evident in his statue of Henry Ward Beecher in Brooklyn's Cadman Plaza.

FEDERAL HALL NATIONAL MEMORIAL

Map p. 620, C3. 26 Wall St (Nassau St). Open Mon–Fri 9–5, closed federal holidays. Free. Visitor information center. Guided tours subject to staff availability. Gift shop. T: 212 825 6888, nps.gov/feha.

In 1699 the British constructed New York's colonial City Hall on this site. After the Revolution, while New York was briefly serving as the nation's capital, the US Congress met there; on April 30, 1789, George Washington took the oath of office on the second-floor balcony, dressed in a plain brown suit—appropriate at a time when the country was chary of the pomp of monarchy. It was renamed Federal Hall to honor New York's status as the nation's capital, and Congress continued to meet there, passing the ten amendments to the Constitution known as the Bill of Rights. The federal government was moved to Philadelphia in 1790, and the old Federal Hall was torn down in 1812.

The present building began as a US Custom House (1842), designed by Alexander Jackson Davis and Ithiel Town, winners of the architectural competition. The design, which combines a Greek Doric portico and an elaborate domed interior, is said to evoke both the democratic ideals of ancient Greece and the power of the Roman Empire.

This severe and elegantly proportioned building is one of the finest examples of Greek Revival temple architecture in the nation. A wide flight of steps leads to eight 32-ft fluted Doric columns of Westchester marble; around the block on Pine St, the back of the building has a second columned portico, unusual in this country. On the steps John Quincy Adams Ward's heroic statue of George Washington (1883) shows the president at the inauguration, lifting his right hand from the Bible on which he swore his oath. Ward relied for historical accuracy on a full-length marble statue made from life in 1786 by French sculptor Jean-Antoine Houdon.

Interior of Federal Hall

The vaulted masonry ceiling of the rotunda was one of the few forms of fireproofing available when the building was constructed. A ring of carved Corinthian columns supports the dome. One of the vaults from the sub-treasury is open for display. In the basement another ring of columns, squat and thickset, supports the upper floors.

On view are models of the original City Hall and the early Federal Hall, and the Bible on which Washington swore the oath. Another exhibit honors John Peter Zenger, the confrontational publisher of the *New York Weekly Journal*, tried here in 1735 for libeling the royal governor. Zenger's acquittal established a precedent for freedom of the press that would later be reaffirmed in the Bill of Rights. On the ground floor old coin vaults (1878) date from the building's period as a US sub-treasury, which at the end of the 19th century contained as much as 1,700 tons of gold and silver coins.

Across the street from Federal Hall at 23 Wall St, the **former Morgan Guaranty Trust Company** (1913; Trowbridge & Livingston) was the bank of J. Pierpont Morgan, who more than anyone epitomized the power of Wall Street and the stupendous acquisition of wealth. The Wall St side of this elegant and restrained building still bears traces of an explosion in 1920 when a carriage loaded with TNT blew up, killing 33 passers-by and injuring 400 others. Anarchists were suspected, but the crime remains unsolved.

FORMER BANKS OF WALL STREET

The Greek Revival bank whose marble façade now stands in the Metropolitan Museum of Art (*see p. 357*) once stood at 30 Wall St (William and Nassau Sts).

At **40 Wall St**, the former Bank of Manhattan (1929; H. Craig Severance & Yasuo Matsui) began ostensibly as a water company, but was in fact a bank, Aaron Burr's response to Alexander Hamilton's Bank of New York. Planned as the world's tallest building during a period when architects were exercising secrecy and cunning to top their competitors, no. 40 Wall St lost out to the Chrysler Building. The uptown architects surreptitiously added a stainless steel spire to their structure (previously 2ft shorter than the bank tower), thus becoming the world's tallest until the completion of the Empire State Building two years later. Its green pyramidal tower and spire are familiar features of the downtown skyline. The present owner, Donald Trump, has added his name in large letters to the façade.

At **48 Wall St** is the former Bank of New York (1927; Benjamin Wistar Morris), recognizable on the skyline by its Georgian-style cupola. Founded by Alexander Hamilton in 1784, it is the oldest commercial bank in the country. The **Museum of American Finance** (*open Tues–Sat 10–4; admission charge; tours; T: 212 908 4110, financialhistory.org*), upstairs in the banking hall, has exhibits on markets, money, banking, and entrepreneurship, with a small room devoted to Hamilton's career. Rotating exhibits have focused on major figures in financial history, the credit crisis, and the role of the Federal Reserve. A gold and bejeweled Monopoly set, weighing 32 pounds and estimated at $2 million, is on long-term display.

Across the street at **55 Wall St** is the venerable former National City Bank building, constructed in two stages. The first (1842; Isaiah Rogers), a three-story Ionic temple with an imposing domed central hall, belongs to the same architectural tradition as Federal Hall. The 16 granite columns, quarried in Quincy, Massachusetts, and hauled up Wall St by 40 teams of oxen, make an impressive façade for the building that first served as the new Merchants' Exchange. Later used as the custom house, the building was remodeled by the firm of McKim, Mead & White in 1907, when the Custom House at Bowling Green opened. The architects doubled the volume of the building by adding the upper stories, which are surrounded by a tier of Corinthian columns. Today it houses a restaurant, event space, and luxury condominiums.

Bas-relief nautical motifs decorate the façade of round-arched **74 Wall Street** (1926; Benjamin Wistar Morris), once the headquarters of the Seamen's Bank for Savings. **No. 70 Pine St** (1932; Clinton & Russell), near Pearl St, is topped off by a spiky Gothic crown and spire. The lavish Art Deco lobby, with brown and beige tones of marble and polished aluminum decoration, still bears the logo of the Cities Service Oil Company, its original owner; the large building models near the Pine and Cedar St entrances date from the era before computer-aided design, when architects used such models to help visualize projects. Today 70 Pine is being converted to luxury apartments.

AROUND BROADWAY AND ZUCCOTTI PARK

CHASE MANHATTAN PLAZA
One Chase Manhattan Plaza (1960; Skidmore, Owings & Merrill, principal designer Gordon Bunshaft), which occupies the enlarged block bounded by Pine, William, Liberty, and Nassau Sts, is an ordinary skyscraper today, but was remarkable when built. Its presence testifies to the bank's decision (and that of its president, David Rockefeller) in the late 1950s to remain downtown when the financial community seemed on the brink of flight, a decision that stimulated the growth of the area in the late 1960s. With its severe, unembellished forms and surfaces of glass and silvery aluminum, the building became Lower Manhattan's first International Style office tower.

The **outdoor plaza** was also the first in the area, a gratuitous act at the time, since the building predates the Zoning Resolution of 1961, which offered developers additional floor space in exchange for such amenities. The black basalt rocks in Isamu Noguchi's sunken Japanese garden (1961–4) were brought from Japan by the sculptor. In 1972 Chase Manhattan Bank installed the *Group of Four Trees* by Jean Dubuffet, a 43-ft, 25-ton fabrication supported by a steel skeleton and constructed of fiberglass, aluminum, and plastic resin, materials the artist hoped would withstand air pollution; the polyurethane paint used on the surface is essentially the same kind used to paint lines on streets. The sculpture, owned by the Museum of Modern Art, has been called handsome, humane, amusing, and ominous; critics were quick to point out the ironic juxtaposition of an institution that epitomized the moneyed establishment and a work by an artist who called himself anti-bourgeois and claimed children, criminals, and psychotics as his influences. In 1966, Chase relocated its headquarters to Park Ave and in 2013 the building was sold to Shanghai-based Fosun Property Holdings.

FEDERAL RESERVE BANK OF NEW YORK

33 Liberty St (Maiden Lane). Free tours weekdays at 1 and 2pm, except bank holidays. Online reservations required; see ny.frb.org/aboutthefed/visiting.html.

The Federal Reserve Bank of New York fills the entire block bounded by Maiden Lane, Liberty, William, and Nassau Sts with its massive institutional stolidity. Philip Sawyer, of York & Sawyer, the lead architect for the building (1924), had studied in Italy, and his design reflects the fortified palaces of the great Renaissance families whose wealth and power made them institutions in their own right. The Palazzo Strozzi in Florence is the bank's principal model, and the superbly-crafted wrought-iron lanterns flanking the doorway on Liberty St are almost exact replicas of their Florentine predecessors. They were executed by Samuel Yellin, whose work also adorns the former Cunard Building on lower Broadway. Beneath the bank five subterranean levels contain offices and bullion vaults, where gold from foreign countries is stored. International transactions are consummated by simply moving the gold from one vault to another without its ever seeing the light of day.

THE EQUITABLE BUILDING

This 1915 tower at 120 Broadway (*Pine and Cedar Sts*) has gone down in history for provoking New York's first restrictions on skyscraper design. In order to maximize rental space and hence profits, the architect Ernest R. Graham designed the Equitable Building to rise 39 stories straight up, filling an entire block and darkening adjacent streets and buildings. It was the largest office building in the world, its floor area more than 30 times its footprint. The following year the City passed the Zoning Resolution of 1916, which insured that such blockbuster buildings would not be built again.

"WEDDING CAKE" SKYSCRAPERS

The 1916 zoning law accounts for the "wedding cake" silhouettes of so many older New York towers. The amount of setback required was determined by running an imaginary plane up from the center of the street at a predetermined angle and requiring the profile of the building to remain within this boundary. After setbacks had reduced the building size to 25 percent of the site, the tower could rise straight up. (In 1961 amendments allowed buildings to rise straight up without stepping back if they covered no more than 40 percent of the site; the law also established absolute limits on building size and offered incentives for including public amenities.)

140 BROADWAY AND ZUCCOTTI PARK

Originally the Marine Midland Bank Building, **140 Broadway** (at Liberty St) soars 51 stories straight up without setbacks. Designed by Gordon Bunshaft of Skidmore, Owings & Merrill (1967) during the 1960s downtown building boom (he also designed the Chase Manhattan Tower; *see above*), it is New York's first dark-glass office tower. More famous than the building is the sculpture on the Broadway sidewalk, Isamu Noguchi's red steel and aluminum **Red Cube** (1968), actually a three-dimensional parallelogram poised on one vertex.

Across Broadway is **Zuccotti Park** (originally Liberty Plaza). Heavily damaged on 9/11, it reopened in 2006, redesigned and renamed for civic activist and real estate mogul John Zuccotti. The park has been landscaped, paved with pink granite, and provided with in-ground lighting, benches, and tables. In the northwest corner, closest to the World Trade Center, sits J. Seward Johnson's bronze *Double Check* (replicated after 9/11 from the 1982 original), the figure of a businessman inspecting a memo. Nearby is a more recent arrival: Mark Di Suvero's heroically scaled *Joie de Vivre*, a towering intersection of red I-beams (1998), which came here from the entrance to the Holland Tunnel. The park is a privately owned public space (POPS in the local real estate argot), required to remain open 24/7. In 2011 the Occupy Wall Street protesters set up camp in the park, using it as a base of operations.

One Liberty Plaza, on the northwest corner of Liberty St and Broadway (1972; Skidmore, Owings & Merrill) replaced the much-admired Singer Building (1908; Ernest Flagg), which at 41 stories was the tallest building in the world for 18 months; it was the last of the early slender downtown towers, replaced by massive bulk of such behemoths as the Equitable Building (*see p. 71*).

JOHN STREET METHODIST CHURCH

Map p. 620, C3. 44 John St (Nassau and William Sts). Open Mon, Wed, Fri 11–5 (subject to change). T: 212 269 0014, johnstreetchurch.org.

The John Street Methodist Church, which has occupied this property since 1768, is the oldest Methodist congregation in the country. The present building (1841), the third on the site, incorporates wide-board flooring, an entrance stairway, pews, and light brackets along the balcony from an earlier building demolished when John St was widened in 1817.

Peter Williams, a black man whose parents were slaves of a family living on Beekman St, converted to Christianity and became sexton here. When his owner returned to England after the Revolution, the church trustees, embarrassed that a well-known Christian was to be sold publicly at auction, bought Williams privately for 40 pounds, a sum he repaid over the years; he was formally emancipated in 1785. Williams went into the tobacco business, prospered, and eventually founded the Mother Zion Church, the first black Methodist church in New York. In the basement of the church is the **Wesley Chapel Museum**, with the church's first altar rail, a clock sent by John Wesley, and other artifacts.

EATING AND DRINKING IN THE FINANCIAL DISTRICT

The Financial District, once the exclusive haunt of Wall Street traders and other type-A personalities, now has a 24/7 resident population. Consequently the dining scene has broadened, and while the neighborhood is not the city's gastronomic center, it offers more options than the power-lunch scene of yore.

$$$$ **Delmonico's**. This Gilded Age steakhouse, where Baked Alaska and Eggs Benedict were (allegedly) invented, still serves up fine prime beef and trimmings, and yes, Baked Alaska. Lunch weekdays, dinner Mon–Sat, closed Sun. *56 Beaver St (William St). T: 212 509 1144, delmonicosny.com. Map p. 620, C4.*

$$$$ **MarkJoseph**. Steakhouse with seafood and chicken, simple and straightforward. Bar menu. Near South Street Seaport. Lunch weekdays, dinner nightly. *261 Water St (Dover St). T: 212 277 0020, mark josephsteakhouse.com. Map p. 621, D3.*

$$$ **North End Grill**. ■ In Battery Park City, this outpost of Danny Meyer's restaurant empire has a wood-burning grill for duck breast, free-range chicken, squab. Also charcuterie, a classic raw bar, seasonal produce (sometimes from the rooftop garden), and fine desserts. Drinks list includes many Scotches. Lunch, afternoon snacks, dinner every day. *104 North End Ave (Murray St). T: 646 747 1600, northendgrillnyc.com. Map p. 620, B3.*

$$ **Fraunces Tavern**. Pub food and more from the building in which Washington bade a tearful farewell to his officers. Known for the historic setting as much as the cuisine. Many craft beers. Lunch and dinner daily. *54 Pearl St (Broad St). T: 212 968 1776, frauncestavern.com. Map p. 620, C4.*

$ **Adrienne's Pizzabar**. On cobbled Stone St, this highly rated pizzeria serves thin-crust rectangular pizzas at lunch and traditional round ones at dinner. Also some pastas and sandwiches, beer and wine. Large local lunchtime crowd. Lunch and dinner daily. *54 Stone St (Coenties Alley). T: 212 248 3838, adriennes pizzabarnyc.com. Map p. 620, C4.*

$ **Dead Rabbit Grocery and Grog**. Popular Irish bar in fine old building; two stories of food and drink. Prize-winning cocktail menu, beers and wines, and Irish whiskey. Named for a 19th-century street gang, it offers better than usual bar food in the Taproom and a few groceries that you can buy and eat with a drink. Lunch weekdays, brunch weekends, dinner nightly. *30 Water St (Broad St and Coenties Slip). T: 646 422 7096, deadrabbitnyc.com. Map p. 620, C4.*

$ **Luke's Lobster**. Lobster, crab, and shrimp rolls, as well as other New England treasures from the sea. Wine and beer, plus homey desserts. Other locations. Take out, order for delivery, or eat in. Microbrews at some branches. Open daily. *26 South William St (Broad St). T: 212 747 1700, lukeslobster.com. Map p. 620, C4.*

The World Trade Center

*Rising from the rubble of Ground Zero, the new World Trade Center is a memorial
to those who died, a 21st-century center of commerce, and a site of pilgrimage for
millions of visitors every year.*

The original World Trade Center (*map p. 620, B3*)—six imposing buildings on a five-acre plaza bounded by Vesey, Liberty, West, and Church Sts, plus a seventh north of Vesey St—was part of a huge urban renewal project undertaken by the Port Authority of New York and New Jersey beginning in the 1970s, though the idea was bandied about as early as the 1950s. Its signature buildings, the Twin Towers, two boxy 110-story office buildings designed by Minoru Yamasaki, rose high over everything in the city and became famous the world over. All of the original buildings (1970–88) were destroyed or catastrophically damaged on September 11, 2001, when Al Qaeda terrorists crashed two fully fueled Boeing 767s into the Towers, which burned and collapsed, taking neighboring buildings with them. The attack killed nearly three thousand people, devastated the city, and reverberated around the world.

The mountain of debris was cleared away by the following spring. Rebuilding, which began in 2002, continues today 15 years after the tragedy.

HISTORY OF THE WORLD TRADE CENTER

By the standards of the 1970s, the first World Trade Center (WTC) was gigantic. Its campus occupied 16 acres; its seven buildings offered ten million square feet of rentable space; 1.2 million cubic feet of earth were excavated for its foundations. Five streets were closed and 164 buildings destroyed in order to build it. The Twin Towers (1350 ft) were the world's tallest buildings; the construction tab, originally estimated at $355 million, eventually came to more than $1 billion.

The WTC was the brainchild of David Rockefeller and other business leaders who hoped in the 1950s to revitalize Lower Manhattan as a center for finance and trade; the Port Authority of New York and New Jersey came on board in 1961. The first building opened in 1970, the last in 1988.

Minoru Yamasaki, relatively unknown at the time, designed five of the six original buildings, including the North and South Towers (1970–1). The five-acre plaza was

ONE WORLD TRADE CENTER
Completed in 2014, it was the city's tallest skyscraper at the time of writing.

home to public artworks including Fritz Koenig's *Sphere* (1968–71); battered by debris from the collapsing buildings, it now stands in Battery Park). Works by Alexander Calder, James Rosati, and Masayuki Nagare did not survive.

The towers were initially unpopular: "stolid, banal monoliths," said the *AIA Guide to New York City*, "General Motors Gothic" wrote *New York Times* architecture critic Ada Louise Huxtable. But as urban lore accreted to the towers, opinion softened. In 1974 Philippe Petit shot a steel cable between them and walked back and forth eight times across the 131-ft gap. Three years later George Willig, a toy designer and mountaineer from Queens, scaled the South Tower using equipment he had devised that hooked into the tracks for window-washing equipment. In time observers noticed that the Towers' shiny aluminum cladding glowed and shimmered when the sun was low in the sky.

Since 9/11, rebuilding has been slow. In 2003 Daniel Libeskind was chosen to design a master plan but as negotiations dragged on and prices soared, his ideas were largely discarded or ignored. For years the site remained a 16-acre, 70-ft-deep hole, but today the final form of the Center is apparent.

THE NATIONAL SEPTEMBER 11 MEMORIAL: "REFLECTING ABSENCE"

Map p. 620, B3. World Trade Center Plaza. Subway: A, C, 4 or 5 to Fulton St; E to World Trade Center; 1 or R to Rector St. Bus: M5, M20, M22. Outdoor memorial open daily 7:30am–9pm. Free. 911memorial.org.

Two 30-ft-deep reflecting pools, each about an acre, fill the footprints of the former towers; water cascades down into their deeper, darker, central holes. Around the pools bronze balustrades bear the names of the 2,983 people who died on 9/11 at the World Trade Center, in Shanksville, Pennsylvania, and at the Pentagon, plus the six people killed in the World Trade Center attack of February 26, 1993. The names of those who died are arranged on the balustrades together with their companions of that day: members of flight crews of the planes are together, as are first responders, and so on.

Groves of swamp white oak trees soften the hard-edged minimalist design of rock and metal. The design, called "Reflecting Absence" (2013; Michael Arad, architect; Peter Walker, landscape architect), was chosen from more than five thousand competition entries.

THE NATIONAL SEPTEMBER 11 MUSEUM

World Trade Center Plaza, near Greenwich and Fulton Sts. Open daily 9am to 9pm, restricted hours in winter. Admission charge, but 9/11 families and first responders free; Tues evening free for everyone, but tickets required; check the website. Often crowded; book ahead: online at 911memorial.org, by phone at 212 266 5211, or at the ticket booth at the museum entrance near Greenwich-Fulton Sts. Some same-day tickets available on a first-come first-serve basis. Guided tours (reservations online); app for mobile devices. Airport-style security at museum entrance. Café and gift shop.

The September 11 Museum, much of it dark and somber, is a stark reminder of the events of that day; it overwhelms both in its scale (occupying the footprint of one of the towers) and in its multitude of detail. Four months after the museum opened, it welcomed its millionth visitor.

In the atrium of the **Museum Pavilion** (2014; Snøhetta) stand two seven-story steel tridents salvaged from the ground-level arcade of the Twin Towers, set in place (2010) before the building was constructed. Inside the Pavilion a ramp descends to bedrock. At the foot of the ramp the raw concrete "slurry wall," studded with steel anchors, dominates **Foundation Hall**. As part of the original foundation, the slurry wall formed a barrier between the basement levels of the Trade Center and the Hudson River, maintaining its integrity even when the Towers collapsed. Foundation Hall accommodates big artifacts: a fire engine whose cab was crushed by debris; 36-foot Column 1001-B, the last removed from Ground Zero during the recovery; a huge rusted grappler claw with debris spilling from its maw.

Within the larger hall is the **Historical Exhibit**, follows a labyrinthine path through the 9/11 narrative, beginning with the construction of the first World Trade Center and ending with ramifications of the tragic event. Many of the exhibits are poignant, even wrenching: a chunk of airplane fuselage framing a window opening; videos of people jumping or falling from the Towers; voices of those who would shortly die as the buildings burned around them; a looping video of the terrorists passing through security in Boston. (There are exits for visitors who want to leave before the exhibit concludes.)

AROUND THE PLAZA

This description begins at the corner of Vesey and West Sts and moves clockwise around the perimeter of the site, which is still a jumble of completed and uncompleted buildings, construction equipment, and traffic barriers. Some parts of the master plan—St. Nicholas Greek Orthodox Church, 5 World Trade Center, and the Performing Arts Center—remain on the design boards; others have been put on hold.

One World Trade Center. *Northwest corner of the site, intersection of West and Vesey Sts. Observatory open daily 9–8, extended hours in summer. Box office opens at 8:30am. Timed entry; tickets available online, by phone or at box office. Admission charge (expensive). Cafés and restaurant. Shop. T: 844 696 1776 (844 OWO 1776), oneworldobservatory.com.* At 1,776 feet (counting the antenna), One World Trade Center (2014; David M. Childs of Skidmore, Owings & Merrill) is the city's tallest skyscraper. An object of contention from the very beginning, the building, first designed by Daniel Libeskind (architect of the WTC master plan), was re-designed several times and renamed once: originally the Freedom Tower (2003), it became One World Trade Center in 2009.

Its windowless, concrete, bomb-proof base, 200ft on a side and 200ft tall, occupies a footprint comparable to those of the Twin Towers. Laminated glass fins and stainless steel slats sheathe the concrete podium, softening the building's bunker-like appearance; LED lights behind the panels illuminate the base day and night. A faceted tower rises 1,368 ft and finishes in a 408-ft spire that gives the building its symbolic height and thrusts it into fourth place (at least temporarily) in the ongoing competition for the world's tallest tower. While One WTC is not the architectural marvel many people had hoped for, it has been accepted as a decent if uninspired occupant of the city's skyline.

The Observatory, occupying floors 100–102, offers all the benefits of 21st-century technology from a viewing point 1,268 ft in the sky: elevators with LED TVs that show a time-lapse panorama of the city's skyline rising through history; 360-degree views; a Sky Portal that lets you see the street below (live in HD); and City Pulse, a high-tech information system that explains the sights visible from the observatory.

Two World Trade Center. *200 Greenwich St, corner of Vesey and Church Sts.* In 2015 Bjarke Ingels, who replaced Norman Foster as architect of the Center's fourth tower, announced a design resembling a stack of boxes or an immense ziggurat, to be constructed on the foundations, which were laid in 2013.

The Transportation Hub. Just south of the Museum pavilion, Santiago Calatrava's Transportation Hub (slated, at the time of writing, to open December 2015) spreads its wings, its swooping steel-ribbed form intended by the architect to suggest a bird taking flight. Daniel Libeskind's original site plan (2003) called for a smaller, underground train station and stipulated that the site remain empty allowing the sun to shine without shadow on the plaza every September 11. In 2004, however, the Port Authority overrode that decision and commissioned what will be New York's most expensive subway station to date, with construction costs nearing $4 billion, double the original estimate. At the concourse level, pedestrian tunnels connect the Hub to the World Financial Center (Brookfield Place, formerly the

World Financial Center) across West St, eleven subway lines, the Port Authority Trans-Hudson (PATH) rail system, and the ferry terminal in Battery Park City, as well as the towers and the Memorial. Shops and restaurants will serve an estimated 220,000 people who will use the facility daily.

Three World Trade Center. *175 Greenwich St, south of the Transportation Hub.* A Richard Rogers-designed 80-story office tower (*under construction at the time of writing*).

Four World Trade Center. *150 Greenwich St (corner of Liberty St).* The second completed building of the new WTC, (2013; Fumihiko Maki), this 977-ft minimalist tower faced with reflective glass achieves "an appropriate presence, quiet but with dignity," according to its architect.

Ten House. *(Ladder Co. 10, Engine Co. 10), 124 Liberty St (Greenwich and Church Sts).* The fire station closest to the WTC, Ten House lost six firefighters in the attacks. On the west wall a 56-ft-long bas-relief (2006; Joseph A. Oddi, Joseph Petrovics, and Biggo Bech Rambusch) depicts scenes from September 11 and the names of the 343 firefighters who perished.

St. Nicholas Greek Orthodox Church and Meditation Center. *Corner of Liberty and Greenwich Sts.*Construction of the new building, designed by Santiago Calatrava, began in 2014. The former church, a quiet presence among gargantuan skyscrapers, stood at 155 Liberty St from c. 1919 until 9/11, when the collapsing South Tower crushed it.

130 Liberty Street (*Washington and Greenwich Sts*) was the site of the Deutsche Bank Building (1974), which suffered a 24-story gash from falling debris. Two firefighters were killed during demolition in 2007.

NORTH OF THE WORLD TRADE CENTER

The Verizon Building. *40 West St between Barclay and Vesey Sts*. Predating the Twin Towers by half a century and originally called the Barclay-Vesey Building (1927), this landmark, filled with offices and switching equipment, dwarfed its low-rise neighborhood, filled with offices and switching equipment of the New York Telephone Company. The first major work by Ralph Walker, the building was New York's first Art Deco skyscraper and the first high-rise to brilliantly deploy the restrictions of the 1916 Zoning Law (*see p. 71*). The arcaded sidewalk along Vesey St (intended as a shopping arcade) resulted from a compromise between the City, which wanted to widen Vesey St, and the phone company, which wanted as much floor space as possible. Lavish Art Deco ornament inside and out includes plant forms, aborigines, baby flutists, and elephants whose ears spiral into nautilus shells and bells. Ceiling paintings (Mack, Jenney, & Tyler) illustrate the history of human communications. Badly damaged by the collapse of World Trade Center (and later inundated by Hurricane Sandy) it underwent a $1.4 billion restoration. The upper floors are now condos.

Seven World Trade Center. *250 Greenwich St*. Designed by Skidmore, Owings & Merrill, this is the only WTC building (2006) finished in the decade after 9/11. Its predecessor, which housed a supposedly bomb-proof, fireproof, hurricane-proof command center ("The Bunker") for the mayor and emergency personnel, collapsed at 5:21pm on 9/11 after burning all day. In the new building's lobby a moving stream of LED text (Jenny Holzer and James Carpenter) offers snippets of poetry and prose chronicling New York history.

In the landscaped triangle east of 7 WTC, Jeff Koons's nine-foot, candy-apple-red, stainless steel ***Balloon Flower*** (?1995) cheerfully sits in a bubbling fountain.

THE OLD NEIGHBORHOOD

Before the World Trade Center existed, the area was low-rise and low-key. Ecclesiastical supply shops clustered around St. Peter's Church on Barclay St. The remnants of a Syrian quarter hung on south of the Trade Center site, while on Radio Row along Cortlandt St dozens of small stores sold radios, televisions, and old phonograph records. Store owners blasted music into the street through speakers mounted on the store fronts. But in 1963, the Port Authority used its powers of eminent domain to acquire the land on which the shops stood; by 1966 Radio Row had disappeared.

THE WOOLWORTH BUILDING
Sculpture in the lobby depicting the building's architect Cass Gilbert
holding an architectural model of his skyscraper.

St. Paul's Chapel, City Hall, & The Civic Center

This is the city's administrative heart, with government buildings of the Civic Center and magnificent City Hall, as well as the beacon of survival that is St. Paul's Chapel.

St. Paul's Chapel is Manhattan's only remaining colonial church (1766), built as a chapel of ease by Trinity Church for worshipers who couldn't or wouldn't walk downtown to Trinity. During the Revolution, when the British occupied the city, other churches saw hard use as stables, prisons, and hospitals, but St. Paul's became the house of worship for British officers. It survived the fire of 1776 (as Trinity did not) thanks to vacant land surrounding it and a bucket brigade that carried water from the Hudson. Because Trinity had not yet been rebuilt in 1789, George Washington held his post-inaugural service at St. Paul's and continued to worship here until the federal government left New York for Philadelphia.

Spared on 9/11, the chapel served as a place of refuge for workers struggling with the smoldering wreckage at Ground Zero, and the iron fence outside became a shrine onto which were fastened handwritten messages and drawings, photos, flowers, teddy bears, and candles. Since 9/11 the chapel has become a site of pilgrimage for visitors to the World Trade Center memorials.

VISITING THE CHAPEL AND CHURCHYARD
Map p. 620, C3. Broadway between Fulton and Vesey Sts. Subway: A, C, 2, 3 4, 5 to Broadway-Nassau; 6 to Brooklyn Bridge-City Hall; E to Chambers St. Bus: M5. Chapel open Mon–Sat 10–6, Sun 7–6; churchyard closes at 4pm on Sat and at 3:30 on Sun. Free. Organ concerts (free) on Wed at 1pm. T: 212 602 0800, trinitywallstreet.org. Free app.
St. Paul's Chapel was built by Andrew Gautier on a design from James Gibbs, architect of St. Martin-in-the-Fields, London, but of homely materials—rough, reddish-gray Manhattan schist and smooth brownstone. The Georgian-style church originally faced the Hudson across a wheat field, but as Broadway became an important thoroughfare, the rear entrance became the principal one. The wooden steeple by James Crommelin Lawrence was added in 1794.

THE MONTGOMERY MONUMENT

On the east porch stands the nation's first official monument (commissioned 1776), a tribute to Brigadier General Richard Montgomery, mortally wounded in the Battle of Quebec on December 25, 1775. Benjamin Franklin, ambassador to France, selected Jean-Jacques Caffieri, royal sculptor to Louis XV, to design the work; Caffieri complained about his fee, but completed the monument in 1777. It moldered on the docks at Le Havre for a couple of years before it was shipped to the US, where after another delay it was installed here in 1788. Restored in 2011, the monument consists of a central marble column, topped with a funerary urn. Flanking it are symbols of freedom: a Phrygian cap (given to freed Roman slaves), broken swords, bent spears, and a club of Hercules with a ribbon inscribed "Libertas Restituta" ("Liberty Restored").

The interior of the church, painted in pale colors, is graced by a clear Palladian window, and 14 Waterford crystal chandeliers (1802) that survived the shock waves of the collapsing Twin Towers. The chandeliers, organ case, and the elaborately carved pulpit and communion rail date from before the Revolution. Pierre L'Enfant, known for his work in Washington, DC, designed the wooden "Glory" altarpiece, a stylized representation of Mt. Sinai surrounded by clouds (probably executed by a ship's carver) from which emanate jagged shafts of light, pointing down to the Tablets of the Law. The pew where George Washington worshiped, originally canopied, is in the north aisle. At the rear of the church the memorial to the lawyer John Wells (d. 1823) is the earliest known marble portrait bust by an American sculptor (1824; John Frazee).

An exhibit documents the role of the chapel in the aftermath of 9/11, when it remained open around the clock for eight months. On view are photos, a pew scarred by workers' boots, scribbled prayers, and an outpouring of origami "Peace Cranes" sent by Japan, some folded by survivors of Hiroshima and Nagasaki.

AROUND ST. PAUL'S

The former American Telephone and Telegraph Building (1915–22; William Welles Bosworth) now known as **195 Broadway** (*Fulton and Dey Sts*), is said to have more columns than any other building—eight tiers of Ionic resting on a tier of Doric. In the monumental lobby (with its own forest of massive marble columns) a wall sculpture, *Service to the Nation in Peace and War* by Chester Beach, recalls the phone company. The central figure, his hair frizzled by lightning, poses before a map of the US whose major cities are linked by long-distance telephone wires. On top of the building stood a 24-ft gilded statue (1916; Evelyn Beatrice Longman): a winged male, clutching a fistful of lightning bolts, girded by a golden telephone cable. Called "Genius of Telegraphy" by the sculptor, its official name evolved, along with its corporate owner, to "The Genius of Electricity" and then "The Spirit of Communication," but the figure was known familiarly as "Golden Boy." After sojourns at the former AT&T building on Madison Ave, and stops in New Jersey, he now glitters at AT&T headquarters in Dallas, Texas.

St. Peter's Church (1838; John Haggerty and Thomas Thomas) at 22 Barclay St, overshadowed by skyscrapers, stands on the site of its predecessor, the city's first

Roman Catholic church. Since the regulations outlawing Catholicism in Britain applied to the US during the colonial period, only in 1785 could the congregation purchase land from Trinity Parish. The present granite church is Greek Revival at its most imposing, its Ionic portico with six massive columns supporting a wood-framed pediment. St. Elizabeth Ann Seton converted to Catholicism here, and Pierre Toussaint attended Mass daily for 66 years. On 9/11 firefighters laid the body of the Rev. Mychal Judge, chaplain of the NY Fire Department, before the altar; like nearby St. Paul's Chapel, the church ministered to Ground Zero workers.

THE WOOLWORTH BUILDING

Map p. 620, C3. 233 Broadway. Admission by guided tour of 30, 60, or 90mins; weekend tours sometimes sold out. Admission charge. Tickets and info online at woolworthtours.com.

The Woolworth Building was the world's tallest when completed (1913; Cass Gilbert), and though it was eclipsed in 1930 by the Chrysler Building, it remains one of the city's most luxuriantly detailed skyscrapers.

F.W. Woolworth enjoyed a classic 19th-century rags-to-riches career, starting out as a farm boy and beginning his life's work clerking in a general store. During this apprenticeship Woolworth became convinced that customers would patronize a store where they could see and even finger the merchandise and buy without having to haggle over prices. After a few false starts he proved himself right in a grand way, opening his first successful five-and-ten-cent store in 1879 and developing it eventually as a chain. By 1913 he was able to pay $13,500,000 in cash for this building.

The care and attention that Woolworth devoted to the smallest details (he personally picked out the bathroom fixtures and the mail chutes), the extravagant expenditures for materials and craftsmanship, and the grandiose conception of the whole make the building a monument to its owner's career as well as a visual delight. When the Woolworth Building officially opened, the Rev. S. Parkes Cadman, a Brooklyn minister and radio preacher known for the intensity of his sentiments, noted that the building inspired "feelings too deep even for tears" and dubbed it "The Cathedral of Commerce." Until 1998 the building was owned by the Woolworth Company; today it houses offices and luxury condos.

Predating the 1916 zoning restrictions (*see p. 71*), the building covers its entire site and rises straight up from the street; the tower above the blocky base ends in a crown (total height 792ft). Carved figures of diligently working men and women surround the **street-level doorway arch**—earning the money, according to some early observers, to shop at Woolworth's. Masks above the second floor represent four centers of civilization—Europe, Africa, Asia, and America—a motif Cass Gilbert had used earlier on the Custom House at Bowling Green.

The lobby reveals Woolworth's love of spectacle: marble-covered walls, vaulted mosaic ceilings intended to recall the mosaics of Ravenna, and murals in the side hall-

8 SPRUCE STREET
Apartment tower by Frank Gehry (2011) clad in electronically designed illusionistic panels.

ways by C. Paul Jennewein representing *Commerce* and *Labor*. The only relief in all this magnificence (neither Gilbert nor Woolworth was known for a sense of humor) is offered by a set of sculpted figures beneath the arches leading to the side hallways; they depict building principals in appropriate poses: Woolworth clutching a big nickel, Cass Gilbert peering through a pince-nez at a model of the building, and so on.

PARK ROW

Park Row (*map p. 620, C2–C3*), formerly the theater district, became the center of the newspaper industry in the mid-19th century. Close to City Hall (political news) and to the slums of the Lower East Side (sensational human interest stories), "Newspaper

Row" ran from Ann St (where James Gordon Bennett's marble New York Herald Building had replaced P.T. Barnum's American Museum in 1866) to Chatham Square. The row was divided by the approaches to the Brooklyn Bridge into a northern section for the foreign-language press and a southern section for the English-language dailies. In one grand line-up facing City Hall Park stood four great papers: Joseph Pulitzer's *New York World*; Charles Anderson Dana's *New York Sun*; the *New York Tribune*, founded by Horace Greeley; and the *New York Times*, revitalized by Adolph Ochs. When Joseph Pulitzer died in 1911, New York had 14 daily newspapers, twelve of them published on Park Row.

The **Potter Building** (1886; Norris G. Starkweather), at 38 Park Row, was built to be fireproof. Its developer, Orlando B. Potter, owner of the previous building on the site which burned in 1882, understandably wanted its replacement to avoid the same fate and clad the brick with architectural terra cotta, which also allowed the elaborate decoration. Today the building houses upscale apartments.

At 41 Park Row between Beekman and Spruce Sts is the **former New York Times Building** (1889; George B. Post), now owned by Pace University. Imposing in its day, the building reflected the aspirations of its owners and the rising status of the industry. Moses King in his 1892 guidebook called it "a masterpiece of the Romanesque style... discreet, moderate, bold, vigorous, perfect in every detail," adding that the building was "the *New York Times* in stone." The *Times* went further and declared it "a masterpiece of architectural art" and "the finest newspaper building in the world."

Frank Gehry's first skyscraper (2011), **8 Spruce Street**, soars above the 19th-century buildings of Park Row. The shimmering 76-story apartment tower, once dubbed "New York by Gehry" by realtors, is clad in more than ten thousand computer-designed stainless-steel panels that make the façade appear to twist and ripple in the light. On the ground floor is an elementary school.

The area around Nassau and Spruce Sts and Park Row was known as Printing House Square in 1872 when Ernst Plassman's **statue of Benjamin Franklin**, publisher of the *Pennsylvania Gazette*, was placed on its pedestal next to the former Times Building.

CITY HALL PARK

Map p. 620, C3–C2. Bounded by Broadway, Park Row, and Chambers St. Subway: R to City Hall; 2, 3 to Park Pl.; 4, 5, 6 to Brooklyn Bridge-City Hall; J, Z to Chambers St; R to City Hall. Bus: M5, M9, M103.

City Hall Park (8.8 acres) is one of the oldest public gathering places in the city, filled with monuments of its historic past.

The Dutch used the area as a commons—shared land for pasturing livestock and holding public ceremonies—and for a windmill (1691). By the early 18th century the area, at the outskirts of the city, seems to have been relegated to use for people on the fringes of society. Between 1736 and 1760 a poor house and a debtors' prison were constructed, as well as a barracks and a powder house. Just to the north the city's blacks, many of them slaves, were permitted to bury their dead (*see p. 90*).

As tensions rose before the Revolution, the presence of the barracks inflamed hostilities between local patriots and the British soldiers garrisoned in the park. At 6pm on July 9, 1776, the Declaration of Independence was read to George Washington's troops assembled there along with a large crowd. After the reading, the raucous pack headed downtown to the Bowling Green to pull down the statue of George III.

Since then the park has hosted both celebrations and protests. It is the destination of the traditional ticker-tape parade through the Canyon of Heroes (the section of Broadway beginning at Bowling Green and ending here). New Yorkers have demonstrated against police violence (1849, 1998), the high price of flour (1837), same-sex marriage (2004), and teacher layoffs (2011), and in favor of labor unions (1836, 1850), and immigrant rights (2006). Excavations during the $34.6-million restoration of plantings and monuments (1999) uncovered coins, pot shards, long clay pipes, intact skeletons, and jumbled bones.

MONUMENTS IN CITY HALL PARK

In the center of the park stands a reconstructed **fountain** (1871) by Jacob Wrey Mould (*see p. 316*), which in 1920 was shipped off to Crotona Park in the Bronx where it was vandalized. The **perimeter fence** replicates an 1820s' original torn down in 1865 to make space for a large post office, which itself was torn down in 1939. Contrasting paving stones mark the perimeters of long-gone buildings, including the windmill and the British barracks, and the aforementioned post office.

Among the various monuments in the park, some are remarkable. Just south of City Hall is a **bronze statue of Nathan Hale** (1890; Frederick W. MacMonnies), the Revolutionary spy best remembered for the words "I regret that I have but one life to give for my country," allegedly uttered just before the British hanged him. The portrayal represents MacMonnies' romantic conception of Hale as a handsome youth (he was 21) in an impassioned attitude of defiance. One of Hale's contemporaries, however, described him as having "shoulders of moderate breadth, his limbs straight and very plump."

On the west lawn stands a monument to the "**Liberty Poles**," erected in the years before the Revolution by the Sons of Liberty, a group of tradesmen, workers, and army veterans, who harassed the British government and propagandized against taxation policies. The poles, ancient symbols of resistance to tyranny, deliberately provoked the British garrison. Five successive poles stood on private property in sight of the barracks; the most impressive was one erected in 1770, an 80-ft pine ship's mast sunk in a 12-ft hole and girded with iron hoops.

North of City Hall on the east side of the park, a bronze **statue of Horace Greeley** (1890; John Quincy Adams Ward) shows the famous newspaperman relaxing in an upholstered chair, a newspaper draped over his right knee. Greeley, who founded the *New York Tribune* and guided it to eminence, is famous also for his advice to an unknown fortune-seeker, "Go West, young man." The editor is known to have been careless about his dress and personal appearance, a quality Ward has captured.

THE SUBWAY BENEATH THE PARK

Sealed behind concrete doors under City Hall Park is the city's first subway station (1904), out of service since December 31, 1945, by which time subway cars had become too long to navigate the tight loop of track. Designed by Heins & LaFarge, whose work includes the Cathedral of St. John the Divine, the elegant appointments—chandeliers, leaded skylights, a vaulted Guastavino ceiling, and decorative tile work—are legacies of the City Beautiful movement. (*The New York Transit Museum sponsors tours of the station for museum members only; admission charge; tickets go fast; T: 718 694 1600, mta. info/mta/museum/programs.*)

CITY HALL

Map p. 620, C2. In City Hall Park. Subway: 2, 3 to Park Pl.; 4, 5, 6 to Brooklyn Bridge-City Hall; J, Z to Chambers St. Bus: M5, M9, M15, M103. Open only for free guided tours given by the Public Design Commission: Thur at 10am (reserve in advance at T: 212 788 2656 or online at nyc.gov/html/artcom) or Wed at noon (first-come-first-serve, sign up the day of the tour at NYC Official Information kiosk, southern end of City Hall Park across from the Woolworth Building). Kiosk open Mon–Fri 9–6, Sat and Sun 10–5.

City Hall (1811), one of the New York's architectural treasures, a gleaming white marble confection, was the third building to house the municipal government after the Stadt Huys on Pearl St and the 18th-century City Hall on Wall St that later became Federal Hall (*see p. 68*). Inside are a beautiful rotunda with a sweeping double staircase, the mayor's office, the City Council chambers, and the historic Governor's Room housing a fine collection of portraits.

The building

The novelist Henry James, born in New York, praised City Hall for its "perfect taste and finish... reduced yet ample scale... harmony of parts... and modest classic grace." Less articulate observers have called it the best city hall in America; it is also one of the oldest in continuous use for government functions. Constructed during the opening decades of the 19th century (1803–12), when the nation was searching for an architecture that would reflect its youthful republican ideals, the building is an outstanding example of the Federal style. Though similar in its Classicism to the government buildings then on the drawing boards or under construction in Washington, D.C., City Hall is unusual in its adoption of French classic details, notably the garlanded swags, the arched windows, and the flat pilasters on the façade, which make it less austere than many of its contemporaries. One of the architects, Joseph François Mangin, was a French immigrant; the other, John McComb Jr., was a native New Yorker brought up in the tradition of master builders. The two won a $350 prize for their design.

The cost of the marble on the façade distressed the city fathers, who wanted to economize with brownstone, but McComb lobbied successfully for marble on the front and sides, leaving only the rear façade a dull brown. (Alabama limestone replaced both brownstone and the original marble in 1956.) The figure of *Justice* on the cupola replaces a wooden original by sculptor John Dixey, who earned $310 for the work. In 1858, when New Yorkers were acknowledging the completion of the Atlantic Cable with a "most thorough and systematic display of popular joy," sparks from the fireworks ignited the statue, which, according to the *London Illustrated News*, "stood wrapt for a length of time in the flames of the grand illumination, and serenely endured the fiery glow for more than an hour, until at length she was observed to totter and fall into the flames." The present statue (1887), like the Statue of Liberty, is constructed of hammered sheets of copper attached to an internal armature, but painted to resemble stone.

CITY HALL

City Hall is as beautiful inside as out, the lobby walls covered with the original white Massachusetts marble, the rotunda, probably designed by McComb, with a beautiful circular staircase and a dome illuminated by a clear glass oculus and supported by ten Corinthian columns. Upstairs, the Governor's Room first served as an office for the governor when he visited and as a reception room; now it also serves as a museum celebrating New York's civic history.

The art collection

In 1790, while New York was enjoying its brief fling as the nation's capital, the Common Council, the city's chief legislative body, commissioned John Trumbull to paint portraits of George Washington and of George Clinton, the state's first governor. The portraits, painted at the height of Trumbull's powers, show Washington as commander-in-chief of the Continental Army on Evacuation Day (*see p. 52*) and Clinton, brigadier general in Washington's army, on the Hudson highlands against a background of burning American ships.

In 1805 the Council expanded the program to include all governors and mayors since the Revolution. Seven years later, with the country embroiled in the War of 1812, the Council added the likenesses of several war heroes. The tradition of officially sponsored portraits continued through the mayoralty of Fiorello La Guardia (1934–45), with subsequent portraits donated as gifts. The collection chronicles changing styles of American portraiture during the 19th century and includes noteworthy first-generation post-Revolutionary artists: John Wesley Jarvis, Thomas Sully, Samuel F.B. Morse, John Vanderlyn. (*See nyc.gov/html/artcom/html/portrait/gallery.shtml for an online catalogue of the collection.*)

THE "TWEED" COURTHOUSE

Map p. 620, C2. 52 Chambers St. Subway: 2, 3 to Park Place; 4, 5, 6 to Brooklyn Bridge-City Hall; J, Z to Chambers St. Bus: M5, M9, M15, M103. Open only for free guided tours given by the Public Design Commission: Fri at noon (reserve in advance at T: 212 788 2656 or online at nyc.gov/html/artcom).

The former New York County Courthouse (1861–72, John Kellum; enlarged 1877–91, Leopold Eidlitz; interiors restored 1990), infamous as the "Tweed" Courthouse, enshrines in marble the excesses of William M. "Boss" Tweed and his cronies, who embezzled impressive sums of money during its construction.

The main section, an imposing Italianate palazzo facing Chambers St, is by John Kellum. After Kellum's death in 1871, Eidlitz added the neo-medieval wing to the south (instead of matching Kellum's building) and developed many of the interior spaces, including the polychrome brickwork in the famous rotunda. In the 1990s the interiors were gloriously restored; today the building houses the NYC Department of Education.

FINANCIAL HISTORY OF THE "TWEED" COURTHOUSE

In 1858 the city Board of Supervisors authorized $250,000 for a new courthouse, the cornerstone of which was laid in December 1861. The Supervisors soon realized that the initial estimate was inadequate, but they could not have dreamed that by the time the building was finished, twenty years later, the cost would rise to more than $11 million, of which an estimated $8.5 million ended up in the pockets of Tweed and his associates. Tweed's hirelings signed up contractors who padded their accounts and then kicked back most of the difference between what the work actually cost and what the City paid for it. Thus Andrew J. Garvey, a plasterer, appeared in the records as receiving $45,966.89 for a day's work, a sum that earned him the title "Prince of Plasterers."

Tweed rose from humble beginnings to wealth, power, and fame through the machinery of Tammany Hall (*see p. 185*), the most powerful organization in Democratic Party politics. He never held a high city office himself, but as a kingmaker profited from friends in high places. Although he and his "Ring" fleeced the city in other ways, the disclosure of the cost overruns of this courthouse precipitated Tweed's exposure and ultimate imprisonment. His fall was swift and spectacular; he was tried in an unfinished courtroom in this building, and he died in prison, poor and friendless, in 1876.

AROUND CHAMBERS STREET

The **former Emigrant Industrial Savings Bank** at 51 Chambers Street (*Broadway and Elk St*) was founded in 1850 by the Irish Emigrant Society with the blessing of Archbishop John Hughes to provide Irish immigrants a secure place to stash their money and to teach the virtues of thrift and industry. The opulent Beaux-Arts building (1908–12; Raymond F. Almirall) was the first in the city constructed in the shape of a three-dimensional H to provide natural light and air to most of the offices; inside, the opulent fittings—marble floors, bronze grilles, stained-glass skylights—suggested security and fiscal probity to the depositors. It is slated for residential conversion.

The building on the northeast corner of Broadway and Chambers St (*280 Broadway*) originally housed the nation's first department store, the **A.T. Stewart Marble Palace** (1846; Trench & Snook). Alexander Turney Stewart did for merchandising at the upper end of the economic scale what F.W. Woolworth did at the lower end, offering different types of merchandise under a single roof, selling clothing in fixed sizes at fixed prices, and freeing shoppers from the psychological demands of bargaining. Furthermore, Stewart shrewdly turned shopping into entertainment and to that end built this store, which initially drew shoppers in droves. By 1862, however, fashionable society had begun shopping further uptown, so Stewart built a new palace, the Cast Iron Palace, further up Broadway between 9th and 10th Sts, retaining this Chambers St store as a warehouse. Stewart's own mansion on Fifth Avenue at 34th St, a $3-million extravagance, set the standard for younger generations of millionaires.

The Marble Palace is an early example of the Italianate style that replaced the Greek Revival as the dominant architectural fashion. Admired for its palatial dimensions, white marble façade, and elegant details (for example the classical masks in the keystones over the second-story windows), it was, according to wealthy diarist Philip Hone, "magnificent beyond anything in the New World or the old either." Originally the slender Corinthian columns on the ground floor framed display windows so large that Stewart had to order the plate glass from France.

From 1919–52 the *Sun*, a politically conservative newspaper, occupied the building, its motto still displayed on the four-faced bronze clock on the Chambers St corner: "The Sun, it shines for all." The paper is remembered today for the 1897 editorial beginning "Yes, Virginia, there is a Santa Claus," which has entered American holiday folklore.

AFRICAN BURIAL GROUND NATIONAL MONUMENT

Map p. 620, C2. Subway: 4, 5, 6, R, W, M, or Z to Brooklyn Bridge-City Hall; A, C, Z to Chambers St; 2, 3 to Park Place. Bus: M5, M15, M22. Visitor Center at 290 Broadway (Duane and Reade Sts): open Tues–Sat 10–4. Bookshop. Outdoor monument on Duane St at Elk St: open Mon–Sat 9–4 in season; closed Nov–March. Both sites closed Thanksgiving, Christmas, federal holidays. Free. T: 212 637 2019, nps.gov/afbg.

In 1991 during excavations for the Ted Weiss Federal Building, archaeologists digging with trowels under a former parking lot unearthed human skeletons that had been wrapped in shrouds, buried in coffins, and laid to rest with their heads toward the west, according to African custom. Construction halted; vehement campaigning by the black community became a nationwide effort to preserve the site. The archaeological dig that followed uncovered 419 sets of remains, 40 percent of which belonged to children. The entire graveyard, indicated on a map of 1755 as the "Negros Buriel Ground," filled about five city blocks and is believed to contain the remains of more than 15,000 African Americans, both free blacks and slaves, buried in layers. The bones were sent to Howard University for forensic and anthropological study and in 2003 were re-interred according to ancestral customs. The site became a National Historic Monument in 2006, a potent reminder of a people brought to America in bondage and against their will.

HISTORY OF THE BURIAL GROUND

The Dutch introduced slavery to New Amsterdam in 1626, using slave labor to clear land, build Fort Amsterdam and the wall at Wall St, widen Indian trails, lay roads (including Broadway and the Bowery), and perform domestic labor. When the British took over in 1664, the city became central to the African slave trade, and by 1711 a slave market stood on Wall St at the East River. In 1697 Trinity Church ordered that "no Negroes be buried within the bounds and limits of the church yard," and the Burial Ground on the desolate outskirts of the city came into heavier use, continuing to receive the dead until 1794, when the Chamber of Commerce acquired part of the land to lay out Chambers St. The neighborhood was leveled and filled for building construction, and as development continued through the centuries, memory of the Burial Ground faded.

The outdoor memorial

The imagery of the monument (dedicated 2007), designed by Rodney Léon, a Brooklyn-born architect, recalls traditional African burial practices. A circular ramp, its walls engraved with African signs and symbols, leads down to a hull-like Ancestral Chamber sited at the level where the remains were rediscovered. A map of the world with Africa at the center is carved into the granite floor. At ground level, between the memorial and the Ted Weiss Building, seven earthen mounds flanked by seven trees cover the reinterred skeletons.

Art in the Weiss Building

Artworks commissioned for the lobby include Clyde Lynds' *America Song* (1995), a stone, steel, and fiber-optic wall sculpture (*exterior, right of entrance*); Barbara Chase-Riboud's *Africa Rising* (1998), a bronze female figure reminiscent both of Umberto Boccioni's Futurist females and the Louvre's *Winged Victory of Samothrace*; *The New Ring Shout* (1994), a floor mosaic by Houston Conwill, Joseph DePace, and Estella Conwill Majozo; Tomi Arai's silk-screen *Renewal* (1998); *Unearthed* (2002), three bronze African-American faces by Frank Bender, a sculptor known for his forensic reconstructions; and *Untitled* (1994) by Roger Brown, a glass mosaic the artist described as "a tapestry of human faces...in memory of those of all races who have suffered and died too soon."

The Visitor Center
The center (opened 2010; *entrance mid-block at 290 Broadway*) powerfully memorializes the African-American experience in New York during the period when the graveyard was in use. A central tableau with life-size figures recreates a burial like those that took place here centuries ago. Photos of the graves as they were opened show disintegrating coffins and bones marked by malnutrition and deformed by heavy labor. An exhibit traces the life of Peter Williams (1749–1823), who paid off his slave price and became a moving force in religion (*see p. 72*); another shows Cuffee (d. 1741), burned alive for allegedly taking part in a rebellion. Beads, buttons, and a ring found in the graves suggest Africa's artistic heritage. Photos and documents record the political struggle to preserve the burial ground.

THE CIVIC CENTER

Map pp. 620, C2–621, D2. Subway: 4, 5, 6 to Brooklyn Bridge-City Hall; J, Z to Chambers St; R to City Hall. Bus: M1, M5.

North and east of City Hall lies the Civic Center, an assortment of government buildings dating from the late 19th century to recent times. The location was chosen almost by default, the boggy ground making the neighborhood unsuitable for high-rise commercial construction and the nearby slums during the early years of the 20th century making it unattractive for anything else.

THE MUNICIPAL BUILDING
1 Centre St (Chambers St). Open Mon–Fri 9–5, closed federal holidays. CityStore (open Mon–Fri 10–5, closed federal holidays) has NYC books, gifts, and memorabilia (used horseshoes from NYPD mounted police, manuals of the New York building codes). Store telephone: within NYC, T: 311; outside NYC, T: 212 NEW YORK (212 639 9675).
This 40-story civic skyscraper (1907–14; McKim, Mead & White) was built when the need for government office space ballooned after the boroughs were consolidated (1898) into a single city. The firm of McKim, Mead & White, known for their mastery of the Beaux-Arts style but not for skyscraper design, won the design competition. The building has an elaborate base (impressive to pedestrians) and a monumental top (conspicuous on the skyline). The central arch in the ground-level colonnade formerly straddled Chambers St, creating a colossal gateway to the slums of the Lower East Side; it now serves as a grand entrance to Police Plaza. Shields above bear the insignia of Amsterdam, Great Britain, New York City, and New York State. Winged figures flanking the arch represent *Guidance* (*left*) and *Executive Power* (*right*). The panels

over the smaller arches are (*left*) *Civic Duty*, depicting the city conferring law upon its citizens and (*right*) *Civic Pride*, showing the citizens returning the fruits of their labors to the city. Above, relief medallions depict *Progress* (*left*) and *Prudence* (*right*).

Adolph A. Weinman's 25-ft *Civic Fame* (1913–14), on top of the building, holds a laurel branch and a five-turreted crown symbolizing the five boroughs. Made of copper hammered over a steel frame (like the Statue of Liberty), it stands 582ft above the street.

The central arch has an imposing coffered ceiling; bronze ornamental work decorates the lobby. On the south side of the building the vaulted ceiling finished with Guastavino tile dignifies the subway entrance.

POLICE PLAZA AND NYC POLICE HEADQUARTERS

Beyond the central arch of the Municipal Building, Police Plaza is bounded by the Avenue of the Finest, Madison St, Pearl St, and Park Row. The site recommended itself to planners because the City could inexpensively purchase many small land parcels in what had long been a warehouse district, but the project took a decade to build, wending its way tortuously through the bureaucracy. **Police Headquarters** (1973; Gruzen & Partners), a Brutalist building of brown brick and concrete, is a ten-story cube with offices above a base containing police facilities. The five interlocking disks of Bernard (Tony) Rosenthal's sculpture *Five in One* (1971–4) symbolize the five boroughs.

SURROGATE'S COURT

31 Chambers St (Centre St). Lobby and Visitor Center open Mon–Thur 9–4:30, Fri 9–1. The Municipal Archives (Room 103) has exhibits on New York City history drawn from its rich collection of photographs, documents, and objects (nyc.gov/html/records). Online gallery of more than 900,000 photos (nycma.lunaimaging.com).

Formerly known as the **Hall of Records** (1899–1907; John R. Thomas and Horgan & Slattery), the Beaux-Arts Surrogate's Court was built as an expression of civic pride, primarily as a repository of historical documents. Somewhat faded today, it remains a grand building. Statuary on the exterior honors the city's history and extols its eminence. Two sculptural groups by Philip Martiny flank the Chambers St entrance: *New York in Revolutionary Times*, a helmeted female figure flanked by a despondent British soldier and a fresh-faced young woman carrying flowers; and *New York in Its Infancy*, a woman wearing a feathered headdress, stepping forward between an Indian and a Dutchman. The frieze above the portico bears eight figures representing prominent early New Yorkers, including Peter Stuyvesant (third from left), and DeWitt Clinton (third from right). The cornice figures facing Reade and Centre Sts represent the arts, professions, and industries.

Inside, the foyer is faced with yellow-toned Siena marble. Above the doorways at each end of the room sculptural groups by Albert Weinert represent *The Consolidation of Greater New York* (east door) and *Recording the Purchase of Manhattan Island* (west door). On the ceiling a mosaic by William de Leftwich Dodge, a Paris-trained muralist, is organized into panels depicting Greek and Egyptian deities. The Greek divinities in the corners are *Themis* (Justice), *Erinys* (Vengeance), *Penthos* (Sorrow), and *Ponos* (Toil). On the end walls are mosaics, also by Dodge, with unimaginative but descriptive titles: *Searching the Records* and *Widows and Orphans Pleading Before the Judge of the Surrogate's Court.* Above the central landing of the grand staircase in the lobby is a stucco relief of the seal of New York City (*see below*).

In the Municipal Archives are such treasures as an indictment accusing Mae West of obscenity; a letter from "Typhoid Mary" Mallon begging to be released from quarantine on North Brother Island; James Cagney's birth certificate; and one of Frederick Law Olmsted's paychecks for his work on Central Park.

THE CITY'S SEAL

The first version of the present seal, adopted in 1686, recounts the city's early history. Windmill sails on the shield recall New York's beginnings as New Amsterdam; the beavers and flour barrels represent the fur trade and milling industry, crucial to the city's early economy. A sailor and Native American support the shield, which rests on a horizontal laurel branch bearing the date 1625, though the first boatload of settlers had arrived in 1624 (in 1977 the date was changed, apparently for political reasons). Above the shield is an American eagle (a post-Revolutionary replacement of the Imperial Crown); a ribbon encircling the lower half reads "Sigillum Civitatis Novi Eboraci" ("Seal of the City of New York"). *Eboracum* was the Roman name for York in England; James, Duke of York, was the first proprietary ruler of New York under the English.

FOLEY SQUARE AND THE COURTHOUSE DISTRICT

North of Centre St lies Foley Square, named after saloon keeper and Tammany boss Thomas ("Big Tom") F. Foley (1852–1925), a kingmaker but never an office-holder. Foley helped Al Smith become governor and prevented William Randolph Hearst—who had attacked him in his newspapers—from becoming either governor or senator.

In the center of the square stands Lorenzo Pace's *Triumph of the Human Spirit* (2000), a 50-ft black granite sculpture inspired by the antelope forms of West African art. The monument honors all Africans brought to America, and the boat-shaped base alludes to the "Middle Passage," the transportation of slaves across the Atlantic.

At 40 Foley Square (Pearl and Worth Sts) the **Thurgood Marshall United States Courthouse** (1932–6; Cass Gilbert; completed by Cass Gilbert Jr.) was the elder Cass Gilbert's last building, after the US Supreme Court in Washington, D.C., which the two Gilberts also designed. It has a gilded top, like the Municipal Building to its south, and a heroic portico (50-ft Corinthian columns), like the County Courthouse to its north. The building houses the US District Court and the Federal Court of Appeals. In 2003 it was renamed to honor Thurgood Marshall, the first African-American Supreme Court justice, famous for his work on civil rights.

On the northeast corner of Pearl St at Foley Square is the **New York County Courthouse** (1913–27; Guy Lowell), home of the New York State Supreme Court. The grand portico in the Roman Corinthian style is three columns deep and about 100ft wide. The carving in the tympanum above the portico (sculptor Frederick W. Allen) shows *Justice with Courage and Wisdom*. Surmounting the pediment are statues representing *Law* (center) flanked by *Truth* and *Equity*. The niches of the porch shelter two female figures (by Philip Martiny) removed from the Surrogate's Court on Chambers St in 1961 when the City widened the street. The figure with the City's shield and coat of arms (left) is *Authority*, while her companion, *Justice* (right), rests her foot upon a bundle of records.

Inside the **rotunda**, Attilio Pusterla's brightly restored murals (1934–6) illustrate the History of the Law; the panels represent Assyrian and Egyptian, Hebraic and Persian, Greek and Roman, Byzantine and Frankish, English and American civilizations, the last embodied by Washington and Lincoln. Portraits of lawgivers include Hammurabi, Moses, Solomon, Justinian, Blackstone, and John Marshall. (*You must pass through security, but the building is open to the public.*)

GETTING MARRIED "AT CITY HALL"

141 Worth St. Mon–Fri 8:30–3:45; closed legal holidays. Shop. T: 311, cityclerk.nyc.gov. The Manhattan office of the City Clerk, i.e., the Marriage Bureau, where couples tying the knot "at City Hall" take their vows, has been relocated from the Municipal Building to 141 Worth St, across from the New York County Courthouse. One chapel has a photo mural of City Hall, so you can marry "in front of" City Hall. The shop carries Married in New York T-shirts, "emergency" bow ties, and even wedding rings—just in case.

THE COLLECT POND

Until the early 19th century most of Foley Square lay beneath the Collect Pond (from the Dutch *kolch*, a small body of water), a deep (60ft) spring-fed pond draining into the Hudson. On its western side were the marshy Lispenard Meadows. In the 18th century tanners, brewers, and potters settled nearby because water was essential to their trade. Industrial waste poisoned the pond, a primary source of drinking water, and by the end of the 18th century it had become "a very sink and common sewer." Although Pierre L'Enfant proposed draining it and creating a park, his plan went nowhere. The City gained title to the pond in 1791.

Around 1800 the city began filling the pond and draining the meadows. By 1807 dirt and garbage were being dumped, creating a foul-smelling island 12–15ft above the water. In 1809, Canal St was laid out and a sewer built to drain the springs which formerly fed the pond; by 1811 the pond had disappeared altogether. The stench, the sinking land undermined by springs, and the encroachment of trade in nearby streets drove out anyone who could afford to live elsewhere. The area became a slum, inhabited by immigrants, freed slaves, and the poverty-stricken. By 1840, it was notorious for crime, its worst area called Five Points at the intersection of Park, Baxter, and Worth Sts. Houses were rotten and overcrowded, with people living in windowless basements or relegated to "back buildings" hastily erected in dark rear yards by eager landlords.

Today Collect Pond Park (formerly Civil Court Park; *open 8–8*) on Leonard St (*Centre and Lafayette Sts*) occupies part of the 18th-century site of the former pond.

Across from Collect Pond at 100 Centre St (*White St and Hogan Place*) looms the bulk of the **New York City Criminal Courts Building** (1939; Harvey Wiley Corbett), formerly the Manhattan Detention Center for Men but better known as "The Tombs." The name originated with an earlier prison (1838) on the site, which hunkered down in a gloomy hollow so deep that the walls hardly rose above the level of Broadway some hundred yards to the west. Officially known as "The Halls of Justice," it exemplified the Egyptian Revival style, with trapezoidal windows, lotus columns, and emblems of the sun god. "The Tombs" got its name partly because of the funereal associations of the architectural style and partly because of its dismal function. It served as the city jail until 1893, when a second prison, Romanesque Revival in style but still called "The Tombs," replaced it.

EATING AND DRINKING NEAR THE CIVIC CENTER

The Civic Center is not prime dining territory; both Chinatown and Tribeca offer more options and are within walking distance (*for listings, see pp. 103 and 127*). But if you are looking for a bite during the day, you might try the eateries where jurors and government workers go on lunch break—simple places for quick meals.

$ **New Sau Voi**. Just north of Foley Square, this is not a restaurant, but a celebrated Vietnamese sandwich shop that looks more like an overstocked convenience store. You can pick up Asian CDs, cigarettes, ladies' underwear, and Lotto tickets, along with your *banh mi*, stuffed with various pork products and pickled vegetables and doused with fiery *sriracha*. Columbus and Tom Paine parks are nearby for eating your sandwich. Open daily, morning until early evening. Cash only. *101 Lafayette St (Walker St). T: 212 226 8184. Map p. 620, C1.*

$ **Nish Nush**. The name is Hebrew for "snack," and this place serves hummus, falafel, salads, and other vegetarian specialties with Middle Eastern flair. Plenty of options for gluten-free diners, too. Lunch and dinner every day. *88 Reade St (West Broadway and Church St). T: 212 964 1318, nishnushnyc.com. Map p. 620, C2.*

$ **Sole di Capri**. Italian home-style cooking, with good pasta dishes, ample *antipasti*, homey desserts. Lunch and dinner Mon–Sat; closed Sun. Cash only. *165 Church St (Reade and Chambers Sts). T: 212 513 1113, soledicapriny.com. Map p. 620, C2.*

The Architecture of New York City

by Francis Morrone

New York's architecture, from earliest Dutch days to the beginning of the 19th century, wore the unaffected look of a vernacular evolved in accord with the basic needs of rugged colonial life and—before electricity or gaslight—the natural rhythms of the day. But it also evolved in accord with the sense of rightness of the ordinary builder, his matter-of-fact taste and pride in the thing well made, attaining an affectless handsomeness and comeliness that appeals to us no less today than it did to the man or woman of the 17th or 18th centuries.

Our earliest extant buildings are the very few that date from the period of New Netherland, a colony of the Dutch West India Company, and these are outside Manhattan. In Brooklyn, the **Pieter Claesen Wyckoff house** (5816 Clarendon Rd; *wyckoffmuseum.org*) has a part going back to 1652, near to the earliest settlement of Brooklyn's interior; additions to the house date to 1740 and 1820. Here we see the classic Dutch farmhouse style, with the distinctive gambrel roof, overhanging eaves, and clapboard walls. What's missing is the surrounding farmland. The oldest part of the **John Bowne house** (*see p. 523*) dates to 1661 with additions made in 1680, 1696, and c. 1830. Flushing, then a town and now part of the Borough of Queens, was a center of Quaker life in the Dutch period. The **Flushing Friends' Meeting House** dates to 1694, with an addition in 1716–19, making it the oldest house of worship in continuous use in New York City today (*see p. 523*). Note the date, however: by 1694, the Dutch had long ceased to rule a place now called New York, so named when in 1664 New Netherland passed to James, Duke of York and Albany and brother of King Charles II of England.

The new British colonial administration of 1664 chose to respect all Dutch property rights, with the result that few of the Dutch left. That is why most of what we regard as "Dutch colonial" among New York's very old buildings is actually from the British colonial period, which lasted until 1783. An example is the **Wyckoff-Bennett house** at 1669 East 22nd St in Sheepshead Bay, Brooklyn, built c. 1766. From the **Dyckman house** (c. 1785), on Broadway at 204th St in Upper Manhattan (*see p. 465*), we see the persistence of Dutch ways even after America gained its independence. Both the Wyckoff-Bennett and the Dyckman are classic Dutch farmhouses.

THE BRITISH COLONIAL PERIOD (1664–1783)

On Staten Island, on Hylan Boulevard in the Tottenville section, **Bentley Manor**, built by Christopher Billopp, a captain in the Royal Navy, in c. 1675 represents the earliest appearance of distinctively British, as opposed to Dutch, houses in the present bounds of New York City. A simple, handsome house, with rhythmically patterned multi-pane windows, it is built of local fieldstone, unlike the clapboarded Dutch dwellings, and is a colonial variation on the Christopher Wren house type from the time of Charles II. (It is also known as "Conference House," as the site of ill-fated negotiations among American and British representatives in 1776; *see pp. 539–40*).

A city house of the Wren type is **Fraunces Tavern** (54 Pearl St; *map p. 620, C4*). This is a speculative reconstruction from 1904–7 of the 1719 townhouse of Étienne De Lancey, a Huguenot whose family was the richest in 18th-century New York (but which chose the wrong side in the Revolution). In later years the house was made an inn and a tavern by Samuel Fraunces, and it is there that General Washington bade formal farewell to his officers in 1783. The house then served a variety of uses, was remodeled, decayed, suffered fire damage, and, while never having technically been pulled down, bore, by 1900, not the faintest resemblance to its 18th-century appearance. At that time, the Sons of the Revolution engaged one of their number, the Staten Island architect William Mersereau, to rebuild the house to what it may—or may not—have looked like. It is, in any event, a good approximation of c. 1720 taste.

In the 1760s, on Broadway between Fulton and Vesey Sts, **St. Paul's Chapel** rose to serve Trinity Parish's "uptown" congregants. By the time it was built, James Gibbs, architect of London's St. Martin-in-the-Fields, had replaced Wren as the principal form-giver to British architecture. That is to say, he designed buildings and produced "pattern books" that suggested to local vernacular builders how they might build—or provided them with detailed plans for buildings. Thus we say that St. Paul's is a Georgian church in the Gibbs mode. The exterior walls are of local schist. Inside, the pastel color scheme, the original Waterford chandeliers, and the large Palladian window all testify to the non-sacramental Anglicanism that the later Gothic Revival rebelled against. This could as easily be the setting of a cotillion as of a worship service. In 1789, after George Washington took the oath of office as America's first president, he and his party attended a service at St. Paul's; needless to say, the *Te Deum* in those days was recited not sung—the architecture would suggest as much. (At the 1865 memorial service for President Lincoln at the Gothic Trinity Church on Broadway at Wall St, the *Te Deum* was sung.)

The so-called **Morris-Jumel Mansion** is a country house on 160th St at Edgecombe Ave in Harlem. In 1765, when the original house was built, the countryside around here possessed all the sylvan majesty we still experience north of the city in the lower Hudson River valley. The estate's grounds stretched all the way from the Harlem to the Hudson rivers. An Englishman, Roger Morris, built the house; like the De Lanceys, he and his family fled New York at the end of the Revolution. Later, Stephen Jumel, a wealthy importer, purchased the property. His wife was the notorious former courtesan Eliza Jumel (*see p. 454*). The porch of this lovely clapboarded house takes the same basic form as St. Paul's Chapel: four full free-standing columns supporting a broad triangular pediment. A feature of the house is its abundance of intricate balustrades, an emblem of high class. Today the mansion is a "historic house museum" and well worth visiting.

THE FEDERAL STYLE

A fascinating glimpse of changing tastes may be had at **7 State Street** in Lower Manhattan, where a man named James Watson built his house in 1793. Though the British had ceded New York to the Americans ten years before, most New Yorkers were of British extraction, and to British taste did they cling. The Gibbs-Georgian style of the house was of a type that had remained virtually unchanged in New York for 30 or more years. By 1806, when the house was roughly doubled in size, the new taste had made its way across the Atlantic from Britain to America. Though we chose to call it "Federal," acknowledging it as the dominant style of the new republic, the changes introduced to the Georgian architecture of Gibbs came from the Scots-born brothers Robert and James Adam, architects of Chiswick House, Kenwood House, and other outstanding buildings in England from the late 18th century. The Adams introduced curving forms and delicate notes like slender, attenuated columns. At 7 State St, the later half of the façade curves, like a movement in a waltz, and bears a screen of skinny columns. It's a thrilling house, certainly the best thing of its period remaining in the city (*pictured on p. 44*).

New York is famously a city of row houses (or terrace houses as they are called elsewhere in the English-speaking world), and perhaps the earliest surviving example in the city stands at **18 Bowery**, built in 1785–9 as the home of Edward Mooney (*see p. 120*). The red-brick house is in the Gibbs mode. The lintels are "splayed" and paneled, the doorway is flanked by twin marble columns supporting a tight triangular pediment, and the double-hung windows are of six-over-six sash, which would remain standard in New York for many years. The use of marble rather than brown sandstone (i.e. "brownstone") for trim indicates that this was a grand house in its day. Today the Georgian façade bears Chinese characters—for this is in Chinatown—and they somehow seem not the least out of place.

The city's most famous country house of the years of the young republic is Archibald Gracie's waterside cottage located at the present-day East End Ave at 88th St (*map p. 615, F3*). Gracie began building his house in 1799, at a time when the countryside around there lured the city's mighty families the way the Hamptons does today. The sight that most impressed the Frenchman de Tocqueville when he visited New York in the early 1830s, before writing his classic *Democracy in America*, was that of the grand country houses lining the East River waterfront of Manhattan north of the built-up part of the city. **Gracie Mansion**, as we call it, has a very broad porch and a simple, graceful interplay of shuttered six-over-six windows, slender columns, and "chinoiserie" balustrades that make this a splendid example of the Federal country-house style. It seems built for relaxation and delight. We see in the inland addition, the Susan B. Wagner Wing of 1966, the persistence of architects' interest—amounting to mastery—of the Georgian vocabulary. Gracie Mansion has since Fiorello La Guardia in the 1940s been the official residence of the Mayor of New York. (One mayor, Michael Bloomberg, chose to remain in his own East 70s townhouse, perhaps because he was the first mayor for whom a move to Gracie Mansion did not represent a step up in living standards.)

Gracie Mansion is probably our oldest extant Federal-style country house. Perhaps the oldest townhouse in the Federal style is the **Stuyvesant Fish house** of 1803–4 at 22 Stuyvesant St (*map p. 619, E3*), on what was once the estate of the Dutch West India Company manager Peter Stuyvesant. Here we see the characteristics common to all the Federal-style city houses of New York: Flemish-bond brickwork (alternating headers and stretchers), six-over-six windows, doorway practically flush with the housefront, low stoop, the elegant columns and sidelights, a semi-elliptical fanlight, and dormers. For 30 years the New York house façade changed very little. This was a high-class townhouse in its day, built by Peter Stuyvesant's great-grandson for his daughter, Elizabeth, and son-in-law, Nicholas Fish.

The Stuyvesant-Fish house was completed while New York's finest public building of the period was under construction. **City Hall** (*map p. 620, C2*) was built in 1802–11, and—remarkably considering the growth of the city—remains New York's city hall, where the mayor has his office and the City Council convenes. The exterior architecture we credit to a Frenchman, Joseph François Mangin, and is in the Louis XV style, expertly executed by an architect who obviously had had thorough training. Though today it may appear quaint and diminutive, surrounded as it is by towering skyscrapers, City Hall in 1811 had a majestic presence. It may have been New York's first building meant not merely to be convenient and comely but to excite us with beauty and grandeur—a work of "architecture," so to speak, as opposed to "building." There had, before Mangin, been a French architect in New York, Pierre L'Enfant, whose surviving work includes the altar decorations in St. Paul's Chapel (which is just down Broadway from City Hall). L'Enfant befriended George Washington and won the commission to plan the new capital city on the Potomac River. But Mangin's work really represents the introduction into New York of a French influence that would in time overtake the British influence. Inside City Hall, it's all Federal-style Georgian. The interior architect was the son of an Ulster Scot, John McComb Jr. He and Mangin dominated the architectural profession in the newly independent city. McComb also designed the country house of Alexander Hamilton, now the **Hamilton Grange National Monument** in Harlem (*map p. 612, B1*). The house was completed in 1802; Hamilton was killed by Vice President Aaron Burr (his political rival) only two years later. McComb's City Hall interior is among the most elegant the Federal period has to show us in New York. The "flying staircase," with its sweeping curves and no visible means of support, rising up through a splendid rotunda, is pure Adamesque exuberance, and one of the loveliest things in New York.

A fine institutional building in the Federal style is the **former Roman Catholic Orphan Asylum** (32 Prince St; *map p. 619, D4*) of 1825–6, established by the American Sisters of Charity. The doorway of this building, as with so many Federal-style buildings, bears special mention, with its typically elegant, slender columns, sidelights, and arched fanlight. Each style of architecture through the ages seems to do one thing better than any other, and the Federal had mastery of the doorway treatment, a simple and lovely arrangement that no one thought superfluous even in so humble a building as an orphanage.

Few buildings until the late 1820s deviated from Federal orthodoxy. And it is not surprising that the style should have had such staying power—or that it would be revived (along with other Georgian styles) in the late 19th and throughout the 20th centuries. In 1899, New York's most important architecture critic, Montgomery Schuyler, would say of the early 19th-century Federal-style houses of Manhattan that they were "the most respectable and artistic pattern of habitation New York has ever known."

One rather remarkable deviation occurred in 1809–15 when Mangin designed the city's first Roman Catholic cathedral. **St. Patrick's Old Cathedral** (so-called nowadays to distinguish it from the later, vastly larger St. Patrick's on Fifth Ave) stands on Mott St right across Prince St from the former Orphan Asylum, with which it was associated. Mangin, daringly for the time, chose a Gothic design, several decades before the mature Gothic Revival set in. Truth be told, Mangin's Gothic was—albeit intriguing—picturesquely awkward, and though the church we see today bears the appearance of a substantial rebuilding that occurred following an 1860s fire, the Mott St façade nevertheless retains its striking strangeness. This is not the Gothic that would later devour the 19th century.

THE GREEK REVIVAL

When a style finally overtook the Federal it was the Greek Revival, which though it bore superficial similarities to the Federal (they both may be called "Neoclassical"), nonetheless gave expression to a city that by 1830 or so had become a significantly different place from the city of Federal days. Projects undertaken by a great New York mayor and governor, DeWitt Clinton, affected forever the appearance—and the architectural pretensions—of the city. In 1811, Clinton's appointed commissioners issued their plan to guide the city's growth northward up Manhattan island. Where, London-style, the city had grown organically in a tangle of often crooked streets, henceforward the entirety of the island not yet developed (roughly north of Houston St) would take form on a topography rigorously denuded of any of its natural features (hills leveled, forests felled, streams and lakes filled, marshes drained) and platted in a rectilinear "gridiron" of north–south avenues and east–west streets divided into uniform lots of (usually) 25ft by 100ft. Federal houses, typically built in small clusters of three or four, diminutive in size and modest in appearance, related well to the short blocks and bending byways of the old city. The new city suggested grander treatments.

Clinton's other city-changing achievement was the **Erie Canal**, which opened in 1825. At 363 miles in length it more than doubled the length of the longest canal yet built, and may have been the largest public-works project undertaken since ancient times. Certainly the world was startled to see what America (in fact, what New York) was capable of. By linking New York Harbor via the Hudson River to the Great Lakes, and the rich agricultural lands of the American interior, the canal ensured that New York's port would for more than a century be the nation's most important. Before the canal New York had at most handled nine percent of the nation's exports. By 1860, that number had risen to more than 60 percent. The canal may be said more than anything to have made inevitable New York's rise to commercial pre-eminence in America. With that pre-eminence came breathtaking growth and the historic churn of New York architecture, the constant tearing down and building up of the city, its relentless growth northward, then its doubling back and reaching into the sky as no city had done—or would, for some time, do or dare to do.

The Greek Revival buildings of New York speak to us of Erie Canal days, of a city's lofty aspirations, and of the values of an increasingly self-confident people. Grecian forms had in fact entered New York architecture in the 1790s following publication of James Stuart and Nicholas Revett's seminal *Antiquities of Athens*. The high **tower added to St. Paul's Chapel** in 1793 adapted its design from the Choragic Monument of Lysicrates, as drawn by Stuart (it is perhaps the oldest example of "Grecian" architecture in New York). Yet it was Roman forms—or at least the arch, the dome, the curving bulge, and the treatment of the orders as ornamental appurtenances without pretense of structural purpose—that prevailed in the Federal style. At 29 East 4th St stands a remarkable townhouse (now the outstanding **Merchant's House Museum**; *see p. 167*) that demonstrates how the Federal transitioned to the Grecian (and how marvelously they could be combined). On the outside the house (built in 1831–2) is largely Federal, though the elaborate iron fence bears Grecian motifs and also signals a change in the nature of New York residences toward an increasing separation of public and private realms. Most Federal houses were built in a time when transportation was primitive. There was as yet not such a thing as "suburban" living. People worked very close to where they lived—often, for example in the artisans' quarter that grew up west of Broadway where the World Trade Center would later rise, in the same or adjacent buildings. An extant example is the marvelous Federal-style frame house at **17 Grove Street** (*map p. 618, C4*), where a sashmaker named William Hyde lived and, in the adjacent wooden structure, practiced his craft. But the Erie Canal era saw the introduction first of the horse-drawn omnibus—which rode rockily on the block-paved streets of the city—and then of the revolutionary horsecar, or horse-drawn street railway, in which the cars' wheels were fitted onto iron rails. These provided smooth, swift transport and placed less stress on the horses. Thus New Yorkers clamored to settle the newly gridded uptown streets—in so doing to create ever greater distance between homes and workplaces.

This in turn created or fed a cult of domesticity that is often expressed in our Greek Revival row houses, with their elaborate passages from sidewalk to inside the house. Look for example at the houses at **1–13 Washington Square North** (*map p. 619, D3*), a celebrated row erected in 1832–3 shortly after the former paupers' burial ground the houses face had been remodeled into a public square, from which time the area boomed. First there is the iron fence, as at the Merchants' House Museum, with anthemion-crested posts and fretwork such as we see painted on Greek vases. The fence opens to an areaway prior to the first step of the stoop. The stoop itself is a wide thing, with thickly balustraded railings terminating in stout stone blocks. At the top of the stoop a landing leads to full fluted columns—chubby ones, not the attenuated things we see in Federal houses. What's most important is that the Grecian columns are pushed out from the front of the house—not set into it, as in the Federal style. Here the columns rise up to a full, heavy entablature that creates a second, sheltered landing past which we finally come to the front door. Four distinct parts make up this passage, which involves opening a gate and standing on a roofed landing before ever going inside. In Federal houses, on the other hand, like the typical examples from the 1820s at **4–10 Grove Street**, you could often in a single bound (sometimes a single step) make your way from inside the house to the sidewalk. With the Greek Revival this was no longer so.

The term "Greek Revival" conjures images not of row houses but of temple-front structures. What we see on Washington Square North, or more typically in the **"Cushman Row"** on 20th St between Ninth and Tenth Aves (*map p. 618, B2*), where sandstone pilasters replace marble columns, is an adaptation of the temple front to a building type—the 25-ft-wide urban house—that would at first seem ill-suited to such a treatment. In New York the architect most responsible for the spread of Grecian taste was Minard Lafever. No Greek Revival houses he may have designed in Manhattan remain. But many of the thousands of extant houses in that style were drawn by builders from the several "pattern books" through which Lafever spread the Grecian gospel. When the English-born architect Calvert Vaux, who co-designed Central Park, called Lafever the "Sir Christopher Wren of America," it was because Lafever, like Wren, developed house types that were readily reproducible by humble builders, yet that also helped to form a congenial style for city streets.

Of Lafever's designs outside Manhattan, we have the outstanding examples (at last authoritatively attributed to Lafever by the architectural historian Barnett Shepherd) at **Snug Harbor** on Staten Island (*see p. 535*). Lafever's buildings form a grand ensemble of fully temple-fronted marble structures. Other survivors of the city's Greek temples include the former Custom House of 1833–42, now the **Federal Hall National Memorial**, on Wall St (*map p. 620, C3*). This was designed by the outstanding architects of the time, Alexander Jackson Davis (who was Herman Melville's friend), Ithiel Town, and Samuel Thompson, with a stunning rotunda we may credit largely to the sculptor John Frazee.

Across the river, Brooklyn was incorporated as a city in the midst of the Grecian era; consequently, Brooklyn City Hall (now **Borough Hall**; *map p. 622, C3*) bears the temple-front style. It was built in 1845–8 though derives from designs of fully a decade earlier. At Snug Harbor, on Wall St, and in Brooklyn the buildings are imposing (which is the point of the temple front) and austere; note the absence of ornamentation. Especially striking in each example is the broad triangular pediment supported by the free-standing colonnades. The pediments have raked cornices, which in Classical architecture served as frames. The ancient Greeks themselves filled in these frames with elaborate figure sculpture. Yet the Americans left them bare. It's like going into a gallery and seeing empty picture frames adorning the walls. Why is this? Partly it's to do with the romanticism of the times, expressed not only in nature-worship but in worship of Antiquity, which itself was accessed by intellectuals through the cult of ruins. It may be said that we patterned our Grecian buildings less after how the Greeks built, than by how nature decayed the Greek buildings, stripping them of their color and ornamentation, leaving them as somber totems of ancient civilizations. Then again, we see in all the arts and crafts of early America a striving after humbler forms than those to be found in European work—our fabled "republican simplicity," which found a profound outlet in our "Grecian" architecture, not to mention in the Greek dresses our ladies wore to garden parties, the fretted patterns on our ceramic dishes, and countless town names (Athens, Georgia; Syracuse, New York).

THE GOTHIC REVIVAL AND MEDIEVALISM

The Romantic era gave New York not only its cult-of-ruins Greek architecture but also the passionate Medievalism we imported from Britain. Here again Mr. Lafever led the way. Mangin valiantly if strangely essayed the Gothic in his St. Patrick's Old Cathedral (*see p. 12 above*). But that is really an eccentric work, a stylistic outlier. The real Gothic Revival doesn't start up until the late 1830s. This is the "archaeologically correct" Gothic—sometimes serving deep liturgical strivings—that Augustus Pugin developed in Britain. An Englishman, Richard Upjohn, is generally credited with introducing the style in New York, at **Trinity Church** (1839–46) on Broadway. However, Lafever designed the Washington Square Reformed Church, on the east side of Washington Square, before Upjohn designed Trinity; and the Lafever building, not the Upjohn, may be said to have inaugurated the mode that with variations persisted well into the 20th century. Alas, Lafever's church is gone, but we can see his approach to Gothic if we go to Brooklyn Heights (*map p. 476*). **Holy Trinity Church**, on the corner of Clinton and Montague Sts, was built in 1844–7, and his First Unitarian Church (**Church of the Saviour**), on Pierrepont St at Monroe Place, in 1842–4. Holy Trinity's English Gothic has a lacy exuberance that we also find in the Gothic designs of James Renwick Jr., such as **Grace Church** in Manhattan, completed in 1846 (*map p. 619, D3*). Both Lafever and Renwick were aesthetes, interested in Gothic as one among several historical styles from which to choose for its appropriateness to a given project. Upjohn, by contrast, belonged to the New York Ecclesiological Society, which sought to import the values of Britain's Cambridge Camden Society, which promoted the Gothic as part of a broad-based reform movement seeking to restore the Catholic liturgy to the Anglican (or, in America, Episcopalian) rite. The Ecclesiologists, whose hero was Pugin, were dedicated churchmen. When Upjohn designed a church—an outstanding example besides Trinity is **Grace Episcopal Church** (1847–9) on Grace Court at Hicks St in Brooklyn Heights (*map p. 476*)—he wished for every stone, every rib of the ceiling vault, every piece of glass to play its proper and approved role in the liturgical pageant of the Mass. Renwick and Lafever merely acceded to clients' wishes and Lafever, especially, helped spread the Gothic to denominations that found it beautiful but had no historical claim on it or liturgical interest in it—after all, the Unitarians of Brooklyn Heights did not debate transubstantiation!

We call the 1840s and 1850s the period of the "Early Gothic Revival." The Gothic, in many variations drawn from many sources, remained a dominant note thereafter in New York architecture. French and Italian Gothic influences soon joined the English. Renwick's **former St. Ann's Episcopal Church** (1867–9) at Clinton and Livingston Sts in Brooklyn Heights (*map p. 476*) is an outstanding example of what was often called—much to the consternation of the man for whom it was named—"Ruskinian Gothic." The English writer John Ruskin, whose magnificent prose transfixed Victorian readers in both Britain and America, had written, in his *Stones of Venice* and other works, of the richly ornamented, polychromatic Gothic of Venice, suggesting that no building in the world merited emulation more than the Doge's Palace of the 14th century. Many architects, each in his own way, employed the style, or at least the tics, of the 14th-century Venetians so admired by Ruskin, whose Medievalism replaced Pugin's. This was an idealized Medievalism to be sure. The chivalric knight, the pious peasant, and the monastery were storybook antidotes to the increasing harshness of life in the industrialized cities of the 19th century, with their pollution, appalling labor and housing conditions, constant epidemics of deadly diseases, and massive infestations of vermin. Romanticism was in general a looking back or away from these pestilential conditions, in hopes of forgetting or remedying them—and in hopes of reclaiming or retaining noble values (however spurious) that the present age had no use for (piety, for example). Ruskin's Medievalism became a full-on political movement that eventuated in, among other things, the creation of Britain's Labour Party. So all of that is implicit when you look at the 1870s and 1880s buildings with their pointed windows, spiky towers, studied asymmetry, zebra stripes, exotic masonry, and so on.

This strain of Medievalism extended to all types of buildings, not just churches. Two Englishmen, Calvert Vaux and Frederick Clarke Withers, both followers of Ruskin, designed the Third Judicial District Courthouse (also known as Jefferson Market Courthouse, now **Jefferson Market Library**) of 1874–7 on Sixth Ave at 10th St in Greenwich Village (*map p. 618, C3*). It has polychromatic masonry, a picturesque skyline with high conical towers, stained glass, and relief sculptures of scenes from *A Midsummer Night's Dream*. At the time, it was voted by architects as one of their most admired buildings in America; a generation later, a reaction set in against "Victoriana," and such buildings as this were demolished in waves. The just-a-bit-over-the-top, exuberantly picturesque Gothic romanticism of Jefferson Market Courthouse is—like London's St. Pancras Station—very much the sort of thing we imagine when we think "Victorian architecture." A private house in the same vein is the one on the south side of Gramercy Park, just west of Irving Place (now the **National Arts Club**; *map p. 619, D2*), remodeled from two ordinary brownstone row houses in 1881–4 by Calvert Vaux and George K. Radford for New York governor Samuel J. Tilden. A commercial building in this style, and perhaps the city's finest work in "Venetian Gothic," is the modestly scaled building at **8 Thomas Street** (1875–6; *map p. 620, C2*), designed by a very talented architect, J. Morgan Slade, who died tragically young.

The prestige of the Gothic may be inferred from its use in three of the city's greatest building endeavors of the 1860s and 1870s: St. Patrick's Cathedral, Central Park, and the Brooklyn Bridge. **St. Patrick's**, on Fifth Ave between 50th and 51st Sts (*map p. 617, D3*), was built between 1858 and 1879, with its fantastic twin towers coming in 1888. Renwick (an Episcopalian) designed this replacement for the old cathedral downtown, and turned to a combination of English and French Gothic forms for the exterior, which is in white marble from Westchester County, just north of the city. His lacy ornamentation, exuberant free-standing gables like those found in France, the soaring towers (which taper more dramatically than any cathedral towers of the Middle Ages), made this perhaps the most extraordinary building that had been erected in New York up to its time. Renwick was forced into many compromises, for he had to squeeze the church into a single lot of the Manhattan grid, and his ingenious adaptations made this one of the most original Gothic buildings of the 19th century. The interior is dazzling as well, patterned partly after Westminster Abbey and York Minster; alas, it is too brightly and harshly illuminated most of the time. The enamel-painted aisle windows, in a Renaissance classical style by Lorin of Chartres, are perhaps the finest of their kind in the city.

The **Brooklyn Bridge** was built in 1870–83. The original design was by a German-born engineer—actually, a great polymath—named John Roebling, who pioneered the manufacture of steel wire cable and already had to his credit the longest suspension bridge in the world, the Cincinnati–Covington Bridge across the Ohio River. The new bridge would have a central span half as long again. As the longest suspension bridge ever built, and the greatest work of steel construction ever undertaken—and not least for its haunting beauty—the bridge outclassed even the Erie Canal as a monument of New Yorkers' ingenuity and ambition, and the world's attention was riveted. Note that in the design of the great granite towers of the bridge, at the time the most skyline-dominating structures in New York, Roebling chose the pointed arch of the Gothic (*see illustration on p. 469*).

Central Park grew out of a public parks movement led by the newspaper editor and poet William Cullen Bryant and the influential landscape gardener Andrew Jackson Downing. Their devotees included a journalist named Frederick Law Olmsted, who visited England in 1850 and was deeply impressed by Sir Joseph Paxton's Birkenhead Park in Liverpool. An English devotee of Paxton, the London architect Calvert Vaux emigrated to America to work in Downing's firm. Eventually, Olmsted, who had been hired to superintend the clearing of the land for Central Park, and Vaux, who had taken over Downing's firm following the master's tragic death in a steamboat accident, teamed up on the "Greensward Plan," which won the 1858 competition for the park's design. Here we see the English ideal of *rus in urbe* magnificently transplanted to American soil. Closely related to romantic Medievalism, Central Park embodies the notion that the antidote to the harsh city is to get rid of some of it and make it over into a verdant fairyland of compacted landscapes that could not possibly follow one upon the other in nature itself, but which in the hands of artists might serve to brighten the souls of otherwise benighted denizens of the great, monstrous metropolis. The park also follows the romantic landscape painting of the time, the Hudson River School of Thomas Cole, Frederic Church (one of Ruskin's favorite artists), and others, whose pictures often served as models for the intricately composed vistas of Vaux and Olmsted's park, which has itself rightly been characterized as one of the greatest works of art of the 19th century. Note that nearly all of Vaux's park structures—service buildings, bridges, etc.—are in the Gothic style. An exception would be the flamboyantly Moorish Bethesda Terrace, that Vaux helped to design but that we credit largely to yet another Englishman, the eccentric genius Jacob Wrey Mould (*see p. 316*), a former assistant to the British designer Owen Jones.

A later, highly original strand of American Gothic is represented by a Bostonian influenced by Henry Adams, the American patrician pessimist and lover of the Middle Ages. Ralph Adams Cram was responsible for the reworking in Gothic of the originally Romanesque **Cathedral of St. John the Divine** (1911–41; *map p. 612, B4*), while he and his brilliant partner Bertram Grosvenor Goodhue designed **St. Thomas Church** on Fifth Ave at 53rd St (1905–13; *map p. 617, D3*), its neo-Gothic reredos one of the world's greatest. St. Thomas may well be the finest Gothic building in America. Goodhue also gave New York such masterpieces of "Modern Gothic" (highly original works in a Gothic idiom) as the **Church of the Intercession** (1915, Broadway and 155th St) and the **Church of St. Vincent Ferrer** (1918, Lexington Ave and 66th St; *map p. 617, E1*).

Two things need noting before we go on. The first is that this roster of names—Upjohn, Renwick, Vaux—tells us that the age of the professional architect had dawned in New York. Henceforward, all important buildings would be designed directly by architects, not put up by builders based upon pattern books. Second, the Greek Revival, the Gothic Revival, and the contemporaneous Italian palazzo style brought us the earliest stone-faced buildings. Such works as the former Custom House on Wall St, Grace Church and St. Patrick's Cathedral, and the **A.T. Stewart dry-goods emporium** (built 1845–6 with several later add-ons) on Broadway between Reade and Chambers Sts, which took after the Pall Mall club-house style of Sir Charles Barry, all bore white marble façades. The marble was from local sources, as was the other principal stone that came into use for full façades at this time, the soft sandstone, brown or reddish-brown in color, quarried in New Jersey, New York State, and, especially, Connecticut. Trinity Church wears an earthen coat of New Jersey **brownstone**, which often suited the somber purposes of the Ecclesiologists. The soft stone also suited the speculative developers of the row upon row upon row of houses revetted in it. The red-brick Greek Revival front yielded to the brownstone front when changing fashions in the 1850s dictated richly carved stone ornamentation. The middle class demanded houses with intricately carved console brackets and elaborate window enframements, and such houses could be built rapidly enough to keep pace with the frenetically growing city only if a soft stone could be used—soft making it easier (and cheaper) to quarry, and easier (and cheaper) to carve. Again for ease and cheapness a great deal of the stone was mishandled, with the result that water absorption caused severe scaling of the stone fronts of many New York houses over the years. It is likely that the speculators who built these houses did not foresee that they would be valued and preserved by future generations.

APARTMENT HOUSES

Multiple-unit dwellings first came to New York in the form of "tenements," built for the very poor, especially the Irish and German immigrants who flooded the city in the 1840s and 1850s. At first several families of Irish would cram together in a Federal-style house that had been erected for a single family then abandoned in the northward trek of fashion. Then purpose-built multi-family dwellings came in. For several decades, multi-family dwellings were considered suitable only for the very poor. But in the second half of the 19th century, as the final, complete covering of Manhattan island's gridded streets appeared imminent, apartment houses for the middle and upper classes became an economic necessity.

The first apartment house was the Stuyvesant, on East 18th St between Third Ave and Irving Place, designed by Richard Morris Hunt and built in 1869. Unfortunately, it no longer stands, though several noteworthy examples of "first generation" apartment houses still do survive. The famous **Dakota** was completed in 1884 (72nd St at Central Park West; *map p. 614, B4*). The **Osborne**, at 205 West 57th St (*map p. 616, C2*), was built in 1883-5 (with later additions). Its architect, James E. Ware, also devised the prototype of what we call the "old-law tenement" (*see p. 135*). In 1879, Ware's prototype for a slightly more healthful tenement design was adopted as law by New York City. This coincided with the most extensive wave of tenement construction in the city's history, such that by the turn of the century a majority of New Yorkers resided in old-law tenements, of which block after block remain—the Lower East Side and the west Midtown neighborhood called Hell's Kitchen particularly abound in them.

Before such laws, the only decent tenements were those constructed by philanthropists as "model tenements." Men like Brooklyn's superb Alfred Tredway White, who was born into great wealth and devoted his life to the physical reform of his native city, attempted to show that decent housing for the working class could be built and still yield modest profits. **White's Tower** and **Home Buildings** and **Workingmen's Cottages**, built in 1876-9 on Hicks St between Warren and Baltic Sts in Cobble Hill, Brooklyn (*map p. 622, A4*), and his **Riverside Buildings**, built in 1890 on Columbia Place at Joralemon St in Brooklyn Heights (*map p. 476*), are the city's outstanding examples of model tenements. The architects of both developments, William Field & Son, were, like White, a product of Brooklyn's influential community of Unitarian social reformers. (White incidentally also helped found the splendid Brooklyn Botanic Garden, where there stands a monument to him designed by Daniel Chester French.)

Buildings such as the Dakota, with their generous interior courtyards, electricity, elevators, high-ceilinged rooms, and so on provided not only more amenity than the tenements but often more than single-family row houses. The Upper West Side of Manhattan did not begin to develop in earnest until the 1880s, when the steam-powered elevated railway made the area swiftly accessible to the business centers downtown. From the time of the Dakota onward, the area took shape as perhaps the first apartment-building neighborhood in America. When the Interborough Rapid Transit subway supplemented the Els in 1904, a wave of speculative apartment house construction ensued, and many of the city's most classic and beautiful examples of the type rose in rapid succession. The **Ansonia Hotel** (1899-1904) on Broadway at 73rd St (*map p. 614, B4*) was built by the eccentric developer William Earl Dodge Stokes, who is credited with its flamboyant design together with the French architect Paul Émile Duboy, possibly the first major French architect in the city since the days of Mangin. The Ansonia bears the hallmark lavish ornamentation of the Belle Époque, though it is well to note that at 17 stories it would have been by a monstrous margin the tallest building in Paris at the time. Arguably the most beautiful of the Upper West Side buildings is the **Apthorp** (1906-8), on Broadway at West 78th St (*map p. 614, A4*). Designed by Clinton & Russell, the full-block building has a magnificent vaulted entryway on

Broadway leading to a large interior courtyard. The entry is designed as though it were a triumphal arch, with figure sculpture as fine as any in the world. With most apartment buildings we do not know the names of the sculptors who embellished them with work unvaryingly of the highest refinement. We only know that the anonymous craftsmen of this era were often Italian immigrants, many descended from long lines of carvers—thus establishing the direct link between the Renaissance in Italy and the "American Renaissance" of the late 19th and early 20th centuries.

THE ROMANESQUE REVIVAL

We must step back for a moment at this point and round out the story of Victorian architecture in New York before looking at the revolution in taste of the late 19th century. Besides the Gothic, the earlier medieval style of the Romanesque also gained traction. Its earliest instances include Richard Upjohn's Church of the Pilgrims on Henry St at Remsen St in Brooklyn Heights (1844–6; now **Our Lady of Lebanon Church**; *map p. 476*), where the Congregationalist parishioners wished a simpler style than the Gothic of the Anglo-Catholic revival, with which they wanted nothing to do. In Manhattan, the Astor Library at 425 Lafayette St (now **Joseph Papp Public Theater**; *map p. 619, D3*) was built in three phases (southern wing 1849–53, central section 1856–69, northern wing 1879–81) with each part perfectly mated to what came before, all in the popular German Romanesque style, or Rundbogenstil (round-arched style). Italian Catholics, who came to New York in large numbers toward the end of the 19th century, found a cool welcome at best in the Irish churches of the city, so, in forming their own parishes, rejected the dominant Gothic of the Irish in favor of an Italian Romanesque such as we see at the **Church of St. Anthony of Padua**, designed by Arthur Crooks and built in 1888 on Sullivan St between Prince and Houston Sts in the southern, once heavily Italian, part of Greenwich Village (*map p. 618, C4*). The inspiration for this and so many other Italian churches in New York was the 13th-century San Francesco, in Assisi.

But America made the Romanesque its own when in the 1870s and 1880s the architect Henry Hobson Richardson, who was based in New York in his early career but grew to prominence after moving to Boston, worked his own refinements on French Romanesque models and created the "Richardsonian Romanesque," which dominated American architecture of the 1880s and early 1890s. Only minor early works by Richardson survive in New York City, but his acolytes abounded here, especially in Brooklyn, which experienced rapid growth during the heyday of the Richardsonian style. Two architects merit note. Frank Freeman designed masterpieces of the Richardsonian Romanesque (sometimes borrowing elements directly from Richardson designs, both built and unbuilt). Examples are the **mansion of the industrialist Herman Behr**, on Pierrepont St at Henry St in Brooklyn Heights (1888–90; *map p. 476*), and the **former Brooklyn Fire Headquarters** (1892) at 365 Jay St in downtown Brooklyn (*map p. 622, C3*). Between 1887 and 1892 C.P.H. Gilbert designed 20 of the 46 houses on the exquisite one-block-long **Montgomery Place**, between Prospect Park West and Eighth Ave, in Park Slope, Brooklyn, all in inventive variations of the Richardsonian Romanesque. The house at 46 Montgomery Place, in particular, is a symphony in elegant, golden Roman brick. Hallmarks of this style include walls of rough masonry blocks, often sensuously contrasting with elegant brickwork and delicate terra cotta adornments. This was the style dominant in American cities during the era of westward expansion depicted in most of Hollywood's Westerns, which evoke similarly to the architecture a combination of raw, urgent power and the civilizing grace notes of refined ornamentation.

One of the first New York architects to use ornamental terra cotta was George B. Post in his **Brooklyn Historical Society** of 1878–81 (*see illustration on p. 479*). Because a single mold could yield literally countless instances of a particular ornamental form, terra cotta answered to its era's penchant for lavish embellishment, which would have been impossible to achieve on such a wide scale if all the ornament had to be carved. Another—and earlier—form of molded ornamentation was cast iron, from which whole building façades were made beginning in the 1840s and 1850s. One of the city's earliest extant examples is the beautiful **Haughwout Building** in SoHo (*map p. 620, C1*). That building also had the first steam-powered passenger elevator (1857) in the world. SoHo has America's largest concentration of cast-iron façades (*see p. 109*).

THE BEAUX-ARTS ERA AND GEORGIAN REVIVAL
The Richardsonian style yielded to a new Classicism that marked a definitive end to Victorian experimentation and historical Romanticism. The first American to attend the École des Beaux-Arts in Paris was Richard Morris Hunt, already mentioned as the designer of the city's first apartment house—a building type he was familiar with from the eight years he lived in the Paris of Louis-Philippe. In New York Hunt established a practice where his employees were also pupils, who received training as though in a Beaux-Arts atelier in Paris. George B. Post, for example, apprenticed in Hunt's atelier. Hunt himself helped lead the charge to the new Classicism, and was heavily involved in the World's Columbian Exposition in 1893 in Chicago, where the grand-manner Classicism of the white buildings, arranged harmoniously along broad boulevards and piazzas and lagoons, provided the public with a vision of beautiful cities that was very different from the *rus in urbe* of Central Park. For the next half century or so America's native Jeffersonian anti-urbanism yielded to an urban grandeur that made of New York a classical city to compare with the likes of St. Petersburg, Vienna, Dublin—and even Paris.

Yet it was not Hunt so much as a firm called McKim, Mead & White, formed in the late 1870s, that led the way. White and his partner Charles Follen McKim met when they both worked for Henry Hobson Richardson. Richardson had, like Hunt, been to the École des Beaux-Arts, as had McKim; White, for financial reasons, was unable to attend. Their first New York masterpiece (begun in 1882) was the ultra-refined Italian Renaissance-style **Villard Houses**, grouped around a courtyard on Madison Ave between 50th and 51st Sts (*map p. 617, D3*). Joseph M. Wells, a brilliant designer in the firm (he died very young and never became a partner), was in charge of the exteriors. It is almost inconceivable that this scrupulously sober ensemble followed by only five years the drunken gallimaufry of Vaux and Withers's Jefferson Market Courthouse. Change was in the air.

The Villard Houses were faced in brownstone, which was *de rigueur* at the time. The stone is expertly handled and a joy to behold. Nonetheless, Wells had specified Indiana limestone, a light-colored metamorphic rock that young architects had begun to think suited the brilliant skies of New York—a city on Rome's southern latitude that had always been treated as though it were on London's northern latitude. The client, Henry Villard, overruled Wells, and went with the conventional material. Soon, however, McKim, Mead & White would lead the way out of the brownstone era. Stanford White excelled at the combination of golden Roman brick with light-colored terra cotta to achieve sumptuous effects even on tight budgets, as at **Judson Memorial Baptist Church** (1888–93, with later additions) on Washington Square South (*map p. 619, D4*), and the **clubhouse of the Century Association** (1889–91) at 7 West 43rd St. For his **Metropolitan Club** at 1 East 60th St (1891–4) White turned to gleaming marble. The Italian Renaissance supplied McKim, Mead & White's models, though the firm adapted them in often strikingly original ways, not least in the manner of applying the models to new building types like the tall apartment house or railroad station.

We call this the Beaux-Arts era because Parisian values ruled. Many of the architects had not only studied in France, as we have seen, but were intense Francophiles. Yet the British influence was not thrown off so easily. McKim and White were in the vanguard of the rediscovery and reappraisal of America's colonial architecture, and they largely begat the Georgian Revival that has, since the 1890s, not shown any signs of going away. It may in the end be the most enduring contribution of this firm to American architecture. An outstanding New York example of McKim's work in that vein is his house for James J. Goodwin, built 1896–8 at **11–13 West 54th St**. An example by White would be the former Colony Club (now **American Academy of Dramatic Arts**) of 1904–8, at 120 Madison Ave (*map p. 619, D1*).

For many years McKim, Mead & White was without question New York's most prestigious—and busy—architectural firm. Other leading Beaux-Arts firms included Carrère & Hastings, who designed the **New York Public Library** (1898–1911) on Fifth Ave at 42nd St, arguably the city's greatest building (*see p. 241*); Warren & Wetmore, architects of **Grand Central Terminal** (1903–13, in association with Reed & Stem) on 42nd St at Park Ave; and York & Sawyer, specialists in awe-inspiring banking interiors such as that of the **Central Savings Bank** (1926–8) on Broadway at 73rd St (*map p. 614, B4*). The outstanding architect in this vein was the Philadelphian Horace Trumbauer, whose sometime partner in design, Julian Abele, was the first African-American to attend the École des Beaux-Arts. They gave us the superb **mansion of James B. Duke** on 78th St at Fifth Ave (*see p. 337*), a limestone beauty of such refined proportion that it claims few rivals among French classical houses—even in France.

We often—and, often, not incorrectly—associate the Beaux-Arts with lavish display, whether in civic buildings (Cass Gilbert's **United States Custom House**, 1899–1907, on the south side of Bowling Green; *map p. 620, C4*) or rich men's mansions (Carrère & Hastings's house for Henry Clay Frick, 1913–14, later remodeled into the **Frick Collection**, on 70th St at Fifth Ave; *map p. 617, D1*). The Georgian Revival, on the other hand, shows a quiet, refined sensibility. In 1897 Edith Wharton and her architect friend Ogden Codman Jr. wrote *The Decoration of Houses*. It influenced a decorator named Elsie de Wolfe (later Lady Mendl), whom Stanford White hired to create the interiors for the Colony Club. Not one for mahogany and gilt, she used light-painted walls, chintz fabric, and trellises to create airy, almost whimsical rooms. The new spirit announced by the limestone architecture of the 1890s was becoming ever brighter, lighter, and more carefree, unshackled by opulent display, made for living. The period of 1910 to 1925 may be the most delicious in all the architectural history of New York. It is also the period of female emancipation (and the end of constraining clothing for women), of "free love" and lifestyle experiments to which the 1960s are a mere footnote, and of the birth of a new popular music in New York—itself the perfect accompaniment to the new architecture.

THE AGE OF "GENTRIFICATION"

When Manhattan island filled up and residences began to be stacked one on top of another, a concomitant phenomenon was the first-ever return of the bourgeoisie to their abandoned downtown homelands, which had in the interim become working-class areas. Not until a British sociologist coined a word—"gentrification"—in 1964 did we have a name for the phenomenon, but this was the golden age of it. In 1909 Frederick J. Sterner, a prominent architect from Denver, completely remodeled an 1840s Greek Revival brick row house at **139 East 19th Street**, a block south of Gramercy Park (*map p. 619, D2*). He removed the, in his word, pompous stoop; stuccoed over the brick façade and painted it a cream color; installed red roof tiles; gave the new basement entrance art-pottery accents; gutted and remade the interior with wood paneling in a linenfold design; and made the small rear yard into a fantasy of the Tuscan countryside. At around the same time, artists were discovering the joys of living and working in stables (or mews houses), as at **MacDougal Alley**, off MacDougal St half a block south of 8th St in Greenwich Village (*map p. 618, C3*). It was in MacDougal Alley that Gertrude Vanderbilt Whitney, who had grown up in a 137-room house on 57th St (where Bergdorf-Goodman now stands), kept a tiny house and sculpture studio (*see p. 203*) and founded the Whitney Museum of American Art. The First World War gave further momentum to the new spirit as New York society ladies such as Anne Vanderbilt and Anne Morgan, whose Francophilia led them to volunteer their services in French military hospitals during the war and who as a consequence had witnessed up-close the most horrible carnage, found that after the war the old opulent way of life was no longer what they wanted. They and other ladies, including Elsie de Wolfe, hired Mott B. Schmidt, a young architect of the Georgian Revival whose wife was a decorator in Miss de Wolfe's firm, to design an ensemble of simple but elegant houses in an East Side slum called **Sutton Place** (*map p. 617, F2*), where the ladies were, for a few years at least, surrounded by tenements and gritty factories. Around the same time, the British Garden City ideal promoted by Ebenezer Howard influenced the design of an exquisite planned community in the old town of Newtown, which had become part of the Borough of Queens. Called **Forest Hills Gardens** (*map p. 609, C3*) and masterfully laid out by Frederick Law Olmsted Jr. (a more talented designer than his famous father), it and similar developments in New York and elsewhere caused the historian John Lukacs to label this the period of the "breeze of beauty" in American life.

THE AGE OF THE SKYSCRAPER

While the domestic ideal became ever more relaxed and intimate, on the commercial side everything was about size in New York. We'd begun putting elevators (first steam-powered, then hydraulic, then electrical) in buildings in the late 1850s. First with iron then with steel framing we eventually created building frameworks that relieved external walls of any load-bearing function, rendering them "curtain walls" draped over steel frames. And the New York skyline shot up in the air. We had a quick succession of "tallest buildings in the world": the Park Row Building in 1899, the Singer Building (since demolished) in 1908, the Metropolitan Life Insurance Company Tower in 1909, the Woolworth Building in 1913, the Bank of the Manhattan Building in 1929, the Chrysler Building in 1930, and the Empire State Building in 1931. By the First World War, New York had so many really tall buildings that the city was visually unique; perhaps not since medieval Constantinople had any city's appearance so awed the first-time visitor. After the war, the city took on a global prominence—in finance, industry, shipping, and selling—commensurate with its growing scale.

As had earlier happened with tenements, a lack of regulation in the design of tall buildings led to overbuilding of lots. A number of tall buildings in a row cast whole sections of the city into darkness. In 1916 the city adopted the first comprehensive municipal zoning legislation in American history. Among the code's provisions was the requirement that tall buildings step back at prescribed intervals to allow sunlight to penetrate to the streets. From 1916 until 1961, when the code was changed, all of New York's tall buildings bore the stepped silhouette that architects soon came to see not as an aesthetic hindrance but its opposite, as allowing for plays of volumes and indentations that resulted in dramatic forms. A Beaux-Arts firm like Warren & Wetmore expertly applied classical detailing to the stepped-back skyscraper with their brilliant New York Central Building (later **Helmsley Building**) of 1927–9, at 230 Park Ave (*map p. 617, D3*). But by this time the classical skyscraper had begun to yield to modern forms, at first in the guise of Art Deco, though that term (like "gentrification") would not be coined until the 1960s. Ralph Walker, a highly individualistic architect with the firm of McKenzie, Voorhees & Gmelin (later Voorhees, Gmelin & Walker), designed the ex-New York Telephone Company Building (1923–7) on West St at Vesey St (now the **Verizon Building**; *map p. 620, B3*). He applied to the stepped-back skyscraper the fashionable modern ornamentation that originated in France and was promoted by the French government at the 1925 Exposition Internationale des Arts Décoratifs et Industriels in Paris. The result was a kind of "jazz architecture," what we later would call the Art Deco skyscraper. At **One Wall Street** Walker went further, experimenting with the limestone "skin" of the building, folding it in wavy patterns that recalled the linenfold paneling Frederick J. Sterner designed for the interior of his house at **139 East 19th Street** in 1909—and that foreshadowed the textile-like curtain walls of such Frank Gehry buildings as the nearby **8 Spruce Street**.

Ely Jacques Kahn designed the **Bricken Casino Building** (1931) on Broadway at 39th St with a kind of bias-cut pattern to the stepped-back massing, recalling a Vionnet gown. The skyscraper had entered a period of high inventiveness. The most stunning of all was the **Chrysler Building** (42nd St at Lexington Ave; *map p. 617, E4*), the tallest in the world in 1930, topped off by a stylized version of a Mycenaean helmet. As unlike anything else in architecture as the top of the Chrysler Building was, so the same could be said of the building's lobby, an eccentric triangular space with a rich palette of red Moroccan marble, Mexican onyx, Siena marble, and elaborate wood marquetry. The **Empire State Building** (Fifth Ave at 34th St; *map p. 618, C1*), 202ft higher than the Chrysler, was completed in 1931, altogether in a more sober style but still characteristically Art Deco, again with the signature use of varied marbles in the lobby, and with a distinctive crown meant at first to be used as a dirigible mooring mast. Throughout the 1930s, John D. Rockefeller Jr. built **Rockefeller Center** on the Midtown site bounded roughly by 48th and 51st Sts and Fifth and Sixth Avenues (*see p. 274*). The ensemble originally comprised 13 buildings (later extended) grouped harmoniously around formally designed open spaces, one of them being the dramatic Promenade leading west from Fifth Ave with the tall Comcast Building terminating its vista: it was one of the first instances of terminating a vista with a skyscraper, something that because of the grid it was hard to do in Manhattan.

THE LATER 20TH CENTURY

After the Second World War, it may be said that New York, however briefly, stood in importance among the world's cities as no city had since ancient Rome—it was the undisputed capital of just about everything. As though to signal that New York had at last become a truly international city, the builders of skyscrapers turned to the so-called International Style. Where Art Deco was modern because it employed modern ornamentation, the new style was modern in that it dispensed with ornamentation altogether, offering up stark metal and glass. Competently handled, the new style yielded its share of winners. **Lever House**, designed by Gordon Bunshaft of Skidmore, Owings & Merrill, rose at 390 Park Ave in 1950–2, the first glass-walled skyscraper built in the dense masonry core of the city. It seemed to float, a shimmering, light-as-a-feather building that showed how exciting the new style could be. The **Seagram Building**, cater-corner to Lever House at 375 Park Ave (*map p. 617, E3*), went up in 1956–9, designed by the German Ludwig Mies van der Rohe. Faced in bronze and tinted glass, and set behind a generous marble plaza, the building evoked the austere glamour of a self-important (though perhaps not self-confident) city. The rapid proliferation of these Modernist buildings, however, drawn from the repertoire of world-weary 1920s intellectuals, were, the philosopher Allan Bloom once said, like Bobby Darin singing "Mack the Knife." The architects knew the words, but not their nihilistic meaning. By the time of the **MetLife Building** (the former PanAm Building) at 200 Park Ave (*map p. 617, D3*) by Emery Roth & Sons, with exterior styling by the Bauhaus panjandrum Walter Gropius, New Yorkers were proud to hate the new architecture.

Worst of all was how federal government money was put to use ripping down old neighborhoods of tenements and row houses and replacing them with brick or concrete high-rises set within parklike "superblocks"—a supposed solution to mass housing based on 1920s prototypes by the Swiss-French architect called Le Corbusier. Corbusier built nothing in New York, but like Henry Hobson Richardson his acolytes were everywhere either doing his bidding or—as Ruskin felt about his acolytes—getting it all wrong. Whichever the case, the Corbusian virus spread across the world's cities, not least New York, in a pandemic of destruction. New York's "master builder" since the 1930s, Robert Moses (none of whose official titles betrayed that he held such power as Haussmann held over mid-19th-century Paris), built in accord with this vision, creating a city of vast high-rise housing estates and automotive high-speed roadways. The bulldozing and rebuilding went by the name "urban renewal." Its orthodoxy was challenged in the late 1950s and early 1960s by a brilliant writer named Jane Jacobs, and also by a historic preservation movement that succeeded in passing the 1965 Landmarks Preservation Law, such that by the early 2000s some 25,000 buildings in the five boroughs were legally protected from demolition or inappropriate alteration.

Public interest in architecture reached a high level in the 1980s, a creative and often confused decade in which architects questioned everything they had been doing. Philip Johnson, one of the major figures of the mid-century Modernist revolution, designed a skyscraper that looked like a Chippendale dresser (the **ex-Sony Building**; *map p. 617, D2*). Architects began using veneers of luscious masonry—cut paper thin, like deli roast beef, because developers weren't willing to pay the cost of whole blocks of the stuff. The result wasn't a return to the look of the old masonry city but a kind of weird, flimsy stage-set version of it. That we remain amply capable of the real thing—solid masonry construction, classical style—is evidenced by the **Carhart Mansion** (2006) on 95th St just east of Fifth Ave, designed by Zivkovic Connolly (*map p. 615, D2*).

THE AGE OF THE STARCHITECT

New York has always had rather an insular architectural culture. We have one Mies van der Rohe building, a façade by Walter Gropius, nothing by Le Corbusier, a single interior by Alvar Aalto, one building by Louis Sullivan, one art museum and one pre-fab house by Frank Lloyd Wright. In the 1990s, and especially in the new millennium, all this began to change as New York embraced the chi-chi world of "starchitects," the globe-trotting celebrity architects many of whom had longed to work in New York and now had their chance. The French architect Christian de Portzamparc's **LVMH Building** (1999) on 57th St just west of Madison Ave is an exciting exercise in wavy glass that seems in part a homage to Ralph Walker and Ely Jacques Kahn. The same architect's 1000-ft-high **One57** apartment tower (2014), on West 57th St across from Carnegie Hall (*map p. 616, C2*), typifies a new breed of super-tall, super-skinny Midtown condominium buildings where the apartments are conceived less as places to live than as safe places (as Swiss banks were once thought to be) for the global financial elite to park their money. Another French architect, Jean Nouvel, is responsible for another such building, **53W53**, on West 53rd St, connecting to the Museum of Modern Art. Nouvel's **100 Eleventh Avenue** (2010), at 19th St (*map p. 618, A2*), is one of the more interesting of the many recent exercises in exploiting revolutionary innovations in glass production. Across 19th St from 100 Eleventh Avenue stands another example of the new glass aesthetic, the celebrated Californian Frank Gehry's **IAC Building** (2007). Gehry has also contributed to New York what is by far his tallest building, **8 Spruce Street** (2010), a downtown apartment tower (*map p. 620, C3; illustrated on p. 84*). Other recent buildings to have received a great deal of attention include the Englishman Norman Foster's **Hearst Tower** (2006; Eighth Ave and 57th St; *map p. 616, B2–C2*); the Italian Renzo Piano's **Whitney Museum of American Art** (2015; Gansevoort St and Washington St; *see p. 202*); and the Californian Thom Mayne's **41 Cooper Square** (2009), built for Cooper Union (*see p. 170*). Of special note are two buildings by the Japanese architect Fumihiko Maki: **51 Astor Place** (2013; *map p. 619, D3*) and **4 World Trade Center** (2013; *map p. 620, C3*) are so sleek and seamless they make almost every other glass-curtain-wall building in the city look like something that fell off the shelf of a hardware store.

The rebuilding of the World Trade Center is, of course, the major architectural news of recent years. The Polish-born, Bronx-bred, Berlin-based architect Daniel Libeskind won a much-publicized 2003 competition for the rebuilding of the site, to be dominated by a 1,776-ft-high "Freedom Tower." For a variety of reasons, design of the tower, now more prosaically titled **One World Trade Center**, devolved upon David Childs of Skidmore, Owings & Merrill (though Libeskind remains the author of the overall site plan). The tower's completion in 2014 marked a major milestone in the city's collective recovery from the traumatic events of September 11, 2001. It is also the tallest building in the United States. It will be several years before the site is completely rebuilt, but thus far we also have the aforementioned 4 World Trade Center by Maki; a dramatic (and almost unimaginably costly) new station, designed by the celebrated Spanish architect-engineer Santiago Calatrava, for the Port Authority Trans-Hudson railroad, featuring a concourse as vast as that of Grand Central Terminal; and the moving **National September 11 Memorial**, by Michael Arad and Peter Walker, incorporating the footprints of the "twin towers."

Finally, mention must be made of New York's surprising rise as an international showcase for new landscape architecture. This followed in large part from the three-term mayor Michael Bloomberg's dedication to redeveloping the disused or derelict waterfronts of New York City. In the process, New York acquired, in all five boroughs, dramatic new waterfront parks, of which by far the most impressive is **Brooklyn Bridge Park**, by Michael Van Valkenburgh Associates, occupying the site of disused piers between Atlantic Ave and the Brooklyn Bridge at the foot of the bluff of Brooklyn Heights. It and the city's most celebrated new landscape, the three-mile-long **High Line** (by the landscape architects James Corner Field Operations and the architects Diller Scofidio + Renfro; *see p. 204*), built atop a disused waterfront-railroad viaduct on the west side of Manhattan between Gansevoort St and 34th St, exemplify the early 21st-century fashion for "Landscape Urbanism." This approach seeks, among other things, to honor both the natural and man-made histories of sites, and accounts for all the rusting gantry cranes set amid fields of native grasses now to be found all across the country, and not least in New York (see **Erie Basin Park**, in Red Hook, Brooklyn, by Lee Weintraub, and **Gantry Plaza State Park**, in Long Island City, Queens, by Thomas Balsley and Lee Weintraub). Other notable major landscapes include **Freshkills Park**, on Staten Island, by James Corner Field Operations, which will occupy 2200 acres by the time it is completed in 2035 on the site of the Fresh Kills Landfill. Unexpectedly and improbably, New York now is a city where tall swaying wild grasses foreground our views of the world's most famous skyline.

Chronology

1524 Giovanni da Verrazzano, working for Francis I of France, explores New York Bay and the North American coastline.

1609 Henry Hudson, seeking a water route to the Orient for the Dutch East India Company, explores the harbor.

1613 Adriaen Block and crew winter in Lower Manhattan, helped by Native Americans, building a new ship after their first, the *Tyger*, burns.

1614 Block explores Long Island Sound and creates the first map showing Manhattan as an island.

1624 Thirty Dutch and Walloon families sent by the Dutch West India Company settle in New Netherland, a territory reaching from the Delaware to Connecticut rivers.

1625 First permanent settlement is made in Lower Manhattan and named New Amsterdam.

1626 Governor General Peter Minuit "purchases" Manhattan Island from the Native Americans.

1636 Governor Wouter van Twiller, whose tenure is disastrous both for the settlers and the Native Americans, "buys" land in Brooklyn, and eventually owns huge tracts there and on Wards, Randalls, Roosevelt and Governors Islands.

1639 Jonas Bronck, a Dane, buys part of the Bronx from Native Americans. David de Vries and others settle on Staten Island but are driven out by Native Americans a few years later.

1643 Native American uprisings in New Amsterdam, New Jersey, and Staten Island; they continue intermittently until 1655.

1645 Lady Deborah Moody, fleeing religious intolerance in Massachusetts, establishes a community at Gravesend, near Coney Island.

1647 Peter Stuyvesant becomes governor.

1653 Peter Stuyvesant builds a fortified wall, river to river at the present latitude of Wall St, to keep out the British, trading rivals of the Dutch.

1654 First permanent Jewish settlement; Asser Levy and 22 others arrive, fleeing persecution in Brazil.

1662 John Bowne is arrested for allowing Quakers, whose religion is outlawed, to meet at his house. He is arrested, sent to the Netherlands, tried, and acquitted, establishing a legal precedent for religious freedom.

1664 The British capture New Amsterdam and rename it New York after James, Duke of York, brother of King Charles II.

1673 The Dutch recapture New York and rename it New Orange.

1674 Treaty of Westminster brings Anglo-Dutch War to a close; New York becomes British once again.

1686 The Dongan Charter gives the city a form of municipal government that remains in force until modern times.

1693 Frederick Philipse builds King's Bridge across the Harlem River, joining

Manhattan island to the mainland.

1713 First Staten Island chartered boat service to Manhattan.

1754 King's College, now Columbia University, founded as city's first college.

1763 French and Indian War closes with Treaty of Paris, confirming British control of North America.

1765 British Parliament passes Stamp Act, raising revenues to support British troops in America. Delegates from nine colonies meet in New York and denounce the Act.

1766 Stamp Act repealed in England. St. Paul's Chapel dedicated.

1767 British again increase taxes and restrict colonial self-government. Anti-British sentiment grows.

1776 Declaration of Independence marks beginning of Revolutionary War. British occupy Brooklyn after Battle of Long Island and take control of all of Manhattan by Nov 17.

1783 Treaty of Paris concludes Revolutionary War as Britain recognizes independence of the 13 colonies. British Army leaves New York.

1785 New York City becomes the capital of the state and nation.

1789 US Constitution ratified. George Washington becomes nation's first president.

1790 Federal capital moves to Philadelphia. First census puts city population at 33,131.

1792 Buttonwood Agreement leads to formation of New York Stock Exchange.

1797 Albany becomes state capital.

1799 State legislature passes the Act for Gradual Emancipation, stipulating that every male slave born after July 4, 1799 will be freed at age 28 and every female at 24.

1803 Cornerstone laid for present City Hall.

1806 First New York free school opens.

1807 Robert Fulton demonstrates his steamboat on the Hudson River.

1808 John Randel Jr. begins survey of Manhattan's 11,400 acres in preparation for Commissioners' Plan.

1811 Commissioners' Plan lays out Manhattan's rectilinear street grid, imposing regularity on the island's natural topography.

1812 City Hall opens. US declares war on Britain; port suffers in trade war and is fortified against possible British attack.

1815 War of 1812 ends. Port begins to recover.

1820 New York becomes nation's largest city, with population of 123,706.

1822 Smallpox epidemic, one of many.

1825 Erie Canal opens, greatly enhancing the importance of New York as a port and making it the gateway to the Midwest.

1827 State legislature ends all slavery in New York State.

1831 New York University founded as University of the City of New York.

1832 New York and Harlem Railroad, a horsecar line, opens along the Bowery and Fourth Ave from Prince St to 14th St.

1834 Village of Brooklyn incorporated as City of Brooklyn.

1835 "Great Fire" destroys 674 buildings near Hanover and Pearl Sts.

1837 Business panic; city losses total some $60 million.

1842 Croton Aqueduct brings water to a reservoir on the site of Bryant Park.

1840s Potato famine in Ireland swells immigration.

1847 Madison Square Park laid out. Referendum calls for creation of City College, founded as the Free Academy.

1848 Political uprisings spur immigration from Germany.

1849 Astor Place Riot demonstrates incompetence of police force.

1850 Giuseppe Garibaldi arrives in Staten Island during period of exile.

1851 *New York Daily Times*, now the *New York Times*, begins publication. Harper's publishes Herman Melville's *Moby-Dick*.

1853 State legislature authorizes Central Park. World's Fair held in Bryant Park.

1855 Castle Garden becomes immigrant station. First model tenement built (block between Elizabeth and Mott Sts).

1858 Calvert Vaux and Frederick Law Olmsted chosen to design Central Park. Macy's founded.

1859 Cooper Union opens. Otis passenger elevator installed in Fifth Avenue Hotel.

1860 City's population reaches 813,669, including 383,717 immigrants; Brooklyn, still a separate city, has 279,122.

1861 American Civil War begins.

1863 Draft Riots against conscription into the Union Army (those who could pay a $300 fee were exempted) paralyze the city for three days. Union Army regiments restore order.

1865 Civil War ends. Municipal fire-fighting system replaces volunteer companies.

1867 Prospect Park opens in Brooklyn. First tenement house law attempts to set standards for ventilation, sanitation, and room size.

1868 Experimental elevated railroad opens on Greenwich St from the Battery to Cortland St, a cable system with both moving and stationary engines.

1869 Rutherfurd Stuyvesant builds city's first known apartment houses, on East 18th St.

1870 Work begins on Brooklyn Bridge. Alfred Ely Beach, editor of the *Scientific American*, opens experimental one-block pneumatic subway under Broadway from Warren to Murray Sts. Ninth Avenue El reaches 30th St.

1871 Grand Central Depot opens. "Boss" Tweed arrested, closing a period of inefficiency and corruption in city government.

1872 Metropolitan Museum of Art opens on Fifth Ave between 53rd and 54th Sts.

1874 Part of the Bronx annexed to New York City, first addition since 1731.

1877 Alfred Tredway White opens model tenement houses in Brooklyn.

1879 Tenement House Law enacted. "Dumbbell" plan by James F. Ware wins a competition for a model tenement. Condemned by reformers, it is nevertheless widely adopted.

1880 Part of Broadway illuminated by Brush electric arc lamps.

1881 Elevated railway reaches 155th St.

1882 Thomas Edison opens generating plant at 257 Pearl St, making electricity commercially available.

1883 Brooklyn Bridge opens.

1886 Statue of Liberty inaugurated. Elevated railway connects Manhattan and Bronx.

1888 Great Blizzard paralyzes city.

1889 First building with steel skeleton erected (Tower Building at 50 Broadway).

1891 Carnegie Hall opens. New York Botanical Garden created by state legislature, will open in the Bronx in 1895.

1892 Immigration station opens on Ellis Island.

1895 First section of Harlem River Ship Canal opens joining Harlem and Hudson Rivers, enabling ships to circumnavigate Manhattan. Rest of Bronx annexed to New York City.

1898 Greater New York created, joining the five boroughs under a single municipal government. Population of 3.4 million makes it the world's second largest city behind London (4 million).

1899 Croton Reservoir in Bryant Park razed for construction of NY Public Library.

1900 Subway construction begins. Census shows tenements house about 70 percent of city's population.

1901 Tenement House Law institutes "New Law" tenements, superseding dumbbell plan.

1903 Williamsburg Bridge opens, making northern Brooklyn accessible to the poor of the Lower East Side.

1904 IRT subway opens from City Hall to West 145th St. Harlem real estate market collapses and African Americans begin moving into unfilled apartment buildings.

1905 City takes over Staten Island Ferry and runs it as a municipal service.

1908 East River subway tunnel links Manhattan and Brooklyn. First Hudson tunnels link Lower Manhattan and New Jersey. IRT Broadway line reaches Kingsbridge section of the Bronx.

1909 Queensboro and Manhattan Bridges open.

1910 Pennsylvania Station opens.

1913 The present Grand Central Terminal opens. The Armory Show introduces New York to "modern art."

1916 Nation's first comprehensive zoning resolution divides city into residential and commercial areas and restricts height and bulk of buildings.

1929 Stock market crashes; Great Depression begins. North Beach Airport opens on site of Gala Amusement Park, owned by Steinway family.

1931 Empire State Building and George Washington Bridge open. Floyd Bennett Field, now a park, opens as city's first municipal airport.

1932 Mayor James J. ("Beau James") Walker resigns after Seabury investigations reveal rampant corruption.

1933 Fiorello La Guardia elected mayor. IND subway opens to Queens.

1934 New York City Housing Authority formed to clear slums and build low-rent housing.

1936 Triborough Bridge (now RFK Bridge) opens.

1938 La Guardia's city charter goes into effect, centralizing municipal power.

1939 North Beach Airport, enlarged by the City, re-opens as LaGuardia Field. New York World's Fair opens in Queens.

1940 Queens–Midtown tunnel opens. Brooklyn–Battery Tunnel (now officially the Hugh L. Carey Tunnel) begun.

1941 US enters World War II. New York becomes major Atlantic port. Brooklyn Navy Yard operates at full capacity.

1943 New York City Opera founded, described by Mayor La Guardia as "the people's opera."

1945 World War II ends. United Nations charter passed.

1946 UN selects New York as permanent headquarters.

1947 Stuyvesant Town opens, providing middle-income housing for returning war veterans and their families, built along East River Drive.

1948 New York International Airport, originally called Idlewild, officially opened; renamed John F. Kennedy International Airport after assassination of president.

1950 Brooklyn–Battery Tunnel opens after construction delay caused by war. City population at new high: 7,891,957.

1952 Lever House opens, first of the glass-box skyscrapers.

1957 Fair Housing Law outlaws racial discrimination.

1959 Ground broken for Lincoln Center.

1960 Completion of Chase Manhattan Bank marks beginning of construction boom in lower Manhattan.

1961 New zoning law offers incentives for public amenities including plazas and arcades.

1963 Pennsylvania Station demolished.

1964 Race riots in Harlem and Bedford-Stuyvesant. World's Fair of 1964–5 opens in Queens. Verrazano-Narrows Bridge opens, ending relative isolation of Staten Island.

1965 Landmarks Preservation Commission established to save city's architectural heritage. New laws allow increased Asian, Greek, Haitian, Dominican immigration. Major power blackout.

1966 Ground broken for World Trade Center (estimated cost of $250 million).

1970 First New York City Marathon is run; 126 men and 1 woman participate. A court ruling requires McSorley's Old Ale House to admit women.

1973 Construction of Twin Towers at World Trade Center completed.

1974 City's financial position worsens as loss of middle class and departure of businesses erode tax base while costs of social services increase.

1975 Cash-flow problems and inability to sell more municipal bonds bring city to verge of insolvency. South Bronx becomes symbol of urban despair as 13,000 fires break out in twelve-square-mile area.

1977 Power blackout, lasting 25hrs, results in widespread looting and vandalism.

1978 Radio City Music Hall saved from demolition. Supreme Court decision preserves Grand Central Terminal. "Pooper scooper" law requires pet owners to clean up after their dogs.

1980 Census assesses population at 7,071,639, with sharp decline in city's white population, moderate increase in black population, and substantial increase in Hispanic population. Blacks and Hispanics account for 48 percent of city's population.

1981 City re-enters long-term municipal bond market. Construction of first residential building begins at Battery Park City.

1982 Andrew Lloyd Webber's *Cats* opens on Broadway.

1983 IBM Building opens on Madison **Ave**. City enacts "antisliver" law to limit height of buildings less than 45ft wide.

1985 First building of World Financial Center opens.

1986 Statue of Liberty celebrates 100th anniversary.

1987 Stock market crashes as Dow Jones average plunges 508 points in one day, losing more than 22 percent of its value.

1988 *Phantom of the Opera* opens on Broadway, another Andrew Lloyd Webber blockbuster.

1989 B. Altman & Company department store closes after 124 years in business.

1990 David Dinkins takes office as city's first black mayor. Ellis Island reopens as a museum.

1991 African Burial Ground discovered near City Hall.

1993 World Trade Center is bombed. Six die, more than 1,000 are injured. Staten Island bids to secede from Greater New York.

1994 High-tech industries reach New York with development of "Silicon Alley" around Broadway in the West 20s.

Staten Island's secession bid quashed.

1996 Lower Hudson River once again able to support life as striped bass return (the good news), along with marine borers (the bad news).

1997 Times Square rehabilitation in full swing. Crime rate continues falling. *Cats* establishes new longevity record (6,138 performances).

2000 City's population tops 8 million, confirming it as nation's largest: 3.6 million whites, 2.2 million Hispanics, 2.1 million blacks, and fewer than 800,000 Asian Americans. *Cats* finally closes after 7,485 performances. "Starchitect" Richard Meier's glassy residential towers in the West Village draw celebrity buyers, kicking off a new wave of ultra-luxury buildings.

2001 On Sept 11, two commercial airliners hijacked by Islamic terrorists deliberately crash into the Twin Towers of the World Trade Center. The towers collapse. More than 2,800 people killed.

2002 Tourism drops and economy shrinks in wake of World Trade Center disaster. Guggenheim Museum scraps plan for Frank Gehry-designed building on downtown waterfront.

2004 Statue of Liberty, closed after Sept 11 attacks, reopens to the public.

2006 World Trade Center rebuilding officially begins.

2008 New Museum of Contemporary Art opens in a new building on the Bowery, sign of a cultural shift downtown. Lehman Brothers, fourth largest investment bank in the US, files for bankruptcy, precipitating fiscal crisis.

2009 Dow Jones average closes at a twelve-year low of 6547.

2010 US Census reports City population at 8,175,133, a gain of 2.1 percent since 2000: 3.7 million whites, 2.3 million Hispanics, 2.1 million blacks, and 977 thousand Asian Americans.

2011 New York City Opera leaves Lincoln Center amid financial stresses.

2012 Hurricane Sandy lashes East Coast, inundating low-lying areas of Manhattan, Staten Island, Red Hook, and the Rockaways. Subways and vehicular tunnels are flooded; massive power outages affect millions; 53 people die.

2013 New York City Opera files for bankruptcy. Mayor Michael A. Bloomberg announces the completion of the Manhattan portion of Water Tunnel No. 3, begun in 1970. Four World Trade Center opens, first building completed on the renovated World Trade Center site. *Phantom of the Opera* has its 10,400th performance, the longest-running show in Broadway history by more than 3,000 performances.

2014 The average sales price for apartments in New York City, estimated at about $1.8 million, continues to soar. National 9/11 Museum opens, attracting one million visitors in the first three months. People's Climate March draws about 311,000 protesters. One World Trade Center officially opens, eight years after the cornerstone was laid.

2015 Apartment building at 432 Park Ave tops out at 1,396 ft, the city's tallest residential tower. One57, a condominium on 57th Street's "Billionaires' Row" (Park Ave to Broadway) sells for $100.47 million, setting a record. Whitney Museum opens in a new home near the foot of the High Line.

A WALK THROUGH TRIBECA

Tribeca (Try-beck-a), an acronym devised in the 1970s to enhance property values in the **Tri**angle **Be**low **Ca**nal St, is a trapezoidal neighborhood known for its intriguing combination of wealth and grit. The grit comes from its days as part of the Lower West Side, when food purveyors roasted coffee or distributed dairy products, and merchants haggled over wool in the district's 19th-century industrial buildings. The wealth is more recent, attributable in part to a spillover from SoHo that began in the 1980s. Today celebrities and other well-heeled people occupy the upper floors of former manufacturing lofts and warehouses. At street level shops offer antiques, boutique clothing, or hand crafted Japanese knives; Tribeca restaurants include those for which reservations are required weeks in advance and small portions of food (albeit exquisitely prepared) command high prices—but there are more modest establishments, too. The Tribeca Film Festival, founded in 2002 by Robert DeNiro (a neighborhood resident) and others to revitalize the area after 9/11, has become a major cultural event (late April–early May). As Lower Manhattan has recovered, so has Tribeca. This walk takes in some examples of Tribeca's 19th-century cast-iron and 20th-century Art-Deco industrial architecture as well as its 21st-century panache.

To reach the starting point by subway: N or R to Canal St (Broadway); 6 to Canal St (Lafayette St). Bus: M6.

LISPENARD STREET, A BLOCK SOUTH of Canal Street, is named for Leonard Lispenard, whose family owned much of eastern Tribeca, while Trinity Church owned much of the west. The two landowners developed their property separately with different street grids, Trinity's streets paralleling the river, the Lispenards' parallel to Broadway. The cast-iron buildings of the east resemble those of SoHo to the north. In the western section brick warehouses from the 1870s and '80s, many in the Romanesque Revival style, serviced the docks. The arrival of the A.T. Stewart Department Store, downtown a few blocks on Chambers St (*see p. 90*), sparked the development of stores, lofts, and houses on and around Broadway. In 1853–9, before he made his mark recording the Civil War, photographer

Matthew Brady ran a portrait studio near Franklin St at 359 Broadway.

Continue down Broadway to White St and turn left (east). Midblock turn right into **Cortlandt Alley**. This narrow alley between Franklin and White Sts is thrown into shadow by the hulking 19th-century warehouses and old residential buildings that line it. A bright spot is **Mmuseumm** (*open late spring– early winter, Fri 6–9, Sat–Sun 11–7; closed late winter–early spring; free; no telephone; mmuseumm.com),* a cube-like space in a former elevator shaft. Self-described as a "modern natural history museum devoted to the curation and exhibition of contemporary artifacts that illustrate the complexities of the modern world," it displays mundane yet bizarre items (e.g. half-squeezed toothpaste tubes) as though they were *objets d'art*. Founded (2012) by filmmakers Josh and Benny Safdie and Alex Kalman, it occasionally hosts special events.

Around the time of the Civil War, industrial buildings began replacing the earlier Greek Revival houses and shops. With its keystone-crowned arches and Corinthian columns (the capitals are now gone), the cast-iron building (1861) at **55 White St** (*Franklin Pl.*) was deemed so handsome by Daniel D. Badger, whose foundry supplied the material, that he featured it in his 1865 catalogue. The building has been home to a saddlery and textile firms; nowadays it houses multi-million-dollar condos.

At 47–49 White St is the **Tribeca Synagogue** (1967; William N. Breger Assocs), originally the Civic Center Synagogue, built to serve the weekday spiritual wellbeing of Jews working in city government but renamed when the demographics of the congregation changed. The seven-inch-thick swooping façade of molded concrete appears to float above the street. (*open weekdays 9–5; early closing Fri; T: 212 966 7141, tribecasynagogue.org*).

A block north of Walker St, 32 Sixth Avenue was originally the **AT&T Long Lines Building** (1930–2; Voorhees, Gmelin & Walker), an irregularly massed Art Deco building with polychrome brickwork. Formerly called the "Tower of Speech," it had direct circuits to several hundred cities, with some 5,000 operators connecting long-distance calls. The lobby lionizes technology, a tile wall map proclaiming "Telephone Wires and Radio Unite to Make Neighbors of Nations" and a ceiling mosaic depicting the continents as female figures linked by golden wires.

On the northeast corner of West Broadway the small two-story Federal house at **2 White St** still has its original gambrel roof and dormers from the early 19th century (1809), but harks back to an earlier style. The man for whom it was built, Gideon Tucker, owned a nearby plaster factory.

Worth the detour if you enjoy cast-iron architecture, **85 Leonard St** (1861) sports a façade made in the works of James Bogardus, generally considered the father of American cast-iron architecture. This building is a catalogue of decorative possibilities: fluted columns (formerly with leafy capitals), lions' heads, rope moldings, bearded faces, dentiled moldings, faceted keystones, egg-and-dart trim, stylized leaves. It is also one of the few buildings in the sperm-candle style, the slender two-story columns resembling candles (which were made from the liquid wax found in sperm whales' heads).

At 60 Hudson St (*between Thomas and Worth Sts*), the **former Western Union Building** (1930; Voorhees, Gmelin & Walker) is an imposing Art Deco building by architect Ralph Walker (a favorite architect of the phone company). Nineteen tons of brick shade the façade, from deep red-brown at the bottom to bright salmon at the top—not unusual for Art Deco brickwork. When it opened, the building housed telephone, telegraph, and ticker machinery, a messenger service, gymnasium, library, and classrooms where Western Union messenger boys could attend high school.

The brown brick lobby gloriously exemplifies Art Deco materials and techniques: recessed lighting, leaded glass windows, geometrically patterned brickwork, and a Guastavino tile ceiling.

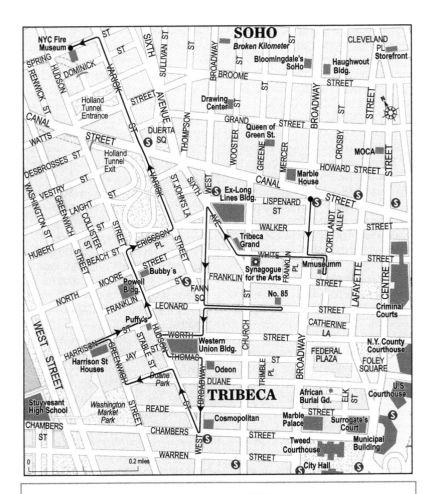

JAMES BOGARDUS

James Bogardus (1800–74), high-school dropout and visionary, foresaw the possibilities of bolting together sections of cast iron into façades or even whole buildings. His importance arises primarily from his patents for constructing buildings with mass-produced cast-iron sections. Between about 1848–60, he promoted iron buildings because they were fireproof and efficient to build. In his *Cast Iron Buildings: Their Construction and Advantages* (1858), he described the method of supporting the weight of construction on columns rather than on masonry walls; it was a first step in the development of skeleton framing, which eventually enabled the construction of skyscrapers. Bogardus was also a prolific inventor, patenting devices for engraving postage stamps, spinning cotton, cutting rubber, and pressing glass.

On the southeast corner of Thomas St (named for Thomas Lispenard, a son of Leonard Lispenard; *see p. 97*) is **The Odeon** (*145 West Broadway; see p. 103*). Converted (1980) from a vintage cafeteria to a bistro, it was the first of many stylish restaurants to follow artists to Tribeca.

Like other early cast-iron buildings, **147 West Broadway** (1869), just off the southeast corner of Thomas St, is designed to imitate stone, down to the incised blocks on the façade and the quoins on the corners. Later cast-iron façades exploited the natural properties of iron, which allowed for more elaborate decoration.

The **Cosmopolitan Hotel**, at 95 West Broadway (*Chambers St*), is said to have opened around 1850 as the Gerard House, when, according to the 1939 *WPA New York City Guide*, its proximity to the piers made it attractive to gold miners returning from California, who "staggered into the lobby after a trip around the Horn, dumped their gold-dust, went out to the barber, and came back un-recognizably clean."

Walk uptown on Hudson St to **Duane Park**, a small triangle with benches and plantings, the first land bought by the City specifically for parkland. The history of the plot can be traced back to 1636 when it belonged to a Dutch farming couple, Roeloff and Annetje Jans. The farm was later sold to the English governor and then confiscated by the Duke of York (later James II), who gave it to Trinity Church. The City bought it back in 1795 for five dollars. James Duane (1733–97) was New York's first mayor after the Revolutionary War and later a federal judge.

Late 19th-century buildings surround the park. **No. 173–5 Duane St** (1879; Babb & Cook) is one of the area's earliest Romanesque Revival buildings. The cast-iron front of **171 Duane St** (1859) was grafted onto an earlier Federal house. The large brick Romanesque Revival building on the northwest corner of Hudson St, **165 Duane St** (1881; Stephen Decatur Hatch), was built as a factory and warehouse for Leopold Schepp (*see box opposite*).

The name of **Washington Market Park** (1983) recalls the city's largest food market, which dominated this neighborhood for almost 150 years. The market building occupied a block bounded by Fulton, Vesey, Washington, and West Sts in what is presently the northwest corner of the World Trade Center site, but its activities as a distribution center for produce, cheese, butter, eggs, and candy spread into the surrounding neighborhood along West St as far north as Canal St. The market, which offered everything from codfish cheeks to bear steaks, was supplanted by the Hunts Point Market in 1967, as plans for the World Trade Center took shape.

Near Greenwich St on Harrison St, the nine 18th-century Federal-style brick **Harrison Street houses** (1796–1828) remain from the first time this was a fashionable residential area, before the advent of commerce and industry. Nos. 25, 37, 39, and 41 Harrison St were built by John McComb Jr., New York's first native-born architect (he designed City Hall), who lived in one of them. The street takes its name from Harrison's Brewery, which stood near the river in pre-Revolutionary days.

At 6 Harrison St is the **former New York Mercantile Exchange** (1886; Thomas R. Jackson), a five-story, gabled brick Queen-Anne-style building with a handsome tower facing the river and rusticated granite pillars at the base. The tall second-story windows opened onto the trading floor, where on a good day at the turn of the 20th century $15,000 worth of eggs changed hands in a single hour. Founded in 1872 as the Butter and Cheese Exchange, for commercial aims (fostering trade, reforming abuses), the organization also had social goals (promoting good fellowship, providing for the widows and orphans of members).

LEOPOLD SCHEPP

Leopold Schepp (1841–1926), the child of immigrants, quit school when he was ten to support his widowed mother. He spent his initial capital, ten cents, on palm leaf fans, which he peddled on horse cars; by the time he was 27, he owned a successful business importing coffee, tea, and spices. Schepp devised a process for drying coconuts, which boosted him into the financial elite, and at the height of his career his sailing vessels brought coconuts from Cuba and the Caribbean. Schepp's instincts for business were perhaps keener than his understanding of human nature, for when he was 83 he announced through the Associated Press that he wanted to give away his fortune before he died and requested suggestions from the public. The next day a crowd so large showed up at his office that he was forced to flee. Before decamping, he issued a statement that the newspapers had exaggerated his wealth, that he did not wish to be referred to as the "Cocoanut King," and that he had no desire to waste money, perhaps an indication of a temper that the *New York Times* had earlier described as capable of causing "the north pole to melt." Nevertheless Schepp established a foundation to help adolescent boys, provided they abstained from intoxicating drink and gambling, a charity he later expanded to include "worthy girls." The Leopold Schepp Foundation still exists, providing scholarships to young men and women.

Puffy's Tavern, on the southwest corner of Harrison and Hudson Sts, dates back to Prohibition (*see p. 104*).

Formerly the Pierce Building (1892; Carrère & Hastings), the **Powell Building** (*105 Hudson St at Franklin St; subway: 1 at the intersection of Franklin St, Varick St, and West Broadway*) was named for its developer, Henry Pierce, who headed the firm that made Baker's Chocolate. It is an early work by the architectural firm that went on to design the New York Public Library on Fifth Ave at 42nd St and the Frick mansion.

After Pierce's death, Alexander Powell, a candy manufacturer, bought it and enlarged it top-to-bottom and side-to-side. The ground floor is occupied by luxury Japanese restaurant **Nobu** (*see p. 103*); though it was purported to be relocating to the Financial District at the time of writing, its presence here since 1994 has helped make Tribeca a culinary destination .

Less rarified and more moderately priced is **Bubby's** at 102 Hudson St (*see p. 104*). You can either end the walk here or continue north on Varick St to visit the **New York City Fire Museum** at 278 Spring St (*Hudson and Varick Sts; open daily 10–5, closed major holidays; admission charge; shop; T: 212 691 1301, nycfiremuseum.org*). Located in the Renaissance Revival firehouse of former Engine Company 30, the museum has one of the nation's most important collections of fire equipment and memorabilia, including horse-drawn vehicles and hand pumpers dating back to the colonial era, a 19th-century hose carriage beautifully appointed with plumes and fancy lanterns, and steam-powered motorized vehicles. Paintings on view illustrate the city's most famous fires. Also exhibited are tools, uniforms and equipment, and an exhibit of fire marks, formerly attached to buildings to show that they were insured (and to advertise for the insurance companies). The museum has a memorial to the 343 members of the FDNY who lost their lives on 9/11, with a timeline of the day's events and a display of tributes sent from all over the nation. (*Subway: 1 at Canal or Houston St, or C or E at Spring St at Sixth Ave.*)

THE HOLLAND TUNNEL

Two blocks north of Franklin St are the ramps (packed at rush hour with bumper-to-bumper traffic) for the Holland Tunnel (1927), the first Hudson River vehicular tunnel, named after its original chief engineer, Clifford M. Holland. The tunnel was heralded as a triumph of engineering, largely because Ole Singstad, who headed the project after Holland's death in 1924, solved the ventilation problems of a long vehicular tunnel by creating a mechanical system that can exchange the air in the tubes every 90 seconds. The roadway occupies the middle third of each circular tube, with an air intake chamber below and an exhaust chamber above. Four ventilation buildings, two on each side of the river, are equipped with 8-ft fans to draw in fresh air from outside and exhaust the foul air. The interiors of the tubes are finished with white glazed ceramic tile, the color chosen because a "color psychologist" reported that blue, green, or red tiles would have had "depressing effects" on drivers. The Port Authority of New York and New Jersey operates the tunnel, which carries about 32 million vehicles annually.

EATING AND DRINKING IN TRIBECA

Restaurants in Tribeca range from the chic and staggeringly expensive to the humble and homey, though the latter are more difficult to find than the former.

$$$$ Atera. This 18-seat restaurant proves the law of supply and demand while dazzling the critics and offering exquisite food, which is also beautiful to look at. The *prix fixe* tasting menu (the only way you can order), at more than $200-per without the wine pairings, still fascinates adventurous eaters; the surroundings are dramatic. Notable cocktails and a non-alcoholic paring. Dinner only, Tues–Sat, reservations essential. *77 Worth St (Church St and Broadway). T: 212 226 1444, ateranyc.com. Map p. 620, C2.*

$$$$ Bouley. ■ Classic French restaurant, with beautiful service, fine food, lovely surroundings. Five-course lunch tasting menu the best bargain, but the wine pairings double the price. Also *à la carte*. Fine wine list. Dress accordingly. Lunch and dinner Mon–Sat. *163 Duane St (Hudson St). T: 212 964 2525, davidbouley.com. Map p. 620, B2.*

$$$$ Nobu. The flagship restaurant of what has become a global empire, directed by chef Nobu Matsuhisa and one of the chief reasons for the evolution of Tribeca, (slated to move to the Financial District in 2017). It is famous for its Japanese cooking with Western nuances. Sushi bar, many seafood dishes, friendly service, and a downtown crowd. Lunch weekdays, dinner nightly. *105 Hudson St (Franklin St). T: 212 219 0500, noburestaurants.com. Map p. 620, B2.*

$$$ City Hall. This neighborhood standby for seafood and straight-forward American dishes in an attractive cast-iron building is close to City Hall. Good wine list. Lunch and dinner six days, closed Sun. *131 Duane St (Church St and West Broadway). T: 212 227 7777, cityhallny. com. Map p. 620, C2.*

$$$ Khe-Yo. Recently opened Laotian restaurant with a Laotian-American chef. If you like things hot, try the grilled meat dishes piqued with Thai hot sauce. Some diners love the coconut rice with spicy Kaffir lime sausage; the adventurous even enjoy the pig's face entrée. Plenty of protein dishes, but not a wide choice of desserts. Lunch and dinner daily. *157 Duane St (Hudson St and West Broadway). T: 212 587 1089, kheyo. com. Map p. 620, B2.*

$$$ The Odeon. Once hip, now a dependable neighborhood brasserie; outdoor dining in season.Breakfast and lunch weekdays; brunch weekends, dinner nightly. *145 West Broadway (Thomas St). T: 212 233 0507, theodeonrestaurant.com. Map p. 620, B2.*

$$$ Pepolino. Popular Italian *trattoria* draws a neighborhood crowd and others in the know with its many pastas, straightforward cooking. Fabulous cheesecake. Lunch and dinner daily. *281 West Broadway (Canal and Lispenard Sts). T: 212 966*

9983, pepolino.com. Map p. 620, C1.

$$$ **Puffy's Tavern**. Prohibition-era watering hole retaining its old-fashioned bar, tile floor, jukebox, and dart board. Snacks, sandwiches, bar food; big TVs for sporting events. Open daily 4–4. 81 Hudson St. T: 212 227 3912, puffystavernnyc.com. Map p. 620, B2.

$$$ **Tamarind Tribeca**. ■ Formerly located in the Flatiron District, now downtown in this bright two-story space, with the dining room and a lounge on the main floor, plus a mezzanine. Upscale Indian specialties include kababs (meat and seafood), vegetarian dishes, and tandoori dishes, accompanied by Indian breads and chutneys, as well as beer, wine, or a cocktail from an imaginative list. Lunch and dinner daily. 99 Hudson St (Franklin St). T: 212 775 9000, tamarindrestaurantsnyc.com. Map p. 620, B2.

$$$ **Tribeca Grill**. The exposed-pipe décor and lively crowd give this informal place its vibe. Whether you indulge yourself with California caviar and grilled filet of beef or hold back with salmon tartare and pan-roasted chicken, you can expect a well-prepared meal. Partially owned by Robert de Niro, the restaurant is remarkable for its longevity (opened 1990) and for its notable wine list. Lunch Sun–Fri, dinner nightly. 375 Greenwich St (Franklin St). T: 212 941

3900, myriadrestaurantgroup.com/restaurants/tribeca. Map p. 620, B2.

$$ **Blaue Gans**. Austro-German cuisine includes such old standbys as schnitzel and wurst, spätzle and goulash, but updated for modern tastes. Pleasant surroundings, with a downtown feeling. Popular bar with cocktails and German beer. Lunch weekdays, brunch Sat, dinner Mon–Sat. 139 Duane St (Church St and West Broadway). T: 212 571 8880, kg-ny.com. Map p. 620, C2.

$$ **Bubby's**. American cooking in all its avatars—from matzo ball soup, to shrimp tacos, to burgers and fries. The weekend brunch scene is hectic. Breakfast, lunch, and dinner daily; open all night Fri and Sat. 102 Hudson St (North Moore St). T: 212 219 0666, bubbys.com. Map p. 620, B2.

$$ **Macao Trading Co**. Portuguese-Chinese fusion food in a setting designed to suggest the exotic and sinister ambiance of 1930s Macao. From the Portuguese side come churiço with fries and from the East, steamed vegetable dumplings and Macanese chili prawns. Downstairs there's a club-like scene, upstairs a more laid-back restaurant. Can be crowded and loud. Portuguese wines and exotic cocktails. Dinner nightly. 311 Church St (Lispenard and Walker Sts). T: 212 431 8750, macaonyc.com. Map p. 620, C1.